CURRENT ISSUES IN THE PHONE

Volume 9
Parts I & II

Harry & Patricia Hollien (ed)

Current Issues in the Phonetic Sciences

CURRENT ISSUES IN THE
PHONETIC SCIENCES

Proceedings of the IPS-77 Congress,
Miami Beach, Florida, 17-19th December 1977

Edited by

Harry and Patricia Hollien

University of Florida
Gainesville, Fla.

PART I

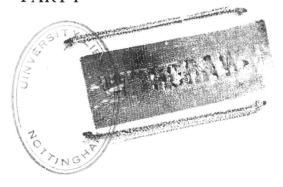

AMSTERDAM / JOHN BENJAMINS B.V.

1979

C

EDITORS' PREFACE

IPS-77 originally was planned as a small Phonetic Sciences congress which, while international in scope, would bring together only a modest number of participants for an intensive interchange. Hence, it was designed in such a manner that those individuals involved could spend a long weekend discussing issues, within our discipline, that were of particular interest to them. However, soon after the first announcement was published, it became apparent that the need for broader and more formal interactions within the Phonetic Sciences was far more acute than we had anticipated. By then, however, it was too late to convert the congress to a regional plan even though one of the reasons for its organization was to test the notion that the quadrennial ICPhS Congresses needed to be bisected with regional efforts in order to better meet the needs of phoneticians on a world-wide basis. However, as stated, this refocusing proved impossible to carry out — for IPS-77 anyway — and had to be deferred to subsequent conferences. In any case, the Florida Congress grew and grew, both in quantity *and* in quality; its success far exceeded our expectations.

This two-volume set of articles is one consequence of the IPS-77 change in scope. As was obvious from the program, many major papers were presented at Miami; the bulk of them can be found between these covers. We regret only that many of the fine presentations from the panel sessions could not be included. Where the contents of the present volumes are concerned, several items should be noted here.

In one or two instances, IPS-77 sessions spawned (or probably will result in) other books; Wayne Lea's effort in
Speech Recognition is one example in this regard. Further,
most of our authors have chosen to expand their papers into major articles. Indeed, since we had to seriously limit
the space allotted to each contributor (excepting the plenary speakers, of course), a number of them chose to with-
draw their second paper in order to concentrate their efforts on a single major article. Moreover, our Publisher
— John Benjamins — graciously expanded the size of this
enterprise letting us utilize every millimeter of space he
could. As a result we have been able to pack some 120 articles into this effort — most of these articles being, we
believe, of major importance and at a state-of-the-science
level.

     Of course, much more needs perhaps be said about these
two volumes. However, in keeping with our attempts to include as much content as possible, most of these discussions will have to be left unwritten. It seems necessary
however, to make mention of several stylistic decisions we
made in order that the reader understand how best to utilize the materials contained in these volumes. First, we
converted all papers to a simple format as follows: a) paragraph divisions and headings were restructured to be as
uniform as possible; b) all tables and figures were placed
at the end of the article; c) references and notes were
combined (in most cases) and, also, placed at the end of
the article; d) abstracts and summaries of papers were deleted; some editing and text reduction was carried out when
required; f) phonetic symbols were standardized wherever
possible, and g) all brackets, parentheses and slash-lines
pertaining to phonetic/phonemic symbolization were converted to slashes only. Moreover, we reduced all references

uniformly to include only author(s)/publishers or author(s)
/journal plus date of publication. In this regard, we were
of the opinion that the reader needing to locate a particular
reference could do so anyway with a little effort — or at
least obtain it by writing to the author for more information. This policy resulted in a substantial saving of
space; most authors cheerfully cooperated with these viola-
tions of the sanctity of their manuscripts. In general, we
hope to have done justice to their fine contributions. Last-
ly, it needs to be mentioned that we recognize the manner
in which we have grouped the papers may not please all authors and readers. Indeed, some papers could have been ac-
commodated in any of several categories. We nevertheless
hope that the sections we have established will prove of
some use in the finding of the information sought after.

    In closing, may we utilize a few lines in order to
thank the individual authors for their kind cooperation and
— especially — for the high quality of the papers they
submitted. The style of presentation is of secondary importance; it is the content of the article that matters.
We also wish to thank the many people whose efforts made
the IPS-77 Congress a success. Except for the plenary
speakers (whose contributions are identified as such in the
Proceedings), the names and responsibilities of these individuals appear on the pages immediately following the Pre-
face. Without them, the Congress would never have become a
reality. Further, we wish to thank Professor E. F. Konrad
Koerner, University of Ottawa, for his substantial help with
these volumes; without his editorial assistance, we could
not have brought this task to a successful conclusion. Finally, our thanks go to Mrs. Voncile Sanders and Mrs. Susan
Gates; they typed the entire text of the Proceedings.

Gainesville, Florida, April 1979   Harry & Patricia Hollien

Sponsors of the IPS-77 Congress

INTERNATIONAL SOCIETY OF PHONETIC SCIENCES

INSTITUTE FOR ADVANCED STUDY OF THE COMMUNICATION
PROCESSES, UNIVERSITY OF FLORIDA

AMERICAN ASSOCIATION OF PHONETIC SCIENCES

UNIVERSITY OF FLORIDA
OFFICE OF ACADEMIC AFFAIRS
GRADUATE SCHOOL
SPEECH DEPARTMENT
TEACHING RESOURCES

ACADEMY FOR FORENSIC APPLICATION OF
THE COMMUNICATION SCIENCES

UNIVERSITY OF NEBRASKA

U.S. DEPARTMENT OF COMMERCE

NATIONAL INSTITUTES OF HEALTH

* * * * *

Honors of the Congress
JAMES F. CURTIS, UNIVERSITY OF IOWA

VIII

IPS-77 COMMITTEES

EXECUTIVE COMMITTEE

HARRY HOLLIEN, Secretary General

ROBERT E. McGLONE, Program Chairman

GILBERT C. TOLHURST, Program

GERALD T. BENNETT

W. S. BROWN, Jr.

JAMES T. FITZGERALD

JENS-PETER KÖSTER

WALTER MANNING

RONALD TIKOFSKY

SPECIAL SESSIONS CHAIRMEN

JOHN K. DARBY, U.S.A.

R. PRAKASH DIXIT, U.S.A.

THOMAS GAY, U.S.A.

W. J. GOULD, U.S.A.

ALAN W. HUCKLEBERRY, U.S.A.

E. F. K. KOERNER, Canada

JOHN LAVER, United Kingdom

WAYNE A. LEA, U.S.A.

ALAIN MARCHAL, Canada

FERNANDO POYATOS, Canada

KLAUS SCHERER, W. Germany

CARL-GUSTAV SÖDERBERG, Sweden

RUDOLF WEISS, U.S.A.

HONORARY COUNCIL

Wolfgang Bethge, W. Germany   Robert A. Bryan, U.S.A.

John W. Black, U.S.A.   Franklin S. Cooper, U.S.A.

Gunnar Fant, Sweden   Betty Goodfriend, U.S.A.

Moti Lal Gupta, India   Gene Hemp, U.S.A.

Martin Kloster-Jensen, W.Germany   Leigh Lisker, U.S.A.

André Martinet, France   Paul Moore, U.S.A.

Masao Onishi, Japan   Harry H. Sisler, U.S.A.

Milan Romportl, Czechoslovakia Kenneth N. Stevens, U.S.A.

Gilbert C. Tolhurst, U.S.A.   Hans-H. Wängler, U.S.A.

Max Wajskop, Belgium   F. Michael Wahl, U.S.A.

E. T. York, U.S.A.

LOCAL ARRANGEMENTS

Ronald Tikofsky, Chairman

W. S. Brown, Jr., Vice Chm. & Treasurer

Sylvan Bloch, AFACS Liaison

James T. Fitzgerald, Physical Arrangements

Anthony Holbrook, Scientific Exhibits

Patricia Hollien, Registration

Stuart I. Ritterman, Commercial Exhibits

Howard B. Rothman, Awards

Thomas Shipp, AAPS Liaison

Faculty Associates

E. Thomas Doherty, Gerard Chollet & Elaine Brown

Student Assistants

Glory Ann Coomer, Russell Crowder, Lynne Harshman

James W. Hicks., Jr., Charles C. Johnson, Christine Johnson

Brian Klepper, Sue Newman, and Donna Tate

ORGANIZING COMMITTEE

Muhammed H. Bakalla, Saudi Arabia   Heinz Balkenhol, Japan
Michelle Berthier, France   Jean Casagrande, U.S.A.
Moses J. Chayen, Israel   John Delack, Canada
Franco Ferrero, Italy   Knut Fintoft, Norway
F. V. Peixoto da Fronseca, Portugal   Thomas Gay, U.S.A.
Samir K. Ghosh, India   William Hardcastle, England
W. J. Gould, U.S.A.   Alan W. Huckleberry, U.S.A.
Wiktor Jassem, Poland   Franciszek J. Kapelinski, Nigeria
Heinrich Kelz, W. Germany   Martin Kloster-Jensen, W. Germany
Jens-Peter Köster, W. Germany   Georg Liiv, U.S.S.R.
Leigh Lisker, U.S.A.   André Malécot, U.S.A.
Wojciech Majewski, Poland   F. Gomez de Matos, Brasil
Robert E. McGlone, U.S.A.   K. M. N. Menon, India
Susana Naidich, Argentina   Rose Nash, Puerto Rico
Milan Romportl, Czechoslovakia   Howard B. Rothman, U.S.A.
William A. Sakow, Japan   Laurent Santerre, Canada
Klaus Scherer, W. Germany   Carl-Gustaf Söderberg, Sweden
Thomas Shipp, U.S.A.   M. D. Steer, U.S.A.
Marcel Tatham, England   Nina Thorsen, Denmark
Ronald Tikofsky, U.S.A.   J. W. Vaca, Equador
Sibylle Vater, Switzerland   Areta Voroniuc, Romania
Kalevi Wiik, Finland   F. Weingartner, Taiwan (Rep. of China)
François Wioland, France

* * * * *

TABLE OF CONTENTS

Editor's Foreword   V
List of Congress Sponsors, Committees and other Organizational Matters VII

PART I

A. HISTORY OF PHONETICS

Muhammed H. BAKALLA: Ancient Arab and Muslim Phoneti-
   cians: An appraisal of their contribution to phonetics   3
Arthur J. BRONSTEIN and Lawrence J. RAPHAEL: Phonetics and Other Disciplines: Then and now   13
E. F. Konrad KOERNER: Toward a Historiography of
   Phonetics 23
Jens-Peter KÜSTER: Giulio Panconcelli-Calzias Beitrag
   zur Geschichte der Phonetik   37
Elbert R. MOSES: Looking Back: Memories of 40 years
   in phonetics 49

B. ISSUES OF METHOD AND THEORY IN PHONETICS

Uzbek BAITCHURA: On the Necessity of the Introduction
   of Technical Principles into Instrumental-Phonetic
   Investigations   57
R. A. W. BLADON: Some Control Components of a
   Speech Production Model 63
E. A. KRASHENINNIKOVA: Phonetic Aspects of Lingua-

Informatics 71

Morteza MAHMOUDIAN: Dimension statistique de la structure linguistique et distinction phonétique/phonologie 77

Mehra M. MEHAN: Linguistics and Systems Theory . . . 85

Marcel A. A. TATHAM: Some Problems in Phonetic Theory 93

C. Laryngeal Function

Louis-Jean BOË et Bernard GUÉRIN: Caractéristique de forme de l'onde de débit des cordes vocales: Productions vocaliques 109

Gérard F. CHOLLET and Joel C. KAHANE: Laryngeal Patterns of Consonant Productions in Sentences Observed with an Impedance Glottograph 119

Osamu FUJIMURA: Physiological Functions of the Larynx in Phonetic Control 129

Hajime HIROSE, Hirohide YOSHIOKA, and Seiji NIIMI: A Cross Language Study of Laryngeal Adjustment in Consonant Production 165

John LARGE and Thomas MURRY: Quantitative Analysis of Chant in Relation to Normal Phonation and Vocal Fry 181

Magnús PÉTÚRSSON: Jointure et activité glottale . . 191

Peter J. ROACH and W. J. HARDCASTLE: Instrumental Measurement of Phonation Types: A laryngographic contribution 201

Ingo R. TITZE: Variations of Pitch and Intensity with Pre-Phonatory Laryngeal Adjustments 209

Idem: Physical and Physiological Dimensions of Intrinsic Voice Quality 217

D. Temporal Factors and Questions of Intonation

Keith O. Anderson: Applied Prosodic Analysis: A pedagogical model for English and German intonation . . 227

Heinz BALKENHOL: Rhythm and Pause as Means of Expression in the Japanese Arts of Storytelling, with special regard to Rakugo 235

Ivan FÓNAGY: Artistic Vocal Communication at the Prosodic Level 245

Herbert GALTON: Syllabic Division and the Intonation of Common Slavic 261

Sarah HAWKINS: Processes in the Development of Speech Timing Control 267

J. W. HICKS, Jr.: An Acoustical/Temporal Analysis of the Effect of Situational Stress on Speech 279

D. R. HILL, Wiktor JASSEM, and I. H. WITTEN: A Statistical Approach to the Problem of Isochrony in Spoken British English 285

E. F. JAMES: Intonation through Visualization . . . 295

Bienming JOU: Tonal Spelling 303

Elisabeth L'HOTE: Quelques problèmes posés par l'élaboration de règles prédictives de l'intonation . . 309

Anatoly LIBERMAN: Prephonological Views on the History of English Syllable Accents 321

D. Kimbrough OLLER: Syllable Timing in Spanish, English, and Finnish 331

Yvette SZMIDT: Le registre mélodique de l'attaque dans un parler franco-ontarien 345

Anne-Marie Ferrand VIDAL: "Mélodie-langage" des chorals de Jean-Sébastien Bach 357

Max WAJSKOP: Temporal Cues in French Intervocalic Stops 363

François WIOLAND: Principes d'une méthode d'enseignement de la prononciation du français à partir du rythme de la langue parlée non méridionale . . . 383

E. Physiological and Acoustic Phonetics

D. AUTESSERRE and B. TESTON: Description of an

Electropalatographic System   407
R. Prakash DIXIT: Inadequacies in Phonetic Specifica-
tions of Some Laryngeal Features: Evidence from Hin-
di   423
Solomon I. SARA: Vocalic Variability in Palatographic
Impressions   435
S. SHIBATA, A. INO, S. YAMASHITA, S. HIKI, S. KIRITANI,
and M. SAWASHIMA: A New Portable Type Unit for
Electropalatography   443
Cynthia R. SHUKEN: Aspiration in Scottish Gaelic
Stop Consonants   451
Peter S. VIG and James B. McLAIN: The Effect on For-
mant Patterns of Differential Volumetric Change in
the Oral Cavity   459
Robert L. WHITEHEAD and Kenneth O. JONES: Character-
istics of Oral Air Flow during Plosive Consonant Production by Hearing-Impaired Speakers   475

F. Speech Production

John W. BLACK, Yukio TAKEFUTA, and Elizabeth JANCO-
SEK: The Production and Recognition of Sounds in
English Words Spoken by Young Japanese Adults . . .   489
R. A. W. BLADON: The Production of Laterals: Some
acoustic properties and their physiological impli-
cations   501
G. H. BRECKWOLDT: African Click Sounds: Early des-
criptions and symbols   509
E. Dean DETRICH: Nasal Consonant Epenthesis in
'Southern' French   521
W. J. HARDCASTLE and Peter J. ROACH: An Instrum-
ental Investigation of Coarticulation in Stop
Consonant Sequences   531
Pierre R. LÉON: Standardisation vs. diversifica-

tion dans la prononciation du français contemporain   541

John M. LIPSKI: On Vowel-Diphthong Transitions . .   551

Leigh LISKER: Speech across a Linguistic Boundary:
Category naming and phonetic description   563

William A. SAKOW: Comparative Analysis of Syllable
and Accent between English and Japanese   573

Roman STOPA: Original Vowels in African Languages   577

László SZABÓ: Vowel Length in Micmac and Malecite   583

PART II

G. NEUROPHONETICS AND PSYCHOPATHOLOGY

Arnold E. ARONSON: Differential Diagnosis of Neuro-
logic and Psychogenic Voice Disorders   591

John K. DARBY and Alice SHERK: Speech Studies in
Psychiatric Populations   599

Harry HOLLIEN and John K. DARBY: Acoustic Comparisons of Psychotic and Non-Psychotic Voices   609

Torgny JENESKOG and Carl-Gustaf SÖDERBERG: The Physiology of Cerebellar Involvement in Motor Control   615

Peter F. MacNEILAGE: Neural Mechanisms in Speech
Productions   621

Catherine A. MATEER: Impairment of Verbal and Non-
Verbal Oral Movements after Left Hemisphere Damage   639

Peter F. OSTWALD: Psychiatric Implications of
Speech Disorder   647

Clyde L. ROUSEY: Phonetic Indications of Psychopa-
thology   657

Carl-Gustaf SÖDERBERG and Torgny JENESKOG: Cerebellar Involvement in Motor Control: A concept . . .   669

H. SPEECH PERCEPTION

Ana María BORZONE de Manrique: On the Recognition
of Isolated Spanish Vowels   677

G. H. BRECKWOLDT: Experiments in Voice Confrontation 683

Glen L. BULL: The Effects of Several Linguistic Factors on the Magnitude of Error in the Location of Extraneous Sounds Embedded in Speech 691

Conrad LaRIVIERE: Normalization Influences in the Perception of Speech 699

Herbert R. MASTHOFF: Some Physiological Interpretations of the Perception of Vowel Duration above and below the One-Period Boundary 707

John OAKESHOTT-TAYLOR: Prosodic Expectancies in Speech Perception: Implications of an Experiment on the Perception of Segmented Speech 713

James M. PICKETT: Perception of Speech Features by Persons with Hearing Impairment 721

Herbert PILCH: Auditory Phonetics 737

Irwin RONSON: The Effect of Labov's Five Phonological Variables on Perceived Listener Judgement . . . 743

Willy SERNICLAES and Pierre BEJSTER: Cross-Language Differences in the Perceptual Use of Voicing Cues . 755

Willy SERNICLAES and Max WAJSKOP: Prevoicing as a Perceptual Cue in French 765

Debra M. VAN ORT, Daniel S. BEASLEY, and Linda L. RIENSCHE: Intelligibility of Time-Altered Sentential Messages as a Function of Contralateral Masking 775

Michel VIEL: The Perception of Distinctive Features 787

I. SPEECH AND SPEAKER RECOGNITION

R. D. GLAVE: Some Steps in Performance Evaluation of the Dawid Speech Recognition System 803

Kathleen HOULIHAN: The Effect of Disguise on Speaker Identification from Sound Spectrograms 811

Charles C. JOHNSON, Jr.: Speaker Identification by

Wojciech MAJEWSKI, Janusz ZALEWSKI, and Harry HOLLIEN:
Some Remarks on Different Speaker Identification
Techniques 829
Howard B. ROTHMAN: Further Analysis of Talkers with
Similar Sounding Voices 837
Donna A. TATE:` Preliminary Data on Dialect in Speech
Disguise 847
Oscar TOSI, R. PISANI, R. DUBES, A. JAIN: An Objective
Method of Voice Identification 851

J. THE TEACHING OF PHONETICS

F. O. BENNETT: Phonetics and Second Language Teach-
ing in Africa 865
Jacqueline L. BROWN: Teaching Beginning Phonetics in
the United States: Some basic considerations 871
Raphael M. HALLER: Non-English Phone Imitation and
General Academic and IPA Transcription Performance
by Monolingual Adults 877
Telete Zorayda LAWRENCE: The Teaching of English
Phonetics in the U.S.A.: Issues related to speech
pathology and theatre 883
Audrey O'BRIEN: The Teaching of English Phonetics in
the U.S.A.: Foreign dialects 891
Betty R. OWENS: Teaching Phonetics in the Voice
and Diction Course 893
Sadanand SINGH and Jeffrey L. DANHAUER: The Teaching
of English Phonetics in the United States 899
Rudolf WEISS: A Perception Test as a Diagnostic Tool
in Teaching German Pronunciation 905

K. CHILDREN'S SPEECH AND LANGUAGE ACQUISITION

George D. ALLEN, Sarah HAWKINS, and Margaret R. MORRIS:
Development of 'Nuclear Accent' Marking in Children's
Phrases 919

George D. ALLEN and Sarah HAWKINS: Trochaic Rhythm
in Children's Speech 927
W. S. BROWN, Jr.: Supraglottal Air Pressure Varia-
tions Associated with Consonant Productions by Chil-
dren 935
E. Thomas DOHERTY and Harry HOLLIEN: An Indicator of
the Onset of Puberty in Males 945
Raphael M. HALLER: Some Competencies Influencing
Phoneme Acquisition in Children 955
E. Charles HEALY: Timing Relationships and Strategies
Used by Normal Speaking Children in the Self-Regula-
tion of Speaking Rate 961
Jo Ann Williamson HIGGS and Barbara Williams HODSON:
What the Child's Perception of the Word-Final Obstru-
ent Cognates Tells Us about His Perceptual Mastery
of English Phonology 967
Walter H. MANNING and Linda L. LOUKO: A Right Ear
Effect for Auditory Feedback Control of Children's
Newly-Acquired Phonemes 977
Stuart I. RITTERMAN and Ulla E. M. RICHTNÉR: An Ex-
amination of the Articulatory Acquisitions of Swedish
Phonemes 985
Ida STOCKMAN, David WOODS, and Abrahan TISHMAN: Ob-
server Reliability in Making Impressionistic Judg-
ments of Early Vocalization 997
Harris WINITZ and Betty BELLEROSE: Interference and
the Persistence of Articulatory Responses 1009

L. SPECIAL ISSUES IN PHONETICS

George D. ALLEN: Transcription of the American /r/ . 1019
Uzbek BAITCHURA: Alphabets, Orthographies, and the
Influence of Social-Historical Factors 1027
Simon BELASCO: Visible Speech Cues and Sandhi Varia-
tion Rules in French 1039

Curt HAMRE and William HARN: Effects of Masking on Sub-
vocal Speech and Short-Term Memory 1053
Idem: The Effects of Masking on Apraxia: Evidence from
spectrographic data 1057
Antti IIVONEN: Experiments and Observations Made Us-
ing a Real-Time Spectrum Analyzer (RTA): One formant
vowels and formant merger 1065
Frances INGEMANN: Speech Synthesis by Rule Using the
Fove Program 1075
Anatoly LIBERMAN: On the History of Quantity in Ger-
manic 1085
Philippe MARTIN: Automatic Location of Stressed Syl-
lables in French 1091
Frank PARKER: Acoustic Cues and Consonant Clusters . 1095
Fernando POYATOS: Phonetic and Interdisciplinary New
Perspectives in Paralinguistic Studies 1105
Mario ROSSI: Interactions between Intensity Glides and
Frequency Glissandos 1117
Laurent SANTERRE: La fusion des voyelles en frontières
inter-syntagmatiques et intra-syntagmatiques 1131
Gladys E. SAUNDERS: Speculations on a Contact-Induced
Phonological Change in Gallo-Italian 1139
James Monroe STEWART and Carol BARACH: A Short Memory
Strategy with Distinctive Features 1149
Ana TATARU: The Analysis of the Combinations of Dis-
tinctive Sounds 1161
Sibylle VATER: La spectrographie et la segmentation
acoustique au service de la poétique expérimentale:
Des analyses fondées sur le dictionnaire de poétique
.et de rhétorique de Henri Morrier (éd. de 1975) . . 1171
Areta VORONIUC: Prosodic Features and Speech Acts . 1187

* * * * *

A. HISTORY OF PHONETICS

ANCIENT ARAB AND MUSLIM PHONETICIANS: AN APPRAISAL OF THEIR CONTRIBUTION TO PHONETICS

MUHAMMED HASAN BAKALLA
University of Riyadh

Arabic and Muslim contribution to Phonetics (using phonetics here in a broader sense) has not been properly acknowledged in modern history of general phonetics. Holger Pederson's remark (in his Linguistic Science in the Nineteenth Century: Methods and Results, Cambridge, Mass., 1931) about Muslim contribution stands as a stumbling block in the way of those who are interested in Islamic culture. What do we expect from a student of linguistics and phonetics when he reads the Professor's remark: "Modern linguistic science owes much to Buddhism." And he then reads his remark in a footnote: "We have nothing to thank Mohammedanism for in this respect." Forty three years or so later a similar observation was reiterated by J. C. Greene (in Hymes, 1974): ". . .curiously enough, the Arabs seem to have contributed nothing to the study of language comparable to the additions and improvements they have made in mathematics, astronomy, physics, medicine, and natural history." This kind of statement is based on the fact that there is still a lack of serious research work in the field of early Arabic linguistics and phonetics, and therefore, some attention and joint effort must be paid to this gap in our knowledge of the Muslim world. Also, this situation reflects the lack of knowledge of what had already been published in the West even as early as 1911 (see Schaade, 1911; Bravmann, 1934).

This paper attempts to contribute to our understanding of some aspects of traditional Arabic phonetics and evaluate the

efforts made. No detailed analysis is worked out here, but
I hope that this study will arouse some interest in this
field about which so little is known in Western Scholarship.

THE ORIGIN OF ARABIC PHONETICS

It is very difficult to establish the exact date for the
beginning of Arabic phonetics. The Arabs' interest in this
area goes back to the pre-Islamic era when the Arabic script
was worked out on some form of phonetic or phonological basis.
But it was not until the advent of Islam and the revelation
of the holy book, the Koran, that Arabic phonetics emerged as
one of the important subjects for the Koranic studies and,
later on, it developed into a discipline of its own. The
earliest extant work containing phonetic information was compiled by Al-Khalil Ibn Ahmad al-Farahidi (ca. 717-791 AD).
His lexicon al-ʕayn, apparently the first Arabic lexicon of
its kind, is arranged according to a phonetic ordering of the
Arabic consonants from the throat upward to the lips. Influenced by the morphophonemic changes of the Arabic consonants,
he chose ʕ rather than ʔ to begin his lexicon and hence it
was given the title al-ʕayn (i.e., the sound or letter ʕ).
Al-Khalil himself is well known as the founder of a number of
Arabic subjects such as Metrics, rhythm, and mathematics. The
proposed phonetic statements made by Al-Khalil suggest a long
and wealthy tradition behind them.

Although the influence of Indian scholarship upon Arabic
studies is evident in a number of Arabic and Islamic disciplines
such as mathematics, it is not easy to prove it insofar as
Arabic phonetics is concerned. The paralellism of the Indian
and Arabic Scholarship here can be interpreted in terms of the
similarity in the point of departure. That is to say each centres around a book which is considered holy to its believers.
The emphasis on rendering each of them in a correct form brought
about independently a wealth of information relating to phonetics, grammer or lexis, etc. This kind of paralellism is not
unique in general scholarship. However and even in the absence
of any convincing evidence, one cannot rule out totally such
an influence or even the influence of both upon each other.

Al-Khalil was succeeded by his student, Sibawaihi
(d. 793 A.D.) who wrote the first comprehensive book which
is still extant on Arabic grammar. In this book Arabic
grammar was presented from syntax to phonology or phonetics.
One can state here that both Al-Khalil and his student
Sibawaihi laid down the foundations of Arabic Phonetics.
Sibawaihi, on the other hand, did not only differ slightly
from his professor but also he added and introduced, probably
for the first time in the history of Arabic phonetics, a number of phonetic categories. For example: voicing, trill,
stop, emphaticness, lateral. Sibawaihi and Al-Khalil both
agree on the number of Arabic sound-units which are basically
consonant phonemes. The ordering of the 29 phonemes by the
two scholars are found in Table 1. A close look at the two
orderings shows that Al-Khalil does not follow the strict
phonetic ordering of the phonemes. While he lists the semi-
vowels and the glottal stop right at the end, Sibawaihi,
on the other hand, follows a strict ascending phonetic order.
It is to be noted that the Arabic letter ﺱ stands for the
semivowel y and the vowel i:, ﻭ for w and u: Also while
Al-Khalil describes the Arabic sounds in terms of place of
articulation or ma×raj, Sibawaihi gives a more detailed
description of the sounds by place and also by manner of
articulation. ·In addition, Sibawaihi lists 13 other sounds,
some of which are either stylistic, dialectal, contextual or
free variants.

Two centuries later, Ibn Jinni (d. 1001) wrote his monumental work Sirr al-Sina:'ah (Mustafa al-Saqqa, 1954) among
other books. Born at Musil in Iraq from a Greek father this
very renowned Muslim scholar in Arabic linguistics gathered
most of the phonetic information in one book and introduced
for the first time the name of the Arabic phonetics:
ʕilm al-ASwa:t wal-Huru:f. He devoted his book to this science
and, therefore, he was able to organize all the phonetic data
known to him with explanations and examples. This work is not
very well known as only a small part of it has been published.

Ibn Jinni begins his work with a definition of speech
sounds as follows: "The human voice is an accidental property
which issues out together with the pulmonic air along the vocal
tract until it is checked at a point in the throat, mouth or

lips with the articulators which can completely stop the air
from passing beyond that point. The sound which is produced
at each point of articulation is called Harf, i.e. speech
sound." He also reformulated a number of statements made by
his predecessors, such as al-Khalil and Sibawaihi. Unlike
them, he devotes a large section to the treatment of the
Arabic vowels where he discusses the following points: (a)
The vowels as a group of speech sounds which are independent
of the consonants on the basis of differences in manner of
articulation; (b) The differences between the vowels themselves in terms of quality and (c) The quantitative differences
between the vowels. He divides the Arabic vowels into long
and short. He also states that the long vowels can be elon-
gated further in certain contexts.

Another new observation in this work is the comparison
between the articulation of speech sounds and the notes made
by musical instruments such as the nay and the lute. According
to him this comparison is valid because phonetics and music
have something in common. That is, they are both involved in
the making of sounds (aSwa:t) and tunes (navam) (pp. 9-10).
He follows the same phonetic ordering of the phonemes from the
throat to the lips except with some slight modifications.
Ibn Jinni places _G before k and orders _D immediately after
y and before l (p. 50). Like Sibawaihi he recognizes for
Arabic 16 points of articulation and lists under each the
speech sounds which are articulated in that position. He also
deals with the variants in greater detail than Sibawaihi,
giving more examples and clearer exposition throughout. Ibn
Jinni also touches upon the vocalic harmony in Arabic. His
account of the distribution of the phonemes in Arabic and
the various phontactic statements is more lucid and precise
than either Al-Khalil's or Sibawaihi's. Ibn Jinni's treatment
of the syllable in grammatical analysis is scanty. The detailed
study of the Arabic syllable structure normally takes place in
the analysis of metrics or poetic metre. As far as I know,
grammatical works edited so far do not mention any analysis
of the stress, pitch, intonation, rhythm in Arabic. However,
Ibn Jinni seems to be aware of the effect of the stress on
the lengthening of vowels in certain contexts (p. 20).

One of the more interesting aspects of the traditional
phonetic analysis is that it is based on a form of binary
distinctive feature analysis. This can be noticed in the
work of al-Khalil and Sibawaihi too. But Ibn Jinni seems to
use this approach more extensively. Unlike al-Khalil, he and
Sibawaihi do not make use of the articulatory features only
but also they employ auditory features as well. Quite readily
one can encounter such descriptive terms as: maDmu:m(rounded),
maftu:H (open), Halqi (guttural), ∫afahiyy (labial), and
majhu:r (voiced), maxmu:s (voiceless), ʔaʁann (nasal), etc.
Also note the following statement where Ibn Jinni (following
Sibawaihi) distinguishes between the emphatics and non-
emphatics in Arabic: "Without ʔiTba:q (emphaticness) D would
become d, S would become s and ẟ would become ð . . .
(p. 70)."

Another important aspect of traditional Arabic phonetics
is its emphasis on experimentation in both theoretical and
applied fields. Many of the statements are based on very
close observation of the articulatory processes. Since this
is not readily available, resort was made to a testing procedure to verify certain statements. Note Ibn Jinni's remark
(following Sibawaihi) where he wants to prove that n is nasal:
"The evidence which proves that n is nasal is that if you hold
your nose while you are articulating this sound, its enuncia-
tion will not be perfect (p. 53)."

It is also interesting to note that Ibn Jinni mentions
some types of speech defects such as laθɣ (lisping), rattah
(inability to pronounce r). This defect was widely acknowledged and attempts were made to treat it. Abu Ali al-Farisi,
Ibn Jinni's Professor for about 40 years, is known to have
developed a technique for treating this defect. The following
anecdote was related by al-Suyuti: "Ibn Jarw could not
articulate r and pronounced it as uvular ɣ. Abu Ali said to
him: insert the nib of your pen under your tongue and push
your tongue up with it and do it frequently while repeating
a word containing r. He did as his teacher advised and the r
came forth faultlessly."

Now we come to Avicenne, Ibn Sinna (d. 1037) who wrote
his scientific work "A treatise on the points of articulation

of the speech-sounds" known in Arabic as <u>Asba:b Hudu:th
al-Huru:f</u>. This work consists of six chapters written very
briefly (see Semaan, 1963): (1) On the Cause of the Generation of Sound; (2) On the Cause of the Formation of Speech-
Sound; (3) On the anatomy of the Larynx and Tongue; (4) On
the Particular Causes of Production of the Arabic Speech-
Sounds; (5) On non-Arabic Speech-Sounds; and (6) On how these
Sounds can be Heard as a result of Activities other than those
of Speech Articulation. I shall select some passages to show
an example of the great interest of the Arabs and Muslims in
phonetic studies: "The immediate cause for the generation of
sound is the wave motion (vibration) of the air expelled
rapidly and with force (as a result of a knocking of two
bodies against one shoulder, or extraction as when one solid
body is withdrawn from another). . . . These undulations
reach the still air in the earhole setting up vibrations
therein which are felt by the aural nerves spread over its
upper surface. . . . It is the vibration itself that produces
the sound. Some speech sounds are simple entities whose formation is the result of complete obstruction of the sound, or
of the air which produces the sound, followed by a release
impulsion. Others are complex entities produced by incomplete
obstruction of the air though with release.

    Among the speech-sounds which are not found in Arabic
there is <u>f</u> which is almost like <u>b</u>. It occurs in the Persian
language as in <u>vzoni:</u> meaning "increase." "excess," but differs
from <u>b</u> in that the obstruction of the air therein is incomplete
and it differs from <u>f</u> in that the narrowing for the exit of the
sound from the lips is greater, while the pressure of the air
is stronger so much so that it almost produces vibration in
the inner part of the lips. Also among them is the harder <u>b</u>
which occurs in Persian as in the word <u>pe:ru:zi:</u> meaning
"victory, success." This harder <u>b</u> is produced by forceful
compression of the lips during the obstruction of the air,with
a somewhat violent release and expulsion of the air. . . .
Similarly there is a velarized <u>L</u> the relation of which to <u>l</u> is
the same as that of <u>T</u> to <u>t</u>. This velarized <u>L</u> is common in the
language of the Turks, and is considered as an independent
speech-sound, but those (among them) who commonly use the
Arabic languages treat it as the one and the same <u>l</u>. Moreover,
<u>g</u> is produced in the same vowel areas as <u>x</u>, but more inward
and with complete obstruction of the air stream. As for the
vowels, <u>a</u> and <u>a:</u> are produced by a smooth emission of the

air-stream without any interference, whereas u and u: are
produced with little interruption of the air-stream, and
narrowing of the lips, along with a slight gentle propulsion
upwards on the way out, and in i and i: the gentle propulsion is little downward. Each short vowel is produced
during a shorter period of time than the long ones which are
produced during a period of time the length of which is twice
as much."

CONCLUSION

The above presentation of Arabic Phonetics is very
sketchy and only some of the salient features have been incorporated here for a number of reasons. First, to show the
deep interest of the Arab and Muslim phoneticians in this
field. Second to point out their contribution to our knowledge of Arabic phonetics at a time when the Middle East was
leading the learned world in this field as well as others.
Third, to arouse interest in this direction in order to bridge
a gap in the history of general phonetics. Fourth, to emphasize the importance of traditional Arabic phonetics to modern
Arabic in particular as well as general phonetics, and to
stress its relevance for those interested in phonetic methodology in the Middle Ages.

Needless to say, the wealth of phonetic information as
well as the richness of technical terminology can be employed
and in fact has been employed by modern Arab and Muslim
phoneticians in their studies of Arabic and Islamic languages.
It is to be noted that such important grammatical works have
been consulted for many centuries and have influenced various
Arabic sciences such as rhetoric, lexicology, Tajwi:d or the
science of Koranic reading. Some of the statements have been
quoted ad verbatim for generations. It is not easy to assess
here the impact of traditional Arabic phonetics upon other
sciences and such a topic deserves a thorough investigation.

In conclusion, the present study is only an attempt to
arouse the interest of historiographers of general phonetics
in this area which has been almost completely forgotten. Also
to arouse an interest in Arabic synchronic and diachronic
studies. If this has been successful, then the paper has
achieved its object.

Bakalla, M. H. (1975). London, Mansell.
Bravmann, M. (1934). Göttingen, Kaestner.
Saqqa, Mustafa et al. (eds.). (1954). Cairo, Halabi Press.
Schaade, A. (1911). Leiden, Brill.
Semaan, K. I. (translator). (1963). Lahore, Pakistan, Ashraf Press.

Table 1. Ordering of 29 phonemes by Al-Khalil and Sibawaihi.

Al-Khalil's

   ʕ   H   h   X   ɣ   -   G   k   -   J   ʃ   D   -   S   s   z   -   T

   d   t   -   ð̵   ð   θ   -   r   l   n   -   f   b   m   -   w/u:

   a: y/i: ʔ

Sibawaihi's

   ʔ   a: h   -   ʕ   H   -   ɣ   X   -   k   G   -   D   j   ʃ   y/i:

   -   l   r   n   -   T   d   t   -   S   z   s   -   ð̵   ð   θ   -

   f   b   m   w/u:

The symbols used above represent certain Arabic sound units. ʕ stands for the voiced pharyngeal fricative; H for the voiceless pharyngeal fricative; x for the voiceless uvular fricative; ___ the voiced uvular fricative; G the voiced uvular stop; the capital letters represent the emphatic counterparts of the non-emphatics; ʔ the glottal stop; ð̵ the emphatic counterpart of ð which is the voiced interdental fricative; θ the voiceless interdental fricative; the colon after the short vowels indicates vowel lengthening. ʃ is a voiceless palatoalveolar fricative. ⱡ is a voiced fricative lateral emphatic (see the following diagram which was made by Al-Sakkaki in the 13th century).

Points of articulation

A DIAGRAM OF THE POINTS OF ARTICULATION AS DISPLAYED
BY AL-SAKKAKI IN THE THIRTEENTH CENTURY A.D.

PHONETICS AND OTHER DISCIPLINES: THEN AND NOW

Arthur J. Bronstein and Lawrence J. Raphael
Herbert H. Lehman College

How pleasant it would be were we able to state at this
(or any) meeting of phoneticians that our investigations
indicate that the Renaissance Men and Women of Academia are
obviously those (or at least many of those) whose interests
are deep in the phonetic sciences. The temptation to do so
is perhaps not so wide of the mark if one does examine who
(or what) phoneticians are and what many do and have done.
There is more than slight justification for the statement
that reasonable numbers of phoneticians bring, and have
brought, to this discipline a wide background of interests
and expertise in many, many fields of scientific and humanis-
tic endeavor. Even a cursory study of those current journals
in which studies in phonetics appear demonstrates a trend for
such contemporary studies to become more and more interdisciplinary in nature. Phoneticians increasingly rely, it seems,
on the work of, or collaborate with, sociologists, psychologists, biologists, poets, physicists, anthropologists, neurolo-
gists, and others. And a look at the history of phonetics
reveals that this seemingly recent trend has deep roots.
Earlier phoneticians seemed no less prone to incorporate into
their work the ideas and findings from other areas of investigation or other disciplines. It is possible, in fact, to draw
parallels between the nature and direction of interdisciplinary
influences on the work done by those we identify as contributors to phonetics both in the current scene as well as in
earlier scenes.

Consider the effect of the following passages upon a
beginning student of phonetics (or a phonetician unaware of

the history of his discipline). The first passage is taken
from the Journal of Phonetics Volume 4 (1976) and is concerned
with the description of the articulation of English /ℓ/. It
appears in an essay by David Leidner. We quote from the third
paragraph of that essay: "METHODS--Bipolar hooked-wire electrodes (0.002 in. diam., platinumiridium alloy) were threaded
through the cannula of a hypodermic needle and inserted into
the following tongue muscles of two subjects, both speakers
of standard American English:[1] genioglossus (GG), medial
intrinsics (MI) two-thirds down from the tongue tip, the most
anterior portion of the superior longitudinal muscle located
at the tongue tip (TT), and the styloglossus (SG).[2] The
entire assembly was inserted directly into the muscle, after
which the cannula was withdrawn, leaving the hooked ends of
the wires embedded in the muscle. Prior to electrode placement, topical anesthesia (2°/o Xylocaine solution) was ad-
ministered at the site of needle insertion by means of an air
jet (Panjet-70). Correct electrode placement was verified
by having the subject articulate gestures considered characteristic of contraction of the target muscle while the experimenter monitored the accompanying electrical activity on
an oscilloscope and amplifier-speaker system. For a complete
description of electrode insertion techniques and placement
verification, see Hirose (1971) and the references cited
there."

The second passage is taken from Phonetica, Volume 33
(1976), in an essay by David J. Broad concerned with determining how two different phonetic entities can be shown to be
acoustically equivalent: "The way that this might be done
can be illustrated with a case for which the necessary data
exist, namely the case of determining whether the estimated
targets for the vowels shown in figure 3 are equivalent to
that speaker's /I/ target. For these vowels, the trajectory
for the ith formant frequency of the kth repetition of /I/
preceded by consonant C_a and followed by consonant C_b is given
by /1/:
$$_kF_i^{(ab)}(t) = V_i + G_i^{(a)}(t) + H_i^{(b)}(t) + _kX_i^{(ab)}(t), \qquad (1)$$
where V_i is the target value of F_i, $G_i^{(a)}(t)$ is an initial
consonant transition function defined for C_a and /I/, $H_i^{(b)}(t)$
is a final consonant transition function defined for /I/ and
C_b, and $_kX_i^{(ab)}(t)$ is the value assumed by a random variable

$X_i(t)$ for the k<u>th</u> token of the speaker's productions of the
type $C_a/I/C_b$. The random variable has a nearly normal distribution with a zero mean and a standard deviation in the
range shown in Table 1 for the inter-repetition variation,
which is the dominant component of $X_i(t)$."

The third selection from an essay by William Labov
comes from a study on the stratification of (a) the initial
consonant in <u>thing</u>, (b) the use of postvocalic /r/ in words
like <u>beer</u>, and <u>beard</u>, and (c) the merger of /i/ and /e/:
"In ... (this) city, this phonological trait has been
generalized throughout the _____ group, reflecting the
social processes which identify the group as a whole." And

"Many of the fundamental concepts of sociology are
exemplified in the results of these studies of linguistic
variation. The speech community is not defined by any
marked agreement in the use of language elements, so much as
by participation in a set of shared norms; these norms may be
observed in overt types of evaluative behavior and by the
uniformity of abstract patterns of variation which are invariant in respect to particular levels of usage. Similarly,
through observations of linguistic behavior it is possible to
make detailed studies of the structure of class stratification in a given community."[3]

Now let's return to our student of phonetics who might
have concluded that what he has been referred to were the
efforts of physicists, physiologists, mathematicians, statis-
ticians, psychosociologists, somehow mixed into phonetic
study. And if he is encouraged to read further, he may well
discover healthy doses of neurology, biology, optics,
mechanics, poetics, and psychology. Were he to conclude that
the study of phonetics has become highly interdisciplinary in
or participated in by students from many other disciplines,
he would be correct, in good part. For practitioners and
students of phonetics have come to rely on contributions from
other disciplines. In some instances phoneticians are themselves much more than that, i.e., they are contributors to,
if not experts in, other areas. In still other cases, phoneticians find themselves collaborating in their research with
others whose expertise in different disciplines is essential
to the development of their own phonetic research.

Among the numerous instances of such research partner-
ships we may mention one which developed at Haskins Laboratories in the early fifties. Pierre Delattre was the phonetician and linguist of that research team; Alvin M. Liberman
was the psychologist; and Franklin S. Cooper, then President
of the Laboratories, was the physicist. One is tempted to
include the pattern playback, that ancestor of modern speech
synthesizers, as a fourth member of the team. It was the
playback, in any event, which drew the phoneticians into the
research at the laboratory. Cooper, the physicist, had designed and built the synthesizer as a prototype for the
output of a speech-reading machine for the blind. Liberman,
the psychologist, was working on the perceptual problems and
questions raised by the manipulations of the synthetic speech
signal. When Delattre, on a visit to the Laboratory, saw and
heard the playback in operation, he realized its potential
for phonetic research. And so he stayed on and a research
team came into being. We are, of course, aware of the impact
that this team's research had, and still has, in the fields
of phonetics, psychology and acoustics. However, we must
note that although Cooper may have continued to handle most
of the problems relating to signal generation and transmission and engineering; and Liberman may have isolated the
perceptual strategies needed for speech processing; and
although Delattre contributed most of the thinking which related the acoustic signal to speech production and phonetic
systems--yet after several years of work together it often
became impossible to isolate an individual's contributions
to a piece of research, just as it became impossible to label
any piece of the team's research as belonging to one
discipline or to another. The individuals and their talents
in this case were, to say the least, well-suited to each other
and to the research problems they undertook. And just as the
abilities and interests of each broadened and merged with
those of the others, so, to some extent, did the boundaries
of their disciplines. Individually and collectively, the
writings of these researchers have appeared in Le Maitre
Phonetique, PMLA, JASA, The 3rd and 4th Annual Round Table
Meetings on Linguistics and Language Teaching, American
Journal of Psychology, Word, Psychology Monographs, Journal
of Experimental Psychology, Proceedings of the 8th International Congress of Linguists, Language and Speech, Phonetica,

<u>Proceedings of the Institute of Electrical and Electronic
Engineers</u> and <u>Studia Linguistica</u>. It is no wonder that our
hypothetical student might conclude that the study of phonetics has become highly interdisciplinary. We need hardly
make the obvious point that interdisciplinary collaborations
of the sort we have been discussing are not now unusual.
They occur not only in acoustically and physiologically-
oriented laboratories from Tokyo to Stockholm, and beyond,
but in universities and research centers around the world.
Further, along with the increase in collaborative efforts we
can note an increase in the number of disciplines brought to
bear on the study of phonetics. Now the point we make today
is that one should not confuse collaborative research efforts
with the interdisciplinary nature of phonetic study. The
former is almost certainly on the increase, and has been for
a number of decades. Not that formal collaboration is unknown historically--but it was certainly uncommon. The latter,
however, has been with us for a long time.

A look at the history of this discipline reveals many
figures, both major and minor, whose approaches to the study
of phonetics were influenced and tempered by their (and
others') expertise in other areas of study. There are thus,
in a study of our own roots, clear demonstrations of a long
tradition of interdisciplinary study in phonetic research.
We cite herein a few.[4]

Perhaps among the more obvious of those with other,
interdisciplinary interests would be the 19th Century inventor of the telephone, Alexander Graham Bell, whom we know
also as the author of <u>The Mechanism of Speech</u> (1906) and
"<u>On the Nature and Uses of Visible Speech</u>" (1872). Bell was
a professor of vocal physiology, the founder of a society to
promote the teaching of speech to the deaf--a physicist,
physiologist, musician, speech scientist, inventor. We have
<u>almost</u> as much right to claim him as a contributor to the
phonetic sciences as do those who believe his contribution to
the communication of speech through his invention puts him
among the great inventors of modern times. We do not belittle
their claim by suggesting ours!

Two of this country's leading anthropologists, Franz Boas
and Edward Sapir, also come to mind in this context. Although

it is true, that neither would be identified primarily as a phonetician, one would be wrong indeed not to recognize that each did make a significant contribution to phonetics. Boas' study of the Amerindian languages led to his well known essay on "Alternating Sounds" published in 1889, in which he suggested that the perception of the phonetic shape of identical lexical items by different analysts could lead to different analyses because of the limitations of the investigators' phonological systems. Boas can be aptly described as a student of the natural sciences (his doctoral degree at Kiel was in the natural sciences); a major scholar of Amerindian languages; a linguist, phonetician, anthropologist. He is credited with having been a prime mover in forging the tools of the phonetic and structural description of many Amerindian languages. Thus Boas is claimed by more than one discipline; and if he is perhaps primarily not a phonetician, no student of his work can fairly deny him the title.

Nor can less be said of his student Sapir, whom Boas called, in the obituary he wrote for Sapir in IJAL (1939), "one of the most brilliant scholars in linguistics and anthropology." An investigation of his famous monograph on Southern Paiute shows him as a brilliant student of phonetics. Sapir is credited by some as one of the pioneers in the United States in the development of phonemic analysis. Sapir's disciplines or areas of expertise include Germanic languages, anthropology, Amerindian languages, mythology, and linguistics—to each of which he made major contributions. We too claim him as a phonetician, and recognize his contribution to the discipline as a major one.

No one would think of Benjamin Franklin, at first glance as "one of us" and perhaps he isn't. A founding father of this country, he was a noted world figure of the 18th century—diplomat, author, printer, inventor. Franklin's "Scheme for a new alphabet and Reformed Words of Spelling" (which he wrote in 1768) strongly influenced Noah Webster and others who followed. That "Scheme" was a remarkably accurate phonetic system of spelling. It alone should assure Franklin's place as a contributor to this discipline and no one may really deny us that privilege. If he belongs more obviously elsewhere, as he does, he belongs and is in our history and we are pleased that we can so claim him.

If one moves to the natural sciences, a number of contributors to our discipline come to mind. One of the more eminent figures is Alexander Ellis, who made significant contributions to mathematical theory and analysis in the mid-19th century. Nor can we belittle Ellis' reputation in theoretical/physical music, such stemming directly from his interest in the physical production of vowels. This major contributor to speech and phonetics brought his influence to bear on a number of 19th century figures--school book authors like Richard Soule, lexicographers like Dan Smalley, phoneticians like Henry Sweet. Ellis' monumental work <u>On Early English Pronunciation</u> (in 5 parts, 1869-1889) raised him to major stature in the field of the history of the English language, perhaps eclipsing the contribution he had already made to mathematics, earlier in his life. Ellis is a noted historical figure in more than one discipline, and one of those was ours!

Another eminent contributor to the phonetic sciences was surely Christian Kratzenstein, the 18th century experimental physicist and noted specialist in electromagnetics, metallurgy, geology, navigation, and medicine. Kratzenstein's interests led him into the area we know today as experimental/acoustic phonetics. He is certainly a pioneer in the area of speech synthesis and sound simulation. Our current practitioners, whether they know the history of our discipline or not, are much in his debt.

Our list of phoneticians, who were also noted contributors to other disciplines or of scholars in other areas who made important contributions to the study and application of the phonetic sciences, can be extended at length. We add only a few here: Agostino Gemelli, medical doctor and psychiatrist, founder of the first Psychiatric Hospital in Italy during World War I, acoustician whose contributions to acoustic/experimental phonetics between the 1930's and 1950's are listed in many bibliographies; George Bernard Shaw, major British playwright, music and theatre critic, whose concern with spelling reform led not only to the provision in his will for a reformed English alphabet, but to the development of the I(nitial) T(eaching) A(lphabet) in British schools and elsewhere and whose Pygmalion brought "phoneticians" like "Henry Higgins" to the attention of the world; Sir Robert

Bridges, 16th poet laureate of England, who, with Sir Walter
Raleigh, Henry Bradley, and Logan Pearsall Smith, founded
the Society of Pure English in 1913 and who acted as the
head of the BBC Advisory Committee on Spoken English in the
1920's; George Lyman Kittredge, called "the most widely
learned literary scholar /of his time/ in America" whose
interests ranged from the literatures and languages of the
classical and western European languages to lexicography,
Virgil, Chaucer, Shakespeare, folklore, witchcraft, and
balladry--and who also wrote on the pronunciation of English
and some of its dialects; Sir William Jones, 18th century
comparative legal scholar, judge, noted colonial administra-
tor from Britain to Asia, who was one of the first to methodi-
cally use native informants for a systematic investigation of
unknown languages and whose tranliterating system of Arabic,
Sanskrit, and Persian lexical items was a miniature early
International Phonetic Alphabet.

Add to these people like Charles Hockett whose contributions to linguistics and phonology are known to all of us
here but whose vita also contains references to over 50
musical compositions from sonatas for oboe and piano, to
songs for tenors and baritones, to a concertino for cello and
woodwind, to organ fugues; or Kenneth Pike whose prowress as
a practical and theoretical phonetician is legendary--and who
is no less a scholar of the Old and New Testaments, a published poet, the head of a Bible Society, and surely one of
the truly talented actors/performers on any academic stage.

You add others--they exist all through our profession
from Dionysius of Thrace and Aristotle the Ionian to our
colleagues Lou Gerstman and Katherine Harris, experimental
psychologists from our own City University of New York. Isn't
it nice to be able to say that many of your colleagues were
and are Renaissance Men and Women of Academia? We are indeed
proud to do so.

NOTES

[1]A third subject was studied, but the EMG signals from this
subject's tongue muscles were all well below 100 μ V and
therefore considered too low to permit claims or inferences.
[2]Also studied, for other purposes, were the orbicularis oris,
anterior belly of the digastric, and the internal pterygoid
muscles. Since the results are irrelevant to this investigation of gestural antagonism in tongue movements, they will
not be reported here.
[3]From "The Reflection of Social Processes in Linguistic
Structures," by William Labov, in Readings in the Sociology
of Language, edited by J. Fishman, Mouton (1968), pp. 248
and 250-251.
[4]All of these instances are developed further in the recently
issued Biographical Dictionary of the Phonetic Sciences, ed.
by A. Bronstein, L. Raphael, Cj Stevens, Lehman, 1977.

TOWARD A HISTORIOGRAPHY OF PHONETICS

E. F. K. KOERNER
University of Ottawa

T. S. Kuhn's The Structure of Scientific Revolutions
first appeared in 1962. In the same year, Chomsky made a
number of excursions into the history of linguistics, at
the Ninth International Congress of Linguists held in
Cambridge, Massachusetts. Soon afterwards, scholars concerned with linguistic historiography began to ask whether
observations and theories put forward by Kuhn for the history of science could be applied to the history of a discipline such as the study of language. The discussion
ranged from uncritical application of Kuhnian conceptions
of how one particular view of science is replaced by another
--conceptions largely advocated by linguists with trans-
formational-generative persuasions who felt their understanding of linguistic science eclipsed the one established
by the preceding generation--to an outright rejection of
Kuhn's proposals for the treatment of the history of linguistics. The acceptance or rejection of Kuhn's ideas seems
to hinge largely on the question of whether or not linguistics does in fact qualify as a science in the Kuhnian sense
of the term.

It is interesting to note that historians of linguistics
have almost exclusively concerned themselves with the presentation of the development of the study of language in terms
of grammatical theories and linguistic philosophy; in other
words, they have tended to disregard by and large that branch

of language study that could most likely compare with the
natural sciences and thus support the claim of those in
whose opinion linguistics should be recognized as a science,
namely, phonetics--the study of speech sounds and their
production, control as well as their teaching (Jones, 1948).
The traditional neglect of this aspect of linguistics by
the historians of the discipline appears the more surprising
if we note that human curiosity about the phenomena of
speech production can at least be documented as having a
tradition certainly no shorter than the Indian grammarians'
analysis of Sanskrit (Allen, 1953; Al-George, 1966) and the
Ancients' reflection upon language, its meaning and use
(cf. Robins' (1957) study on Dionysius Thrax). Indeed, it
would appear that the historical and archaeological evidence
available to the present (e.g., from stone carvings) suggests a very early interest in the physiological explanation
of the human voice going back at least three millenia
(Panconcelli-Calzia, 1961). In other words, the fact that
the term 'phonetics' appears to have been first proposed by
the Danish scholar Georg Zoega (1755-1809) only in 1797
(Zwirner & Zwirner, 1966:18) should not be taken to suggest
that the science of sound did not begin much earlier; we
would have to take a similar conclusion from the fact that
'linguistics' is an early 19th-century coinage.

    It must appear still more surprising to see a scholar
pretending to write an historical overview on what he terms
the 'biological basis of language' (Marx, 1967) expressly
leaving aside phonetic studies (p. 465, note 1, where he
refers the reader to Panconcelli-Calzia, 1940, 1941, and
1961). In view of such strange neglect of the field of
phonetics in linguistic historiography one may only
speculate whether an explanation for this should be
sought in the structuralists' tendency (noticeable
already in Trubetzkoy's work, at least on the theoretical
level) to relegate phonetics to the position of a mere
ancillary to linguistics proper (cf. Halliday, 1961).
This tendency leads to extreme claims, as in the case of
Klaus Heger, who suggested, in a heated discussion with a
Scandinavian linguist with strong phonetic leanings at a
linguistics meeting two years ago, that the less a phonolo-
gist knew about phonetics the better for his theory.

Happily neither all modern linguists nor all historians
of linguistics share such an extreme view regarding the place
of phonetics within the science of language. Indeed, it
would seem that in particular those scholars concerned with
the teaching of language in addition to their general interest
in linguistic theory have not only always regarded phonetics
as an integral part of linguistics but have also frequently
concerned themselves with their scientific ancestors. It
may be appropriate in the present context to refer to at
least some of these scholars.

Where the past century is concerned, at least three
linguists come to mind who contributed to the advancement
of phonetics and engaged in the teaching of modern languages
and in addition devoted considerable attention to the history of phonetic studies, namely, Friedrich Techmer (1843-
1891), Wilhelm Viëtor (1850-1918), and Otto Jespersen
(1860-1943). Of these three scholars Techmer appears to
be the least known, and yet his contribution to the history
of phonetics (as well as to the science of phonetics itself)
was by no means small (cf. Seelmann, 1892:1-8 passim;
Koerner, 1973:3-7). It was of Techmer's Beiträge to the
history of French and English phonetics and phonography
(Techmer, 1890) that Viëtor said after the author's death:
"Had the author,. . ., left us only these 'Beiträge', a
grateful remembrance of him with all colleagues would be
secured as a thorough expert and discerning scholar."
(Quoted from an English rendering in Koerner, 1973:7).
Techmer had edited large excerpts from John Wilkins' (1614-
1672) famous Essay towards a Real Character and a Philosophi-
cal Language (1668) and from Jacobus Matthiae Arhusiensis
(alias Jacob Madsen (of) Aarhus, 1538-1586) De Literis Libri
duo (1586) in his journal, Internationale Zeitschrift für
Allgemeine Sprachwissenschaft, adding detailed introductions
to both in which the historical development of phonetics was
sketched. (Panconcelli-Calzia, writing two generations
later, still made frequent reference to Techmer's findings.)

Wilhelm Viëtor was one of the promoters of the practical
study of language in Germany during the late 19th and early
20th century. His interest in the history of the subject
was quite conspicuous; it began with his 1886 edition of

Christoph Friedrich Hellwag's (1754-1835) <u>Dissertatio</u>
<u>inauguralis physicomedica de formatione loquela</u> (1781),
and did not cease before his 1917/18 edition of Johann
Conrad Amman's (1669-1724) <u>Dissertatio de loquela</u> (1700).
In between Viëtor published a number of articles devoted
to the history of phonetics, in his own journal, <u>Phonetische</u>
<u>Studien</u> (cf. Viëtor, 1888/90), as well as in other places,
and encouraged others to do like-wise (e.g., Swoboda, 1891).

Jespersen, as is customary among many phoneticians, in
particular those with Scandinavian or German backgrounds,
added an historical survey of phonetics, from John Hart
(d. 1574) and Mattiae to his own contemporaries, to his
Danish textbook on phonetics (Jespersen, 1897:16-62).
During 1905-06 he revised and extended his account for a
German periodical, republishing it in 1933. (Jespersen's
writings on the history of linguistics are well-known and
need not be referred to here.) Much useful information,
not only on the study of phonetics between 1876 and the
mid-1890s but also on the work devoted to its history, may
be gleaned from Hermann Breymann's (1843-1910) bibliographi-
cal survey of 1897. Scholars well read in the literature
will easily be able to add other names of scholars in the
past century who wrote on the history of phonetics, though
such a list would not be very long (cf. Austerlitz, 1975).

Among the scholars born during the last decades of the
19th century there are at least four scholars who contributed,
all in the later years of their careers, to the history of
phonetics: two Italian-born physiologists, who had turned
their attention to phonetics, namely, Guglielmo Bilancioni
(1831-1935) and Giulio Panconcelli-Calzia (1878-1966),
the British linguist John Rupert Firth (1890-1960),and a
North American scientist who is hardly ever mentioned in
the annals of the discipline, Dayton Clarence Miller (1866-
1941). Next to Miller, whose <u>Anecdotal History of the</u>
<u>Science of Sound</u> of 1935 is certainly worth consulting,
Bilancioni is the least known of these scholars, probably
because he published only in his mother-tongue. He had a
long-standing interest in the work of Dante, particularly
with respect to the poet's references to phonetics and
phoniatrics, and in 1927 Bilancioni published a study on the

conceptions of sound and voice in Dante. In his journal
founded two years earlier, Il Valsalva (named after the
Italian physiologist Antonio Maria Valsalva (1666-1723),
who is best remembered for his work on the ear), Bilancioni
published a series of articles of historical interest (cf.
Panconcelli-Calzia, 1941:88, for details), of which one on
Giorgio Bartoli (fl. 1584) may be mentioned here (Bilancioni,
1931).

Panconcelli-Calzia, Bilancioni's countryman, spent most
of his life in Germany, as a university professor and
director of the Phonetisches Laboratorium in Hamburg (cf.
Wängler, 1959 and Zwirner, 1967, for details), a position
which he handed over to his pupil Otto von Essen in 1950
(cf. Bronstein et al., 1977:56). Panconcelli-Calzia's
mastering of his subject matter was based on a distinguished
background in physiology and speech therapy. His Geschichtszahlen der Phonetik (1941), together with his
Quellenatlas (1940), must still today be regarded as one
of the most important sources of information on the development of the phonetic sciences. (It is therefore to be welcomed that J.-P. Köster of the University of Trier is
currently engaged in preparing a re-edition of these two
volumes, together with a bio-bibliographical account of the
author.) In 1942, Panconcelli-Calzia published two further
studies, one devoted to Leonardo da Vinci as a phonetician,
the other bringing together references to phonetic observations in the work of Aristotle (Panconcelli-Calzia, 1942a
and b). Indeed he continued his labours in this field after
the Second World War (cf. Austerlitz, 1975:1199, for details),
concluding with a 140-page study entitled 3000 Jahre Stimm-
forschung (1961).

The youngest of the four distinguished scholars born
towards the end of the 19th century who contributed to our
understanding of the tradition within which phoneticians
of today are working (particularly in the English-speaking
lands) is J. R. Firth, the first Englishman ever to hold a
chair in General Linguistics in Britain. Both the long-
standing tradition in phonetic work (of which Firth was
very conscious) and the particular impetus given to this
field by the institute with which he was associated (namely,

the School of Oriental and African Studies at the University
of London) explain the emphasis laid on phonetics in his
writings. His two popular expositions of linguistics of
the 1930s. Speech (1930) and The Tongues of Men (1937),
which were reissued thirty years later in one volume (Firth,
1964), already contain frequent references to earlier periods
in the study of phonetics; however, the most informative
account he wrote was that on The English School of Phonetics
(Firth, 1946), which traces the development of phonetic work
in Britain from the 17th century to the first half of the
20th century.

      The mid-thirties did see contributions by a younger
generation of phoneticians and other linguists interested
in the history of phonetic work and adjacent areas of research. These include P. Moore's Short History of Laryngeal
Investigation (1937) and M. Lehnert's Die Anfänge der
wissenschaftlichen und praktischen Phonetik in England (1938)
among others (e.g., Møller, 1931, Abercrombie, 1937). The
most important publication of this period, however, was
E. Zwirner's Bemerkungen zur Geschichte der Phonetik, which
he added, with a view to strengthening his own theoretical
position, to his and K. Zwirner's Grundfragen der Phono-
metrie (1936:6-59). Thirty years later, in 1966, Zwirner
expanded the historical portion considerably, to the extent
that it may be regarded as the most thorough treatment of
the history of phonetics to date. (Curiously enough,
Austerlitz (1975:1209) does not seem aware of this.) Zwirner's
account was made available in English in 1970, and for anyone
concerned with presenting aspects or periods of the development of the phonetic sciences in the Western tradition this
study may be recommended as a good model of how the subject
matter should be treated (cf. Koerner, 1971, for a critical
account).

      Apart from R. B. Lindsay's Historical Introduction
(1945) to a much larger work, Firth's (1946) article (already mentioned toward the end of section 2), and D.
Abercrombie's masterly study of 1948, Forgotten Phoneticians,
the 1940s saw little on the history of phonetics. The 1950s
witnessed a revival of interest in this field, with a definite Anglo-American preeminence. We may refer to a number

of publications that followed H. W. Dudley and T. H.
Tarnóczy's article on The Speaking Machine of W. von
Kempelen in 1950. They include D. Abercrombie's (1951)
essay on Joshua Steele (1700-1791), Monboddo (1714-1799),
and the famous actor David Garrick (1717-1779) and issues
relating to elocution; W. S. Allen's 'appreciation of the
earliest phoneticians,' Phonetics in Ancient India (1953);
the late R. W. Albright's (1913-1972) dissertation of 1953
on the pre-history and the history that led to the establishment of the International Phonetic Alphabet at the
turn of this century (Albright, 1958); J. F. Curtis' article
on The Rise of Experimental Phonetics (1954); Cj Stevens'
paper on John Pickering's (1777-1846) On the Adoption of a
Uniform Orthography of 1821 (1956); and E. J. Dobson's
voluminous study of 1957 on English Pronunciation, 1500-
1700 (cf. Kökeritz' (1961) review), to mention but a few.

   The 1960s, with its awakening interest in the history
of linguistics, saw comparatively little in the area of the
history of phonetics, perhaps simply because most scholars
were busy with carrying ahead phonetic research proper.
Brief historical surveys as found in manuals such as Julius
Laziczius' (1896-1957) Lehrbuch der Phonetik (1961:3-11)
or O. von Essen's Allgemeine und angewandte Phonetik (1963:
2-8) date from the 1940s or 1950s. E. R. Moses' venture
into the history of phonetics (1954), for example, did not
find unanimous acceptance among scholars well read in the
literature (e.g., Abercrombie, 1966). The most important
achievement of the mid-1960s is undoubtedly the revised and
much enlarged Remarks on the history of phonetics (1970;
German original 1966:17-110) by E. Zwirner mentioned above.
Of course, a considerable number of articles appeared in
this decade that concerned themselves with either particular observations made by scholars of earlier periods in the
history of phonetics (e.g., Ricken, 1965, Vértes, 1963) or
with the development of particular branches of the phonetic
sciences (e.g., Scholz, 1966; Mettas, 1964), but these
publications do not differ much from writings that appeared
in previous decades. (Cf. the bibliography in Köster, 1973:
439-536, for details.)

In contrast to the fairly dull 1960s, it appears that
the 1970s are much more promising with regard to work done
in the history of phonetics. Following the appearance of
B. Malmberg's Reflexions sur l'histoire de la phonétique,
which the author included in his survey of the phonetic
sciences (Malmberg, 1971:17-42, the Swedish original appeared
in 1969), 1970 saw the facsimile-reprint of Gerauld de
Cordemoy's (1620-1684) Discours physique de la parole (1677;
cf. Brekle, 1970) as well as Wolfgang von Kempelen's (1724-
1804) Mechanismus der menschlichan Sprachs (1791; cr. ed. by
Brekle & Wildgen, 1970). This was followed in 1972 by
J. A. Kemp's bilingual edition, together with an introductory
article, of John Wallis' (1616-1703) Grammatica linguae
Anglicanae (1653), which Wallis prefaced by a 'tractatus
grammatico-physicus' on the formation of speech sounds.
Brekle provides informative (largely bio-bibliographical)
introductions to his facsimili-editions, and throughout
his comments on Wallis Kemp makes comparisons with other
phoneticians of the period, in Britain as well as on the
Continent (esp. Matthiae, Montamus, and Amman). In 1973 a
540-page study appeared by a promising scholar in the field
which combines a thorough knowledge of the science of
phonetics with a good deal of background information in
this area: J.-P. Köster's Historische Entwicklung von
Syntheseapparaten zur Erzeugung statischer und vokalartiger
Signale devotes large portions (in fact pp. 16-409 passim)
to the delineation of the development of the phonetic
sciences from the late medieval period (cf. Vértes, 1963,
with regard to Albertus Magnus) through the Renaissance
and the next centuries up to the present. Köster presents
in particular detailed accounts of the mechanical speech
synthesizers built by mathematicians and engineers such as
Christian Gottlieb Kratzenstein (1723-95),Abbé Mical (1730-
1789), and Kempelen (see pp. 68-81, 81-93 and 94-127,
respectively). Where the 19th century is concerned, the
work of Robert Willis (1800-1875), the Viennese mathematician
Joseph Faber (cf. Gariel, 1879), and Hermann von Helmholtz
(1821-1894) are treated extensively (pp. 131-39, 142-48 and
159-83, respectively). The past one hundred years have witnessed a considerable advance in many branches of the phonetic
sciences, viz. in acoustic, physiological, experimental, and
many other areas of phonetics, and Köster's narrative

reflects this progress very well through an increase in
density with regard to both the general argument and the
technical knowledge the author displays. (Köster, 1976,
constitutes a summary treatment of subject of his 1973
book.)

In 1974 J. Kramský's book The Phoneme was published.
It includes a chapter on The Prehistory of the Phoneme
(pp. 9-20), which goes back to the Ancients and the classical Indian grammarians, as well as another entitled The
Discovery of the Phoneme (21-31). The latter, however, is
entirely based on secondary sources and does not always
supply the reader with accurate information on the first
coinage (in 1873) of the term 'phoneme' and its involved
subsequent history (cf. Koerner, 1976, 1978). E. Fischer-
Jørgensen's 'historical introduction' of 1975, Trends in
Phonological Theory, by comparison, contains much more
reliable data on the development of the phoneme-concept from
the end of the 19th century to the individual 'schools' of
phonology up to around 1970. In view of the particular
goal of the book, namely, to present the phonological
theories of 20-th century structuralist trends, the pioneers
of 'classical phonetics' such as Sweet, Passy, Jespersen,
and others are presented only briefly, the acknowledged
forerunners of structural phonology, Baudouin de Courtenay,
Kruszewski, Winteler, and Saussure being treated somewhat
more extensively. A particularly valuable feature of Fischer-
Jørgensen's voluminous study is that she has included an
entire chapter on Phonological Theory in the Soviet Union
(pp. 320-63), which offers brief accounts of scholars such
as L. V. Ščerba (1880-1944), E. D. Polivanov (1891-1938),
S. I. Bernštejn (1892-1970), and others, although the bulk
of her survey is devoted to more recent structuralist views,
in particular the theories advanced by S. K. Šaumjan. (Cf.
also Vachek's (1976) review of Fischer-Jørgensen's book.)

Another 1975 publication deserves particular attention
in the present overview, namely, Austerlitz' bibliography,
intended as a basis for 'the future historian of phonetics.'
Austerlitz judiciously includes a number of references to
earlier contributors to the field, e.g., works by Ernst
Brücke (1819-1892), Eduard Sievers (1850-1932), and many

other distinguished 19th century scholars mentioned earlier
in this paper. However, the inclusion of a considerable
number of late 19th and especially 20th century publications, which admittedly have little or no historical content, seems superfluous. Indeed, his 30-page bibliography
containing some 950 titles, has pages with hardly more than
2 items which might be regarded as publications devoted to
the history of phonetics (cf. pp. 1184, 1185, 1187, etc.).
Perhaps rather less would have been more useful, particularly since all items are arranged alphabetically by author
with few crossreferences and often much too brief and un-
helpful (at times even misleading) comments. Several
important entries are incomplete and have been drawn from
secondary sources only and not inspected. Even so, despite
these shortcomings, Austerlitz' bibliography is the fullest
listing to date and constitutes a useful tool for anyone
embarking on research in the history of phonetics.

It may not be unduly hazardous to predict that the
next years will see a revival of interest in the history
of phonetics, though probably not in all branches of this
multifacetted discipline. The appearance of a Biographical
Dictionary of the Phonetic Sciences compiled by A. J.
Bronstein, L. J. Raphael and Cj Stevens, to which scholars
throughout the world have contributed individual entries,
will certainly play an important role in this revival.
Further evidence of this renewed interest is the fact that
the organizers of the International Congress of Phonetic
Sciences to be held in Copenhagen, Denmark, in August
1979 have chosen to include a session devoted to the history
of phonetics in their program. Those who have consulted
the proceedings of the international phonetic congresses
held during the past fifty years will realize that this is
an innovation. But nonetheless progress will be relatively
slow, in spite of these hopeful signs, and it will doubtless
take several years more until the history of phonetics
becomes an established subject within the phonetic sciences.

REFERENCES

Abercrombie, D.   (1937).   London, Pitman.
Abercrombie, D.   (1948).   Trans. Phil. Soc., 1-34.
Abercrombie, D.   (1951).   BBC-Broadcast.
Abercrombie, D.   (1965).   London, Oxford Univ. Press.
Abercrombie, D.   (1966).   Phonet., 15:42-43.
Albright, R. W.   (1958).   Baltimore, Waverly Press.
Al-George, S.   (1966).   Cah. Ling. Theor. Appl., 3:11-15.
Allen, W. S.   (1953).   London, Oxford Univ. Press.
Austerlitz, R.   (1975).   The Hague, Mouton, 1179-1209.
Bilancioni, G.   (1927).   Pisa, M. Pacini.
Bilancioni, G.   (1931).   Il Vale., 7:140.
Brekle, H. E.   (1970).   Stuttgart, Frommann-Holzboog.
Brekle, H. E. and Wildgen, W.   (1970).   Stuttgart, Frommann-
    Holzboog.
Breymann, H.   (1897).   Leipzig, Deichert.
Bronstein, J., Raphael, L. J. and Stevens, C.   (1977).
    New York, Press of Lehman College.
Curtis, J. F.   (1954).   New York, Appleton-Century-Crofts,
    348-69.
Dobson, E. J.   (1957).   London, Oxford Univ. Press.
Dudley, H. W. and Tarnóczy, T. H.   (1950).   J. Acoust. Soc.
    Am., 21:151-66.
Essen, O. von.   (1963).   Berlin, Akad.-Verlag.
Firth, J. R.   (1946).   Trans. Phil. Soc., 92-132.
Firth, J. R.   (1964).   London, Oxford Univ. Press.
Fischer-Jørgensen, E.   (1975).   Copenhagen: Akademisk
    Forlag.
Gariel, C. M.   (1879).   J. Phys. Pod., 8:274-75.
Gombocz, Z.   (1909/11).   Nyelvtudómány, 2:241-57 and 3:
    32-38.
Gupta, M. L.   (1972).   The Hague, Mouton, 521-31.
Häusler, F.   (1968).   Halle/S., Niemeyer.
Heepe, M.   (1928).   Berlin, Reichsdruckerei.
Jespersen, O.   (1897).   Copenhagen, Schubothe, 16-62.
Jespersen, O.   (1933).   Copenhagen, Levin & Munksgaard,
    40-80.
Jones, D.   (1948).   Zeit. Phon. All. Sprach., 2:127-35.
Kemp, J. A.   (1972).   London, Longman.
Kneiser, E.   (1930).   Vox, 16,41-52.
Koerner, E. F. K.   (1971).   Phonet., 26:247-52.

Koerner, E. F. K.   (1973).   Amsterdam, Benjamins.
Koerner, E. F. K.   (1976).   Phonet., 33:222-231.
Kökeritz, H.   (1961).   Lang., 37:150-161.
Köster, J.-P.   (1973).   Hamburg, Buske.
Köster, J.-P.   (1976).   Pol. Acad. Sci., 4:41-104.
Köster, J.-P.   (1979).   Amsterdam, Benjamins.
Kortlandt, F. H. H.   (1970).   The Hague, Mouton.
Krámský, J.   (1974).   Munich, Fink.
Laxiczius, J.   (1961).   Berlin, Akad.-Verlag, 3-11.
Lehnert, M.   (1938).   Arch. Stud. Neuer. Sprach. Lit.,
     173:163-80 and 174:28-35.
Lindsay, R. B.   (1945).   New York, Dover.
Malmberg, B.   (1971).   Paris, Presses Univ. de France,
     17-42.
Marx, O.   (1967).   New York, Wiley & Sons, 443-69.
Mettas, O.   (1965).   Trav. Ling. Litt., 3:185-200.
Miller, D. C.   (1935).   New York, Macmillan.
Møller, C.   (1931).   Aarhus, Stiftshostrykkeriet, 41-66.
Moore, P.   (1937).   Quart. J. Speech, 23:531-54.
Moses, E. R.   (1940).   Quart. J. Speech, 26:615-25.
Moses, E. R.   (1964).   Englewood Cliffs, N. J., Prentice-
     Hall.
Panconcelli-Calzia, G.   (1940).   Hamburg, Hansischer
     Gildenverlag.
Panconcelli-Calzia, G.   (1941).   Hamburg, Hansischer
     Gildenverlag.
Panconcelli-Calzia, G.   (1942a).   Hamburg, Hansischer
     Gildenverlag.
Panconcelli-Calzia, G.   (1942b).   Hamburg, Hansischer
     Gildenverlag.
Pipping, H.   (1890).   Helsingfors, Frenckell, 1-15.
Protogenov, S. V.   (1970).   Taškent, "Fan."
Ricken, U.   (1965).   Bucharest, Editura Academiei, 761-65.
Robins, R. H.   (1957).   "Dionysius Thrax and the Western
     Grammatical Tradition." Trans. Phil. Soc., 67-107.
Raudnitzky, H.   (1911).   Marburg, Elwert.
Scholz, H.-J.   (1966).   Phonet., 15:110-21.
Seelmann, E.   (1895).   Krit. Jab. Fort. Roman. Phil.,
     1:1-24.
Stevens, Cj   (1956).   Quart. J. Speech., 42:139-43.
Swoboda, W.   (1891).   Phon. Stud., 4:1-36 and 147-82.
Sweet, H.   (1884).   Trans. Phil. Soc., 84:100-105.

Techmer, F.   (1890).   Ulm, Kerler.
Vértes, À. O.   (1963).   Phonet., 10:80-91.
Viëtor, W.   (1886).   Heilbronn, Henninger.
Vietor, W.   (1888/90).   Phon. Stud., 1:257-61 and 3:43-55.
Vietor, W.   (1917/18).   Berlin, Fischer;   Hamburg, Friede-
   richsen & Co.
Vachek, J.   (1976).   Lingua, 39:165-66.
Wängler, H.-H.   (1959).   Orbis, 8:529-39.
Wildgen, W.   (1973).   Lang. Sci., 24:7-10.
Zemlin, W. R.   (1968).   Englewood Cliffs, N. J., Prentice-
   Hall, 161-69.
Zinder, L. R.   (1960).   Učen. Zap. Leningrad. Univ., No. 237,
   5-25.
Zwirner, E. and Zwirner, K.   (1936).   Berlin, Metten, 6-59.
Zwirner, E. and Zwirner, K.   (1966).   Basel, Karger, 17-110.
Zwirner, E.   (1967).   Phonet., 16:111-15.
Zwirner, E.   (1970).   University, Ala.; Univ. of Alabama
   Press.

Note added in proof

A revised version, with a much more detailed bibliography, of the present article, and subtitled "A Brief Survey of the State of the Art",
appeared in *Festschrift für Otto von Essen* ed. by Hans-Heinrich Wängler and others, 221-37 (Hamburg: Buske, 1978).

Koerner 1978 (inadvertendly omitted in the above References) stands
for my contribution to *Sprache in Gegenwart und Geschichte: Festschrift für Heinrich Matthias Heinrichs* ed. by Dietrich Hartmann
and others, "Zu Ursprung und Entwicklung des Phonem-Begriffs: Eine
historische Notiz" (Cologne & Vienna: Böhlau, 1978), pp.82-93.

GIULIO PANCONCELLI-CALZIAS BEITRAG ZUR GESCHICHTE DER PHONETIK

JENS-PETER KÖSTER
Universität Trier

Fällt bei einer Untersuchung früher klassischer deutscher Phonetiken wie Brückes "Grundzüge" (1856), Sievers' "Grundzüge der Phonetik" (1876), Techmers "Phonetik" (1880), Viëtors "Elemente" (1884) oder gar Grassmanns "Sprachlehre" (1890) mit ihrem fünfzig Seiten starken phonetischen Teil wie auch Sütterlins "Lehre" (1908) auf, dass Fragen zur Geschichte der Phonetik einen recht unterschiedlichen Raum in den Werken einnehmen, so darf dies nicht darüber hinwegtäuschen, dass die Mehrzahl der Vertreter einer sich im Kampf um Autonomie von den etablierten Wissenschaften befindlichen Phonetik historischen Fragen grundsätzlich grosses Interesse entgegenbrachte. Dies bezeugen beispielhaft einmal Brückes, Grassmanns und Sütterlins geschichtliche Darstellungen zu Beginn ihrer Abhandlungen, des weiteren Techmers Einbeziehung früher und frühester phonetischer Erkenntnisse in seine wissenschaftlichen Erörterungen, eine Tendenz,die sich mit besonderer Deutlichkeit in seiner späteren Arbeit von 1883 zur "Naturwissenschaftlichen Analyse und Synthese der hörbaren Sprache" fortsetzen wird, und schliesslich die nach der Jahrhundertwende erschienenen historischen Beitrage Viëtors / Neudrucke von Hellwags "Dissertatio" (1781), Helmonts "Entwurff" (1667) und Ammans "Dissertatio" (1700) / und Techmers / Neudrucke von Wilkins "Essay" (1668) und Matthiaes "De literis" (1586); "Beitrag zur Geschichte der französischen und englischen Phonetik und Phonographie" /.

Wenngleich diese Beobachtung dazu führen muss, den
deutschen Phonetikern des ausgehenden 19. und beginnenden 20.
Jahrhunderts eine relativ einheitliche positive Haltung dem
geschichtlichen Studium ihrer Disziplin gegenüber zu konze-
dieren, so ist andererseits ebenso unübersehbar, dass in
keiner Veröffentlichung dieses Zeitraumes der Versuch eines
umfassenden und systematischen Überblicks über die Leistungen
der phonetischen Forschung früherer Jahrhunderte noch eine
klare Methode zur Erschliessung solcher frühen Erkenntnisse
nachweisbar ist. Das durchweg eklektische Vorgehen legt
deutlich Zeugnis dafür ab, dass sich bei der Phonetikergeneration des späten 19. Jahrhunderts ein neues, his-
torisches Bewusstsein zu entwickeln begann, dessen Impulse
erst im 20. Jahrhundert in systematische Bahnen gelenkt
werden sollten.

Techmers Ansatz nimmt hier eine Sonder- und Brücken-
stellung ein: Einerseits sich historischen Fakten nur
selektiv zum Zwecke der Dialektik in der wissenschaftlichen
Erörterung bedienend, macht er andererseits den Rückgriff auf
frühere Forschungsergebnisse zu einem durchgängigen Prinzip
seines Erkenntnisstrebens und verbindet damit den Eklektizis-
mus seiner Zeitgenossen mit der sich an die Grenze
zur selbständigen Disziplin begebenden phonetischen Geschichtsforschung des 20. Jahrhunderts. Für die Übernahme
des Erbes des letzten Jahrhunderts, seine Weiterentwicklung
und letzliche Ausformung zu einem heuristischen Prinzip
phonetischer Forschung steht in Deutschland ohne jeden
Zweifel ein einziger Name: der Giulio Panconcelli-Calzias!

Als Student hatte der aus seiner italienischen Heimat
nach Paris gelangte junge Panconcelli-Calzia noch regen
Anteil an den Gründerjahren der französischen Experimentalphonetik genommen. Hier leitete der Abbé Rousselot seit 1897
das Laboratorium für experimentelle Phonetik des Collège de
France, und hier war 1899 die erste phonetische Zeitschrift
Frankreichs, "La parole," ins Leben gerufen worden. In
dieser durch steigendes Selbstbewusstsein, Expansionsdrang,
Missionsbedürfnis und Dynamik geprägten Atmosphäre ent-
wickelte sich der Studiosus rasch zu einem engagierten und
habilen Vertreter der Experimentalphonetik. Nach der
Promotion auf Grund einer wissenschaftlichen Abhandlung

über die Nasalität des Italienischen verliess Panconcelli-
Calzia Paris und ging, nach kurzem Zwischenaufenthalt als
Lektor für italienische Sprache und Kultur in Marburg, wohin
er einer Einladung Viëtors gefolgt war, 1910 nach Hamburg.
Am dortigen Seminar für Kolonialsprachen des Kolonialin-
stituts hatte Carl Meinhof in Verbindung mit seinem Lehrstuhl
für Afrikanische Sprachen und Kulturen ein phonetisches
Laboratorium einrichten können, dessen Leitung er dem
zweiunddreissigjährigen Rousselotschüler nur allzugern
anvertraute.

Aus diesen bescheidenen Anfängen führte Panconcelli-
Calzia das Hamburger Phonetische Laboratorium zu einem
Institut von Weltruf. 1919 setzte er seinen Status als
selbständiges Institut durch, verschaffte ihm (zusammen mit
Hermann Gutzmann) in der Vox ein Publikationsorgan, das bis
zu seinem letzten Band ein Forum der deutschen und inter-
nationalen phonetischen Diskussion war, organisierte das
erste grosse internationale Treffen in der Geschichte der
Experimentalphonetik und gab vor, während und nach seiner
Zeit als a.o.pl. Professor der Phonetik und Direktor des
Phonetischen Laboratoriums der Phonetik wesentliche Impulse
auf den Gebieten der phonetischen Analyse romanischer und
afrikanischer Sprachen, der Physiologie, Pathologie und
Therapie der Stimme und Sprache sowie der Reflexion über das
Selbstverständnis der Disziplin, der er sein berufliches und
einen wesentlichen Teil des privaten Lebens gewidmet hatte,
deren Leistungen und Ansprüche.

In inniger Verbindung mit diesen Elementen des
ausserordentlich fruchtbaren Wirkens für die phonetischen
Wissenschaften steht die besondere Leistung Panconcelli-
Calzias auf dem Gebiet der phonetischen Geschichtsforschung.
Eberhard Zwirner (1967) würdigt diese Leistung in seinem
Nachruf mit den Worten: "In dieser Tendenz zu geschichtlicher
... Selbstbestimmung liegt das Besondere an Panconcelli-
Calzia und dasjenige an seinem Lebenswerk, was vorbildlich
bleiben wird." Die Sammlung geschichtlicher Notizen,
Hinweise, Zitate und Dokumente aus dem Bereich der Phonetik
geht bis in die Pariser Periode zurück und ist über die lange
Zeit vor der ersten Veröffentlichung im Jahre 1925 und
darüber hinaus mit Eifer und Hingabe betrieben worden. Im

Gegensatz zur Kontinuität der Datensammlung erfolgten die
Publikationen zu geschichtlichen Themen jedoch ausgesprochen
schubartig. So veröffentlichte Panconcelli-Calzia nach
seinem Aufsatz von 1925 (zur Laryngo-Endoskopie) erst 1931
die folgenden historischen Beiträge, d.s. Ausführungen über
Geronimo Mercurialis Beziehungen zur Phonetik und Phoniatrie
(1931a) sowie Dokumente zur Geschichte der Phonoskopie(1931b)
und Diaphanoskopie (1931c). Den ersten Schwerpunkt stellen
die Jahre 1934 und 1935 mit insgesamt sechs Aufsätzen zu
unterschiedlichen Themen dar, gefolgt von den veröffent-
lichungsreichen Jahren 1937/38. Die Vierzigerjahre bringen
dann in schneller Abfolge vier historische Monographien
hervor, die den hervorragenden Ruf Panconcelli-Calzias als
phonetischen Historiker endgültig begründen. Die Zwischen-
phasen der geschichtlichen Arbeiten fallen somit in die Jahre
1926-1930, 1932/33, 1936 und 1939. In seinen letzten
Arbeiten (1957/61) schöpft der Emeritus erneut aus seiner
reichhaltigen historischen Belegsammlung, muss hier jedoch
bereits vielfach auf veröffentlichtes Material zurückgreifen,
so dass diesen Arbeiten ein sekundärer Rang im Gesamtschaffen
zugewiesen werden muss.

Eine thematische Analyse erlaubt, das historische
Gesamtwerk Panconcelli-Calzias in drei Gruppen zu fassen.
Dabei ist das zentrale Anliegen der ersten, einen so umfassenden wie systemmatischen Überblick über die Entwicklung der
Phonetik von den frühen Hochkulturen bis in die Neuzeit zu
geben; die zweite stellt Persönlichkeiten in den Mittelpunkt,
in deren Werke bedeutende Aussagen zu Problemen der phonetischen Forschung gemacht werden, deren Auswirkungen die
Entwicklung der phonetischen Wissenschaften teilweise
nachhaltig beeinflusst haben; die dritte Gruppe schliesslich
umfasst alle übrigen Veröffentlichungen, welche sich
vornehmlich auf Untersuchungstechniken und Instrumente
beziehen, die im Rahmen der Experimentalphonetik Verwendung
fanden und in weiterentwickelter Form auch heute noch als
Hilfsmittel benutzt werden. Bei dem durchaus naheliegenden
Unterfangen, in die Fülle des gesammelten historischen
Materials zu einem gegebenen Zeitpunkt Ordnung zu bringen
und dem gewählten Ordnungsprinzip entsprechend darzustellen,
hat Panconcelli-Calzia zwei Wege beschritten, die sich
gegenseitig sinnvoll ergänzen. Der erste führt über die zum

Zeitpunkt des Erscheinens des Werkes kaum bestrittene
klassische stoffliche Ordnung des phonetischen Wissen-
schaftsbereiches und trägt somit zur Festigung einer auf
naturwissenschaftlicher Einsicht gegründeten gewachsenen
Systematik bei (Quellenatlas zur Geschichte der Phonetik,
1940), der zweite orientiert sich am trivialen Prinzip
chronologischer Ordnung, die ihre eigentliche Sinngebung
jedoch durch die Verbindung der historischen Ereignisse mit
kulturhistorischen Sternstunden erfährt (Geschichtszahlen
der Phonetik, 1941).

Der Autor war sich bei der Veröffentlichung des
"Quellenatlas" und der "Geschichtszahlen" der Gefahr der
Unvollständigkeit und der Schwierigkeiten, die die Gewichtung
der Eintragungen mit sich bringen musste, vollauf bewusst,
und so bezeichnet er diese Arbeiten (freilich in viel zu
grosser Bescheidenheit) als "anspruchslose Stichproben"
(1941).   Natürlich haben spätere Beiträge zu geschichtlichen Ereignissen in der Phonetik manche Lücke geschlossen
und auch Verbesserungen vorgeschlagen (Essen, 1966; Koerner,
1978; Köster, 1973; Martens, 1972; Wängler, 1960 and 1972),
aber dies schmälert in keiner Weise das wesentliche Verdienst,
welches sich Panconcelli-Calzia mit der Vorlage eines Gerüsts
für 3000 Jahre phonetischer Geschichte erworben hat. Der den
Phonetikern, Linguisten, Sprachphysiologen, -pathologen und
-therapeuten an die Hand gegebene geschichtliche Überblick
ist nämlich mehr als eine blosse Sammlung von ca. 450
Eintragungen: es handelt sich vielmehr um eine durch
kritische Gewichtung wohlselektierte Anzahl von Belegen und
durch "geistige Verarbeitung" (1941) gewertete Ereignisse aus
der Geschichte der Phonetik. Durch eben diese Selektion und
geistige Bewertung aber erhalten die Sammlungen zur
Geschichte der Phonetik einen über den historischen Belang
hinausgehenden Anspruch, zur Selbstreflexion und Abgrenzung
des Faches und indirekt auch zum Problem seiner Erkennt-
niserschliessung einen wesentlichen Beitrag geleistet zu
haben. Auf Grund dieser Zielsetzung dürfte auch der
Entschluss gefallen sein, die geschichtlichen Übersichten
nicht auf Fachteile zu begrenzen, sondern "die Phonetik in
ihrer Gesamtheit ... (zu berücksichtigen) ..., d.h. vom
normalen und pathologischen, sowie vom theoretischen und
angewandten Standpunkt aus" zu beleuchten.

Entsprechen die beiden letzten grösseren Arbeiten
Panconcelli-Calzias (1957-1961) zum geschichtlichen
Problemkreis sowohl in bezug auf die Intention, in der sie
geschrieben wurden, als auch hinsichtlich ihres Charakters
dem "Quellenatlas" und den "Geschichtszahlen," so gilt dies
nicht für die frühe Monographie "Phonetik und Kultur" (1938).
Was die o.g. Klassifizierung der Veröffentlichungen Panconcelli-Calzias zum Bereich der Geschichte der Phonetik
anbelangt, ist dieses Werk eher ein hybrides Gebilde. In
ihm deuten sich die grossen geschichtlichen Übersichten
genauso an wie die Abhandlungen zu Aristoteles und Leonardo.
Ausserdem ist die Idee der Verbindung phonetischer historischer Ereignisse mit Entwicklungen des allgemeinen
kulturellen Rahmens - ein wesentlicher Charakterzug der
"Geschichtszahlen" - direkt auf diese Veröffentlichung
zurückzuführen: "In den nachfolgenden Arbeiten habe ich mich
bemüht zu zeigen, welch lebendiges Bild fachgeschichtliche
Darstellungen ergeben, wenn die betreffende Wissenschaft in
Beziehung zu den übrigen Erscheinungen des kulturellen Lebens
gebracht wird." Es wird hier, ungebunden von den für die
geschichtlichen Überblicke so charakteristischen Prinzip der
extremen stofflichen Begrenzung, am Beispiel der Interaktion
zwischen Kenntnissen über den phonetischen Aspekt beim Singen
und Sprechen und der bildenden Kunst (exemplifiziert an der
Kirchenplastik und Malerei des Mittelalters, Leonardo da
Vinci, Tizian, Raphael, del Piombe, Hals, Brouwer, van
Ostade, van Steen, Schwind, Doumier, Degas, Busch, Högfeld,
Petersen) wie auch literarischen Werken die enge Verbindung
der Phonetik mit dem sie umgebenden kulturellen Rahmen im
historischen Aufriss dargestellt. Die Abhandlungen "Zur
Geschichte der Stimmgabel und ihre Verwendung in der Ex-
perimentalphonetik" sowie "Über Entstehung und Entwicklung
der Sprechschreibmaschine" setzen die in den geschichtlichen
Aufsätze bis 1938 ausgebildete Tradition der Darstellung der
Entwicklung phonetischer Techniken und Instrumente fort.

Den Kern der zweiten Gruppe historischer Schriften
Panconcelli-Calzias stellen die Monographien über
Aristoteles (1942) und Leonardo da Vinci (1943) dar.
Beide finden sie ihre indirekte Vorankündigung in den
Ausführungen zu Geronimo Mercurialis (1931) die letztere
ausserdem und in direkter Weise durch den Beitrag zu

Leonardo. In seiner Arbeit über Aristoteles hat Panconcelli-
Calzia nicht nur ein neues, vollständiges und objektives
Bild von den phonetischen Erkenntnissen des griechischen
Gelehrten gezeichnet, sondern auch die bis dahin gemachten
Äusserungen über Aristoteles' Verdienst als Phonetiker
einer entscheidenden Korrektur unterzogen. Die Erörterung
bleibt auch nicht auf Aristoteles beschränkt, sondern
spiegelt in Vorgängern (Hippokrates, Plato) und Nachfolgern
die Evolution bestimmter Themen in ihrer Gesamtheit wider:
z.B. das Hören, die Atmung, die Phonation, die Artikulation,
der Schall.

Angeregt durch die Vorstudien zu dem 1938 unter dem
Titel "Leonardo glottologo" erschienenen Aufsatz, konzen-
trierte sich Panconcelli-Calzia in den nachfolgenden Jahren
auf die Herausarbeitung der phonetischen Anteile im Werke
Leonardo da Vincis. Die Ergebnisse dieser Arbeiten sollten
ursprünglich als dritter Band einer Trilogie "Aristoteles,
Galen, Leonardo da Vinci" erscheinen, jedoch "übte (Leonardo)
eine derartige Anziehungskraft auf (ihn) aus, dass (er) Galen
übersprang." Der Plan, auch Galen eine Monographie zu
widmen, ist übrigens auch später nicht mehr realisiert worden.
Die in Verbindung mit dem Werk über Aristoteles genannten
Vorzüge gelten uneingeschränkt auch für seine Abhandlung über
Leonardo. Das Vorgehen ähnelt stark dem Ansatz von 1940, d.h.
auch hier werden erst nach einer eingehenden Besprechung der
Arbeiten über Leonardo als Phonetiker, deren Würdigung und
Kritik (z.B. Ablehnung der Theorie von der Existenz eines
gesonderten Werkes über die Stimme; Feststellung, dass
Leonardo die Stimmlippen weder beschrieben noch gezeichnet
hat), die breit verstreuten Bemerkungen des italienischen
Universalgenies zu Fragen der Phonetik gesammelt und unter
den Punkten des von Panconcelli-Calzia bekannten stofflichen
Ordnungsschemas abgehandelt. Wie bei Aristoteles, wird
besonderer Wert auf erkenntnistheoretische Grundlagen und
die Einbettung der besonderen Leistung Leonardos im Rahmen
des geschichtlichen Wandels der Einsichten über aufgegriffene
Themen gelegt. Dabei war naheliegend, dem Verhältnis
Leonardos zu seinem Zeitgenossen Vesal besondere Aufmerk-
samkeit zu widmen. An Hand einer Reihe gewichtiger Gründe
wird eine direkte gegenseitige Beeinflussung der aus beider
Feder stammenden Anatomien ausgeschlossen.

		Von den Artikeln der dritten Gruppe befassen sich viele
mit physiologischen Untersuchungsmethoden (und hier vor
allem dem technischen Aspekt), deren Geschichte und deren
Anwendungsmöglichkeiten im experimentalphonetischen Bereich
diskutiert werden. Diese Aufsätze stellen den Beginn des
stark geschichtlich geprägten Teils des schriftlichen
Lebenswerkes Panconcelli-Calzias dar. Einen zweiten
Schwerpunkt bilden solche Beiträge, in denen Themen der
Sprech- und Sprachstörungen aufgegriffen werden. Die sich
in Artikeln widerspiegelnde Sicherheit der Erörterung von
Problemen aus dem Grenzgebiet der Phonetik zur Medizin ist
nicht verwunderlich. Schon als Student hatte sich Pancon-
celli-Calzia stark für die medizinischen Fächer interessiert
und wohl auch zeitweilig den Wunsch gehegt, Arzt zu werden.
Die Vorliebe für medizinische Fragen durchzieht sein ganzes
Lebenswerk und fand ihre gerechtfertigte Anerkennung in der
Verleihung des medizinischen Doktorgrades ehrenhalber. Das
Aufgreifen sprachpathologischer Fragen ist aus der Sicht der
Hamburger Schule eine selbstverständliche Aufgabe des Phone-
tikers, dessen Forschungsgegenstand die normalen und anomalen
Verhaltnisse der gesprochenen Sprache sein sollen. Aber auch
die institutionelle Verantwortlichkeit des phonetischen
Laboratoriums für die Betreuung der Gehörlosen-, Hörge-
schädigten- und Sprachbehindertenpädagogik steht als Motivation hinter den Veröffentlichungen dieser Thematik. Eine
dritte Konzentration von historischen Artikeln ergibt sich
schliesslich für den gennematischen Bereich.

		Das geschichtliche Werk Panconcelli-Calzias liegt vor
unseren Augen. Es zeugt von ungeheurem Forschungsdrang und
unerschöpflicher Arbeitskraft und hinterlässt der nachfolgenden Phonetikergeneration einen so reichhaltigen Schatz wie
ein gewichtiges Erbe. Der Rahmen dieser Betrachtung erlaubt
es nicht, die gefällten Urteile über seinen Stellenwert im
einzelnen zu begründen. Dies muss einer kommenden
Veröffentlichung vorbehalten bleiben (Köster, 1978). Die
Herausforderung, die das Werk darstellt, wurde in der
Folgezeit angenommen, ja, es darf durchaus als Auslöser einer
neuen Bewegung der phonetischen Historiographie angesehen
werden (Koerner, 1978). Diese Strömung erbringt in immer
deutlicherem Masse Leistungen für ein besseres Selbstverständnis der phonetischen Wissenschaften und wirkt sich im

Sinne Panconcelli-Calzias immer fruchtbringender auf die
Suche nach neuer Erkenntnis aus: "Wer sich nämlich
einbildet, seinem Fach zu neuen Wegen zu verhelfen, ohne
die Entwicklungsgeschichte desselben gründlich zu kennen,
der wird Nacherfindungen leicht, Neues dagegen selten und
dann nur zufällig zustandebringen" (1942).

GIULIO PANCONCELLI-CALZIAS HISTORISCHE SCHRIFTEN

(1925). Über den heutigen Stand der Laryngo-Endoskopie in
Deutschland vom experimentalphonetischen Standpunkt aus. Zs. Lar. Rhin. Otol. 14:137 ff.

(1931a). Geronimo Mercurialis Beziehungen zur Phonetik und
Phoniatrie. Vox 17:13 ff.

(1931b). Zur Geschichte der phonoskopischen Vorrichtungen.
Ann. Physik 5/10:673 ff.

(1931c). Über Diaphanoskopie des Kehlkopfes im Dienste der
experimentellen Phonetik. Mschr. f. Ohrenh. 11:
1307 ff.

(1933). Die Erforschung der Stimmlippentätigkeit mit Hilfe
der Kinematographie. Deutsche med. Wschr. 23:891
ff.

(1934a). Das Hören durch die Zähne. Vox 20:820-823.

(1934b). Die tuba sphaerica von Kircher und die Resonatoren
von Helmholtz. Zs. Lar. Rhin. Otol. 25:162 ff.

(1934c). Das Sprechen ohne Zunge und eine bisher unbekannt
gebliebene Zungenprothese von Paré (1561).
Zahnärztl. Rundsch. 42:1723-1726.

(1935a). Dichterische Spielereien und phonetische
Angstzustände (Phthongophobien). Med. Welt
14:507-508.

(1935b). Zur Geschichte des Kymographions. Zs. Lar. Rhin.
Otol. 26:196 ff.

(1935c). Der erste Kehlkopfspiegel: Babingtons "Glottiskop"
(1829-1835). Med. Welt 48:1752-1757.

(1936). Keim- oder Fruchtschädigung als Ursache von
Lippen- und Gaumenspalten, eine grundlegende Frage
auch für den Zahnarzt. Zahnärztl. Rundsch. 4:
145-151.

(1937a). Der "Wilde Knabe" (homo sapiens ferus, Linné) in
seiner Beziehung zu manchen Sprachstörungen im
Kindesalter und zu der Entstehung von Mythen.
Med. Welt 12:410-414.

(1937b). Das Zungenbändchen, ein Belang auch des Zahnarztes.
         Zahnärztl. Rundsch. 32:1397-1405.
(1938a). Wilhelm Weber als gedanklicher Urheber der
         glyphischen Fixierung von Schallvorgängen (1827).
         Arch. vgl. Phon. 2:1-11.
(1938b). Phonetik und Kultur. Hamburg, Hansischer Gilden-
         verlag.
(1938c). Untergang und Wiederaufleben der Nasenplastik im
         Spiegel der Kulturgeschichte. Zahnärztl. Rundsch.
         52:2185 ff.
(1939). Leonardo glottologo. In: Mostra, Leonardo da Vinci,
         Novara, pp. 399 ff.
(1940a). Quellenatlas zur Geschichte der Phonetik. Hamburg,
         Hansischer Gildenverlag.
(1940b). Vom Alter des künstlichen Velums. Eine geschicht-
         liche Feststellung. Zahnärztl. Rundsch. 19:657-661.
(1941). Geschichtszahlen der Phonetik. 3000 Jahre Phonetik.
         Hamburg, Hansischer Gildenverlag.
(1942). Die Phonetik des Aristoteles. Hamburg, Hansischer
         Gildenverlag.
(1943). Leonardo als Phonetiker. Hamburg, Hansischer
         Gildenverlag.
(1948). Phonetik als Naturwissenschaft. Berlin, Wiss.
         Editionsgesellsch.
(1951). Erfindungen und Nacherfindungen auf dem Gebiete
         der Stimmforschung. Marburg (Lahn), N.G. Elwert.
(1954). Leonardo da Vinci und die Frage vom sprechenden und
         weinenden Fötus im Märchenmotiv vom "starken
         Knaben." Münchn. med. Wschr. 49:1456 ff.
(1955). Das Motiv vom "wilden Knaben." Zur Sprache verwil-
         derter Kinder. Sprachf. 1:272 ff.
(1956). Die Stimmatmung. Das Neue - das Alte. Nova Acta
         Leop. 18/123, Leipzig.
(1957a). Earlier History of Phonetics. In: Manual of
         Phonetics, ed. L. Kaiser, Amsterdam, North-Holland
         Publ. Co., pp. 3-17.
(1957b). Entstehung und Entwicklung der bildlichen Dar-
         stellung des Kehlkopfes. Folia Phoniatrica 9:1 ff.
(1957c). Leonardo de Vinci als Zeichner von Deformationen
         der peripheren Sprechwerkzeuge. Münchn. med. Wschr.,
         pp. 1960 ff.

LITERATURANGABEN

Amman, J. C. (1700). Diss. de Loquela, Amsterdam, J. Wolters.

Brucke, E. (1856). Wien, C. Gerold's Sohn.

Essen, O. von. (1966). Berlin, Akademie Verlag.

Grassmann, R. (1890). Stettin, R. Grassmann.

Helmont, F. M. van. (1667). Kurzer Entwurff des eigentlichen Naturalphabets der heiligen Sprache.

Hellwag, C. F. (1781). Diss. de Form. Loquela, Tubingen.

Koerner, E. F. K. (1978). Hamburger Phon. Beitrage.

Koster, J. -P. (1973). Hamburg, Buske.

Koster, J. -P. (1979). Amsterdam, Benjamins.

Martens, P. (1972). Hamburger Phon. Beitrage.

Madsen, J. (1586). De literis libri duo. Basel, C. Waldkirch.

Sievers, E. (1876). Leipzig.

Sievers, E. (1901). Leipzig.

Sutterlin, L. (1908). Leipzig, Quelle and Meyer.

Techmer, F. (1880). Leipzig.

Techmer, F. (1883). Int. Zs. f. allgem. Sprachwiss, 1:6-128.

Techmer, F. (1890). Int. Zs. f. allgem. Sprachwiss, 5:145 ff.

Vietor, W. (1884). Leipzig, O. R. Reisland.

Wangler, H. -H. (1960). Marburg, N. G. Elwert.

Wangler, H. -H. (1972). Marburg, N. G. Elwert.

Zwirner, E. (1967). Phonet. 16:111-115.

LOOKING BACK: MEMORIES OF 40 YEARS IN PHONETICS

ELBERT R. MOSES, JR.
Clarion State College

After considerable thought regarding what particular
phase of the history of phonetics I might discuss, after
reading numerous publications, reviewing already familiar
ones, and also previewing Dr. Koerner's presentation, I concluded that anything of a scholarly nature that I might contribute would, in a sense, be somewhat of a re-hashing nature.
I have, however, in my forty-odd years of work in the field
of dynamic phonetics had the privilege of working with, or of
knowing personally, several of those persons whose contributions to the field have added much to the history, and the
controversies of phonetics, particularly dynamic phonetics;
so I have decided rather to reminisce, and to let others know,
at least to a certain degree, these phoneticians as persons,
as was my privilege.

Quite naturally, as a graduate student at the University
of Michigan, one of my first contacts was with Dr. John H.
Muyskens, a big, burly Dutchman, whose name (little mouse)
belied his personality. John Henry, as he was called by his
students, came into the phonetic field via the door of
foreign languages. He began his career as a teacher of
French at the University of Michigan. At that time he was
a rather timid young professor, who, with his friend Meader
(later the well-known psychologist of the Pillsburg-Meader
team), felt very shy in their first convocation processional
and chose for themselves a spot in what appeared to be the
very end of the line. As the procession began to move, however, the line was reversed, and they found themselves two

very embarrassed young men, marching at the head of the procession immediately behind the officials.

By the time it was my privilege to know these two each
had become well known through their teaching and works, John
Henry an impressive figure in his height, breadth, and whis-
kers, Meader in his ill-fitting old overcoat and battered hat.
Meader frequently, especially at the close of the Saturday
lab period, came wandering in looking for Muyskens. Before
we learned who he was my wife and I took him to be a member
of the janitorial staff trying to hurry the tarrying Muyskens
and students out of the lab so it could be closed for the
weekend!

John Henry's classes were informal, for those days, and
discussions ranged far and wide over many topics which sometimes seemed at the moment to be a far cry from dynamic
phonetics, but usually very neatly ultimately fitted into
the scheme of things. John Henry himself was dynamic--and
controversial--and embued his students with a keen interest
in phonetics. We were allowed to think and to experiment
freely, but he always was there to guide gently and offer
comment--or argue.

Muyskens' laboratory assistant provided a decided contrast. Hide Shobara, a native of Tokyo, had come to the
University of Michigan as a student, but remained as a professor there to the end of her days. Diminutive, quiet,
always serious, she went about her work in a methodical,
scholarly manner that won her a place of distinction in the
phonetic field. She contributed to Muyskens' research and
to his book, conducted research on her own, and ultimately
her work led her into the linguistics field, where in later
years she made her name in the teaching of English as a
second language.

Dr. Meader continued through the years his collaboration
with Muyskens and Shohara, teaching a course in Hermeneutics,
an evaluation of many phases of science and literature that
contributed to understanding speech and linguistics and aiding
in the publication of the rather monumental publishing project
of Muyskens.

Both John Henry and Hide are gone now, but my wife and
I often think back to those Depression days when our life
centered around a phonetics laboratory and two widely diver-
gent personalities--the burly Dutchman with the deep chuckle,
and the wee Japanese girl and her quiet, unobtrusive manner,
who gave to the phonetics world the theory of the hypha, and
the later definitive work on the relation of specificity in
the origin and development of speech.

It was a year or so later that I first met Dr. Stetson
of Oberlin College, and through him came to know Dr. C. V.
Hudgins of Clark Institute for the Deaf and also Professor
Doctor Louise Kaiser of Amsterdam, the Netherlands. My
acquaintance and ultimate collaboration with Dr. Stetson
came about in a unique manner. An aunt of mine, who had
had a laryngectomy, was referred to him for aesopageal speech
training. She, in turn, mentioned to Dr. Stetson that she
had a nephew who no doubt would be interested in her work,
and arranged a meeting. I then was living in North Carolina,
but was spending the summer in Ohio. Thus our first meeting
came about. The following summer, at Stetson's invitation,
I joined him and Dr. Hudgins in their experiment with the
changes in palatograms that take place with changes in rates
of articulation, linking in this experiment the sciences of
palatography and kymography. Hudgins was one of the leading
kymographers of his time. Out of this summer's work grew
an article later in the Archives Neerlandaises de Phonetique
Experimentale, a periodical edited by Madame Louise Kaiser
of Amsterdam University, and out of this incident a life-long
association with Louise Kaiser. Almost until her death at
an advanced age Louise Kaiser continued to write, read papers,
and participate in many ways in her field. She will be
remembered for her editorship of Archives, and of A Manual of
Phonetics.

Dr. Stetson's life was his work, and he expected the same
dedication from his associates. We were in the old Peter's
Hall laboratory, high up on the last floor, almost with the
dawn until late at night, often battling the bats that in-
habited that third-floor lab. The country was still
struggling out of the Depression and money was scarce in the
colleges and universities, but if Professor Stetson wished

to hire assistants or to buy equipment, he freely used his
personal resources rather than slow the progress of his work.
Many a graduate assistant's salary came not from the college
coffers, but from Stetson's own pocket. Yet to many Stetson
was a cold, scholarly person. To those of us who knew him
and worked with him he was, if a taskmaster, also a warm,
kindly human being. I remember one particular incident
which impressed not only me, but others who never had known
Dr. Stetson before. I had arranged to have a young couple,
friends from Wooster, Ohio, and my wife, come to Oberlin for
a Sunday to act as subjects for our palatographic experiments
The women had planned a picnic supper to be eaten on the way
home, but the weather did not cooperate, so we figured that
we would just eat our picnic supper in the lab. Somehow,
Dr. Stetson learned of our predicament, and absolutely insisted that we have the picnic in his home. He and his
housemate, Dr. Artz, simply walked out and turned over the
house to virtual strangers. We were not only astounded, but
appalled, when we found ourselves surrounded by his beautiful
antiques, fine china, travel treasures, and other exquisitely
tasteful possessions. The women were almost afraid to touch
anything, but we did have our picnic in super style. The
couple who shared this experience never did forget Dr. Stetson's hospitality; to them it was a marvel that a renowned
professor should make students and total strangers so welcome
to his home. But that was Stetson, the man.

That same summer Dr. C. V. Hudgins, one of the best
kymographers of his time, worked with us. He was neither
so well known nor so colorful an individual, but a scholar
from whom I, a neophyte, also learned much in the field of
kymography. By the end of that summer we three had devised
a new type of pseudo-palate and also through our experiment
had established that palatograms do change with rates of
articulation. Besides, we had most successfully linked the
sciences of palatography and kymography.

From this summer's work there ultimately grew another
friendship. The article resulting from our experiments,
Palatograms Change With Rates of Articulation, was published
in Archives Neerlandaises de Phonetique Experimentale, editor,
Madame Louise Kaiser of Amsterdam. We had ordered offprints

of the article but they had never reached us. They had been
mailed on the day the Nazis occupied Holland. Madame Kaiser
did manage to get through to each of us one copy of the
Archives, with the request that we defer payment until after
the war. Throughout the years following the war we kept in
touch with Louise Kaiser through correspondence until we felt
that we wanted to pay that small debt in person. Twenty
years later, while in Amsterdam my wife and I sought out
Madame Kaiser. After numerous unsuccessful telephone calls
one evening, the proprietor of the small private hotel where
we were staying asked us the address of the person we were
trying to contact. "That," he exclaimed, "is on the next
canal, just around the corner from here." We were on the
Kaisersgracht; she was on Prinsensgracht, with just one
street between, and our house numbers were almost the same.
At about nine o'clock the next morning we walked around to
792 Prinsensgracht, and to the astonished Madame Kaiser, who
answered our ring from a second-story window, announced our
names and purpose. Her reply, "You are always so astound-
ing!" In her typically Dutch home, about a door and a small
room wide and three stories high, with a cork-screw staincase
reaching straight upward from floor to floor, we spent a
delightful morning in the second-story parlor, drinking
coffee and reminiscing about Dr. Stetson and others, while a
sudden thunderstorm rolled and rumbled outdoors. That was
our one and only personal contact with Louise Kaiser, although
until her death we continued the correspondence we had begun
years before. When we received a death announcement from her
family we realized that our last link with the older group of
phoneticians was broken. We are the one living link between
them and the younger, upcoming group whose names and works
were to become the leaders. Madame Kaiser will be remembered
for her editorships and her individual research, but to us
she will always remain a kindly, excitingly but quietly
brilliant, elderly lady, playing hostess to two somewhat
unorthodox Americans in her old-style Dutch parlor.

Within two years of my first contact with Dr. Stetson,
I found myself once more working with a well-known, if highly
controversial, figure in the phonetics world, Dr. G. Oscar
Russell (God Oscar to his irreverent students). I had joined
the staff of the Ohio State University. Although my teaching

assignment was not at first in Dr. Russell's department, our mutual interest in phonetics, and my efforts to publish, brought us together. I submitted an article to Russell, who then was editor of <u>Journal of Speech Disorders</u>. Twenty-five times that article was returned for revisions, some seemingly so slight as to be absolutely unnecessary, but always so placed that each necessitated retyping the entire article. When finally he pronounced the article suitable, he said, "You know, all those revisions weren't really necessary. I just wanted to see if you had the fortitude to stick it out." But, irritating (he had the habit of phoning at dinner time and holding hour-long conversations) and controversial as G. Oscar Russell may have been, he did, nevertheless, establish the vowel triangle, a definite contribution to the phonetic field, and I am happy that he was a part of my professional experience. My last contact with Russell, if such it might be called, was during World War II. As I was driving up 14th Street in Washington, D. C. one day, I spied G. Oscar standing on a traffic island awaiting a trolley. He by then had severed connections with Ohio State, and on my return to the University I found his position filled by another staff member.

It is to Dr. John W. Black, whom I consider one of the foremost experimental phoneticians of today, that I owe not only the encouragement to venture into the textbook field some years ago, but the very thought underlying this paper. He came to Ohio State just as I was leaving for Illinois, but throughout the years we have had rather close contact, although we never have worked together. Once, in conversation, he remarked, "You--do you realize it?--are the one living link between the older and the younger group of experimental phoneticians. Only you have worked with all the men such as Stetson, Russell, etc. who still is here." That remark haunted me, and it is the reason that I have chosen to make this a paper of reminiscence and thumbnail character portraits instead of a scholarly paper. It is a kind of swan-song to a former day.

B. ISSUES OF METHOD AND THEORY IN PHONETICS

ON THE NECESSITY OF THE INTRODUCTION OF TECHNICAL PRINCIPLES INTO INSTRUMENTAL-PHONETIC INVESTIGATIONS

UZBEK BAITCHURA
Leningrad, USSR

The introduction of mathematical and physical-technical methods into linguistics has produced among those who were not versed in techics an illusion of absolute precision of some instrumental-phonetic methods and a fashion to require the absolute exactness (accuracy) according to which instrumental methods were devided into exact and that is why reliable as, e.g., electroacoustic methods and non-exact and that is why unreliable, e.g., pneumographic.

Thus, in his brochure <u>The Laboratory of Experimental Phonetics and Psychology of Speech</u>, Moscow, 1950 and the booklet <u>Experimental Phonetics</u>, Moscow, 1956 (both in Russian), professor of psychology, V. A. Artemov, an honorary vice-president of The ISPhS, wrote that all pneumographic, cymographic and palatographic methods are unreliable and unfit for instrumental investigation because they are not precise enough, and he proposed to replace them by electroacoustic methods and X-ray photography of speech organs, which he considered to be absolutely exact although until now only static X-ray photographs have been used in the USSR but not films.

It is noteworthy that, at that time, the instruments which were proclaimed as the only exact and reliable were either only possession of Artemov's laboratory or at the Institute for Röntgenology and Radiology in Moscow with which

Artemov collaborated but these instruments, at that time, were unavailable to other laboratories in the USSR, and this reveals the real cause of the preference of these methods.

Rejecting the pneumographic and other methods of instrumental phonetics, Artemov, however, does not reject the method of acoustical perception by ear applied by the vast majority of linguists of our time although this method is less exact than any one depending upon cymographic and pneumographic instruments. On the contrary, Artemov uses the acoustic method on a large scale, combining it with the electroacoustic methods. And just this fact shows his tendentiousness because, according to his way of raising the problem, as he strives for abstract and absolute exactness, disregarding the task and object of investigation, he ought to reject the method of acoustic perception by ear in the first place, and only after that he would have been entitled to speak of insufficiency of this or that sort of instrumental methods because the latter are always much more exact than the former presented by our ear and, besides, give us documentation in the shape of cymograms, palatograms, etc.

In contrast to Artemov's views, the position of the Laboratory·of the Leningrad University was more objective and scholarly because they considered methods of study in connection with the task of investigation, as it was, e.g., at the time when Professor M. I. Matusevič was the director of the laboratory.

But nowadays, the very same tendency as that of Artemov's appears also in the Leningrad laboratory, which, by now, has also acquired some modern instruments (NB). However, there is a difference because, in Leningrad, they are careful not to blame other laboratories openly in press, but leave it to their students coming from some national republics, as it was, e.g., with the objections to some cymographic investigations performed at Professor Bogorodickij's study in Kazan (in the symposium N.I.Ašmarin-- osnovopoložnik čuvašskogo jazykoznanija, Čeboksary, 1971, p. 56) although no objection was raised against cymographic investigations performed at the Leningrad laboratory, in spite of the fact that the error of registration of Bogorodickij's cymograph comprised only 2.0% (the cymograph being a product of the famous firm 'Verdin' in France), whereas the home-made cymograph of the Leningrad laboratory, although also reliable, still had the error of registration equal to 2.8%. (CF., e.g. the fact that the electromagnetic recorder of the Alma-Ata laboratory at the Institute of Linguistics of the Academy of Sciences of the Kasakh SSR has the error of regis-tration equal to 2.0%, as it was established a few years ago.) But these critics never refer to any figure substantiating their objections against this or that method, which can be explained by the inconsistency of their criticism, and the figures would have revealed this. However, this does not prevent them from repeating as their own of the conclusions drawn from the cymographic data by those whom they criticize (See e.g., Voprosy Čuvašskoj Fonetiki i Leksikologii, Čeboksary, 1976, pp. 41-54, and many other works, e.g., from Alma-Ata, etc.).

All this does not at all mean that the work of the laboratories named was useless. Quite the contrary. With the help of the instruments made in the Moscow, Leningrad and other laboratories, as well as in Kazan, many useful instru-mental investigations have been carried out first of all by different postgraduate students (mainly coming from different national republics), which contributed to study of different languages belonging to several linguistic groups. But it is surprising to see how the views of some linguists (or psycho-logists) change whenever the matter concerns the evaluation of works done at some laboratory other than their own. Tenden-tiousness combined with the ignorance of elementary technical principles accompanied, as a rule, by unfitness of learned councils to form a competent judgement in this field because of complete (or almost complete) absence of specialists in instrumental phonetics in their bodies or even in the insti-tutions bring about the possibility of desinformation which leads to practical resolutions hampering the development of instrumental phonetics.

It is quite clear that all these methods and criteria mentioned do not answer the requirements of exact research, namely, the requirements of physical-technical and mathe-matical methods.

As it is known, the degree of exactitude, i.e., accuracy achieved by means of different methods is different. It is usually assumed that the least exact instrument which is represented by our ears has the error rate of registration ca. 20%, which is still quite sufficient for understanding speech, whereas in the pneumatic apparatus, the usually tolerated error is equal to 5%, and in electroacoustic instruments, the exactness (accuracy) can be (but is not always) higher by one degree. All these methods can be used and are applied by linguists to study the sound structure of a human speech, but their applicability in each individual case depends upon the object and the task of investigation. Thus, investigation of the length of speech sounds can be carried out by means of acoustic perception. But in this case, mainly data on phonological length of sounds will be reliable. In order to investigate the length of sounds on the phonetic (not phonologic) level, it is necessary to apply the pneumographic or electroacoustic methods which are to one degree more exact. But the degree of accuracy (of exactness) can be limited also here by the object and the purpose of the investigation. It is known that every sound has two transitional (intermediate) parts which are at the beginning and at the end of it, and the length of these parts usually comprises from 10 to 20% of the total length of the sound, whereas the deviations in the total length of the sound can amount to 20 or 30% in analogous positions and for the same informant. Under these conditions, an error of registration amounting to 5% is unessential, whereas attempts at more exact measurements (to within milleseconds) will result only in quasi-exactness (quasi-accuracy) because the character of the object limits the degree of attainable accuracy. But though attained, the degree of accuracy (exceeding 1%) would be redundant in most cases, which technically has no sense, and for this reason it is considered a fault because a railway carriage is not weight with accuracy to within one milligram, and this is not possible.

Nevertheless, there are some linguists engaged in experimental phonetics who have no idea of technical tolerance as well as of the fact that any instrument, including the most accurate ones makes always some error in registration, and that the task of the experimenter is to find out which degree of accuracy is tolerable for his task and attainable for the object of his investigation and which is not. And from this point of view, even some modern instruments can sometimes be less exact and less reliable in comparison to some older methods, or they even may be totally unfit in this or that respect. Thus, although electroacoustic methods are to one degree more exact (accurate) than the pneumographic ones, and can replace the latter in some respects, still the pneumographic methods give us information about aerodynamics of speech (which is of much importance for investigation of consonants) whereas the elctroacoustic methods cannot give us any information on this question.

Thus, we can draw the general conclusions that all methods of experimental (and non-experimental) phonetics are good, only one must know to what object, under what conditions and to what degree can be applied this or that method, and what kind of data are to be expected in every case.

SOME CONTROL COMPONENTS OF A SPEECH PRODUCTION MODEL

R. A. W. BLADON
University College of North Wales

The object of this paper is to assemble evidence from coarticulation relevant to modelling the speech production process. We therefore omit all reference to other areas of speech motor control, including for example any distinction between planning and execution phases, the role of a possible simulation component or of auditory feedback loops. We assume, for the purposes of this discussion, a target specification for each allophone, and the space coordinate systems in terms of which these are defined. Furthermore, in reviewing a rather wide range of evidence, space does not permit us here to report any one experiment in detail.

It is our belief that coarticulation evidence is currently posing interesting problems for theories of speech motor control because of its diversity, on the one hand, and on the other, its suspect predictive capacity. Information relevant to the direction and domain of coarticulatory effects seems to derive from a wide range of different sources, some quasi-universal, some language particular, some context sensitive. We have discussed some of these in recent publications (Bladon & Al-Bamerni, 1976; Bladon & Nolan, 1977), and these discussions have provoked Kent and Minifie (1977) to write: "Perhaps the solution to coarticulation is as complex as this multiplicity of factors suggests, but . . .(they) represent the contributions of many unknown, or poorly known effects." Our current view is that Kent and Minifie's comment is perfectly valid, but that it in itself constitutes no criticism

of our position. It seems to be inescapable that the control of coarticulation in speech is indeed governed by a
multiplicity of factors. The hope, implicitly expressed in
many early coarticulation studies, of finding one or a small
number of determinants regulating the control of coarticulatory domain and direction, seems to be a vain one.

    First, then, we propose today to review some factors
which are known already, from our own work or that of others,
to have an effect upon the motor control of coarticulation,
and which, as such, are represented in the control components
of a speech production model. Figure 1 is a preliminary and
highly simplified arrangement of these.

    Of the determinants of coarticulation, several are
clearly referable to components of the phonological system
of a language, as outlined by Chomsky and Halle (1968) in
their presentation of generative phonology. Accordingly,
the large box in Figure 1 is a diagrammatic representation
of that phonological component. Firstly, and importantly,
it is well established that there are constraints on coarticulation which are referable to syllable structure rules,
ones for example which would define a unit C_0V (where C_0
stands for any number of consonants). This unit has often
been called the "articulatory syllable," and many investigators, notably Kozhevnikov and Chistovich (1965), have
uncovered evidence that coarticulation tends to be maximal
within the C_0V unit but minimal across its boundaries. However, we referred in our introductory remarks to this paper
to dubious predictive capacity, and indeed, if the C_0V theory
is set up as a component of a model to predict coarticulatory
behaviour, counterexamples are readily found. The anticipatory nasalization of vowels before nasals (in English and
other languages) is by now a well known counterexample (cf.
Moll & Daniloff, 1971); a less well known one would be
American English /r/ which coarticulates with the adjacent
vowel quality much more readily in the final position than
in the initial C_0V position (cf. Lehiste, 1964). Other
cases from our own data include "vowel+nasal+vowel" sequences which, in both Hindi and Brazilian Portuguese, show
greater nasalization of the first than of the second vowel;
and, again in Hindi, there is an analogous situation with

"nasalized vowel+oral fricative+nasalized vowel" sequences
where the orality of the fricative overlaps further into
the first vowel than into the second.

A second component contributing to coarticulatory control seems to be the lexical representation of the inventory
of phonological items in a language. The degree to which a
lateral for instance undergoes vowel-quality coarticulation
varies according to the number of laterals in a language's
phonological system: in our data, Irish, with three laterals
to be kept distinct, shows very little quality coarticulation in comparison with American English, with only one
lateral but highly coarticulated; and Swedish, with two
laterals -- an alveolar and a retroflex, falls in between
with respect to coarticulation. However, contrary to this
principle is the coarticulatory behaviour between trans-
consonantal vowels in VCV sequences, which has been attested
for Swedish (Öhman, 1966), but explicitly is not present in
Russian (Purcell, 1977). This cannot be because Russian has
a more densely populated vowel system which in some sense
needs to preserve its perceptual spacing; because the Russian
vowel system is markedly less complex than that of Swedish.
Again, this component has a limited predictive ability.

Thirdly, some constraints on coarticulation seem to be
referable to universal marking conventions (which assign
marked or unmarked values to certain feature combinations).
As an example, take the boundary of an intonation-group
(or tone-group), which is widely observed to act as a strong
barrier to the segmental spread of coarticulated features.
On the other hand, some of the control of coarticulation, far
from being of universal or quasi-universal applicability,
may be speaker-specific, as has been suggested for example
by Su, Li and Fu (1974), who found that coarticulated vowel-
quality in English initial nasals could have a speaker-
identifying function.

A fourth component of the control of coarticulation
resides in the phonetic representation, for there is evidence
that the speech control mechanism has access not just to
details of the segmental composition of the utterance but
also of the feature being coarticulated. Thus, for example,

it has been shown that English /s/ occurring in CCC clusters
blocks the spread of coarticulatory jaw-opening anticipating
/æ/ (Amerman, Daniloff & Moll, 1970); and that /s/ resists
any shift in its tongue-bladeness towards a tip articulation
adjacent to /t d n l/; but that this resistance to coarticu-
late cannot be ascribed inherently to the English /æ/
phoneme per se, because /s/ freely allows coarticulated
labialization anticipating an /u/ vowel (Daniloff & Moll,
1968) or an /r/ (Bladon, 1977). However, yet again, this
phenomenon of sensitivity to phonetic feature is also
limited in its predictive capacity, since it is not borne
out for example in British English "clear" l, which is
free in coarticulation with any of the features vowel-
quality, lateral-quality and voicelessness indiscriminately
(Bladon & Al-Bamerni, 1976).

Fifthly, some language-particular phonological rules
seem to be relevant. Ladefoged (1967), for instance, reported that while French and English both show a /k/ co-
articulatorily advanced before an /i/ vowel, only French
shows the similar effect after /i/. At the same time, however, we also have to provide for dialect-specific control
of coarticulation, as is evidenced for example by the smaller
degree of anticipatory nasalization shown by British English
vowels than by American English vowels.

Other determinants of coarticulatory control fall outside the phonological component in its traditional sense.
The control mechanisms must be sensitive, firstly, to
speaking rate. Gay (1977) shows that at a fast speaking
rate a vowel F_2 transition effectively begins at a point of
greater overlap with the preceding consonant than is the
case with normal speaking rate.

Among acoustic constraints we might for example hypo-
thesise the favouring of coarticulatory effects whose articulatory perturbations are quantal in that they result in relatively invariant acoustic consequences.

Motor constraints of compatibility would include for
example the prediction that jaw opening is incompatible with
/s/ for the probable reason that it would necessarily deform
the friction passage.

As an example of a perceptual constraint we could instance the maintenance of phonemic distinctiveness which
(short of the point of incipient sound change and phonemic
restructuring) has widely been held to place an upper bound
on the extent of coarticulatory behaviour. .Even this principle appeared to make the wrong predictions in the data of
Benguerel and Cowan (1974), however, who found that lip protrusion anticipating French /u/ could extend transconsonan-
tally into a preceding /i/ vowel, despite the apparent threat
to the perceptual contrast /i - y/ in French.

It remains to be seen how many more determinants of
coarticulatory control come to light. It may be interesting
at this point to summarize some recent findings of ours regarding the possibility that coarticulatory control might
have to be sensitive also to the phonetic <u>strength</u> of the
feature being coarticulated. That is, it could be hypothesized that for example the labialization which accompanies
RP English /r/ might be anticipated less early in a multi--
consonant sequence than that which accompanies /u/, since
it can be shown that /u/ labialization is phonetically a
"stronger" gesture than that present in /r/. Our EMG experiments did not support that hypothesis, showing instead
that /r/ labialization did extend just as far leftwards as
that of /u/. Hence, there is no evidence yet that the components supplying the coarticulatory control mechanisms need
include the additional determinant "feature-strength."

To summarize so far: good evidence exists for each of
the factors discussed as determinants of the domain and direction of coarticulatory effects. The testing of these model components (a major concern in the recent coarticulation literature) by predicting from them onto new data, turns out to be
partly unsuccessful and partly successful, for each component.
Clearly, no one component will explain all or even a large part
of observed coarticulatory behaviour. How then to assign a
weighting to the separate contribution of each component, and
indeed what a full inventory of these components is, remain
open questions.

Where we can reasonably make progress, it is suggested
here, is to integrate these disparate sources in the following
way: let us suppose that the numerous factors constraining the
domain and direction of coarticulatory effects can be described
as we have suggested elsewhere (Bladon & Al-Bamerni, 1976).

by postulating the notion of <u>coarticulation</u> <u>resistance</u> (CR)
as the central principle of articulatory control. The speech
production mechanism is hypothesized to have continuous access
to CR information, which can be considered to be initially
stored linguistically as a scalar feature specification like
any other - i.e., of the form <u>n</u> CR - and attaching to each
allophone and boundary condition. Thus, for instance, English
/h/ which is highly susceptible to coarticulation, and English
/θ/ which is much more resistant, might be provided with specifications such as 1 CR and 5 CR, respectively. The numerical
value of the CR index is re-computed at a level of articulatory planning by what might be termed a CR compiler to take
account of the wide range of constraints imposed by the
factors surveyed in this paper. It is further suggested
that coarticulation may proceed freely in either direction
(left-to-right or right-to-left) in time, until impeded by
a specification of CR on some segment. It is important to
realize also why an initial CR specification is tabulated
for each allophone. A classic demonstration of whis is
afforded by the RP English /l/ allophones, of which dark
syllabic ɫ is highly resistant to coarticulation, dark
nonsyllabic ɫ ('feel') is somewhat less so, and clear
nonsyllabic l ('leaf') is very much less resistant. We
are aware of no explanation of this behaviour in terms of
the fringe components connected to the compiler by dotted
lines in Figure 1: the idiosyncracies can only be handled
by assuming something like an allophone-specific assignment
of a CR value.

   Further evidence, not presented here, is currently becoming available which lends further support to the CR
aspects of the proposed model; but we do not pretend that
the search for that evidence does not need to continue.

REFERENCES

Amerman, J. D., Daniloff, R. G. and Moll, K.   (1970).
     <u>J. Speech Hear. Res</u>. 13:147-161.
Benguerel, A.-P. and Cowan, H. A.   (1974).   <u>Phonet</u>. 30:41-55.
Bladon, R. A. W.   (1978).   <u>ARIPUC</u> (University of Copenhagen),
     11:13-26.
Bladon, R. A. W. and Al-Bamerni, A.   (1976).   <u>J. Phonet</u>.
     4:137-150.

Bladon, R. A. W. and Nolan, F. J. (1977). J. Phonet. 5:185-193.

Chomsky, N. and Halle, M. (1968). New York: Harper and Row.

Daniloff, R. G. and Moll, K. (1968). J. Speech Hear. Res. 11:707-721.

Gay, T. (1977). J. Acoust. Soc. Amer. (in press).

Kent, R. D. and Minifie, F. D. (1977). J. Phon. 5:115-133.

Kozhevnikov, V. A. and Chistovich, L. A. (1965). Joint Publications Res. Ser., US Depart. Commerce.

Ladefoged, P. (1967). Phon. 6, Los Angeles: UCLA.

Lehiste, I. (1964). Bloomington: Indiana UP.

Moll, K. L. and Daniloff, R. G. (1971). J. Acoust. Soc. Amer. 50:678-684.

Öhman, S. E. G. (1966). J. Acoust. Soc. Amer. 39:151-168.

Purcell, E. T. (1977). 94th Meeting, Acoust. Soc. Amer., Miami Beach.

Su, L. S., Li, K. P., and Fu, K. S. (1974). J. Acoust. Soc. Amer. 56:1876-1882.

FIGURE 1.   Some control components of a speech production
            model, showing sources supplying the CR compiler.

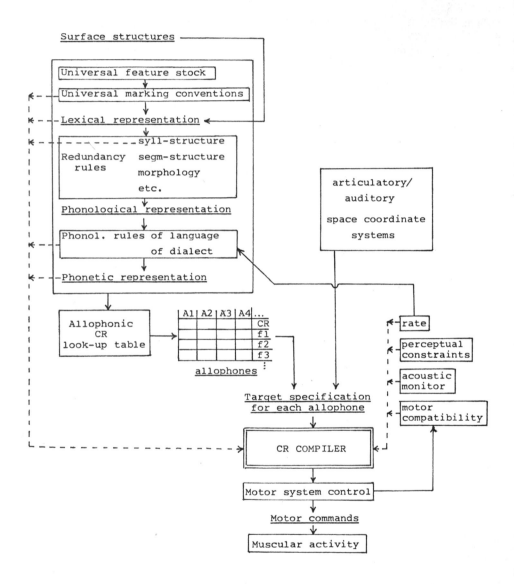

PHONETIC ASPECTS OF LINGUA-INFORMATICS

E. KRASHENINNIKOVA
Moscow, USSR

Modern Informatics is characterised by the growing use of related sciences data, which are influenced more and more by Informatics, resulting in the rise of new branches of science. Today we can talk of the emergence of a new science of Lingua-Informatics. This does not mean simply using linguistic data for the purposes of Informatics. There has appeared a new, "hybrid," branch of knowledge, with its specific point of view on language phenomena and common facts, with its object, method and its peculiar problems.

According to common view, Informatics is nothing but a general theory of programming while Lingua-Informatics deals with theoretical and practical linguistic problems, arising in the process of information retrieval. We refer to the various and complex problems of text linguistics, language study problems of processing the text by man and by machine, studying the laws of coherent speech units distribution, measuring the text semantic information in different languages, linguistic models retrieval for information curtailment, creation of thesaurus, information retrieval systems and other aspects. This science may be subdivided into written and oral Lingua-Informatics. The written Lingua-Informatics, i.e., one of written speech, studies linguistic aspects of text abstractions and annotation, construction of information retrieval languages, information storage and supply, creation of documental and data retrieval systems and other problems of written information reception and transfer.

Oral or sound speech Lingua-Informatics deals with pre-documental information. It is often more important than the recorded information, especially in discussing the new technological ideas, hypothesis and prognoses of great and immediate importance. Here the problems arise of verbal information reception, transfer, organization, classification, systematization and evaluation. Informatics has three main components: the message (i.e., concrete combination of signs which serve to transfer the information); the fixing (i.e., methods of recording the message), and the notification (i.e. in the form of essays, documents, annotations, etc.). Oral Lingua-Informatics deals with messages only in the form of oral speech. Messages always take the form of signs perceived by our senses. Graphemes are used in written speech, while oral messages are sequences of meaningful phonetic units--phonemes. Both phonemes and graphemes are symbols making up certain finite sets and strictly defined within each language limits.

The main function of oral speech phonetics is to shape and form linguistic information transfer signs. Oral audio-messages, expressed as a sequence of signs perceived by the ear, presuppose the ability and readiness of a listener to break up these sound signals and reveal their sense. As a result of the listener's effort, the message proves to be understood and received. To correctly understand the sound speech contents, one cannot simply limit oneself to perceiving the sounds and their combinations. The listener must also consider the information act situation, information speech context, shades and accents of intonation and their distribution, meaningful intervals, tempo of speech and its emotional coloring. In some cases however, the phonetic aspect of oral message may be so indistinct, erased or distorted that it does not help but hinders the reception and understanding of information. It happens when: (1) the speaker does not articulate the sounds well because of his speech defects; (2) his use of foreign language is phonetically imperfect, i.e., when the native tongue is strongly felt in the pronunciation and (3) the information is being transferred along deficient communication lines, with various noises and other interference.

The above types of hindrances, arising on the way of receiving oral audio-messages, refer to sound speech only. The written Lingua-Informatics has no such problems. It presupposes the possibility of adequate reading of documents "silently," on the basis of micro-articulation. The basic relations of phonetic structures in oral Informatics are of a syntagmatic and paradigmatic nature. Phonetic units of oral speech appear in time consecutively and are unequivocally located to each other in syntagmatic plane. The linear disposition of speech sounds is the basis of speech perception. It presupposes, on the one hand, remembering what is said, and on the other hand--a certain apperception towards what will be said, i.e., while waiting. Paradigmatic, i.e., systematic organization and phonematic contrasting of sound structures make the basis of catching information by the ear. As the basic, associative relations, paradigmatic ties of oral speech sounds help reveal the logical structure of sound speech and messages in the form of lexical units.

Oral information has specific laws of its own. From the point of view of grammar, verbal speech is substantially different from the written one. For example, in the German language it provides for a phrase, laconical enough and easy to perceive by ear; it avoids using widely spaced components of frame structures,etc. Newspaper titles and advertisements often omit articles,which are reestablished when reading the same text aloud: "Lehrling gesucht," etc. Sentences equal in their sense and purpose have different syntactical form in oral and written speech. We say: "Der Werktätige will sich in den Werken des Künstlers sehen und nicht irgendeine erdachte Gestalt," and we write otherwise: "Der Werktätige will nicht irgendeine erdachte Gestalt in den Werken des Künstlers sehen sondern sich."

The phonetic reality of oral speech as a means of existence, formation and transfer of information is also very specific. There arises therefore a number of particular problems to be elaborated further. (1) The problem of prevalence in Lingua-Informatics of standard phonetic form and possibilities of sounds dialectal coloring should be solved from purely pragmatic positions. In cases when dialectal shades of pronunciation appear in words of weak informational weight,they do not interfere with understanding and receiving

of basic information. Then phonetical discrepancies in the
"Norm-Dialect" system are irrelevant from the point of view
of Informatics. For example, the German modal word combination "kann sein" in the oral Schwab dialect turns into
"kesei," and "nicht wahr?" in Hamburg is often substituted
by the casual "nech" or "nöch." However such deviations from
standard pronunciation are inadmissible once they involve
meaningful, weighty morphemes and hinder the adequate perception of information. For example, in literary German the
word "die Sühne" means "expiation, confession." If the
phrase is pronounced with dialectal coloring, as "sine dre
Sühne" (seine drei Söhne), its sense is not clear at first
and misinformation occurs.

(2) Foreign shades of sounds may also be irrelevant and
not interfering with understanding and reception of oral
information, especially in regard to form-words. A Russian
student would often pronounce the English conjunction "with"
with certain deviations: Consonants "th" sometimes sound
not like /ð/ but as /θ/ or even /s/, but it does not distort
the sense of the word. Pronouncing "with" as "wit" may be
a greater obstacle and may cause some misunderstanding, since
"wit"--mind, intellect, has quite a different meaning. It is
a different case when we speak of a possible misinformation
when someone's name is mispronounced with foreign coloring.
The German word "Börne" will sound "Pörne" for a Frenchman,
since voiced consonants in German are less voiced compared
with similar voiced consonants in the French language. And,
since the sound "B" is here positioned at the beginning of
the word and is rather important in finding the name, this
proves to be a substantial mistake in pronunciation. Or, for
example, the Russian name of "Orekhov" in Moscow dialect
begins with /ʌ/, so to avoid a mistake its bearer would often
dictate it with /o/ (especially when filling out documents).

(3) The arrangement of intervals is often of great importance in information transfer. A wrong position of interval
may cause the distortion of contents and misinformation.
Thus, in A.S. Pushkin's verse there is a phrase:"On iz Ger-
manii tumannoi privez uchennosti plody." The verse is "Eugene
Onegin." The above sentence was transliterated from Russian
by the translator, it sounds like: /on iz ger'ma:nii

tu'ma:nnoj pri'və:z u'tʃə :nosti plo'dy"/ and is translated
"From hazy Germany he brought with him the fruits of scientific study." Should we place the interval not after
"Germany" but after the word "tumannoi" (hazy), the sense
will be distorted since the author means not "a foggy
Germany," but a hazy, obscure erudition (the knowledge of
the German idealistic philosophy that Lensky learnt and
brought from Germany). Information distortion is particularly clear in such cases when learning foreign languages,
e.g., a person about to start the study of German, would
often err in placing intervals in negations: "Ich habe das
Buch nicht / gekauft." Such location of interval refer the
denial not to "Particip II" "gekauft" but to the verb "haben,"
which is then perceived not as an auxiliary verb, but as a
full-meaning verb "to have."

(4) The phonetic aspect of audio-messages has a granular,
quantum, structure. Similar to the text, where meaningful
words alternate with little-informative units, in oral speech
phonetics we can also trace an uneven distribution of information weight. The granular, quantum, structure of phonetic
units in German is manifest not only in the stressed meaningful syllables and unstressed syllables which are devoid of
informational weight or carrying excessive information. The
granular quantum structure is also manifest in that little-
informative units are capable of changing their phonetic
structure: German "haben" ⟶ /hamn/ "sie kamen" ⟶ /zi:
ka:m / with long "m." Sometimes unimportant syllables and
even whole words are reduced: "mal sehen" instead of
"Wollen wir einmal sehen!," or "Ich hab" instead of "Ich
habe." Lexical components carrying the greatest information
load have quite stable phonetic characteristics.

(5) Within the sentence, intonation is an important vehi-
cle for message sense transfer. The informational weight of
intonation is especially great in radio and TV broadcasts,
in telephone and audio-visual communication. Thus the German
phrase "komm zurück!," put in the imperative, depending on
the intonation may imply an order, request, or entreaty, with
differences not only in the tone height, voice movement,
emotion and stress but also in the speech tempo itself. An
order demands a quicker tempo, clear and curt tone. A request

has a more even melodic and calm tone. An entreaty possesses
rather effective coloring and flexible musical modulation, the
purpose of which is to influence the listener's feelings.
In written speech the corresponding meanings are usually conveyed by a special set of lexico-grammatical means: "Komm
doch zurück!" (order), "Komm, bitte, zurück!" (request),
"Oh, komm mal zurück!" (entreaty). The oral messages, as
distinct from written ones, play a double role. They supply
information both on the real content of speech, on its material content, and on the speaker.

It is typical in this case that intonational aspects of
oral speech, as its sounding properties, are usually manifested unconsciously, and spontaneously. Intonation conveys
the mood of the speaker, his emotional attitude towards what
he is saying. It creates a kind of informational plane of
secondary order which is superimposed on the main informative
content of speech. Specifics of speech sounds and shades of
pronunciation show the person's sex, nationality, age, tem-
perament, health, place of birth, artistic and cultural level.
The phonetic form of oral information may also distort its
text contents, bringing it to naught, since intonation can
contradict the sense of words. For example, if the sentence
"Schade ist's, das er nicht kommt" be pronounced sadly, with
a feeling of vexation or grief,its meaning has been definite-
ly implied. While should the same sentence, contrary to the
meaning of words, be pronounced playfully, ironically or with
evident pleasure (="I am pleased, I am glad he has not come,
but express my sorry out of courtesy"). Here the intonation
carries greater informational load than the word, thus changing the sense of the whole phrase.

Sound speech has great psychological advantages over the
written information. It is easier and quicker perceived,
makes a fuller use of language possibilities to transfer information. We can now say that phonetics, stripped of its
individual peculiarities, will be introduced into information
retrieval systems to transfer information inquiries in oral
form. Verbal statements may also be used to obtain answers
from IRS (Information Retrieval Systems) to informational
inquiries of consumers. The possibility is likewise not excluded that phonetical aspects of Lingua-Informatics will
be widely used for special purposes of collecting and storing
information.

DIMENSION STATISTIQUE DE LA STRUCTURE LINGUISTIQUE ET DISTINCTION PHONETIQUE/PHONOLOGIE

MORTEZA MAHMOUDIAN
Université de Lausanne

Par-delà leurs diversités, les courants structuralistes
en linguistique partent tous - y compris la grammaire généra-
tive transformationelle - de certains principes communs. Le
plus fondamental de ces principes est - nous semble-t-il - la
conception d'une langue comme un tout organisé (ou une structure) et la primauté de cette structure sur les unités constitutives de la langue. Ainsi concues, les unités d'une
langue - telles que les unités phoniques - ne peuvent etre
identifiées sur la seule foi de leurs caractéristiques
positives. En tant qu'éléments linguistiques, les unités
phoniques ne sauraient etre assimilés à une somme de propriétés physiques; elles incorporent des caractéristiques
structurales: les relations qu'elles entretiennent avec les
autres unités, et la place qu'elles occupant dans la langue.
La relation d'opposition est l'une des plus importantes d'entre elles, et c'est sur la foi de ce rapport oppositif (ou
distinctif) que sont identifiés les phonèmes (pour ne parler
que d'un type d'unités phoniques). La procédure d'analyse -
commutation ou dans la terminologie américaine substitution -
est fondee sur cette fonction distinctive: deux sons /p/
et /b/ par exemple, sont deux phonemes en francais dans la
mesure où ils sont capables de distinguer /pul/ de /bul/,
/pa/ de /ba/, etc.

Le succès qu'a remporté la théorie phonologique est dû
au fait qu'à cette procédure formelle correspond une contre-
partie dans le comportement des sujets parlants; en ce sens

que les usagers ont conscience des faits phoniques de leur
langue, et les reconnaissent pour autant que ces phénomènes
assument une fonction linguistique. Alors que la différence
"sourde"/"sonore" est perçue par le francophone dans /p/ et
/b/, elle lui échappe dans /l/ et /l̥/ dans ongle et oncle,
respectivement. C'est que la différence de "voix" n'a pas
le même statut dans le cas de la latérale et des bilabiales.
Dans ce dernier cas, la vibration glottale a une fonction
distinctive, et relève donc de la phonologie. Dans l'autre,
elle est du ressort de la phonétique, puisque la latérale
reste le "même" phonème, qu'elle soit sourde, sonore ou à
mi-chemin des deux. La distinction entre phonologie et
phonétique est ainsi conçue: la phonologie serait le domaine
des unités phoniques, la phonétique celui de la réalisation
de ces unités, étant entendu que les unités constituent un
systeme formel, et leur réalisation un continuum caractérisé
par des variations multiples (individuelles, sociales,
stylistiques).

Or, si la distinction phonétique/phonologie et la procédure de la reconnaissance des phonèmes sont valables dans
les grandes lignes, elles laissent à désirer dans certaines
zones de la structure phonologique. Ces insuffisances ont -
pensons-nous - des implications pour la conception de la
structure linguistique et des unités qui en relèvant, ainsi
que pour la distinction entre phonétique et phonologie.

Si l'on s'interrogeait sur le rapport de deux sons comme
/nj/ et /ɲ/ en francais, la réponse ne serait pas aussi simple
que dans le cas de /p/ et /b/. Les difficultés auscquelles
on est confronté dans un cas de ce genre, peuvent être de
deux types: (1) d'ordre mental. L'identité ou la différence
phonologiques de deux éléments phoniques peuvent ne pas être
évidentes pour l'informateur que nous sollicitons. Ses ré-
actions pourraient alors révéler des hésitations (ou contra-
dictions) quand on lui demande s'il fait une différence dans
la prononciation de nous peinions et nous peignons. (2) d'ordre
social. Interrogés sur le même point, différents informateurs
peuvent émettre des avis opposés: les uns pourraient admettre
l'identité des deux sons alors que d'autres y verraient une
différence. Nous avons ici affaire à des cas de dissension.

Si nos informateurs sont choisis parmi les Parisiens, nous avons de fortes chances de rencontrer les deux phénomènes d'hésitation et de dissension. A noter que pour les mêmes informateurs, l'interrogation sur /bul/ et /pul/ ne susciterait pratiquement ni hésitation ni dissension; ce qui tend à prouver que l'intuition du sujet parlant n'est pas nécessairement floue ou non fiable, puisque pour certains faits phoniques, les usagers d'une langue disposent d'une intuition nette sur le plan individuel, et font montre d'un haut degré de consensus au niveau collectif. La conclusion qui semble s'imposer à la suite de cette constatation, c'est que tous les faits phonologiques n'ont pas le même statut dans le psychisme du sujet, et ne revêtent pas la meme importance dans la communauté. Cela revient a remettre en question le caractère formel et homogène de la structure phonologique (ou de facon générale, de la structure linguistique).

Reprenons l'exemple des sons /ɲ/ et /nj/. Que peut-on en dire dans une description de la phonologie du francais? Doit-on négliger /ɲ/ dans une étude phonologique? Faut-il reconnaitre /ɲ/ comme un phonème, distinct de la suite /nj/? Des deux solutions, l'une paraît aussi difficile à soutenir que l'autre. Dire que /ɲ/ n'a aucun statut phonologique est aussi arbitraire que de le considérer sur le même plan que des phonemes comme /p/, /b/ ou /m/. Dans les deux cas, on se décide à ignorer les habitudes linguistiques d'une partie non négligeable de la communauté francophone. Force est d'admettre l'existence de variations et d'une hiérarchie dans les systèmes phonologiques. Dans des travaux récents et moins récents - de Martinet à Bailey & Shuy en passant par Labov - ces concepts ont été présentés et développés. Il nous est apparu cependant que ces notions sont riches en implications pour la théorie linguistique; implications qui n'ont pas retenu toute l'attention qu'elles méritent. En voici quelques unes: (1) Une langue n'est pas un système formel constitué d'unités discrètes et de règles explicites. En ce sens, les variations ne portent pas uniquement sur la réalisation des unités, mais affectent les unités elles-memes. Le nombre et les caractéristiques définitoires des unités varient d'un usage à l'autre. Comme nous venons de voir, la question n'est pas seulement de savoir si la nasale palatale se réalise de telle facon ou de telle

autre facon. Il s'agit aussi de savoir s'il existe un
phonème nasal palatal distinct du phoneme nasal dental suivi
de /j/.

(2) C'est mal poser la question que de se demander si
une langue est douée d'une structure formelle ou aleatoire.
Toute réponse unilatérale conduit à l'impasse. Si l'on se
refuse à reconnaitre à l'aléatoire le droit de cité dans les
langues, la délimitation das systèmes sera arbitraire, et
restera à la discrétion du descripteur. En effet, peut-on
fonder la distinction entre systèmes (qu'il s'agisse de
langues ou de dialectes) exclusivement sur la différence du
nombre des unités et de leur combinaison? Si oui, peut-on
alors dire que l'on a affaire à deux systèmes phonologiques
selon qu'il existe ou non un phonème nasal palatal dans
l'usage considéré; même si aucun autre trait différenciateur
ne sépare les usages à l'étude? Quand on considère le nombre
des variables susceptibles de distinguer différents systèmes
(ou sous-systèmes) linguistiques dans une communauté, on se
rend compte d'un danger: celui d'arriver à autant d'usages
(ou de dialectes) qu'il y a de sujets parlants. Et la dimension sociale du langage s'en trouvera réduite à zéro. On
pourrait naturellement éviter cette fragmentation outrancière
en opérant un tri parmi les critères de différentiation.Mais
sur quel(s) principe(s) théorique(s) pourrait-on fonder ce
tri si l'on ne voulait pas avoir recours a l'arbitraire du
descripteur? On se trouverait dans l'impasse si l'on optait
pour l'autre réponse à la question "formel ou aléatoire?";
réponse qui voudrait qu'on caractérise les phénomènes
linguistiques par leurs seules propriétés statistiques.Cette
conception ne serait défendable que si les faits dont on
étudie les caractéristiques statistiques étaient préalable-
ment déterminés, et les unités délimitées d'avance. Or, il
n'en est rien dans les langues.

(3) Toute langue réunit le formel et l'aléatoire. Une
langue est structurée, mais cela n'implique pas que cette
structure soit formelle ou homogène. C'est une structure
hiérarchisée qui comporte des variations. Pour bien saisir
le fonctionnement d'une langue, il faut tenir compte de ces
variantions inhérentes. La communication linguistique est
assurée malgré ces variations; et nous dirons volontiers en

raison de ces variations. A ce propos, on remarquera que:
(a) la communication n'est jamais totale; (b) deux usages
(ou dialectes) d'une langue ne sont pas imperméables;
l'intercompréhension est très souvent possible; (c) l'usager
d'un dialecte social ne peut opérer l'adaptation nécessaire
pour comprendre un autre dialecte social que dans la mesure
où il a conscience de l'existence des différences et resem-
blances (d) et enfin, si les possibilités d'évolution et
d'utilisation poétique sont inscrites dans la structure même
d'une langue, cela tient à ce que certaines parties de cette
structure sont d'une laxité telle qu'un remodelage est
possible, et que ce remodelage ne portent nullement atteinte
à l'essentiel de la fonction communicative d'une langue.

      (4) Les variations linguistiques ne sont pas illimitées
dans une communauté donnée. Ces dernieres années, l'accent
a été mis souvent sur l'existence de variétés au sein d'une
langue. L'intérêt porté à ces variations ne doit pas faire
oublier qu'il existe aussi des constances, ne serait-ce que
de nature statistique. L'originalité de notre travail consiste en la recherche des limites de variation, et à vérifier
une corrélation entre divers types de variation.

      (5) Il y a corrélation entre variations mentales et
variations sociales. Les hésitations individuelles sont
groupées dans les zones de structure linguistique où l'on
trouve une forte dissension sociale. Si la distinction
/ɲ/~/n+j/ est très incertaine pour l'individu, c'est ici
aussi que les réponses de la communauté révèlent un très
grand désaccord. Le jugement sur l'identité ou la différence
de la prononciation de l'agnelle et la nielle divise les
francophones en deux camps sensiblement égaux. De la même
façon, là où la réaction individuelle est nette et sans bavure
le consensus dans la société est aussi grand. Cela est
tellement vrai que personne ne s'est avisé - et àjuste titre -
de faire une enquête sur l'identité ou la différence de l'initiale de pont de bon en français. C'est que l'intuition individuelle atteint un tel degré de certitude, qu'une confusion de
/p/ et /b/ semble hautement improbable. Cette corrélation
entre variations mentales (individuelles) et variations
sociales apparaît comme résultat de l'interaction entre l'individu parlant et la collectivité linguistique. Si cette

corrélation est vraie, nous pourrons ramener les variations
a une dimension unique: laxité et rigueur de structure. Le
pôle de structure rigoureuse sera caractérisé par un haut
degré de certitude individuelle et un fort consensus social;
l'autre pôle - laxité de structure - correspondant à une
hésitation indivuelle très élévée ainsi qu'a une très grande
dissension sociale. Les faits linguistiques peuvent atre
hiérarchisés selon leur rigueur très élevée - comme /p/∼ /b/
ou leur laxité très marquée comme /ɲ/∼ /n+j/.

(6) La hiérarchie que nous venons d'esquisser est extrin-
sèque, en ce qu'elle est fondée non sur les critères internes
de la structure, mais sur le statut de cette structure dans
l'intuition de l'individu et sur son extension dans la communauté. Une hiérarchisation intrinsèque est possible compte
tenu de la fréquence d'usage des unités les unes relativement
aux autres dans le cadre d'un corpus. On peut ranger les
unités selon leur plus ou moins grande fréquence d'occurrence
dans le texte on constate alors que plus un fait est fréquent,
plus la structure en est rigoureuse: sinsi l'opposition
/p/∼ /b/ en francais. Moins un phénomène linguistique est
utilisé, et plus la structure en est lâche; ce qui se vérifie
pour /ɲ/∼ /n+j/. Cela est dû au rapport dialectique entre la
structure et l'usage: l'une conditionne l'autre, et est con-
ditionnée par lui. (Soit dit en passant, la fréquence n'est
qu'un aspect d'un phénomène plus vaste que nous appellerions
généralité dont l'autre aspect pourrait être l'intégration au
sens où l'entend Martinet.)

En conclusion, nous dirons que la distinction entre
phonétique et phonologie n'est pas aussi simple qu'on a pu le
croire. Cette distinction ne peut être assimilée à la
différence entre une structure et sa réalisation; puisque le
système phonologique comporte des zones peu ou non structurées.
On ne peut non plus fonder la distinction phonétique/phonologie
sur le caractère indivuel de l'une opposé au caractère social
de l'autre, ne serait-ce que parce les faits phonétiques ne
sont pas totalement dépourvue de caractère social. Enfin et
surtout, il n'est pas possible d'arriver à une distinction
claire entre phonétique et phonologie par l'opposition con-
stance/variation.

En fait, notre critique vise moins ces critères de distinction que l'utilisation absolue qui en est faite. Tous
ces critères peuvent et doivent être utilisés dans une
délimitation des domaines phonetique et phonologique. Mais
le recours à ces critères ne conduit pas à une réponse oui ou
non; de multiples gradations sont à prévoir.Et cela n'a rien
d'étonnant: si la phonologie vise à cerner l'utilisation
fonctionnelle qui est faite des éléments phoniques, il est
normal que cet emploi soit variable et présente des différence
de degré. Des lors, la pertinence phonologique peut être plus
ou moins considérable selon le statut psychique, l'extension
sociale et la fréquence des phénomenes à l'étude.On ne pourra
déterminer le statut phonologique d'un élément dans une langue
de quelque extension sans préciser le cadre social auquel on
se réfère.La longueur vocalique est-elle pertinente en finale
du mot en francais? La réponse varie selon la population qu'on
considère. Cette longueur a un statut phonologique en Suisse
romande, mais n'en a guère dans la région parisienne. Elle
relève partant de la phonologie dans un cas, de la phonétique
dans l'autre. Ce sont ce va et vient entre phonétique et
phonologie et ce chevauchement des deux domaines que rendent
possibles le fonctionnement d'une langue malgré l'évolution
constante, et permettent l'intercompréhension en dépit des
divergences.

NOTES

Nous essayons de vérifier empiriquement notre hypothese
concernant la double corrélation: entre le psychique et le
social comme entre l'intrinseque et l'extrinseque. La
vérification vise les domaines de la syntaxe et des unités
phoniques. Les travaus sont en cours; pour le domaine
phonologique les recherche ne sont pas suffisamment avancées
pour pouvoir en tirer des conclusions. En revanche, dans le
domains syntaxique les résultats partiels tendent à confirmer
la corrélation "mental/social."

Cette recherche bénéficie de l'appui financier du Fonds
national suisse de la recherche scientifique.

BIBLIOGRAPHIQUE

Pour plus de détail, on se reportera à:
Jolivet, R.   (1976). Etudes de lett., 1:81-119.
Mahmoudian, M.   (1976). Etudes de lett., 1:65-80.
Mahmoudian, M.   (1976). Paris, Press. Univ.de France, 121-
     139.
Mahmoudian, M.   (1978). Bull., Sect. de Ling., Fac. de
     Lausanne, No. 1.

LINGUISTICS AND SYSTEMS THEORY

MEHRA M. MEHAN
Solna, Sweden

The static (invariance, structuralism, mechanical) view
of linguistics which seeks explanations exclusively within
the existing structure of a linguistic system on the highly
dubious assumptions of oppositional stability and nearly
perfect functional integration seems--as we shall see be-
low--clearly to be giving away, in this century at least,
to a dynamic orientation which focuses attention on the
linguistic processes (phonological and semantic) by which
such systems come into being and succeed one another over
time. This concept makes it impossible to speak of linguistic structure in the singular. Analysis in terms of
distinctive feature is incapable of presenting whole linguistics; nor, which means the same, can any conceptual
system be said to exhibit an embracing, coherent linguistic
structure as we understand the term and its implication.
There are always dissociations, decompositions. . . ,so that
any description alleged to present a single structure will
in fact present only a fragmentary or one-sided picture.
Hence, a perennial critic of the structural conception we
argue that it is from the process of phonological interaction (viz. Composition-Disjunction; "CD") itself that a
phonological unit (a syllable) gets its main features, which
cannot be adequately analyzed in terms of fixed structural
assumptions-the distinctive features, minimal pairs, etc.
In this sense, the linguistic system is not swept along as
an indifferent unit by the operation of the environmental

systems thus social, cultural, etc., or various norms, status, role relationships, ... The linguistic system then is a <u>dynamic open system</u>, manifesting varying degrees of order and disorder. . .which is defined merely as a complex of elements in mutual interaction in accordance with the physiological, psychological, social, cultural. . .and individual attributes. Under this assumption, we must note that the most general and fundamental property of a dynamic open system is the interrelation of parts (phonemes) with regards to (a) the physiological energy, (b) the linguistic interaction, and (c) psychological and social relations. Unfortunately, structuralism calls for a great deal of caution by the user, for which it may serve to eliminate the systemic nature and complexities of linguistic, societal or organizational processes, any attempts at con-crete application warn us against the hope of an easy breakthrough. In other words, such a static model seems valid as a generalized picture of what factors <u>should</u> occur in a language; but these factors are just what <u>prevent</u> the analyst from any concrete use of the model.

Unlike traditional theories in dealing with V-C classi-fication, we distinguish in the total linguistic system two analytically separable subsystems, the independent and the dependent, and relate them in terms of the concept of CD. These two subsystems refer to the <u>relations</u> between activi-ties viewed as responses by members to the necessities of surviving in an environment. In this manner we argue, for instance, that an independent variable has to have some division of labor and some chain of command to the extent that we have explained the existance of these features of group sounds by the assumption that the system of dependent sounds could not survive without them. On this basis, sounds--independent and dependent variables--are thus to be conceived as states of occurrences within the linguistic system of any language; what we need to recognize is that we are dealing with the <u>relationship</u> of the independent variable to the environment selected by its own sensitivity. Hence, in accordance with linguistic data we consider that independent variables may occur in isolation. For instance, /o/, /e/, etc., occur in isolation and simultaneously have

meaning, while /s/, /p/, etc., neither occur in isolation
nor do they have meaning. Accordingly, we can safely assume
the following: independent variables occur in isolation
while dependent variables do not; dependent variables are
functions=variables and thus unstable. On the other hand,
by considering various allophones of dependent variables
(e.g., /ki/, /ku/, etc.), we discover that a change in
the independent variable leads to a change in the dependent
variable. We may now assume, in accordance with the systems
theory, that these two categories of sounds are to be taken
as components of a system. This, then, suggests that these
two categories of sounds are irreducible parts of each other.
But to be irreducible parts of each other does not mean
that independent variables are to be taken as variables=
functions. This cannot be true simply because each category
of sounds has specific density and property unequal but
related with the other categories. So to speak, a sound
acquires plausibility only because it is treated as independent and dependent variables, as independent when it
contributes to a process of a certain kind of energy dis-
ruption, as dependent when it is made into conditions by
the independent variables; if dependent, it cannot be
independent, and if independent, it cannot be dependent--
yet it must be both if the concept of dynamic open system
is to be retained.

In this manner, it is no longer a question of independent variables vs. dependent variables; it is no longer
relevant to ask how sounds behave in isolation, and so on.
For, as we said above, sounds are not entities but relations
such that the behaving sounds (syllable and word) is essentially an organization that is developed and maintained only
in and through a continually ongoing linguistic, social,
cultural, psychological and physiological relation with
other sounds and components of the environment. Some of
these relations (entities) become independent in certain
structures and refer to a structure of relatively stable
linguistic interrelationships comprizing linguistic organizations. It is these interactionally developed and supported webs of components of varying degrees of permanance
that give linguistics some degree of wholeness, or make it

an "entity" in its own right, to be studied by techniques
and perspectives different from those used in studying the
entity called "structuralism." In other words, the linguistic processes with which we are endowed, according to
various criteria, are less solid and less multiply confirmed
of less sharp boundaries such that most importantly, we
have evolved in an environment in which the identification
of certain relations (entities) are the only relevant
features in sound processing. Needless to say, as a product of this evolutionary systemicness we have the mechanism
of psychological, social, cultural, and physiological processes which, within a limited range of relations, analyze
sounds and sound-features so vividly that other static
theories and assumptions seem in contrast, incomplete and
illegitimate. Thus, linguists who view sounds as related
primarily in terms of DF, formant structures, etc., will
use a more or less artificial kind of sound analysis as the
basis of a theory of the linguistic phenomenon they are
studying. If the DF goes relatively far back into the past,
the theory may not only be inefficient or ineffective but
also illegitimate. More importantly, when we are dealing
with perception and conception, we must insist that semantic
units are consequences of the individual's environment such
that the meaning system is the matching of external events
or objects against internal test criteria. But neither external events nor internal criteria are representations of
isolated sounds to be put into opposition; they are consequences of environmental occurrences in terms of values and
relations. Values and relations refer to the degree to
which any process permits a given type of "behaviour."
Obviously, behaviour is the result of the subject's experiences of the environment whether objectively legitimate
or illegitimate, composing an associational and distinct
world. The "world" then becomes processes of differentiation or permutation of "interests" (see below) within
the individual. Characteristic to this pursuit of purposes,
and to the process of adjustment between objects (or objects
and their components) which results, the individual enters
into certain more or less persistent structural relationships
with the object, to be called as "internal institutions,"
and into certain more or less permanent directions of effort
to be called "internal functions." These internal functions

are, in the first instance, results of the previous
"personal" experiences. It is, then, the general principle
of mutual development of the environmental components which
make the individual like a system.

In dealing with the individual as a system, we need a
new method to analyze processes contributing to the actual
behaviour, whether linguistic or non-linguistic. This is
apparently due to the search for demand requirements of
the individual's relatively fixed structures based on maintenance mechanisms. Thus for us the linguistic system is
synonymous with the environmental and structural (innate)
propositions such that the specification of conditions
essential for the persistence of any linguistic system can
tell us about the particular "structures" developed to
satisfy them. In effect, there are relatively fixed well-
defined and comprehensive structures (values, etc.) upon
certain concepts related to personal experiences. A cowboy
knows more about cows than an ordinary man. As we noted
earlier, we cannot regard isolated sounds as meaningful components to a conceptual system. Here we shall try to probe
somewhat deeper into the intricacies of analysis of the
nature of relation of parts and components which characterize any system. First of all there are a number of theoretical and empirical weaknesses in traditional linguistics.
To begin with, theories determine various states of sounds
without paying the slightest attention to the physiological
factors thus brain and states of perception and conception.
Instrumental investigation, DF, etc., for instance, are all
based on some "evidences" as assumed theoretically by some
linguists. Within this conceptual framework DF goes on to
define sounds, meaning, and communication in a generalized
way without any scientific investigation. However, observation is not satisfactory and legitimate for presenting a
theoretical model in sounds' perception and conception. We
have already seen how meaning is conceived as a whole and
not in terms of isolated sound or sounds to be put into
opposition. As MacKay put it, "the meaning of an indicative
item of information to the organism may now be defined as
its selective function on the range of the organism's possible states of orientation, or for short, its organizing
function for the organism. It will be noted that this too

is a relation. . . .A solitary organism keeps its orienting
system up to date in response to physical signs of the state
of the environment, received by its sense organs. This
adaptive updating of the state of orientation we call perception." In this sense, we cannot develop a theory without
a comprehensive knowledge of sense organs connected to the
brain. And this cannot be done by linguists, as such a
study needs many years experiences with physiological
studies (and a well established mathematical background).
The logical and beneficial starting point for a linguistic
theory would therefore seem to be the analysis of relations
(entities) between sounds and the sounds and the environment. But to do this, one needs a theoretical framework
which has demonstrated accuracy and relevance in other
branches of the natural and social sciences.

Consideration of the nature of linguistic, social,
cultural, . . .structures leads us to regard the greater
part of the current discussion of sounds and meanings in
linguistics embarrassingly naive and out of date in the
light of modern systems research. Hence, to be able to
study linguistic elements, we need to develop a theory
based on "feedback" theory in a dynamic open system.
Processes to be studied are, then, linguistic elements
(sounds) and their limit, viz., relations found between
the environment of the types individual, social, psychological, cultural, economical, political and so forth. In
this manner, and as it can be expected, we are interested
in the processes of the environment and various relations
in terms of interactions of components not in a reciprocal
manner, but merely interactions between all relevant components and variables of contributing subsystems and systems.
Of particular interest to us in dealing with the evolution
of the linguistic system in an individual is, however, the
notion of feedback systems which are referred to as "goal-
directed" and not merely "goal-oriented" simply because it
is the deviations from the goal-state itself that direct
the behaviour of the system, rather than some predetermined
internal linguistic mechanism that aims blindly. In such
a way, linguistic behaviour, like any organization and
system, can be determined as a hierarchy of occurrences in
terms of "organizational goals." Hence the semantic units

involved are at various stages in their frequency and
occurrence have their own bounded goals, references, implications, . . .and assume the linguistic behaviour with
differential significance. This is true because factors
which govern the meanings of the semantic units are different
in different cultures.

    Nonlinguistic features and processes presented here
point up the need for a more adequate conceptual understanding, exemplifying especially well the argument that linguistics must of necessity make greater use of psychological,
social. . .variables if it is to progress. Hence, as we
suggested earlier, in accordance with systems theory,
emphasis on structural concepts like DF, formants, etc.
(with an occasional mention of centralization), carry us to
wrong conclusions. A more concerted effort to relate sounds--
and not isolated ones--to the propositions stemming from
psychological, social and physiological interactions of processes is the only possible way of studying the elements
of communication. It is as certain as anything can be in a
situation like this that a workable theory of linguistics
must invoke the principle of interactionalism. What we mean
in arguing for an interaction of linguistics in terms of
psycho-linguistics, socio-linguistics, etc., theory is not
that all semantic portions contain only psychological and/or
social values, but that some of the components of each
semantic unit contain a number of such concept. Accordingly,
our general theory of linguistics is psychological, social
. . .only in the sense that each linguistic system contains
components to be called psychological, social and so forth.
We believe, however, that interactional explanations containing propositions about the relations between components
of the environment thus the individual's experiences, his
physical and psychological mode. . .social norms and values
. . .cultural significances. . .are general explanations in
our theory. This, then, would suggest that linguistic
elements are to be served as means of individual and social
demand requirement (needs). So to speak, the basic interaction model focuses on the complementarities of various
needs of environmental processes, each component acting in
terms of social, cultural. . .need. Our theory does not
focus on a simple linear relation but types of relations

whereby a variable has' no appreciable effect on other elements until its values are experienced by the member of the
society.

If the adaptive system in question is a (relatively high
level) psychological or cortical system, we refer to "learning," whereby the significant environmental variety is transmitted via sensory and perceptual channels and decodings to
the cortical centers where, on the basis of selective criteria
(for example, "reward" and "punishment") related to physiological and/or other "needs" or "drives," relevant parts of
it are encoded and preserved as "experience" for varying
periods of time, and may promote adaption. Or, on the level
of the symbol-based sociocultural system, where the more or
less patterned actions of individuals and groups are as
crucial a part of the environment of other individuals
and groups as the non-social environment, the behavioural
variety and its more or less normatively defined constraints
is culturally encoded, transmitted, and decoded at the receiving end by way of the various familiar channels and
intragroup processes, with varying degrees of fidelity. In
time, again by a selective process--now much more complex,
tentative, and less easily specified--we note the selective
elaboration and more or less temporary preservation of some
of this complex social and physical variety in the form of
"culture," "social organization," and "personality structure."

SOME PROBLEMS IN PHONETIC THEORY

M. A. A. TATHAM
University of Essex

In this paper I want to highlight some of the difficulties which arise when one considers phonetics as a part
of linguistic theory. Several researchers have argued that
phonetics should be viewed as following on from the phonological component of a transformational generative grammar,
accepting as input the output from that component. Others
have sought to relate phonology and phonetics by making
suggestions about details of the phonology where consideration of such details is phonetically motivated--as, for example, attempts to provide a phonological feature set relating
more closely than that proposed in, say, Sound Pattern of
English, to alleged phonetic facts. Indeed, many see phonology as in danger of being too abstract and seek to relate its
abstractions to the real world by incorporating phonetic
observations. For myself, I don't want to do anything to
phonology--or at least not very much: I would rather make
proposals concerning phonetic theory. As I see it, phonetic
theory is at odds with phonological theory: not only are the
data sets of each different in type, but the formats of the
current theories are so incompatible as to at least run the
risk of technically rendering vacuous any 'corrections' to the
phonology which might come from phonetic theory. I shall try
to show why I think there are problems of mismatch between the
two theories and make some suggestions to improve compatibility

Let us consider some data: In French there is a vowel
/u/. This vowel is characterized in the phonology by being
high and back and at the same time by being round. There is
another vowel /y/ which is characterized by being high and

front, whilst also being round. There is also the vowel /i/
which is high and front like /y/, but differs from /y/ by
being non-round. Notice that /u/ differs from no other
vowel along the rounding parameter alone: all other vowels
in French have a different high/low-front/back characterization. In the case of /y/, however, there is distinction
from /i/ only along the rounding parameter.

Now, moving to phonetics, suppose we examine the lip-
rounding of /u/ and /y/. This is a relatively simple task
using the technique of electromyography which enables us to
examine the degree and duration of contraction of muscles--
in this case the orbicularis oris which is a sphyncter muscle
running around the lips and responsible, in one of its modes
of contraction, for lip-rounding. As with all physiological
parameters, measurements of the contraction of a muscle over
repetitions of a phonologically 'same' utterance show a certain degree of variation. That is, if, for example, I repeat
the word in French doux (/du/) several times, some variation
from example to example will occur in the contraction of
orbicularis oris. However, if we compare the range of
variation exhibited by this muscle over repetitions of doux
with the range of variation in repetitions of, say, du
(/dy/), we notice that the range is significantly less for
/y/ than for /u/. This difference in range exists notwithstanding the overall increased rounding of /y/ and the lip-
protrusion associated with the articulation of that sound.
It has been suggested that this narrowing in range can be
interpreted as reflecting an increase in the precision with
which any one of the repetitions was articulated. If this is
the case--that is, if a native-speaker of French articulates
/y/ on the lip-rounding parameter with more precision than
when he articulates /u/, then we might well ask ourselves the
question Why? A possible explanation might be that since the
difference between /y/ and at least one other vowel, /i/ is
carried only by the lip-rounding feature it becomes crucial
to get the lip-rounding right to avoid confusion at a perceptual level between different morphemes; for example:
/dy/ and /di/ in j'ai dû--'I had to,' and j'ai dit--'I said.'
It may be that the difference in meaning between these two
phrases rests entirely on the precision of contraction of a
single muscle.

Another piece of data: Take the minimal pair in English cap and cab. At an underlying level in the phonology these two morphemes are distinguished only in the third segment and on the feature /voice/. They may also be differentiated on the feature /tense/ if that feature is not vacuous: /p/ being /+tense/ and /b/ being /-tense/. A phonological rule operates, lengthening the vowel segment before the /+voice/ consonant in cab, and this is followed at some stage in the phonology by a rule which changes /+voice/ to /-voice/ in voiced obstruents in final position. Thus, cap and cab are differentiated at the underlying level on the final segment, but (and still in the phonology) at the derived level of systematic phonetics, on the penultimate segment. The phonetic data is in accord with the surface phonology in this case (but see below): vocal cord activity is indeed prolonged during that portion of the utterance which may be said to correspond to the vowel segment in the phonology and is noticeably absent during the part of the utterance corresponding to the final phonological segment--this is in the word cab. In cap we also note the absence of vocal-cord activity at the end of the utterance and that its duration during the identified vowel section is less. Certainly in my English when either of these words is in sentence or phrase final position the final bilabial occlusive is often unreleased, and it would follow that at least from an acoustic viewpoint the morphemic difference between the words is carried by the relative duration of the vocal-cord activity. I imagine that one would note in this example a relatively high degree of timing precision on this parameter.

Yet a third piece of data: Consider in my English the utterance /man/--man. Phonologically at the underlying level we have a nasal consonant /m/ followed by a non-nasal vowel /a/, followed by nasal consonant /n/. At the systematic phonetic level, specification of the nasal feature would not have changed--though some may argue with this. An examination of the actual articulation of this nasal-non-nasal-nasal sequence, however, reveals a certain degree of phonetic nasality in the vowel--that is, the velum does not quite close at any time between the two consonants. Several dialects of English have rather more phonetic nasalization of the vowel segment than I do--and they have this greater degree of nasalization consistently. Since there is no

contrastive nasal feature on vowels in any dialect of
English--that is, since the feature /nasal/ is always
marked minus at the underlying level in the phonology in
vowels, and since there is no phonological rule transferring
any contrast from an adjacent segment onto this feature of
vowels, precision at the phonetic level with respect to
opposing oral vowels and nasal vowels is unnecessary.

Now, let us look back at this data and try to fit it
into a theoretical framework which integrates both phonology
and phonetics. The output of the phonology--that is, at the
level of systematic phonetics--can be taken as a characterization of the requirements to be imposed on the phonetics. As
such there clearly is going to be nothing there which is
utterly impossible for the phonetics to carry out on the one
hand, and on the other it is said that all information will
be there for the phonetics to proceed as an automatic, that
is, non-linguistic component: nothing linguistically determined can be added during the phonetic realization of the
phonological requirement.

Now, note that phonetically /y/ is realized with more
precision than /u/: how does the phonetics know that more
precision is required?

Take the second piece of data: vowels before voiced
obstruents are to be phonetically lengthened and voiced
obstruents in final position are not to have vocal cord
activity. Let me say that last part again: if the systematic phonetic level characterizes the phonological requirement
to be imposed on the phonetics then a marking of /-voice/
on the final obstruent should mean 'do not vibrate the vocal-
cords'. I have some further data derived from an experiment
observing electromyographically the behaviour of the laryngeal
muscles during these phonologically devoiced segments. The
data clearly shows that although the vocal-cords were not
vibrating the laryngeal muscles were doing all the right
things to bring about vibration--the vocal-cords did not
vibrate because of the fact that the air-pressure differential above and below the vocal-cords was incorrectly
balanced to allow spontaneous vibration to take place. In
other words the data suggests not that there was no intent
to voice but that on the contrary there was every intent to

voice. This is a demonstration of the classical mistake of making incorrect deductions from surface observations.

If we revise the phonology and do away with the de-voicing rule on the grounds that, whatever happens phoneti-cally, voicing is signalled as a requirement, we give our-selves quite a problem. Voicing is required: it does not happen. A coarticulatory influence has prevented vibration, and this is of no consequence because phonologically the morphemic contrast is redundantly signalled by the vowel length. But look at final phonologically voiced obstruents in a language like French: there is vocal-cord vibration. The phonetic action taken in French to obtain vocal-cord vibration for these /+voice/ obstruents must be different from that taken in English or the results would be the same in both languages.

On to the third example: the phonological requirement for the vowel segment in man is that there should not be nasality--there usually is, however--but in different dia-lects there is more or less; and this more or less is per-fectly consistent. It must surely follow that what is re-garded often as an artifact of coarticulation is nevertheless systematic in a way which is not determined by the mechanical or other considerations which determine that the artifact shall occur. In other words, it is clear that control is being exercised over the artifact--just as it is clear that in French control is being exercised over the air-pressure balance artifact--and just as it is clear that control is being exercised over the variability artifact in the case of French /y/.

I hope it is by now obvious where I'm going in my argu-ment. What may not be obvious is why I chose those three examples: there are several others which could have been chosen. I selected these because they are indicative of the control of different artifacts for different reasons. My lip-rounding example is about maintaining precision to pre-serve morphemic contrast and shows phonetic attention to the most fundamental use to which the features of a segment can be put. My voiced obstruent example--besides showing that the inclusion of a devoicing rule in the phonology of English

is probably wrong--is about maintaining at the phonetic
level a different interpretation of a phonological requirement seemingly identical across two languages as far as the
linguistic contrast is concerned. My oral-vowel-between-
nasal-consonants example is similar to the voiced obstruent
one, but is about different interpretations of the phonological requirement in different dialects of the same language.

In each of these cases we are talking about adjustment
of a property which is essentially phonetic for a specific
linguistic aim: to maintain contrast dictated from a high
level, to maintain a low-level not crucially contrastive
variant operating differently in different languages, and to
maintain a variant operating differently in different dialects of the same language. To include these operations in
the theory we must decide at what levels they are introduced.

Let us backtrack a little. At the input to the phonology
morphemes are correctly strung together to provide a linguistic encoding of a high-level concept or idea otherwise
non-transferable between human beings. I am saying something
quite obvious and uncontroversial. Language is an encoding/
decoding system enabling the copying of ideas between brains.
These ideas are encoded into soundwaves which exit from one
human being and transfer to another human being where a
decoding process takes place. Such an encoding/decoding
system must have several properties, one of which is that
the encoding and decoding algorithms must be complementary
in some sense. One unfortunate property of this type of
encoding/decoding system is the spurious introduction all
along the line of noise, distortion or error. In the abstract
various techniques are in principle available to minimize the
introduction of errors or to detect and inversely filter--that
is, negate--errors when they occur.

In principle when designing an encoding/decoding system
the designer predicts the occurrence of such errors and
either avoids those situations where they will occur or
takes steps to minimize or cancel them as completely as
possible--or rather, as completely as necessary: the distinction between 'as completely as possible' and 'as completely as necessary' is an important one as I shall try to
show in a moment.

Up to the input to the phonology there have been constraints at work dictating in a sense some of the format
of the syntactic strings able to be generated. These constraints can often prove extremely revealing as to the
nature of the brain and its workings, and linguists go to
considerable lengths to highlight classes of constraint
and hierarchies of constraint. The constraints to this
point--the underlying level of the phonology--have been
essentially neurological or psychological and have been revealed to the linguist by adopting a metatheoretical stance
which begins by setting up a too-powerful model and successively limiting that power.

The constraints imposed on a phonology are often,
though, of an essentially different nature. Not only are
we dealing with neurological and psychological limitations
on the encoding process--but also with phonetic constraints:
that is, motor, mechanical and acoustic constraints at least.
And, picking up a phrase I used earlier, the phonology is
not going to require a phonetic impossibility.

Phonological encoding is about transforming strings of
morphemes into strings of phonetic requirements--that is,
into strings of objects (in the abstract sense) which, when
phonetically encoded into soundwaves, will sufficiently
enable a decoding device to extract all the relevant information from the signal. The phonology is, however, doing a
double task. Whilst attempting error minimization (and we
shall look at at least one way it does this in a moment) it
is in addition required to introduce variants into underlying
strings--merely for the hell of it. The classical example of
this is the introduction of the palatal and velar alternates
of an underlying /l/ in English. Some researchers claim that
this serves to aid perception, but I doubt if that is the
reason.

One major error minimization device is redundancy. A
given piece of information is stated and restated in different ways. An essential property of this redundancy in
phonology is that it is patterned--that is, predictable. The
values of certain features in the specification of segments
may be predicted from the values of other features, or indeed
whole segments may be predicted from their context.

At any rate, we exit from the phonology at the derived
or systematic phonetic level with a string of segments designed to take account of the possibilities of phonetic
realization and which has as accurately as possible encoded
the input ready for conversion to soundwaves, and which has
already built in the possibility of correcting some errors
which might arise later in the encoding/decoding process,
and which has catered for any idiosyncratic alternations.
All of these phenomena we may call linguistic and all
transformations occurring during phonological encoding are
systematic or rule-governed.

Now, and only now as far as we are concerned today, do
the real problems begin, and central to those problems is
the one of <u>precision</u>. Neural control of the organs of speech
is not entirely precise even under ideal conditions--or rather
perhaps I should say the results of neural control (the actual
positioning and movement of the organs of speech) are not precise. The degree of precision varies--but is particularly
vulnerable to the constraint of time, and vulnerable also to
the constraint of context: that is, the precise achievement
of a desired configuration of the vocal-tract may be particularly difficult (or impossible) given preceding and following configurations. When a human being constructs a mechanical system where precision is of importance he generally
builds in some kind of monitoring device which can adjust
the system if it begins to run wild. As you know, there has
been much discussion in the phonetics literature as to
whether there are such devices in speaking, what their exact
role is, and so on. I don't wish to extend that particular
discussion here, except to say that I believe that such devices do exist but that they have a limited role to play
inasmuch as they often operate too slowly to be effective on
a segment-by-segment basis.

<u>Time</u> is our big problem. Notice that phonology seems
to have forgotten about time. Notice also that it works
perfectly well without it (since it is abstract)--or rather,
in the human being, if it has to take account of time in its
own operation, then the temporal constraints <u>it</u> suffers are
those imposed by the time required for the transmission of
neural impulses and for computations <u>within</u> the brain. When

we're talking about transmission of neural impulses to
muscles, the time it takes them to contract and the time it
takes the articulators to move--then we have entered a quite
different area of problems.

The organs of speech assume different configurations for
different phonological requirements, and the accuracy of
these configurations is constrained firstly by the fact that,
all other considerations (including time and context) being
optimum, precision is not 100%, and constrained in addition
by time and segmental or spacial context.

But notice--now back to my original data--that degree
of precision varies. Lip-rounding for /y/ is more precise
than for /u/; spontaneous vocal-cord vibration during final
phonologically voiced obstruents is more carefully controlled
in one language than in another; nasalization of phonologically non-nasal vowels is allowed more in one dialect of a
language than in another. So the precision is controlled
and is therefore controllable. Two questions immediately
spring to mind: how is it controlled? and why is it controlled? And two further questions: at what stage in the
encoding process does this control take place? and what are
the limits of the control?

To the question 'why is it controlled?,' I have in a
sense already provided some kind of answer. It is controlled
to maintain morphemic contrast, or to maintain some idiosyncratic surface output. The other questions are more difficult to answer. Firstly, how is it controlled? For short-
term precision, say within a segment, I don't believe the
degree of precision is controlled by monitoring followed by
subsequent adjustment: the known monitoring systems, from
the slow auditory feedback through to the comparatively fast
gamma-loop servo system, are just not fast enough--in any
case there is every evidence that we go to a particular configuration directly without a semi-oscillatory onset which
would be a property of a servo-controlled system. And also
in any case the servo system would have to be set, and setting the system would depend on knowing just what setting
is required.

Now, that last remark leads me straight into a suggestion
as to how we control precision: we control precision by prior

computation, and of necessity the prior computation must
involve consideration of the imprecision which is going to
occur unless steps are taken. So, spontaneous vocal-cord
vibration will not occur unless the right balance is obtained between supra- and sub-glottal air-pressures, and
this fact must, of course, be available for inclusion in the
computation to obtain vocal-cord vibration. What also must
be known is that in obstruents, as opposed to, say, vowels,
the air-pressure balance will be disturbed because the free-
flow of air out of the mouth will be interrupted. In other
words the system must have knowledge of firstly that /+voice/
as an abstract phonological requirement involves vibration
of the vocal-cords, and secondly that vibration of the vocal-
cords will not occur if other features specify interruption
of the air-flow (the abstract phonological features are
mutually exclusive if the 'normal' algorithm for obtaining
vocal-cord vibration is followed), and thirdly what to do
about it if necessary.

But that is not all. We see from the data that sometimes we do not get vocal-cord vibration with phonologically
voiced obstruents and that sometimes we do--so that it must
be the case that a decision has been taken as to whether or
not to overcome the effects of the predicted constraint. Such
a decision occurs with predictable outcome--in French it goes
one way, in English the other. The decision is therefore
principled.

There is an alternative model possible. I have assumed
so far that the phonological requirement for vocal-cord
activity is signalled by marking the voice feature as /+voice/
at the level of systematic phonetics in both languages. I
have done this on the basis of similarity of function of the
segments in question in English and in French. I went on to
assume that despite similarity of function an idiosyncratic
(or contrastively unmotivated) decision was taken to disregard the predictable non-occurrence of vocal-cord vibration
in English, but not to disregard it in French. The alternative model would suggest that the phenomenon was akin to the
velar/palatal /l/ alternation in English and that somehow the
voiced obstruents in French were marked at the end of the
phonology in a special way allowing the automatic realization
of those segments <u>with</u> vocal-cord vibration. I do not believe

this alternative model to be appropriate--at least not on
those grounds. Surface variants accounted for in the
phonology seem to me to be properly those which do <u>not</u>
involve the containing within limits of a phonetic constraint.

   Now I seem to have contradicted myself, for I said
earlier that I believed that the phonology took into account
phonetic constraints. If it does not seem too much like playing with words, let me explain that I mean the phonology
takes account of phonetic constraints on the phonology, whereas the phonetics takes account of constraints on the phonetics.
Some constraints cannot be overrideen or modified in any
linguistically useable way: obviously the phonology must
take account of this. But some constraints can be modified
and the extent to which they can be modified will determine
their phonological 'usability'--but the decision as to just
what degree of overriding is to be executed is taken by the
phonetics. To do this the phonetics would need to know the
phonology.

   So you could imagine a series of phonetic questions:
what is the phonological feature to be executed? what does
this involve? what constraints will be encountered? do
these matter? if yes, then how are they overcome?   Notice
that if the answer is 'yes,' then by definition they are able
to be overcome--or the phonology would never have made such
demands on the phonetics.

   Now, even if you do not agree with me, bear with me
because if all this <u>is</u> an adequate model then one or two
interesting questions arise. How <u>does</u> the phonetics decide
whether or not overcoming constraints is necessary?   In
what sense could the phonetics be said to know the phonology?
--to know, for example, that precision in the lip-rounding
of /y/ is more important that in /u/? Well, some writers have
suggested a sort of summary of the phonology--particularly of
redundancy--somewhere around the end of the phonology or beginning of the phonetics. Their reasons have varied, sometimes concerned with accounting for diachronic sound change,
or sometimes accounting for syncope (i.e., segment deletion),
etc. Postal (1968) was rather emphatically concerned to

avoid any what he called 'independent level of autonomous
phonological representation' on the grounds that such a
level would involve spurious duplication of rules and perhaps loss of generalization. However, I believe that to
involve the phonology proper in anything non-phonological
in the strictest sense would be ill-motivated, and this
leaves us with a <u>non</u>-automatic phonetics. And a non-
automatic phonetics means a phonetics which is <u>linguisti-
cally sensitive</u>.

I have been treating the phonetics as an encoding system. One kind of encoding system can be identified as a
passive system--that is, for any given input a well-defined
and invariant algorithm is operated to give the output. The
passive encoding system is, however, a special case of what
might be called <u>active</u> systems. An active encoding device is
sensitive to its input in a rather interesting way. In the
particular case of phonetics a passive encoding would entail
segment-by-segment (or feature-by-feature) scanning of the
input and segment-by-segment execution of the encoding. An
active phonetic encoding would scan more than one segment
(or feature) at the input, and, as a consequence of seeing
this segment (or feature) in a particular context would
adjust the encoding algorithm. Note that the trigger for
adjustment has not come from the input segment or feature
itself, and note further that the same segment or feature
introduced in a different environment would be encoded by a
different algorithm. When scanning the input what the
phonetics would be looking for is difficulty of execution of
individual segmental requirements. How a particular phonological feature is to be encoded varies with the marking of
other features associated with that segment and with the
marking of those features in surrounding segments. Clearly,
such an active encoding would be unnecessary if the phonology
had anticipated all the problems and specified each systematic
phonetic segment exhaustively--and that is a position some
researchers may care to take. I believe, however, that a
solution of <u>this</u> kind does not accord with the facts or provide as much insight into speech as the former solution.

I favour the active encoding solution for a number of
reasons. Let me give just one example. It is clear that on

many occasions we can choose alternate phonetic encodings.
I can say, for example, cap with a released /p/ or cap'
with an unreleased /p/--the most the phonology might signal
is that it is linguistically unimportant whether there is
release of the obstruent or not. If release is either to
occur or not, then, despite the fact that it doesn't matter
which, a decision must be taken as to which to do, since
both involve active motor control of the articulation.
Such a decision could hardly be phonological if there is no
phonological interest in the outcome. Some researchers
have suggested that degree of phonological interest might be
signalled to the phonetics by arranging the features in segments at the systematic phonetic level hierarchically, with
crucial features higher than less crucial features. Note
that how crucial a feature is will vary with phonological
context.

I am trying to show, of course, that we cannot have an
autonomous automatic phonetics. And if we are to have
phonetics integrated with linguistics then we are up against
the metatheoretical problem of format. One cannot legiti-
mately integrate two differently formatted theories. I propose a reappraisal of the format of phonetic theory and adjustments to bring it in line with phonological theory, or
with linguistics in general. Linguistics is a statement of
what a native speaker/hearer knows about language in general
and about his language in particular. Syntax, for example,
therefore characterizes classes of sentence--rather than
produces individual one-off sentences; and phonology characterizes classes of abstract phonetic shapes. Formatted along
these same lines phonetics would be a statement of what a
speaker knows of the implementation of phonological inten-
tions and as such would characterize classes of articulatory
or acoustic outputs--rather than describe the waveshape or
articulatory configuration of any particular utterance.

With such compatibility phonetics would more transparently
relate to phonology. Phonetic explanation of certain phonological phenomena would be more meaningful and self-evident,
and problems thrown up by phonological theory more readily
investigated by phonetic methods.

There is another aspect to linguistic theory which
I alluded to much earlier. Formally linguistics proceeds
by successively constraining a too powerful device. Constraints are identified according to type and hierarchically
imposed on the unconstrained device. This formal technique
might usefully be adopted into phonetics and, in a sense,
we have already begun to do so. We talk of mecanico-inertial
constraints, of temporal constraints, of missed targets and
the like. I do not see any difficulty in principle in
formally organizing these ideas with a vew to optimizing
insights into how human beings work phonetically.

I began by quoting some relatively simple data at you,
and I have ended by talking about metatheoretical problems,
formalism and a phonetic theory that is as abstract as
phonology--the way between the two may not have come out as
clearly as I would have liked: I excuse myself by saying
that I set myself a non-too-easy task. I do firmly believe,
however, that linguistics and phonetics are not to be treated
as distinct, but that they have a mutually revealing role to
play. I further believe that currently phonetics is lament-
able in its inbuilt to capture significant generalizations
about speech, and I hope that even if my tentative proposals
prove valueless in themselves, they will nevertheless have
indicated that a different approach from the one we have now
is worth considering.

C. LARYNGEAL FUNCTION

CARACTERISTIQUES DE FORME DE L'ONDE DE DEBIT DES CORDES VOCALES: PRODUCTIONS VOCALIQUES

L. J. BÖE ET B. GUÉRIN
Institut de Phonetique de Grenoble et E.N.S.E.R.G.

Dans ce travail nous avons tenté d'obtenir des précisions concernant l'influence du couplage source-conduit vocal sur la forme de l'onde de débit glottique, dans le cas des productions vocaliques. Pour ce faire nous avons utilisé le modèle à deux masses d'Ishizaka et Matsudaira (1968) (Figure 1), qui semble présenter une bonne simulation du fonctionnement du larynx. En nous servant de l'étude d'Ishizaka et Flanagan (1972) pour la mise en oeuvre numérique, nous avons déjà montré (Guérin et Boë, 1977; Guérin et al., 1977) qu'il était possible de se limiter à deux commandes, la pression subglottique P_S et un paramètre Q qui rend compte à la fois de l'étirement et de l'amincissement des cordes vocales sous l'effet de l'action conjuguée des tensions passive et active. Ce facteur est relié aux variables mécaniques du système par les relations: $m_1 = M/Q$; $k_1 = K.Q$; $m_2/m_1 = k_2/k_1 = 0,15$; $k_{12} = 5Q + 10$ avec comme valeurs de base: M = 380 mg et K = 20 kdynes/cm Q variant de 1 à 3 pour le registre de poitrine et une voix d'homme. Pour P_S nous nous sommes référés aux valeurs moyennes relevées par de nombreux auteurs par de multiples procédures. Nous avons donc, pour chacune des trois voyelles, donné aux deux paramètres les valeurs suivantes: Q : 1, 1,5, 2, 2,5, 3 et P_S: 6, 8, 10, 12,cm d'H_2O soit un total de 60 simulations. Pour mettre en jeu le couplage de la source avec le conduit vocal, celle-ci est connectée sur un circuit qui représente

l'impédance d'entrée d'une disposition articulatoire donnée.
Sa valeur dépend essentiellement des deux premiers formants
(Mrayati, et al., 1976) c'est-à-dire de leurs fréquences et
bandes passantes. Les valeurs que nous avons adoptées sont
les suivantes en Hz (Table 1). La simulation a été réalisée
sur PDP 11/20, un ensemble de sous programmes permettant de
dessiner les déplacements des deux masses m_1, m_2, l'onde de
débit, son spectre (échelles logarithmiques) (Boë et Guérin,
1977).

RESULTATS

La forme de l'onde de débit est, en général,
caractérisée par les paramètres suivants (Figure 2). Le
quotient d'ouverture Q.O $=(t_1 + t_2)/T$ c'est-à-dire le temps
d'ouverture des cordes vocales ramené au temps de la période
et le quotient de dissymétrie Q.D $= t_1/t_2$ rapport du temps
d'écartement des cordes vocales au temps de rapprochement.
Pour caractériser le spectre nous avons mesuré sa pente
moyenne α en dB sur les trois premières octaves.

1. Le quotient d'ouverture. En valeur moyenne Q.O est
rigoureusement le même pour les trois ensembles de simula-
vocalique: 0,64; les valeurs extrêmes sont aussi très
voisines (Table 2). Il dépend de P_S et de Q de façon
différente: si la pression croit Q.O décroît, alors que
c'est l'inverse pour Q. Les relations sont assez bien
décrites par des droites de régression: /i/: Q.O =
$-0,72 \cdot 10^{-2} P_S + 1,22 \cdot 10^{-2} Q + 0,68$; /a/: Q.O = $-0,82$
$10^{-2} P_S + 1,90 \cdot 10^{-2} Q + 0,68$ et /u/: Q.O = $-0,83 \cdot 10^{-2} P_S$
$+ 2,30 \cdot 10^{-2} Q + 0,67$.

Ces influences peuvent s'expliquer ainsi: si P_S
augmente, l'effet Bernouilli est plus important, les cordes
vocales s'accolent plus rapidement et plus longtemps; si
elles sont plus tendues, l'effet d'aspiration ne peut agir
autant. Ces valeurs correspondent bien aux mesures effectuées avec la parole naturelle (Fant, 1968; Linqvist, 1965,
1970; Takasuqi, 1971; et Zemlin, 1959). Pendant la phonation il a été constaté que le quotient d'ouverture diminue
avec l'intensité (qui dépend essentiellement de P_S) et

augmente avec la fréquence de vibration des cordes vocales
(à intensité constante) c'est-à-dire quand leur tension
évolue (Cederlund et al., 1960; Sonesson, 1960; Timcke,
1956, 1957; et Timcke et al., 1958). On voit que la
nature de la voyelle n'a pratiquement pas d'influence sur
le Q.O: c'est aussi l'observation qu'avait faite Takasugi
qui, pour les voyelles du japonais, avait relevé des valeurs
de 0,69 pour /i/ et /a/ 0,70 pour /u/.

   2. Le quotient de dissymétrie. Pour cette variable,
les écarts extrêmes et les valeurs moyennes présentent de
nettes différences pour les trois voyelles (Table 3). La
mise en évidence des influences de P_S et de Q n'aurait pas
grande signification sous la forme de régression linéaire,
comme on peut le constater (Figure 3). S'il se dégage des
tendances: Q.D augmente plutôt avec P_S et Q, on peut constater que les relations ne sont pas linéaires. Les variations du quotient de dissymétrie avec la pression subglottique et la tension des cordes vocales sont aussi modi-
fiées par le couplage source-conduit vocal. Comme cela a
déjà été mis en évidence, en particulier avec un modèle à
deux masses (Guérin et al., 1976), l'impédance d'entrée
du conduit vocal, pour laquelle le 1^O formant joue un rôle
important, provoque une suroscillation de l'onde glottique;
on retrouve d'ailleurs dans le spectre des zéros qui sont
situés à la fréquence des formants. Le déplacement de cette
ondulation par rapport à la forme de base provoque une
variation importante pour l'évaluation de Q.D (Figure 4).

   Pour la parole naturelle, les relevé de Q.D effectués
par Lindqvist évoluent autour de 2 et ceux de Takasugi entre
1,32 et 2,13. L'action de la pression subglottique et de la
tension des cordes vocales ne semble pas clairement apparaître (comme pour la simulation). Quant aux variations d'une
voyelle à une autre, les mesures de Takasugi montrent
qu'elles sont plus faibles que celles d'un locuteur à un
autre, mais pour le japonais, c'est aussi /i/ qui a le Q.D.
le plus (Carr et Trill, 1964; Linqvist, 1970).

   3. La pente du spectre. Exprimée en dB/octave, elle
évolue dans les limites, présentées à la Table 4. Il n'y
a pas de très nettes différences pour les trois voyelles et

ces valeurs sont tout à fait comparables à celles qui ont
été mesurées au cours de la phonation (Carr et Trill, 1964;
Flanagan, 1958; Miller, 1959; Takasugi, 1971) mais inféri-
eures aux relevés de Cederlund et al., Monsen et Engebretson
(1977) (18 dB/octave) (Figure 5).

Les influences de la pression subglottique et du
facteur Q sont très nettes pour les trois ensembles de
simulation: /i/-- a = 0,35 P_S + 0,95 Q - 15,3; /a/-- a =
0,32 P_S + 0,74 Q - 15,3 et /u/-- a = 0,45 P_S + 1,54 Q -
17,1. Si ces deux paramètres croîssent, la pente du
spectre devient moins négative, c'est-à-dire que l'intensité
des composantes diminue plus lentement en fonction de la
fréquence. En fait, ce résultat est prévisible dans la
mesure où P_S et Q, nous l'avons vu, influencent la forme
de l'onde glottique, ce qui a été évalué avec les variations des quotients d'ouverture et de dissymétrie. Pour
l'onde glottique, Takasugi a proposé une relation empirique
permettant de relier la pente de son spectre aux deux
quotients: a = k(Q.0/Q.D) avec k = - 30. Cette évaluation s'explique assez facilement: si la phase de fermeture
et la dissymétrie du signal augmentent, le spectre aura
d'autant plus de composantes de fréquences élevées. A ceci
s'ajoute une caractéristique propre au signal glottique:
le forme de l'onde est généralement plus arrondie lorsque
le Q.0 est grand.

Nous avons évalué séparément les valeurs de k pour
les trois voyelles (Table 5). Pour l'ensemble des valeurs
confondues k = - 28, ce qui est très voisin du relevé de
Tagasugi. Les variations de k sont essentiellement dues
à Q et une estimation donne: k/i/ = + 3,0 Q - 37; k/a/ =
+ 1,9 Q - 29 et k/u/ = + 4,4 Q - 37.

CONCLUSION

Cette simulation de l'onde glottique visait à obtenir
des précisions sur: (1)-sa forme, décrite par les quotients
d'ouverture et de dissymétrie; (2) son spectre, caractérisé
par la pente moyenne; (3) les influences de la pression
subglottique et de la tension des cordes vocales, approchée

par le facteur Q; et (4) le phénomène de couplage avec le conduit vocal, dans le cas des trois productions vocaliques /i, a, u/.

En ce qui concerne les trois premiers points les résultats correspondent tout à fait aux mesures effectuées pour la parole naturelle. Cette étude permet de préciser le peu de différence entre les simulations pour les trois voyelles, ce qui confirme les relevés de Takasugi. Seul le quotient de dissymétrie, directement affecté par la position des suroscillations dues au couplage, permet d'opérer un regroupement /i/, /u/ par rapport à /a/. Cette manifestation du phénomène de couplage confirme bien l'influence prépondérante du 1° formant. Tous les résultats confirment la bonne adéquation du modèle à deux masses et le bien fondé de son utilisation pour faire progresser la connaissance du fonctionnement interne du larynx.

REFERENCES

Boë, L. J. and Guérin, B. (1977). Bull. l'Inst. Phon. Grenoble VI. 1-56.

Carr, P. B. and Trill, D. (1964). J. Acoust. Soc. Am., 36:2033-2040.

Cederlund, C., Krokstad, A. and Kringlebotn, M. (1960). STL. RIT. QPSR., 1:1-2.

Fant, G. (1968). North Holland Pub. Co., Amsterdam, 173-277.

Flanagan, J. L. (1958). J. Speech Hear. Res., 1:99-116.

Guérin, B. and Böe, L. J. (1977). IEEE Inter. Conf. ASSP, 583-586.

Guérin, B., Degryse, D. and Boë, L. J. (1977). Symp. Artic. Modèles Grenoble, 263-277.

Guérin, B., Mrayati, M. and Carre, M. (1976). IEEE. Int. Conf. ASSP, 47-50.

Ishizaka, K. and Flanagan, J. L. (1972). BSTJ, 51:1233-1268.

Ishizaka, K. and Matsudaira, M. (1968). 6th Int. Cong. Acoust., B.13.

Linqvist, J. (1965). 5th Int. Cong. Acoust., A-35.

Linqvist, J. (1970). STL. RIT. QPSR, 1:3-9.

Miller, R. L. (1959). J. Acoust. Soc. Am., 31:667-677.
Monsen, R. B. and Engebretson, A. M. (1977). J. Acoust.
Soc. Am., 62:981-993.
Mrayati, M., Guérin, B. and Boe, L. J. (1976). Acust.,
35:330-340.
Sonesson, B. (1960). Acta Otolaryn., S156:1-80.

Takasugi, T. (1971). J. Radio Res. Lab., 18:97, 209-220.
Timcke, R. (1956). Ztschr. Laryng. Otol., 35:331-335.
Timcke, R. (1957). Rev. Laryn., 78:619-624.
Timcke, R., Leden, H. Von and Moore, P. (1958). Arch.
Otol., 68:1-19.
Zemlin, W. (1959). MA Thesis, Univ. Minn.

Table 1.

	/i/	/a/	/u/
F_1 (B_1)	244 (99)	578 (37)	296 (98)
F_2 (B_2)	2250 (19)	1300 (63)	783 (21)

Table 2.

Q.0	/i/	/a/	/u/
valeurs extrêmes	0,61 - 0,68	0,60 - 0,68	0,60 - 0,70
valeurs moyennes	0,64	0,64	0,64

Table 3.

Q.D	/i/	/a/	/u/
valeurs extrêmes	1,81 - 2,22	1,20 - 1,92	1,32 - 2,08
valeurs moyennes	1,97	1,47	1,82

Table 4.

a	/i/	/a/	/u/
valeurs extrêmes	- 7,5 à - 12,0	-8,3 à -13,2	-7,6 à -13,1
valeurs moyennes	-10,3	-10,9	-10,0

Table 5.

	k/i/	k/a/	k/u/
valeur moyenne	-31	-25	-28
écart type	2,9	3,2	4,8

Position de repos

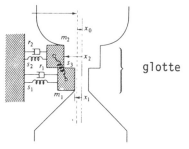

glotte

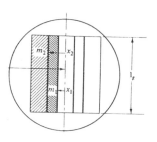

Vue de face

Vue de haut

figure I

Modèle à deux masses d'après
Ishizaka and Matsudaire (1968).

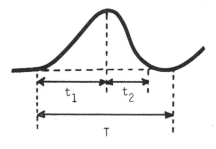

figure 2

Forme schématisée de l'onde de débit

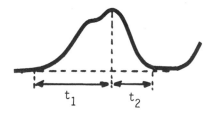
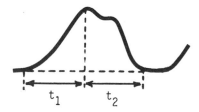

figure 4

Suroscillation de l'onde glottique due au couplage
avec le conduit vocal

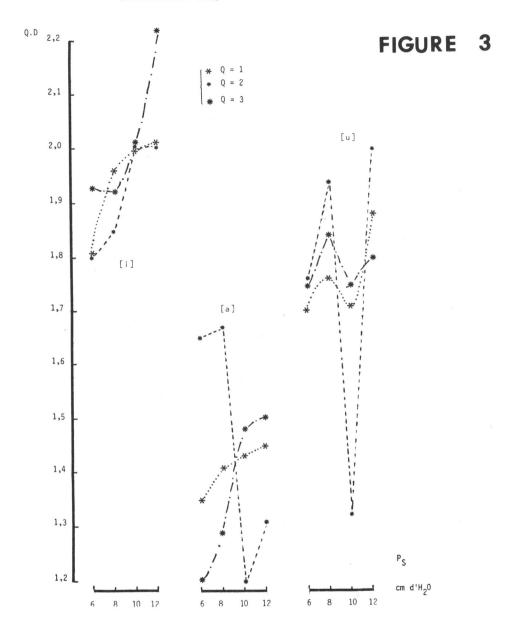

FIGURE 3

Relation entre le quotient de dissymétrie Q.D et la
pression subglottique P$_S$, pour différentes valeurs du
paramètres Q en fonction de la nature de la voyelle.

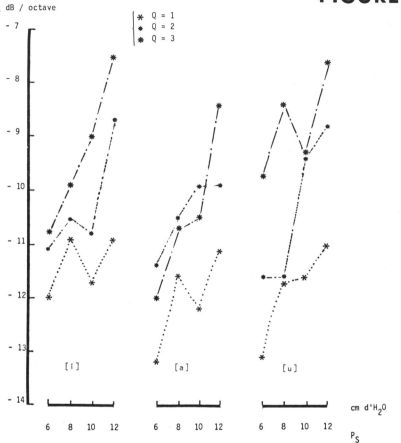

Relation entre la pente α du signal source et la pression subglottique P_S, pour différentes valeurs du paramètre Q et en fonction de la nature de la voyelle.

LARYNGEAL PATTERNS OF CONSONANT PRODUCTIONS IN SENTENCES OBSERVED WITH AN IMPEDANCE GLOTTOGRAPH

GÉRARD F. CHOLLET AND JOEL C. KAHANE
University of Florida and Memphis State University

The transillumination technique, one of the more widely used alternative methods for the measurement of vocal fold activity, records glottal area changes by measuring the amount of light passing through the glottis(Weiss,cited in Sonesson, 1960). While there is no uniform agreement among investigators regarding the validity of this method,most researchers suggest that glottal area changes as determined from photoelectric glottographs are comparable to similar measures obtained from ultra high speed photography (Harden, 1975; Sawashima, 1972). Data from Coleman and Wendahl (1968) appear to indicate, however, that absolute measures of glottal area cannot be obtained via this methodology. Various methodological diffi- culties encountered in the early use of this technique have been largely resolved through the substitution of minute photosensors attached to the end of thin flexible plastic tubes for the stiff light conducting rod used in Sonesson's version of this method(Frøkjaer-Jensen,1967;Sawashima, 1972). The modification of this method has enabled speakers to main- tain the normal configurations of the supraglottic cavities attained in continuous speech. As a result of these modifi- cations experimenters have employed the transillumination technique to study vocal fold vibratory patterns during con- tinuous discourse as well as in the more conventional examina- tion of individual vibratory cycles of sustained vowels employed in transillumination, stroboscopic, and high speed photographic studies (Cooper et al., 1971; Lisker et al., 1969; Sawashima, 1970).

Electroglottography is a technique which has traditionally been used to study the motion of the vocal folds
during sound production; specifically in quantifying the
temporal characteristics of each vibratory cycle. The relative merits of this technique include the fact that it is the
least invasive of all methodologies previously discussed and
its adaptability to the study of vocal fold vibratory activity
during continuous discourse. While the validity of this technique in studying the temporal characteristics of the vibratory
cycle is not universally accepted, equivalence of the electroglottographic method to the transillumination and high speed
photographic methods has been demonstrated by several authors
(Frøkjaer-Jensen, 1969; Köster, 1970).

Frøkjaer-Jensen (1968) has pointed out that the differences between the photoelectric glottograph and the electroglottograph are best explained in terms of their respective
abilities to illustrate different aspects of the vibratory
cycle. He maintains that the photoglottograph best illustrates the opening phase while the electroglottograph best
illustrates the closing phase of the vibratory cycle and the
effects of vertical contact of the mucous membranes of the
vocal folds. Van den Berg (1974), on the other hand, noted
that the transglottal impedance measurements obtained via
electroglottography were ". . .highly qualitative. . .and the
results were very poor in falsetto voice." This observation
appears to question the ability of the electroglottograph to
illucidate very subtle vibratory events of the vocal folds.

A thorough review of the literature has not unearthed
an electroglottographic study of the larynx during continuous
speech. Hence, the purpose of the present investigation is
to study laryngeal behavior during continuous speech and to
identify specific laryngeal adjustments during obstruent
production.

METHOD

Equipment. Figure 1 represents the arrangement of equipment used in this study. Changes in glottal impedance and
contours reflecting changes in vocal intensity and airflow
were made concurrently during phonation. Acoustic signals

were monitored by a microphone incorporated into a hand held
mask placed over the speaker's face. The mask also contained
an aerometer which monitored oral airflow during phonation.
An Frøkjaer-Jensen (F-J) intensity meter (1M340) was used to
generate intensity contours and a duplex oscillographic
record of voicing was used as a microphone tracing. Electro-
glottograms were made from F-J electroglottograph, Type EG830.
A weak voltage, high frequency signal (.5V and 13mHz) was applied with maximum amperage (10mA) to plate electrodes placed
over each thyroid lamina. Permanent records of all data were
made on separate channels of an F-J ultraviolet recorder
(Type R1200) at a recording speed of 100 mm/sec.

Subjects and Tasks. Ten adult male speakers, ranging in
age from 20-29 years served as subjects. All subjects were
native speakers of English and were free from laryngeal pathology. Each subject was seated erectly with his occiput
stabilized and asked to utter three repetitions of four test
sentences used by Lisker et al. (1969) to study glottal articulation of plosives, fricatives and affricates. A total of 120
sentences were collected.

Analysis. Electroglottographic (EGG) records were
examined to determine if any systematic patterns would be
assigned to amplitude changes in the waveforms obtained from
the four test sentences. Identification of these patterns was
made without the benefit of phonetic transcription. Four distinct patterns of transglottal impedance were consistently
identified. Each pattern type was operationally defined as
follows (Figure 2): (1) Type 1 or "free pulsing" was characterized by a sustained level of suprabaseline transglottal
impedance. (2) Type 2 or "constrained" pulsing was characterized by an abrupt drop in transglottal impedance which
decreased but did not reach baseline levels. (3) Type 3
pulsing was characterized by a prominent drop in transglottal
impedance which often reached baseline levels and was associated with a "short" period of non-vibration of the vocal
folds (no concurrent activity in voicing channel). (4) Type
4 pulsing was characterized by a "long" period of baseline
impedance associated with a "long" period of non-vibration of
the vocal folds.

The duration of non-vibration of the folds was measured for all consonants that showed cessation of glottal vibration for longer than 2 cycles. The acoustic signal is clearly inadequate to get this information for obstruents because the entire closure duration shows up as a silence. A caliper was used for the measurements and the readings were translated to msec. Histograms of these data were obtained using a bin size of 5 msec. The temporal characteristics of consonants were compared by computing the overlap of the corresponding distributions. A probability distribution was obtained by normalizing a histogram to unity. This was required to correct for discrepancies in the number of samples between groups.

RESULTS

Phonetic segments have been grouped per pattern types as shown in Figure 3. All vowels, diphtongs, glides, and liquids were classified as type 1 patterns. All unvoiced fricatives, plosives, and affricates were recognized as type 4 patterns. The voiced consonants were subdivized to show their distribution in types. Dental flaps, weak voiced fricatives, voiced plosives, and strong voiced fricatives were shown in that order to reflect increasing difficulty of the folds to vibrate during their production (a drop in amplitude was more acute and observed more frequently for strong voiced fricative than voiced plosives, for voiced plosives than weak voiced fricatives, etc.). The closure of a dental flap is so sudden that the vibratory pattern of the folds was not affected in 36% of the cases. Tense and lax voiced fricatives showed different laryngeal behavior. These differences may be related to the increased air flow and turbulence for tense fricatives compared to their lax counterparts which may have some dampening effect upon the vibration of the folds. Transglottal impedance for inter-vocalic voiced plosives and strong voiced fricatives were always reduced (Types 2, 3, or 4) compared to those of adjacent vowels, glides or liquids (Type 1). This dramatic drop in transglottal impedance is further emphasized by the finding that in 22% of the voiced consonant productions, either a type 4 or a type 3 was found with a duration of non-vibration larger than two pitch periods. Type 3 patterns should be

viewed as limit cases where the folds hardly vibrate. Non-
vibration of the folds is certainly a major characteristic
of unvoiced consonants. It was, therefore, important to compare the distributions of the duration of non-vibration for
voiceless and voiced consonants when this duration is longer
than 2 pitch periods. The two distributions are obviously
distinct as expected, but their overlap (11%) is quite considerable. This characteristic seems specific to continuous
speech as other studies using VCV syllables have shown that
the glottis is continuously vibrating through all voiced
consonants.

DISCUSSION

Data from this study suggest that electroglottography
is a useful method to describe laryngeal activity during
continuous speech, although it is not without limitations.
This instrumentation provides a non-invasive method to make
detailed analyses of laryngeal behavior. The EGG waveforms
enable the investigator to use more than a binary system--
interrupted vs. non-interrupted--to classify pulsing conditions of the larynx during speech production. It must be
pointed out that the amplitude of EGG waveforms may have been
significantly affected by the upward and downward movements
of the larynx during connected speech. Such factors would not
have played such a potentially critical role in studies where
data on vocal fold vibratory behavior were obtained using
sustained vowels or monosyllabic productions. In future EGG
research, controls for monitoring laryngeal displacement
should be incorporated in research designs.

Results from the present investigation illustrate that
four distinct pulsing conditions associated with specific
classes of phonemes can be abstracted from EGG tracings. It
was not possible, however, to state whether the glottis was
open or closed in the way that photoglottography or fiberoptic
instrumentation can. It was only possible to infer about the
movement of the vocal folds from EGG impedance variations.
Before statements regarding the degree of opening or closing
of the vocal folds can be made with precision from EGG
tracings future research must be undertaken to synchronize
EGG recordings with laryngeal motion pictures. This will allow

precise statements to be made regarding the relationship between transglottal impedance and glottal arcs.

The exclusive use of fiberoptic instrumentation to study laryngeal behavior during speech appears to be limited in its value, as well. The careful study of English obstruents by Sawashima (1970) enabled the author to classify these phonemes /b,g,p,k,ð,v,z/ grossly on the basis of whether the arytenoid cartilages were separated and whether the vocal folds were concomittantly vibrating or non-vibrating. He did not differentiate different patterns of laryngeal vibration for the obstruents studied. The only previous study of English obstruents in continuous speech using glottography was reported by Lisker et al. (1969). They used photoglottography to study laryngeal adjustments during plosive, fricative and affricate productions in continuous speech. Each phoneme was described according to whether the glottis was open or closed and if the vibrations of the vocal folds were interrupted or noninterrupted. Though direct comparisons regarding open-closed gestures of the glottis as described by Lisker et al. cannot be made with data from the present study, comparative statements regarding pulsing conditions can.

The EGG data appears to better describe gradations in vocal fold vibratory activity during connected speech than photoglottography (Lisker et al.). The binary classification of interrupted vs noninterrupted pulsing used by Lisker et al. can be improved upon with EGG from this study. Instead of a single classification for uninterrupted pulsing, two EGG conditions were found--free pulsing (Type 1) associated with vowels, semi-vowels glides and voiced weak fricatives (v,ð) in certain contexts and constrained pulsing (Type 2) associated with voiced fricative, affricate and plosive productions. Similarly, instead of a single classification for interrupted pulsing, two EGG conditions were found--short non-pulsing (Type 3) observed for voiced plosives in certain contexts and a long non-pulsing (Type 4) condition associated with productions of unvoiced obstruents. EGG data from the present study are in general agreement with the trends reported by Lisker et al. for laryngeal behavior during obstruent productions. However, results from this study permit further refinements to be made in their classification.

Coarticulatory effects could often be seen in the EGG tracings in the form of altered durations of the vibrations of the vocal folds. Thus /p/ in "pleasure" tended to take on the EGG appearance of /b/ in that the duration of non-vibration became shortened such that it tended to approximate the temporal laryngeal characteristics of the voiced cognate. Unfortunately, an acoustic study of coarticulation cannot be done adequately on a single parameter as many phonetic, prosodic, lexical, syntactic and semantic factors can influence the values observed. These factors should be quantified and varied systematically. Acoustic phonetic studies have taught us that such investigations should be performed on large speech corpuses. Further validations of the electroglottographic techniques are necessary before such large scale studies can be launched.

REFERENCES

Coleman, F. R. and Wendahl, R. W. (1968). J. Acoust. Soc. Am., 44:1733-1735.

Cooper, F. S., Sawashima, M., Abramson, A. S., Lisker, L. (1971). Ann. Otol., 80:678-682.

Frøkjaer-Jensen, B. (1967). ARIPUC 2:5-19.

Frøkjaer-Jensen, B. (1968). ARIPUC 3:9-16.

Frøkjaer-Jensen, B. (1969). Nord. Kong. XVII Otol.

Harden, R. J. (1975). J. Speech Hear. Res., 18:728-738.

Koster, J.P. (1970). Folia Phon., 22:92-99.

Lisker, L., Abramson, A. S., Cooper, F. S. and Schvey, M. H. (1969). J. Acoust. Soc. Am., 45:1544-1546.

Malécot, A., and Peebles, K. (1965). Phon., 18:545-550.

Sawashima, M. (1970). Haskins Lab., SR 21/22:187-200.

Sawashima, M. (1972). Mouton, The Hague, 69-115.

Van den Berg, J. W. (1974). North-Holland Pub. Co.

Weiss, D., cited in Sonnesson. (1960). Acta Otol., 5-156.

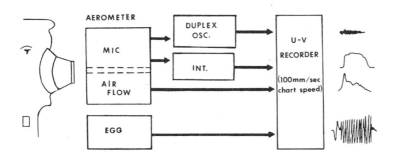

FIGURE I: The equipment

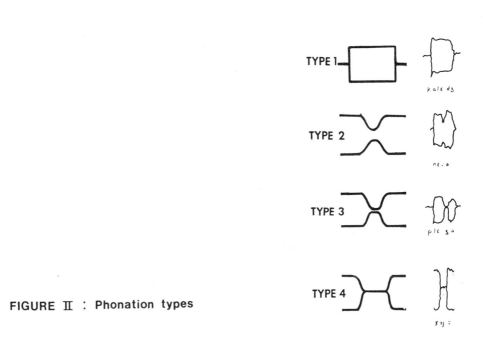

FIGURE II : Phonation types

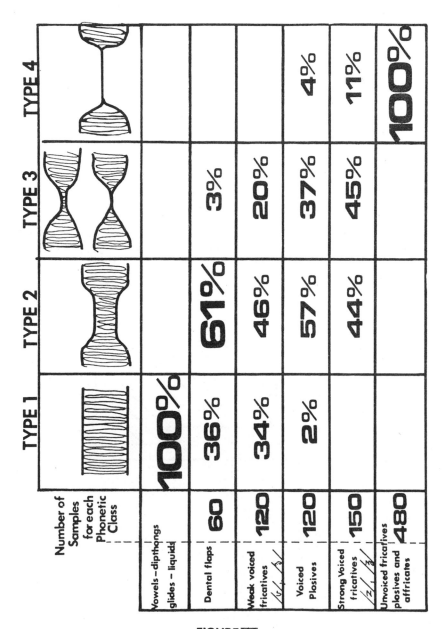

FIGURE III

Laryngeal types corresponding to phonetic segments.

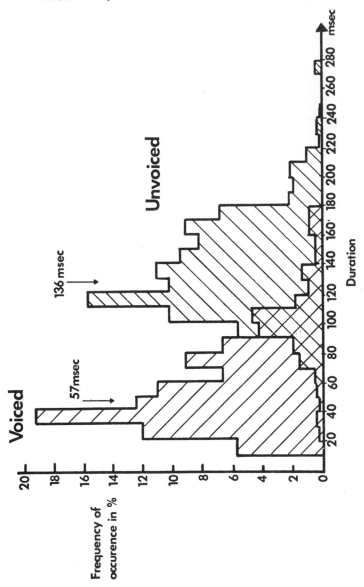

FIGURE IV :

Normalized histograms of the duration of non-vibration of the folds for voiced and voiceless consonants.

PHYSIOLOGICAL FUNCTIONS OF THE LARYNX
IN PHONETIC CONTROL

O. FUJIMURA
Bell Laboratories

Let us examine how the larynx behaves during speech
utterances. We all know that speech organs such as the
tongue, the lips and the velum move characteristically for
specific articulatory purposes. Not much was known about the
movements of the larynx until recently. The most direct way
of observing such movement is actually to see it, but this
obvious technique was not conveniently available until we
succeeded in using a special fiberscope inserted through the
nasal passage, so the oral pathway was left free for articulatory movements. There have been many interesting findings
about phonetic control of the larynx using this technique
(which was created by Sawashima and Hirose, 1968), some of
which I would like to discuss later in this paper. In addition to the expected laryngeal actions with respect to glottal
adduction - abduction, we find, using this technique, extensive
movements of the larynx in the vertical direction. Also, considerable contraction-expansion of the larynx in the front-
back direction may be noticed.

When the larynx moves vertically as it changes its
shape, we encounter difficulty in quantitative measurements
of the dimensions of the laryngeal structures by use of a
fiberscope, for we do not know the distance between the objective lens of the fiberscope and the object, the part of
the larynx we are interested in. We recently obtained a
solution to this problem, by designing a special stereoscopic

fiberscope. The two glass-fiber cables are inserted through
the two nostrils, and as their tips appear out of the velum
opening in the pharynx, we snap them together by a magnetic
bridge via the mouth opening, so the entire system constitutes a well-calibrated stereoscopic system. By using such a
system, we can measure the distance between the fixed objective lenses and the object, and thereby the exact dimensions of the object. Two images through the two objective
lenses are obtained side by side. By comparison of exact
positions of selected points on the object structures, a
computer program gives us the height of each point and distance between each pair of points on its object. In the case
of the laryngeal gestures, we cannot only measure the height
of the glottal orifice, for example, but also any tilting of
the laryngeal structures (Fujimura, 1976), which is crucial
for clarifying the physiological mechanism of pitch control,
etc., as we will discuss later. This new experiment is being
conducted in cooperation with Drs. Thomas Baer and Seiji Niimi
at Haskins Laboratories and we expect to obtain more extensive data in the very near future. I should mention also at
this point that there are some other techniques for measuring
larynx height, notably due to Kakita and Hiki (1976), and to
Ewan and his coworkers (1972). They both measure the movement of the apparent prominence of the thyroid cartilage.
Shipp (1977) also uses a direct optical method for measuring
vertical movement.

Vocal Cord Vibration and its Acoustic Consequence. The
larynx, housing the vocal cords, acts as a rapidly moving
valve that modulates the airflow from the pulmonary system
into the vocal tract. The vocal tract is the acoustic tube
extending from the glottis to the mouth opening. Its cross
sectional area changes from point to point along the direction
of wave propagation, and we can represent its acoustic characteristics by its resonant pattern, particularly, for our present discussion of voiced vowel-like sounds, a set of formant
frequencies. The shape of the vocal tract, and consequently
the formant characteristics, are determined by articulatory
gestures.

If we specify the airflow modulation by the vibrating
vocal cords in the form of time variation of the volume
velocity of air flowing through the glottal orifice, we can
compute the output speech waveform, that we would hear as

different stationary vowels, given the shape of the vocal tract. If we change the waveform of the modulated airflow, simulating different modes of vocal cord vibration, we will hear different voice quality. In some languages, such voice quality changes may be crucially related to phonological distinctions (Henderson, 1975).

If we use a simulation model for the vibrating vocal cords as a myoelastic system with aerodynamic interaction with the airflow, a physical interpretation due to van der Berg (1958), then we can compute the glottal modulation as the result of specifying certain physical parameters for the laryngeal adjustments as well as pulmonary variables. This problem was discussed in detail by Rothenberg (1968). Ishizaka and Flanagan (1968), using a so-called two-mass model for the vocal cords, experimented with a combined vocal-cord vocal-tract system, showing effects of interaction between the vocal-cord vibration and articulatory conditions. Such an approximate system is capable of reproducing natural involvement of turbulent noise that is generated at the point of constriction along the vocal-tract, as the result of relative abduction of the glottis accompanying voice cessa- tion. Also, it demonstrates that voice pitch is affected by an articulatory constriction when pulmonary and laryngeal conditions remain constant. Their model involves several degrees of freedom which could be used for adjusting the state of the vocal cords, affecting the resultant voice quality. One of those is the transglottal air pressure difference. Abduction-adduction is represented in this model by a parameter that determines the gap between the left and right sets of masses when there is no flow and the vocal cords are at rest. The rest of laryngeal adjustments are reflected in the control of a set of physical parameters such as masses and spring constants of the model, which may not necessarily represent "real" physical quantities that pertain to natural parts of organs in a direct way. Never- theless, a functional model with an appropriate number of controlled variables can serve as an excellent means for simulating gross overall characteristics of the speech production system, especially for applications such as speech synthesis with an effective set of time-varying con- trol parameters.

From a physiological point of view, it is crucial to
be able to identify physical components and relate them to
different channels of neural control. In particular, we
would like to be able to identify specific muscles, the
states of which are quantitatively represented in the model.
This is necessary in order to understand the inherent and
basic mechanisms involved in the complex phenomena of speech
behavior in general, and phonetic control for linguistic
distinctions in particular. It is also important for understanding pathology and exploring remedies for various
problems.

The Anatomical Structure of the Vocal Cords. Much has
been done quite recently with respect to vocal fold anatomy,
notably by Hirano (1974). He examined both human and canine
larynges using a number of advanced techniques. He determined that the vocal folds should really be considered a
composite structure of what he calls "cover" and "body,"
the connection between these two substructures being loose
both mechanically and biologically. As for biological evidence, he showed, for example, that the blood circulation
system is appropriate for their relatively independent
functions, allowing the cover to slide freely relative to
the body. Fig. 1 summarizes his findings. Roughly speaking,
the cover is a strong thin mucous membrane, whereas the body
mainly consists of the so-called vocalis muscle. In the
human larynx, there is a transition phase in between the
two structures from an anatomical point of view.

Vocal Cord Vibration. There have been proposed several
different models for the vocal cords in vibration. Svend
Smith, years ago, with admirable insight, advocated the idea
that it was the mucous membrane of the vocal fold that
played crucial roles in determining the vibration pattern of
the vocal folds (see Smith, 1961). He made a mechanical
model, called 'munyo,' which consisted of a solid orifice
for blowing air, from which a pair of thin rubber membranes
forming an open-ended flat tube extended. The tube naturally
collapses, two sheets of rubber coming in loose contact with
each other, but can be blown apart slightly as air pressure
is applied at the orifice. Then, however, because of the
Bernoulli's effect which sucks the membranes inwards, in

addition to the elastic restoring force of the membranes,
the membranes come in complete contact to block the airflow.
This causes excessive air pressure to be built up in the
blowing orifice, and the process of opening up the membranes
starts again to repeat the entire cycle. Voice pitch, i.e.,
the fundamental frequency of vibration, is controlled by
manually stretching the rubber membranes transversely near
the open end, altering the elastic restoring force. This
corresponds to controlling the spring constants in the two-
mass model we discussed before.

In the natural system, it is known that the cricothyroid muscle when it contracts causes a similar stretch
of the vocal cords (cf. Fink, 1975, for a detailed account).
The blowing orifice opens toward the trachea in the natural
case. The vibrating membranes of the "munyo" model then
represent the medial surface of the vertically extended vocal
folds up to the upper edges of the glottis. This munyo model
is, we might say, an exaggeration. It helps visualize, however, the essence of the natural system as a pair of thin
membranes with appropriate longitudinal tension, interacting
with airflow receiving Bernoulli's sucking force over the
relatively large surface areas. The wave-like motion of the
membranes, the wave propagating in the vertical direction
along with the airflow, was discussed by Kirikae (1943) in
relation to register control, based on his stroboscopic
motion picture data on human vocal cords in combination with
a carbon particle technique for tracking the movements of
specific points on the membrane. Many high--speed motion
picture films, including the one dating from 1940 by
Farnsworth of Bell Laboratories, later notably those of
van der Berg, Moore, Lieberman, Hiroto, Hirano, and Gould,
all with somewhat different techniques, showed such three-
dimensional movements of the vocal cords.

Recently, Baer (1975) examined quantitative details of
such vibration modes by using excised dog larynges. He also
used carbon particles attached on the vocal fold surface in
order to observe local movements. Since he could accurately
measure three-dimensional positions as functions of time
using a stereoscopic microscope from both above and below
the glottis, unlike in any of the preceding studies, he

discovered many interesting characteristics of vocal fold
vibration in "phonation" (by the dog larynx). Out of such
measurements, he produced an animation film of the frontal
section of the vocal fold surfaces during an episode of
phonation, which demonstrates an apparent propagation of a
surface wave along the medial vertical surface of the vocal
fold upward. His measurements of movements of selected
points on the mucous membrane also showed a considerable
amount of local stretch/shrinkage of its surface during the
vibration cycle. Since the membrane is to a large extent
elastic with respect to surface stretch, this finding suggests that the physics of vocal fold vibration may involve
significant energy transfer between the potential energy
due to surface tension and the kinetic energy of vocal fold
movement in the vertical tangential direction. Fig. 2 is a
drawing by Hirano (1975), showing a wave propagation type
movement of the vocal fold surface in frontal section.
Little deformation of the inside structure, in particular
the thyroarytenoid muscles (vocalis muscles) can be assumed
for such a mode of vibration.

It is interesting to note that the importance of
asynchronism between the upper and lower parts of the
glottis was first theoretically pointed out by Ishizaka
and Matsudaira (1968). This was why they proposed the two-
mass model, deviating from the previous simulation work by
Flanagan and Landgraf (1968) using one mass and one spring.
A single mass-spring system with interacting airflow could
not account for observed readiness of vocal cord vibration
under varied conditions. Separation of the glottal orifice
into upper and lower sections seems to make the model vibrate
under a more reasonable range of parameter values. This
point has been further clarified by Stevens (1977). It must
be cautioned, however, that literal visualization of such a
model as a mechanical model can be quite misleading. For
example, the springs are not intended to represent only the
direct restoring force due to the elastic stiffness of the
body, which could be affected by contraction of the vocalis
muscle. They are intended to represent the complex of contributions, in particular that from the external tension of
the vocal fold in the longitudinal direction that is created
by the cricothyroid muscle contraction (see _supra_ and _infra_).

They may also reflect negative contributions due to the
tracheal pull (Maeda, 1976) and surface stiffening due to
forces from the upper structures (Ohala, 1972), negative
effects of the lower pharyngeal sphincter action (Lindquist-
Gauffin, 1972) as well as the effects of the vocalis contraction. The vocalis contraction actually should contribute to reduction of stiffness of the cover (as well as
increase of the effective mass), since the vocal cords are
shortened by such contraction, other conditions being equal,
and the cover becomes less stretched and more slack (and
thicker). On the other hand, the stiffness of the body will
increase by the vocalis contraction. Therefore, in order
to accurately predict the modes of vibration under different
muscular conditions, it is necessary to know exactly what
the roles of the cover and body are in actual vibration of
human vocal folds. We do not have the necessary information
at present.

The correct interpretation of the two separate masses
is not clear either, at the moment. Even though Hirano's
account of the anatomy is clear in terms of the functional
separation of cover and body, we just don't know how much
of the body mass participates in the vibration. As Hollien
and others (1969) clearly showed by x-ray tomography, and
as Hirano's dissection with contracting muscles directly
demonstrates in the case of animal larynges, there is no
doubt that body is important in determining the mechanical
parameters of the vibration system, such as the extent of
adduction and the stiffness of the internal wall against the
movement of the cover (see Hirano, 1975, for description of
relevant experiments, using electric stimulation of the
vocalis muscles). Perhaps, the two masses should represent
two vertically dissected parts of the cover, the property
of the body being entirely neglected, or being only
indirectly represented via its influence on the effective
spring constant for each of the sections. Perhaps, as
Titze (1976) suggested in his work using a more complex and
realistic model of the vocal folds as a three-dimensional
system, one of the two masses as a crude approximation should
be related to the body and the other to the cover constituting
the upper surface of the fold. The latter interpretation is
tenable if the movement of the body mainly determines the

vibtation of the lower part.

Baer (1975) demonstrated, in this connection, that
the excised larynx, when the vocalis muscle, or the body,
was entirely removed, vibrated almost normally in chest
register, but failed to simulate head register. Smith's
model of course demonstrates the feasibility of the cover-
only system. In any case, it seems generally accepted that
the head register, with high membrane tensions and thin and
stiff body can be simulated, in effect, by a one-mass system.
In this sense, visualization of the vocal "cords" as elastic
strings or bands delimiting the glottal slit, captures some
truth only in the case of a high pitched, more sinusoidal
mode of vibration, in either the so-called head register or
falsetto.

Adduction/Abduction of the Glottis for Phonetic
Distinctions. The glottal adduction and abduction, i.e.,
the adjustment of the gap between the vocal cords, is
achieved to a large extent by the control of the displacement and rotation of the arytenoid cartilages relative to
the cricoid cartilage. The distance between the vocal cord
edges at the vocal processes which represent the boundary
between the so-called cartilaginous part and the membranous
part of the vocal cord, often gives a convenient measure of
the degree of adduction or abduction. In addition, different
conditions of the membranous portion affect the apparent
shape of the glottal slit. Depending on such aerodynamic and
elastic membranous conditions, the folds may vibrate even
with a slightly but distinctly open glottis at the cartilaginous portion, leaving a glottal gap all through the
vibratory cycle. This causes an additional DC-flow of air
superimposed on the rapidly modulated airflow which represents voice. The constant flow through the cartilaginous gap
causes an /h/-like turbulent sound, and the voice may be
called breathy. Particularly when there is no severe supraglottal constriction, the fast airflow enables otherwise
fairly widely separated membranous portions to maintain
vibration, as often observed for intervocalic /h/'s in many
languages.

Specifications of physical quantities describing the vocal fold conditions are thus relatively complicated. In order to understand the control mechanism, we need to know about physiological specifications, since at any rate, what one adjusts in speech is the contractile patterns of the set of relevant muscles. Of course, here again one has to be cautious about the considerable roles of various feedback loops. In fact, there seems to be evidence that muscle contractions are in some cases even primarily caused by motor commands to special feedback devices rather than directly via commands to the main muscle fibers. But even so, the contraction pattern of muscles as a whole determines the physical conditions of the entire system, and therefore, specification of such contractile states of muscles and their temporal changes does give us a complete description of the entire speech production system. Unfortunately, available techniques are limited in their applicability to measurement of such contractile states of various muscles. Nevertheless, electromyographic studies in very recent years have brought us some substantive knowledge about speech physiology in general, and laryngeal adjustment in particular. The cartilaginous adduction/abduction is a good example. Fig. 3 shows EMG activities of a pair of laryngeal muscles, the interarytenoid and posterior cricoarytenoid, as reported by Hirose and Gay (1972). In the figure at the top, the EMG signals from the vocalis muscle are also shown. As we can see, reflecting the phonetic voicing distinction between /p/ and /b/ (presumably in American English), clear antagonistic functions of these two muscles are demonstrated, revealing the adducting function of the interarytenoid and the abduct- ing function of the posterior cricoarytenoid. The peak of activity in the PCA muscle for /p/, accompanied by an inhibi- tion of the INT muscle, takes place within the voiced vowel portion a few tens of milliseconds before the implosion. The peak of the INT muscle, accompanied by a somewhat slower relaxation of the abducting activity of PCA, takes place 60-70 msec before the voice onset for the schwa vowel. In contrast, nothing drastic happens for the word with inter- vocalic /b/, except that the PCA acts to abduct the glottis, anticipating the end of the utterance. The vocalis muscle does not seem to contribute much to the consonantal distinc- tion in this environment.

    Fig. 4 from the same paper, exemplifies a similar
distinction between /s/ and /z/. It may be noted, however,
that for the voiced /z/, there is a slight dip in the INT
activity, which we did not see clearly in the case of the
voiced stop /b/ in the previous figure. This reflects the
tendency for the glottis to be somewhat abducted for the
voiced fricative, causing a breathy voice with a fair
amount of airflow for generating the turbulence at the
apical constriction. Note also that the vocalis does not
show much change for the consonantal gesture.

    Fig. 5 shows similar EMG records for the three muscles:
PCA, INT, and VOC. The utterances are Japanese words in
isolation, and this figure was published by Sawashima et al.
(1975) (also see Hirose, 1975). In addition to the EMG
records, a fiberscopic film was simultaneously taken, and
the figure shows glottal width as measured at the vocal
processes. These data show several interesting points.
First, the PCA curve qualitatively resembles the temporal
change of glottal width, but the muscle activity, the cause
of change, always precedes the corresponding change in
glottal width, the effect of the muscle contraction. The
apparent amount of the lead in time, however, varies from
case to case (see infra). Secondly, when we compare the
initial stop consonants /p/ and /b/ in subject MS, glottal
width approaches zero more rapidly for /p/, and corres-
spondingly, the activities of the abductor PCA and the
adductor INT slightly overlaps for /b/, but not at all for
/p/. In other words, there is a totally inactive period
preceding the articulatory release of the utterance initial
/p/. The other subject HH, however, shows somewhat different
temporal characteristics of the activity switching in this
environment. The physiologic strategy concerning the transition from a non-speech mode to the beginning of speech
gestures in general seems to vary considerably from subject
to subject (see Sawashima et al., 1975; Hirose, 1975; and
also Hirose and Ushijima, 1976).

    Another interesting point about these data by Sawashima
et al. is the comparison between the two medial consonants,
single /p/ and geminate /pp/. Sawashima and his co-workers

have studied extensively glottal width for Japanese voiceless consonants, including the geminate consonants, and
the devoicing phenomena for high vowels surrounded by tense
voiceless consonants (see Sawashima et al., 1971; Weitzman
et al., 1976). According to these previous studies, intervocalic tense stops always show only a small glottal opening for the articulatory closure, even though the vocal
folds stop vibrating completely. In comparison, the
geminate stop shows a slightly larger glottal aperture as
well as longer stop period of the articulatory closure
accompanied by voice cessation. This point is borne out
clearly in the data here. In the EMG record, we can see
also that the abductor (PCA) is active not only for the
opening process of the glottis but also, probably to a
lesser extent, for maintaining the opening throughout the
long closure period, if we consider the general lead of EMG
in comparison with its physical effect to be about 50-100
msec for this muscle under the pertinent condition.

There is something special about the so-called geminate
consonants in Japanese. Hattori (1961) describes them by a
phomeme /Q/, which is supposedly characterized by a kind of
laryngeal tension. Voice characteristics near voice onset
following the articulatory release seem to differ significantly from nongeminate tense consonants, in my informal
experience from syllable concatenation experiments. The
physiological interpretation for such characteristics is
not yet clear. Such difference in voice quality may be
found in the preceding vowel as well, and the apparent
difference in the vocalis activity between /p/ and /pp/
(/Qp/) immediately to the right of the vertical line in the
figure may reflect such a difference. In any case, it should
be noted that this intuitively "tensified" or somehow
"laryngealized" (geminate) consonant, in comparison with the
plain consonants, seems to reveal about equal or even weaker
vocalis activity (compare the broken lines for MS during the
period for which PCA shows isolated peaks (dotted)). On the
other hand, it can be shown that at least for some types of
glottalization, including glottal stops at voice onset and
the momentary disturbance of vocal fold vibration in Danish
stød, the vocalis activity does show a peak, according to
Fischer-Jørgensen and Hirose (1974). The Korean forced

type stops, often transcribed by capital P, T, and K, also
show such vocalis activity (see intra).

As we see in Fig. 5, the intervocalic /h/ shows strong
activity of the abductor (PCA), considerably stronger than
that for /p/ or geminate /pp/. Correspondingly, glottal
width also shows much wider opening for /h/ than for /p/ or
/pp/. According to fiberscopic studies by Sawashima and
Hirose (see Hirose, 1975), this wide opening for /h/ is a
typical situation as far as the glottal width at the vocal
process is concerned. That is, the arytenoid cartilages
are fairly widely abducted, undoubtedly by an active role
of PCA, even when the vocal folds maintain vibration resulting in voiced /ɦ/. The glottis, particularly when there is
no voicing, may be as open as for /s/, for example. However, the membranous portion of the vocal fold takes a very
different shape in comparison with /s/, as we see in Fig. 6.
For a given cartilaginous position, the cover seems more
medially displaced for /h/ than for /s/. This is presumably
due to the faster airflow and a larger Bernoulli effect, but
it also could well be the case that the physiological adjustment for the vocal folds is different, causing membranous
folds to approach each other. The vocalis activity, according to the Sawashima data, seems low for /h/, however. The
lateral cricoarytenoid, another adductor running to the
sides of the vocal folds, does not seem to participate in
/h/-gestures either, according to Hirose and Gay (1973),
who reported on an EMG study of vocal attack which I will
discuss in a moment. Other physiological control may have
to be examined. In particular, it seems that /ɦ/ is often
associated with a higher larynx. See the comparison in
Fig. 6 between /se'se/ and /he'he/. In spite of the requirement for a low-pitched second vowel in both cases due
to the accent kernel, the larynx for the final /e/ in
/he'he/ is not low, apparently, nor constricted in a
longitudinal direction. The supralaryngeal structure
seems to pull the larynx upward. This may also be related
to heightened subglottal pressure, as well as lower supraglottal pressure. Lee and Smith reported on a higher subglottal pressure for the aspirated stop in Korean in comparison with others. Weitzman et al. (1976) discussed a

higher larynx in stage whisper. More data about laryngeal
and respiratory control, including vertical movement of the
larynx and related muscle activities, are necessary in order
to clarify this issue.

Hirose and Gay succeeded in obtaining useful EMG
signals from five laryngeal muscles at the same time, as
shown in Fig. 7, in their study of vocal attacks. They
used a comparison of monosyllabic words /ha/, /ba/, and
/ʔa/ in isolation as the material, and named the different
manners of voice initiation in these utterances breathy,
soft and hard attacks, respectively. The five muscles were
identified as the lateral cricoarytenoid (LCA), interarytenoid (INT), posterior cricoarytenoid (PCA), the cricothyroid (CT) and the thyroarytenoid or vocalis (VOC)
muscles. We may note that for /ha/, to the left of the
vertical line which represents voice onset, LCA is inactive.
On the other hand, PCA is activated well before the voice
onset in /ha/, showing a positive abduction of the arytenoid
cartilages for /h/. INT, CT, and VOC, and to a lesser extent LCA also, all show well-defined peaks around the voice
onset, showing that a positive action is taken as a set of
concurrent activities for voicing of the vowel, in this
environment. The lack of activity in CT for the aspiration
proper, to the left of the peak, is particularly interesting, because it indicates a relaxed longitudinal tension as
an inherent gesture for aspiration in spite of the fact that
pitch near voice onset is usually relatively high. For some
reason, it seems as though an increased longitudinal tension,
as well as adduction, is required for voice initiation in
the /h/-context. This tension, however, as far as the cover
of the vocal fold is concerned, is more or less counter-
acted by the vocalis activity observed here, and there may
not be much lengthening of the cords in actuality. Instead,
the body is thickened and stiffened for voicing. This suggests that for /h/, the lower parts of the vocal folds are
far apart, and when voice is required, they have to be
brought together by a special maneuver in addition to the
usual adduction of the arytenoid cartilages in the upper
part of the structure. In the case of /ba/, a similar effort

is observed to a much smaller extent, presumably because
the sudden increase in airflow caused by the articulatory
release triggers the initiation of vibration, rather than
because of a strong adduction. The glottis is gradually
closed beforehand for /b/ (see Fig. 5).

In a glottal stop preceding a vowel gesture, we need
a different strategy (see broken lines). There we have a
wide open stationary supraglottal channel for the airflow.
A simple adduction strategy as in the voiced stop context
does not seem to guarantee an abrupt voice onset. Rather,
the strategy seems to be to prepare a tight contact of the
folds as a whole by means of a very strong glottal adduction by LCA from the sides at a relatively low vertical
level, without involving much positive adduction of the
cartilages by INT. This effort for tight closure is aug-
mented before its release for voice onset by a peak in the
CT-VOC activity pair. At the moment of voice onset,
together with a sudden release of adduction by LCA, the
CT-VOC activity is also released, resulting in particular,
for this subject, in a remarkable trough of VOC activity.
This relaxation gesture is assisted at the cartilaginous
level by a small but distinct peak of PCA activity. But,
in this case, contrary to most cases of phonetic adduction-
abduction processes, INT is also slightly activated, con-
tradicting the abducting effect by PCA. This indicates a
rather peculiar strategy in terms of displacement and
rotation of the arytenoid cartilages. This peculiarity,
however, may vary depending on the subject.

There is another interesting point about this datum
for this subject. The momentary relaxation of the tight
glottal closure by the relaxation of the CT-VOC and the
small activity of PCA is seen to be effected around the
actual voice onset, rather than preceding it. In particular, the PCA activity peak, though small, seems limited to
a range of about ±40 msec. Note that there is no other
change of articulatory conditions than voice initiation in
this utterance. This PCA peak must be pertinent to voice
onset. It seems to be generally the case that a small

activity affecting the physical state only for small movement and serving as a triggering mechanism rather than as
a direct cause for movement of a relatively large mechanical
structure shows little lead in time. In the case of the
CT-VOC strategy, also, the longitudinal length of the cords
is relatively fixed, causing little movement of the cricoid
and thyroid cartilages, and the change is more or less
limited to the local stiffening of the muscles themselves.
When there is no massive structure involved in the movement,
time discrepancy is of course small.

According to Hirose et al. (1969) who experimented with
a supramaximal electric stimulation of the pertinent motor
nerves of cats under isometric twitch conditions, the contraction time (up to the peak force from the beginning of
force development) was on the average about 40 msec for the
cricothyroid and about 20 msec for the posterior cricoarytenoid and the thyroarytenoid muscles. For the muscle
fibers responsible for smaller force, the delay may be
smaller. In addition, there was a relatively constant
7-msec. latency between onsets of the EMG signal and force
development. The remaining part of the delay we observe
(after adjusting for the difference between cat and human
muscles) between EMG and physical effects depends on the
inertia of the mechanical system involved. We should
emphasize here, that the so-called adductors, i.e., LCA,
INT, and VOC, behave very differently from each other,
showing different activity patterns depending on what
exactly the speaker intends to do. In contrast to the
relaxation of VOC activity for the voice onset after a
glottal stop, as observed in this vocal attack study, a
momentary peak in VOC activity observed in emphatic utterances in Swedish /Gårding et al., 1970) seems related to
the voice onset after the glottal stop rather than to the
implosion into the glottal stop. In this case, the peak
vocalis activity seems to precede voice onset by 20-40
msec. Also, a sharp and momentary peak of VOC activity is
reported related to the voice onset after the forced type
unaspirated voiceless stop in Korean. Before we examine
how the muscles behave for Korean stops, however, we should

learn what happens to the glottis for the rather unusual
manner contrast in this language.

Kagaya (1974) studied Korean stops, as well as affricates and fricatives, by using the fiberscope, and submitted
a clear account of the phonetic distinction using two Seoul
subjects. Fig. 8 plots glottal width at the vocal process
as a function of time. The glottis is wide open before
voice onset (right extreme of the time scale) and around the
articulatory release (large circles) for the aspirated type
/p^h/ etc. For the forced type /P/ etc., the glottis is
closed by the voice onset, which coincides with articulatory release. At voice onset, voice is breathy for /p^h/ etc.
and a small opening is often observed between the cartilaginous parts of the vocal cords. The glottal width during the
articulatory closure of the lax type /p/ etc. in utterance
initial position fluctuates from utterance to utterance,
and the consonant is voiced in intervocalic position, whereas wide opening of the glottis characterizes the aspirated
type and a tight closure preceding the release and voice
onset is invariably observed for the forced type even in
different contexts such as word medial position.

Fig. 9 shows a figure from a paper published by Hirose,
Lee and Ushijima (1974). See the sharp peak of the VOC
activity for the forced /P/. The longitudinal tension is
also given by a broader peak of CT activity, reflecting high
pitch immediately after voice onset. In this experiment,
test words of a CV-type are embedded in a carrier sentence
/ikəsi ___ ita/. Note that much the same patterns are
shown for the aspirated type (denoted /p^h/) at the top for
both VOC and CT. Apart from the apparently somewhat weaker
activity for VOC in this case, the main difference is in
timing of the peaks with reference to the vertical lines,
which represent the articulatory release of the stops. In
contrast, the weakly aspirated lax stop, denoted by /p/,
shows a lack of VOC peak even though the CT-pattern is very
much like that for the aspirated stop /p^h/. This is interesting because the lax type usually is associated with lower
pitch immediately after voice onset. As far as the longitudinal tension of the cover is concerned, the pitch

difference has to be accounted for by the different timing
of the CT-activity peak relative to voice onset. The peak
in CT activity /p/ has an effect of raising pitch only in
the middle portion of the following vowel, voice onset
being close to articulatory release, whereas in the case
of /p^h/, a similar pitch rise happens to be effected near
voice onset (60-80 msec to the right of the vertical line,
cf Fig. 10). The VOC activity may or may not contribute
to the higher pitch for /p^h/ than for /p/ immediately after
voice onset. In contrast, in the case of the forced unaspirated type P, the CT-peak does occur earlier causing
a higher pitch value near voice onset.

Fig. 10 compares INT with VOC. Interestingly enough,
INT shows a peak activity near stop release only for the
aspirated type /p^h/. This peak immediately precedes voice
onset, and is obviously necessary because the glottis is
wide open during the closure for this type of stop. In
contrast, in the case of the forced type, the sharp VOC
peak is not accompanied by any appreciable INT activity,
except for the earlier low peak which reflects the glottal
adduction, well before the stop release, from the open state
for the preceding voiceless /si/. Thus, the quick and
momentary vocalis contraction combined with high cricothyroid activity does seem to characterize the forced type
stops. The high voice pitch immediately after the articulatory release reflects high longitudinal tension and relatively stiff body, a generally difficult condition for
voice initiation. A transient slackening of the cover by
the VOC activity is probably very effective as a trigger of
vibration in cooperation with the sudden drop in supraglottal
pressure due to the articulatory release, under these circumstances. The body is also considerably adducted for the
forced stop, by a sharp activity of LCA, according to the
EMG data illustrated in the same paper, and this is probably
part of the reason INT is not strongly active for this type.
The vocal fold must be more strongly adducted at the lower
level than for other types, resulting in a voice quality
rich in high frequency components (Kagaya, ibid). I suspect,
however, that part of the pitch difference for the inherent

distinction between the stop types may have to be accounted
for by factors other than activities of those muscles discussed above. The aspirated type may be associated with a
higher larynx position, whereas the lax type may be associated with a constricted and relaxed larynx due to other
external conditions. There may also be considerable difference between subjects, particularly those from different
dialectal regions, in details of phonetic implementations
of features.

Another interesting topic with respect to laryngeal
control is the rich consonantal paradigm in Hindi and other
languages. In Hindi, we observe four manners of articulation for stop consonants with the same place of articulation, and these four are often transcribed as (e.g., for
labial stops) /p/, for voiceless unaspirated, /ph/, voiceless aspirated, /b/, voiced unaspirated, voicing always
preceding the articulatory release, and /bh/, voiced
aspirated. Ladefoged (1971) described the fourth type as
distinct from the other three in having murmured voice, a
condition intermediate between breathy voice and soft voice,
showing a slight opening in the cartilaginous portion of the
glottis while the membranous portions vibrate. There are
two recent systematic and experimental studies on this topic,
one by Dixit with McNeilage (1974), and another by Kagaya
and Hirose. They both disagree with Ladefoged, and place
more emphasis on the temporal patterns. They both also
disagree with Kim (1970) on his theory of aspiration in this
case. Kim had stated that the extent of aspiration is determined by the glottal aperture at the moment of articulatory release.

Figure 11 is from the paper by Kagaya and Hirose (1975),
comparing the three types; voiced and voiceless aspirated,
and voiceless unaspirated, in terms of glottal width as time
functions. The voiced unaspirated stop, of course, shows no
glottal aperture all through the time course. It is seen
clearly, at least for this native speaker of Hindi, that
the voiced aspirate is to be described as a sequence of
voice and aspiration in that order. Articulatory release
occurs around the transition between the two laryngeal

gestures, at least as far as the glottal width at the vocal
process is concerned. It is probably true, however, that
after the aspiration phase of /bʰ/ etc., the voice is still
characteristically aspirated, as Ladefoged describes. The
point is that the distinction between the consonant types is,
phonetically at least, really a matter of different syllables.
Consonantal features are intermixed with vowel characteristics to a large extent, and this "intermixing" cannot be
prescribed by a general principle of segmental concatenation,
but has to be specified as specific temporal organizations
(Fujimure and Lovins, 1977). It seems that the unaspirated
voiceless /p/ is quite different from the Korean forced /P/,
showing no tight closure preceding voice onset. The vocalis
muscle does not show any peak of activity either. These investigators, after Dixit (1975), also emphasize the importance of longitudinal tension of the vocal folds, based on
EMG records of CT activity, specifically for unaspirated
voiceless /p/.

    Pitch Control for Accent Patterns. The pitch raising
function is better understood than pitch lowering mechanism,
in the sense that we have located a muscle, the cricothyroid,
that plays a primary causal role in pitch raising. Figure 12
exemplifies temporal patterns of muscle activities, in relation to the control of pitch descent that reflects the so-
called accent kernel (indicated by a hook-shaped diacritic
in the phonemic transcription) in Japanese. The position of
such a pitch descent distinguishes lexical accentual patterns.
The bottom curves show the fundamental frequency contours,
and next to the top, we see cricothyroid activities. With a
lead by around 100 msec., the CT activity clearly predicts
the two pitch patterns.

    Figure 13 shows a similar comparison of muscle activi-
ties for a pair of word accent patterns, the words involving
voiceless /s/. Because of segmental effects on pitch, particularly the pitch disturbance due to the voice cessation, the
actual pitch contours are not simply related to the abstract
pitch changes. The CT-activity, however, manifests the
underlying pitch patterns, i.e., for the first three syllables, high-low-low (thick lines) vs. low-high-low (thin

lines). In this case at least, the sternothyroid muscle
also gives a good indication of pitch lowering, but its
activity does not seem to lead the physical effect of pitch
descent. These figures are from Simada and Hirose (1971).
       Fink (1975, in his recent book, described the
vocalis muscle as an antagonist to CT. This is true, as I
discussed before, in the sense that the tension of the so-
called vocal ligament is relaxed by its contraction. However, the pitch raising function, the primary function of the
CT, is not opposed by the vocalis muscle, and therefore, it
is a misleading notion to pair the vocalis muscle and the
cricothyroid muscle as antagonistic muscles. Hirano (1975)
studied the effects of the CT and VOC contractions on the
shape of the vocal fold by using electrical stimulation of
motornerves in the dog. His deep frozen frontal sections
suggest an intricate three dimensional effects of the two
muscles. The vocalis muscle stiffens the body as it slackens
the cover. According to Hirano, the net-effect of its contraction on pitch is slightly positive in heavy register,
presumably also in normal speech. In spite of the apparently
important function of pitch lowering, both for accentual
marks -- prosodic features --, and for phrasal boundary marks
or configurational features in the Jakobsonian terminology
(Jakobson et al., 1952) --, we have many theories for pitch
lowering mechanisms and do not have one theory everyone agrees
on. The problem is that many muscles even far from the
larynx, such as the geniohyoid muscle connecting the chin and
the hyoid bone, seem to be relevant in the laryngeal conditions affecting pitch. Table 1 shows Hirano's summary of
physiologically observed effects of a variety of muscles on
laryngeal conditions (Hirano, ibid.) To supplement this, for
the geniohyoid, for example, Mark Liberman (personal communication) has found negative correlation between the activity
of this muscle and pitch lowering. There are other muscles,
notably the so-called strap muscles such as the sternothyroid, as I referred to above, that seem to be related to this
dimension of control. Often, however, these activities
appear to be a response to change of conditions rather than
the cause, lacking the lead in time in relation to physical
effects of pitch change, in spite of the relatively massive
structure involved.

Concluding Remarks. We have discussed some of the
issues concerning physiological control for phonetic distinctions in language. Of course, this paper is not given
for a comprehensive survey, but for pointing out some topics
of our concern in current research. Conclusions are mostly
of a highly tentative nature at the moment. Different
languages reveal different linguistic distinctions, some of
which may sound foreign to most of us. Often, however, the
features used for phonetic distinctions in those languages
reveal available physiological capabilities which we tend to
overlook, but nevertheless are important in understanding
the overall picture of our daily speech behavior, because
there are various aspects of control that have to be sub-
tracted from observed effects as nondistinctive use. Also,
interaction between different control dimensions is common
in reality, and we have to be at least aware of possible
physiological dimensions that come into the picture under
discussion.

The world of physiological control may seem formidably
complex. It is clear, however, that different muscles
effecting allegedly the same function, such as glottal
adduction, have in reality different functions in some crucial cases of phonetic distinction. Also, the same muscle,
such as the vocalis muscle, serves in different manners giving rise to various effects. In order to obtain the true
understanding of phonetic dimensions, we will have to take
the pain of determining functions of individual muscles,
trying to construct an overall model of the complex system,
and then simplify the system for comprehensive approximation
for a given purpose.

REFERENCES

Baer, T.   (1975).   Unpub. Doctoral Diss., MIT.
Dixit, R. P. and MacNeilage, P. F.   (1974).   J. Acoust. Soc.
    Am., 55(S):580.
Dixit, R. P.   (1975).   Unpub. Doctoral Diss., Univ. Texas.
Ewan, W. G. and Krones, R.   (1973).   J. Acoust. Soc. Am.,
    53:345(A).

Farnsworth, D.   (1940).   Bell Lab Rec, 18:203-208.

Fink, B. R.   (1975).   New York, Raven Press.

Fischer-Jorgensen, E. and Hirose, H.   (1974).   Haskins,
    SR Speech Res., 39-40:225-259.

Flanagan, J. L. and Landgraf, L.   (1968).   IEEE Trans Audio
    Electroacoust AU-16:57-64.

Flanagan, J. L., Ishizaka, K. and Shipley, K. L.   (1975).
    Bell Syst Tech J, 54(3):485-506.

Fujimura, O.   (1977).   Tokyo, Univ. Tokyo Press, 133-138.

Fujimura, O. and Lovins, J. B.   (1977).   Proc. Symp. Segment
    Org. and Syll., Univ. Colorado.

Gauffin, J.   (1977).   Phonet., 34:307-309.

Hattori, S.   (1961).   Bull. Sum. Inst. Ling., 1:1-27.

Hattori, A. S.   (1961, 1966).   Tokyo, Iwanami Pub. Co.

Henderson, E. J. A.   (1977).   Phonet., 34:256-263.

Hirano, M.   (1974).   Folia Phon., 26:89-94.

Hirano, M.   (1975).   Tokyo: Otologia.

Hirano, M.   (1977).   Tokyo, Univ. Tokyo Press, 13-30.

Hirose, H., Ushijima, T., Kotayashi, T. and Sawashima, M.
    (1969).   Ann. Atol Rhin. Lary., 78:297-307.

Hirose, H. and Gay, T.   (1972).   Phonet., 25:140-164.

Hirose, H. and Gay, T.   (1973).   Folia Phon., 25:203-213.

Hirose, H., Lee, C. Y. and Ushijima, T.   (1974).   J. Phon.,
    2:145-152.

Hirose, H.   (1975).   Ann. Bull. Univ. Tokyo, BILP, 9:47-66.

Hirose, H. and Ushijima, T.   (1976).   Ann Bull. Univ. Tokyo,
    BILP, 10:101-112.

Hollien, H., Coleman, R. F. and Moore, P.   (1968).   Acta
    Oto-Lary., 65:209-215.

Hollien, H. and Colton, R.   Folia Phon., 21:179-198.

Ishizaka, K. and Matsudaira, M.   (1968).   J. Acoust. Soc. Jap.
    Jap., 24(5):311-312.

Kagaya, R.   (1974).   J. Phon., 2:161-180.

Kagaya, R. and Hirose, H.   (1975).   Ann. Bull. Univ. Tokyo,
    RIIP, 9:27-46.

Kakita, Y. and Hiki, S.   (1976).   J. Acoust. Soc. Am., 59:
    669-674.

Kim, C. W.   (1970).   Phonet., 21:107-116.

Kirikae, I.   (1943).   J. Jap. Soc. Oto-Rhino-Laryn., 49:
    236-268.

Ladefoged, P.   (1971).   Chicago: Univ. Chicago Press.

Lindqvist-Gauffin, J.   (1972).   KTH OPSR, 2/3:10-27.

Lindqvist-Gauffin, J.   (1972).   KTH OPSR 2/3:1-9.

Maeda, S.   (1976).   Ph.D. Diss., MIT.

Ohala, J. J.   (1972).   J. Acoust. Soc. Am., 52(1,1):124.

Ohala, J. J.   (1977).   Phonet., 34:310-312.

Rothenberg, M.   (1968).   Bib. Phon., 6.

Sawashima, M. and Hirose, H.   (1968).   J. Acoust. Soc. Am., 43:168-169.

Sawashima, M.   (1971).   Ann Bull. Univ. Tokyo, RILP., 5:7-13.

Sawashima, M., Hirose, H., Ushijima, T. and Niimi, S.   (1975).   Ann Bull., Univ. Tokyo, RILP, 9:21-26.

Shipp, T.   (1978).   Blenery Paper: IPS-77, Miami, Fla.

Shimada, Z. and Hirose, H.   (1971).   Ann. Bull. Univ. Tokyo, RILP, 5:41-49.

Smith, S.   (1962).   Proc. 4th Int. Cong. Phon. Sci., Helsinki: Mouton & Co., 96-110.

Stevens, K. N.   (1977).   Phonet., 34:264-279.

Titze, I. R.   (1976).   J. Acoust. Soc. Am., 60:1366-1380.

van den Berg, J.   (1958).   J. Speech Hear. Res., 1:227-244.

Weitzman, R. S., Sawashima, M., Hirose, H. and Ushijima, T. (1976).   Ann Bull. Univ. Tokyo, RILP, 10:61-80.

MUSCLE STIMULATED	ENTIRE LARYNX				VOCAL CORD			
	UP	DOWN	FORE	BACK	ELONG.	SHORTEN.	ADDUCT.	ABDUCT.
STYLOHYOID	(+)							
DIGAST. (ANT.)	(+)							
DIGAST. (POST.)	(+)							
MYLOHYOID	+		+					
GENIOHYOID	+		+			+		
THROHYOID	+		+		+			
STERNOHYOID		+		+				
STERNOTHYROID		+	+		+			+
HYOPHARYNG.	+						+	
THROPHARYNG.						+	+	
CRICOPHARYN.G		+				+		+

TABLE 1. Changes in the states of the canine larynx as a whole and the vocal folds caused by electric stimulation of each of the extrinsic laryngeal muscles as observed under a suspension laryngoscope (Hirano 1975, p. 289).

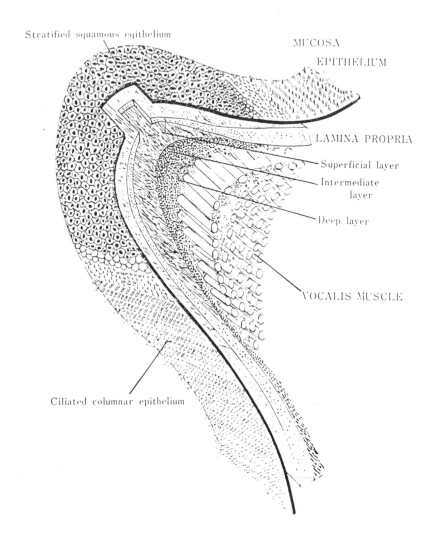

FIGURE 1

Internal structure of the human vocal cord (Hirano 1975).

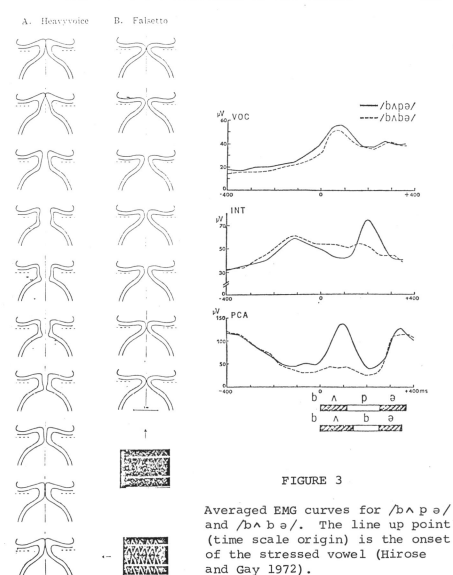

FIGURE 2

Two representative pat-
terns of vocal and vibra-
tion (Hirano 1975).

FIGURE 3

Averaged EMG curves for /bʌpə/
and /bʌbə/. The line up point
(time scale origin) is the onset
of the stressed vowel (Hirose
and Gay 1972).

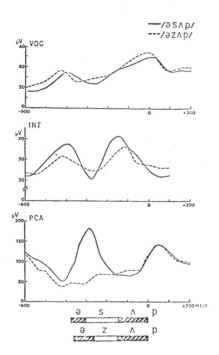

FIGURE 4

Averaged EMG curves for /ə s ʌ p/ and /ə z ʌ p/
(Hirose and Gay 1972).

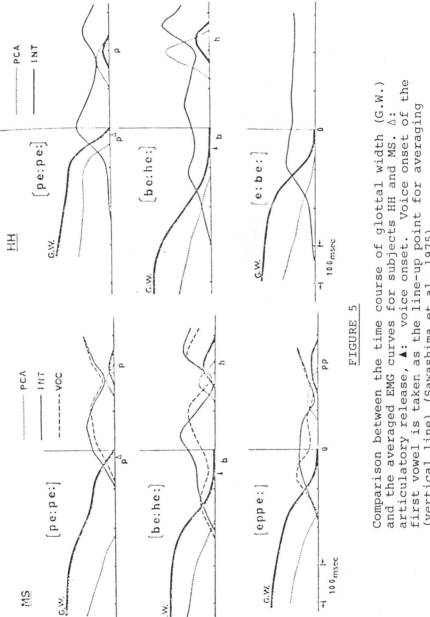

<u>FIGURE 5</u>

Comparison between the time course of glottal width (G.W.)
and the averaged EMG curves for subjects HH and MS. Δ:
articulatory release, ▲: voice onset. Voice onset of the
first vowel is taken as the line-up point for averaging
(vertical line) (Sawashima et al. 1975).

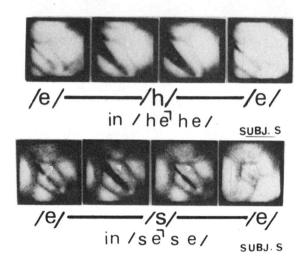

/e/————/h/————/e/

in /he˺he/

SUBJ. S

/e/————/s/————/e/

in /se˺s e/

SUBJ. S

FIGURE 6

Comparison of [h] and [s] in intervocalic position
(nonmeaningful Japanese words). Frame samples from
a fiberscopic film (by Sawashima, personal communication). The pitch accent pattern high-low is used for
both cases.

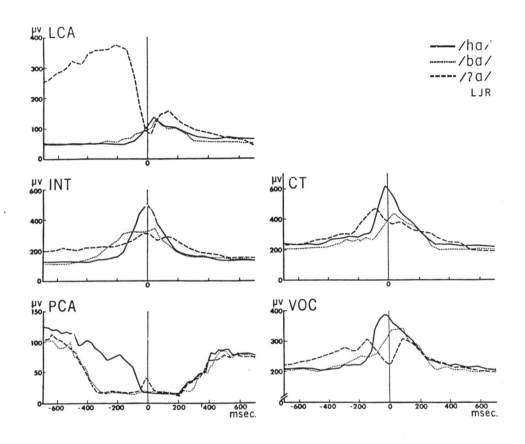

FIGURE 7

Averaged EMG curves (in microvolts) of the intrinsic laryngeal muscles of an American native. Zero on the time axis is the onset of voicing. Muscle identifications are LCA: lateral cricoarytenoid; INT: interarytenoid; PCA: posterior cricoarytenoid; CT: cricothyroid; VOC: vocalis (Hirose and Gay 1973).

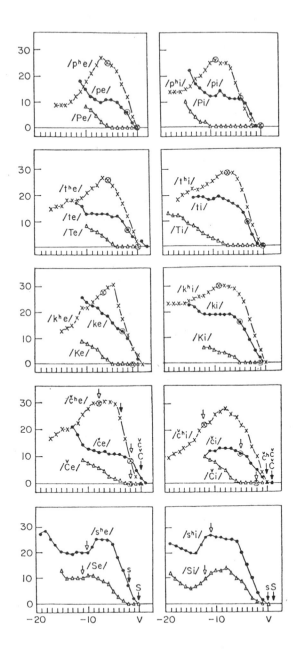

<u>FIGURE 8</u>

Glottal width (ordinate, arbitrary scale) as functions of time (abscissa in frame number, 20 ms./frame). Large circles denote articulatory releases, and the mark V on time scale represents voice onset. See Kagaya (1974) for details.

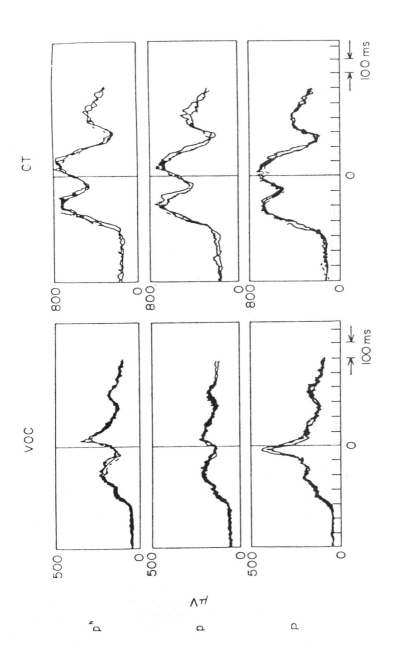

FIGURE 9

Average EMG curves of the vocalis (left) and the cricothyroid (right) muscles.
For each of the three stop types in Korean in word initial position. Curves for
three vowel contexts (__i, __a, __u) are superimposed (Hirose et al. 1974).

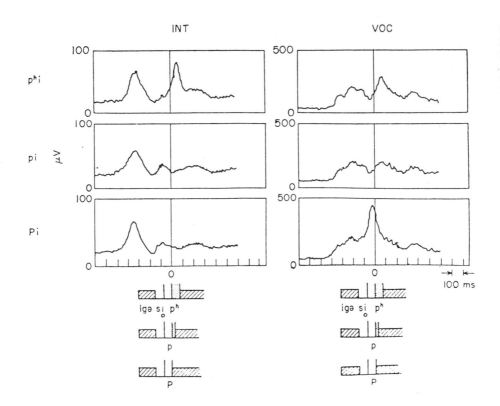

FIGURE 10

Averaged EMG curves for the three stop types of the
interarytenoid and the vocalis muscles. Acoustic
events are depicted below the curves. Striped areas
represent voiced intervals (Hirose et al., ibid).

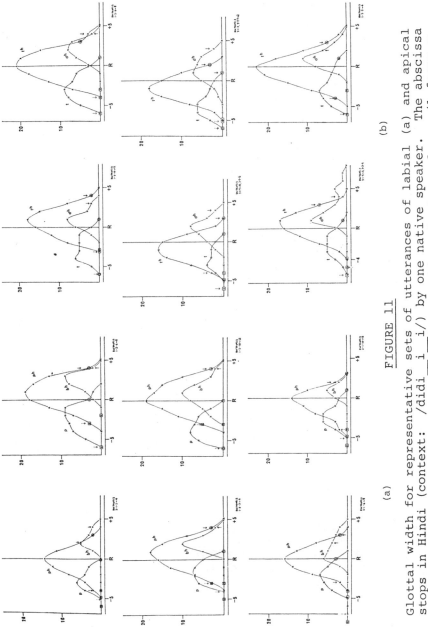

(a)

(b)

FIGURE 11

Glottal width for representative sets of utterances of labial (a) and apical stops in Hindi (context: /didi i i/) by one native speaker. The abscissa represents frame numbers with the reference time at stop release (1 frame = 20 msec.). Large open circles represent voice onsets, open squares articulatory implosions (Kagaya and Hirose 1975).

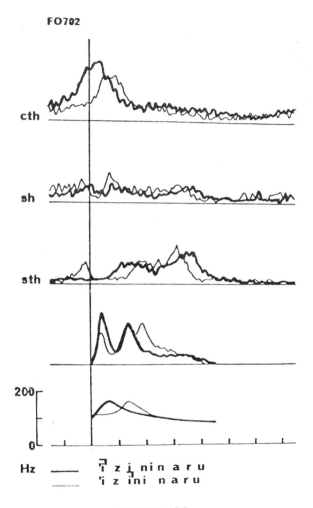

FO702

<u>FIGURE 12</u>

Averaged EMG curves for a pair of Japanese words with
different accent patterns in sentence initial position.
The accent kernel is denoted by the mark ⌐ . Abscissa
is marked off every 200 msec. The lowest curve represents
typical pitch contours (Simada and Hirose 1971).

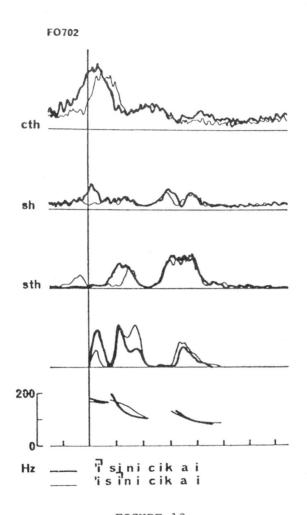

FIGURE 13

EMG records for Japanese words with a voiceless palatalized fricative /s/. See Fig. 12 for explanation (Simada and Hirose, ibid.).

A CROSS LANGUAGE STUDY OF LARYNGEAL ADJUSTMENT IN CONSONANT PRODUCTION

HAJIME HIROSE, HIROHIDE YOSHIOKA AND SEIJI NIIMI
University of Tokyo and Haskins Laboratories

Recent electromyographic (EMG) and fiberoptic studies have revealed that there is a reciprocal activity pattern between the adductor and abductor muscle groups of the larynx during consonant production; and that the posterior crico-arytenoid (PCA) is particularly important for the active vocal fold abduction for those speech sounds produced with an open glottis. The reciprocity between the PCA and the adductors, and the interarytenoid (INT) in particular, has been observed for different languages including American English, Japanese, Danish and French.

Figure 1 shows an example of EMG traces of the PCA and the INT for a pair of test words /əpʌp/ and /əbʌp/ produced by an American English speaker. It is shown that PCA activity is suppressed for the voiced portion of the test words, while it increases for the production of the inter-vocalic voiceless stop /p/ as well as for word final /p/. On the other hand, the INT shows a reciprocal pattern when compared with that of the PCA, in that its activity increases for the voiced portion and decreases for the voiceless portion of the test words.

Figure 2 illustrates the reciprocal pattern between these two muscles more clearly. These curves were obtained by computer-averaging the EMG signals in reference to the line-up point on the time axis, which was taken at the voice offset of the stressed vowel. The solid lines show the EMG pattern for the production of /əpʌp/, while the dotted lines

show the pattern for /əbʌp/. PCA activation and INT suppression for voiceless /p/ are clearly demonstrated.

In Figure 3, an averaged pattern of PCA activity is compared for the pairs /p/ vs. /b/ and /s/ vs. /v/ in the same
American English speaker as in the previous figure. The comparison was made in different phonetic environments, namely,
in prestressed position in the left half of the figure and
in poststressed position in the right. Zero on the time
axis indicates the line-up point for the averaging. A
marked elevation of PCA activity is always noted for the
production of voiceless consonants. For voiced consonant
production, on the other hand, PCA activity is generally
suppressed. However, the PCA shows a relatively higher
activity for the segment /z/, particularly in the poststressed position, when compared to the neighboring vowel
segments. This finding would suggest that the glottal
closure is less tight for voiced /z/ than for vowel segments.

Figure 4 shows averaged EMG curves of the PCA and the
INT in a Japanese subject for the test utterance "soreo
Keekee to yuu," where the four mora meaningful word "keekee"
with initial and medial voiceless stops is embedded in a frame
sentence. The PCA shows an increasing activity for /k/ in
the test utterance but the peak value is clearly higher for
the word-initial /k/ than for the word-medial /k/. Incidentally, PCA activity also increases for the voiceless /t/
in the frame. In the same Japanese subject, a fiberoptic
movie of the glottis was taken for various kinds of test
utterances, in order to investigate the relationship between
glottal dynamics and PCA activity. It was always observed
that there were separation of the arytenoids and widening of
the glottis for the voiceless portion of the test utterances,
including voiceless stops and fricatives, geminates and devoiced vowels. Figure 5 shows the relationship between peak
values of averages PCA activity and maximum glottal width
for all types of voiceless segments used in the experiments.
It is shown that the maximum glottal width is generally
larger when the peak PCA activity is higher. A statistical
test shows that a significant positive correlation exists
between these two parameters at the 0.01 level of confidence
(r = 0.86). It is also shown here that PCA activity is
higher and glottal width is larger for voiceless stops in

word initial position, which are marked with the letter "I,"
than those in word medial position, which are labelled "M."
However, there is no appreciable difference for voiceless
fricative /s/ with regard to the difference in phonetic
environment.

Figure 6 compares activity patterns of the five intrinsic laryngeal muscles for the production of a pair of
Japanese test words, /keNri/ vs. /geNri/, embedded in a
frame sentence 'sore wa --- desu." The reciprocal relationship between the PCA and the INT can be seen again in this
figure. For the lateral cricoarytenoid (LCA) and thyroarytenoid (VOC), muscle activity increases at the initiation of each utterance, namely, for the carrier portion preceding the test word, and decreases for word initial consonant
production, where the degree of suppression is similar regardless of the voiced-voiceless distinction in the paired consonants. The activity increases again after the suppression,
apparently for the nuclear vowel following the initial consonant. In the case of the VOC, muscle activity sharply
increases after the voiceless consonant particularly when
the accent kernel is attached to the vowel following the
voiceless consonant, whereas the increase is less marked
after the voiced pair. The pattern of LCA activity in terms
of suppression for the initial consonant and increase for
the following vowel is essentially uniform regardless of the
voiced-voiceless distinction in the initial consonant.
Similar findings were also obtained from American-English
speakers, in that both the VOC and the LCA appeared to be
suppressed for consonantal segments regardless of voiced-
voiceless contrast.

For most voiced-voiceless pairs, the general pattern of
cricothyroid (CT) activity is similar and characterized by
two peaks separated apparently by suppression for the initial
consonant of the test words. It should be noted, however,
that the degree of suppression is different depending on
whether the initial consonant is voiced or voiceless, in that
the suppression is less marked for the voiceless cognate than
for the voiced. The difference is also related to the degree
of reactivation after the suppression, and it is apparently
more marked for the voiced cognate. The pattern of the CT in
relation to the voicing distinction will be discussed again
later.

EMG and fiberoptic experiments were also performed with a Canadian subject who speaks Swiss-French. Figure 7 illustrates an example of averaged EMG curves for the PCA and the INT in the /t/ vs. /d/ contrast in word initial position. It can be seen that there is a reciprocal pattern between the two muscles in this case too, and that PCA activity increases for voiceless /t/. It should also be noted here that there is PCA activation and INT suppression for the postvocalic /r/. A fiberoptic study made on the same subject showed that the vocal folds were abducted for the production of /t/ and other voiceless segments, and for /r/, as well. Figure 8 compares the pattern of the PCA for the voiceless /t/ sound in the three-way contrast between liaison, non-geminated and geminated conditions. The contrast appeared to be evidenced primarily by the duration of oral closure and thus reflected in the timing of laryngeal gestures and of the corresponding EMG activity. In other words, the PCA peak occurred earliest, and duration of PCA activation is longest, for the geminated voiceless stop, while the peaking is latest, and the duration is shortest, for the liaison stop. The order exactly corresponds to that of glottal gesture in terms of the timing of vocal fold abduction. Fiberoptic studies also showed that the maximum glottal aperture during the oral closure of a geminated stop was not a function of the duration of glottal separation. The finding is also consistent with these EMG patterns, where the peak PCA activity for the geminated stop is similar to that for the non-geminated stop, while the duration of PCA activation is longer for the geminated case.

A similar finding was obtained for Danish. In this language, both "p,t,k" and "b,d,g" groups are voiceless in word initial position but the degree and timing of glottal opening is different for the two groups. Figure 9 compares the time course of the glottal opening for /p/ vs. /b/ embedded in a frame. Glottal aperture is much larger for /p/ and the glottal width becomes widest near the oral release, whereas the glottis is less open and the peaking is earlier for /b/. Figure 10 compares the Danish words /pʰaːnə/ and /baːnə/ preceded by a carrier /han sa/. It can be seen here that there is a large dip for s and p and a somewhat smaller dip for b in averaged INT activity. In the PCA curves, there are peaks corresponding to the INT dips. It should be noted that PCA activity lasts longer and the peak is higher for p

than for b. These EMG patterns seem to be consistent with
the glottal gestures presented in Figure 9.

Reciprocity between the PCA and the INT was found to
exist even for a five way distinction using the same manner
of articulation examined with the aid of an American English
speaker, a phonetician who produced labial stops of five
phonetic types. Figure 11 illustrates the averaged PCA and
INT activity for, from the top to bottom, voiced inaspirates,
implosive voiced inaspirates, voiced aspirates, voiceless
aspirates and voiceless inaspirates. It can be seen that
PCA activity sharply increases for the bottom three types,
namely for voiced aspirates, voiceless aspirates and voiceless inaspirates, whereas reciprocal suppression is found
in the INT curves. Supplemental fiberoptic observation of
the same subject revealed that separation of the arytenoids
was always observed for these three types and there was a
good agreement in both timing and degree between PCA activity
and the opening gesture of the glottis, both factors being
considered physiological determinants of different phonetic
types in greater than two-way distinction.

There are certain cases where another physiological
dimension must be taken into consideration. Figure 12 shows
an example of the averaged EMG curves of the VOC and the INT
for three types of Korean stops in word initial position.
For all types, an opening gesture of the glottis was evidenced by fiberoptic observation. It can be seen for type I
or forced stop, which is illustrated in the bottom of the
figure, that there is a sharp increase in VOC activity before
the articulatory release. This vocalis activity presumably
results in an increase in the inner tension of the vocal fold
and can be taken as a physiological correlate of so-called
laryngealization.

A similar type of VOC activity is also found in the
case of Danish stød. In Figure 13, we are comparing stød
vs. non-stød opposition in meaningful Danish words. For the
stød group, there is a sharp increase in VOC activity. Although the nature of the increasing VOC activity in these
cases still seems to be open for discussion, we do need an
additional dimension independent of glottal constriction.

Going back to the topic of the activity patterns of
the VOC and the LCA in the voiced-voiceless contrast, a
recent EMG study on a Swedish subject showed that these two
muscles appeared to be less suppressed for the voiced cognate
than for the voiceless. As can be seen in Figure 14, both
the VOC and the LCA are more clearly suppressed for short and
long voiceless consonants given in the left half of the
figure, when compared to their voiced counterparts. A
similar tendency is also observed in our recent study on
Danish consonants in which VOC is more suppressed for
strongly aspirated stops, namely, so-called p, t, k, group,
than for less aspirated b, d, g group, even though, as mentioned previously, both groups are produced as voiceless.
It can also be seen in this figure that CT suppression is
less marked for voiceless consonants than for the voiced.
As suggested by Dixit, the CT can contribute to the increase
in tension of the vocal fold which might eventually be relevant for eliminating voicing. In this sense, it might be
plausible to consider the relatively high CT activity in the
production of voiceless consonant in certain cases as one
possible factor of enhancing voicelessness. However, our
recent observations on Danish consonant production revealed
that a relatively high CT activity was also seen for voiced
/h/, which was produced with an open glottis, where F_0 was
rather low and CT activation did not seem to be related to
a pitch rise. Thus, the correct interpretation of the
apparently higher CT activity in certain consonantal segments is still unresolved, and further investigation of the
physiological and physical parameters in connection with
acoustic phenomenon in speech is warranted.

In summary, our EMG and fiberoptic investigations on
laryngeal behavior in consonant production have revealed the
followings:

1.   The intrinsic laryngeal muscles participate actively
in laryngeal control in speech articulation.

2.   A reciprocal pattern between the PCA and the
adductor muscles, the INT in particular, is almost always
observed in subjects of different languages and can be taken
as an important physiological correlate controlling the
timing and degree of the glottal opening gesture.   PCA

activity increases for those speech sounds produced with an
open glottis, and there is a positive correlation between
maximum glottal width and peak PCA activity.

3.   It is suggested that there is a functional differentiation in the adductor group. In particular, the VOC
can be regarded as a specific muscle working to control an
additional dimension independent of glottal constriction
in some specific languages.

4.   The contribution of the CT in the voicing distinction seems plausible in some cases but further investigation
is necessary for a definite interpretation of pattern of CT
activity in speech.

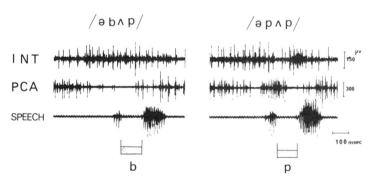

Fig. 1 Raw EMG traces of PCA and INT for a pair of

test words /əpʌp/ and /əbʌp/

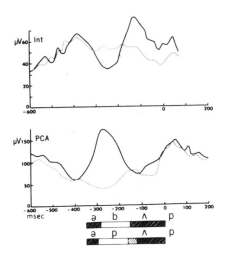

Fig. 2 Computer-averaged EMG curves of PCA and INT

for the same type of test words as in Fig. 1

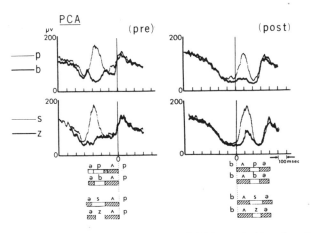

Fig. 3 Averaged EMG pattern of PCA activity for the

pairs /p/ vs. /b/ and /s/ vs. /v/

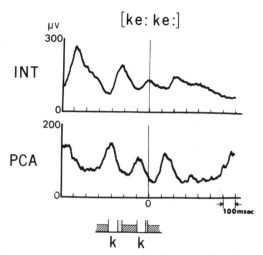

Fig. 4 Averaged EMG curves of PCA and INT in a Japanese

subject producing a test utterance "soreo kee

kee to yuu"

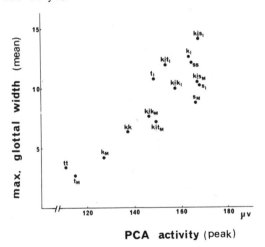

Fig. 5 Relationship between peak values

of averaged PCA activity and

maximum glottal width

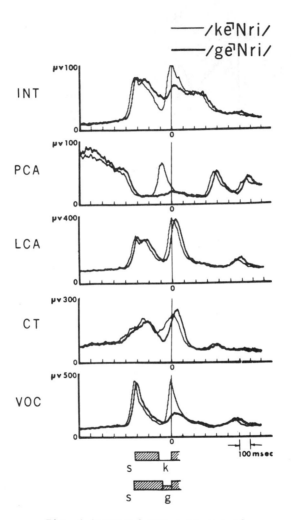

Fig. 6 Averaged EMG patterns of

five intrinsic laryngeal muscles

for the production of paired

Japanese test utterances.

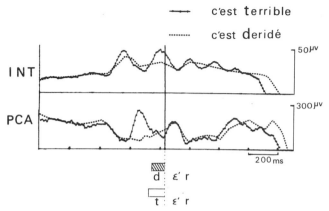

Fig. 7 Averaged EMG curves of PCA and INT for /t/ vs. /d/

contrast in French

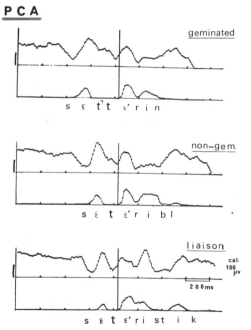

Fig.8 Comparison of PCA patterns for voiceless /t/ in French

in different phonetic environments

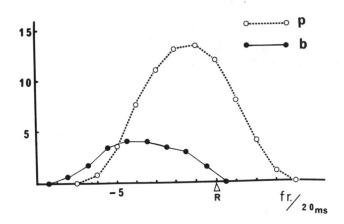

Fig. 9 Time course of glottal width for /p/ vs. /b/

contrast in Danish word in a frame sentence.

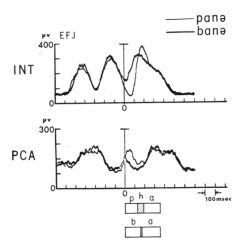

Fig. 10 Averaged EMG curves of PCA and INT for Danish

test words

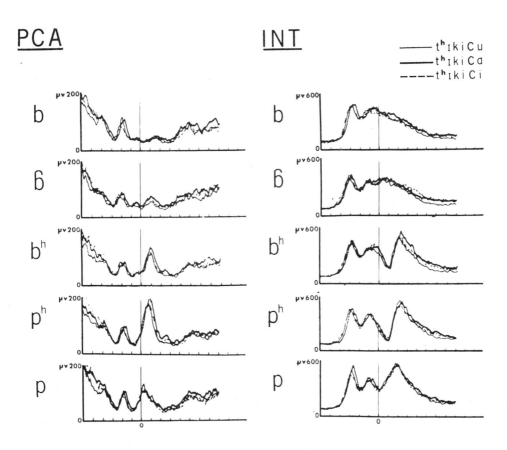

Fig. 11 Averaged EMG activities of PCA and INT for five

different types of labial stops

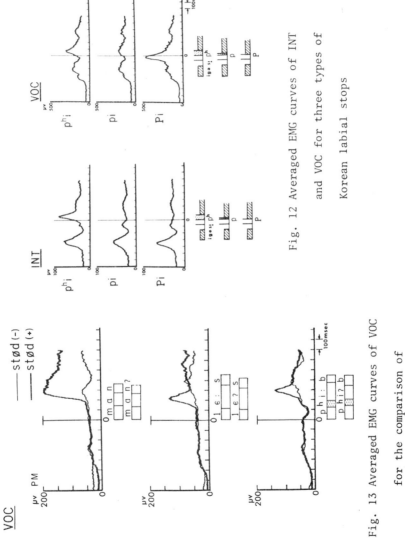

Fig. 12 Averaged EMG curves of INT
and VOC for three types of
Korean labial stops

Fig. 13 Averaged EMG curves of VOC
for the comparison of
stød vs. non-stød contrast
in Danish

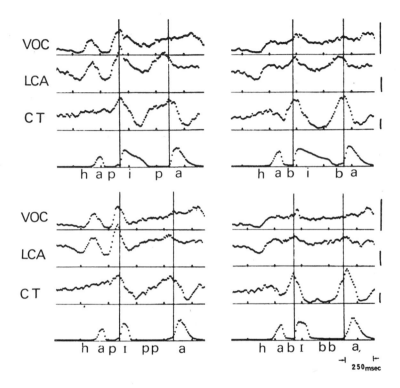

Fig. 14   Averaged EMG curves of VOC, LCA and CT for the production

of Swedish labial stop pair /p/ and /b/ in different

phonetic environment

QUANTITATIVE ANALYSIS OF CHANT IN RELATION TO NORMAL PHONATION AND VOCAL FRY

JOHN LARGE AND THOMAS MURRY
North Texas State University, Veterans Administration
Hospital and University of California

The use of chanting as a mode of voice production has been generally limited to religious ceremonies. In 1967, Smith et al. reported a study of the chanting of certain Tibetan lamas trained to make overtones audible in such a way as to yield the impression of a single lama singing a chord. Within relatively recent times, certain Western composers have begun to borrow vocal sounds, including chant, from non-Western cultures to use in their musical compositions. To investigate these possibilities and other new vocal resources, an Extended Vocal Techniques Ensemble was formed at the Center for Music Experiment on the campus of the University of California at San Diego. The members of the group have learned to produce a reasonable facsimile of Tibetan chant.

In this paper we have attempted to evaluate the chant produced by members of the EVTE in relation to "normal" phonation and vocal fry (Hollien et al., 1966) on the basis of the performers' subjective sensations (Large and Murry, 1978) that chant represents a combination of light Western singing with vocal fry.

METHOD

Two female and three male subjects were selected from the UCSD Extended Vocal Techniques Ensemble on their ability to produce the required sounds. Two sets of recordings were

obtained from each subject. The first set was produced in an
IAC sound-treated room. The subjects stood approximately
25 cm from an Electrovoice 654 Microphone. The microphone
output was directed to a Revox A-77 Magnetic Tape Recorder
with a speed of 7.5 ips. Next to the Electrovoice Microphone
was positioned a B&K sound level meter. The meter was set to
the A-weighted scale. The meter was in full view of the subject and one of the experimenters who was also in the sound-
treated room.

The subjects were instructed to produce one of the desired phonatory samples--either vocal fry, chant, or normal
sustained phonation using the vowel /ʌ/. The subject sustained the vowel at a comfortable effort level and observed
that value on the sound level meter. Then, without stopping
or interrupting the phonation, the subject shifted to the
next predetermined phonatory sample while maintaining the
sound pressure level equivalent to the first sample. In
most instances, there was some variation in SPL during the
shift from one sample to another. As many samples were taken
as deemed necessary by the two experimenters and the subject
in order to obtain a steady state sample of both voice
qualities at a sound pressure level within 2dB. Six diads
were produced by each subject: fry-chant, chant-fry, chant-
normal, normal-chant, fry-normal, and normal-fry. Based on
the sound pressure level readings and the experimenter's
subjective judgments, one sample of each of the six diads
was selected for subsequent acoustic analysis. This same
procedure was followed in order to obtain pneumotachographic
data on the three types of voice production--chant, normal,
and vocal fry. Figure 1 shows a block diagram of the air flow
recording apparatus. The subject's face was positioned inside
a full face mask. The sound level meter was located in a
direct line of sight of the subject. Each subject produced
one of the voice samples; when he held it satisfactorily, he
shifted to the second sample of the diad. The diad which was
ultimately accepted for pneumotachographic analysis showed no
greater than a 2dB difference between members of the diad, and
it was acceptable to the experimenters as the voice qualities
desired.

Acoustic Analysis. Sound spectrograms of the six diads
of each subject were made on a Kay Sonagraph. The experimenter produced each sonogram so that it showed the first
voice quality, the shift, and the second quality. In addition, a section was taken at a point approximately one-half
second on either side of the shift. Waveform records for
each type of phonation were obtained from a Honeywell 1508-C
Visicorder. Aerodynamic Analysis. The location of the shift
was identified from the acoustic trace on the visicorder output. Approximately one-half second on either side of the
shift, the air flow curve was sampled five times during a
one-half second duration. From these five data points, a
meal air flow rate was obtained for each voice quality.

RESULTS

The acoustic records for all subjects were similar. A
typical series (Subject 3) of wide band Sonagrams with superimposed amplitude sections (displayed below) is shown in
Figures 2-4. Task 1, fry to chant, is illustrated in Figure
2; note the variable pulse rate for fry and the regular
repetition rate for chant. Task 3, fry to normal, is illustrated in Figure 3; note again the shift from the slow irregular pulse rate of fry to the regularized fundamental frequency of roughly F_3-sharp, 185 Hz. Task 5, chant to normal,
is illustrated in Figure 4. On shifting from chant to normal
the record shows the usual picture of vocal fold vibration
in the clean vertical striations at approximately F_3-sharp,
185 Hz. Tasks 2, 4 and 6 were the reverse of tasks 1, 3 and
5. Several subjects find it easier to produce the task going
in one direction rather than the other. Nonetheless, the
acoustic results did not differ depending on the direction of
the task.

Additionally, the recorded samples were processed on the
Honeywell 1508-C Visicorder. The three samples--fry, chant,
and normal, each showed a distinctive waveform. That is, the
sample of the chant showed a tendency towards damping prior
to repeating itself; the vocal fry waveform damped sufficiently prior to repeating and the normal sample showed the
characteristic waveform of normal voice.

Figure 5 shows the air flow data for the chant-normal and normal-chant trials. The data for subject five were not available. In addition, one subject could not produce the chant to normal condition satisfactorily. It can be seen that the mean air flow rates for the normal samples are considerably higher than those for the chant. There is little difference in the air flow rates regardless of whether the subject went from chant to normal or normal to chant. There is, however, considerable variation from subject to subject for each voice quality. This may be due to the amount of effort or control expended by each subject in order to produce samples that were within 2dB of each other.

Figure 6 shows the fry-chant and chant-fry conditions for four of the subjects. There was little difference in the overall mean air flow rates whether the subject began in vocal fry or in chant. While there was substantial individual variation in the chant air flow rates, there was no more than a 60 cc/sec air flow range for the vocal fry samples.

Figure 7 summarizes the mean air flow rates for the six conditions. The vocal fry samples had the lowest mean air flow rates; the normal conditions always had the highest mean air flow rates. An examination of the data revealed no individual reversals. The mean air flow associated with the chant samples was approximately midway between the vocal fry and normal samples.

DISCUSSION AND CONCLUSIONS

The data presented in this paper are somewhat inconclusive in that they were derived from a small number of subjects and in that the investigators relied on each subject to produce chant as the Tibetan monks produce it. Individual differences in the renditions offered by each subject were present; however, each sample of chant was auditorily similar to that produced by the Tibetans and felt subjectively like chant to the subjects. Thus, the authors offer a tentative framework for the further study of chant.

Chant is produced at frequencies generally located in the male modal register. In addition, there is a degree of damping of the vocal tract between glottal excitations but not as great as the damping that occurs in vocal fry. Physiologically, chant appears to be produced at air flow rates greater than vocal fry but less than those of the normal register. The subjects in this study, with the best controlled samples of chant, produced air flow rates approximately twice those of vocal fry. Those same subjects were also able to shift from chant to normal and produce the normal phonation with generally accepted normal air flow rates. The nature of vocal cord vibration for chant has not yet been investigated. Our subjects, trained to produce chant in a manner which they feel is similar to that produced by the Tibetan monks, content that subjectively they are combining Western normal phonation with vocal fry. From our air flow data, chant does indeed appear to be physiologically intermediate with regard to "normal" and vocal fry. This appears to be a fruitful area of investigation in order to understand the physiological basis of vocal chant in greater detail.

ACKNOWLEDGEMENT

Supported by Medical Research Service of the Veterans Administration.

REFERENCES

Hollien, H., Moore, R., Wendahl, R. W., and Michel, J. (1966). J. Speech Hear. Res., 9:245-247.
Large, J., and Murry, T. (1978). The NATS Bulletin, 24/4:30-33.
Smith, H., Stevens, K. N., and Tomlinson, R. (1967). J. Acoust. Soc. Am., 41:1262-1264.

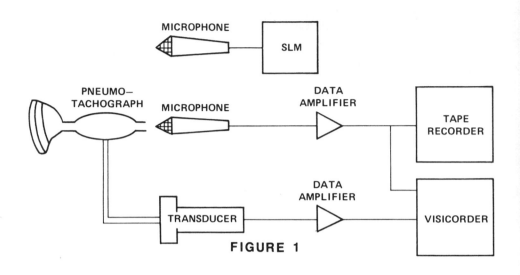

FIGURE 1

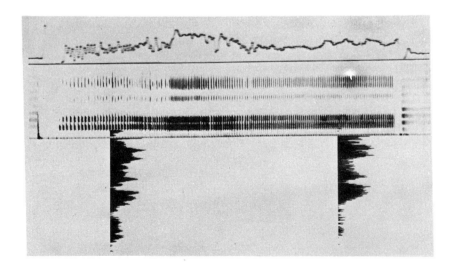

FRY   **FIGURE 2**   CHANT

TYPE B/65 SONAGRAM® KAY ELEMETRICS CO. PINE BROOK, N. J.

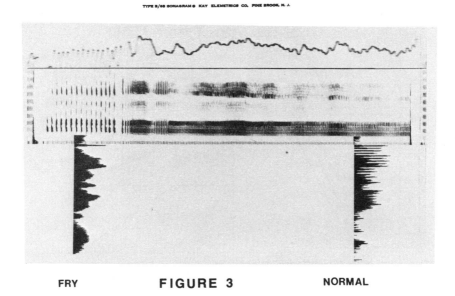

FRY   **FIGURE 3**   NORMAL

TYPE B/65 SONAGRAM® KAY ELEMETRICS CO. PINE BROOK, N. J.

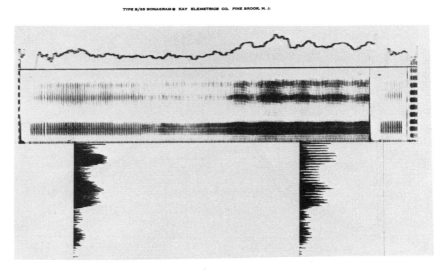

CHANT   **FIGURE 4**   NORMAL

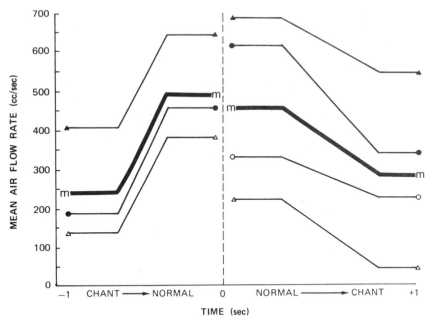

FIGURE 5

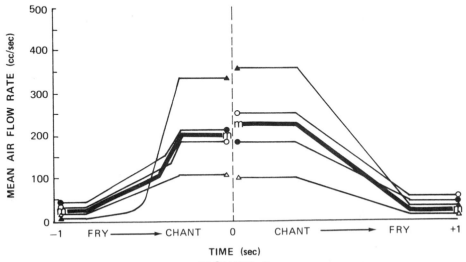

FIGURE 6

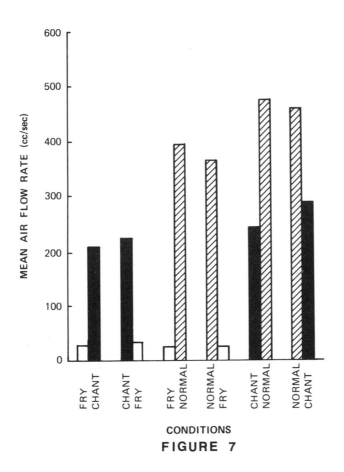

CONDITIONS

FIGURE 7

JOINTURE ET ACTIVITÉ GLOTTALE

MAGNÚS PÉTURSSON
Universität Hamburg

Dans les langues germaniques une consonne aspirée peut seulement suivre un /s/ ou une autre constrictive sourde si une jointure sépare les deux consonnes, c'est-à-dire les deux consonnes doivent appartenir à des mots différents. Si les deux consonnes appartiennent au même mot, seules des occlusives non aspirées sont admises après /s/. Pour cette raison la présence d'aspiration après /s/ a été interprétée comme signe de jointure (Lehiste, 1960; Trubetzkoy, 1962). On est même allé jusqu'à affirmer que l'absence d'aspiration après /s/ constituait un trait phonétique universel (Lindqvist, 1972, p. 20) et on a proposé plusieurs explications de ce fait. De celles-ci la plus sérieuse nous semble être celle de Kim (1970) Il propose une explication en termes d'économie des mouvements de la glotte.

Mais l'absence d'aspiration après /s/ ne constitue aucunement un trait phonétique universel. Dans plusieurs langues de l'Inde l'aspiration après /s/ est courante et il y a une opposition entre consonnes aspirées et non aspirées dans cette position (Aoyagi, 1963, p. 14; Elizarenkova, 1974, p. 172; Doi, 1974).

Le but de notre recherche, qui se situe dans le cadre d'un vaste programme de recherche sur l'aspiration en tant que phénomène phonétique, était de contribuer à l'étude d'un aspect peu étudié de l'aspiration et simultanément de poser la question de la réalisation de la jointure au niveau glottal. Autant que nous le sachions ce dernier problème n'a pas été examiné expérimentalement.

Méthode et matériaux linguistiques

Les matériaux linguistiques sont des mots islandais
et des combinaisons de deux mots dont le premier se termine
par un -s et le deuxième commence par une occlusive aspirée.
Ces mots ont été lus 26 fois par un sujet islandais, précédés
par le mot-clé segðu "dis," impératif du verbe segja "dire."
Par comparaison nous avons également enregistré les mots
suédois en viss tid /en vIs: t^hi:d/ "un certain temps" lus
par M. Anders Lofqvist qui nous a aidé dans la réalisation
des enregistrements (Fig. 4).

Les mots ont été enregistrés avec le photoglottographe
Frøkjær-Jensen (Frøkjær-Jensen et al., 1971). Simultanément
nous avons enregistré le débit d'air et l'oscillogramme. Sur
les tracés nous obtenons donc trois lignes sur lesquelles
nous avons mesuré les paramètres suivants: (1) durée de la
consonne /s/; (2) durée de l'occlusion; (3) durée de l'explo-
sion de l'occlusive non aspirée; (4) durée de l'aspiration;
(5) le moment de l'ouverture glottale maximale à l'intérieur
du /s/; (6) le moment de l'ouverture glottale maximale à
l'intérieur de l'occlusive aspirée.

Le moment de l'ouverture glottale a été mesuré à partir
du début de la consonne respective. Les mots ont été lus avec
un rythme naturel. En particulier on a fait attention à ne
pas faire une pause entre les deux consonnes. Dans cette
communication nous nous sommes limité aux groupes de s suivi
d'une occlusive alvéodentale. Les groupes que nous considérons sont donc les suivants:

Groupe	Exemple
# st-	stími "je progresse," présent de stíma
-s#t	laus dýr "des animaux libres"
-s#t^h-	laus tími "un moment libre."

Résultats de l'analyse

Les résultats de l'analyse sont résumés dans le Tableau 1.
Dans le tableau la durée est mesurée en millisecondes. La
durée du /s/ est la plus longue dans le groupe /#st-/ et la

plus brève dans le groupe /-s#t-/. Le groupe /-s#t^h-/ prend
une position intermédiaire. Ces faits s'expliquent comme
conséquence de la position du /s/ dans la syllabe. Dans le
groupe /#st-/ les deux consonnes se trouvent au début de la
syllabe et portent un accent fort initial qui allonge le /s/.
Dans les deux autres groupes le /s/ ferme la syllabe et se
trouve par conséquent dans une position plus faible par
rapport à l'accent ce qui a comme conséquence que sa durée
diminue. Quant au groupe /-s#t^h-/ en suédois ses données ne
peuvent pas être comparées avec celles des mots islandais,
mais il est évident que la même relation prédomine dans les
deux langues, à savoir que le /s/ est toujours plus long que
l'occlusive subséquente. L'aspiration est plus longue en
suédois qu'en islandais. L'aspiration en suédois dépend
quant à sa durée largement de celle de l'occlusion (Lofqvist,
1975, pp. 101-103), alors qu'en islandais une corrélation
semblable entre la durée de l'occlusion et celle de l'aspiration n'a pas été observée (Pétursson, 1976b, pp. 127-128).
Pour le groupe /-s#t^h-/ nous avons pu observer deux maxima
d'ouverture glottale, un maximum correspondant à chaque
consonne. Mais tant en suédois qu'en islandais il est
également possible d'observer un seul maximum d'ouverture
glottale pour les deux consonnes. Dans ce cas le maximum
d'ouverture glottale est localisé soit dans la deuxième partie
du /s/ soit à l'intérieur de l'occlusive subséquente (Figure 5)
Pour les autres groupes il y a toujours un seul maximum
d'ouverture glottale pour lex deux consonnes. Ce maximum est
localisé à l'intérieur de la consonne /s/ (Figures 1 et 2).
Un changement dans la position de la jointure ne change pas
la localisation du maximum d'ouverture glottale. Ceci est
un argument en faveur de l'interprétation de la jointure comme
frontiere entre deux séquences (Lehiste, 1960, p. 48). Une
jointure ne peut donc pas être phonème, mais elle est liée à
des variantes de position, lesquelles a leur tour correspondent
aux phonèmes.

Discussion

     Une interprétation des données que nous venons d'exposer
n'est pas sans certains problèmes. Si on analyse les glottogrammes d'une seule consonne il apparaît qu'il n'y a jamais
plus qu'un seul maximum d'ouverture glottale (Pétursson, 1975;

Uchita, 1974). Ce même fait est également observé pour les
groupes de constrictive et occlusive. Pourtant il ne faut
pas en conclure qu'au niveau glottal ces groupes sont traités
comme une seule consonne. La localisation du maximum
d'ouverture glottale ne peut pas intervenir à n'importe quel
moment, mais elle est au contraire soigneusement coordonnée
selon les consonnes qui forment le groupe, c'est-à-dire elle
n'intervient jamais à un moment trop tardif pour que la
glotte ne puisse pas être pratiquement fermée au moment de
la rupture de l'occlusion.

Pour les groupes dans lesquels le /s/ est suivi d'une
occlusive aspirée il y a deux maxima d'ouverture glottale dans
à peu pres 70% des cas. Li il n'y a donc pas de doute que
l'activité glottale est organisée en fonction des deux consonnes qui forment le groupe. Mais dans 30% des cas nous
observons qu'il y a un seul maximum d'ouverture glottale.
Ce maximum est situé soit à l'intérieur du /s/, soit à
l'intérieur de l'occlusive aspirée subséquente. Si l'économie
des mouvements articulatoires était le seul principe sous-
jacent de l'acte de la parole, nous aurions pu espérer trouver
toujours un maximum d'ouverture glottale pour les groupes
/-s#t^h-/. Le seule différence avec les autres groupes de s
suivi d'une occlusive non aspirée serait alors le décalage
temporel entre les maxima d'ouverture glottale.

Les cas où il y a deux maxima d'ouverture glottale dans
les groupes /-s#t^h-/ montrent de toute évidence que l'économie
des mouvements articulatoires--bien qu'important, personne
n'en doute--n'est pas le seul principe gouvernant les mouvements des organes articulatoires. Il faut supposer l'existence
d'un autre principe additionnel et nous suggérons que ce
principe soit le phonème. Le phonème est une unité fonctionnelle, mais pas une manifestation dans une substance sonore.
Il est par conséquent logique et ne parle aucunement contre
le phonème que la recherche des invariants correspondant au
phonème a été un échec complet. On ne peut jamais esperer
trouver autre chose qu'une variation infiniment grande dans
la substance sonore. C'est en effet cette variation elle-même
qui est le meilleur argument en faveur du phonème. Une
recherche phonétique qui cherche des invariants correspondant
au phonème dans une substance sonore est sur la fausse piste,

car le phonème est une unité fonctionnelle appartenant au
niveau de la forme linguistique. La phonème est pourtant le
fondement qui rend possible l'interprétation de la grande
variation observée dans l'analyse des mouvements articulatoires et de la substance conore. Nous croyons avoir apporté
des arguments dans notre analyse en faveur du phonème comme
unité sous-jacente de l'acte de la parole. Ceci ne signifie
pas que nous n'accordions aucune valeur à des facteurs comme
l'économie des mouvements articulatoires et le principe du
moindre effort. Ce que nous affirmons c'est qu'à eux seuls
ces principes mécaniques ne peuvent pas expliquer toutes les
particularités des mouvements articulatoires. Si nous
admettons le phonème comme unité sous-jacente nous serons en
mesure d'expliquer certaines particularités restées jusqu'ici
sans explication véritable dans l'analyse expérimentale.

BIBLIOGRAPHIE

Aoyagi, S. (1963). Bull. Fac. Lit., Tokyo Univ. Ed., 39:1-18.

Doi, K. (1974). Tokyo, Phon. Soc. Jap., 725-730.

Elizarenkova, T. J. (1974). Issl. Diax. Fono. Indo. Jazy.,
     166-183.

Frøkjær-Jensen, B.; Ludvigsen, C. and Rischel, J. (1971).
     København, Akad. Forl., 123-140.

Lehiste, I. (1960). Phonet. Suppl., 5.

Lindqvist, J. (1972). KTH, Quart. Prog. Status Rep., 2/3:
     10-27.

Lofqvist, A. (1975). Work. Pap. Phon. Lab., Lund Univ.,
     12:99-106.

Pétursson, M. (1975). Work. Pap., Phon. Lab., Lund Univ.,
     12:107-130.

Pétursson, M. (1976a). Phonet., 33:169-198.

Pétursson, M. (1976b). Hamb. Phon. Beit., 17:121-150.

Trubetzkoy, N. S. (1958). Gottingen, Vandenhoeck & Ruprecht.

Uchita, S. (1974). Tokyo, Phon. Soc. Jap., 709-718.

Tableau 1. Résultats de l'analyse.

Groupe	Nombre d'ex	1	2	3	4	5	6
#st-	40	147,5	97,5	13,5		60,5	
-s#t-	52	109,5	88,5	12,0		65,0	
-s#t^h-	60	123,0	90,0		33,0	64,0	73,0
-s#t^h-l	6	148,0	81,0		60,0	80,0	42,0

1. Le groupe /-s#t^h-/ en suédois.

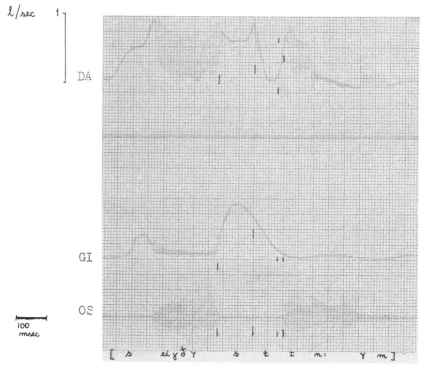

Fig. 1.

Glottogramme des mots islandais <u>segðu stinnum</u> [seiɣðY stIn:Ym] "dis rigides" (dat. pl. de <u>stinnur</u> "rigide").
DA = débit d´air; GL = photoglottogramme; OS = oscillogramme
Il y a un seul maximum d´ouverture glottale pour ·le groupe [∦ st-].

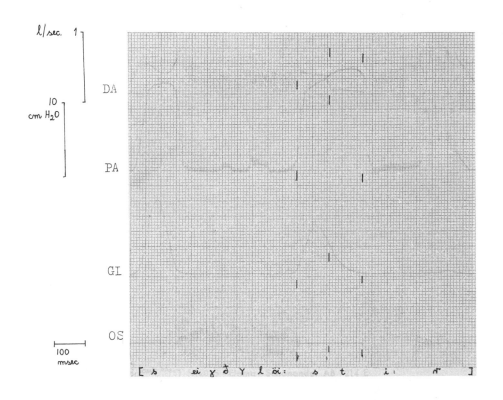

Fig. 2.

Glottogramme des mots islandais <u>segðu laus dýr</u> [seiɣðʏ
löi:s ti:r] "dis animaux libres". Il n´y a aucun changement
sur le glottogramme par rapport à celui de la fig. 1, bien
qu´une jointure sépare les deux consonnes [-s#t-].
Pour cette série la pression intrabuccale (PA = pression d´air)
a été enregistrée.

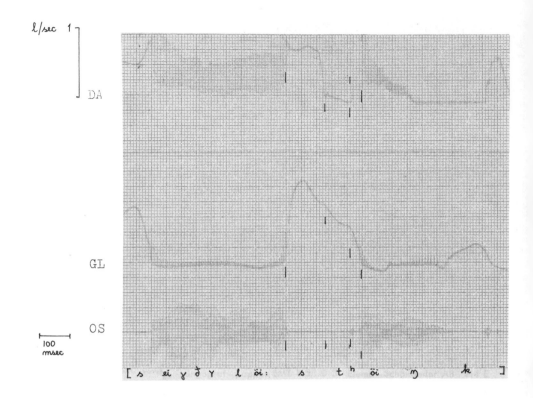

Fig. 3.

Glottogramme des mots islandais <u>segðu laus töng</u> [seiχðY
löi:s tʰöiŋk] "dis tenailles non attachées". On peut observer
deux maxima d´ouverture glottale, chacun correspondant à une
consonne. Le deuxième maximum d´ouverture est moins prononcé
comme ceci est presque toujours le cas dans nos enregistrements.

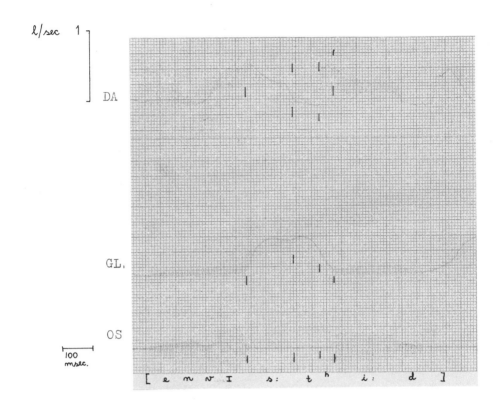

Fig. 4.

Glottogramme des mots suédois <u>en viss tid</u> [en vɪs: tʰi:d] "un certain temps". On peut observer deux maxima d'ouverture glottale, lesquels correspondent à chaque consonne [-s#tʰ-].

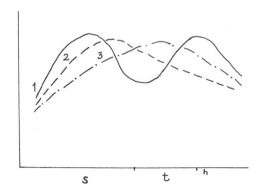

Fig. 5.

Schéma des glottogrammes observés pour le groupe con-
sonantique [-s#t^h-].
1. Deux maxima d´ouverture glottale, chaque maximum
   correspondant à une consonne.
2. Un seul maximum d´ouverture glottale à l´intérieur du [s].
3. Un seul maximum d´ouverture glottale à l´intérieur de la
   consonne occlusive.

INSTRUMENTAL MEASUREMENT OF PHONATION TYPES:
A LARYNGOGRAPHIC CONTRIBUTION

P. J. ROACH AND W. J. HARDCASTLE
University of Reading

An area of undoubted importance in phonetic research is the study of phonation types, both in the study of normal speech at segmental and suprasegmental levels, and in relation to the diagnosis and remediation of phonatory disorders. For the purposes of this paper we use the term phonation type to refer to a mode of vibration of the vocal cords, this being one component among others which together constitute voice quality. In this we follow Catford (1964) and Laver (1968).

While we recognize the value of an auditory/kinaesthetic analysis which attempts to resolve the complex range of possible phonation types into a limited number of components with possibilities of co-occurrence with each other (see for example Catford, 1964, 1977; Laver, 1968, 1976 and forthcoming), we feel that it is important at the same time to look for corresponding physical instrumentally measurable characteristics of vocal cord vibration. Many instrumental techniques are currently available for measuring aspects of vocal cord vibration (see Sawashima, 1974); almost certainly, no single instrumentally measurable variable in isolation will be found adequate to discriminate among all perceptually different phonation types, so some suitable combination of variables must be sought. Recent research, for clinical purposes, using several acoustic parameters is described in Fritzell, Hammarberg and Wedin (1977) and Gauffin and Sunberg (1977).

One instrument which because of its simplicity and ease of application seems to have considerable potential from the point of view of studying a wide range of speakers, in conjunction with other measures, is what various authors have called an <u>electrical glottograph</u> or an <u>electroglottograph</u> and which in Britain is now widely called a <u>laryngograph</u> (Fourcin and Abberton, 1971). An unpublished cinephotographic/laryngographic study by Fourcin, Donovan and Roach (referred to in Fourcin and Abberton, 1971; Fourcin, 1972 a and b and Fourcin, 1974a) and work using a similar but not identical instrument by Ondráčková (1972), as well as parallel comparisons of electroglottographic and photoelectric glottographic recordings (Frøkjaer-Jensen, 1969) have more or less confirmed the expected relationship between vocal cord vibratory movement and variations in trans-glottal electrical impedance. An important aspect of the laryngograph waveform is the indication of the open phase of the vibratory cycle. The study by Fourcin <u>et al</u>. referred to above showed that glottal opening generally occurs before the laryngograph trace reaches its lowest point, though as a generalization the low part of the trace from this particular instrument is associated with glottal opening. However, for the purpose of the small experiment to be described here it was found more suitable, in attempting to produce a measure of variation in the open phase, to measure from the lowest part of the trace to the highest; in effect this represents slightly less than the actual open phase, but since we shall be concerned principally with relative and comparative, not absolute measures this should have little effect; this measuring technique has the advantage that it will make the computer measurements planned for later experiments easier.

It is known that the proportion of the vibratory cycle of the vocal cords taken by the open phase varies with phonation type, and (except at high pitches) with intensity (see Timcke, von Leden and Moore, 1958 and 1959; Zemlin, 1968). It is not possible to derive separate measurements of opening and closing times (as did Timcke <u>et al</u>. from film) from the laryngograph waveform, but it is hoped to make use of the measure used in the present experiment, that is, the proportion of the laryngogram cycle taken by the time from base to peak. This measure (abbreviated as BP/T) is illustrated in Fig. 1;

the waveform shown (which was digitized by computer and
plotted on an X-Y plotter) is of P.R.'s voice during sustained low-pitch phonation with high intensity and a degree
of glottal constriction sufficient to give the unusually low
BP/T value of approximately .35.

The experiment was carried out using only one subject
(P.R.). It seemed simplest and most convenient to take as a
starting point the system proposed in Ladefoged (1971), where
a single continuum of glottal stricture (the physiological
basis for which is admittedly dubious) is set up with seven
different phonation types. The instruments used were a
laryngograph and a photoelectric glottograph (the latter
being included in the experiment to see if any interesting
comparisons emerged--in fact there were no discrepancies
between the two traces). The outputs of these instruments
were reported at 37.5 i.p.s. on an FM data recorder and then
replayed at one-tenth of that speed into a Mingograf oscillo-
graph running with a paper speed of 100 mm./sec.

For the first part of the experiment the subject
phonated for 10 seconds at a steady pitch (approximately
120 Hz.) attempting to keep intensity constant while gradually
changing the phonatory quality from minimal glottal constriction (extreme breathiness) through normal voice to maximal
glottal constriction (extreme creakiness). Each cycle was
measured and BP/T, averaged over 3 cycles, was plotted against
time (Fig. 2). It can be seen that apart from a certain instability at about half a second from the beginning, BP/T
decreases fairly steadily up to about 3.5 seconds from the
beginning and from then onwards there is very little further
decrease and more variability among measurements.

For the second part of the experiment the subject, having
practised phonation with seven distinct qualities which he
felt to be reasonably close to the descriptions given by
Ladefoged, recorded steady phonation at approximately constant pitch and normal intensity with each of these qualities
for about 10 seconds. The waveforms for these were again
recorded via FM tape recording on to paper. For each example
of phonation, every third cycle was measured and the mean BP/T
value calculated. On Fig. 2 lines have been produced from the

point on the BP/T axis at which each mean is located, to
transect the continuous trace plotted after the first part
of the experiment. It can be seen that normal phonation (D)
and the three types of breathy phonation (A,B,C) are ordered
as expected, but that for the three qualities with greater
glottal constriction than normal voice the progression does
not continue. Considerable variability from cycle to cycle
was found during measuring and the BP/T value for quality G
is in fact slightly higher than that for E and F. (The
photoelectric glottograph traces for qualities E, F and G
were of very low amplitude and practically impossible to
measure.)

The measure discussed would appear, on the basis of this
very limited experiment, to have some use in characterizing
different types of breathy voice and in distinguishing these
from normal voice and from qualities produced with greater
degrees of glottal stricture, but not to be useful in dis-
criminating among (auditorily and kinaesthetically) different
qualities of the latter type. It seems that measurement of
cycle-to-cycle variability (Fourcin, 1974b) used in conjunction
with the BP/T measure discussed would be very valuable and it
is hoped to calculate this in future experiments.

In conclusion, it should be noted that measurements of
sustained phonation are much easier to make than measurements
of phonation in running speech; some of the former can even
be done in real time by computer, while the latter generally
has to be done by detailed 'after-the-event' analysis. There
are further problems in the rapid changes in phonatory quality
associated with distinctions used in various languages at or
around the segmental level, as described for example by
Ladefoged (1971) and by Halle and Stevens (1967, 1971). In
such cases (e.g., the various laryngeal adjustments for which
it is common to use the cover term "laryngealization") it
may well be that the perceptually important characteristic of
the vocal cord vibratory pattern is the rapid change in waveform rather than any "steady state" quality; in cyclic laryngeal manoeuvres such as those described by Rothenberg (1968,
1972) the vocal cords may well pass into and out of a state in
which vibration is either not sustainable or is inherently
unstable. This being so, it would perhaps be misguided to

attempt to bring these laryngeal phenomena into the same
classificatory system as that used for phonation types as
described earlier in this paper.

REFERENCES

Catford, J. C.   (1964). Longman.
Fourcin, A. J.   (1972a). Proc. Inter. Cong. Phon. Sci.,
     Mouton.
Fourcin, A. J.   (1972b). Proc. Inter. Cong. Phon. Sci.,
     Mouton.
Fourcin, A. J.   (1974a). O.U.P.
Fourcin, A. J.   (1974b). Proc. Inter. Cong. Acoust., London,
     1:225.
Fourcin, A. J. and Abberton, E.   (1971). Med. Biol. Ill.
     21:172-182.
Fritzell, B., Hammarberg, B., and Wedin, L.   (1977). STL,
     QPSR, Stockholm, 2-3.
Frøkjaer-Jensen, B.   (1969). Nor. Cong. Otolaryn., Denmark.
Gauffin, J. and Sundberg, J.   (1977). STL, QPSR, Stockholm,
     2-3.
Halle, M. and K. N. Stevens (1967). QPR, RLE, M.I.T., 85:
     267-271.
Halle, M. and K. N. Stevens.   (1971). QPR, RLE, M.I.T., 101:
     198-213.
Ladefoged, P.   (1971). Chicago.
Laver, J.   (1968). Brit. J. Dis. Comm., 3:43-54.
Laver, J.   (1976). Univ. Essex Occas. Pap., 17.
Laver, J.   (forthcoming). C.U.P.
Lindqvist, J.   (1969). STL QPSR, Stockholm, 4:1-4.
Ondráčková, J.   (1972). Proc. Inter. Cong. Phon. Sci.,
     Mouton.
Rothenberg, M.   (1968). Basel, Karger.
Rothenberg, M.   (1972). Proc. Inter. Cong. Phon. Sci.,
     Mouton.
Timcke, R., von Leden, H. and Moore, P.   (1958, 1959).
     Arch. Otol., 68:1-19 and 69:438-444.
Zemlin, W. R.   (1968). N.Y., Prentice-Hall.

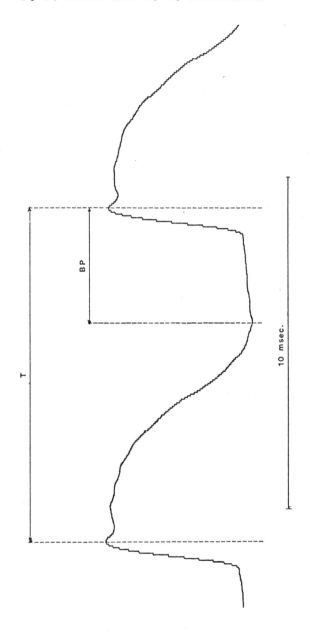

Fig.1 Laryngograph Waveform:

Period and Base-to-Peak Time

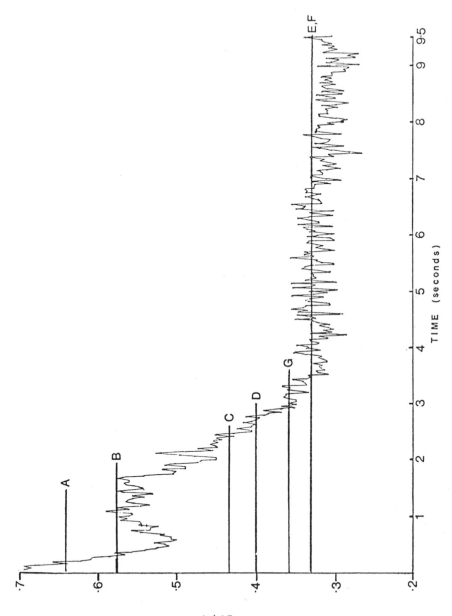

Fig.2 Laryngographic Measurements of Phonation Types

VARIATIONS OF PITCH AND INTENSITY WITH PRE-PHONATORY LARYNGEAL ADJUSTMENTS

INGO R. TITZE
Gallaudet College

INTRODUCTION

Experimental data on the mechanism of pitch and intensity control have not been entirely conclusive. This paper reviews briefly the experimental techniques and attempts to point out some fundamental reasons for the lack of consistency in measurement. The importance of the laryngeal configuration in the unique specification of phonatory acoustics is stressed, and some directions for further research in the study of pitch and intensity control are suggested.

ANALYSIS OF LARYNGEAL FUNCTION

Major contributions to the understanding of the laryngeal mechanism and its control of fundamental frequency and intensity, along with various aspects of vocal quality, have been made in five basic areas. (1) Kinematics of hard and soft laryngeal tissues; (2) Electromyographics of soft laryngeal tissues; (3) Aerodynamics of the respiratory and phonatory systems; (4) Acoustics of speech production; and (5) Viscoelasticity in human tissues. The first of these areas, the kinematic studies, have been primarily epxerimental, although some attempts have been made to treat the motion of hard structures on a theoretical basis (Broad, 1968). High speed cinematography, techniques involving x-rays, indirect and direct laryngoscopy, fiber optics, particle tracking, and ultrasonics have afforded us a detailed description of the motion of laryngeal tissues during a variety of phonation

types. The second major area, electromyographics (EMG),
provides us with a link between neurophysiology and pure
mechanics, however loose that link may be at this point.
Not having been developed into a concrete theory, EMG is
presently not more than a technique, but will ultimately
allow us to study cause-effect relationships in voice production. It still faces many quantitative limitations.
Heavy usage is made of signal averaging, over repeated small
time segments, over various tokens of an utterance, and
preferably over many speakers. On a theoretical basis, EMG
is just beginning to be understood, but not without formid-
able, almost heroic, mathematical efforts (DeLuca, 1975).
The third area, aerodynamics, is reasonably well understood,
both from a theoretical and an experimental point of view.
Major problems seem to be the miniaturization and attachment
of transducers, interference with the normal speech mechanism,
and clinical safety. The fourth area, acoustics, has provided us with major insights into voice production, although
in many cases in terms of a byproduct of a more general analysis of speech production. Both theory and experimentation,
especially via the current techniques of signal processing,
are highly developed. In some cases, too much has in fact
been expected in the line of basic research from this most
reliable workhorse. Finally, the fifth area, viscoelasticity,
is a new, more-or-less unknown, discipline to most speech
scientists. As a fundamental theory of biomechanics, this
area has seen an upsurge of activity in the past ten years.
Much has been learned about the functioning of the heart,
blood vessels, the brain, and many other internal organs by
studying the viscoelasticity and rheology of human tissues.
In my opinion, this field has great potential for basic research in speech production, both on a theoretical and on an
experimental plane. It provides the only framework for
kinetic investigations of speech production, where tissue
stresses and inertial effects can provide unique causality
for phonatory and articulatory events.

THE LARYNGEAL CONFIGURATION

Turning now to the specific problem of pitch and intensity control in phonation, much of the controversy about
which muscles are involved in pitch raising and lowering, or
which muscles increase and decrease vocal intensity, could be

eliminated if we were more precise about the <u>configuration</u>
which these muscular contractions produce. A number of
electromyographic investigations have been conducted in an
effort to relate muscular activity and acoustic output
directly (Hirano <u>et al</u>., 1969; Gay <u>et al</u>., 1972; Shipp and
McGlone, 1971; Collier, 1973). The fact that sometimes
little or no attention was paid to vocal fold configuration,
i.e., length, thickness, glottal shaping, longitudinal and
transverse tissue stress, vibrational amplitude, and in many
cases even glottal volume flow and subglottal pressure, makes
these studies inconclusive especially with respect to the
control of intensity. Cricothyroid contraction seems to be
the only quantity which can be reliably correlated with an
acoustic consequence, namely pitch raising.

In order to specify accurately the pre-honatory laryngeal configuration, ten configurational parameters have been
identified in our computational model of the vocal folds and
their surrounding boundary structures (Figure 1). Geometric
parameters, such as length L, thickness T, depth D, glottal
shape factors w, s, and q, as well as the viscoelastic parame-
ters μ_o, η_o , μ_L' , μ_M' can all be affected by muscular contractions. μ_o and η_o represent the average isotropic shear elasticities and viscosities of the tissues, while μ_L' and μ_M'
represent additional elasticities along the length of the
tissue fibers in the ligament and muscle, respectively. Detailed discussion of these parameters is given elsewhere ·
(Titze & Talkin, 1979).

We have learned that the majority of these configurational parameters can affect pitch and intensity. The overall problem is illustrated graphically in Figure 2. The left
column symbolizes muscular contraction consisting of sterno-
hyoid (SH), sternothyroid (ST), thyrohyoid (TH), cricothyroid
(CT), vocalis (VOC), lateral cricoarytenoid (LCA), interarytenoid (IA), posterior cricoarytenoid (PCA), and subglottal
pressure (PS). The middle column represents the configuration already mentioned, and the right column shows the two
most often discussed acoustic variables, pitch and intensity.
Solid lines represent positive correlations, and dashed lines
represent negative correlations. The thickness of the lines
is a qualitative measure of the strength of the correlation.

It is clear that a given configuration will generate a
unique combination of pitch and intensity. (We are neglec-
ting, for simplicity, subglottal and supraglottal effects.
These could, of course, be included in the overall configuration.) A large variety of configurations have been studied
by computer simulation (Titze & Talkin, 1979). We are now
beginning to understand some of the complexities of phonatory
control based on laryngeal configuration. For example, the
isotropic elasticity μ_o and the longitudinal tension μ_l' in
the ligament have been found to be the primary pitch control
mechanisms, followed, in order of significance, by tension
in the vocalis, tissue viscosity, and vocal fold length.
Surprisingly, vocal fold thickness has an insignificant effect
upon pitch. Additional glottal shape factors, such as w, s,
and q, have smaller affects on pitch control, but play an important part in regulating intensity. Primary intensity regu-
lators are subglottal pressure, thickness, the glottal shape
factors s and w, tissue viscosity, and both ligament and
vocalis tension. Note that certain pairs of these work in
opposite directions. For example, an increase in ligament
tension produces a decrease in intensity, but an increase in
vocalis tension produces an increase in intensity. Simultaneous increase in both, in proper proportions, could possibly leave the intensity unchanged. Is it any wonder, then,
that EMG data on intensity control without careful monitoring
of laryngeal configuration are inconclusive? As another
example, consider the much debated subject of pitch control
by subglottal pressure. We have found no convincing evidence
that volume flow, and the so-called Bernoulli effect, have a
substantial effect on fundamental frequency. Excepting perhaps very small amplitude vibrations near the onset of aspirate phonation, the fundamental frequency seems to be governed
by the normal modes of the tissues, by tissue nonlinearity,
and by the boundary conditions. We believe that the subglottal
pressure increases the phonation _amplitude_, and therewith the
effective ligament elasticity μ_l' (Figure 2). Therefore,
without direct or indirect determination of static and dynamic viscoelastic properties and the associated geometric configuration, inconclusive EMG measurements on pitch and intensity control are likely to be continued. This is especially
true for the extrinsic muscles SH, ST, and TH. We know so

little about their effect on the configuration, that even speculative correlations in Figure 2 are difficult.

What steps should be taken, then, to eliminate these possible misinterpretations. In my opinion, more work is needed to relate EMG to laryngeal tissue mechanics, rather than phonatory acoustics. Less than a handful of studies have been attempted in an effort to relate static configurations to isolated and well controlled muscular contractions, the most noteworthy being the recent one by Hirano (1975). Barring perhaps the correlation between cricothyroid contraction and ligament stress, all of the correlations indicated in the left hand side of Figure 2 are still speculative. If we had more experimental data showing what perturbations in laryngeal configuration result from contractions of these muscles, some of the hypotheses could be tested by modelling. At present, the almost universally accepted myoelastic-aerodynamic theory of voice production has been subject to investigation on a myoacoustic basis, with relatively little emphasis on aerodynamics, and even less on myoelastics.

REFERENCES

Broad, D. J. (1968). SCRL Mono, No. 3, Santa Barbara, Cal.
Collier, R. (1973). J. Acoust. Soc. Amer., 58:249-255.
DeLuca, C. J. (1975). Biol. Cybernet. 19:159-167.
Gay, T., Hirose, H., Strome, M., and Sawashima, M. (1972).
    Amer. Otol. Rhinol. Laryngol. 81:401-409.
Hirano, M., Ohala, J., and Vennard, W. (1969). J. Speech
    Hear. Res. 12:616-628.
Hirano, M. (1975). Annual Convention of Oto-Rhino-Laryng.
    Soc., Japan.
Shipp, T. and McGlone, R. (1971). J. Speech Hear. Res.
    14:761-768.
Titze, I. R. and Talkin, D. T. (1979). J. Acoust. Soc. of
    Amer. (in press).

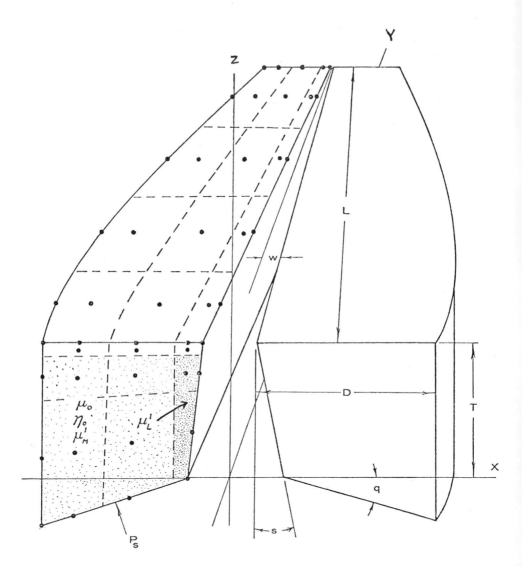

figure 1

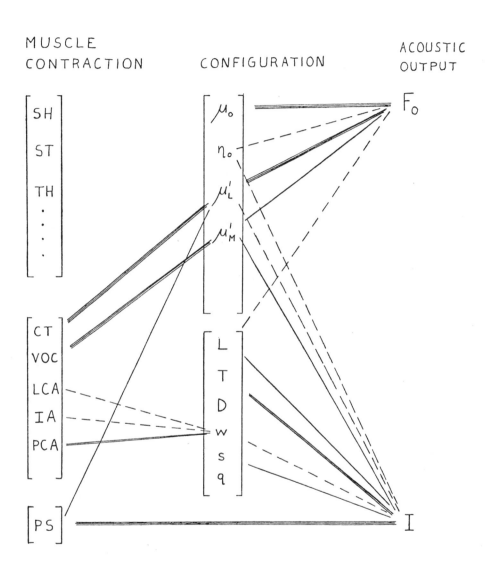

figure 2

PHYSICAL AND PHYSIOLOGICAL DIMENSIONS OF INTRINSIC VOICE QUALITY

INGO R. TITZE
Gallaudet College

Of the many laryngeal adjustments which are apparently used in speech and singing, few seem to be well understood physiologically. We are beginning to develop an understanding of voice initiation and voice release. (See the review discussion by Fujimura in these proceedings.) We have some ideas about the mechanisms of pitch and intensity control, but considerable uncertainty still exists in relating these acoustic variables to physical and physiological states. I discussed some underlying reasons for this uncertainty in another paper at this IPS meeting. When we search for a physical and physiological basis of voice quality, the picture becomes quite fuzzy in a hurry. One reason is that quality, almost by definition, encompasses everything that remains un-known about voice production after we have accounted for pitch and intensity. To complicate matters even further, there is no clear distinction between subcategories of quality which can be attributed to the larynx itself and those which can be attributed to the immediate environment of the larynx, i.e., the pharynx and the trachea. We know that often in speech the acoustic coupling between the larynx and the vocal tract is small (in comparison with source-system interaction in brass and woodwind instruments, for example). But does that con-dition prevail in singing, or even in all types of phonation encountered in speech? Sundberg (1972) has made a good argu-ment against this by demonstrating that a resonating cavity in the upper laryngeal region of the vocal tract could, in effect, create a rather firm coupling between the source and

the resonating system. Unfortunately, Sundberg's synthesis
is based on a linear model of speech production, allowing no
freedom for source-system feedback. Thus, the so-called
ringing quality of the singing voice, which is presently
attributed solely to the lower vocal tract, may in fact have
contributions from both source and tract. Similar arguments
can be made for larynx lowering. There is no question that
the formant structure is altered by an increase in vocal
tract length, but it has been argued that such a maneuver
will also affect the boundary and internal stress conditions
of the laryngeal soft tissues (Ohala, 1972) creating a
perturbation upon pitch and intensity, and very likely
quality. Thus we are left with the uncomfortable feeling
that voice quality may be related to a large number of complex interactions of laryngeal, sublaryngeal, and supralaryngeal adjustments.

By careful physical modelling of the larynx and its
subglottal and supraglottal environment, we hope to be able
to make a contribution to the eventual untanglement of various
phenomena related to voice quality. For example, if there are
certain intrinsic laryngeal qualities, described often with
such words as tense, raspy, strident, gravelly, creaky, shrill,
grating, harsh, breathy, flat, wobbly, bleeting, etc., they
can perhaps be identified apart from those qualities which are
sometimes associated with the laryngeal environment, that is,
the extrinsic laryngeal qualities, which are given such labels
as twangy, covered, dark, focused, ringing, lifted, lilting,
chesty, robust, etc.

So far we have begun to focus only on the intrinsic
qualities. Figure 1, which shows our computer model of the
vocal folds, illustrates the configuration and various
parameters we have chosen to systematically vary the configuration. For the purpose of this discussion, we point out
that the mechanical action of two sets of opposing laryngeal
muscles, the adductor-abductor combination, and the cricothy-
roid-vocalis combination, are represented by the parameters
W, μ_L, and μ_M. w is the angular glottal separation
at the arytenoid processes, μ_L is the longitudinal stress in
the ligament, and μ_M is the longitudinal stress in the
vocalis. The other parameters are discussed elsewhere (Titze
and Talkin, 1979).

Figure 2 shows a table of tense-lax phonatory features
which can account for some intrinsic laryngeal qualities.
The table is a modification of the one proposed by Stevens
in the 1975 conference at Leeds (Stevens, 1977). The primary
difference is the tense-lax distinction in the body and
cover of the vocal folds. Rather than describing the elastic
state of the vocal folds simply as tense, neutral, and lax,
it appears that a distinction based on opposing muscles, the
cricothyroid and the vocalis, which, incidentally, are also
innervated distinctively, appears more appropriate. Thus we
are led to posit four states, (1) tense ligament and lax
vocalis, (2) tense ligament and tense vocalis, (3) lax
ligament and lax vocalis, and (4) lax ligament and tense
vocalis. The odd-combination tense/lax states are considered
the extreme states. According to our simulations, these tend
to produce saturation effects, especially with respect to
vocal fold length. Tense ligament and lax vocalis results in
hyper-elongation, whereas tense vocalis and lax ligament
results in a reduction in length. These odd-combination extremes tend to create vastly different stiffness ratios in
the body and cover of the vocal folds, as discussed by Hirano
(1975). Smaller stiffness ratios are possible with well coordinated control of the vocalis and circothyroid muscle
(columns 2 and 3). This seems to be the region where efficient voicing can occur for a large range of frequencies.
The central two blocks encompass the two more acceptable
registers of voice in singing, the modal register, and the
middle register (or midvoice). All other blocks around the
perimeter exhibit saturation effects of one type or another.
These are often judged as being less acceptable in quality.
Thus creaky voice is the result of a saturation of adduction,
breathy voice a saturation of abduction, falsetto a saturation
of ligament stress, and various forms of glottalization, voice
inhibition, and aperiodicities a result of saturation in two
dimensions (the corner blocks).

We have begun to synthesize some of these effects.
Figure 3, from Titze and Talkin (1979), shows glottal waveforms for seven different configurations, a neutral (or
nominal) configuration, three tense and three lax conditions.
None of these are extreme, however, in that they show no
marked saturation effects. The general trends can readily be

noticed, however. Waveform (b) demonstrates inefficiency of
vocal tract excitation with high average flow rate, resulting
in somewhat breathy voice. Waveform (c), characterized by
tense adductors, is approaching creaky voice as seen by the
reduction in opening quotient. Waveform (d), the case for
lax ligament, shows flow irregularities. Waveform (e) shows
a drastic amplitude reduction and pitch increase, both of
which are falsetto characteristics. Waveform (f) shows both
an amplitude and an efficiency reduction. It is essentially
a low-pitched falsetto, as one would expect from a relaxation
of the vocalis muscle. Finally, waveform (g), the tense
vocalis situation, shows a slight increase in pitch, an increase in intensity, as indicated by the speed quotient, and
a slight trend toward vocal fry, as indicated by the decreased
opening quotient. It must be pointed out again, however, that
none of these conditions represent the true saturations indicated in the former table. More cases need to be investigated
to validate our hypotheses about laryngeal tense-lax features.
Speculations with regard to quantal aspects in voice production
and perception are indeed tempting at this point, but we shall
not yield to that temptation until further investigations have
been conducted.

REFERENCES

Hirano, M.   (1975).   Rep. Oto-Rhino-Laryn. Soc. Japan.
Ohala, J.   (1972).   Month. Intern. Memo., Univ. Cal., 25-42.
Stevens, K.   (1977).   Phon., 34:264-279.
Sundberg, J.   (1972).   STL-QPSR 1.
Titze, I. and Talkin, D.   (1979).   J. Acoust. Soc. Am.
     (in press).

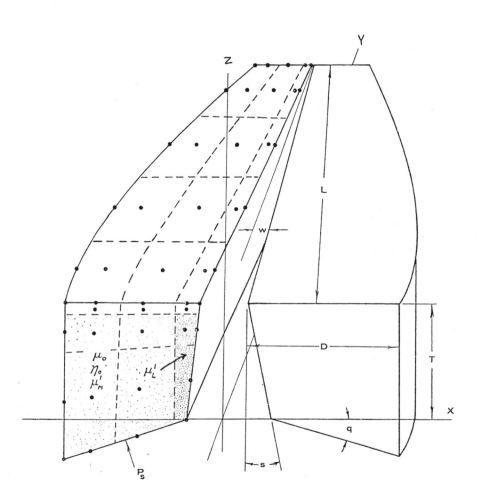

FIGURE 1

PHONATORY QUALITY AND RELATED MUSCULAR

TENSE-LAX FEATURES

	TENSE LIG. LAX VOC.	TENSE LIG. TENSE VOC.	LAX LIG. LAX VOC.	LAX LIG. TENSE VOC.
TENSE ABDUCT. LAX ADDUCT.	INHIBITED	BREATHY (HIGH PITCH)	BREATHY (LOW PITCH)	APERIODIC
NEUTRAL	INEFFICIENT (FALSETTO)	EFFICIENT (MIDVOICE)	EFFICIENT (MODAL)	CREAKY (MEDIUM)
LAX ABDUCT. TENSE ADDUCT.	GLOTTALIZED	CREAKY (HIGH PITCH)	CREAKY (LOW PITCH)	INHIBITED

FIGURE 2

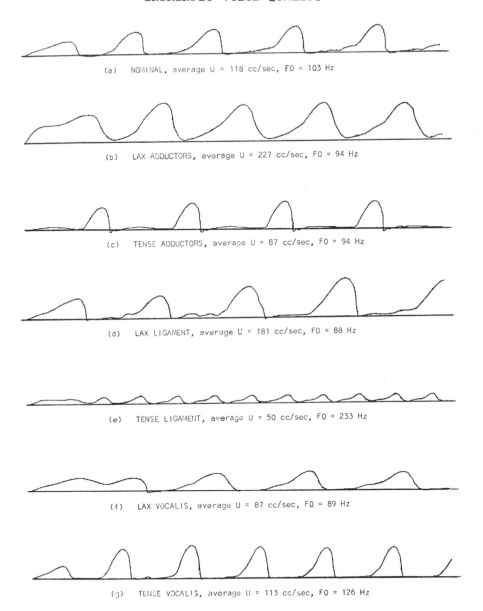

(a) NOMINAL, average U = 118 cc/sec, FO = 103 Hz

(b) LAX ADDUCTORS, average U = 227 cc/sec, FO = 94 Hz

(c) TENSE ADDUCTORS, average U = 87 cc/sec, FO = 94 Hz

(d) LAX LIGAMENT, average U = 181 cc/sec, FO = 88 Hz

(e) TENSE LIGAMENT, average U = 50 cc/sec, FO = 233 Hz

(f) LAX VOCALIS, average U = 87 cc/sec, FO = 89 Hz

(g) TENSE VOCALIS, average U = 113 cc/sec, FO = 126 Hz

FIGURE 3

D. TEMPORAL FACTORS AND QUESTIONS OF INTONATION

APPLIED PROSODIC ANALYSIS: A PEDAGOGICAL MODEL
FOR ENGLISH AND GERMAN INTONATION

KEITH O. ANDERSON
St. Olaf College

In 1962, William Moulton wrote in his handbook for
teachers, The Sounds of English and German: "Until far
more is known than at present about the intonations of
English and German, it will not be possible to make a contrastive analysis of the two systems and to reveal points
of conflict between them." More recently, Wolf-Dietrich
Bald concluded in a 1976 survey of contrastive studies in
English and German intonation that: "On the whole very
little detailed information is as yet available on the intonational contrasts between English and German. . . , no
contrastive analysis is yet possible. . . ." From these
statements it would seem that any contrastive model of
German and English intonation must be, at best, highly
tentative. This is indeed true in respect to the broad
functional level of intonation in the two languages. However, in respect to the phonetic substance of the intonations a great deal of very useful information is available.

Within the last two decades particularly, a number of
investigators have directed their attention to key points
of pitch transition between and within syllables. Especially relevant here is the work of Bolinger (1965a) in the
U.S. and Isačenko and Schädlich (1966) in the German Demo-
cratic Republic. Out of this approach has come a model

which is phonetically detailed enough to reveal some critical English/German contrasts, yet which is simple enough
to be quickly grasped and easily taught. Furthermore, it
agrees with a wide range of observations on the phonetic
substance of German and English intonation, while at the
same time encompassing the patterns of the level and tune
analysts. It was basically this tone-switch model which I
used in an experimental contrastive study in 1970. The same
model was used in the most extensive pedagogical handbook
on German intonation published to date, <u>Deutsche Satzintona-
tion</u> by Eberhard Stock and Christina Zacharias (1971).

The purpose of the following discussion is to attempt
to consolidate a wide range of observations on the phonetic
characteristics of German and English intonation, to demonstrate the ability of a pitch transition approach to reveal
points of English/German conflict which were concealed or
obscured by previous analyses, and to propose some pedagogical guidelines for teaching German intonation to
Americans.

THE PHONETIC SUBSTANCE OF GERMAN INTONATION

<u>A Prosodic Basis</u>. Because it is difficult to quantify,
the term basis of articulation has not been widely used by
American writers. However, as suggested by Heinrich Kelz
(1971), the concept deserves more attention in second language teaching. It is proposed here that a teaching model
of German intonation contain a general phonetic component
parallel to basis of articulation. This component, which
might be called the prosodic basis, would contain such
factors as the relative use of dynamic, quantitative and
pitch accent; overall contour shape characteristics; slope,
direction and range of pitch changes; juncture types; and
rhythmic features relating to stress and syllable timing.

<u>The Phonetic Substance of Syntactic Accents</u>. It is
generally conceded that English and German use similar
phonetic means to create prominence in the sentence, primarily shifts in tonal and dynamic levels. As stated by
Moulton (1962): "Both English and German seem to have the
same stress system; they differ only in the ways in which

they use them." An obvious restriction, of course, is imposed by the phonemic relevance of length in German, which
limits the use of expressive lengthening.

Contour Shape Characteristics. Abundant references to
general characteristics of English and German intonation
are found in the literature. What emerges from them is a
basic pattern for the German declaration sentence, which
consists of a series of rises followed by a final fall.
A high frequency contour contains a secondary rising accent,
a medial high-mid level section and a final fall on the
nuclear stress:
                                  \\   /   ↓
       (1) <u>Frau</u> | Müller ist | <u>Lehrerin</u>. This
rise-level-fall overall pattern has led writers to characterize the basic German pattern as a "Spannbogen." E.g.,
Christian Winkler (1966) writes: "Der Spannbogen eines
Aussagesatzes gliedert sich in einen spannenden Aufast,
der den Gegenstand oder die Voraussetzung der Aussage
enthält und den lösenden Abast der Aussage selbst."

    For American English, we find instead of a "Bogen,"
what Bolinger (1972) has characterized as a "suspension
bridge"; he writes: "We tend to favor the two extremes
of the sentence (or, in longer sentences, the two extremes
of each relatively independent phrase or clause), as if to
announce the beginning and the end. There may be intermediate accents, but they are less prominent. This gives
the sentence the shape of a bumpy suspension bridge:
      snow   ear   to
The   generally comes   ly in Oc ber." The transfer
of this "bumpy" pattern into German is one of the most
salient marks of English intonational interference in the
speech of American students. In approaching a sentence
such as: (2) Wir fliegen nächstes Jahr nach Deutschland.
the American student will typically render it:
                  \\   /
(3) <u>Wir fliegen</u> | nách | stes Jahr nach | Deutsch | land.
instead of the correct
                 \\   /
(4) <u>Wir fliegen</u> | nächstes Jahr nach | <u>Deutschland</u>. The
"error" of the student is the allowing of his voice to drop

to a low pitch level following the rising secondary accent.
With contrastive English-German drills most students quickly pick up the German pattern, although habitual control
in communication will take considerably longer.

   Rhythmic Features. Most writers on English stress and
intonation recognize a tendency toward equal spacing of
stressed syllables. Although this perceived isochrony, as
it has been called, is by no means absolute, it is much
stronger in English than in German. In his work on the
stress system of English, Alvar Goes (1974) formulates the
rule: "The Perceptual Isochrony Rule (PIR) establishes
equidistant points of maximally informative unit nuclei
along the speech chain." Due possibly to the perceived
regularity of stress placement in English, Goes further
postulates the existence of "constraints on the number of
background (low-stress) syllables allowed" (p. 106).

   German speech, on the other hand, seems to be less
limited in allowing strings of unaccented syllables. More
equal weight is given to each syllable. This more pronounced "syllable beat" allows for relatively long series
of weak syllables, particularly in the initial and final
unstressed segments of the sentence. Both von Essen and
Stock-Zacharias correctly recognize this special characteristic of German in their handbooks by providing sections
on "Erweiterung des Nachlaufs" and "Erweiterung des Vor-
laufs." Isačenko and Schädlich (1970) conclude that the
Nachlauf, designated "coda" by them, theoretically "can
include any number of syllables," and "as many as 20
syllables" can occur in practice.

   Syntactic Boundary Markers. In the use of syntactic
boundary markers there is a high degree of similarity between English and German. For immediate practical purposes,
the declarative fall and interrogative rise can be treated
as essentially the same. Serious problems exist, however,
with the continuation contour which marks an incomplete
utterance. Whereas the American English continuation is
typically falling, e.g.:

                    (5)   If it ⌐ rains◣ or falling-

rising:

(6) <u>If it</u> ⌐ rains ⌐ the German pattern is
almost always high and level:

(7) <u>Wenn es</u> ⌐ regnet
In German, the voice can drop down to a low level only
after the end of the entire syntactic unit. When this
occurs, it constitutes a major continuation break as described by Pierre Delattre (1965); this configuration may
be found in Figure 1. Important to note is that all
secondary accents in the German are rising. Only the last
accent, the main sentence accent, is falling. In the
English sentence, all of the accents are falling.

    <u>Accent Type</u>. It is widely conceded that pitch accent
is the primary basis for prominence in both English and
German sentences. Experiments with synthetic speech have
shown that pitch changes alone can produce unambiguous
marking of accented syllables. Accordingly, a number of
investigators, notably Bolinger for English and Isačenko
and Schädlich for German, have turned their attention to
the nature and function of these pitch accents or "tone-
switches." Isačenko and Schädlich (1970) propose a two
dimensional system based on direction of movement and the
placing of the switch before or after the stressed syllable;
this system may be seen in Figure 2. Moreover, Stock and
Zacharias (1971) have expanded this system to include compound rise-fall and fall-rise as seen in Figure 3. Bolinger (1965b) presents basically the same pattern for English,
but lumps both rises (pre-ictic and post-ictic) into one,
his "Accent B."

    Because both languages have a similar inventory of
rises, falls and compound fall-rise and rise-falls, transfer of native habits to the target language is highly
likely and the resulting "foreign accent" is often difficult to diagnose by the ear alone. In his spectrographic
study, Delattre (1965) determined that one basis for perceived differences lies in the place of energy concentration in pitch transitions. German speakers concentrate
energy primarily in the level or rising segment before a

fall, while American English speakers put their main energy
on the falling glide itself. A German imitation of the
American 2-3-1 pattern was compared with the native rendi-
tion; this comparison may be seen in Figure 4. In addition
to the contrasting energy envelope, the statistical
occurrence of rising and falling accents is different in
English and German. As Delattre notes: "It is this constant recurrence of falling glides that characterizes
American intonation for the ear of foreigners." This difference was clearly evident in my own study of English intonational interference. The American college students in
the study used more than three times the number of falling
secondary accents used by the native German control group.

Syntactice Accent Placement. Once the student has
mastered the forms of pitch accents and terminal contours,
he still faces the difficult task of determining which words
should be selected for accentual prominence. As stated previously, the student must resist the pressure to transfer
the English rhythmic stress pattern into German. The German
rhythm is much more syllable-oriented with a greater semantic
load on the accented syllables. Thus, to read aloud correctly, the student must understand the text well. A good
introductory survey of the rules for accent placement in
German is found in the handbook Patterns in German Stress
and Intonation by Hans-Heinrich Wangler (1966).

SUMMARY AND CONCLUSIONS

In conclusion, I hope I have brought some real differences between English and German intonation into sharper
focus. In my experience as a teacher of German, I have
found that intonation is teachable if the student is aware
of the relevant units and points of conflict with his native
language. The typical intonational diagrams found in many
textbooks are of little help because they call for imitation
of an entire pattern. A key to success is to have the
student focus on key points of pitch transition (Tonbrüche)
which mark accents. He must produce secondary accents in
German that are primarily rising. Also, the student must

avoid the American medial pitch dip and strive for the more
unified German "Spannbogen."

In dealing with continuation breaks within the sentence, the voice must remain on a relatively high level
tone. Finally, the student must fight the pressure to locate accents rhythmically, and zero in on the key semantic
elements.

REFERENCES

Anderson, K. O.   (1970). Ph.D. Diss., Univ. Colorado.
Bald, W.-D.   (1976). Poznań, Adam Mickiewicz Univ.
Bolinger, D.   (1965a). Cambridge, Harvard Univ. Press.
Bolinger, D.   (1965b). Cambridge, Harvard Univ. Press.
Bolinger, D.   (1972). Harmondsorth, Penquin.
Delattre, P.   (1965). Philadelphia, Chilton.
Goes, A.   (1974). Stockholm, Upsala Univ.
Isačenko, A. and Schädlich, H.-J. (1966). Berlin,   Akademie.
Isačenko, A. and Schädlich, W.-J. (1970).   The Hague, Mouton.
Kelz, H. P.   (1971). Phonet., 24:193-211.
Moulton, W. G.   (1962). Chicago, Univ. Chicago Press.
Stock, E. and Zacharias, C.   (1971).   Leipzig, VEB Verlag
      Enzyk.
Wängler, H.-H.   (1966). St. Paul, EMC.
Winkler, C.   (1966). Mannheim, Dudenverlag.

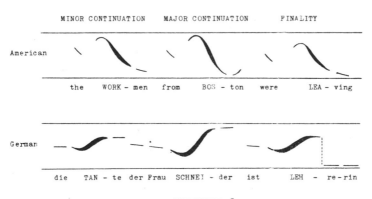

FIGURE 1

	A rising tone-switch	B falling tone-switch
I pre-ictic	die↑Kinder	die↓Kinder
II post-ictic	die Kin↑der	die Kin↓der

FIGURE 2

	Vorakzentintervall	Nachakzentintervall	Form
1.	positiv	negativ	⌐\
2.	neutral	negativ	⌐
3.	negativ	negativ	⌐
4.	negativ	positiv	⌣
5.	neutral	positiv	⌐/
6.	positiv	positiv	⌐/

FIGURE 3

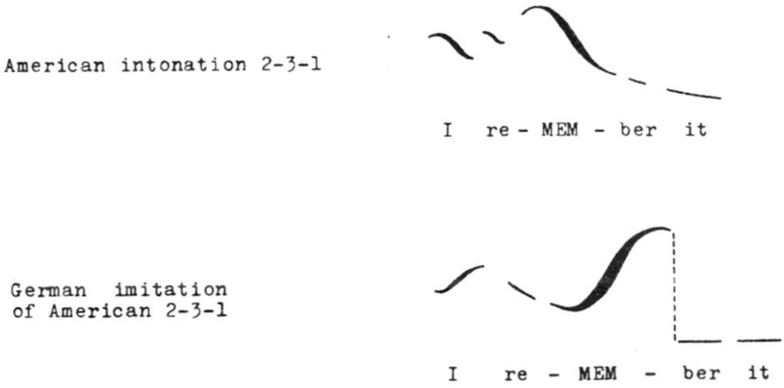

American intonation 2-3-1

I   re - MEM - ber   it

German   imitation
of American 2-3-1

I   re - MEM -   ber   it

FIGURE 4

RHYTHM AND PAUSE AS MEANS OF EXPRESSION IN THE JAPANESE ARTS OF STORYTELLING WITH SPECIAL REGARD TO RAKUGO

HEINZ BALKENHOL
Sophia University, Tokyo

About 15 years ago an almost miraculous revival of the classical Japanese art of storytelling took place. The art of storytelling can roughly be divided into four different types: Utaimono, i.e., chanted recital with musical accompaniment; Katarimono, i.e., spoken recital with musical accompaniment; Yomimono, i.e., reading of long stories of mostly tragic nature; and Hanashimono, i.e., telling of short stories of mostly comic nature. The most popular art of storytelling is RAKUGO, one type of Hanashimono, performed by a single storyteller on a simple stage without scenery except for a six-folded golden paper screen placed behind the Rakugo-teller. Among the four kinds of storytelling Rakugo is least bound to fixed rules of performances. The styles of relating Rakugo are: narrations in the third person (jibanashi), monologues concerning a character in a story (hitorigoto), and dialogues (taiwa). There are no written instructions, but only oral tradition (jishô-kuden) from master to his apprentice learner. Explanations by the masters are vague and one cannot grasp them by scientific concepts. One of the most interesting criteria according to which the quality of all representation is judged is the perfection of the so-called ma. It is said that ma 'enlivens' or 'kills' the whole performance, and the Rakugo-teller's application of ma belongs to the secret tradition (hiden) of Japanese storytelling.

In all Japanese arts the concept ma plays an important role, in recitation and narration as well as in dramaturgy,

music, and the plastic arts. The word ma literally means
'distance between two points.' In the visual arts it indicates the space between two or more objects, and in a broader
sense the rules of spatial distribution. In the aural arts
ma originally denoted the moment of silence between two beats
of a musical instrument. This moment of silence, however, was
not conceived as an interruption or a discontinuity of sounds,
but as a linking unit between two sounds. Thus, ma was felt
to be an element of continuity in the flow of sounds. It is
not said 'to interrupt a recitation,' but 'to maintain the
ma of recitation' (ma o toru, ma o mamoru). As a consequence, in music as well as in the theater, the concept of
ma has developed to a point where it has been adopted as the
technical term for rhythm, a measure of rhythm, a rhythmical
unit, a metrical division (beat), proper timing, and the tempo
of speech. In all cases ma, in itself a negative concept,
is considered a highly positive and meaning bearing element
of expression and communication. The rhythmical unit of a
recitation is called ma-measure (ma-byôshi). The normal unit
(jô-ma) consists of two beats, the front-beat (omote-ma) and
the rear-beat (ura-ma). If all measures are struck by an
instrument (taiko, shamisen), the rhythm is called ko-ma
(small ma); if the measure is indicated at certain intervals,
the rhythm is called ô-ma (big ma).

Different from the usual Western conception of rhythmical
measure, ma-measure (ma-byôshi) does not mean regular time
intervals nor regular alternations of stressed and unstressed
units, as, e.g., in iambic or dactylic verse. Emphasis is
expressed by the lengthening (nobe), non-emphasis by the
shortening (haya) of one or more elements of a ma-byôshi.
Stress might be added to the lengthening as a secondary
element.

In a combined measure unit which consists of two or more
simple measure units, the major emphasis by lengthening and
stress is laid on the initial front-beat (omote-ma) and the
final rear-beat (ura-ma). Instead of lengthening the last
beat, a pause in the length of at least one beat may be inserted. Not only the recitation on the stage, but also most
Japanese popular songs and poems are based on this kind of
emphasis pattern. By a native Japanese it is felt as a .

natural rhythm, to untrained Western ears it might give the
impression of arhythmicality.

If one beat is missing the unit is called han-ma (semi-
ma); combined with the normal unit of a front-beat and a
rear-beat, the resulting rhythm is similar to a three-quarter
measure. If both front-beat and rear-beat are missing in a
sequence where they normally should occur, it is called
nuki-ma (missing-ma). In its broadest sense ma means the
average tempo of recitation and speech; quick tempo is called
haya-ma and slow tempo noro-ma. Expressions from rhythmical
recitations are even found in colloquial speech. 'Rhythm
difference' (machigai) has the meaning of 'mistake,' and a
man of 'slow rhythm' (noroma) or 'missing rhythm' (manuke)
is a fool.

In each of the above mentioned four species of traditional Japanese recitation ma is used in a specific sense.
In chanted recital (utaimono) ma is taken first of all in its
literal meaning as beats and rhythmical sequences of drums
(taiko) or string instruments (shamisen). In spoken recital
with musical accompaniment (katarimono) ma is used both in the
sense of beat-rhythm created by the musical accompaniment, as
well as in the sense of speech rhythm appropriate to a certain
character of a story. Roles like 'samurai,' 'court lady,' or
'supernatural being' are said to have their characteristic ma,
expressed by tempo of speech, tension of the voice, and pauses.

In the art of story-reading (yomimono), ma denotes mainly
the stress rhythm of phrase sequences. Yomimono are actually
not read from a book but told from memory. The little reading-
desk in front of which the storyteller squats is usually empty.
Yomimono consist of descriptive parts and dialogues. The
typical yomimono-ma appears mainly in the descriptive parts,
which consist of sequences of phrases of nearly equal length
and a monotonous stress. In introductions or at dramatic
moments the presentation of the story adopts even elements
of metric rhapsodical recitation, i.e., variations of a
7-5-7-5 syllable rhythm.

The art of telling comical short stories (hanashimono)
is very close to completely free speech. It belongs essentially

to the prose genre and has no direct relation to metric
rhythmical recitation of any kind. It is basically different
from rhapsodical recitation of verbally memorized texts, even
different from the semi-memorized reading texts of the
yomimono. An attempt to give exact measures for the rhythm
in storytelling would be a futile task. Only by comparing
frequently occurring patterns, can one arrive at conclusions
about the form of specific patterns of ma in Rakugo. In
addition to ma-patterns which are specific for Rakugo, ma-
patterns of other genres of recitation incidentally found
their way into storytelling. This fact has two historical
reasons: First, the common root of all types of artistic
narration found in the Buddhistic sermon stories (setsuwa)
and rhapsodical recitations of the 8th - 12th centuries;
second, the strong influence of Kabuki during the 18th - 19th
centuries. Kabuki was originally reserved for the bourgeois
in the bigger cities. When the desire for education and
entertainment grew in the lower classes of employees, storytellers had to take over the social role of Kabuki actors.
They imitated their way of expression and manner of speech.
They took over into the Rakugo stories whole passages from
Kabuki, or made comic parodies on them. There arose a
'Kabuki-complex' in Rakugo, which even today has not been
completely overcome.

In the following paragraphs some frequent ma-patterns
will be listed, beginning with the ones which have been taken
over from other genres of recitation and narration. The first
is the Drama and Orchestra Rhythm (taiko-ma, hayashi-ma). In
this area drama and orchestra rhythm fixes the frame of a
Rakugo story. The orchestra (hayashi) has its place behind
the stage. It consists of a great drum (ôdaiko), a small
drum (shimedaiko), and shamisen, besides sometimes a flute
(fue) and a gong (shô). The first rhythms are beaten, when
the curtain is drawn. This is called ichiban-daiko. This
gives way to twelve slow beats which symbolize the twelve
months of a year. There follow quicker two-stroke beats
which give way to the rhythm of the niban-daiko and a melody
played on the shamisen and flute. A famous master will choose
his own melody by which the audience can tell who will appear
on the stage. The orchestra is also used to enhance the effect
of an extraordinary event such as the emerging of a

supernatural being. When the storyteller leaves the stage,
his withdrawal is accompanied by the rhythms of the hayashi-
orchestra. The same kind of drum and orchestra rhythm is
also found in other types of recitation and narration (wagei),
and this shows how closely they are related to each other.
However, Rakugo might be modernized, the musical frame shows
its affiliation to traditional wagei.

Secondly, ma-rhythm is taken over from utaimono,
katarimono and yomimono. Since Rakugo has not developed in
isolation but in close contact with the three other types of
classical narration, some ma-rhythm patterns have been taken
over from these. Melodies of famous utaimono or imitations
and parodies of them occur in many Rakugo pieces, especially
in the Kamigata-Rakugo of Osaka. In the well-known story
Hayashi-nagaya the storyteller imitates for several minutes in
quick two-stroke rhythm (don-tsuke / ten-tsuke / ...) the
music, dances, and gaiety of a temple feast. When performed
by a skillful storyteller, it can have an irresistible hypnotic
effect on the audience. When the whole atmosphere of the hall
seems to be vibrating with the same rhythm, the storyteller
suddenly stops. The audience awakes from its illusion and
breaks out laughing. Influenced by the 'Kabuki-complex,'
well-known passages of Kabuki-plays are imitated and incorporated into Rakugo-stories. Sanyûtei Enshô (1901 -)
is said to be a master of the imitation of Kabuki roles. In
the descriptive parts (jibanashi) of a Rakugo story the manner
of strong and rhythmical stressing employed in 'story-reading'
(yomimono, esp. Kôdan) is frequently imitated. Ma-patterns
taken over from utaimono, katarimono, or yomimono are like
accessories and do not play a central role in Rakugo. Rakugo
is essentially a 'genuine storytelling' (su-banashi) with the
main purpose of exposing humor.

Next is the Prelude-ma (kanki-ma). A hesitative sound
'eh.....' is the necessary 'upbeat' to each Rakugo performance.
It is a greeting as well as a compliment. Without saying anything else, the storyteller will make the audience laugh, not
about the story which they haven't heard yet, but at the storyteller himself. Similar kinds of 'prelude-ma' are also found
in other types of popular arts, e.g., the loud and gradually
decreasing exclamation 'tôzai-tôzai' (meaning 'east and west'
with the connotation of 'everybody of the audience') in the
traditional Bunraku puppet play.

Fourth, the scenery-ma (jôkei-ma). Different from the puppet play and Kabuki, Rakugo does not have any background scenery, except for the six-folded golden paper-screen behind the storyteller. Changes in the scenes of a story are described by onomatopoetic words and sounds, e.g., the ringing of a temple-bell (bong-bong), the clapper of wooden clogs (karan-koron), the sound of the wind (pyû-pyû), rolling stones (gara-gara), noise in the background (dô-dô, gô-gô). Onomatopoetic insertions can extend over a period of more than one minute when they describe locomotion or movements of other actions, e.g., slow walking (tata-tata, tsun-tsun), running (sai-sai-koro-sai, e-sa-sa-, sowa-sowa, chowa-chowa), walking with heavy baggage on one's shoulders (wasshoi-wasshoi), sounds of work and play (kachi-kachi, pachi-pachi, pochi-pochi, poka-poka, potsu-potsu, sara-sara), heavy exertion (hora-yo, sora-yo, yoshi-oi).

Fifth, the Mood-ma (kimochi-ma). The proper presentation of moods and feelings of the spirit belongs to the more diffi-cult techniques of storytelling. Whether somebody is a master or a mere amateur is revealed by the way the ma of moods and feelings is presented. In Rakugo the description of kimochi (mood of the spirit) is more important than the realistic and objective description of a person. In the course of the narra-tion it sometimes does not matter WHO is speaking and WHAT is being said, if only the HOW of the presentation fits into the frame of the whole. There are several moods which have their specific pattern of expression by means of the height of voice, tempo of speech, and placement of pauses, e.g., anger, pain, jealousy, fright, or 'love-sickness.' The degree of tempo indicates a relation especially to the stereotyped mood of certain characters of Rakugo-stories. For example, the quick-tempered citizen of Edo (edokko) usually speaks in a very excited way; on the other hand, old masters (inkyo) have to show their calmness of mind in a very slow way of talking. Some stories are specially designed for training in fast tempo; delivered slowly, they lose all their attractiveness. In the well-known story 'Jugemu' the most amusing point of the story is the quick pronunciation of the ridiculously long and con-fusing name of the son of an edokko, which occurs in the story again and again, until the storyteller seems to be completely exhausted, and the audience tired from laughing. The extremely

quick way of the presentation of some stories requires high
training not only on the part of the storyteller, but also
on the part of the listener. Otherwise he misses too much of
the text.

Next is the murmuring-ma (tsubuyaki-ma). The Rakugo-
teller is not supposed to change his position, once he takes
a seat on the stage. But merely by the movement of the upper
half of his body he represents all kinds of actions. Walking
from one place to another is expressed by one of the most
amusing stereotypes of Rakugo: The storyteller withdraws his
hands into the wide sleeves of his kimono, his knees, hips,
and shoulders sway rhythmically, and he talks to himself in
short phrases in a murmuring voice, as if lost in thought. The
audience knows that a person is on his way to another place;
they also know that he suddenly will be startled out of his
thoughts by an unexpected event, and they anxiously wait for
that moment.

Seven, far-near-high-low-ma (enkin-kamishimo-ma). The
'far-near-high-low'-figure of expression represents the distances of the characters in a story or the differences in their
ranks. The more distant people are from each other, the more
the storyteller has to turn his face and shoulders in the
direction of the imagined speakers. This causes short pauses,
by which the distance and the change of the role are understood. The rules of this technique are known as the enkin-
technique. According to the rules of Japanese theater, a
person of higher rank has to appear on the right side of the
stage, seen from the audience, the lower rank on the left.
Furthermore, the one higher in rank is usually also sitting
or standing on a higher place than the one of lower rank.
Accordingly, when presenting such a dialogue between people
of different ranks, the storyteller has to ceaselessly move
his head from right-high to left-low, or vice versa. This is
known as the kamishimo-technique. The famous story 'Sangen-
nagaya' is full of changes of distances and ranks. If the
storyteller does not master the enkin-kamishimo-ma, he will
never bring out the point of the story to the audience. Young
storytellers avoid such stories for fear they might fail and
get confused with the distances and ranks.

The telephone-ma (denwa-ma). Sometimes the storyteller
speaks only one part of a dialogue. This technique of representation resembles somewhat a telephone-conversation observed by a third person. The difference is that the pause
in which the non-present partner of the dialogue is talking,
that is to say the ma between the answers, is always of the
same length. The audience usually can guess what is going
on, but sometimes the exact content of the conversation is
left obscure on purpose. In such cases even the audible part
of the conversation consists of only short confirmative or
doubting phrases such as 'yes - yes - what? - impossible -
. . .'. The function of 'telephone-ma' is that of the time-
accelerator or the quick-motion device of a film. It is used
to maintain the tension of the audience.

The missing-ma (nuki-ma). In Rakugo even 'missing
pauses' and 'missing words' are used as a means for representing certain situations. Before one person's part of a
phrase has been completed, another person's phrase breaks in,
as if superimposed on the preceding one. This simple technique gives the impression of a very vehement discussion or
quarrel, and increases the illusion of the real presence of
two partners. The pattern of a 'missing-ma' can be diagrammed
as follows ('1+2' represents the complete phrase, '1' the
actually pronounced part; between '1' and '2' the nuki-ma):

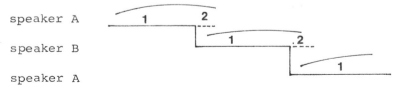

speaker A

speaker B

speaker A

The tenth ma is the group-ma (yajiuma-ma). The 'group-ma'
is a stereotyped variation of the 'missing-ma'. By overlapping
greetings and words of address, the impression of a larger
group of passers-by or spectators (yajiuma) is indicated. A
'group-ma' occurs only at the moment of a change of scene.
During a scene the number of the people present is not so
important. A frequently occurring 'group-ma' is e.g. the
greeting 'ohayô gozaimasu.' The storyteller repeats it the
following way: "ohayôgozai/hayogozai/yogozai/gozai/zaimasu..,"
or "ohayôgo/ohai/ohai/ohai/gozansu..," or similarly.

Finally, there is the mimicry-_ma_ (_shikata-ma_).   The
'mimicry-_ma_' can be an effective element of communication.
The storyteller interrupts the talk and indicates a characteristic point by a short gesture, which would require much
more time and effort if expressed verbally, e.g., a facial
expression, bowing or the lifting of one's head, looking for
something in the neighborhood, or transformation into a ghost.
However, if mimicry is used too frequently, and if it is used
for other purposes than that of saving time and unnecessary
words, then Rakugo will fall into the danger of becoming mere
pantomine and of degenerating from the art of narration.
People watching TV are usually not able to concentrate on
the screen only; they are distracted by family noise or are
simultaneously doing other work. TV Rakugo-tellers sometimes
take this into consideration; they use less difficult words
and more mimicry. Young storytellers especially are said to
be in the danger of falling into mere pantomine. Real Rakugo
fans complain of this kind of deterioration in the moderniza-
tion of the genuine art of storytelling.

Some young storytellers have recently tried to break away
from the classical tradition of _ma_-performance and have tried
to appeal to the public by means of a modernized Rakugo in a
style resembling cheap and shallow comic strips. They have
had some effects in filling time on TV programs and for entertainment at parties, but not on the Rakugo stage, where by far
the traditional way prevails.

ARTISTIC VOCAL COMMUNICATION AT THE PROSODIC LEVEL

IVAN FÓNAGY

C.N.R.S., Antony, France

Plain and Modified Melodic Transfers

All signs, whether grammatical morphemes, punctuation
marks or intonation patterns, can be used metaphorically
(Fónagy, 1971). If a given intonation pattern is placed into
a context which is incongruent to its original functions, the
melodic form acquires additional meaning. In artistic vocal
performances we meet at least four types of transfers:
  (a) transfers of emotive melodic patterns;
  (b) transfers of syntactic intonation patterns;
  (c) transfers of modal intonation;
  (d) transfers of idiomatical melodic patterns.
I shall try to illustrate the first and the last type.

The transposition of _emotive_ patterns is the most likely
to be encountered in artistic interpretations. In the Hungarian version of Arthur Miller's "Death of a Salesman,"
Willy, performed by the Hungarian actor József Tímár, exager-
ates his enthusiasm about his own son's achievements, as he
compliments his son's classmate. The prosodic pattern scarce-
ly reflects the optimistic and confident phrases of the text.
Twenty Hungarian listeners to whom this sentence was played
after low-pass filtering made the text incomprehensible, chose
out of ten emotive attitudes: sorrow and resignation.[1] The
distance between text and prosodic message grows as the scene
progresses. Finally, Willy's true emotion, hidden, but anticipated by the prosody, is expressed in words.[2] In a French

TV play "Appele-moi Rose" (of Youri), the actor, Michael
Lonsdale, playing the role of a high ranking government
official, speaks of his friend, a very talented man whose
promising but surprisingly unsuccessful career recently ended
in suicide. His condescending, yet envious attitude toward
his friend can be felt through the aggressive, attacking
melodic pattern accompanying sympathetic statements, e.g.
Et moi qui accourais a son aide (And me who came to help
him): a melodic pattern regularly associated with hatred
and quarrel. Such cases are no exceptions. The vocal
style which contrasts with the text and forms a counter-
point, is one of the basic tenets of modern theatre.

The great social constraint imposed on French conversational style may account for the large number of melodic
clichés. Melodic clichés almost offer themselves for meta-
phoric use. Clearly, if such a specific intonation pattern
is transferred to a different text, the listeners will
associate to this text the original wording. In a recent
experiment a woman lecturer said the sentence Il a une
voiture with intonations corresponding to sentences eliciting melodic clichés, such as Mais qu'il se débrouille,
Na-na-na. These sentences were recorded simultaneously on
the oral and the laryngeal level with microphone and a
laryngograph. The laryngo graphic recordings were presented to 38 French speaking subjects (university students
of both sexes). These subjects were told that the prosodic
patterns presented corresponded to a set of different sentences which were also given to them (these were the sentences eliciting melodic clichés). They were asked to
assign the sentences to the presented prosodic patterns.
The results indicate that for most laryngographic stimuli
the subjects chose the text associated with the melodic
cliche which the elocutionist lent to the sentence. The
laryngographic projection of the sentence Il a une voiture,
spoken with the melody of Na-na-na, was indeed assigned to
the "sentence" Na-na-na (Figure 1a and b).

Modified Melodic Transfer

A quasi-assertive question melody appears frequently
in French television thrillers: it is the usual questioning
style of police detectives. Its implications are: "in any

case I know the answer"; "are you trying to call me that...?"
or, "I assume that...". In the above quoted French TV play,
Lonsdale characterizes vocally the prominent personality he
is performing by means of the frequent use of quasi-assertive questions during his inquisitorial conversation with the
waitress (Figure 2). His assertive question does not
invariably reproduce the usual assertive pitch. The melody
in the last syllable is mid falling instead of low falling.
The level in the penultimate syllable is considerably higher
than it should be, with a high rise, equally unexpected.
Although the transferred declarative intonation pattern is
dominant, it has not been transposed intact.

In the same play, Lonsdale provides another example of
modified melodic transfer. He gives an enumerative intonation
curve to a sentence which does not contain enumeration: <u>Il
lui fallait sauver les apparences, et m'interroger sur mon
travail, ma famille...</u> 'He had to keep up appearances,
and ask me about my job, my family...' Since redundancy
is inherent in enumeration, the transfer may express a
bored, indifferent attitude, and suggests implied statements
such as 'this is how matters stand.' Compared with the conventional French enumerative intonation, it appears that
Lonsdale's pseudo-enumerative intonation follows a slightly
different melodic line: whilst the usual pattern contains
a recurring, unchanged motive. Lonsdale varies the intervals
which progressively decrease after the second group (Figure
3), as if gradually untuning a violin.[3]

Complex Intonation

Modified melodic transfers could be conceived as the
result of a superposition of two intonation patterns. Such
complex melodic patterns are most easily found in artistic
vocal performances. In the course of an acoustic and
semantic analysis of artistic vocal expression in plays
(Fónagy and Magdics, 1963, pp. 32-48), and poems recited
by the poet and by elocutionists (Fónagy, 1975) it appeared
that in attempting to interpret especially expressive parts
of a performance, subjects produced consistently diverse interpretations. In talking about these sentences their
pronunciation followed their understanding. None of these
reproductions corresponded exactly to the actor's performance,

but they all contained important features of the reproduced pattern. This led to the hypothesis that the melody of such utterances is complex: it is produced by the effective superposition of several everyday intonation patterns. We attempted to verify the hypothesis by using acoustical and semantic techniques.

Level of expression. French and Hungarian subjects[4] were asked to repeat (to "echoe," to "shadow") two types of sentences: (1) sentences selected from recorded conversations; (2) sentences chosen from recordings of artistic performances. The intonation of the first set was supposed to be "simple," that of the second set was expected to be "complex." There was much greater similarity both between the stimulus and response sentences, and between response sentences over subjects for the "simple" conversational stimuli, than for the artistic "complex" stimuli. For instance, in the case of a banal question Il est content? the similarity of the responses is quite apparent on the auditory as well as the visual level (Figure 4). The (voluntarily) ambiguous utterance of a French actor elicited statements expressing evidence or hesitation, on the one hand, and different types of questions on the other (Figure 5).

Similarly, an artistic amalgam of a question and an astonished exclamation of the French actress Laurence Bady, was decomposed in the course of the mimicking test, and appeared either as an incredulous (triangular) rise-fall question intonation, or as a rising exclamatory pattern: see Fig. 6. The prosodically polyvalent sentence Az én hibam volt /az e:n hiba:m volt/ 'Was it my fault' and/or 'It was my fault' of Arthur Miller's salesman, performed by Timár, elicited sharply falling assertive intonation patterns, as well as rising-falling interrogative patterns (Figure 7).

The dissimilarity of these responses is evident for the listener as well as for the reader comparing the F_O curves of the figures. It is less easy, however, to find a suitable measure in order to test our intuitions. We tried subsequently four different measures. One of these defines dissimilarity in terms of melodic distance, in quarter tones, measured either at the frequency peaks of each syllable, or

at the points of maximal sound-pressure. (This measure is
referred to as measure c.) See also Figure 8. Another
measure defines dissimilarity in terms of intersyllabic
melodic changes. The melodic interval between the frequency peaks of subsequent syllables is determined, and the
direction of the change also considered. For instance, a
rise of 2 quarter tones in curve A corresponding to a fall
of 3 quarter tones in curve B is interpreted as a deviation
of 5 quarter tones. (This measure is referred to as measure
a.) We introduced a third measure reflecting intra-syllabic
melodic changes as well. The continuous curve had to be
divided into segments, and the average frequency levels of
subsequent syllables defined in quarter tones. (This measure
is referred to as measure b.) The most reliable measure
proved to be the difference between the integrals of the
curves compared (cf. Figure 8 d).

$$\frac{1}{t} \int_o^t \left| g_1 (x) \rightarrow g_2 (x) \right| dx$$

In practice, we measured the area enclosed by the two curves
in mm^2. In all cases we shifted the curves according to the
speaker's base level. According to the four measures, we
obtained significantly greater values in the case of complex
melodic stimuli (on probability levels ranging from
$p < 0.01$ to $p < 0.0005$) as seen in Table 2.[5]

It appears furthermore that responses to the complex
stimuli, though they varied greatly, could be generally
grouped into few (two, three, rarely four) configurative
categories. Inside these categories the melodic dissimilarity between the individual echoes vary between approximately the same limits and in the same way as the echoes of
simple intonation patterns (Table 3). This seems to confirm
the hypothesis that complex melodies can be considered as an
integration of two or more simple (conventional) intonation
patterns. The subjects, unable to reproduce the unusual
condensed form, shadow one or the other conventional pattern
underlying the complex melody. Shadowing experiments could
be compared to the breaking down of white light.

Level of content. In contrast to the diverse and contradictory semantic interpretations assigned to the complex

artistic pattern, the echoes seem to be semantically
homogeneous. Thus, for instance, one of the echoes of the
salesman's sentence ("Was it my fault?") in the Hungarian
version of Miller's play was consistently interpreted as a
categorical statement, another echo as an astonished question. A sentence in the poem Old Age of a great Hungarian
poet, Milán Fust, read by the poet himself ("Who did once
deem a face so blessed," in Adam Makkai's translation)
suggested in the course of the semantic tests at the same
time sorrow, resignation, tenderness, complaint, strength,
majesty. The individual echoes showed however, no attitu-
dinal ambiguity. One of the echoes provided a melodic expression of sorrow, the other suggested tenderness, a third
one conveyed only strength. In order to express quantitatively the similarities and divergencies between semantic
evaluations of simple vs. complex melodic patterns 20 French
and 10 Hungarian subjects were asked to rate (on seven point
semantic scales cf. Osgood, Suci and Tannenbaum, 1957;
Snider and Osgood, 1969) each of the stimuli and all the
reproductions. As Figure 9 indicates, all the echoes of
the poetic or artistic sentence had clear cut semantic pro-
files with one dominant trait: resignation or complaint or
tenderness or insistance. The stimulus sentence, spoken by
the poet himself, proved to be functionally multivalent: it
was highly rated on scales of contradictory semantic content
(majesty and resignation and complaint and insistance).

   The technique of integration. There is no overlapping
between assertive and interrogative intonation in Hungarian.
How could the sentence of the salesman "was it my fault"
resp. "It was my fault" of the Hungarian artist convey at
the same time assertive and interrogative modality? The
descending melodic line, paired with a strong initial accent,
on Én 'I' seems to justify the subjects shadowing the sentence as a categoric statement (See again, Figure 7). On the
other hand, the ascending tone in the penultimate syllable
is a characteristic feature of the Hungarian question melody:
it is reproduced in a more clear-cut form in echo c. In the
artist's sentence a double rise in the penultimate syllable
could be considered as an unsuccessful attempt to attain the
interrogative melodic peak.

Similarly, the French sentence <u>La raison</u> of Laurence
Bady contained the elements of the triangular melodic cliché
(of questions of doubt) as well as elements of the rising
exclamation pattern. We could try to represent the superposition of the two patterns seen in Figures 6 and 10. In
the present paper, we considered only one prosodic parameter:
pitch. It is quite evident, however, that other prosodic
parameters and articulatory gestures might equally contribute to the semantic complexity of the artistic utterance
(Fónagy, 1975). The modal ambiguity of the stimulus sentence
<u>Il est content</u> might be partly due to a sudden loss of
intensity in the last 3 centiseconds of the final syllable
(See again Figure 5). Needless to say that these are not
the only difficulties posed by the analysis of artistic
vocal performance as attempted in this paper. Among many
other things, I was not even able to mention important questions like the vocal projection of mimics, or the configurative function of artistic intonation (Fonagy, 1975; Fonagy-
Magdics, 1963). The latter strictly divides the elocu-
tioninst's intonation from every-day speech melody which
does not even attempt to represent the world of objects.

Verbal and Vocal Art

Instead of a summary I should like to point to some
striking parallels between poetic verbal art and vocal creation. Since the first century B.C., classical rhetorics
tended to emphasize the expressive function of sounds in
poetry. Today we can state on the basis of statistic evidence that the poet really tries to make his discourse
livelier and more concrete by a remotivation of sounds and
sound-sequences. The vocal artist achieves a similar effect
by the revitalization of gestural vocal communication. It
is easy to find typical examples of the attempted polyphony
in poetry in the art of the elocutionist who tries to enrich
the text with contrapuntal effects. In poetry (especially
since the breakdown of the acceptance of normative classical
rhetorics) the tendency towards achieving a higher degree of
entropy has constantly been increasing. This trend is also
connected, among many other things, with the mounting
importance of the lexical and grammatical metaphor. This
paper was mainly concerned with analogous structures at the
level of intonation. We do not know of an exact parallel

in poetry to the superposition of simple intonation patterns.
The trend towards condensation, however, is equally basic
to verbal art and to vocal art.

FOOTNOTES

[1]The votes were distributed as follows: Joy Ø, Sorrow
12, Anger Ø, Tenderness Ø, Fear Ø, Daring Ø,Enthusiasm Ø,
Resignation 6, Menace Ø, Complaint 1, with 1 abstention.

[2]WILLY (small and alone): What - What's the secret?
BERNARD: What secret?
WILLY: How - how did you? Why didn't he ever catch on?

[3]The conventional intonation pattern presented in a
laryngographic version to a group of 20 students was
correctly identified in an open ended task (by 18 students
out of 20). The filtered version of Lonsdale's sentence,
however, presented to another group of 30 university students
was identified as an enumeration only be 4 students out of
30 (with 4 abstentions).

[4]The Hungarian sentences were presented to 8-10 Hungarian subjects (research workers); the French sentences
to 6-10 French subjects (university teachers and students).
Each sentence was presented twice, and the subject was
asked to "echo" the stimulus sentence after a pause of 5
seconds.

[5]According to t-tests the melodic dissimilarity between
the echoes of complex melodies is significantly more important than melodic dissimilarity between echoes of simple
melodic patterns.

REFERENCES

Fónagy, I.   (1971).   Semiotica, 3:189-222.
Fónagy, I.   (1975).   (In: Towards a Theory of Context),
     The Hague, Mouton, 81-124.
Fónagy, I. and Bérard, E.   (1973).   Stud. Phon., 8:53-98.
Fónagy, I. and Magdics, K. (1963). Ural-Altaische Jahrbücher
     35:1-55.
Osgood, C. E., Suci, G. J. and Tannenbaum, P. H.   (1957).
     Urbana, Univ. Illinois Press.
Snider, J. O. and Osgood, C. E.   (1969).   Chicago, Aldine.

Table 1. Forced choice test based on laryngographic recording of Il a une voiture spoken with intonation
forms implying other sentences. -- II: the
implied sentences. -- I: the suggested sentences.
O = a sentence not implied by any of the intonation forms.

Sentences suggested for choice

		0	1	2	3	4	5	6	7
Sentences implied by pitch	1	1	5	–	–	1	–	4	16
	2	4	–	20	–	–	–	–	2
	3	4	–	–	22	–	–	–	–
	4	–	–	–	–	21	–	–	1
	5	1	–	–	–	–	18	9	–
	6	4	6	–	–	1	2	13	–
	7	–	2	–	–	6	–	–	16

List of the sentences implied: 1. Mais bien sûr! --
2. Quelle voiture! -- 3. Na-na-na! -- 4. Mais oui,
je t'assure! -- 5. Tu crois vraiment? -- 6. C'est
bien ce que tu as dit? -- 7. Qu'il se débrouille!

Table 2. Averages of melodic dissimilarity, according to
four measures between the echoes of simple and
complex melodic stimuli. ($\overline{x}$ = mean of diver-
gency in quarter tones; σ = standard deviation).

| | SIMPLE intonation patterns | | COMPLEX intonation patterns | |
| | Hung.Ott voltál? | | Hung.Az én hibám volt | |
Measures:	($\overline{x}$)	(σ)	($\overline{x}$)	(σ)
(a)	0.905	0.365	2.049	0.916
(b)	0.871	0.209	1.019	0.218
(c)	0.839	0.396	1.740	0.780
(d)	0.721	0.339	2.461	1.408
	French Il est content?		French La raison	
	($\overline{x}$)	(σ)	($\overline{x}$)	(σ)
(a)	0.911	0.396	2.643	1.722
(b)	0.954	0.246	1.767	0.751
(c)	0.943	0.455	1.670	0.968
(d)	1.110	0.617	1.693	0.692

Table 3. Four measures of melodic dissimilarity between the
echoes of the complex melodic stimulus La raison,
inside the same pattern, and between two different
configurations. Q = question pattern (triangular),
A = assertive, exclamative pattern (rising).

| | Melodic dissimilarities | | |
| | Inside the same pattern | | Between two patterns |
Measures	Q vs. Q	A vs. A	A vs. Q
(a)	0.71	1.42	4.08
(b)	1.07	1.22	2.25
(c)	0.81	1.11	2.28
(d)	1.08	1.10	2.15

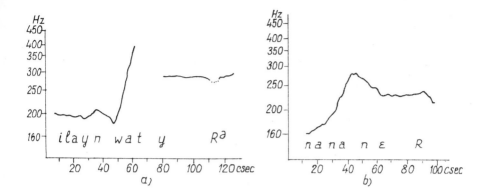

figure 1

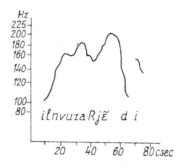

figure 2

Il lui fallait   sauver les apparences,   et m'interroger   sur mon travail, ma famille...

Sauver les apparences,   m'interroger   sur mon travail,   ma famille...

figure 3

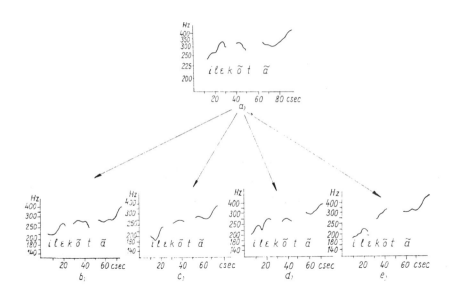

figure 4

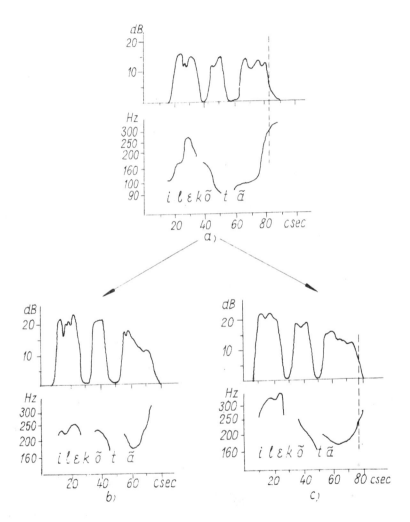

figure 5

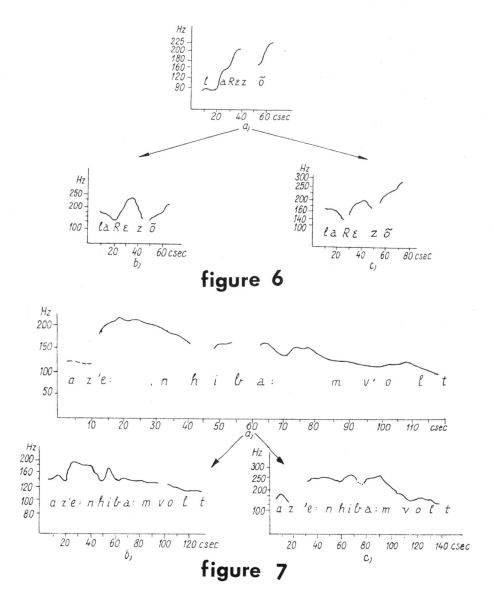

figure 6

figure 7

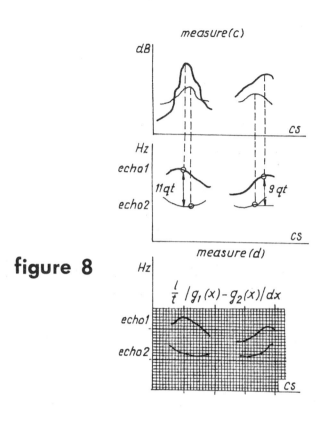

figure 8

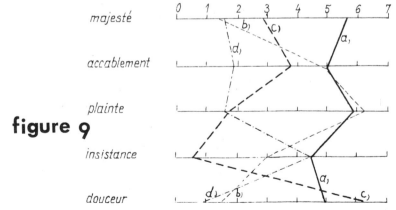

figure 9

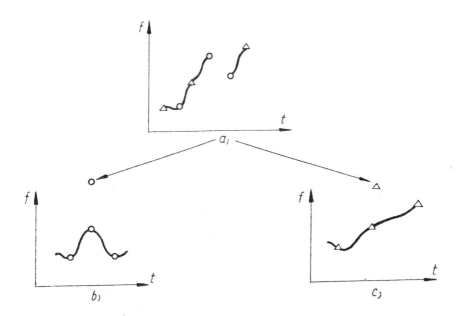

figure 10

SYLLABIC DIVISION AND THE INTONATION
OF COMMON SLAVIC

HERBERT GALTON
University of Kansas

It is said about some people that they are like other
people, only more so. Now I find this characterization also
eminently applicable to the Common Slavic language as it
emerged out of Indo-European. Its peculiarities are mostly
well known, such as precisely the principle of the open
syllable. H. R. Stetson, in his "Motor Phonetics," con-
nects the appearance of the open syllable, that is one that
ends in a vowel, with a fast rate of delivery as a sort of
physiological necessity due to the fact that the chest arrest
of the syllable pulse, as he calls it, works faster than an
arrest by a consonant. I might mention by the way that the
syllable appears as such an incontrovertible fact, among
other things in certain aphasia phenomena or, let us say,
the bound accentuation of certain Slavic and other languages,
that the qualms which some phoneticians like Wheeler
Scripture of Panconcelli-Calzia had regarding its existence,
for lack of a pat definition, need not detain us any further. Stetson's chest pulse may not, of course, be the only
factor underlying its existence.

To revert to the original Slavic open syllable that presided over the genesis of that language, though it has since
then been more or less abandoned by the Slavs, there is indeed no reason to believe that these people were especially
fast speakers. But the point is precisely that a tendency
which quite generally comes to the fore when, e.g., in English,
to take Stetson's example, an utterance like ape, ape or
eat, eat is increased beyond a rate of 3.5 per second,

becoming <u>pay, pay</u> ... <u>tea, tea</u>, came to mold the whole of
Slavic speech regardless of the rate of utterance. Other
languages show the same tendency rather more sporadically,
such as Latin, which has <u>mē</u> with loss of /d/ after long
vowel, but <u>sĕd</u> with /d/ maintained after short, i.e., only
under certain conditions.

    Besides, the Slavs did not only open the end of all
their syllables without exception, without regard to origin,
morphological pattern and paradigmatic association, nay even
to etymology--though it must be said in fairness to them that
they did not single out certain consonants for illtreatment
like the Kelts their /p/'s or the Greeks their /s/'s and
/w/'s, but proceeded quite even-handedly precisely on the
basis of position within the syllable. Moreover,they went
to quite some length in closing the onset of the syllable
where it was vocalic, especially with the more open or
sonorous vowels. Thus, the Indo-European "apple" became a
<u>jäblʹbko</u>, with the feature of syllabic harmony thrown in for
good measure, *<u>ēdmi</u> "I eat" became <u>jämʺ</u>, but *<u>epro-</u> "boar"
<u>veprʹb</u> like *<u>atra</u> "fire" <u>vatra</u>, etc. These examples, which
can easily be multiplied, are also interesting in that they
show that the initial glide which we must originally posit here,
/i̯/ and /u̯/, was not necessarily connected with the front vs.
back character of the following vowel, but itself took the
shape of the sonontal form of the two closest vowels in a way
that sometimes looks quite haphazard, as long as it provided
the syllable initial with a semi-consonantal onset. It is in
my opinion quite vain to attribute this to our good old stand-by
sandhi, but represents rather its opposite--a clear delimita-
tion of syllables.

    Nor is this all. Diphthongs containing precisely the
same /i̯/ and /u̯/ as their second part were without exception
contracted into a sort of compromise monophthong if and only
if they occurred in the same syllable, which belongs to the
essence of a diphthong; those with a nasal consonant yielded
new nasal vowels, and those with liquids were subjected to a
variety of procedures, according to different tribal pre-
ferences, all aiming at the establishment of open syllables,
most conspicuous among which is the South Slavic and
Czechoslovak metathesis exemplified by say <u>branʺ</u> "battle"
from something like *<u>bhorni-</u> which can be explained, without

resort ad hoc to a mysterious schwa-vowel, as a real swap,
maintaining the awareness of the originally closed and therefore long quantity in a compensatory lengthening of the
displaced vowel.

All treatments were strictly limited by the bounds of
the syllable, within which phonetic tendencies known from
other languages operated with an unheard-of degree of consistency. Palatalizations are common in the languages of
mankind; the Slavic ones, which in Common Slavic did not yet
bring about a correlation of palatalization, but only an
unusually high number of palatal consonants--ten, if /j/ is
included, neither spread analogically where they had no
business to on purely phonetic grounds, as e.g., in Sanskrit
1st Sg. Pres. pacāmi and 3rd Pl. pacanti, nor spared some
velars before front vowels under paradigmatic pressure like
Skt. kim "what" like kas "who," or before subsequently arising front vowels like kevalam "merely" with a contracted
diphthong, but when in Slavic the diphthongs were mono-
phthongized to new front vowels and the force of the first
palatalization had apparently been spent, there followed a
second palatalization likewise yielding new palatal, though
different, consonants. These palatals had to be followed by
one of the then still numerous front vowels, and velars only
by back vowels, which on account of this apparent condition-
ing, mutual though it often is, does not, of course, at first
establish a full-fledged correlation of palatalization. This
we only witness later, when, among a majority of Slavic
speakers, palatalized consonants occur regardless of a following front vowel or not--in fact in peripheral Bulgarian only
before back vowel! In this position the vowel transitions
are obviously more audible and, incidentally, also more visible in a spectrogram. This is, then, no longer a feature of
harmony within the syllable--this harmony dies with Common
Slavic or soon after. But when this harmony existed, it also
created the hard Slavic /ɪ/ before back vowel, which owes its
deep resonance to a convex surface of the tongue, thus en-
larging the resonance chamber, while reducing the pharyngeal
passage out of it. Again, we observe a similar feature in
Latin, where the native grammarians distinguished /l/ pinguis
and exilis, but it certainly operated across the syllabic
boundary as say in familia against famul, exilium against
exul.

Nothing of the sort in Slavic--or rather, in Slavic the exception confirms the rule. For where we have transsyllabic effects as against the otherwise autonomous syllable, it is precisely the two least sonorous vowels which are concerned, /u/ and /i/. As regards the first, in a very old development which Slavic shares with Latin, its sonantal form /u̯/ assimilates a front /e/ in the preceding syllable, thus *neu̯os > novъ like Latin novus; the second /i/ in its various shapes palatalizes velars which release the next syllable as in lice "face" against likъ without any such effect, but, as also this example indicates, the change is so much bound up with the quality of the following vowel or consonant, if any, and so irregular, especially in the Slavic North, as to really confirm the rule, as I said in the beginning.

We must also expect, I think, the first major breach in the principle of the open Slavic syllable with its rising sonority to take place precisely where they ended with the least sonorous vowels, the typical Slavic /ъ/ and /ь/. When these broke down all over the Slavic world--its last common evolution--in pursuance of a curious arithmetical principle, i.e., when they were in uninterrupted sequence, dropping out in odd syllables counting from the right in writing, and sounding forth in a newly gained vocalic force in the even-- the spell of the open syllable was broken and, incidentally, the correlation of palatalization entered upon its triumphal march that eventually subjected all consonants, as I see it, to its sway at least in Russia as its center. In so doing, the Slavs also supplied evidence of the strength of the syllabic count, even from the end of phonetic words backward, in the subconscious mind.

The question surely arises as to why the syllable, whose best division--and the syllable is essentially division--is the open one, should have gained such a hold over the Slavic mind, whose motoric commands the articulatory organs obeyed. Again, Slavic is not unique--only more so, as with its palatalization. Even in French, similar features are regular, such as the dropping vs. retention of e muet e.g. in je n(e) te l(e) dis pas. But the closest parallel I am aware of is furnished by Japanese, which at least in its older literary language--all these features are transient human phenomena!--has only open syllables (like Slavic also

in loanwords), including a type ending in short /ŭ/ liable
to disappearance as in Slavic. Now that French has a weak
expiratory stress is known, and so has Japanese, though some
dynamic component is naturally never absent. But the last
mentioned language has an intonation whose tonal range may
amount to a quart or a sext according to sex. Regardless of
their position, vowels in Japanese may be long or short,
exactly as in Common Slavic, and the intonation contour,
which may be rising, falling, or falling-rising, also level,
does not only characterize the main accented syllable which
displays greater force of articulation, according to the
recent Russian investigator T. M. Gurevič, following E. D.
Polivanov. But it is most remarkable that in isolated
syllables, the pitch cannot be distinguished by the native
hearer--an environment is required, at least for short mono-
syllables, because what matters is the position within a
larger contour.

   When I teach Old Church Slavic, I always regret that
Saints Cyrill and Method did not leave us any tapes to
convince our skeptical students. We must, therefore, extra-
polate in our picture of the Common Slavic accent. In view
of the fact that the relatively greatest number of open
syllables among the living Slavic idioms has been preserved
by Serbo-Croatian, which also sports a musical intonation,
this must inform our guess. Now as we have learned from the
exemplary investigation by Ilse Lehiste and Pavle Ivić, the
accentual characteristics cannot be perceived in isolated
Serbo-Croatian syllables as merely suprasegmental features
of the syllabic nucleus, but require a surrounding contour
for this, i.e., the tone movement especially on the following syllables for their identification. It is my contention,
though I regret I cannot "quantify my data," that this kind
of intonation also presided over the genesis of Slavic out
of Indo-European, opening all syllables, providing those in
need with initial glides, and performing all the other operations very briefly referred to before, with one sole aim in
view: the creation of a sequence of basic units or beats,
with an ideal division between them, through which the peculiar
nature of the musical accentuation of Slavic could best assert
itself. I am quite aware that my approach is unashamedly
teleological.

PROCESSES IN THE DEVELOPMENT OF SPEECH TIMING CONTROL

SARAH HAWKINS
University of North Carolina

I would like to discuss some processes evident in the development of timing control for initial clustered consonants. The data come from monosyllabic English words elicited from seven British children with normal speech, aged between 4 and 7 years, and from six of these, plus a child of almost four years, about 14 months later. Figure 1 shows the ages of the children at testing. The words made up sets where, for each word with an initial consonant cluster, there were others with the same vowel but only one of the consonants of the cluster. Examples are spin, with sing and pin, or flit, with fit and lit. All initial consonant clusters of English were included, except for /θr, θw, tw, dw, and kw/. Each child said at least 30 tokens of each word in the first year, and at least 24 in the second year. The durations of the clustered and unclustered word-initial consonants were measured oscillographically and compared with the speech of five adults saying the same words.

I shall briefly present evidence from these data for five principles commonly found in theories of skill learning and development. Then I shall discuss evidence for processes which may be more specific to articulation development. Figure 2 lists the five general processes. The first two, more variable behavior and more stereotyped behavior are opposites, but there is evidence for both in cross-sectional analyses between children within one year. The other three

are evident in longitudinal analyses across the two years.
An overall tendency for gradual refinement of behavior
towards the adult norm may be modified either by the 4th
category, overgeneralization of rules (which also causes
stereotyped behavior, and may involve regression), or by
category 5, periods of rapid change alternating with more
static phases. I will give examples of each of these in
turn. An example of greater variability in the children's
speech compared with the adults' is in the variances of
their distributions of each word. Each variance was divided
by its mean (resulting in the 'relative variance'), to
correct for the children speaking more slowly than the
adults. Figure 3 shows that the children in year 2 have a
wider distribution than the adults, whereas in year 1,
the range is much wider, and the absolute values are much
higher.

The second process is the children's failure to
differentiate between contexts. An example of this is the
difference between adults and children in the relative
durations of the devoiced part of liquids following voiceless stops. On the left of Figure 4 can be seen the adult
pattern of durations for /r/ or /l/ following /p, t, k/, as
a proportion of their respective unclustered durations. The
devoiced section is long compared with the voiced section,
especially for the homorganic /tr/. On the right of Figure
4 are seen the differences between adults and children in
the second year. Note the lack of overall difference for
/r/ after /t/. This is contrary to the general pattern in
the data, in which timing in homorganic clusters like /tr/
is generally less mature than in nonhomorganic clusters.
Comparing the devoiced and voiced columns, we see that the
children do not shorten the devoiced section of the liquids
in nonhomorganic contexts sufficiently. The implication is
that differences between devoiced parts of liquids following
various voiceless stops may be largely learned, and that
children between 4 and 8 years have not yet learned to
differentiate between these contexts.

Many aspects of the children's temporal control seem
to mature gradually towards the adult norm. The pattern
among segments apparently subject to this third principle,

gradual refinement, contrasts with the effects of the
fourth principle, overgeneralization of rules. Overgeneralization can cause regression. This is the case in
stop-liquid clusters of /p/ or /k/ before /r/ or /l/.
Contrary to the general rule for abbreviation of clustered
consonant durations, adults do not shorten /p/ or /k/ in
stop-liquid clusters, although /t/ is shortened. Children
initially follow this pattern, but then go through a stage
of abbreviating both /p/ and /k/ similarly to /t/. Later,
/p/ and /k/ are again unchanged in duration, as with
adults. In these stops then, we see a clear movement away
from the adult norm, in contrast to the pattern for continuants (fricatives and liquids). In all contexts where
adults shorten the clustered continuant relative to its
unclustered duration, the children moved nearer to that
norm over the 14 months. Typically, the degree of change
was only moderate, as from lengthening to no change, or
no change to moderate abbreviation. Major changes were
rare, and changes away from the adult norms did not occur.
Since the data come from only two periods, separated by as
much as 14 months, these patterns for continuants provide
only equivocal evidence for a gradual approximation to
adult norms.

The fifth principle, stages of rapid development
alternating with quiescent phases, is inferred from the
fact that some children matured faster than others between
year one and year two. An example of this comes from an
experiment reported by Hawkins and Allen (1977). Forty-
eight naive judges heard a tape of pairs of children saying
the same word, and judged which child spoke more maturely.
Each of the six children who spoke in both the first and
second years was paired with himself saying the same word
in each year. This was for five words--flit, spring, string,
treat, and ring. If the child was rated as more mature
in year 2 for a given word, he scored 1; otherwise he scored
0. Figure 5 shows the results for all five words, expressed
as a deviation from chance. A bigger deviation represents
a bigger change in judged speech maturity between the two
years. K4 and K7, with scores of +55 and +32, both sounded
appreciably more mature. K6, with -4, hasn't changed much,
while K2, with -54, sounded less mature in the second year.

The data presented suggest that many aspects of the child's developing control of speech timing can be described by processes that are well attested in other areas of skill learning. I will now present possible evidence for a pair of processes that may be more specific to the development of control in articulation. I would like to suggest that when the child begins to integrate the gestures for clustered consonants into cohesive units, the strategy he uses depends upon the segmental structure of the cluster. Clusters involving only continuants require constant monitoring, which I shall refer to as 'concurrent planning,' whereas clusters involving a stop as a non-initial member may be organized in two discrete stages. I refer to this as 'replanning.'

In Figure 6, the durations of each segment in initial 3-segment clusters are shown as proportions of their unclustered durations. KY2 stands for children recorded in the second year, and KY1 for children recorded in the first year. The adults lengthen the stops, except for /t/ and /k/ before /r/. The children exaggerate this tendency to lengthen, and for them it also applies to /t/ and /k/. This contrasts with the stops in initial stop-liquid clusters, for which the children either have similar durations to the adults, or over-abbreviate the stops.

The relative durations of the segments in these clusters for individual children in each year provide evidence suggesting the following pattern for clusters of initial /s/ plus stop, with or without a following liquid. At first, clustered segment durations are unchanged from their respective unclustered durations, or possibly slightly abbreviated. Later, the clustered stops are lengthened. Following this, the durations of /s/ and of the following liquid, if present, become quite adult-like relative to their unclustered equivalents. Later still, the lengthened stop becomes shorter again. Thus the timing of the non-initial stop shows movement away from both the adult norm and from the general pattern of increasing relative abbreviation of segments that characterizes most of the children's development. At the same time, the durations of segments surrounding the stop approach the adult norm more rapidly than the timing of the same segments in different contexts. For example, liquids in three-segment clusters--that

is, after /sp, st/ or /sk/--are more maturely timed than
liquids in most other clustered contexts--that is, in /fl, sl,
sw/ or in initial voiceless-stop-liquid clusters like /pl/ or
/tr/.

I suggest that this uneven development of segments in
clusters with non-initial stops is the result of the child's
applying a particular strategy, 'replanning,' at the time when
he is just beginning to integrate the gestures into single
complex units. In effect, the child divides the cluster into
two parts. Using /spr/ as an example, he executes the /s/
and transition into the /p/ as a well-integrated complex
gesture. He then executes the transition from the /p/ into
the following /r/ as a second integrated complex gesture.
Execution of the first gesture requires concentration of most
of his 'planning resources' in the early part of this stage,
so that preparation for the second and later gestures is
minimal. During the stop closure, these later gestures are
'replanned' in more detail before execution. This is possible
since maintenance of the closure should be relatively easy,
requiring few 'resources' because articulatory overshoot is
possible. But 'replanning' takes time, and leads to a long
closure period. In the later part of this stage, the segments
surrounding the stop closure should be executed more maturely
than the stop itself, and more maturely than the same segments
in clusters to which 'replanning' does not apply. This pattern
occurs later with homorganic clusters--/st/ and /str/--than
with nonhomorganic clusters--/spr, spl, skr, skw, sp, sk/.
This can be taken as evidence that 'replanning' is a strategy
applied during the integration of complex clusters of the appropriate structure since children's timing control of homorganic
clusters generally lags behind their control of the equivalent
nonhormorganic clusters.

The stragegy of 'replanning' contrasts with 'concurrent
planning,' a strategy the child may use for other difficult
clusters which do not include stops as non-initial members.
Clusters such as /sl/, for instance, require constant monitoring of articulatory position so that attempts at increasingly fluent execution of the cluster must occur concurrently with its production. In these clusters, we find

a general slowing of some or all segments and a gradual
approximation to the adult norm, rather than piecemeal and
uneven changes. Conclusive evidence for these strategies of
'replanning' and 'concurrent planning' is as yet scanty, but
it could be fairly easily collected in longitudinal studies.
There is enough evidence in these data however to suggest that
the notions merit investigation.

REFERENCE

Hawkins, S. and Allen, G. D.   (1977).   J. Acoust. Soc. Am.,
        62, Sup. 1, 006.

Child	Sex	Age at start of recording	
		Year 1	Year 2
K1	m	7;0	8;2
K2	f	6;4	7;6
K3	f	5;8	–
K4	m	5;4	6;6
K5	m	4;7	5;9
K6	f	4;6	5;8
K7	m	4;1	5;3
K8	m	–	3;10

Figure 1

1. Greater variability than in adult speech.

2. Failure to differentiate between contexts (stereotyped behavior).

3. Gradual refinement of performance.

4. Overgeneralisation of rules (stereotyped behavior; possible regression).

5. Periods of rapid development alternating with quiescent phases.

Figure 2

Grouped frequency distributions of relative variances.

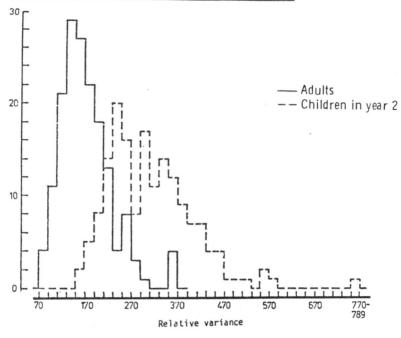

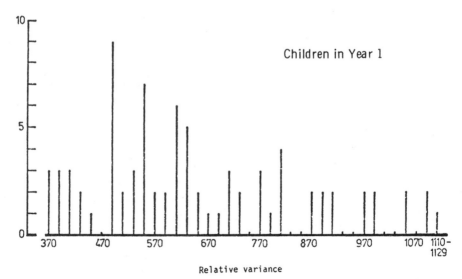

Figure 3

Durations of adult /r, l/ after /p, t, k/ as a proportion of their unclustered durations

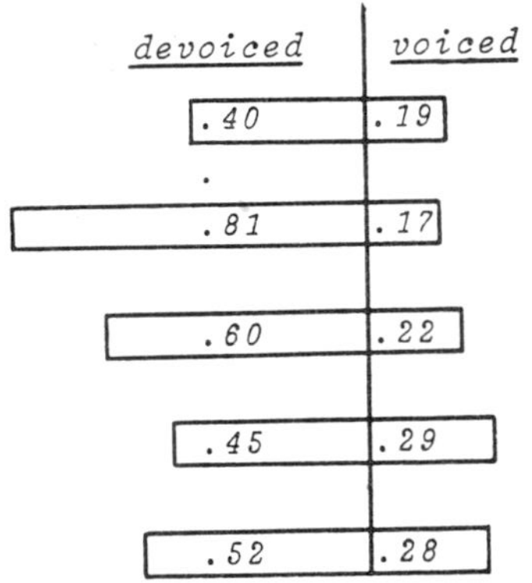

	devoiced	voiced
/pr/	.40	.19
/tr/	.81	.17
/kr/	.60	.22
/pl/	.45	.29
/kl/	.52	.28

Difference between adults and children in year 2. ((Children−Adults)×100).

	devoiced	voiced	total
/pr/	+16	+4	+20
/tr/	−3	+5	+2
/kr/	+2	+3	+4
/pl/	+5	+4	+9
/kl/	+4	+4	+8

Figure 4

Child	Score*
KI	+ 18
K2	- 54
K4	+ 55
K5	+ 21
K6	- 4
K7	+ 32

*Difference from chance score of 120.
(Max. difference = ± 120)

Figure 5

Durational changes in
/spr, str, skr, spl, skw /

Adults

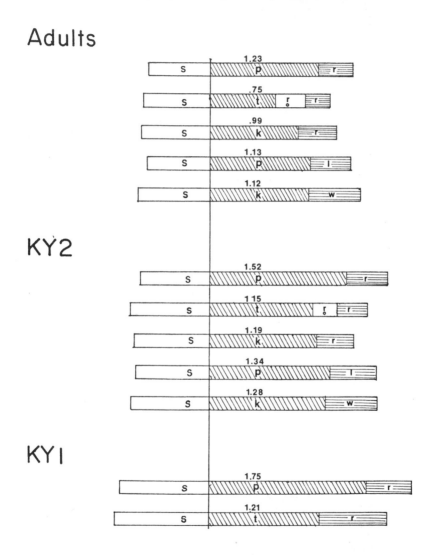

KY2

KY1

FIGURE   6

AN ACOUSTICAL/TEMPORAL ANALYSIS OF THE EFFECT
OF SITUATIONAL STRESS ON SPEECH

J. W. HICKS, JR.
University of Florida

INTRODUCTION

It is well known that speech contains both a linguistic
message and para-linguistic information. That is, speech
conveys data on several levels--including information about
cultural background, regional dislect, foreign origin and
"general feelings" about the statement being made. Perhaps
more important, a speaker can transmit information reflecting
his current health and emotional state.

There are many instances in which knowledge about the
emotional state of an individual would be desirable. Further,
there are situations where it would be advantageous to obtain
this information without any direct physical contact with the
individual; for example, in aerospace or diving operations.
Indeed, research directed at determining the acoustical/
temporal correlates of emotional stress should be useful to
many sub-specialties in the speech communication area; among
these are Forensic, Aerospace and Diver Communications and
Psychology/Psychiatry.

If research is to be carried out on stress, it would
appear that the first step would be to operationally define
this psychological state. Often the terms "stress" and
"emotion" are used interchangably. But, are they synonymous?
When an individual experiences stress, certain emotions are
evoked; however, does this make stress and emotions one and
the same? A given stressful situation may produce dissimilar

emotions in different people as well as diverse emotions in
the same individual at different times. There are many
emotions that are not related to stress (love, joy, delight).
It would appear that a reasonable definition of stress is
that it is a psychological state that is a _response_ to a
perceived threat and that it will be accompanied by specific
emotions such as fear, grief, anxiety or anger.

Situational stress can be defined as a form of stress
that results from a subject being exposed to a particular
setting that is normally stressful. In this case, the experimenter has not induced the stress; rather, the situation is
one that is normally stressful to the subject. This paper
reports the results of a pilot study conducted on the effects
of situational stress on speech. Specifically, the situation
studied is the presentation of a public speech.

METHOD

Recording Technique. Recordings for the present study
were made using an FM wireless microphone/transmitter. A
special headset was built in order to maintain the microphone
in an exact position relative to the speaker--a relationship
important for intensity measures to be made. It was judged
that this technique would allow subjects a natural freedom of
movement and minimize the effect (of the recording procedure)
on the subject's level of stress. This belief was verified
by comments made by the subjects at the conclusion of the
recording sessions.

Subject Population. Subjects were drawn from students
enrolled in a public speaking course at the University of
Florida. All the students in the class were recorded and each
completed the Multiple Affect Adjective Check List (MAACL)
upon finishing their presentation. However, only the ten
students (three males and seven females) with the highest
anxiety scores were used in the present study. Their anxiety
scores ranged from 14 to 19, with the maximum score being 21.
Nonstressed subjects score 4-6 whereas individuals under
stress average about 15.

Speech Materials. Two types of speech materials were
obtained. The stress material consisted of actual speeches

recorded at the time the students delivered them in class.
The normal speech sample consisted of a reading of a modern
adaptation of Robert Louis Stevenson's "An Apology for Idlers"
recorded in an IAC sound treated booth. The recording technique mentioned earlier was used for both speech samples.

Analysis. The first two minutes of the stress and
normal samples were analyzed for: (1) mean fundamental frequency (f_o), (2) fundamental frequency distribution, and (3)
speech/pause-time ratio. The mean fundamental frequency
and distribution were obtained utilizing the Fundamental
Frequency Indicator (FFI), a digital fundamental frequency
tracking device, available at the Institute for Advanced
Study of the Communication Processes. The speech/pause-
time ratio was obtained using a time-energy distribution computer program with an output that includes the percent of the
total speech sample in which the subject was speaking or
pausing.

RESULTS AND DISCUSSION

Table 1 provides the mean f_o measures for the stress
and normal conditions. The individual measures as well as
the group and overall means show an increase in fundamental
frequency for the stress condition when compared to the
normal condition. This finding is indicated by the negative
values for the difference between stress and normal conditions. Only one subject (female C.E.) exhibited a reversal
in this trend. Two-tailed t-tests were conducted in order to
test the hypothesis that the difference between the normal
and stress conditions were significantly different from zero.
The resultant t-value for the males was -1.92 which is significant only at the 0.20 level. Similarly, for the females,
the calculated t-value was -2.05, which is significant at the
0.10 level. Combining the males and females resulted in a
t-value of -2.54, significant at the 0.05 level. Although
the increase in f_o was not highly significant, the negative
values of t indicate that the general trend is for f_o to
increase in speech produced under stress.

On the other hand, this increase in f_o may have been
the result of an increased speaking intensity for the stress

condition. It is to be remembered that the stress condition was recorded while the subjects were speaking before
an audience and the normal speech sample was obtained in
the laboratory with only the subject and experimenter present. In presenting a "public address," the subjects might
have spoken louder in order to "project" their voice and be
heard by the entire audience. Conversely, for the laboratory recordings the subjects may have decreased their vocal
intensity since they were not faced with these problems.
As this research continues, intensity measures will be obtained and analyzed. With this additional information, the
correlation between intensity and fundamental frequency for
the two speech conditions will be determined.

The f_0 distribution obtained from FFI also was compared
between the stress and normal conditions. The output of
FFI includes a tabulation of the individual values of fundamental frequency and the percent of the total sample that
each values occurred. Differences between the distributions
for the stress and normal conditions were tested for each
subject. This analysis yielded t-values ranging from 0.00
to 0.09, none of which were significant of course. From these
data it would appear that no differences occur in f_0 fluctuations between normal speech and speech produced under stress.
However, it is possible that the stress of this situation was
not sufficient to produce high enough emotional levels to
affect changes in the distributions. That is, changes in the
f_0 distribution may only occur under extreme levels of stress,
such as for life threatening situations or for particularly
shocking experiences.

Table 2 shows the speech/pause-time ratios for the stress
and normal conditions. The speech/pause-time ratio is defined
as the percent of speech-time divided by the percent of pause-
time of the total speech sample. Therefore, ratio values
greater than 1.0 indicate that a higher proportion of the
speech sample contained speech as compared to pauses. Note
that one subject (female K.G.) had ratios less than 1.0
indicating that she produced more pauses than speech for the
two minute sample of her speech. Compared to the f_0 data
there was more individual variation in the speech/pause-ratios
However, the overall tendency was for the speech/pause-time

ratio to be greater under conditions of stress than for the normal condition. This finding is reflected in the negative values of t as well as in the negative differences in the group means. These results indicate that, under stress, the subjects produced more speech than pauses. This relationship could be attributed to two possible causes: one being the presence of audible pauses; that is, "ah's" and "um's," which were evident on listening to the tape recordings. The other reason could be an increase in speech rate related to stress. This would result in the subjects speaking so fast that they produced fewer pauses than they would when speaking in a normal or conversational situation. Audible pauses and speech rate are additional measures that will be investigated and taken into account in subsequent examinations of the effect of stress on speech.

Table 1.   Comparison of mean fundamental frequency between stress and normal conditions.

	Normal (Hz)	Stress (Hz)	Difference (N-S) (Hz)
1. Males			
G.H.	89.0	94.3	- 5.3
P.G.	121.8	133.1	-11.3
D.E.	117.0	119.2	- 2.2
Mean	109.3	115.5	- 6.2
t = -1.92. Significant at the 0.20 level.			
2. Females			
K.T.	218.1	235.6	-17.5
*C.E.	228.2	214.1	14.1*
M.B.	194.0	203.4	- 9.4
L.K.	208.6	234.0	-25.4
D.W.	216.4	218.2	- 1.8
K.G.	172.5	191.6	-19.1
S.S.	210.9	232.9	-22.0
Mean	206.8	218.5	-11.7
t = -2.05. Significant at the 0.10 level.			
3. Males and Females			
Mean	177.7	187.6	- 9.9
t = -2.54. Significant at the 0.05 level.			

*The only subject with a lower f_0 under stress condition.

Table 2. Speech/pause time ratios for stress and normal
          conditions.

	Normal	Stress	Difference (N-S)
1. Males			
G.H.	1.8	1.3	0.5
P.G.	1.6	2.8	-1.2
D.E.	2.1	1.7	0.4
Mean	1.8	1.9	-0.1
t = -0.14. Not significant.			
2. Females			
K.T.	1.6	2.0	-0.4
C.E.	2.1	3.1	-1.0
M.B.	1.5	1.5	0.0
L.K.	1.5	2.1	-0.6
D.W.	2.7	1.6	1.1
K.G.	0.8	0.9	-0.1
S.S.	2.5	2.6	-0.1
Mean	1.8	2.0	-0.2
t = -0.70. Not significant.			
3. Males and Females			
Mean	1.8	2.0	-0.2
t = -0.43. Not significant.			

A STATISTICAL APPROACH TO THE PROBLEM OF ISOCHRONY IN SPOKEN BRITISH ENGLISH

D. R. HILL, W. JASSEM AND I. H. WITTEN
Calgary, Poznań and Colchester

It is difficult to reconcile actual measurements of durations in British English speech with text-book statements referring to a "tendency for rhythmic units based upon recurring word stresses to be of equal duration" -- so-called "theories of isochrony." There are a number of theories that attempt to explain these relationships; those of Abercrombie (1967), Halliday (1970) and Ladefoged (1975) for example -- all arise from the teachings of Jones (1918/1960). Moreover, an alternative rhythmic basis for isochrony had been formulated by Jassem (1952). For convenience, these theories will be referred to as the Halliday theory and the Jassem theory respectively.

The basis of the Halliday theory has been stated by Ladefoged (1975). He first introduces the notion of "stress" (or accent) and goes on to emphasize that a word having the potential for stress on a syllable when spoken in isolation may lose that stress in connected speech so that not all words have stressed syllables under these conditions. The rhythmic units in such a theory Halliday terms "feet," and a foot extends from one stress mark to the next. Marks inserted during "pauses," are termed "silent stresses," though it should be noted that we have, so far, found little evidence for their existence in our work. Ladefoged emphasizes that the stresses only tend to recur at regular intervals, but -- as a direct consequence of this -- it is

necessarily asserted that feet tend to be of equal duration. Jassem's theory differs from Halliday's in that
proclitic syllables (those belonging syntactically to the
following foot) are excluded in computing the durations of
his rhythmic units which he terms "rhythm units." Thus, it
should be noted that rhythm units and feet are identical if
there are no proclitic syllables, otherwise rhythm units are
shorter than the corresponding feet. The omitted syllables
in Jassem's terminology are dubbed "anacruses," by analogy
with their counterparts in musical rhythm. Both approaches
to describing the rhythm of spoken British English, however,
postulate a tendency towards isochrony of the rhythmic units,
and estimates of the degree of approximation to isochrony
of rhythmic units might be expected to differ depending on
whether feet or rhythm units were used in the analysis of a
given body of data. Finally, it should be noted that
rhythmic units fall into different classes. In a simple
analysis, four classes may be considered: those falling
at the end of an utterance (final); those subject to both
these conditions (tonic-final); and the remainder (unmarked).

METHOD

A tape-recorded sample of Educated British English
speech -- i.e., Study Units 30, 39 (Halliday (1970) -- was
analysed spectrographically. The spectrograms were segmented by hand according to traditional phonetic criteria
and the whole analysis (217 seconds) was subjected to double
checking by a second reader. The segment identities and
durations, together with certain other information (for
example: tonic stress; syllable, word and foot boundaries;
and syllable and foot types) were composed into computer
readable form. Subsequently, the durations of syllables and
both kinds of rhythmic unit (Halliday's "feet" and Jassem's
"rhythm units") were computed and statistically analysed.
Simple models of syllable and rhythmic unit duration were
also set up and run, the results being compared to actual
measured durations. The qualified results of this analysis
and modelling exercise, reported in our earlier paper (Hill,
Witten & Jassem, 1978) may be summarized as follows: (1)
Computer synthesis of spoken British English may be expected
to produce reasonable approximations to the required rhythm.

(2) At least 25 percent of the determinants of rhythmic structure in spoken British English are unaccounted for in our simple model. (3) Despite a measured 6:1 ratio between the durations of the longest and shortest rhythmic units in our data, we have convincing evidence of a "tendency towards isochrony" that ranks third in importance as a determinant of segment duration assignment. Two questions now may be asked: (a) how can we quantify the notion of "tendency" in this context and (b) is there any reason to prefer one theory over the other.

DISCUSSION

One obvious quantity associated with any isochrony effect is the amount that it contributes to the total variance in mean segment duration, as in the part of this study that led to our formulation of a simple model for rhythm. Such an approach requires one to find out how much the variance in mean segment duration may be reduced by taking account of the size of rhythmic unit into which each segment falls -- assuming that decreasing segment durations are associated with increasing unit size. It was found that 9 percent of the variance could be accounted for by this factor, and that it was the third most important factor in determining segment durations in our model. It was also found that the equivalent syllable level effect did not exist -- we could find no evidence in our data of any syllable timing effect for spoken British English. However, two problems arise.

First, such a measure only tells us about that component of any tendency towards isochrony that arises from adjustment of segment durations -- what we may call "Segment Duration Compensation" or SDC. It is conceivable that spoken English could be strictly isochronous in the absence of SDC, if the speaker selected the semantics, syntax, words and phonetic realization of an utterance appropriately. Indeed, such selection is, perhaps, a large component of what a poet or lyricist does, although by no means always with the intention of introducing a tendency towards isochrony. Secondly, such a measure does not give a good "feel" for the amount of isochrony in utterances, even assuming that SDC

were the only factor at work; and, furthermore, in our
study, the measure does not distinguish at all between the
two alternative formulations of isochrony in rhythmic
structure.

An even more obvious approach would, perhaps, be to
compute simple statistics on rhythmic unit durations.
Table 1 shows the standard deviations for feet, rhythm
units and anacruses as percentages of their respective
means for SU30 and SU39. Again, it is difficult to gain
a feeling for the amount of any tendency expressed by these
figures, nor do they distinguish the two theories in any
convincing fashion. However, the figures do represent all
contributions toward equality of unit durations. We note
here that anacruses show a great deal more variation than
feet or rhythm units; they appear to exhibit very little
"tendency towards isochrony," yet they still exhibit a
marked central tendency by this simple measure. It seems
clear that almost any division of speech into units will
appear more or less isochronous, if normalized standard
deviation of unit size, or some similar statistic, is chosen
as the measure.

A number of measures were investigated involving,
typically, plots of average rate of segment production, or
mean segment duration, against size of rhythmic units.
Some were awkward to interpret because of the reciprocal
relationships involved. The measure of the tendency
towards isochrony finally chosen is based on the idealized
plot found in Figure 1. In this plot, the relation of
rhythmic unit duration to rhythmic unit size is compared for
some class of rhythmic units. To ensure compatibility between plots of different sets of data, both axes are normalized -- the rhythmic unit duration being divided by
mean rhythmic unit duration for the class, and the rhythmic
unit size by mean rhythmic unit size. Thus the point (1,1)
represents the mean of the data distribution, regardless of
the data plotted, and the horizontal regression line must
pass through this point (which implies that rhythmic unit
duration is the same, regardless of size). A line through
the origin, on the other hand, implies that the duration of

rhythmic units changes in strict proportion to the number
of segments that it contains. Looking at this another way,
a zero intercept on the y-axis implies no tendency towards
isochrony based on SDC, while an intercept of 1.0 implies
100 percent isochrony, whatever the mechanism. A negative
intercept would imply a disproportionate increase or decrease in rhythmic unit duration as its size changed, whilst
an intercept exceeding 1.0 would imply that there was
actually a decrease in the duration of rhythmic units as
their size increased (i.e., overcompensation). This measure,
although not entirely satisfactory, has many of the desirable
properties of the required measure.

     Our justification for choosing normalized plots as a
basis for comparing different kinds of rhythmic unit, under
different theories of "tendency towards isochrony," in terms
of the degree of this tendency is simple and, hopefully,
reasonable. The actual durations of rhythmic units under
any theory are likely to be affected by a variety of factors,
including speaking rate. If, as we found in various analyses
of our original data, there are real differences in mean size
and mean durations for different kinds of rhythmic units,
even under the same theory, then some kind of normalization
forms an essential precursor to comparison, or else such
normalization will be implicit and hidden in any comparative analysis attempted. Theories based on the notion of
isochrony merely assert a tendency for units to be more
nearly equal than might be expected. If the average size
and duration of different sets of units vary then it seems
reasonable to express any measure of this tendency relative
to the mean size and duration, just as one may describe the
variation in scatter for different populations by referring
to standard deviation as a proportion of the mean. In fact
the method we have adopted in the proposed measure is very
much of this character since it expresses the isochronous
proportion of a set of rhythmic units as a percentage of
the mean duration of the set.

     Figures 2 to 5 show the plots obtained for each of
the study units according to either theory. Similar type
figures, but broken down by type of rhythmic unit, had to
be omitted from this paper due to space limitations. Table 2

summarizes the degree of "Tendency Towards Isochrony"
(TTI) for SU30 and SU39 as: TTI = I x 100 percent -- where
I is the y-intercept as described above.

Our figures show quite well something that was apparent
in our modelling of British English rhythm -- namely that
marked rhythmic units show a greater isochrony effect than
unmarked units. However, they also show very clearly that
the greatest effect is in final rhythmic units -- 60 to 69
percent of the mean duration in final rhythmic units is
seen as fixed, regardless of size. At the other extreme,
the anacruses (not, strictly, rhythmic units at all, but
well worth analyzing in these terms) show a fixed component
amounting to only 12 to 17 percent of their mean duration.
Broadly speaking, anacruses show no significant SDC effect
at all, and the correlation between length and size is high
(e.g., 0.74 for SU30 as opposed to 0.46 for the final
rhythmic units). However, there seems little other ground,
at this level, for preferring the Halliday theory over the
Jassem theory -- the former showing a slightly greater tendency towards isochrony on tonic feet, the latter on unmarked feet.

Further, it was noted from our plots that, although
the slopes and intercepts for the two formulations are
highly comparable, there is rather less scatter for the
plots based on the Jassem formulation of rhythmic structure.
This almost certainly relates to the exclusion of proclitic
syllables, and may be the one reason, at the strictly
acoustical level, for preferring the Jassem formulation of
British English rhythm over the other. At this stage of
the work, however, it has not proved possible to show that
this, or any other difference between the two, is statistically significant. Nevertheless, the isochrony effect
itself is significant, at better than the 1 percent level,
whichever theory is chosen.

REFERENCES

Abercrombie, D.   (1967). Edinburgh, Edinburgh University
     Press, 96-97.
Halliday, M.A.K. (1970). Spoken English: Intonation,
     Oxford University Press, London, 1-3.

Hill, D. R.   (1975). Proc. 8th Int. Cong. Phon. Sci.
Hill, D. R., Witten, I. H. and Jassem, W.   (1978).
   Res. Rept. 78/25/6, U. Calgary, Canada.
Jassem, W.   (1952). Biul. Pol. Tow. Jezyk., 9:21-49.
Jones, D.   (1960). Cambridge, Heffer, 237-242.
Ladefoged, P. (1975). New York, Harcourt, Brace, Jovanovich,
   102-103.

The present study was supported by a grant from the National
Research Council of Canada.

Table 1.   Standard deviations in rhythmic unit durations
           normalized as percentages of their respective
           means. (Figures in brackets denote mean durations
           in milliseconds.)

	SU30	SU39
Feet	33%	37%
	(383)	(423)
Rhythm units	36%	38%
	(311)	(356)
Anacruses	50%	54%
	(138)	(181)

Table 2 .   Tendency towards isochrony (TTI).

	SU30	SU39
All feet	54%	42%
All rhythm units	48%	44%
Final and tonic-final		
rhythmic units	69%	60%
Tonic feet	55%	50%
Tonic rhythm units	51%	44%
Unmarked feet	33%	28%
Unmarked rhythm units	37%	36%
Anacruses	17%	12%

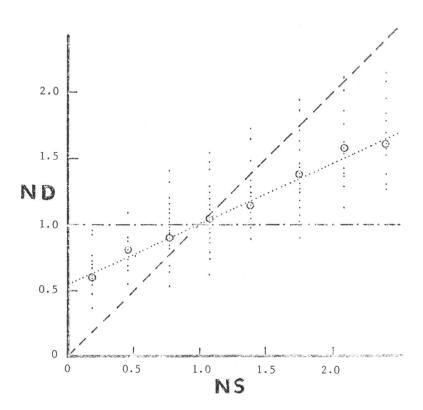

———·——·——·——·   Regression line indicating constant rhythmic unit duration
—— —— —— —— ——   Regression line indicating strict proportionality with size
················   Actual regression line
O   Mean of normalised durations for given size category

(The scattered points represent actual data)

Figure 1:   Generalised illustration of the relationship between normalised size (NS) and normalised durations (ND) for hypothetical data.

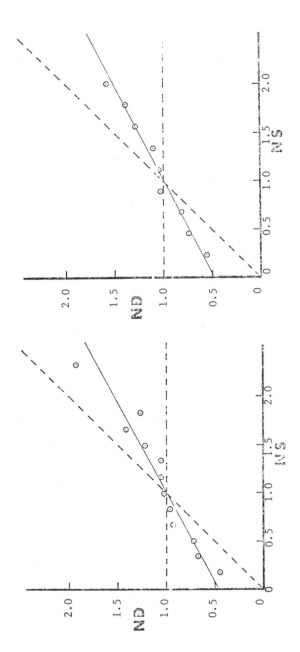

Figure 3: All rhythm units for SU30

Figure 2: All feet for SU30

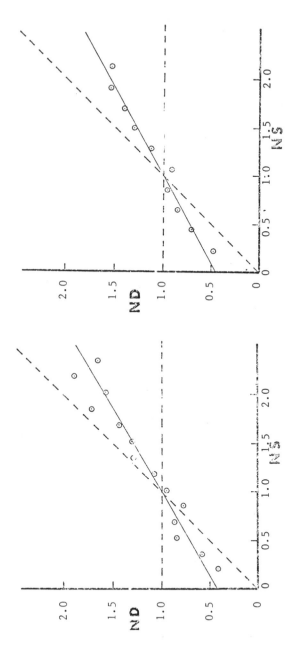

Figure 5: All rhythm units for SU39

Figure 4: All feet for SU39

INTONATION THROUGH VISUALIZATION

E. F. JAMES
University of Toronto

INTRODUCTION

The teaching of prosodic elements of 'speech, i.e.,
speech melody (variation in pitch), stress and rhythm in
the field of second language learning is an area which has
been, until comparatively recently seriously neglected.
This is, however, a very important aspect of language since
incorrect speech melody and accentuation can cause misunderstanding if not a complete breakdown in communication.

Famous pioneers in the field of second-language learning,
such as Varney-Pleasant, Pike, Fries, Delattre, all under-
lined the importance of teaching correct prosody in addition
to correct articulation. The systems they used to present
intonation patterns to their students included (1) snake
like lines with the accompanying words written underneath
(see Figure 1), (2) a system of intonation levels either
represented by numbers from 1-4: If Tom goes, I will too
                                    3   2-4-3 / 2-4 -3   2-4//
or by a kind of musical scale on which the words like notes
in music, are disposed according to the level at which they
are uttered (see Figure 2).

In the field of English intonation, before any of the
above-mentioned linguists published their individual systems
of transcribing intonation, Armstrong and Ward (1926) had
used a transcription which presented, graphically, the
intonation contour and the accented syllables of English

utterances as in Figure 3. Variations of this system (Faure, 1948 and 1962) have since been used to teach English intonation to foreign students.

VISUALIZING THE SPOKEN WORD

As mentioned earlier, the importance of correct speech prosody had been stressed by many leading linguists. Pike (1945) to quote just one, pointed out that we often react more violently to meaning signalled by intonation rather than the meaning conveyed by the words we use. It follows then that a non-native speaker using an incorrect intonation contour could create for himself some embarrassing problems. This is obviously an example taken from the domain of phonostylistics, in which nuances are conveyed by subtle changes in certain parts of the speech melody. However, even in the case of "neutral" utterances, where emotive implication are not present correct intonation is of paramount importance. Again, to quote only one of the many linguists who have studied the question, Faure (1962) finds that speech melody is very often responsible for fixing the sense of the message expressed by the spoken word (p. 67).

Recently Harlan Lane, the well known psycho-linguist of Ann Arbor, Michigan, also tackled the problem of teaching prosodic features of speech. In collaboration with Buiten, Lane (1964) he designed an electronic machine for just that purpose. The machine known as SAID (Speech Automatic Instruction Device), consisted of a tape recorder for playing model utterances, a pitchmeter to extract, in real time, the fundamental frequency (pitch) of the model utterance and that of the student, and a computer for comparing the output of the student with that of the model. This comparison was effected according to data previously programmed into the computer. Using this system a student would hear the model, copy the intonation pattern and, within a matter of micro-seconds the computer would judge his performance and either permit him by means of a system of signal lights, to pass on to the next parameter, intensity, or make him repeat the utterance until the intonation was judged satisfactory. The percentage of error was indicated to the student by the deviation from zero of a needle on a dial.

At approximately the same time Vardanian (1964) in
California was using a much better technique of visualization
for her experiments in teaching English intonation. A pitchmeter extracted the fundamental frequency of the model utterance and displayed it on the upper half of an oscilloscope
screen. The same process was repeated for the student imitation which was displayed on the lower half of the screen.
Vardanian, however, at the conclusion of her brief experimentation, seemed to feel that visual intonation is of little
help in the acquisition of prosodic features. However, our
early attempts with visualized intonation in 1967 seemed to
prove the contrary as we will show below.

THE SPEECH VISUALIZER AT THE
UNIVERSITY OF TORONTO

Using the facilities of the Experimental Phonetics
Laboratory of the University of Toronto, a similar, but
greatly improved, system to the ones used by Lane and Vardanian was devised. This consists of a series of filters,
constructed by Philippe Martin, which in connection with a
special computer programme, written by Martin, are responsible for extracting, accurately and instantaneously, the
fundamental frequency of the utterance being analyzed. The
essential element of this system is a two-track storage
oscilloscope for presenting, visually, on the screen the
intonation curve of both utterances, model and student imitation. Under this system a student hears the model utterance
and sees at the same time the intonation curve being traced
on the upper track of the oscilloscope screen. At a given
signal the student commences his imitation and sees, again
at the same time, his own intonation pattern being traced on
the lower half of the screen. He now has before him, on the
screen, the curve of the model utterance and immediately
below it the curve of this imitation utterance. The student
then examines both, to detect any errors in his utterance
and, if he decides to repeat his attempt, a voice-operated
relay clears the lower half of the screen only, and his new
imitation is traced on the screen, once again in real-time
so that the process of comparison and repetition can begin
again. (For a fuller description of the system, see Leon
and Martin, 1970.)

EXPERIMENTS UNDERTAKEN IN TORONTO

In 1969, using the Martin visualizer, a first set of
experiments was conducted using two groups of students who
were trained in the acquisition of French intonation with
and without visual feed back of individual imitations. These
experiments plus certain technical and psychological problems
have been described elsewhere (James, 1970). In April 1970,
the second set of experiments was started at the Language
laboratory of the Faculty of Education, University of Toronto.
After administering the Modern Language Aptitude Test devised
by Carroll Sapon (1958) and the Seashore Test of Musical
Talents (1939), our 30 subjects (students at the faculty)
were divided into 3 groups of 10 people, each group containing an even distribution of linguistically weak and strong
students.

Group 1, which we labelled TM, used a traditional
approach of listening to and repeating model sentences, each
carrying a typical and common intonation contour; group 2,
called AV 1, was presented with an instantaneous visual presentation of the intonation contour for each model sentence.
This group, however, received no visual feedback of their own
imitations. The third group, however (AV 2), saw not only
the visualization of the model sentences but also that of
each imitation of the model so that after each attempt the
model curve was fixed on the upper half of the screen and the
imitation was fixed on the lower half. In this way each student was able to compare both utterances and to detect any
divergencies from the model. Each time a new attempt was made
the old imitation was instantaneously erased and the new one
was displayed below the model. Each group visited the laboratory 6 times over a period of several weeks and a total of
3000 imitations were recorded on tape.

EXAMINATION OF RESULTS

Each imitation was played to a group of trained phoneticians all of whom, except two, were native French speakers.
The listeners were asked to judge the imitations, from the
point of view of speech prosody only, by assigning to each a
mark according to the following system: "2" - if the   .

imitation was perfect, "1" - if it was acceptable, and "0" - if it was unacceptable.

After all judgments were collated and analyzed it was discovered that group 3 (AV 2) was far superior to the other two groups. Raw scores for each group were calculated for all sessions and progress was charted. This progress was considered negative if the score for the final session was lower than that for the initial one and positive if the reverse was true. The results seem to be quite conclusive as the following figures show:

        Group 1 (TM)   11 negative progressions
                            _9 positive progressions
                          - 2

        Group 2 (AV 1)   25 negative progressions
                            _8 positive progressions
                          -17

        Group 3 (AV 2)   0 negative progression
                            63 positive progressions
                          +63

CONCLUSION

The examination of the results of these experiments seem to prove conclusively that the method which relies on visualization of the model curve only (AV 1) is if anything, little or no improvement on the traditional method of presenting an auditory stimulus and asking the students to respond based on what his ear perceives (TM). However, the method which provides a student with an immediate reinforcement in the form of a visual feedback of his own imitation (AV 2) which permits comparison with the model is vastly superior to both the other methods in terms of actual improvement made by the subjects. This is not surprising in view of the findings of those psychologists who have studied the question of feedback in its various forms. Annett (1969) summarizes many such studies.

A close examination of many oscillogrammes showing the microphone envelope and the intonation curve enabled us to detect danger zones and margins of tolerance along the various contours studied. A discussion of this aspect of the research is outside the scope of this paper but will be reported elsewhere. However, the one fact that did emerge very clearly was the efficacy of visualization of speech melody in the teaching of intonation in second language learning.

REFERENCES

Annett, J.   (1969).   Harmondsworth, Penguin Books.

Armstrong, L. E. and Ward, I. C.   (1926).   Leipzig and Berlin, Teubner.

Carroll, J. B. and Sapon, M.   (1958).   New York, Psychological Corporation.

Delattre, P.   (1946).   Middlebury, Vermont, The French School.

Faure, G.   (1948).   Paris, Hachette.

Faure, G.   (1962).   Paris, Didier.

Fries, C. C.   (1946).   Ann Arbor, U. Mich. Press.

James, E. F.   (1970).   Studia Phon. 3, Paris, Didier, 169-173.

Lane, H. and Buiten, R.   (1964).   Behav. Anal. Lab., PR 5, University of Michigan.

Leon, P. R., Martin, Ph. et al. (1970).   Studia Phon. 2, Paris, Didier.

Pike, K. L.   (1945).   Ann Arbor, U. Mich. Press.

Seashore, C. E.   (1939).   Camden, N. J., R.C.A.

Vardanian, R. M.   (1964).   Lang. Learn., 3-4:109-117.

Vidon-Varney, J.   (1934).   MLJ, 18:516-527.

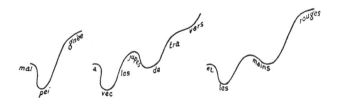

Figure 1

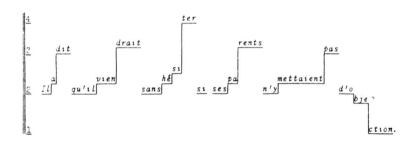

Figure 2

Figure 3

TONAL SPELLING

JOU BIENMING
University of Singapore

A. Tonal Spelling in Chinese Romanization

In international phonetics, linguistic tone being considered a separate entity from sound, it is usually represented by means of diacritics. This approach is highly impractical in romanization for the purpose of printing and typewriting. For sixty years (since the 1920s), the Coterie of Seven of Bamboo Grove fame, under the chairmanship of Professor Y. R. Chao, have advocated "Tonal Spelling," which spells tone as well as sound in letters. This is accomplished by spelling out the tone-class in letters, while the tone-value is marked by diacritics.

For example, in Chinese, the same tone-class in the various dialects can be made out by the same spelling formation, although its tone-value in pronunciation varies from dialect to dialect. For adequate romanization, therefore, the tone-value being implicit in the tone-class, it is necessary and sufficient only to spell out the tone-class.

Take "la, lanc, lan, lam," for example, the eight tone-classes in Chinese may be spelled out in the following manner:

Tone 1	la	T. 3	las	T. 5	laf	T. 7	lac
	lanc		lancs		lank		lak
	lan		lans		lant		lat
	lam		lams		lamp		lap

```
Tone 2  lar     T. 4  laa     T. 6  lav     T. 8  laq
        lang          laang         lanq          lag
        larn          laan          land          lad
        larm          laam          lamb          lab
```
where /-c, -q/ are glottal stops, and the final consonants
indicate tone-classes.

We have already succeeded in the tonal spelling of
Mandarin, Cantonese and Amoy. The result is the integration
of tonal orthography into a regular, striking, neat and
clean-shaven script.

B. Tonal Spelling for Hainanese

Tonal Spelling for Hainanese romanization is worked
out as may be seen in Table 1. Please note that each tone-
class is called either (a) by its name, i.e., im-Peng, yong-
Peng; imSeong, yong-Seong; im-Quf, yong-Quf; im-Jib, yong-
Jib, or (b) by its tone-class number 1, 2; 3, 4; 5, 6; 7, 8.
As a rule, im-tones are short, being numbered ODD: 1, 3, 5,
7;yong-tones are longer, being numbered EVEN: 2, 4, 6, 8.

The actual tone-values for each individual dialect are
identified severally by means of diacritics. These tone-
values are implicit in the tonal spelling. They may be
found in Figure 1 and Table 2.

Tonal spelling for vowels may be found in Table 3; tone
ablaut of medials in Table 4 and tone ablaut in finals in
Table 5. Finally, consider the following passage in
Hainanese romanized in tonal spelling.

Prak'huanc kanc Ziedxaur
North Wind and the Sun

Uv ziag-triau Prak'huanc kanc Ziedxaur tio-tse trianq oy.
  Once   North Wind and the Sun disputed who more capable.
Hof tirhau uv ziag-kair kyalou-nang sianq ziag-tryau nafku
At that time   a traveller   wearing   a   rather
kaw kair
  thick

tror-praur xant hofdic kuef. I nov-nang tsiw samtiang koong:
padded gown by there passed. The two then agreed, saying:
"Naan bo-zionq tio-tse lah. Naki trianq neng-toc hofmoc
  Let's not quarrel.   Whoever can make this
kyalou-nang
traveller
xuot i hof-tryau tror-praur quf, tsiw tuiftoc i oy lah."
take off his padded gown   will be counted the more cap-
able."
Prak'huanc tsiw suot-lad trua xauf. Nativ huanc naa trua,
North Wind then with all might blew. But wind the stronger,
Kyalou-nang ui i hof-tryau tror-praur naa keen. Kauf lof'aw,
traveller wrapped his padded gown the tighter. In the end,
Prak'huanc bo-prat taetoo toc, tsiw kaki bo xauf.
North Wind knew not what to do, and stopped blowing.
Bo-wav-kuu Ziedxaur tsiw suotlai trag'trag ffag. Kyalou-nang
Soon later, The Sun appeared and severely shone. The traveller
zuaq bo-neng naytriet, tsiw xuotkag hof-tryau tror-praur quf.
so hot could not bear it, and took off his padded gown.
Tezef-zianq Prak'huanc tsiw kaki zien Ziedxaur iank oy.
In this manner, North Wind acknowledged the Sun was more
capable.

Table 1. Nomenclature of Tone-classes

	Peng (even)	Seong (rising)	Quf (going)	Jib (entering)	
im	1 iP	3 iS	5 iQ	7 iJ	(upper)
yong	2 yP	4 yS	6 yQ	8 yJ	(lower)

Table 2. Initials.

	Voiced				Voiceless			
(a)	w	m	b		pr	—	ff	(labial)
(b)	y	n	d	l	tr	t	x	(dental)
(c)	h	ng	g		—	k	q	(velar)
(d)				z	—	ts	s	(affricate)

NOTES--/h/ is voiced, used also as a sign of plosive
           aspirated.
      /r/ is sign of implosion.
      /pr/ is the implosive /p/; /tr/ is the implosive of /t/.
      /ff/ is the bilabial /f/, being developed from
           aspirated /ph/.
      /x/ is fricative, being developed from aspirated /th/.
      /q/ is fricative, being developed from aspirated /kh/.

Table 3. Vowels.

(a) In Tonal Spelling	/ a e i o ou u /
(b) In IPA	/ a e i ɔ o u /
(c) Syllabic consonants	ng (nc, nk, nq)
	n (nh, nt, nd)
	m (mh, mp, mb)

Table 4. Tone ablaut of medials: /-i-, -y-, -e-/,
          /-u-, -w-, -o-/.

1	iom	3	eom	5	iomp	7	iop
	ien		een		ient		iet
	uanc		oang		uank		uak
2	yom	4	eom	6	iomb	8	iob
	yen		een		iend		ied
	wang		oang		uanq		uag

Table 5.   Tone ablaut of finals.

(a)	1 -,	-i,	-u,	3 +,	-e,	-o	5 -f,	-if,	-uf		7 -c	
	2 -r,	-ir,	-ur	4 +,	-e,	-o	6 -v;	-y,	-w		8 -q	
(b)	1 -nc			3 +ng			5 -nk				7 -ķ	
	2 -ng			4 +ng			6 -nq				8 -g	
(c)	1 -n			3 +n			5 -nt				7 -t	
	2 -rn			4 +n			6 -nd				8 -d	
(d)	1 -m			3 +m			5 -mp				7 -p	
	2 -rm			4 +m			6 -mb				8 -b	

NOTE--/-/ represents the principal vowel /a, e, i, o, u /;
/+/ represents the vowel doubled /aa, ee, ii, oo, uu /.
/-c, -q/ are glottal stops /-c/ on the im-level and
/-q/ on the yong-level, respectively.

TONAL SPELLING FOR HAINANESE

1	huanc	風	3	koong	講	5	iank	更	7	prak	北
	zien	認		keen	緊		xant	趁		triet	得
	sam	參		kuu	久		tuif	算		suot	出
	trun	大					luef	過		toc	作
2	nang	人	4	naan	咱	6	oy	會	8	zied	日
	xaur	頭		naa	愈		kaw	厚		ziag	一
	kya	行					nov	兩		lad	力
	tror	長					zianq	樣		zuaq	熱
	tiang	詳					trianq	是誰		ffag	曝

1		風	3		講	5		更	7		北
		認			緊			趁			得
		參			久			算			出
		大						過			作
2		人	4		咱	6		會	8		日
		頭			愈			厚			一
		行						兩			力
		長						樣			熱
		詳						是誰			曝

QUELQUES PROBLEMES POSES PAR L'ELABORATION DE
REGLES PREDICTIVES DE L'INTONATION

ELISABETH LHOTE
Université de Franche-Comté

La principale difficulté à laquelle se heurtent les
études sur l'intonation réside dans le choix des unités de
mesure aptes à décrire les faits réels observés. Même si
elle n'est pas le seul élément constitutif de l'intonation,
la variation de la fréquence fondamentale est certainement
le paramètre le plus important - c'est celui que nous avons
choisi d'étudier en priorité dans ce travail. Nous considérons que c'est la vibration des cordes vocales qui est
le phénomène - source à l'origine de la variation de hauteur
de toute intonation de phrase. Si l'on fait prononcer à
quelqu'un une phrase ne comportant que des sons sonores et
aucune pause, on peut dire que la fréquence fondamentale du
locuteur varie de façon continue et que l'auditeur perçoit
une variation continue de hauteur. On peut se demander ce
qui caractérise un phénomène continu. La notion de continuité ne recouvre pas les mêmes concepts suivant les
disciplines; nous dirons ici que la continuité est la
propriété des phénomenes "dont la nature est de ne faire
qu'un lorsqu'ils sont en contact" (Aristote).

Cette façon de concevoir la continuité ne s'oppose pas
au caractère discret des éléments successifs qui composent un
un phénomène, et Faure l'a bien montré pour l'intonation
(Faure, 1967). D'un point de vue formel, le discontinu peut
être considéré comme une étape vers quelque chose de continu;

une surface peut être considérée comme un continuum quand
on peut passer d'un point à un autre de cette surface en se
déplaçant par une infinité de points intermédiaires de telle
sorte qu'on n'ait pas de sauts à faire d'un de ces points
à un autre. Dans le domaine musical, le continu et le
discontinu entretiennent des relations complexes. Exemple:
des notes successives jouées sur un piano sont en elles-
mêmes des éléments discontinus, et cependant chez l'auditeur
chaque note est intégrée et dissoute dans le mouvement
global et continu de la hauteur.

On peu aussi considérer - et ceci est paradoxal - que
la continuité musicale est le fruit d'une reconstruction
mentale : selon BACHELARD, il faudrait apprendre la continuité d'une mélodie: "La continuité du tissu sonore est
si fragile qu'une coupure dans un endroit détermine parfoie
une rupture dans un autre endroit ... il faut apprendre la
continuité d'une mélodie. On ne l'entend pas de prime abord;
et c'est souvent la reconnaissance d'un theme qui apporte la
conscience de la continuité mélodique. La, comme ailleurs,
la reconnaissance a lieu avant la connaissance" (Bachelard).

Ces réflexions sur le caractère continu ou discontinu
d'un fait nous conduisent à proposer deux demarches dans
l'analyse de l'intonation! ou bien considérer la succes-
sivité des notes musicales, c'est-à-dire envisager tout fait
intonatif comme une suite de faits discrets; ou bien considérer la continuité de variation de hauteur. C'est la
première (de ces attitudes) que nous avons choisie pour ce
travail. On pourrait aussi se demander si l'analyse des
faits intonatifs envisagée du point de vue du locuteur ou de
celui de l'auditeur ne privilégie pas dans un cas l'aspect
continu et dans l'autre l'aspect discontinu du même fait de
langage. Nous avons tenu compte de cette double vision des
faits, mais nous considérons dans le cadre de cet exposé
qu'll s'agit d'un phénomène unique.

L'OBJET DE CE TRAVAIL

Nous avions observé que dans la perception des éléments
sonores du langage, certains fait jouent le rôle de déclencheurs, ces déclencheurs pouvant varier selon les individus,

selon les phrases et selon les types de communication. Et
nous pensons que la perception de l'intonation n'échappe
pas à ce mécanisme qui est typiquement humain.

Si l'on ne connaît pas la nature des déclencheurs et
ce qui les fait agir, on sait que leur fonction peut etre
de deux types; soit une fonction de prédiction, c'est-à-dire
que dès le debut d'un énoncé, l'auditeur peut prévoir tout
ou partie de l'ensemble; soit une fonction d'intégration,
c'est-à-dire que la suite des éléments constitutifs d'un
énoncé ne peut être reçue, comprise et intégrée à l'expérience vécue par l'auditeur que dans la partie finale
de l'énoncé.

Ceci suppose une remise en cause de la façon dont
l'auditeur perçoit la suite des notes d'un motif musical
et laisse entendre que notre perception auditive et notre
intégration linguistique ne fonctionnent pas forcément
selon l'axe temporel de défilement des informations
linguistiques. C'est pourquoi nous avons cherché à faire
apparaître des éléments déclencheurs dans la suite d'unités
discrètes au sein de mélodies de phrases. Nous sommes
partie de l'observation de faits réels, faits captés à
leur source par un électro-glottomètre. Les phrases choisies
illustrent des oppositions linguistiques qui ne peuvent être
transmises que par l'intonation. A partir de l'observation
des résultats d'analyse, nous avons construit des hypothèses
qui cherchent à décrire des modèles intonatifs à l'aide
d'unités discrètes. Pour tester ces hypotheses nous avons
utilisé un procédé de synthèse de mélodie et nous avons
soumis les mélodies synthétiques aux jugements d'auditeurs.

PROCEDURE EXPERIMENTALE

Enregistrements. A l'aide d'un glottomètre de type
FABRE nous avons enregistré 11 locuteurs prononçant 4
phrases francaises qui ne diffèrent entre elles que par
l'intonation (Lhote, 1977): Phrase 1: tu viens demain
(finalité). Phrase 2: tu viens demain (interrogation)?
Phrase 3: tu viens demain (ordre)! Phrase 4: tu viens
demain ... (continuation; énoncé non terminé). On a
demandé aux sujets de dire ces phrases aussi naturellement
que possible, et sans faire de pauses.

Analyse de la mélodie des glottogrammes. Nous avons
soumis chacun des énoncés captés par le glottomètre (que
nous appelons glottogrammes) à l'analyse effectuée par un
analyseur de mélodie (Andre and Lhote, 1976) qui donne les
variations de hauteur en 1/4 de ton. De ces analyses se
sont dégagés des traits communs entre les réalisations des
locuteurs et des variations dans les moyens utilisés par
chacun pour différencier les glottogrammes des 4 phrases.

Les hypothèses: ou patrons simplifiés construits à
l'aide d'une suite de notes de musique. A la lumière des
traits communs et des variations individuelles, nous avons
élaboré des hypothèses destinées à sélectionner des indices
participant à la perception et à la reconnaissance des
oppositions prosodiques: finalité $\neq$ interrogation $\neq$
ordre $\neq$ continuation. Les patrons simplifiés que nous
avons construits s'appuient sur les principes suivants:
(1) nous voulions savoir si l'on pouvait décrire ces
phrases de 4 syllabes par 4 notes, ce qui représente une
grande simplification, car les glottogrammes naturels
montraient 10 à 30 notes pour une phrase; nous savions
qu'il fallait alors s'attendre à une impression auditive
de discontinuité entre les notes; (2) la durée de chaque
note n'est pas constante: nous l'avons fait varier de
5 à 25 centisecondes selon la place de la note et selon
l'hypothèse; (3) ayant constaté que nos locuteurs utilisaient
une faible dynamique de la hauteur, nous avons fait varier
l'écart tonal de 1/2 ton à 3 tons; (4) plusieurs locuteurs
commencant les 4 phrases sur la même note, nous avons dans
la plupart des hypothèses neutralisé la hauteur initiale
en commençant les 4 phrases sur la même note, ce qui permet
de neutraliser la voix; (5) la durée totale des 4 phrases
peut être la même: 50 centisecondes, ou au contraire varier
comme dans l'hypothèse 4. Une illustration plus complète
des 5 hypothèses est fournie par la figure qui les résume.
Remarque: pour la commodité de la représentation graphique
nous avons lié les notes entre elles par un trait vertical.

Les stimuli. Les stimuli - que nous appelons des
patrons mélodiques - sont constitués d'une suite temporelle
de sons de forme sinusöidale dont l'amplitude reste constante mais dont la fréquence varie. Cette suite de sons

est assimilée à une suite de notes musicales. Comme 't
Hart et Collier (1976) nous avons choisi nos stimuli de
façon à obtenir un équivalent perceptuel des glottogrammes
naturels que nous avions enregistrés: la note initiale,
les variations de hauteur, la durée totale de chaque phrase
et la durée de chaque note ont été choisies en fonction
des résultats observés chez les locuteurs; exemple: dans
4 hypothèses sur 5 la note initiale est do$_2$ #dont la
fréquence normalisée est de 138 Hz, note la plus fréquemment
utilisée par les locuteurs masculins.

  La synthèse de mélodie. Les patrons simplifiés ont
été transcrits selon un code destiné à la programmation
numérique du synthétiseur. Le synthétiseur de mélodie
utilisé est celui qui a été construit par le Laboratoire
d'Automatique de Besançon (Andre and Lhote, 1976). Les
résultats obtenus sont des patrons mélodiques ou mélodies
synthétiques. Cette synthèse de mélodie, qui par certains
points ressemble à celle de 't Hart et Collier (1975)
diffère de celle qui est faite la plupart du temps: en
effet les patrons intonatifs qu'entendent les auditeurs ne
comportent que l'information véhiculée par la variation de
hauteur; ils sont donc privés du support phonémique, lexical
et syntaxique de la phrase.

  Les tests perceptuels. Nous avons fait entendre les
mélodies synthétiques à 20 auditeurs et leur avons demandé
soit de reconnaître, soit de juger les phrases francaises
synthétisées. Les sujets: parmi les 20 auditeurs, 11
sont français et 9 étrangers d'origine linguistique variée.
Quoique faisant partie de l'Université, ils ne sont ni
phonéticiens, ni entraînés à la pratique des tests, ni
habitués à entendre des glottogrammes. Les tests: nous
avons fait subir 2 tests: (a) dans le premier test nous
demandions aux auditeurs d'identifier et de reconnaître les
phrases selon chaque hypothèse dans des suites désordonnées
de patrons mélodiques. Quand ils le pouvaient, ils devaient
dire quels indices ils avaient utilisés pour la reconnaissance. (b) dans le second test, qui suivait le premier,
nous leur avons fait entendre chaque phrase selon toutes les
hypothèses et ils devaient dire quelle hypothèse leur
semblait la meilleure pour chaque phrase.

Spécificité de la tâche des auditeurs: ceux-ci n'ont jamais eu le support segmental pour reconnaître, identifier et juger les phrases; on suppose donc qu'une grande partie de l'information linguistique différentielle de ces phrases se trouve dans la mélodie seule. Les auditeurs savaient qu'il s'agissait de la phrase phonétique /t y v j ɛ̃ d ə m ɛ̃ / mais ils devaient différencier les 4 oppositions mélodiques: l'affirmation, l'interrogation, l'ordre et la continuation. On a fait appel à leur représentation mentale, ce qui leur a demandé de faire à tout moment une double analyse à deux degrés d'abstraction différents: une analyse auditive des variations de hauteur, c'est-à-dire une intégration perceptuelle de la suite continue des notes; une analyse linguistique qui leur fit associer un patron mélodique à une signification et juger de l'adéquation du modèle à l'idée. Le tableau synoptique qui suit permet de résumer la procédure expérimentale.

RESULTATS ET INTERPRETATION

Nos résultats et nos conclusions ne concernent pas à proprement parler la prosodie de la phrase, mais les relations qui existent entre deux paramètres acoustiques de la parole: la variation de la hauteur de la voix et la variation de la durée. Nous ne donnons ici que les résultats qui nous ont semblé les plus importants, c'est-à-dire ceux qui peuvent apporter quelque chose à la description de l'intonation par des unités discrètes, et ceux qui semblent reflèter la présence d'éléments déclencheurs dans la perception de l'intonation.

(a) Reconnaissance des phrases: contrairement à ce que l'on pourrait croire, les sujets francais n'ont pas mieux reconnu les phrases que les étrangers. 25% ont réussi à identifier les phrases et à les donner dans l'ordre, ce qui représente une belle performance, car la tâche est difficile (ces sujets sont tous musiciens). Les confusions faites par les autres montrent que la continuité et l'ordre sont difficiles à différencier de l'affirmation dans nos hypotheses. (N'oublions pas qu'il n'y a pas de variation d'intensité, paramètre utilisé dans l'expression de l'ordre.)

(b) <u>Hypothèse optimale</u>: malgré la grande diversité des
résultats, on s'aperçoit, quand on fait le bilan pour
chaque phrase et chaque hypothèse, que c'est la
<u>2e hypothèse</u> qui est préférée: cette hypothèse comporte
une note par syllabe, une durée totale identique et la
même note initiale. Par ailleurs les auditeurs n'ont été
gênés par la discontinuité des variations tonales que
quand la variation était trop brusque ou la durée trop
brève - ceci par référence au contenu de la phrase.

(c) <u>Indices pertinents</u>: si nous comparons les patrons
simplifiés entre eux (cf. figure) et les résultats des
tests, nous trouvons des éléments invariants quand les
4 phrases commencent sur la même note; entre la note
initiale n_i et la note finale n_f existe une différence
tonale qui est pertinente pour la reconnaissance de 2
phrases: $n_f - n_i = + 3$ tons: intonation d'interrogation; $n_f - n_i = + 1$ ton: intonation de continuation;
$n_f - n_i = - 1$ ton: intonation de finalité et intonation
d'ordre.

La différence tonale $n_f - n_i$ ne permet pas à l'auditeur de
différencier les phrases 1 et 3 qui toutes deux présentent
une note finale située 1 ton plus bas que la note initiale.
Par contre c'est la 2e note, toujours plus longue et plus
haute, qui permet la reconnaissance de l'<u>ordre</u> par rapport
à l'<u>affirmation</u>. Nous voyons se dégager deux sortes d'indices
pertinents dans la perception de l'intonation: un indice
qui a une <u>fonction d'intégration</u>, l'écart tonal entre la note
finale et la note initiale pour l'<u>interrogation</u> et la <u>con-
tinuation</u>; un indice qui a une <u>fonction de prédiction</u>, la 2e
note plus haute et plus longue pour l'<u>ordre</u> que pour
l'<u>affirmation</u>. Ce dernier indice permettrait à l'auditeur
dès le début d'une phrase de reconnaître le caractère impératif d'un énoncé par référence implicite au même énoncé
affirmatif - ce dernier jouant alors le rôle d'énoncé non
marqué.

CONCLUSION

Nous espérons avoir montré qu'il était possible de
décrire la variation de hauteur propre au mouvement mélodique

continu de phrases francaises non par une courbe mais par
une suite d'unités discrètes, et qu'il était également
possible de dégager par le jeu de ces unités discrètes des
indices pertinents qui participent à la reconnaissance
globale d'une fonction linguistique.

BIBLIOGRAPHIE

André, P. and Lhote F. (1976). Analyseur - synthétiseur de
     fréquences musicales, 14th Conference on Acoustics -
     Pratislava - Octobre 1976.
Aristote: Physique - Chapitre V.
Bachelard G.: La dialectique de la durée.
Faure, G. (1967). Proc. 6th Int. Cong. Ph. Sci., Prague.
Lhote, E. (1977). Mélanges Faure (à paraître).
't Hart, Jr. and Collier, R. (1975). J. Phon., 3:235-255.

     Le travail de synthèse par ordinateur a été effectué
par M. Hamelin au Laboratoire d'Automatique de Besançon,
et nous le remercions particuliérement.

```
┌─────────────────────────────┐
│      Enregistrement         │
│          des                │
│      glottogrammes          │
└─────────────────────────────┘
              │
              ▼
┌─────────────────────────────┐
│      Analyse de la          │
│      mélodie des            │
│      glottogrammes          │
└─────────────────────────────┘
              │
              ▼
┌─────────────────────────────┐
│     Elaboration des         │
│       hypotheses            │
│      sous forme de          │
│    patrons mélodiques       │
│        simplifiés           │
└─────────────────────────────┘
              │
              ▼
┌─────────────────────────────┐
│      Synthèse de            │
│        mélodie.             │
│    Chaque hypothèse         │
│     est traduite en         │
│  mélodies synthétiques      │
└─────────────────────────────┘
              │
              ▼
┌─────────────────────────────┐
│         Tests               │
│       perceptuels           │
│        Audition             │
│          et                 │
│     reconnaissance          │
│      des mélodies           │
│         par les             │
│        auditeurs            │
└─────────────────────────────┘
              │
              ▼
┌─────────────────────────────┐
│    Comparaison entre        │
│   résultats des tests       │
│     et hypothèses.          │
│     Interprétation          │
└─────────────────────────────┘
```

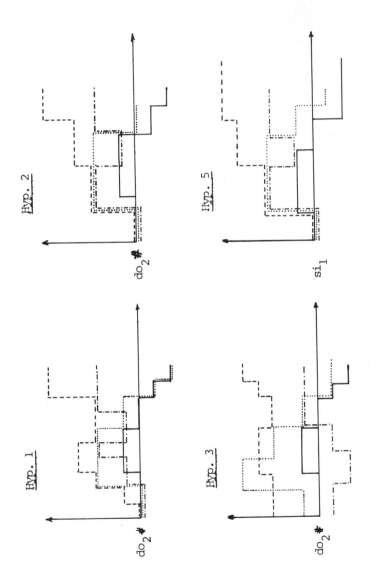

(le dessein est continué à la page prochaine)

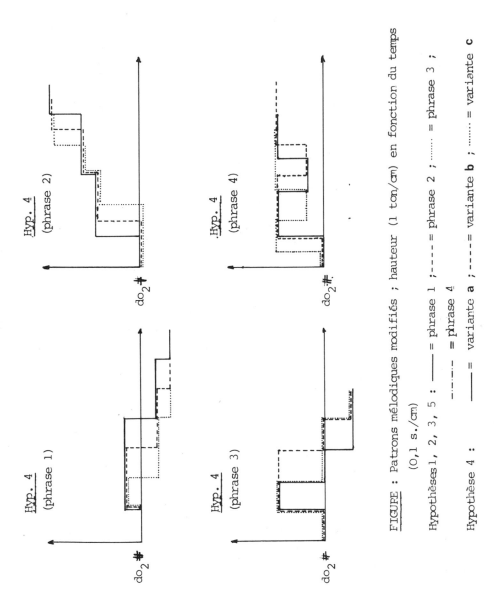

FIGURE : Patrons mélodiques modifiés ; hauteur (1 ton/cm) en fonction du temps (0,1 s./cm)

Hypothèses 1, 2, 3, 5 : ——— = phrase 1 ; ----- = phrase 2 ; .... = phrase 3 ; –·–·– = phrase 4

Hypothèse 4 : ——— = variante **a** ; ----- = variante **b** ; .... = variante **c**

PREPHONOLOGICAL VIEWS ON THE HISTORY OF
ENGLISH SYLLABLE ACCENTS

ANATOLY LIBERMAN
University of Minnesota

The first classification of syllable accents goes back
to Eduard Sievers who distinguished between geschnittener
Akzent, geschliffener Akzent and gestossener Akzent (Sievers,
1876, 113-118). Geschnittener Akzent is one-topped, i.e.,
it only has one peak of intensity and one high. Both
geschliffener and gestossener Akzent are two-peaked: a vowel
affected by them reaches the intensity peak, becomes attenuated
and passes through another reinforcement. If the peaks are not
separated by an interval and the attenuation is gradual, we
have geschliffener Akzent; but if during the vowel articulation
the glottis closes and opens again, this is already gestossener
Akzent. Geschliffener Akzent prefers long vowels, while
gestossener Akzent can fall on long and short vowels alike.
As we see, Sievers differentiated between a smooth and an
abrupt two-peaked accent.

Geschnittener Akzent also subsumes two varieties: strong,
i.e., abrupt (stark geschnittener Akzent) and weak, i.e.,
smooth (schwach geschnittener Akzent). Under a strong accent,
a vowel reaches its peak and is at this moment cut off by a
subsequent strong consonant or juncture. Under a weak accent,
a vowel is allowed to pass its intensity peak and the tonal
high and is only then cut off. The terms stark geschnittener
Akzent and schwach geschnittener Akzent were used by Sievers
as German counterparts to acutus and gravis in Latin, and he
designated them as /´/ (acute) and /`/ (grave), respectively.
The most important idea in his prosodic theory is the connection

he posits between the type of accent and two more characteristics, sc., stress and vowel length. Unstressed vowels, according to Sievers, always have grave (see footnote #1). Since acute requires a strong postvocalic consonant, and unstressed vowels of Germanic languages can hardly satisfy this condition, Sievers is quite consistent. We shall see below that the idea of grave as the only possible accent of unstressed vowels was applied by Karl Luick to English data and became a cornerstone of his reconstruction.

The relationships between the accents and vowel length are also described by Sievers in a very simple way. The old Latin rule runs as follows: the syllable having a short vowel is pronounced with an acute accent. Sievers followed Latin grammarians and believed that a short vowel naturally goes together with acute (and a long vowel with grave). He even went a step farther and taught that short and long vowels are DETERMINED by acute and grave, respectively. Besides, he thought that lengthening presupposes a smooth accent, while an abrupt accent protects vowels from lengthening (Sievers, 1901). It should be noted that acute and grave are ambiguous notions in Sievers. Thus, acute is a characteristic of a vowel (which has not reached its peak of intensity); in modern terms, it is a phonemic distinctive feature. But, on the other hand, acute is also a syllabic characteristic (for it is determined by the type of contact between a vowel and a subsequent consonant), i.e., again in modern terms, a prosodeme. The same is true of grave.

Sievers' rule that lengthening presupposes a smooth accent (=grave) made it possible to trace various quantitative shifts to the change of accents. A model for all investigators of Germanic quantity was an article by Hermann Paul, entirely inspired by Sievers (Paul, 1884). According to Paul, in Middle High German, all short stressed syllables had grave. But, by Sievers' rule, grave must accompany long vowels. Therefore, German tried to avoid the unnatural situation, and, as a result, either the vowel underwent lengthening, as in Vater /-a:-/ 'father,' or the accent was replaced (acute substituted for grave), as in Sitte /-i-/ 'custom.' Paul admitted that he could not explain why in short-syllable words sometimes the vowel and sometimes the accent conformed to the "natural" state of things, but, surprisingly, he was in no way disturbed by a much more puzzling circumstance, viz., why a Germanic language (in his case, Middle High German) happened to have original short syllables under grave.

After Sievers and Paul it became customary to view the history of length as a reflection of the history of accents. We find this approach in the works of two outstanding historians of English: Karl Luick and Lorenz Morsbach. Here are some passages from Luick, 1896. He wrote, "The vowels which stood before a single consonant or a geminate (but not before a cluster) in weakly stressed syllables, as well as the few unreduced vowels in unstressed syllables, were lengthened when they came to be stressed.....We have every ground to suppose that in Old English, as in all old Germanic languages, the accent that primarily reigned supreme was grave. In a stressed syllable, if it remained short, grave was supplanted by acute, but it remained intact in unstressed syllables..... Intermediate stages between stress and no stress could go each way.....As regards the weakest stages, we can safely assume the retention of the old grave in them, even when it had become extinct under stress. If, for some reason, such syllables happened to acquire stress, seeing that in a stressed syllable long vowels usually have grave and short vowels acute, the unusual combination of grave with a short vowel was transformed into either the combination of acute with a short vowel or of grave with a long one" (pp. 233-234, 238).

It will have been seen that, on the whole, Luick's reasoning is the same as with Sievers and Paul. He begins his reconstruction with an epoch when there is only one accent, sc., grave. The idea is self-explanatory: if modern long vowels from short ones have grave and lengthening presupposes grave on short vowels as well, there could be no acute in Old English But later, again as with Paul, acute is suddenly brought into play, and the rule is formulated that acute goes together with short vowels; now short vowels have two ways before them: either to preserve their original length but change the accent or preserve the accent and get lengthened. From a modern point of view, the most amazing thing is Luick's reconstruction of one accent. It is an established fact that Luick was a true precursor of historical phonology (besides Vachek's

article in 1932, see Trubetzkoy's account of his meeting
with Luick in Trubetzkoy, 1975), and one can only wonder
how he reconciled his structural insights with this strange
idea. Obviously, if Old English only had grave (i.e., some
syllable characteristic which, compared with later accents,
can be taken for grave), from a phonological point of view,
in this language there were no accents at all, just as
Modern English does not differentiate between grammatical
genders. Later, as Luick claims, grave could be, in certain
positions, supplanted by acute. But was it a feasible shift
if, given Luick's reconstruction, there was originally no
acute at all? Just as Paul before him, Luick never tried to
answer this question.

Morsbach, Luick's adversary for decades, also made use
of the accentual theory, though in a very peculiar way.
According to Morsbach (1896: 53, Note 4; 54, Note 2; 57 (d),
Note 2; 58, Note 2; 59, 1 and 64), every lengthening is
accounted for by grave replacing acute, while the reverse
process causes shortening. This reconstruction is quite
unlike that of Sievers and Paul. Paul emphasized that old
short vowels had grave and only avoided acute because they
got lengthened. But if, as Morsbach thought, old short
vowels had acute, then, by Sievers' rule, the language,
already at the very start, had attained the ideal combination
of accent and vowel length, and there was no reason for short
vowels to undergo lengthening. Luick was quick to point out
this inconsistency (1897, 441).

Morsbach's mistake is very instructive and helps understand the depth and subtlety of Sievers' theory. Sievers
starts with the statement that short must go with acute and
long with grave. But he immediately adds that lengthening
is only possible under grave; consequently, the vowels which
underwent lengthening, independent of their original length,
had grave, not acute (this is what Morsbach did not understand). As a matter of fact, Sievers divided the entire
history of Germanic vowels into two periods: first, short
vowels had either acute or grave (nothing is said about long
vowels, but it seems that in accordance with the natural state
of things they had in Sievers' opinion, grave: cf. Luick's
reconstruction), then short vowels acquired length under grave

and preserved their original accent, while short vowels under acute remained short, and this is how the modern rule was ultimately formed: short vowels with acute, long vowels with grave. Sievers admitted that modern accentual characteristics of vowels, even though he presented them as something natural and physiologically determined, were different in the past, and realization of this flexibility is the essence of his diachronic theory of length.

Disparate, but often quite interesting remarks on the distribution of accents can be also met with in other works. For instance, Gregor Sarrazin posited that the type of accent could depend on a vowel's tongue height and that /i/ and /u/ had originally had acute (Sarrazin, 1890, 314). Morsbach appropriated this idea and thought that /i, u/ had withstood lengthening in open syllables, because they had always had acute and, in later periods, refused to take on grave.

Let us sum up the most salient points of the accentual theory, as it was once developed by German-speaking scholars (in England this doctrine made no impression). Sievers and his followers believed that the history of length is the reverse side of the history of syllable accents. Sievers stated that in modern Germanic languages vowel length is relevant not in and for itself but only as an indicator of the type of syllable contact and distinguished between acute (strong contact) and grave (weak contact). This idea later found an excellent interpreter in Trubetzkoy, and after him the correlation of syllable cut, Silbenschnitt, has become one of the most popular topics in prosody, but phonological theories will remain outside the present paper. Sievers put forward the hypothesis that Germanic languages had always striven to combine short with acute and long with grave; however, according to the same hypothesis, in the ancient periods short vowels could only have grave, and this abnormal union was the driving force of all subsequent quantitative shifts. Since Sievers presented all lengthenings, among others, lengthening of vowels in open syllables, as a consequence of the accent shift, he discarded the theory of a permanent increase of force in Germanic stress and abandoned all attempts to put down lengthenings to the concentration of "dynamic accent" on the root syllable; moreover, he remarked that such

concentration goes much better with acute and thereby con-
duces to the preservation, rather than disappearance of short
vowels. (Here Sievers was at least a century ahead of his
time, for the absurd concentration theory has managed to
survive the 19th century and made its triumphant way into
most of modern textbooks.) Sievers could not explain why
accents tended to replace one another, but this fundamental
drawback, strange enough, did not seem important to his
disciples.

We have briefly discussed Sievers' main ideas concerning
DYNAMIC accents. The opposition of one-peaked to two-peaked
accents also attracted the attention of Sievers and his school.
It will be remembered that Sievers distinguished between a
two-peaked grave (geschliffener Akzent) and a two-peaked
acute (gestossener Akzent). Very often the term circumflex
is used, and it covers both varieties. Scandinavian dialec-
tologists, who deal with circumflexes more often than other
phoneticians studying Germanic languages, know circumflex 1
(presumably, an abrupt two-peaked accent, i.e., an acute
circumflex) and circumflex 2 (its smooth counterpart, i.e.,
a grave circumflex). In Sievers' terminology, only
geschliffener Akzent corresponded with the circumflex.

In 19th century English studies we do indeed come across
descriptions of two one-peaked and two two-peaked accents,
but it so happened that scholars would usually reconstruct
grave in some type of syllables without specifying the number
of peaks in it; likewise, two-peaked accents would often crop
up in reconstructions without any indications of their dynamic
nature (abrupt or smooth), so that the two lines of accen-
tological research were parallel rather than meeting at some
point. An interesting example of a 19th century reconstruction of two-peaked accents can be found in the same early
book by Sievers (1876, 143). In his discussion of the vowel
lengthening before a resonant followed by an obstruent in
Old English, Sievers says that if in the group like ald the
vowel has acute, it is completely protected from lengthening.
But if the vowel has grave OR A SMOOTH TWO-PEAKED ACCENT
(geschliffener Akzent), even a short delay in the transition
from the vowel to the postvocalic consonant will increase the
duration of the vowel and decrease the duration of the

consonant. The two-peaked accent, originally divided between the vowel and the resonant, will be now concentrated
in the long vowel and may later lose one peak and turn into
a usual grave: ãld > āld > àld. Thus, tint, tilt, etc. had
acute in Old English and have preserved their short vowels,
while kind, mild, etc. had a circumflex (=a smooth two-peaked
accent) and were lengthened. As before, Sievers again insists
that lengthening requires a smooth accent, but he does not
explain why the grave accent which he reconstructed in mild,
kind had two peaks.

It was Luick who tried to fill up the gaps in Sievers'
reconstruction. He believed that the words burg 'fortress,'
wylf 'she-wolf,' etc. had acquired their circumflex as a
result of West Germanic syncope, i.e., that the two-peaked
accent posited by Sievers had arisen by way of compensation
for a lost mora. Under the influence of the two-peaked
accents an epenthetic vowel had appeared between the resonant
and the obstruent: * burug, * wylif. Luick, just like
Sievers, added that later the second peak of the circumflex
had been lost, together with the epenthetic vowels, but an
oblique evidence of their existence is the fate of the words
like bindan 'bind': those, according to Luick, never had
epenthetic vowels, which caused the lengthening of the root
vowel; after the loss of the two-peaked accents length went
over to the vowel, and *biñdan became bindan (Luick 1914-1940,
245-246). To be sure, Luick's and Sievers' circumflex functions very much like deus ex machina, but Luick took his cue
not only from Sievers but also from Streitberg and Wrede, both
of whom (though using different data) traced Germanic and
German circumflexes to syncopes and apocopes. In contemporary
Scandinavian linguistics too the compensatory origin of the
circumflex is a commonplace.

But Luick's explanation did not just complement Sievers'
old hypothesis. For Sievers the most important thing was to
reconstruct a smooth accent which transformed ald into āld;
the two peaks were, in a rather mysterious way, taken for
granted. Luick, on the other hand, shows how the two peaks
came about, but he is not very much interested in the dynamic
properties of this accent. Strictly speaking, Sievers believed that the lengthening had been caused by a SMOOTH accent

(albeit two-peaked), while Luick posited a TWO-PEAKED accent
as the cause of the quantitative change. Besides, Luick
viewed the circumflex as a direct consequence of West Germanic syncope, and Sievers, as it seems, was ready to admit
an original two-peaked accent (though he was not explicit on
this point).[1]

The most striking feature of English historical accentology, as it was developed by old scholars, is an over-
abundance of hypotheses entirely divorced from dialectal
data. If in the course of millenia different accents clashed,
decomposed, replaced one another and caused major sound
changes, where are they today? In Swedish, Norwegian, Danish,
and partly in German and Dutch, all these accents exist and
have been described by phoneticians. Historians of English
are so indifferent to accentology precisely because these
prosodemes are absent from the literary norm, and it is hard
to believe in the grave, acute, and two circumflexes which
seem to have perished without leaving a trace. The achievement of Sievers and his school is practically lost, and there
is not a single article (let alone book) which would examine
the history of English syllable accents from a phonological
point of view. Even S. D. Kacnel'son (1966) does without
English.

A new rise of English accentology will become possible
after a screening of multifarious dialectal phenomena.
Already now we can be sure that some remnants of the once
ramified system of accents are extant. The most obvious
dephonologized accent is the glottal stop which bears a
strong resemblance to the Danish stød (see Liberman, 1972,
and 1973, 122, and the literature cited there). Our present
knowledge of Scandinavian accents and the so-called Rheinische
Schärfung could supply an important clue to the events which
happened in English dialects.

NOTE

[1] I am not discussing here the problematic circumflex of
unstressed syllables in Germanic and Old English. The well-
known reconstruction of acute and circumflex in Germanic final
syllables (Scherer, Hansen, Hirt), the reconstruction which

owes its origin to Bezzenberger, was an attempt to draw
Germanic accents into the Indo-European network. Sievers,
on the other hand, started out from modern pronunciation,
even though his terms are the same as with all other com-
parativists. Nineteenth-century scholars who worked on the
history of English (Luick, Morsbach, Sarrazin, etc.), took
little or no heed of Bezzenberger's doctrine.

REFERENCES

Kacnel'son, S. D. (1966). Moskva, Nauka.

Liberman, A. S. (1972). Kalbotyra (Vilnius), 32(3):45-57.

Liberman, A. S. (1973). Inost. Jazyki v jkole, 3:120-126.

Luick, K. (1896). Strassburg.

Luick, K. (1897). Archiv. Stud. Neuer. Sprach. Lit., 98:
    425-445.

Luick, K. (1914-1940). Leipzig.

Morsbach, L. (1896). Halle.

Paul, H. (1884). Beit. Gesch. Deutsch. Sprache Lit.,
    11:101-134.

Sarrazin, G. (1890). Beit. Kunde Indoger. Sprachen, 16:
    297-322.

Sievers, E. (1876). Bibliothek Indoger. Gramm. 1, Leipzig.

Sievers, E. (1901). Leipzig. (5 Rev.Ed. of Sievers 1876).

Trubetzkoy, N. S. (1975). The Hague, Mouton.

Vachek, J. (1933). Casopsis pro Moderni Filologii, 19:
    273-291.

SYLLABLE TIMING IN SPANISH, ENGLISH, AND FINNISH

D. KIMBROUGH OLLER
University of Miami

"Final-syllable lengthening" is generally defined as
follows: syllables occurring just before utterance, clause,
phrase or word boundaries are longer than phonotactically
similar syllables not occurring before such boundaries. Although the phenomenon has been documented and discussed for
a number of years (cf. Klatt, 1975; Umeda, 1975; Oller, 1973;
Lindblom, 1968; Delattre, 1966; Haden, 1962), little is
known about why final syllables might be lengthened. Several
explanations have been proposed: (1) The boundary cue theory
(Haden, 1962) suggests that lengthening is motivated by the
fact that listeners use lengthened syllables to locate constituent boundaries in perception of conversational speech.
(2) The motoric planning theory (Oller, 1973) suggests that
pre-boundary sullables might be lengthened in order to provide
extra time for the planning of articulation for succeeding
constituents. (3) The constituent review theory suggests that
lengthening of pre-boundary syllables allows the speaker time
for checking back to make sure that the just-uttered constituent has been properly executed, before going on to the next.
(4) Cooper and Sorensen (1977) have proposed that lengthening
is a by-product of a "generalized relaxation response of the
speech-processing machinery as it nears completion of the
processing of a constituent." (5) It is also possible that
final lengthening is attributable to some combination of
factors.

The specific form that any explanation must ultimately
assume depends upon how universal the presumed lengthening

factors are. Consequently it is necessary to investigate
final-position lengthening cross-linguistically. A review
of several previous works (e.g., Delattre, 1966; Lehtonen,
1970; Lindblom, 1968; Pinkerton-Hutchinson, 1973) suggests
that there may be considerable differences among languages
in the degree to which native speakers lengthen final
syllables. The present paper will provide results on three
languages which previous studies suggest may differ widely
in extent of lengthening. Data on one of the languages, Cuban
Spanish, are new and will be presented in as much detail as
space permits. The data on English and Finnish are derived
from a doctoral dissertation (Oller, 1971), the results of
which have not been published previously. These data will
be presented here in summarial form only.

Final and non-final vowel durations in Cuban Spanish

Subjects. Five native speakers of Cuban Spanish participated in the study. Although they are presently residents of
Miami, Florida, all five are Cuban born and four of the five
subjects came to the United States after adolescence. All
five speak English as well as Spanish.

Stimuli. Spanish employs predominantly CV syllables,
especially in Caribbean dialects where low-level phonological
processes delete many underlying final consonants. As a result, in order to study phonotactically typical Cuban Spanish
utterances, it is necessary to employ open final syllables.
The syllable /pa/ was chosen. The first study was designed
to obtain information about final-syllable lengthening in
words which occur in utterance final position. The stimulus
inventory is similar to the ones used in the investigations
of Lindblom (1968) and Oller (1973). Each utterance in study
one included the Spanish carrier phrase "dime" ("tell me")
followed by the key word which was one of five phonotactically
well-formed Spanish sequences of /pa/s /pápa/, /papá/,
/pápapa/, /papápa/, /papapá/. The second study was designed
to offer further possible insight about lengthening of pre-
constituent boundary syllables in words in a variety of
utterance positions. Each utterance in study two (see Table 1)
included either the Spanish word /pápa/ or /papá/. These words
were embedded in paired meaningful sentence frames so that the
key words occurred just prior to either a major constituent

boundary (as in sentences 2 or 5) or a minor constituent boundary (as in sentences 1 or 4). An additional pair of sentences included the key words as the first item in a list (sentences 3 and 6). Assuming that the syntactic structure of the list implies underlying sentential status for each list item, the key words in sentences 3 and 6 can be thought to precede a major constituent boundary.

Procedure. Subjects were seated in a quiet recording room and were instructed to read the sentences as naturally as possible. Each sentence from the two randomized lists was to be read twice with a pause between sentences but no pauses during the utterance of the setences. Subjects were also asked to maintain a constant mouth-to-microphone distance throughout the recording and to pronounce each sentence at approximately the same intensity level. If the subject mispronounced a sentence, the experimenter interrupted. Often the subject could correct the pronunciation without special assistance. If there were repeated errors (as occurred just a few times) the experimenter simply modeled the utterance for imitation.

Instrumentation. The speaker's utterances were recorded on a TEAC 3300 S2T tape recorder through a TEAC ME-120 microphone. The tape recorded utterances were then employed to make wide-band (300 Hz filter) spectrographic recordings via a Kay 6061B Sonagraph.

Segmentation. The "papa" sequences were isolated on the spectrograms and durations of the segments were measured. In most cases the utterances yielded relatively ideal recordings for segmentation since there were clear indications of onset of vocal tract closure (operationally defined here as consonants) and opening (vowels). However, in some instances the high amplitude signal corresponding to vocalic production had a gradual offset, sometimes trailing off into breathy voice especially in absolute final position. In such cases it was hard to tell whether or not the breathy offset should be assumed to be a part of the vowel's duration. Because there are signal ambiguities of this sort, it seems wise to adopt both a conservative (minimizing vowel durations) and a liberal (maximizing vowel durations) criterion for segmentation in

order to offer the reader alternative possible data interpretations. It should be pointed out that the liberal and
conservative criteria yield only minor data differences for
words in non-final position (as in study two) since even the
word-final vowels are followed by consonantal closures of
the following word.

Results. The vowel duration results for the two stimulus sets are presented together in summary form in Table 2.
The reader should keep in mind, however, that data on words
in utterance-final position derive from study one and data
on words in other positions derive from study two. Since
the two studies were not conducted simultaneously and were
not designed as a single investigation, some caution should
be exercised in comparing results for the various positions
of words. In the ratio data, final stressed vowels are compared with non-final stressed vowels (e.g., the last vowel
in /papá/ with the first in /pápa/, and final unstressed
vowels are compared with non-final unstressed vowels.

Final vowels are consistently of greater duration than
non-final vowels as evidenced by ratios greater than one for
all positions of words for both stress conditions and for
both segmentation criteria. However, these ratios are relatively low compared to results from such languages as English
(Oller, 1973), Swedish (Lindblom, 1968) and German (Delattre,
1966). At the same time, the results suggest that Cuban
Spanish lengthening differs little from other Latin American
Spanish dialects (cf. Pinkerton-Hutchinson, 1973). Some subjects showed ratios of less than one for words in some
positions though all five subjects showed overall tendencies
to lengthen final-syllable vowels. Note also that in data
from the liberal segmentation criterion, the higher order
constituent boundaries (utterance, list item, clause) seem
to yield greater lengthening than the lower order boundary
(minor within-clause boundary). The conservative criterion,
however, yields its lowest ratio for the highest order constituent type.

Final vowel lengthening in English
as a function of position-of-word
and contrastive stress

Three studies considered the effects of contrastive
stress and position-of-word on final-vowel lengthening in
English. The first study investigated the stressed vowel in
the words "stándardized" and "understánd." The second considered a non-primary stressed vowel (or diphthong) /ow/ in
the words "télephone" and "phonátion." The third investigated
the non-primary stressed vowel /aj/ in "párasite" and "citá-
tion." The words were embedded in sentence pairs which were
designed to elicit the desired productions in terms of position of key word and contrastive stress. Consider the sentences for English study one presented in Table 3. Notice,for
example, that sentence pairs 1 and 8 yield a possible comparison of final and non-final syllable vowels for the words "understand" and "standardized" in utterance-final position under
contrastive stress. As another example, consider sentence pairs
3 and 9 which yield a comparison of final and non-final syllable vowels in clause-final position but not under contrastive
stress.

All three studies incorporated a similar design with a
paired sentences inventory. The studies included variables of
contrastive stress (contrastive vs. none),position-of-word
(utterance-final, clause-final, phrase-internal) and speakers
participated in study one while six participated in study two
and another six in study three. High fidelity recordings were
made and segmentation was performed from spectrograms.

The results of the three studies are presented in summarized form in Tables 4, 5 and 6. For the data in Table 4 an
ANOVA yielded significant F-ratios (p < .001) for several factors including syllable position (final vs. non-final), the
interaction of syllable position and word position, and the
interaction of syllable position and contrastive stress.
The significant findings indicated that final-stressed-vowel
lengthening occurred in the experiment and that the extent of
final lengthening was substantially affected by contrastive
stress and position-of-word. Thus, it appears that when a
word bears contrastive stress, final-vowel lengthening is
greater than when it does not bear contrastive stress. In

addition, when a word is adjacent to a higher order constituent boundary, it shows greater lengthening than when
it is adjacent to a lower order constituent boundary.
Analysis of the data on non-primary stressed syllables from
Tables 5 and 6 also produces significant F-ratios for syllable position (Table 5, p < .001; Table 6, p < .01) and the
interaction of syllable position and word position (Table 5,
p < .05; Table 6, p < .01). However, the syllable position
by stress interaction is significant for the data in Table 6
(p < .05) only. These significant findings can be interpreted to mean that for non-primary stressed vowels there is
final-syllable lengthening as well as a significant tendency
for words adjacent to higher order constituents to show
greater lengthening than words adjacent to lower order constituents. At the same time the analysis indicates that unstressed vowels in English words bearing contrastive stress
may not always show greater final-position lengthening than
unstressed vowels in words bearing no contrastive stress.

Finnish segment duration as a function of position-in-utterance

A native adult Finnish speaker read a corpus of nonsense
words /tat/, /tatat/, /tatatat/, /tatatatat/, and /tatatatatat/,
each word embedded in three carrier sentences (1. Se oli
sama ____. 2. Sama ____ alkaa tästä. 3. Sama ____ avain
oli tässä.) for a high fidelity recording. Both the author
and a collaborating Finnish linguist monitored the recording
for naturalness of production. The sentences offer the
opportunity to compare final and non-final vowel and consonant
durations for words in three positions: utterance-final,
phrase-final and phrase-internal. Segmentations were made
from spectrographic recordings of the taped utterances. Because Finnish words bear stress on initial syllables, the
comparison of final and non-final vowels is limited for data
in Table 7 to non-initial syllables. Note that the final-
vowel lengthening ratios are extremely low for these Finnish
sequences. Assuming substantial intersubject variation, these
data suggest that some Finnish speakers may not lengthen final
vowels at all. Surprisingly the data on Finnish consonants
from the present subject show considerably more final-syllable
lengthening than the data on vowels. Final, penultimate, and

medial consonant durations are compared in Table 8. It
should be pointed out that the syllables employed in this
study are not typical since Finnish does not widely employ
final consonants. Note that the largest lengthening ratios
apply only to the atypical "final" consonants. Further work
with the same subject also showed that in real sentences
using real Finnish words with final consonants, the average
final vowel lengthening ratio is low (1.16), penultimate
consonant lengthening ratios are also low (1.12) and final
consonant lengthening ratios are comparatively high (1.66).

Comparison of final-vowel lengthening in Spanish, English, and Finnish

The studies presented in this paper were obviously not
designed to offer an ideal comparison of final-syllable
lengthening in three languages. There are considerable
differences among the various studies. However, a comparison
of the results may offer a preliminary perspective on the
possible universality of final-syllable lengthening. The
data are summarized in the Figure. Data on "clause-final"
and "list-item-final" words are included under "major internal
boundary," while data on (clause-internal) phrase-final words
are included under "minor internal boundary." The data included in the Figure are based on liberal segmentation criterion only. Whenever possible, data on stressed and unstressed vowel ratios, as well as data on contrastive and
non-contrastive stress, have been averaged.

Conclusions. The Figure suggests a wide range of final-
vowel lengthening across the three languages. This suggestion
is supported by comparisons of the three languages based on
several previous studies which have shown English with high
lengthening ratios (Delattre, 1966; Oller, 1973), Finnish with
low ratios (Lehtonen, 1970) and Spanish with intermediate
ratios (Delattre, 1966; Pinkerton-Hutchinson, 1973). These
results impose important limits on all the proposed explanations for final-syllable lengthening. The boundary cue
theory should in the face of this evidence be extended to
account for how some languages might use predictable variations in duration (as well as intonational features, cf. Lea,

1972) to mark constituent boundaries, while other languages
might employ different mechanisms, for example, a fixed
position for word stress to mark word boundaries (as in
Finnish). In their present forms the motoric planning
theory, the constituent review theory and the general relaxation theory also fall short in explaining why one language
would have substantially lengthened final syllables and
another would not. Does English require some special
motoric planning that Finnish does not? Does English require some special review of articulation at the end of
constituents that Finnish does not? Why would English speakers
have a generalized relaxation response at the end of constituents to a greater extent than Finnish speakers? Only with
answers to these questions can the proposed theories offer
substantial insight into the lengthening of constituent-final
syllables.

REFERENCES

Cooper, W. E. and Sorenson, J. M. (1977). J. Acoust. Soc.
    Am., 62:683-692.
Delattre, P. (1966). Int. Rev. Appl. Ling., IV:183-198.
Haden, E. (1962). Stud. Ling., 16:38.
Klatt, D. H. (1975). Paper, Am. Speech Hear. Assoc.
Kloker, D. R. (1975). Paper, Acoust. Soc. Am.
Lea, W. A. (1972). Ph.D. Diss., Purdue Univ.
Lea, W. A. and Kloker, D. R. (1975). UNIVAC Rep. PX11239.
Lindblom, B. E. F. (1968). KTH:SR, 2:1-5.
Lehtonen, J. (1970). Stud. Phil. Jyvask. VI.
Oller, D. K. (1971). Ph.D. Diss., Univ. Texas.
Oller, D. K. (1973). J. Acoust. Soc. Am., 54:1235-1247.
Oller, D. K. and Smith, B. L. (1977). J. Acoust. Soc. Am.,
    62:994-997.
Pinkerton-Hutchinson, S. J. (1973). MA Thes., Univ. Texas.
Umeda, N. (1975). J. Acoust. Soc. Am., 58:434-445.

ACKNOWLEDGEMENTS

This research was supported by the Mailman Foundation and by a previous grant NSF-USDP GU-1598. It was conducted at the University of Miami's Mailman Center for Child Development and in the Linguistics Laboratory of the University of Texas at Austin. The author would like to express gratitude for comments and assistance to Peter MacNeilage, Orvokki Heinämäki and Rebecca Eilers.

Table 1. Sentences for Spanish study two.

1. Mi papa tiene mil ojos.
2. Si lo pides al papa, te dirá que no.
3. Son para mi papá, tus hermanos, y los vecinos.
4. Mi papá tiene does ojos.
5. Si lo pides a papá, te dirá que sí.
6. Es para la papa, tu zanahoria, y low melocotones.

Table 2. Ratios of final and non-final vowel durations in Cuban Spanish.

Position of Words	Conservative Segmentation Criterion		Liberal Segmentation Criterion	
	Mean Ratio	SD Sub-jects	Mean Ratio	SD Sub-jects
A. Stressed Vowels				
Utterance-final	1.20	.10	1.30	.19
List-item-final	1.26	.34	1.29	.32
Clause-final	1.17	.23	1.19	.20
Minor-constituent-final	1.05	.17	1.03	.16
B. Unstressed Vowels				
Utterance-final	1.03	.23	1.36	.22
List-item-final	1.24	.27	1.24	.27
Clause-final	1.17	.07	1.16	.09
Minor-constituent-final	1.25	.13	1.23	.10

Table 3.   Sentences for English study one.

1.	Q.	Are these the questions he didn't answer?
	A.	These are the questions he didn't <u>understand</u>.
2.	Q.	Are these the symbols that were standardized?
	A.	These are the <u>numbers</u> that were standardized.
3.	Q.	If he can understand, how will it make you feel?
	A.	If he can understand, it will make me <u>happy</u>.
4.	Q.	He didn't understand a single answer, did he?
	A.	He didn't understand a single <u>question</u>.
5.	Q.	Are these the answers he didn't understand?
	A.	These are the <u>questions</u> he didn't understand.
6.	Q.	If they were differentiated, it would be easy, wouldn't it?
	A.	If they were <u>standardized</u>, it would be easy.
7.	Q.	If he can remember, will it make you happy?
	A.	If he can <u>understand</u>, it will make me happy.
8.	Q.	Are these the numbers that were derived?
	A.	These are the numbers that were <u>standardized</u>.
9.	Q.	If they were standardized, it would be hard, wouldn't it?
	A.	If they were standardized, it would be <u>easy</u>.
10.	Q.	Were they differentiated in every respect?
	A.	They were <u>standardized</u> in every respect.
11.	Q.	He didn't answer a single question, did he?
	A.	He didn't <u>understand</u> a single question.
12.	Q.	Were they standardized in some respects?
	A.	They were <u>standardized in every</u> respect.

Table 4. Stressed vowel durations in English words "under-
          stand" and "standardized."

Position of Word	Final Syllable Duration	Non-Final Syllable Duration	Difference	Ratio
A. Words Bearing Contrastive Stress				
Utterance-final	238	130	108	1.83
Clause-internal	210	129	81	1.63
Phrase-internal	182	130	52	1.40
B. Words Not Bearing Contrastive Stress				
Utterance-final	181	113	68	1.60
Clause-final	175	126	49	1.39
Phrase-internal	113	106	7	1.07

Table 5. Duration of /ow/ in "telephone" and "phonation."

Position of Word	Final Vowel Duration	Non-Final Vowel Duration	Difference	Ratio
A. Contrastive Stress				
Utterance-final	132	71	61	1.86
Clause-final	108	72	36	1.50
Phrase-internal	113	81	36	1.39
B. No Contrastive Stress				
Utterance-final	141	64	77	2.20
Clause-final	117	79	38	1.48
Phrase-internal	83	73	10	1.14

Table 6.   Duration of /aj/ in "parasite" and "citation."

Position of Word	Final Position Duration	Non-Final Vowel Duration	Difference	Ratio
A. Contrastive Stress				
Utterance-final	170	113	57	1.50
Clause-final	141	113	28	1.25
Phrase-internal	135	105	30	1.29
B. No Contrastive Stress				
Utterance-final	145	113	32	1.28
Clause-final	140	114	29	1.26
Phrase-internal	117	104	13	1.12

Table 7.   Vowel Durations in Milliseconds.

Position of Word	Final-Vowel Duration	Medial-Vowel Duration	Difference	Ratio
Utterance-final	93	87	6	1.07
Phrase-final	93	88	5	1.06
Phrase-internal	91	85	6	1.07

Table 8.   Final, penultimate, and medial consonant durations.

Position-of-Word	Final Consonant Durations	Penultimate Consonant Durations	Medial Consonant Durations	Ratio Final to Medial	Ratio Penultimate to Medial
Utterance-final	115	67	57	2.02	1.20
Phrase-final	91	61	57	1.60	1.09
Phrase-internal	87	61	57	1.53	1.09

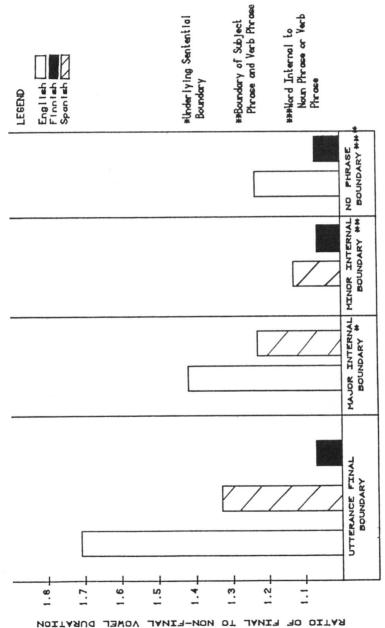

FIGURE: Final Vowel Lengthening in Three Languages

LE REGISTRE MELODIQUE DE L'ATTAQUE DANS UN
PARLER FRANCO-ONTARIEN

YVETTE SZMIDT
York University

Parmi les syllabes constitutives de la phrase française qui ont apparues importantes pour l'analyse des traits pertinents de la prosodie, l'attaque (ou première syllabe prononcée) semble avoir un certain rôle à jouer dans le décodage des divers types intonatifs--voir en particulier les travaux de Pierre Delattre (1966, 1967, 1969), de Denis Autesserre et Albert Di Cristo (1972), de Renée Baligand et Eric James (1973), et de Pierre R. Léon (1975). Dans cette recherche nous avons tenté, de notre côté, de dégager le registre mélodique de l'attaque dans les questions totales d'un parler franco-canadien afin de déterminer si l'attaque dans ces énoncés interrogatifs débute au même niveau que le fondamental usuel de la voix des phrases énonciatives (F_O), interrogatives (F_{INT}), ou si, au contraire, elle se place à un niveau entièrement différent.

CARACTERISTIQUES DES INFORMATEURS

Nos dix sujets franco-canadiens sont nés entre 1911 et 1943 a Lafontaine, en Ontario. Ils ont tous fait des études secondaires et cinq d'entre eux (A,B,C,F,I) des études universitaires. Ces derniers sont instituteurs dans une école bilingue. Quant aux autres informateurs, G,D, et E sont mères de famille, J est gérant d'une coopérative agricole, et H est fermier. Ils parlent tous francais à la maison et sur leur lieu de travail. Leurs familles ont habité la région depuis cent trente ans.

MATERIAUX LINGUISTIQUES

Nous avons extrait, de sept conversations spontanées, deux cents énoncés interrogatifs appartenant à la catégorie des questions dites "totales," c'est-à-dire celles qui appellent une réponse du type "oui," "non," "peut-être." Dans ce type d'énoncé, la fonction interrogative peut être assumée: (1) par la mélodie (question mélodique : "Il est marié?" ou question <u>fragmentaire</u> : "Marié?"); (2) par la structure syntaxique (question <u>inversive</u> : "Est-il marié?"); (3) par l'adjonction d'un morphème interrogatif placé, soit à l'initiale (question <u>locutive</u> : "Est-ce qu'il est marié?"), soit à la finale (question <u>adjonctive</u> : "Il est marié, hein?"). Nous avons examiné le fonctionnement mélodique de l'attaque dans ces cinq formes de questions totales.

METHODE DE RECHERCHE

Nous avons enregistré, à l'analyseur de mélodie du laboratoire de phonétique expérimentale de l'Université de Toronto, toutes les questions totales de ce corpus. Ainsi, pour chacun des locuteurs, nous avons pu mesurer la fréquence du fondamental (en hertz) des syllabes initiales de toutes ses phrases interrogatives et calculer leur moyenne, tant pour l'ensemble des phrases que pour chaque type de question totale.

Dans une deuxième étape, nous avons dégagé les niveaux mélodiques de l'attaque (normalisés par rapport à F_O),suivant les diverses formes syntaxiques de l'interrogation totale, en calculant la valeur de DIFF, pour chaque sujet, selon les formules suivantes:

(i) attaque par rapport à F_O (ii) attaque par rapport à F_{INT}

$$\text{DIFF} = \frac{F_X - F_O}{F_O} \times 100\% \qquad \text{DIFF} = \frac{F_X - F_{INT}}{F_O} \times 100\%$$

où:

F_X : est la valeur de fréquence (en Hz) selon que nous considérons F_{ATT}[1] ou f_{att}[2]

F_O : est la fréquence du fondamental usuel de la voix dans les phrases déclaratives[3] (en Hz)

F_{INT} : est la fréquence du niveau usuel de la voix caractéristique aux énoncés interrogatifs[4] (en Hz)

En outre, nous avons établi la moyenne (M) et l'écart-
type / σ / des données chiffrées de DIFF afin d'obtenir les
valeurs de /M - σ / et /M + σ/. Ces dernières permettent la
délimitation de l'aire de dispersion ou "zone" de variation
des résultats obtenus. Nous en avons étudié les modalités
selon qu'elles dépendent de la structure syntaxique de
l'interrogation totale ou du groupe de locuteurs (femmes
ou hommes). Les tableaux 1 et 2 et les figures 1, 2 et 3
présentent les résultats de ces calculs chez chaque locuteur,
dans le corpus global et pour chaque type de question.

RESULTATS

Niveau d'attaque dans l'énoncé
interrogatif (corpus global)

Le dépouillement des résultats (tableau 1) montre que
l'attaque interrogative se réalise à un niveau plus élevé
que le fondamental usuel de la voix (F_O). La hauteur
mélodique des syllabes initiales dans les questions totales
se situe, en moyenne, à 19% (3.0 demi-tons) au-dessus de F_O.
On voit des tendances similaires pour les voix masculines et
féminines--chaque locuteur ou locutrice commence ses phrases
interrogatives à un niveau qui est, en moyenne, supérieur à
celui de F_O (figure 3). De plus, l'analyse des données
chiffrées démontre que les syllabes initiales dans le parler
des hommes et des femmes se répartissent d'une manière plus ou
moins semblable dans ces deux groupes de locuteurs--de 10%
à 23%, et entre 10% et 30%, respectivement. (C.-à-d., M =
16.7%, σ = 6.5% pour les hommes, et M = 19.6%, σ = 10% pour
les femmes).

D'un autre côté, si on envisage l'attaque de l'interrogation totale par rapport à F_{INT}, on constate que ces énoncés
débutent également à un niveau plus élevé: M = 6% (σ = 7%).
Observons que le niveau habituel de la voix caractéristique
aux questions totales (F_{INT}) est distinct de F_O et se situe
à un niveau supérieur à ce dernier chez tous les informateurs
(tableaux 1 et 2, et fig. 3). En effet, lors d'une étude
récente,[5] nous avons démontré que les valeurs de F_{INT}, pour
l'ensemble des sujets, se regroupent entre 6% et 20% (1.0 et
3.2 demi-tons) au dessus de F_O, c.-à-d., M = 13%, σ = 7%.

Il est intéressant de constater que non seulement tous
les sujets prononcent leurs syllabes initiales a un niveau
bien plus élevé que F_O, mais dans 8 cas sur 10 ce niveau est
également plus haut que celui de F_{INT}.

On remarque enfin que les syllabes initiales de
l'interrogation totale tendent à se répartir dans une zone
relativement étroite de 10% à 28% (1.7 à 4.3 demi-tons) par
rapport à F_O et de -1% à + 13% (-0.2 à + 2.1 demi-tons) en
comparaison avec F_{INT} (figures 1 et 2--"corpus global").

Niveau d'attaque dans les cinq formes syntaxiques de
l'interrogation totale. Cette deuxième partie de notre
recherche met en évidence le fait que l'attaque dans chacune
de ces formes interrogatives s'actualise à un niveau moyen,
supérieur au fondamental usuel de la voix (F_O). Ainsi, pour
l'ensemble des sujets, l'attaque des questions totales se
place nettement au-dessus de F_O, en moyenne à 22% (3.5 demi-
tons) pour les questions "fragmentaires" et "locutives";
à 18% (2.9 demi-tons) pour les interrogations "mélodiques" et
"adjonctives"; et à 13% (2.1 demi-tons) pour les questions
"inversives."

D'autre part, lorsque nous dégageons le niveau mélodique
de l'attaque de chaque type de question et le comparons au
niveau habituel de la voix caractéristique à l'interrogation
totale (F_{INT}) nous voyons que les questions suivant l'ordre
syntaxique: Sujet + Verbe commencent au-dessus de F_{INT}
("locutives": M = 10%; "fragmentaires": M = 8%; "mélodiques":
M = 5%, et "adjonctives": M = 4%). En revanche, si on examine
le répartition des syllabes initiales dans les questions de
type: Verbe + Sujet (questions "inversives") on remarque
qu'elles s'actualisent légèrement au-dessous de F_{INT} (M = -1%)
On ne peut pas accorder une grande importance à ce résultat,
étant donné le grand écart-type (σ = 15%) et le peu de
questions inversives relevées dans ce corpus (6% du nombre
total). Il est à noter, néanmoins, que parmi les quatre
sujets chez qui on retrouve ce type de question, trois
énoncent leurs syllabes initiales à un niveau en général
inférieur à F_{INT} (A: -8%, D et H: -9%).

L'examen des syllabes initiales dans les questions non-
marquées grammaticalement ("mélodiques" et "fragmentaires")

démontre que les niveaux mélodiques de l'attaque recouvrent une zone qui s'étend respectivement de 9% à 27% et de 6% à 38% au-dessus de F_O. Par rapport à F_{INT}, ils ont tendance à se situer de -4% à + 14% et entre -3% et + 19%, respectivement.

Des résultats presque analogues peuvent être observés dans les <u>questions marquées par un morphème interrogatif</u> ("adjonctives" et "locutives"). Les syllabes initiales se regroupent dans une zone de 8% à 28% et de 7% à 37% respectivement, au-dessus de F_O. Elles se réalisent dans une zone limitée par -7% et+15%, et de -3% à + 23% respectivement, en comparison au niveau de F_{INT}. Quant au niveau des <u>questions marquées syntaxiquement</u> ("Inversives") le registre des syllabes initiales s'étend de 1% à 25% au-dessus de F_O, et entre -16% et +14% par rapport à F_{INT}. Il est intéressant de noter que les valeurs des <u>moyennes</u> montrent qu'il existe des différences parmi les cinq types de questions totales, mais leurs "zones" respectives, qui regroupent les variations mélodiques des syllabes initiales, semblent similaires. Ainsi, le chevauche- ment des "zones" nous amène à conclure que le registre mélodique de l'attaque dans les diverses formes syntaxiques de l'interrogation totale ne permet pas de distinguer nettement une forme interrogative d'une autre (figures 1 et 2).

CONCLUSION

Pour terminer cette étude,fondée sur l'analyse d'un corpus spontané de franco-ontarien, il nous reste à évoquer le fait que cette enquête a mis en évidence une certaine instabilité dans les réalisations individuelles à l'initiale des énoncés interrogatifs. En effet, les questions totales commencent rarement au même niveau chez un même locuteur et varient d'un sujet à l'autre (rappelons que nous avons opéré une normalisa- tion fréquentielle des résultats). Chaque informateur semble donc avoir son <u>propre registre d'attaque</u>. Il suffier,pour s'en rendre compte, d'examiner les tableaux 1 et 2 et la figure 3.

Ces résultats paraissent confirmer, ainsi que l'observent Baligand et James (1973), qu'il existe, ". . .en français canadien, une instabilité 'normale' de la hauteur mélodique de l'attaque" (p.138). L'accord des informateurs se manifeste,

toutefois, dans la tendance à réaliser les syllabes initiales
des énoncés interrogatifs à un niveau plus élevé que F_O
et, dans la majorité des cas, que F_{INT}.

Enfin, l'examen de l'ensemble des résultats de cette
analyse instrumentale nous conduit à formuler la conclusion
suivante. L'attaque de l'interrogation totale ne commence
pas au niveau 2 (ou "registre medium"[6] ou F_O) comme le
suggérait Delattre (1966, p. 4) mais se réalise à un niveau
supérieur à ce dernier (M = 19%), ainsi que l'a illustré
Monique Léon (1964, pp. 10-12 et p. 19) dans un ouvrage
pédagogique. La syllabe initiale des questions totales est
marque d'un sommet mélodique qui apparaît chez tous nos sujets
non seulement plus haut que le niveau du fondamental usuel
de la voix des énoncés déclaratifs mais probablement aussi
de celui des phrases interrogatives.

REFERENCES

Autesserre, D. et Di Cristo, A.   (1972).   Actes VII Cong. Int.
    Phon., 842-859.
Baligand, R. et James, E.   (1973).   Stud. Phon. 8, 123-167.
Delattre, P.   (1966).   French Rev., 40(1):1-14.
Delattre, P.   (1967).   French Rev., 4(3):326-339.
Delattre, P.   (1969).   Le fran. dans le monde, 64:6-13.
Faure, G.   (1970).   Stud. Phon. 3, 93-108.
Léon, M.   (1964).   Hachette/Larousse, Paris.
Léon, P. R.   (1975).   Phon. Soc. Japan, 253-280.
Szmidt, Y.   (à paraître).   Stud. Phon. Hommages a Georges
    Faure. Didier, Montreal, Paris et Bruxelles.

FOOTNOTES

[1]F_{ATT}: fréquence moyenne des syllabes initiales pour
l'ensemble du corpus.
[2]f_{att}: fréquence moyenne des syllabes initiales dans
chaque type de questions totales.
[3]F_O : moyenne des fréquences des syllabes inaccentuées
des phrases déclaratives, a l'exception des syllabes
initiales et prétoniques.
[4]F_{INT}: moyenne des fréquences des syllabes inaccentuées des énoncés interrogatifs a l'exception des syllabes

initiales et prétoniques. (F_{INT} a été calculé pour chaque sujet).

[5]Voir a ce sujet, SZMIDT, Y. "Niveaux de voix caractéristiques aux questions totales" (à paraître).

[6]Si l'on peut emprunter ce terme a Georges Faure (1970).

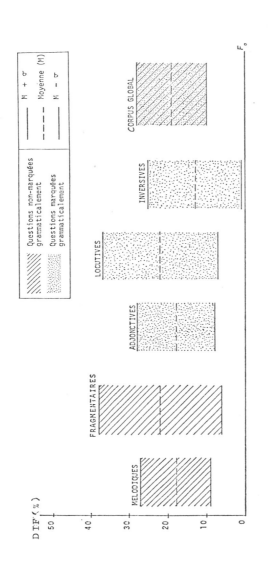

FIGURE I Registre mélodique de l'attaque dans les questions totales par rapport à F_o (valeurs normalisées)

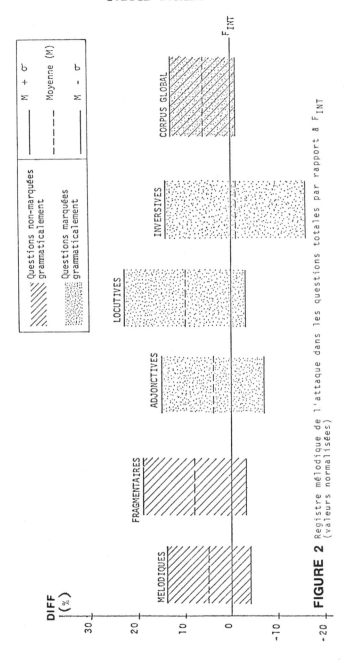

FIGURE 2 Registre mélodique de l'attaque dans les questions totales par rapport à F_{INT} (valeurs normalisées)

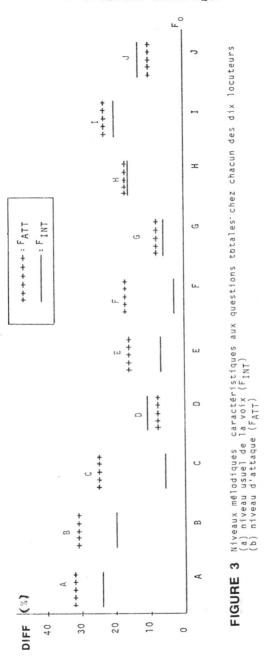

FIGURE 3 Niveaux mélodiques caractéristiques aux questions totales chez chacun des dix locuteurs
(a) niveau usuel de la voix (F_{INT})
(b) niveau d'attaque (F_{ATT})

Sujet	F_0 (Hz)	MELODIQUE f_{att} (Hz)	DIFF (%)	FRAGMENTAIRE f_{att} (Hz)	DIFF (%)	ADJONCTIVE f_{att} (Hz)	DIFF (%)	LOCUTIVE f_{att} (Hz)	DIFF (%)	INVERSIVE f_{att} (Hz)	DIFF (%)	TOUTES LES QUESTIONS F_{ATT} (Hz)	DIFF (%)
QUESTIONS TOTALES													
Voix fém.													
A	180	244	36	236	31	235	31	232	29	210	17	238	32
B	162	210	30	212	31	210	30	220	36	—	—	212	31
C	219	252	15	230	5	250	14	298	36	—	—	273	25
D	175	208	19	195	11	187	7	—	—	178	2	189	8
E	140	163	16	—	—	160	14	150	7	180	29	162	16
F	203	244	20	—	—	250	23	218	7	—	—	237	17
G	160	175	9	170	6	—	—	—	—	—	—	172	8
Voix masc.													
H	89	104	17	110	23	100	12	95	7	95	7	104	17
I	99	105	6	148	49	102	3	—	—	—	—	122	23
J	89	101	12	—	—	113	27	120	35	—	—	98	10
Moyenne: (M) (%)			18		22		18		22		13		19
Ecart-type: (σ) (%)			9		16		10		15		12		9

Tableau 1 : -Différences de hauteur mélodique entre le fondamental usuel de la voix (F_0) et :
(a) l'attaque des questions totales (F_{ATT})
(b) l'attaque dans les diverses formes syntaxiques des questions totales (f_{att})
-Valeurs de DIFF normalisées par rapport à F_0.

	F_{INT}	QUESTIONS TOTALES										
		MELODIQUE		FRAGMENTAIRE		ADJONCTIVE		LOCUTIVE		INVERSIVE		TOUTES LES QUESTIONS
Sujet	(Hz)	f_{att} (Hz)	DIFF (%)	f_{att} (Hz)	DIFF (%)	f_{att} (Hz)	DIFF (%)	f_{att} (Hz)	DIFF (%)	f_{att} (Hz)	DIFF (%)	F_{ATT} (Hz)	DIFF (%)

Sujet		F_{INT} (Hz)	MELODIQUE f_{att} (Hz)	DIFF (%)	FRAGMENTAIRE f_{att} (Hz)	DIFF (%)	ADJONCTIVE f_{att} (Hz)	DIFF (%)	LOCUTIVE f_{att} (Hz)	DIFF (%)	INVERSIVE f_{att} (Hz)	DIFF (%)	TOUTES LES QUESTIONS F_{ATT} (Hz)	DIFF (%)
Voix fém.	A	224	244	11	236	6	235	6	232	4	210	-8	238	8
	B	194	210	10	212	11	210	10	220	16	—	—	212	11
	C	232	252	9	230	-0.9	250	8	298	30	—	—	273	19
	D	194	208	8	195	0.6	187	-4	—	—	178	-9	189	-3
	E	150	163	9	—	—	160	7	150	0	180	21	162	9
	F	209	244	17	—	—	250	20	218	4	—	—	237	14
	G	170	175	3	170	0	—	—	—	—	—	—	172	1
Voix masc.	H	103	104	1	110	8	100	-3	95	-9	95	-9	104	1
	I	119	105	-14	148	29	102	-17	—	—	—	—	122	3
	J	101	101	0	—	—	113	13	120	21	—	—	98	-3
Moyenne: (M) (%)				5		8		4		10		-1		6
Ecart-type: (σ) (%)				9		11		11		13		15		7

Tableau 2 : Différences de hauteur mélodique entre le niveau usuel de la voix caractéristique à l'interrogation totale (F_{INT}) et :
(a) l'attaque des questions totales (F_{ATT})
(b) l'attaque dans les diverses formes syntaxiques des questions totales (f_{att})
-Valeurs de DIFF normalisées par rapport à F_o

"MELODIE-LANGAGE" DES CHORALS DE JEAN SEBASTIEN BACH

ANNE-MARIE FERRAND-VIDAL
Paris

Nous observerons le plan suivant: (I) La langue parlée est avant tout une mélodie. (II) Le Choral de Bach est un langage. (III) Le Choral de Bach pour la Thérapie mélodique du langage. Le Langage oral est une combinatoire de deux structures : une structure mélodique S I et une structure signifiante (S 2). S.1. est chronologiquement la première et toujours préservée, même dans les cas les plus graves de pathologie du Langage (aphasie, autisme, psychose-traumatique ....).

La langue parlée est avant tout une prosodie. Par prosodie nous entendons les pauses, les accents, les tons et l'intonation ou scheme mélodique (La prosodie varie d'une langue a l'autre bien sûr). Insistons sur le fait que notre communication première se fait au moyen de l'intonation. Il n'est qu'à observer les jeunes enfants en période pré-linguistique et nous nous apercevrons, apprès une écoute attentive que leurs "modulations" sont signifiantes (il ne leur manque que les mots). Langage oral = S.2 (mots signifiants); S.I(mélodie). Il est donc possible de transcrire une phrase, en tenant compte de $S._I + S._2$. Cette transcription sera très utile pour la méthode de Thérapie mélodique du Langage que nous examinerons brièvement à la fin de cet exposé.

Si le langage oral est avant tout une mélodie, la musique ellemême peut être considérée dans bien des cas comme le SI de la langue parlée. Notons aussi que: pause, accent, ton sont également des termes musicaux. Puisque la langue parlée

est avant tout une mélodie, prenons un des meilleurs exemples
de mélodie langage "qui nous est donné, à savoir les Chorals
de Jean-Sébastien BACH et voyons pourquoi il est possible de
parler de "Mélodie-Langage" pour ces Chorals. Les Chorals
de BACH ne s'expliquent qu'en fonction du texte sur lequel ils
sont bâtis. Ce n'est pas en vain que BACH, au témoignage
de son élève ZIEGLER, enseignait qu'accompagner un Choral ou
improviser à son sujet, n'était pas seulement appliquer des
règles d'harmonie ou des procédés de composition, mais surtout
pénétrer l'esprit du texte et s'appliquer à le traduire de
son mieux (Cf. Les Chorals pour orgue de Jean-Sébastien BACH
"par Jacques Chaillet, Professeur d'Histoire de la Musique à
la Sorbonne et Directeur de la Schola Cantorum).

   Qu'est-ce qu'un Choral? En soi, l'expression "un Choral"
n'a aucun sens. Le mot n'est qu'une abréviation imposée par
la paresse de l'usage. Il représente tout aussi bien le
CHORALLIED ou CANTIQUE d'ASSEMBLEE QUE LE CHORAL VORSPIEL ou
PRELUDE d'ORGUE préparant l'exécution de ce cantique, ou encore
la CHORALFASSUNG qui désigne l'utilisation de ce répertoire de
cantiques dans un morceau quelconque, vocal ou instrumental.
Jusqu'au XIX-siècle, "choral"-adjectif abusivement substantivé--
est un mot passe-partout qui désigne à la fois le cantique
d'assemblée des églises luthériennes(et à la rigueur anglicanes)
et tout ce qui touche à l'utilisation de ce cantique, y compris
et principalement les morceaux d'orgue bâtis autour de ce
répertoire. Ces derniers ont un double but: - ou bien préluder
à l'exécution du cantique,- ou bien donner un sens liturgique à
des morceaux libres en les rattachant, par allusion musicale
aux paroles sous-entendues connues de tous, aux sentiments de
la fête du jour. On voit que dans tout ceci, l'élément commun
est exclusivement le répertoire, donc d'ordre beaucoup plus
culturel que musical. La musique y est un support du texte
et la mélodie construite par Jean-Sébastien BACH n'est pas un
choix gratuit puisqu'elle "colle" au cantique en question.

   Le Choral de BACH n'est nullement une forme musicale, mais
un genre, doté d'un esprit particulier et faisant appel aux
formes les plus différentes, don't les unes lui sont propres
et les autres non. Mais pourquoi le Choral se présente à nous
sous des aspects aussi divers ? C'est originellement le
cantique d'assemblée, et d'une assemblée de langue et de

culture germaniques - d'où son style propre de scansion syllabique, coupée d'arrêts en fin de phrase que l'on notera par
des points d'orgue sans que ceux-ci aient forcément le sens
solfégique qu'ils ont pris dans la théorie. Ce point d'orgue
est la pause du langage oral, le point de l'écriture. Ce cantique, l'organiste l'accompagne, sans autre but ni obligation
que de soutenir le chant, d'où le choral harmonisé syllabique,
restant monodique dans l'assistance. Si la paroisse comporte
une maîtrise, celle-ci soutiendra ou représentera l'assemblée,
en chantant de la même manière qu'elle, mais la monodie chantée
se fera polyphonie vocale, et ce qui se jouait à l'orgue se
repartira tout aussi bien aux voix: le choral harmonisé, sans
changer de nature, est devenu choral vocal, parfois avec la
même graphie. Le choral, quel que soit son mode d'expression,
organistique, vocal ou orchestral, n'est pas de la musique
pure. C'est avant tout une musique religieuse, liée à sa
fonction liturgique. Il a pour but de communiquer un message.
Le point d'orgue n'est-il pas le point d'une phrase ou la
pause du Langage oral! Et cette scansion syllabique ne symbo-
lise-t-elle pas le schème mélodique? Le Choral de BACH est
donc une "mélodie-langage" dans la mesure où il communique un
message (essentiellement liturgique) et ou les mots sont in-
timement imbriqués au rythme scandé de la musique,ce qui correspond au rythme et à l'intonation de la langue allemande.

     Illustrons cette théorie par de brefs exemples. Choral
paraphasé (Les parties accompagnantes au lieu de posséder leurs
thèmes propres'empruntent leur développement au cantique
lui-même, le plus souvent à son incipit). Transcrit par Jean-
Sébastien BACH pour le Lundi de Pâques. Le texte, inspiré de
l'épisode des Disciples d'Emmaus, Evangile du Lundi de Pâques,
paraphrase dans la bouche du chrétien la parole des disciples
à Jésus ressuscité qu'ils n'avaient pas reconnu, lorsqu'il eut
cheminé quelque temps avec eux en conversant= Mane nobiscum,
Domine (reste avec nous,).

     CHORAL CONTINU COMMENTÉ: Le cantique, orné ou non, est
exposé d'un bout à l'autre à l'une des voix - souvent au so-
prano - tandis que les autres développent un ou plusieurs thèmes
differents qui sont tres souvent le commentaire descriptif des
idées évoquées par le texte. Cette forme caracterise principale
ment l'Orgelbuchlein, don't elle affecte 38 chorals sur 4 5.

Celui-ci est l'avant-dernier choral de l'ORGELBUCHLEIR, où
il forme comme un prologue au choral final sur la brièveté
de la vie. Une image traverse en gros tout le commentaite
une figure brève, couple de silences, qui tombent à inter-
valles réguliers comme la faux du moissonneur. Mais cette
mort n'est que la renaissance à une nouvelle vie, la faux
n'est pas encore retirée que déjà la plante se relève pleine
de force vitale.

Flétrissure et corruption; nous les devinons à travers
ces harmonies qui nous glacent, et dont la fausse relation
do-dièse do bécarre de la dernière mesure est l'exemple
le plus voyant. Mais pourquoi cette insistance sur les
tierces - sixtes parallèles, indiquant l'importance que
BACH a attachée à une idée d'union, d'assimilation ? Sans
doute estce ce rapprochement intime, indissoluble, entre
la mort et la nouvelle vie, qui fait que l'une est inexpli-
cable sans l'autre, et que, comme le dit le texte d'après
Saint Paul et tous les ésotéristes, la mort est la condition
nécessaire sans laquelle le chretien ne pourrait renaître à
la vie éternelle. Une fois de plus, la musique de BACH est
une véritable prédication.

En conclusion, nous constaterons que: (1) Si le langage
oral est avant tout une mélodie, (2) Si le choral de BACH
est une mélodie-langage, (3) Les chorals de BACH peuvent avoir
une application directe dans la "Thérapie mélodique du Langage'
qui consiste à construire des phrases items sur une mélodie se
rapprochant le plus possible de la prosodie de la langue.
Cette nouvelle forme de Thérapie s'appuie sur la structure S.I
du Langage oral et nous offre un moyen efficace et plus rapide
de rééducation du Langage pour les cas graves de pathologie,
tels que l'Aphasie, la Psychose traumatique, et l'Autisme...
(etc....). Bien que les chorals de BACH aient été créés par
un musicien de langue germanique, il est à remarquer que
certaines formes conviennent également très bien à la prosodie
française. Cette remarque peut s'appliquer également aux chants
grégoriens. C'est pourquoi notre équipe de Musicologues de la
Sorbonne et moi-mê-me faisons des Recherches sur ce point.

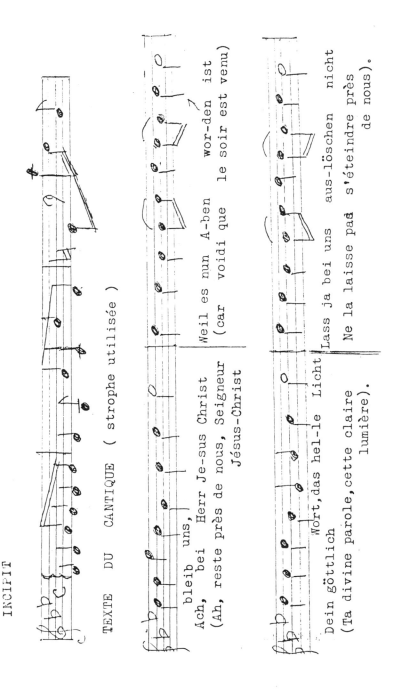

"ACH, BLEIB BEI UNS"
(Schübler No. 5)

INCIPIT

TEXTE DU CANTIQUE (strophe utilisée)

Ach, bleib uns, bei Herr Je-sus Christ
(Ah, reste près de nous, Seigneur Jésus-Christ

Weil es nun A-ben wor-den ist
(car voidi que le soir est venu)

Dein göttlich Wort, das hel-le Licht Lass ja bei uns aus-löschen nicht
(Ta divine parole, cette claire lumière). Ne la laisse pas s'éteindre près de nous).

"ALLE MENSCHEN MÜSSEN STERBEN"
(Orgelbüchlein No. 44)

TEXTE DU CANTIQUE

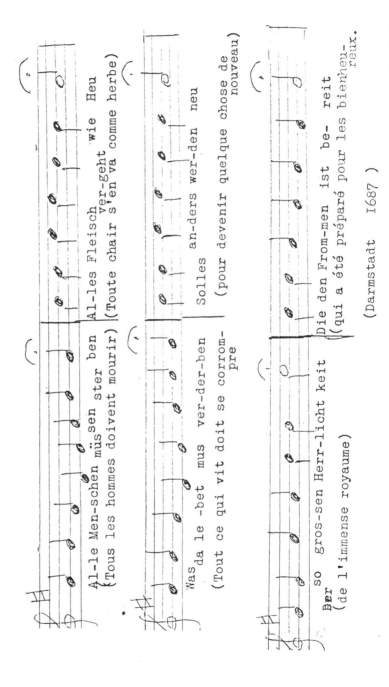

Al-le Men-schen müs sen ster ben
(Tous les hommes doivent mourir)
Al-les Fleisch ver-geht wie Heu
(Toute chair s'en va comme herbe)

Was da le -bet mus ver-der-ben
(Tout ce qui vit doit se corrom-
pre)
Solles an-ders wer-den neu
(pour devenir quelque chose de
nouveau)

Der so gros-sen Herr-lich keit
(de l'immense royaume)
Die den From-men ist be- reit
(qui a été préparé pour les bienheu-
reux.

(Darmstadt 1687)

TEMPORAL CUES IN FRENCH INTERVOCALIC STOPS

MAX WAJSKOP
Institut de Phonetique, Université Libre de Bruxelles

Since the capital study by Lisker and Abramson (1964),
investigation into the voicing dimension has seen considerable growth at all levels of phonetic research. The quasi
universal nature of this opposition, the dichotomy which it
allows across almost the entire range of consonant categories together with the fact that it convincingly illustrates the role of distinctive features in linguistic
analysis has obviously accounted for this preferential
treatment. The debate has been periodically enlivened by
the many suggestions aiming to substitute the fortislenis
opposition for the voiced-unvoiced distinction. The value
of Lisker and Abramson's work lies in the importance given
to VOT as the major cue for the articulatory and acoustic
separability of the class of plosives in several languages, at
least in initial position.

If the publications devoted to this problem are numerous,
they are chiefly of a perceptual and physiological nature.
On the other hand, in-depth descriptive studies are very
small in number. This is even more to be regretted since
the voicing opposition is supported by a large number of cues
which tend to be neglected in favour of VOT alone. Furthermore, most of the perceptual studies have used synthetic
stimuli based on manipulations of this cue. As we don't have
precise data for French, this study was undertaken to describe
the temporal relationships between voiced and voiceless intervocalic stops in function of symetrical vocalic contexts, and

under different conditions˙of stress.

PROCEDURES

Subjects

In order to eliminate sources of heterogeneity as much
as possible the choice of subjects was determined by a series
of factors: (a) age: between 20 and 30, (b) sex: male,
(c) dialect origin: French speakers from the Brussels area
whose parents were also French speakers who had lived in the
area since early childhood, and (d) socio-cultural origins:
subjects were university people whose families belong to the
middle class (teachers, civil servants or liberal profes-
sions).

From the 40 subjects selected on the basis of a sociolinguistic questionnaire distributed amongst 150 potential
candidates, 10 were retained for the purpose of the experiment. This kind of selection was made in order to avoid
unnecessary dispersal of the results. For it has recently
been noted that far too many earlier descriptions (1) tended
to mix speakers with highly varied sociolinguistic backgrounds.

Stimuli

The utterances consisted of six French plosives /p, t, k/
and /b, d, g/ inserted into a symetrical vocalic context
using the three vowels /i, a, u/ and presented under three
different conditions: (a) "VCV" isolated; (b) the logoteme
is inserted into the sequence "Dites VCV," i.e. in accentuated
position /dit a'ka/ (-VCV) and (c) the logoteme was inserted
into the sequence "Dites VCV pour moi," i.e., in unstressed
position /dit aka pur'mwa/ (-VCV-).

Measurements

For each VCV sequence, four measures were taken: (a)
length of V_1, (b) length of V_2, (c) length of consonant occlusion, and (d) the length of the burst: the interval between
the release of the consonant and the appearance of the first

regular laryngeal vibrations (2).

The segmentation criteria were based on principles
established in several earlier studies, notably those by
Fant (1960), Peterson and Lehiste (1960) and M. Naeser (1970).
The burst is measured from the wide band impulsion terminating
closure which is not synchronous with the laryngeal impulses
that follow. Most of the measures were taken with the help
of the Oscillominck Siemens, notably for all the sequences
consisting of voiceless plosives. Most of these presented
no major problems. Certain sequences required the addition
of spectographic analysis and visualisation on a storage
oscilloscope.

RESULTS

The raw results confirm and render more precise certain
tendencies which are already well established: (a) the
initial vowel is reduced before unvoiced consonants. Over
the whole set of conditions, the average for this reduction
is 10 msec. (71 msec. as opposed to 81 msec.), (b) the temporal difference between voiced and unvoiced closure may
reach 40 msec. (86 msec. as opposed to 124 msec.) for isolated logotemes but is reduced to 13 msec. (62 msec. as
opposed to 75 msec.) in unaccented position -VCV- and (c)
Average length of Burst for voiceless consonants is 30 msec.
whereas that for voiced consonants is 10 msec. The general
tendencies of temporal behavior for the four parameters
studied appear in Figures 1 to 4. The configurations reveal
important contextual variations.

The initial vowel (VI - Figure 1)

From the isolated logoteme to the unstressed logoteme
embedded into a sentence the difference of length between the
voiced and the unvoiced group decreases on the average from
15 msec. to 10 msec. with a reduction in absolute values
which reflects the influence of the accent. These values
(table 1) are less than those noted for French by Chen (1970)
but maintain almost identical ratios. It should also be
noted that VI lengthens in function of its degree of aperture
(Fischer-Jorgensen, 1964). However, this is not valid to

the same extent in all cases. The degree of vocalic aperture
intervenes chiefly for non-isolated logotemes.

If the hypothesis remains plausible of a motor command
of vowel lengthening before voiced consonant (Raphael, 1975)
independent of the place of articulation of the consonant in
spite of the effect of coarticulation (the movement of closing operating more rapidly at the lips than at the velum)
it is none the less true that the point of vocalic articulation and aperture upset this command and prevent the detection of a clear tendency.

Closure (Figure 2)

(a) Isolated logotemes: VCV. For isolated logotemes,
the temporal difference between voiceless and voiced Closure
is about 40 msec. Further, it is noted that Closure shortens
with the draw back of the place of articulation of the consonant. In the case of voiceless consonants, length of
Closure may also vary as a function of the vocalic environment. The closed vowels /i/ and /u/ reduce the Closure of
/k/ to 111 msec. for corresponding average values of 124 and
127 msec.

If we compare the contextual variations (the place of
articulation of consonant and vowel) of Closure and of VI
within each class (voiced or unvoiced) it can be seen that
the two types of modification are mirror images (Figs. 1
and 2). Inside each class, the duration of one of the
parameters is in inverse proportion to the duration of the
other. If the total is made of the duration of VI and of
Closure, two relatively stable values are obtained: voiced:
205 msec. and unvoiced: 183 msec. (difference: 22 msec.),
indicating that the contextual variations of Closure follow
the same program of those of VI but where the difference
indicates that there is no strict temporal compensation
between the two modifications. In that case, lengthening
of Closure with unvoiced consonants would not depend entirely
on non-lengthening of the preceding vowel. On the contrary,
there would be a specific command of lengthening of Closure
of the unvoiced consonant which concurs with the palatographic observations of Fujimura (1975).

(b)   Logotemes in context: -VCV and -VCV-. The insertion of logotemes into a sentence and the stress clearly reduce the length of Closure but this reduction is mitigated by symetrical modifications of V 1. Desaccentuation and the embedding of the logoteme into a sequence consisting of a greater number of syllables (-VCV = 3 syllables; -VCV = 5 syllables) bring us nearer to the conditions to be encountered in continuous speech. Their effect is to somewhat destabilise the differences in duration between voiced and unvoiced consonants and, in the case of -VCV-, lead to a quasi temporal compensation.

It would be highly tempting to consider the sum of these two parameters as a good predictor of the nature of the consonant, voiced or unvoiced. In effect, of the 3 x 9 pairs of sequences, only two cases are to be noted /iki - igi/ and /upu - ubu/ in condition, -VCV- where this sum is slightly superior for the voiced consonant. However, we are here dealing only with mean differences in which the variance of the measures do not intervene. A more efficient predictor would be in the relationship Closure/Vowel 1 (Serniclaes, 1974) which shows even clearer tendencies. The relationship is in every case greater for the sequence vowel + unvoiced consonant and must contribute to some extent to the perception of the voicing opposition (Wajskop, 1974).

Burst (Figure 3)

(a) Isolated logotemes: VCV. Average BURST for voiceless stops for the totality of vocalic contexts and the three places of articulation is about 30 msec. as opposed to 10 msec. for the voiced cognates.

(i)   Contextual effects for unvoiced consonants. A lengthening of BURST is noted as a function of the moving back of the place of articulation: p   t   k (Lisker-Abramson, 1964) due to the difference of mobility between the articulators (Klatt, 1973). The relative slowness in moving the body of the tongue in relationship to that of the lips also slows down the decrease in pressure inside the oral cavity and thereby the introduction of a difference in transglottal pressure indispensable to laryngeal vibration. Moreover, lengthening

of BURST in closed vocalic contexts can be explained
by a decrease in the speed of escape of the flow of
air which in turn slows down the appearance of aerodynamic conditions necessary for voicing. The fact
that BURST in /ti/ and /pu/ is longer than in /tu/ and
/pi/ can be explained: (a) be the extreme anteriority
of the place of articulation of /i/ and the restriction
imposed on the displacement of the tip of the tongue
in the free space between the alveolars and the spread
lips; (b) by the antagonism between the closing of the
lips for /p/ and the protruding and rounding required
for /u/.

(ii) Voiced plosives. An average difference of
20 msec. has been noted between the two phonetic
categories. On the average, fluctuations in length are
considerably less important for voiced consonants.

(b) Non isolated logotemes: -VCV and -VCV-. When the
logotemes are embedded into sentences, stress or lack of
stress has little effect on the duration of the BURST which
in this respect shows remarkable stability. This is a completely different pattern of initial position plosives under
stress as noted by Lisker-Abramson (1967). The decrease in
the BURST duration within the framework -VCV- is due not
only to loss of stress but probably also to the increase in
the number of syllables in the sequence. If this category
of utterances is representative of natural discourse it can
be said - in spite of the slight fluctuations due to crossed
contextual variations - that the BURST presents a strong
resistance to the pressure of its environment in spie of the
decrease in temporal difference which goes from 19 msec.
(31 msec. c/12 in VCV) to 16 msec. (26 msec. c/10 in -VCV-).

Final vowel: V2 (Figure 4)

Five points will be noted here: (a) there is an effect
of voicing on the length of vowel V2 (141 msec. c/125 msec.),
that is an average difference of 16 msec. which is maintained
in the three conditions in spite of, (b) the drastic effect
of loss of accentuation which reduces the length of vowel
V2 by an average of about 70 msec., (c) that moving back the
articulation of the consonant lengthens the vowel in the

case of voiced consonants, (d) that in the case of the final
vowel, vowel aperture does not seem to have any effect on
its length and (e) that in conditions of VCV and -VCV, V2
is notably longer than V1 which underlines the influence of
stress on the last syllable of the group.

DISCUSSION

From the results it can be seen that none of the four
parameters alone allows for a clear differentiation between
the two phonetic classes of French plosives. On the
descriptive level, this lack of distinction is clearly observable in figure 5 where the distribution of the four
parameters is presented under all conditions: vowels, consonants, stress. It serves some purpose to take several
parameters together into consideration in order to arrive at
a separation which remains valid across the different conditions, the more so in that the parameters are divergingly
sensitive to each of these conditions. Thus, the duration of
the BURST which varies according to the place of articulation of vowels and consonants remains stable in the presence
of stress effects. Inversely, the Closure is first of all
sensitive to stress but offers a better resistance to the
vocalic contexts.

The difficulties that may arise in looking for a good
differential device may be due to many sources: (a) the
speech wave is made up of a variable intermingling of acoustic segments, (b) contextual influences: vocalic and consonantal places of articulation, stress, number of syllables,
tempo of speech, etc., and (c) subjects present a considerable degree of latitude in their speech. The Burst range
of duration extends from 8 to 72 msec. (voiceless) and from
2 to 31 msec. (voiced). But, the principal difficulty perhaps arises from the fact that we are still looking for an
invariant assimilated most often to the concept of a major
cue. We have previously shown (Wajskop, 1974; Wajskop and
Sweerts, 1973) the importance of the global acoustic pattern
in perceptual behavior. This is in accordance with the
emphasis placed on the syllable (Liberman, 1970) which,
not only conveys the coarticulation information at the level
of production but also supports, on the perceptual level, a
framing function which reduces the number of sound segments

and at the same time allows free play to their contrasts,
which is so important for the action of auditive discrimination (Fant, 1968).

One is confronted by a similar problem when one is looking for an efficient separation between voiced and voiceless
plosives. Thus, the question is to know how many and which
parameters it is necessary to bring together in order to
obtain this differentiation. Different combinations have
already been proposed: the ratio of the duration of vowel
to closure (Wajskop and Sweerts, 1973; Denes, 1955;
Serniclaes, 1974); the sum of the average duration - differences between vowels and closures before voiced and
unvoiced stops (Raphael <u>et al.</u>, 1977). These combinations
are not very efficient in that they discard the variance
due to the subjects. Yet, we know that three temporal
parameters at least (V_1, Closure, BURST) reveal sufficient
differences to be taken into account. Hence, we looked for
a linear relationship between them in order to obtain a
better distinction between voiced and voiceless stops.

We saw before that V_1 and Closure covariate inversely
with a relation of the form of a quasi temporal compensation.
The sum of V_1 + Closure is relatively stable for the two
classes. In. Fig. 6, we see that the first bissectrice of
the equation V_1 = Closure divides fairly well the two clouds
of points corresponding to the voiceless (V_1 < Closure) and
to the voiced (V_1 > Closure) stops. Thus, we have retained
this value (V_1 - Closure) as a good marker for this opposition for these two parameters. The overlap is nevertheless
large and logically requires the intervention of the BURST
duration.

By the same procedure, we visually adjusted a boundary
dividing at best the voiceless and voiced values obtained
by plotting the V_1 - Closure data relative to BURST. The
resulting separation is very satisfactory (P of errors < 10%)
above all, if one remembers that the diagram puts together
all the conditions and all the contextual variations and
takes only account of the temporal parameters which are
certainly not the sole relevant ones. In order to allow
a direct comparison with the histograms relative to the

isolated parameters (Fig. 5), we have clustered the three
parameters according to the equation V_1 - Closure - 4 x
BURST (3) defined by the direction of the line-boundary.
The diagram (Fig. 8) shows an obvious advantage in the
division of the two classes. The coefficients peculiar to
each parameter in this equation permit to estimate their
relative weight provided that we take into account their
standard deviation.

Table 4 confirms that it is also necessary to take
into account the two other parameters, which combined, have
a weight nearly as important as the BURST. From this analysis, it is clear that only a combination of parameters can
function as an efficient separator in the presence of fluctuations due to speakers, context and stress. This claim
does not mean, of course, that only the temporal parameters
are efficient.

CONCLUSION

Our approach has led us to retain a combination of
parameters rather than one alone in order to differentiate
better, on the descriptive level, the two classes of intervocalic stops in French. Our results confirm the insufficiency of a descriptive procedure which would be based on an
isolated cue. It would seem to us, indeed, illusory to
reduce such a complex phenomenon as the voice distinction
to a single acoustical correlate, based only on perceptual
investigations themselves limited most often to the initial
prevocalic stop. It has been clearly shown that prevoicing
(negative VOT) and VOT (voicing lag) cannot be clustered
together into a single dimension (Serniclaes, 1975 and 1977;
Serniclaes and Bejster, 1977).

In 1967, Lisker and Abramson insisted on the lack of
parallelism between physical and perceptual data: "But
these data can only be taken to demonstrate the relevance of
our measure for analysis, for the physical characterization
of the stops as linguistic elements. In no sense can they be
equated with data from experiments in synthesis, for only
data of the latter kind could show the perceptual significance of the VOT dimension" (p. 7). Such a claim has as a
result that it widens the gap between the acoustic image

of speech production and its perception. As a matter of
fact, the emphasis given to VOT is essentially due to
results coming from perceptual investigations using "speech-
like segments" whose principal characteristic is to present
to the subjects stylized situations, devoid of any redundancy
(i.e., all other cues being neutralized), during which only
one cue is manipulated at a time. This procedure has the
great advantage of leading to a better understanding of the
basic perceptual mechanisms associated with this sort of
stimuli. It is in this way that emphasis may be given to
the subjects sensitivity to the simultaneity or the non-
simultaneity of two complex sounds (4), to the duration of
a silent interval followed by a sound (Stevens and Klatt,
1974), to the combined modulation of amplitude and frequency
of a burst, or to the duration of a noise followed by a
periodic vibration (Miller et al., 1976), etc. But, important as these results may be, they cannot be mapped directly
onto the psycho-phonetic mechanisms associated with natural
speech, i.e., phonetically structured sound complexes. In
the same way that the production of the voice opposition
needs a combination of parameters in order to be described
with efficiency, it appears to us that the identification
or the discrimination of this feature must be based on a
complex of cues whose variations make it impossible at the
present time to set up a single specificaion in terms of the
signal. It is likely that the decoding of the phonetic
feature is the result of an integrative processing of the
different cues present in a given phonetic context.

Future work will need to take account of the overall
acoustic pattern for the purpose of establishing a perceptual configuration in which all the cues suitably weighted
would (Fant, 1967) lead to a vector determining the subject
response. Where phonetic research is concerned, such an
approach requires two stages: in-depth large-scale
descriptive studies which can only lead to more refined
perceptual investigations.

FOOTNOTES AND REFERENCES

(1)   Cf. Nordstrom and Lindblom, "A normalization procedure
      for vowel formant data" and their comments about the
      large dialectal spread in the Peterson-Barney data –

8th IC Phon. Sci., 1975 (paper 212c). The spread of dialects, ages, sociolinguistic levels is also visible in Debrock et Forrez "Analyse des voyelles du néerlandais et du francais – Méthodes et résultats" in Rev. Phon. Appl., 37:27-72.

(2)   Burst or "open interval" is not identical to VOT, in particular in the case of the voiced plosives where an uninterrupted weak voicing is generally superimposed during the transient phase, the fricative and aspirative segments. It may also happen that this voicing is absent during a short interval after the transient release. A French intervocalic stop would thus be labelled with a VOT = zero by the Lisker-Abramson 1964 definition.

(3)   The coefficient four results from a visual and empirical adjustment of the best separating boundary between the two classes.

(4)   This is the cases for stimuli constructed with and without F1 - cutback in order to simulate the distinction between voiced and voiceless stops as in the Haskins procedure.

(5)   The equation of the boundary provides the weighting coefficients ω relative to each variable only if they have been normalised:

$x = Burst/SD_{Burst}$ $y = V1 - closure/SD_{V1 - closure}$

This equation may be written:

$$Y \omega_{V1-closure} + x \omega_{Burst} = c^{te}$$

If a comparison is made with the same straight line equation before normalisation (Fig. 7).

$$C1 (V_1 - closure) + C_2 Burst = c^{te}$$

then

$\omega_{V1 - closure} = C_1 SD_{V1 - closure} = 32.73$

$\omega_{Burst} = C_2 SD_{Burst} = 55.76$

ratio $\dfrac{Burst}{V_1 - closure} = 1.70$

Chen, M. (1970). Phonet. 22:129-159.

Denes, P. (1955). J. Acoust. Soc. Am., 27:761-764.

Fant, G. (1960). La Haye, Mouton.

Fant, G. (1967). Proceed. 6th Inter. Cong. Phon. Sci.

Fant, G. (1968). Amsterdam, North-Holland, 173-277.

Fischer-Jorgensen, E. (1964). Zeit. Sprach. Kommun., 17:175-207.

Fujimura, O. (1975). Proceed. SCS-74, 2:33-43.

Klatt, D. H. (1973). J. Speech Hear. Res., 18:686-706.

Liberman, A. (1970). Cognit. Psych., 1:301-323.

Lisker, L. and Abramson, A. S. (1964). Word 20:384-422.

Lisker, L. and Abramson, A. S. (1967). Lang. Speech, 1-28.

Lisker, L. and Abramson, A. S. (1970). Proceed. 6th Inter. Cong. Phon. Sci., 563-567.

Lisker, L. (1957). Lang., 33:42-49.

Miller, J. D., Pastore, R. E., Weir, C. C., Kelly, W. J., and Dooling, R. J. (1976). J. Acoust. Soc. Am. 60:410-417.

Naeser, M. (1970). Tech. Rep. 124, U. Wis.

Peterson, G. E. and Lehiste, I. (1960). J. Acoust. Soc. Am. 32:693-703.

Raphael, L. J. (1975). J. Phon., 3:25-33.

Raphael, L. J., Dorman, M. F. and Geffner, D. (1977). Haskins Lab. S.R., 50:115-122.

Serniclaes, W. (1974). GALF, 5me Journ. e'Etude Groupe Comm. Parlée, 1:10-18.

Serniclaes, W. (1976). Rapp. d'Act. l'Inst. de Phon. 10/1:83-104.

Serniclaes, W. and Wajskop, M. (1977). Amsterdam, Jour. Benjamins, AG, 1978, in press.

Stevens, K. N. and Klatt, D. H. (1974). J. Acoust. Soc. Am. 55:653-659.

Wajskop, M. and Sweerts, J. (1973). J. Phon., 1:121-130.

Wajskop, M. (1974). Hamburg, Helmut Buske Verlag, 245-282.

ACKNOWLEDGMENTS

This investigation was supported by a FONDS de la RECHERCHE FONDAMENTALE COLLECTIVE contract nr. 2.4522.76. The autor wishes to thank Willy Serniclaes, Renaud Beeckmans and Yves Caldor for their helpful comments and technical assistance in collecting and preparing a statistical analysis of the data.

Table 1. Mean durations of VI.

	PTK	BDG	$\overline{m}$ difference	ratio
VCV	81	96	15	Ø.84
-VCV	70	82	12	Ø.85
-VCV-	63	67	4	Ø.94
$\overline{m}$	71(N-270)	82(N=270)	11	Ø.86

The effect of place of articulation is significanct at .005;
stress, voicing and vowels are significant at .001. The
interaction of voicing and stress is significant at .001
and the interaction of voicing and place is significant at
.05.

Table 2. Mean duration of V 1 + Closure for each stress
          condition.

	p t k	b d g	$\overline{m}$ difference
VCV	205	183	22
-VCV	178	156	22
-VCV-	137	130	7

Table 3. Averaged ratios: Closure/Vowel 1.

	PTK	BDG
VCV	1.54	Ø.89
-VCV	1.54	Ø.91
-VCV-	1.17	Ø.91

Table 4. Weighting coefficients of the three parameters (5)

	Eq. C Coeff.	S.D.	Weight Coeff.
Burst	4	13.94	55.76
V1-Closure	1	32.73	32.73

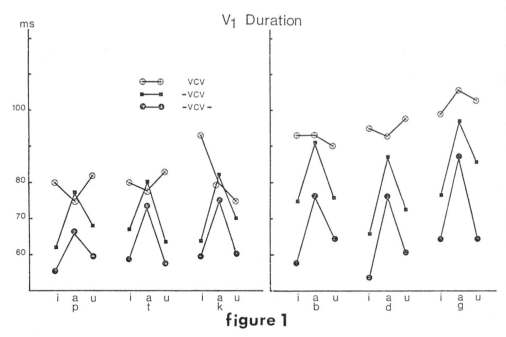

figure 1

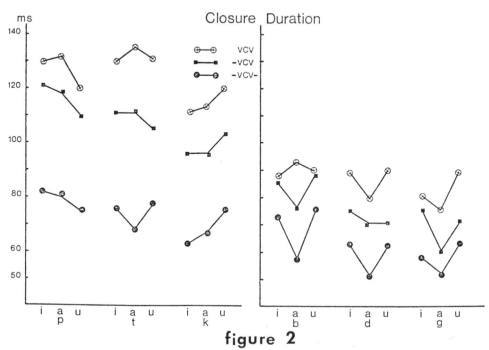

figure 2

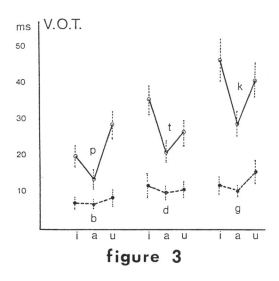

figure 3

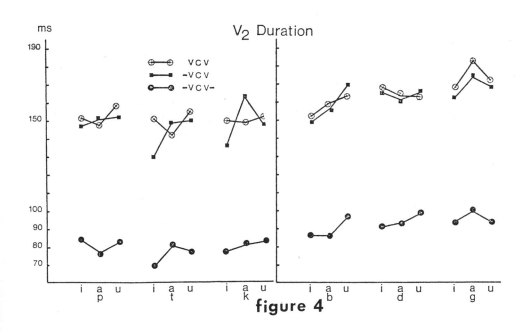

figure 4

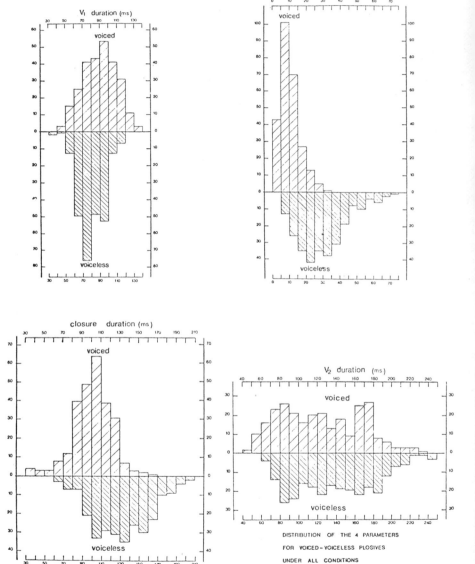

figure 5

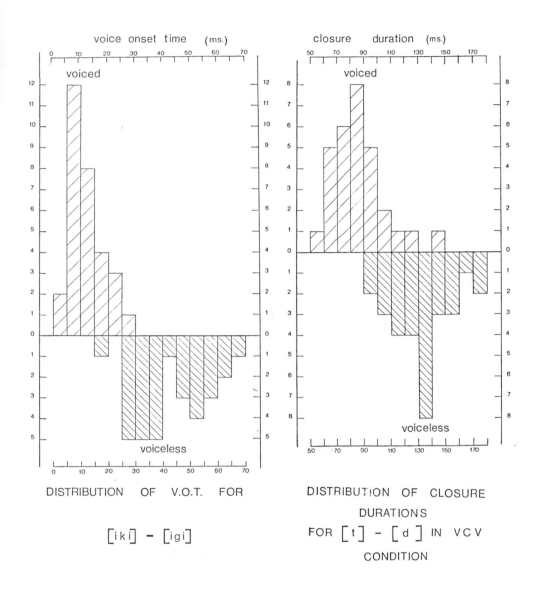

DISTRIBUTION OF V.O.T. FOR

[iki] – [igi]

figure 6

DISTRIBUTION OF CLOSURE
DURATIONS
FOR [t] – [d] IN VCV
CONDITION

figure 7

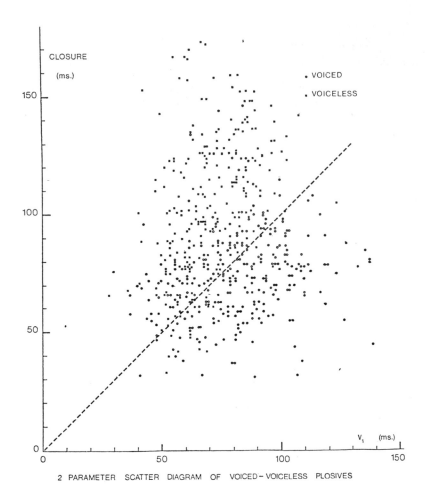

2 PARAMETER SCATTER DIAGRAM OF VOICED–VOICELESS PLOSIVES

figure 8

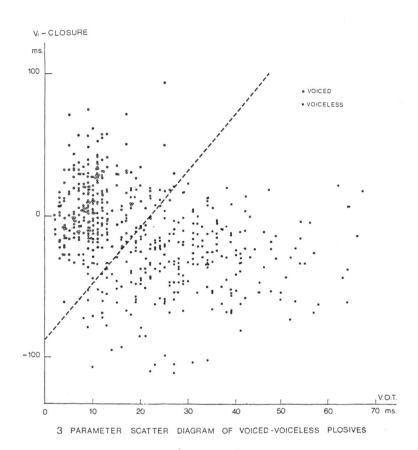

3 PARAMETER SCATTER DIAGRAM OF VOICED-VOICELESS PLOSIVES

figure 9

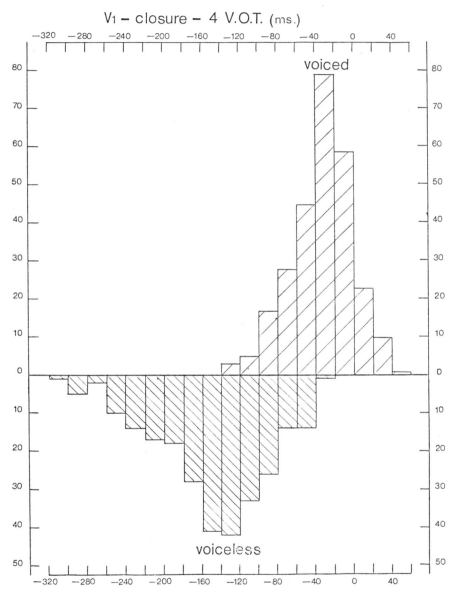

DISTRIBUTION FOR VOICED-VOICELESS PLOSIVES
IN RELATION TO A 3 PARAMETER LINEAR COMBINATION
figure 10

PRINCIPES D'UNE MÉTHODE D'ENSEIGNEMENT DE LA PRONONCIATION DU FRANCAIS A PARTIR DU RYTHME DE LA LANGUE PARLÉE NON MÉRIDIONALE

FRANÇOIS WIOLAND
Institut de Phonétique, Strasbourg

La variété des francais parlés peut être schématique-
ment présentée en fonction du modèle suivi: (1) francais
parlé sans référence au modèle écrit; (2) francais parlé
construit sur le modele écrit. Il n'en demeure pas moins
que, quelle que soit la variété de francais parlé considérée, c'est l'unité rythmique de base qui est fondamentale en prononciation puisqu'elle regroupe une suite
de sons en leur conférant une importance relative les uns
par rapport aux autres.

UNITES RYTHMIQUES DU FRANCAIS

Matérialisons par des lignes courbes les suites de
sons qui peuvent former une unité rythmique dans les
réalisations correspondant successivement aux deux modeles.

à. Modèle non écrit: Il s'agit de quelques extraits de
dialogues spontanés:
Les frites oh la la j'aime ça.

Demain ça va être bourré hein.

Alors on y va.

Oui bon tout droit et puis au feu à droite.

Le trouver allons donc c'est pas difficile.

b. Modèle écrit: Considérons par exemple les structures syntaxiques minimales de type déclaratif: Fonction sujet:

1. A. S_2 x V x S_1

  B. Il faut travailler

2. A. S_2 x V x Adj. x S_1

  B. Il est important de s'exprimer

3. A. Il y a x S_1 x qui ....

  B. Il y a un avion qui décolle

  C.

Fonction attribut:

1. A. S x V x Attribut

  B. Cette femme est belle

2. A. S x V x O x Attr.

  B. L'altitude rend le climat supportable

  C.

  D.

3. A. S x V x Attr. x Compl. d'agent

  B. Mon ami parait satisfait de son travail

  C.

  D.

Fonction objet:

1. A. S x V

  B. Le vent souffle

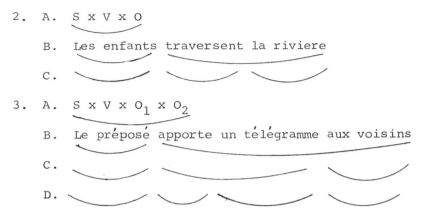

2. A. S x V x O

    B. Les enfants traversent la riviere

    C.

3. A. $S \times V \times O_1 \times O_2$

    B. Le préposé apporte un télégramme aux voisins

    C.

    D.

   Constatations. Le francais parlé spontané se caractérise
par une suite d'éléments syntaxiques de nature très variée
qui peuvent correspondre chacun a une unité rythmique:
nominaux, verbaux, adverbiaux, phatiques etc. Les phrases
minimales ne comportent qu'un nombre limité de distributions
rythmiques, 4 au plus. Prenons comme exemple la phrase
"Les enfants traversent la rivière."

   Comme d'une part les unités rythmiques correspondent à
des unités syntaxiques d'un niveau plus ou moins élevé, les
unités rythmiques du rythme A correspondraient à la phrase
toute entiere; celles du rythme B correspondent: au syntagme nominal sujet, et au syntagme verbal; celles du rythme
C correspondent: au syntagme nominal sujet, au verbe, et au
syntagme nominal objet.

   Comme d'autre part ces mêmes unités rythmiques reflètent
la hiérarchie de la structure syntaxique, l'importance de la
jointure entre deux unités rythmiques est fonction de leur
relation syntaxique. C'est ainsi que dans l'exemple choisi
(rythme C) la jointure est plus marquée entre les deux
premières unités rythmiques qu'entre les deux dernières.
Malgré le nombre très restreint de découpages rythmiques par
phrase, il est bien connu que la locuteur francais n'a pas
la liberté de choisir l'un quelconque des rythmes théoriquement possibles. En fait, le rythme lui est imposé par la
situation dans laquelle il se trouve.

Le rythme A entrainerait obligatoirement un débit
rapide, car le locuteur prononcerait en une seule unité
rythmique un nombre relativement important de syllabes;
dans l'exemple choisi 8

8 syllabes

un seul groupe rythmique
En réalité, ce rythme est une vue de l'esprit car il est
impossible de réaliser un groupe rythmique aussi long.

Le rythme B qui découpe la même suite sonore en deux
unités rythmiques oblige à une élocution plus lente.

3 syllabes   5 syllabes

1er groupe   2e groupe
rythmique   rythmique

Comme la tendance du français est de répartir de façon égale
dans le temps chaque unité rythmique, la vitesse d'élocution
a l'intérieur de chaque unité est proportionnelle au nombre
de syllabes qu'elle contient: plus le nombre de syllabes
contenu dans une unité rythmique est different de celui
contenu dans une autre, plus la vitesse d'élocution variera
d'un groupe à l'autre. C'est ainsi que la deuxième unité
rythmique de l'exemple ci-dessus qui contient 5 syllabes
nécessite une vitesse d'élocution plus rapide que celle que
demande le premier groupe qui ne se compose que de 3 syllabes.
La différence de débit serait encore plus marquée pour le
rythme B dans la phrase "Mon ami parait satisfait de son
travail" puisque le rapport des syllabes contenu dans chaque
unité est de 3 contre 8. Ces rapports n'expriment qu'une
tendance et ne correspondent pas a des valeurs absolues.

Le rythme C fait apparaitre toutes les unités rythmiques
que peut comporter la phrase (unités rythmiques de base).
Le debit d'élocution est relativement lent du fait de la
multiplication des unités rythmiques et du petit nombre de
syllabes contenu dans chaque groupe. Les variations de
vitesse d'élocution d'un groupe à l'autre sont de ce fait
bien moins importantes que dans le découpage précédent.

3 syllabes   2 syllabes   3 syllabes

1er groupe   2e groupe   3e groupe
rythmique   rythmique   rythmique

Lorsqu'il s'agit de structures syntaxiques complexes les
modificateurs a savoir: l'adverbe, l'adjectif, la relative,
le complément déterminatif, l'apposition etc... peuvent
également former des unités rythmiques à des niveaux
différents selon la structure syntaxique de la phrase.

Exemple

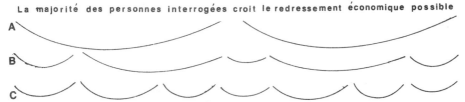

La majorité des personnes interrogées croit le redressement économique possible

     Seul le nombre d'unités rythmiques augmente en fonction
de la longueur et de la structure de la phrase. Dans cet
exemple le rythme A est évidemment théorique. Les possibilités rythmiques d'une phrase française sont donc. Très
clairement définies puisqu'elles sont conditionnées par la
syntaxe; limitées en nombre pour une phrase donnée.

     Tout locuteur francophone adopte le rythme qui convient
à la situation concrète de parole dans laquelle il se trouve.
Ces diverses situations de parole auxquelles correspondent
des distributions rythmiques différentes sont tout aussi
clairement caractérisées que les différentes situations
d'écriture.

     Point de vue pédagogique. Faut-il enseigner les
différentes possibilités rythmiques d'une même séquence ou
ne retenir que l'une d'elles? Le rythme A, le plus souvent
fictif, est à l'évidence bien trop rapide pour pouvoir être
correctement réalisé par un étudiant même avancé. De toute
façon, la rapidité d'élocution n'est pas un idéal a atteindre.
Il est possible de s'exprimer parfaitement dans une langue,
sans être obligé de parler vite. Le rythme B est tout aussi
difficile à maîtriser du fait des constantes variations de
débit qu'il nécessite d'un groupe à l'autre. Même un
étudiant averti a toujours tendance a prononcer trop rapidement les unités rythmiques de peu de syllabes (c'est facile)
et à ralentir son débit lorsque leur nombre augmente, alors
que le francais procède à l'inverse. Le locuteur qui, dans
l'exemple suivant:

"Nice est une jolie ville"

1 syllabe   5 syllabes

1er groupe   2e groupe
rythmique   rythmique

prononce trop rapidement le premier groupe formé d'une seule
syllabe s'interdit automatiquement une variation correcte
de la vitesse du débit pour la prononciation du deuxième
groupe composé de 5 fois plus de syllabes. Il lui sera en
effet matériellement impossible d'augmenter suffisamment la
vitesse d'élocution pour conserver un rapport "francais."

     C'est à l'évidence le rythme C qui doit être retenu pour
l'enseignement de la prononciation française, pour les raisons
suivantes: (1) C'est un rythme français à part entière, qui
correspond par ailleurs le plus souvent à celui du français
parlé spontané. Il ne s'agit pas d'une étape intermédiaire.
(2) C'est celui qui est le plus facile à appréhender par
l'étudiant. (3) C'est celui qui demande la prononciation
la plus lente, donc la plus facile a réaliser. Le locuteur
prend son temps pour s'exprimer, tout en possédant un rythme
"français." A titre d'exemple, la moyenne des syllabes par
groupe est d'environ 2,5 pour un corpus composé de discours
enregistrés. (4) C'est celui qui entraine le moins de
variations de vitesse du débit puisque le nombre de syllabes
par groupe varie dans des proportions relativement faibles.
(5) C'est celui qui permet à l'étudiant, dans un grand nombre
de cas, de réaliser une pause entre deux unités rythmiques,
sans pour autant que l'unité rythmique de la phrase soit
rompue, dans la mesure où il respecte la hiérarchie syntaxique. Si l'étudiant ne sait pas qu'il peut s'arrêter
en des endroits bien définis de la phrase, lorsqu'il
éprouvera une difficulté de prononciation, il ne respectera
forcément plus le rythme et achoppera sur la difficulté
où elle se trouve, c'est-a-dire en n'importe quel point
d'une unité rythmique. Si, au contraire, il est convaincu
de la nécessité de prononcer en une seule unité rythmique
de petits groupes après lesquels une pause est toujours
virtuellement possible, il pourra aisément relâcher
régulièrement son effort et réaliser s'il le faut une pause,

tout en conservant le rythme du français parlé. Ce point
nous paraît fondamental. (6) Un francais qui n'emploierait
que ce rythme se ferait évidemment remarquer. Mais celui
qui apprend le français et qui emploie ce même rythme dans
n'importe quelle situation se fait au contraire très bien
comprendre et ne donne pas l'impression de "faire un discours." C'est un fait d'expérience.

La difficulté à ce niveau concerne les unités rythmiques
exceptionnellement longues formées soit par des unités
lexicales de plus de 4 syllabes soit par des groupes du
type: Déterminant x Adjectif x Substantif, soit par tout
autre groupe figé.

Exercices d'application. Le premier exercice consiste
a découper n'importe quelle séquence de francais parlé en
un nombre le plus grand possible d'unités rythmiques,
autrement dit, en unités rythmiques les plus courtes possibles entre lesquelles une pause est réalisable si le
locuteur en éprouve le besoin.

SPECIFICITE DE CHAQUE UNITE RYTHMIQUE

Il est évidemment bien connu que chaque unité rythmique
doit son existence a la prédominance de sa dernière syllabe
prononcée qui est dite "accentuée" par rapport aux autres
qui sont dites "inaccentuées."

Rappel succinct des caractéristiques de la syllabe
accentuée. (1) Au niveau articulatoire: L'effort articulatoire particulier ne concerne pas systématiquement
l'ensemble de la syllabe, mais uniquement: la voyelle
(1 seule voyelle par syllabe), et la (ou les) consonne(s)
qui la précède(nt). Il n'intéresse jamais la (ou les)
consonne(s) qui suit(suivent) la voyelle.

Soient les structures syllabiques suivantes où V ne
représente qu'une voyelle et C une ou plusieurs consonnes
prononcées:

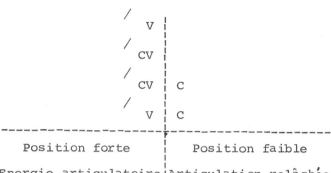

Position forte   Position faible

Energie articulatoire Articulation relâchée

(2) Au niveau acoustique: Les manifestations de l'accent à
ce niveau sont caractérisées par un ensemble de relations
"françaises" entre les trois paramètres que sont l'intensité,
le temps et la fréquence. Rapports établis par le francais:
Intensité sonore: à la différence d'un grand nombre d'autres
langues, l'intensité sonore est extrêmement faible, moins
importante parfois que celle enregistrée pour une même
voyelle en position inaccentuée. Temps: la voyelle accentuée est nettement plus longue en temps objectif que la
meme voyelle inaccentuée car l'intensité articulatoire est
toujours importante. Fréquence: les variations de fréquence
qui se réalisent sur les voyelles accentuées sont en relation
avec la durée vocalique. Mais ces variations de fréquence ne
seront "françaises" que si elles sont mises en relation avec
la durée.

    Il existe une corrélation entre durée et variation de
fréquence, en ce sens que la mélodie française ne peut être
obtenue sans allonger plus ou moins la durée vocalique.
Car l'augmentation ou la diminution de la fréquence est
linguistiquement pertinente en français dans la partie
finale de la durée vocalique.
(3) Au niveau perceptuel: Tous les locuteurs francophones
articulent avec un soin particulier et donc de façon précise
les sons qui tombent sous l'accent rythmique. Ces mêmes
personnes en tant qu'auditeurs perçoivent toujours dans
cette position des sons articulés avec une énergie et une
précision particulières. Leur "oreille" est de ce fait
devenue très exigente. Tout petit écart de prononciation
sous l'accent rythmique est donc obligatoirement perçu
comme non conforme au français. A l'inverse, comme la

prononciation des sons en syllabes inaccentuées est plus
ou moins relachée, la perception de ces mêmes sons est plus
grossière et autorise des écarts bien plus prononcés que
sous l'accent rythmique. Ces écarts ne sont évidemment pas
reconnus comme tels.

   Point de vue pédagogique. Il est recommandé de faire
porter l'effort de prononciation sur les sons en position
accentuée puisque, pour une "oreille française," ils
participent dans une large mesure à la compréhension du
message linguistique. Si un français n'a pas correctement
indentifié la syllabe accentuée de chaque unité rythmique
de base il lui est pratiquement impossible de comprendre ce
qui lui est dit. La correction phonétique une fois obtenue
sous l'accent rythmique, la majorité des problèmes de
prononciation concernant les consonnes et le timbre des
voyelles seront résolus. Il faut éviter d'attirer
l'attention de l'étudiant sur les syllabes inaccentuées
pour échapper à la syllabation. C'est également le moment de
caractériser articulatoirement, acoustiquement et au niveau
perceptuel les différents sons sous l'accent rythmique ainsi
que leurs différentes formes graphiques. L'effort articulatoire ne porte pas seulement sur la voyelle accentuée,
mais déjà sur la (ou les) consonne(s) qui précède(nt) la
voyelle. Habituer l'étudiant à cette structure syllabique
de base:CV. Par contre, le mettre en garde contre un effort
articulatoire trop important sur les consonnes finales de
syllabes accentuées. L'étudiant non averti a tendance a
confondre l'accent final de groupes et la (ou les) con-
sonne(s) finale(s) de syllabes accentuées de groupes
rythmiques. Les variations de fréquence linguistiquement
significatives n'affectent que les voyelles effectivement
accentuées dans le discours. Pour faciliter une prononciation correcte des sons de la syllabe accentuée et la
variation correcte de la fréquence, nous pensons qu'en
pratique il est utile de faire prendre conscience à
l'étudiant que les voyelles accentuées qu'il prononce n'ont
pas toujours la durée requise. L'effort articulatoire qu'il
porte en général sur les consonnes finales de syllabe
(influencé en ceci par l'orthographe le plus souvent) a pour
conséquence d'abréger la voyelle précédente, alors que

l'allongement de la voyelle accentués favorise de façon
quasi automatique et la variation mélodique et le relâche-
ment articulatoire des consonnes finales de syllabe.

   Exercices d'application. Le deuxième exercise consiste
à identifier correctement les sons qui composent la syllabe
accentuée dans chaque groupe rythmique. Bien que cela
paraisse rébarbatif à certains, l'utilisation de la transcription à cet effet ne peut que ˙faciliter cette identification et, par voie de conséquence, la réalisation correcte
des sons concernés.

   L'homme a un an de plus chaque année et la femme tous les
     ˊlɔm   ˊnɑ̃   ˊply   ˊne   ˊfam
   trois ans seulement
     ˊzɑ̃   ˊmɑ̃

On ne saurait trop insister sur la signification concrète
du signe de l'accent en transcription du français et par
conséquent sur les exercices pratiques concernant:
l'unité manifestée par un effort articulatoire sur le
groupe CV aux dépens systématique des consonnes finales de
syllabe;
l'allongement de la voyelle accentuée;
la variation mélodique en rapport avec la durée;
le peu d'intentisé sonore malgré l'effort articulatoire.

              IMPORTANCE DE LA POSITION DE LA VOYELLE
                 DANS LA SYLLABE ACCENTUEE

   Si nous parlons une langue c'est dans le but de nous
faire comprendre. Puisque les "oreilles françaises" ne
comprennent pas, ou comprennent mal, ce qui est dit si la
dernière syllabe de chaque unité rythmique n'est pas
correctement prononcée, le maximum d'effort articulatoire
doit être consacré à cette même syllabe. Nous ne parlerons
que de la prononciation de la voyelle. Or il est bien
connu que la prononciation de la voyelle accentuée est
fonction de sa position dans la syllabe. Des quatre
structures syllabiques possibles:

              A - ˊCV
              B - ˊV
              C - ˊCVC
              D - ˊVC,

il resort que la voyelle accentuée peut se trouver: (1) en position finale (A et B), (2) en position devant consonne(s) prononcée(s) (C et D).

Conséquences au niveau de la durée et du timbre des voyelles. (1) Conséquences de la position au niveau de la durée vocalique: L'allongement de la voyelle accentuée par rapport à la même voyelle inaccentuée n'est qu'une première étape, indispensable, vers la réalisation correcte des articulations vocaliques accentuées. Mais cet allongement peut etre multiplié par 2, 3 voire 4 en durée objective d'une voyelle accentuée à une autre en fonction de la position de la voyelle. Sans entreprendre une analyse de détail, rappelons les variations de durée objective qui ont une influence sur la compréhension du francais parle: En position finale, les voyelles accentuées ne sont que très légerement allongées.

Quels sont les cas où la voyelle accentuée est très allongée sans exception possible? En position devant consonne(s) prononcée(s):
(a) lorsque la voyelle est nasale:
    /ɑ̃ˈfɓɑ̃:s/
(b) lorsque la voyelle orale est suivie des consonnes
    /ɓ/, /z/, /v/, /ʒ/ finales et du groupe /vɓ/, exemple:
    / ləˈnɔ:ɓ/ mais /eˈnɔɓm/ car /ɓ/ n'est pas final.

En réalité, la durée est fonction de la nature des consonnes qui suivent la voyelle et l'on peut établir un classement des consonnes qui allongent plus (les sonores) ou moins (les sourdes) la voyelle précedente. L'expérience montre qu'au niveau de la compréhension seuls sont vraiment indispensables les allongements indiqués ci-dessus (y compris ceux dont il est question ci-dessous en 2 et 3).

(2) Conséquences de la position au niveau du timbre des
    voyelles /E/ /OE/ et /O/.
    (a) En position finale: le timbre est fermé
        /e/ exemple: /ilamaɓˈʃe/
        /o/ exemple: /ilaˈʃo/
        /ø/ exemple: /ilˈplø/
Mais il existe une exception a cette loi de position en ce qui concerne le timbre ouvert /ɛ/ pour des graphies du type

AI: le lait, je marchais, etc...
ET: le soufflet, etc...
è,ê: l'accès, etc...

Actuellement, ce point est en évolution et l'on peut constater une prononciation fermée /e/ chez un certain nombre
de locuteurs a des degrés très divers selon les graphies ou
même les unités lexicales concernées. C'est un fait. Cette
réalisation soit ouverte /ɛ/ soit fermée /e/ pour les graphies
du type AI, ET,Ê, Ê ne doit surtout pas donner l'impression
à l'étudiant d'une indétermination générale du timbre quelles
que soient les graphies. L'évolution ne se réalise que dans
le sens d'une généralisation plus ou moins rapide du timbre
fermé, autrement dit d'une tendance à l'élimination de
l'exception aux lois de position. Cette évolution n'affecte
en rien la prononciation du timbre fermé dans tous les
autres cas. Imposer le timbre fermé de façon générale est
tout aussi répréhensible car non conforme à la réalité. Il
faut informer l'étudiant de la situation actuelle en lui
faisant comprendre que le remplacement du timbre ouvert par
un timbre fermé dans un certain nombre de cas n'a pas de
conséquences pratiques sur la compréhension, alors que le
remplacement inverse dans cette position est des plus
fâcheux.

(b) En position devant consonne(s) prononcée(s) le
    timbre est habituellement ouvert
    /ɛ/ exemple: /laˊsjɛst/
    /ɔ/ exemple: /sɔ̃ˊɔs/
    /œ/ exemple: /dˊybœf/

Si cette voyelle est suivie de /b/, /z/, /v/, /ʒ/ ou /vb/,
elle sera également très allongée. Le /ɛ/ sera également
allongé lorsqu'il est graphié - ê, aî, exemple: ei, ai +
/m/, /n/ ou /ɲ/, exemple: /ˈʒɛ:m/. C'est dans cette
position que l'étudiant rencontre les plus grandes difficultés de prononciation du fait des exceptions aux lois de
position liées dans ce cas à des allongements très importants
de la voyelle. Il s'agit des timbres /o:/ et /ø:/. /o:/
dans les cas suivants: (a) graphie o: exemple: le vôtre,
(b) graphie AU, EAU, sauf Paul: exemple: elle est haute
(c) /o/ + /z/: exemple: la chose, (d) devant les nasales
dans: arome, atome, axiome, brome, chrome, idiome, fibrome,
hippodrome, vélodrome, etc..., cyclone, incone et zone.

/ø:/ dans les cas suivants: (a) graphie eû: exemple: il
jeûne, (b) /ø/ + /z/: il creuse, (c) et neutre, feutre, la
meute, une émeute, il ameute, pleutre, il calfeutre, un
neume, Polyeucte, le Pentateuque, Eudes, Maubeuge ... Ces
deux points sont actuellement en évolution. La tendance
est à la suppression des exceptions aux lois de position.
Mais comme cette évolution n'a pas encore abouti, il faut
émettre les mêmes réserves que précédemment.

(3) Conséquences au niveau du timbre de A. Un certain
nombre de francophones possèdent encore deux A. Le /a/
dit antérieur et le /a/ dit postérieur. Mais d'un point de
vue pédagogique, on peut considérer que l'opposition de
timbres n'est plus pertinente au profit d'une opposition de
durée /a/ et /a:/ en position devant consonne(s) prononcée(s).
Comme en position finale l'allongement très important n'est
plus possible, un terme comme "las" a pratiquement disparu
du français parlé à cause de son homophonie avec "là." Mais
en position devant consonne(s) prononcée(s) un certain nombre
d'anciens /ɑ:/ sont actuellement réalisés comme des /a:/
surtout lorsque la graphie est "â". S'il n'en était pas
ainsi, aucun parent n'oserait donner à sa fille le prénom
d'Anne par peur de la confusion avec âne.

Point de vue pédagogique. Pour se faire comprendre en
parlant francais il n'existe pas d'autre solution que de
prononcer avec un soin particulier la syllabe accentuée.
Habituer l'étudiant à distinguer le plus rapidement possible
les positions vocaliques finales des positions devant con-
sonne(s) prononcée(s). L'un des exercices les plus utiles
à ce niveau concerne la prononciation ou non des consonnes
finales des unités lexicales écrites. Insister sur
l'allongement très important de la voyelle accentuée en
position devant consonne(s) prononcée(s) dans les différents cas envisagés ci-dessus malgré le peu d'importance
apparente de ce paramètre.

En effect, plus la durée de la voyelle est grande, plus
l'articulation de la (ou des) consonne(s) finale(s) est
relâchée. De plus, l'allongement oblige l'étudiant à prononcer avec plus de précision encore la voyelle concernée.

Quelle que soit la langue maternelle de l'étudiant, il est
indispensable d'insister sur les exceptions aux lois de
positions. Elles sont en général l'objet de deux erreurs
de sa part, d'une part le timbre plus ou moins ouvert et
d'autre part la réalisation trop brève. Quant aux pro-
nonciations qui suivent les lois de position, l'étudiant
sait très rapidement comment il devrait prononcer. Une
simple correction phonétique en fonction de ses difficultés
propres est alors nécessaire. L'apprentissage de la prononciation du francais parlé c'est pour une bonne part celui
de la prononciation de la syllabe accentuée rythmiquement.

   Exercices d'application. Ils peuvent se réaliser sous
la forme d'un jeu. A toute voyelle accentuée de n'importe
quelle séquence de francais parlé correspond une case du
tableau récapitulatif de la prononciation des voyelles
accentuées (d'après M. G. Straka) présenté à la page 23.
La prononciation de la voyelle accentuée dans: "C'est deux
heures" par exemple est indiquée dans la case Al 6.

DANGERS DE LA MISE EN RELIEF AU NIVEAU DE L'APPRENTISSAGE DU FRANCAIS PARLE

   Si l'on écoute objectivement parler les français, il
faut admettre que ce n'est pas la derniere syllabe des
unités rythmiques qui paraît la plus importante, mais bien
au contraire celle placée en général au début des mots et
qui se manifeste par une augmentation instantanée de
l'intensité, de la fréquence et de la durée par rapport aux
syllabes voisines. C'est cet accent qualifié soit d'accent
de mise en relief, soit d'accent d'insistance que tout un
chacun percoit sans équivoque possible. Cet accent peut
frapper n'importe quel début de mot suivant le désir de
celui qui parle. A la différence de l'accent rythmique, il
n'est pas obligatoire, mais son emploi a pour effet de
multiplier les unités rythmiques. Les manifestations de
cet accent sont très différentes de celles de l'accent
rythmique et leurs places respectives ne peuvent se confondre que pour les monosyllabes.

   Paradoxe. Cette mise en relief, phénomène extrêmement
courant en francais parlé est un piège pour l'étudiant

étranger pour les raisons suivantes: (1) Du fait de sa
prédominance du point de vue perceptuel, et de son influence
sur les syllabes voisines au niveau de l'intensité, de la
fréquence et de la durée, il masque en quelque sorte à
l'oreille de l'étudiant la présence de l'accent rythmique
bien moins intense que lui. Comme l'accent de mise en relief
ne supprime ni l'accent rythmique, ni l'unité rythmique de
base, considérer cet accent de mise en relief comme un accent
rythmique serait une grave erreur. Or, c'est la tendance
qu'ont la plupart des étudiants étrangers ayant dans leur
langue maternelle un accent rythmique qui se manifeste par
une augmentation de l'intensité. Habitues qu'ils sont dans
leur langue à percevoir le rythme sous la forme, entre autre,
d'une augmentation d'intensité et d'une variation mélodique
il est presque impossible qu'ils ne retrouvent pas à l'occasion des accents de mise en relief du français ce qui pour
eux correspond à un accent rythmique. (2) L'étudiant ne
réalise que très difficilement de façon correcte dans un
même groupe rythmique deux accents de nature aussi différente. Privilégier articulatoirement deux syllabes aussi
proches l'une de l'autre relève de l'exploit surtout sur
des dissylabes où deux syllabes successives se verraient
accentuées de manière particulière chacune. L'incapacité
dans laquelle se trouve pratiquement l'étudiant de réaliser
la mise en relief sans porter préjudice au rythme et le fait
que la mise en relief n'est absolument pas nécessaire à la
compréhension du message, à la différence de l'accent
rythmique, nous font opter pour une suppression pure et
simple de cet accent au niveau de l'enseignement, tant que
l'intégrité de l'unité rythmique n'est pas respectée.
C'est un paradoxe de l'enseignement du français parlé.

   Point de vue pédagogique. Changer de rythme en passant
d'une langue à une autre est l'une des plus grandes difficultés rencontrées lors de l'apprentissage. L'étudiant doit
être persuadé que, malgré la présence de nombreux accents
de mise en relief dans le français qu'il entend parler
autour de lui, celui du professeur entre autres, il ne
doit pas essayer de les reproduire. Il doit s'attacher à
retrouver les unités rythmiques telles qu'elles ont été
décrites précédemment. S'il n'emploie que la mise en

relief, il risque de ne pas être bien compris. L'expérience
prouve en effet qu'il est inutile d'insister sur la première syllabe d'un mot si la dernière n'est pas correctement prononcée. Nous serions tenté de dire que dans la
bouche d'un étudiant qui apprend le français plus la mise
en relief est importante plus il a tendance à négliger la
syllabe accentuée. La compréhension de ce qu'il dit s'en
trouve souvent affectée, sauf bien évidemment s'il s'agit
de monosyllabes qui peuvent être accentués rythmiquement.

    Exercices d'application. A partir d'enregistrements
comprehant des accents de mise en relief, l'étudiant répète
les mêmes phrases, en ne réalisant que les accents rythmiques
et en supprimant par conséquent les mises en relief exception
faite des monosyllabes en fin d'unités rythmiques.

LA PRONONCIATION DE L'INTERIEUR
D'UNE UNITE RYTHMIQUE

    La prononciation des voyelles inaccentuées. Une voyelle
inaccentuée est par nature brève.

    Deux types de voyelles inaccentuées: (1) Soient les
exemples suivants: (a) "Faisons le pause" et "Faisons la
pause café," (b) "J'aime les pommes" et "J'aime les pommes
de terre," (c) "Elle chante" et "Elle chante bien." Nous
constatons que dans la première phrase: "pause," "pomme"
et "chante" sont accentués, alors que dans la deuxième
phrase, ces mêmes syllabes peuvent être inaccentuées.
Autrement dit, la dernière syllabe prononcée d'un même mot
peut être dans un cas accentuée, dans l'autre inaccentuée.
(2) Soient les exemples suivants: (a) "C'est une erreur,"
(b) "La France est un beau pays." La voyelle de la première
syllabe de "erreur" et de "pays" est toujours inaccentuee
en français. Elle ne peut jamais porter l'accent rythmique.

    Il est donc indispensable de distinguer deux types de
voyelles inaccentuées: (1) celles qui pourraient être
accentuées (syllabes finales de mots); (2) celles qui ne
peuvent jamais etre accentuées (syllabes non finales de
mots). Les premières, mêmes inaccentuées, conservent le
timbre qu'elles auraient sous l'accent. En effet, que

"pause" soit accentué ou non, il conserve le timbre /o/,
que "pomme" soit accentué ou non, il conserve le timbre /ɔ/.
La seule différence concerne évidemment la durée et la
variation de fréquence. Les lois de prononciation sont donc
semblables à celles de la position accentuée, l'allongement
et la variation de fréquence exceptées.

	Voyelle devant consonne(s) prononcée(s)		Voyelle finale	
Voyelles à 1 timbre	/ã/ /i/ /a/		/ã/ /i/ /a/	
Voyelles à 2 timbres	/ɛ/ /ɔ/ /œ/	/o/ /ø/	/e/ /o/ /ø/	/ɛ/

Les secondes subissent des influences diverses puisqu'elles
se trouvent toujours en position faible. Selon leur position, les syllabes dans la chaîne parlée sont dans des
rapports de force différents. On ne peut plus parler de lois
mais uniquement de tendances et chaque cas à la limite est
un cas particulier.

   Point de vue pédagogique. Puisque toutes les voyelles
qui peuvent être accentuées (même si elles ne le sont pas
dans tous les cas) ont un timbre très clairement défini et
un seul, il est indispensable de rendre l'étudiant attentif
à la prononciation de la derniere syllabe prononcée de tous
les mots qui peuvent porter un accent rythmique. Cet état
de fait justifie une fois de plus l'adoption du rythme le
plus soutenu pour l'apprentissage du français. Car tout
locuteur, même lorsqu'il utilise un rythme différent,
privilégie néanmoins les dernières syllabes des mots qui
pourraient être accentuées. Par contre, il est à notre avis
parfaitement vain de vouloir imposer à l'étudiant un timbre
/e/ ou /ɛ/, /o/ ou /ɔ/, /ø/ ou /œ/ pour les voyelles toujours
inaccentuées. La voyelle de la première syllabe de "erreur"
a-t-elle un timbre ouvert /ɛ/ ou fermé /e/? Du point de vue
pédagogique, c'est un faux probleme car: Le timbre respectivement ouvert ou fermé d'une voyelle toujours in accentuée

n'est pas aussi ouvert ou aussi fermé que celui d'une
voyelle accentuée. Il serait préférable de parler de
tendance à l'ouverture ou à la fermeture. L'"oreille"
francaise n'est pas très sensible à une différence de timbre dans cette position. Le problème ne se pose que si l'on
syllabe ce qui revient à accentuer chaque syllabe. Or,
c'est justement ce qu'il faut éviter pour ne pas donner aux
syllabes inaccentuées une importance qu'elles n'ont pas dans
la langue parlée. Dans un premier temps, il ne faut surtout
pas donner trop d'importance aux syllabes toujours inaccentuées. Il suffit de rappeler la tendance générale du francais: à savoir que si la syllabe inaccentuée à l'intérieur
du mot est ouverte (structure CV) le timbre sera plutôt
fermé, alors que si elle est fermée (structure CVC) le
timbre sera plutôt ouvert: par exemple le "é" dans des
unités lexicales comme abrégement, crémerie, événement,
etc... est plutôt ouvert malgré l'accent aigu parce qu'il
se trouve en syllabe fermée. Il faut également évoquer les
phénomènes d'analogie du type allegre/allégrement, etc.

   La structure syllabique. (1) La cellule rythmique de
base: La structure syllabique du francais est à plus de
80% formée de syllabes ouvertes. 11% environ seulement
de structures syllabiques ne possèdent pas de consonne en
début de syllabe. (2) Point de vue pédagogique: Il faut
habituer l'étudiant à unir systématiquement a l'intérieur
d'une unité rythmique la (ou les) consonne(s) initiale(s)
de syllabe à la voyelle suivante et à ne pas donner en
conséquence une trop grande importance aux consonnes
finales de syllabes

    CV(C)   CV(C)   CV(C)   CV(C)

   syllabe   syllabe   syllabe   syllabe

              Unité rythmique
C'est cette tendance fondamentale qui explique les phénomènes
de liaison en français à l'intérieur d'une unité rythmique.

   Exercices d'application. Ne jamais proposer d'exercices
sur les seules syllabes inaccentuées: elles risquent d'être
trop bien prononcées par rapport à la syllabe accentuée.

Les exercices devraient se situer dans le cadre de l'unité
rythmique. Au lieu de corriger l'étudiant sur des mots
isolés, il est préferable de lui apprendre tout d'abord les
règles de prononciation pour ne plus avoir qu'à faire
appel à l'une de ces règles lors d'une correction particulière. Si par exemple la dernière voyelle dans "il a
chaud" est mal prononcée il est préferable de rappeler a
l'étudiant qu'en position finale seul le timbre fermé est
possible au lieu de lui donner l'impression de ne corriger
que la prononciation d'un seul mot. En ce qui concerne les
phénomènes dits de liaison il convient de les présenter
comme faisant partie intégrante de la structure syllabique
de base. La consonne dite de liaison est initiale de
syllabe et a exactement la même importance que toute autre
consonne initiale de syllabe, à plus forte raison s'il
s'agit de la voyelle accentuée. Ce qui n'exclue évidemment
pas les exercices touchant les cas de liaison interdite.

CONCLUSION

     Nous préconisons lors de l'apprentissage du français
parlé:

(1)   la multiplication des groupes rythmiques parce que
      l'unité rythmique de base est un <u>cadre</u> qui conditionne:
      les caractéristiques articulatoire, acoustique et
      perceptuelle de la suite de sons concernés; les lois
      de position des voyelles accentuées ou qui pourraient
      l'être; la structure syllabique du français; les faits
      d'assimilation; la plupart des phénomènes dits de
      liaison; et en partie la prononciation des /ə/.

(2)   l'allongement plus ou moins marqué de la voyelle accen-
      tuée, qui facilite: la variation de fréquence sur cette
      même voyelle; la réalisation correcte du timbre
      vocalique; le relâchement articulatoire des consonnes
      finales de syllabe s'il y a lieu.

(3)   la suppression de la mise en relief - exception faite
      des monosyllabes - qui permet à l'étudiant: de
      s'exprimer dans un rythme français; de ne faire porter
      son effort que sur ce qui est important pour "l'oreille"

d'un francophone, et de savoir pourquoi il s'est mal
fait comprendre.

La prononciation du français repose sur un petit nombre
de règles générales qui trouvent leur justification au niveau
des unités rythmiques de base. Les conclusions auxquelles
nous avons abouti sont le fruit de dix années d'enseignement
du français parlé à l'Institut Internationl d'Etudes Françaises et de dépouillement de documents expérimentaux au
Laboratoire de Phonétique de Strasbourg.

BIBLIOGRAPHIE

Boudreault, M.   (1967).   Press. l'Univer. Laval.
Brichler-Labaeye, C.   (1970).   Paris, Klincksieck.
Clas, A., Demers, J. et Charbonneau, R.   (1968).   Montréal,
    Lib. Beauchemin.
Delattre, P.   (1938).   French Rev., 12:141-145.
Delattre, P.   (1938).   Le Maître Phon., 64.
Delattre, P.   (1938).   French Rev., 12:49-50.
Delattre, P.   (1940).   Le Francais mod., 8:47-56.
Delattre, P.   (1940).   PMLA, 55:579-595.
Delattre, P.   (1956).   Middleburg.
Duez, D.   (1976).   Bull. l'Inst. Phon. Grenoble, 5:39-53.
Fouché, P.   (1959).   Paris, Klincksieck.
Goldman-Eisler, F.   (1968).   New York, Academic Press.
Goldman-Eisler, F.   (1972).   Lang. Speech, 15:103-113.
Grammont, M.   (1926).   Paris, Delagrave.
Grammont, M.   (1960).   Paris, Delagrave.
Grosjean, F. et Deschamps, A.   (1973).   Phonet., 28:191-226.
Leon, P. R.   (1966).   Paris, Didier.
Leon, P. R. et Martin, P.   (1970).   Paris, Didier.
Leon, P. R.   (1971).   Paris, Didier.
Lucci, V.   (1973).   Bull. l'Inst. Phon. Grenoble, 2:139-161.
Lucci, V.   (1974).   Bull. l'Inst. Phon. Grenoble, 3:139-152.
Malmberg, B.   (1962).   Proc. 4th Int. Cong. of Phon. Sci.,
    456-475.
Malmberg, B.   (1968).   Lyon, Simep-Editions, 35-45.
Martinet, A. et Walter, H.   (1973).   Paris, France-Expansion.
Mettas, O.   (1963).   Paris, Klincksieck, 143-149.
Mettas, O.   (1964).   Paris, Klincksieck, 99-105.
Morier, H.   (1975).   PUF.

Rochette, Cl. E. (1973). Paris, Klincksieck.
Roudet, L. (1910). Paris, H. Welter.
Simon, P. (1967). Paris, Klincksieck.
Simon, P. (1969). Le Français aujourd'hui, 8.
Straka, G. (1950). Bull. Fac. Lett. Strasbourg, 1:1-43.
Straka, G. (1952). Bull. Fac. Lett. Strasbourg, 1:1-47.
Straka, G. (1959). Phon. Allge. Sprach, 12:276-300.

Prononciation des voyelles accentuées

Voyelles accentuées	Voyelles devant consonne(s) prononcée(s)			Voyelle finale		Code
	A	Al	Aex	F	Fex	
Voyelles Nasales /ɑ̃/ /ɔ̃/ /ɛ̃/ /œ̃/		ɑ̃ː		ɑ̃		1
Voyelles Orales /i/ /y/ /u/	i			i		2
à /a/ 1 Timbre	a	aː	aː	a		3
Voyelles Orales /e/ - /ɛ/	ɛ	ɛː	ɛ	e	ɛ	4
/o/ - /ɔ/	ɔ	ɔː	oː	o		5
2 Timbres /ø/ - /œ/	œ	œː	øː	ø		6

A   = position antéconsonantique
Al   = position antéconsonantique avec allongement
Aex   = position antéconsonantique: exceptions aux lois de position
F   = position finale
Fex   = position finale: exceptions aux lois de position.

E. PHYSIOLOGICAL AND ACOUSTIC PHONETICS

DESCRIPTION OF AN ELECTROPALATOGRAPHIC SYSTEM

D. AUTESSERRE AND B. TESTON
L'Université de Provence et C.N.R.S.

After more than a hundred years of palatography, interest among linguists for techniques, the principles of
which up until recent years had hardly evolved at all,
might have been expected to be on the decline. In fact this
is not the case. The readily interpretable nature of a pa-
latogram is perhaps sufficient to explain the continuing interest for this type of document even among those linguists
who are put off by the extreme sophistication of much physiological research. No doubt the ease with which palatographic documents can be interpreted, resulting in a certain superficiality, has been responsible, in some cases,
for an excessive use of cues of place of articulation in
phonetic descriptions, the foundations of which, today,
seem somewhat doubtful when the linguist has not taken into account the general form of the tongue at the moment of
articulation. Furthermore, it has become traditional to
decompose the overall palatographic image in order to reconstruct the sequence of lingual contacts by comparing the palatograms of phonic sequences where for example the same
consonant appears in a variable vocalic environment.

Despite the precision of these interpretations, the
need was felt for a less static system which would enable
the investigator to follow directly the temporal sequence
of the regions of contact between the tongue and the palate,
without limitations of any kind. This has been made

possible by the development of electropalatography which, after a slow start some fifteen years ago can now be considered one of the most advanced techniques of physiological phonetics. One can readily imagine the incredible wealth of data on the functioning of spoken language, particularly concerning the phenomena of lingual coarticulation which will become available in the years to come thanks to the simultaneous use of electropalatography and X-ray films. The recording of the sound source synchronised with each X-ray picture will make it possible to follow up with any desired acoustic or perceptual analysis.

This vast research programme which has been undertaken at the Institut de Phonetique d'Aix (laboratoire associé du C.N.R.S.) is now well under way, after the development of an electropalatographic system of which, in the rest of this paper, we shall outline the technical characteristics, the operating conditions and the various modes of treatment of the data thus obtained, particularly where these differ from other existing electropalatographic systems. We shall also point out, as we go along, various improvements which we intend to make to this material without changing its basic conception.

The electropalatograph consists of two main parts connected to each other: (a) a palatal plate equipped with electrodes connected to electric wires and (b) an electronic system comprising of a sine-wave generator and a palatal-electrode signal detection and processing unit.

The Palatal Plate

The electronic circuits used in various types of electropalatography are often described in abundant detail, information concerning the palatal plate however is generally given far more sparingly. And yet, as was shown by the discussion between proponents of direct palatography (by painting the tongue) and indirect palatography (using an "artificial palate"), the fact of placing a plate of a certain thickness against the hard palate is not without effect on the production of speech. While the majority of phoneticians today are convinced of the superiority of direct examinations, particularly considering the

considerable progress made in the field of intrabuccal
photography, electropalatography brings up once more the
delicate problems concerning the use of palatal plates.
The conditions of construction of "artificial palates"
have of course changed considerably in recent years, taking
advantage of the progress made in dentistry in general.
It is nonetheless a fact that one of the biggest obstacles
for the development and diffusion of electropalatography
comes from the difficulty of perfecting palatal plates.
Before an intensive and reliable use can be made of these
techniques, a number of questions need to be answered:

(a) Do the "artificial palates" fit the palatal (and
     if necessary dental) morphology of the subject
     perfectly, without compressing the palatal mucous?

(b) Does the thickness which is necessary for the plate,
     to prevent it from being deformed in use, give rise
     to compensatory positions and movements when the
     subject speaks (including any possible modifica-
     tions of jaw-positions)? The fact that patients
     get used to artificial dentures, with variable
     modifications to their voice, seems to imply the
     existence of a process of adaptation.

(c) Does the technique used for fixing the plate
     (usually by means of metal hooks) hold the plate
     securely in position during the experimentation,
     even when the subject swallows?

(d) Do the plates need to be replaced frequently due
     the ageing of the material used and resulting
     deformations?

(e) Is the join between the electrodes and the plate
     sufficiently waterproof to prevent any eventual risk
     of infiltration of saliva by capillarity along the
     electric wires?

(f) Is it possible to achieve perfectly hygienic condi-
     tions of use without damaging the plate? If not,
     does the re-use of the plate in experiments at
     different times present a danger for the subject
     (risk of mouth infections)?

     In order to answer these crucial questions unambigu-
ously, we decided to undertake a first phase of

experimentation during which several prototypes manufactured in various different ways were submitted to a
series of detailed examinations (Fig. 1).

Technique for the production of the palatal plates
(Fig. 2). Based on the results obtained from the above-
mentioned experiments, and following several tests the results of which were positive, we finally decided to adopt
the BIOSTAR technique for the production of the "artificial
palates." This process is the result of a collaboration
between two West-German companies: BIOS GESELLSCHAFT
OSNABRUCK and SCHEU DENTAL LETMATHE. It consists of thermo-
plastic modelling by compression of plates of sheets of
variable thickness, dimensions and hardness. Our final
choice was of extra-hard transparent plates of 0,5 mm
thickness in prepolymerised acrylate, totally exempt from
any monomeric residue, designated by the term IMPRELON.
The model of the upper dental arch, obtained by extremely
precise impression with OPTOSIL using the XANTOPREN method
is placed on the work-plate of the BIOSTAR APPARATUS. The
sheet of IMPRELON is blocked with a bayonet-joint against
the compression chamber and heated by means of an infra-red
diffuser on the side which is to be applied to the model
thus making it possible to obtain extremely precise moulding.
The frame holding the plastic sheet is swung over with its
pressure-chamber onto the model which is already in place
on the work-plate. Looking it into place lets compressed
air into the tank automatically moulding the sheet of
plastic against the model. The opening of an outlet-valve
releases the pressure and allows cool air to circulate and
cool down the plate.

At this point in the production of the plate, the sheet
of IMPRELON entirely covers the teeth of the model, both on
their palatal and on their vestibular faces, as well as the
complete vestibular zone. There is no good reason not to
make use of this fact since the under-cut of the neck of
the teeth and the vestibule constitute the best possible
means of holding the plate in place and make the use of
metal hooks unnecessary. It seemed, however, important
not to cover the vestibular face of the incisors in order
to reduce any possible interference with the closing of the

mouth. The cutting-line for the plate was consequently as
follows: it stops, at the front of the plate, at the level
of the middle third of the palatal face of the incisors
(this can be extended to the free edge of the incisors).
The line then runs, at the level of the canines fairly high
up into the vestibule, up to approximately 10 mm above the
neck of the premolars and molars, covering the tuberosities
at the back, and on the palate itself follows the line of
the postdam (Fig. 2A).   The advantages of these sheets of
Imprelon moulded according to the Biostar technique and cut
as described above are numerous. First of all the artificial palates which are produced in this way reproduce the
palatal morphology extremely faithfully, particularly in the
front alveolar region where the palatal palpillas are
reproduced with great precision, which is a considerable
progress compared to artificial palates in acrylic resin.
The fact that the teeth are covered provides a satisfactory
solution to the otherwise delicate problem of the passage
from the neck to the palatal face of the teeth, where it is
difficult to avoid both excessive thickness of the material
used (particularly in the case of acrylic resin) a detach-
ment of the plate near the teeth. This explains why the
cut which is generally adopted stops at the level of the
necks. This lack of covering for the teeth deprives certain users of electropalatography of information which
could otherwise be of interest to them. This is particularly the case for orthodontic specialists who are concerned
with the relationship of tongue to teeth during speech and
during swallowing: the use of palatal plates covering the
teeth could give them the means of following minor inter-
positions and protusions of the tongue during speech which
are not always easy to detect. While this single palatal
plate gave us entire satisfaction so that we were led to
adopt it as "artificial palate" for indirect palatography,
with excellent results, the development of the electrodes
presented us with a number of difficulties.

Construction and positioning of the electrodes (Fig. 2).
Within the framework of the research-programme E.L.P.A.I.,
three palatal plates were developed: the construction of
the plates followed the same principle in each case, the
only difference being in the positioning of the electrodes

which varied from one prototype to another. The first
prototype ELPAI I. 1., Fig. 2D., had only twelve electrodes
which were positioned to record the maximum number of
tongue-contacts for the articulation of French consonants
(based on the results of the preliminary experimentation).
The second plate, ELPAI I. 2. Fig. 2E., was fitted with
thirty-eight electrodes in order to allow a more detailed
exploration. The purpose of this second plate was above
all to check whether it was possible to increase the number
of electrodes without abandoning the Biostar technique: the
results were positive in all respects. The third prototype,
ELPA I. 3. Fig. 2B, C., was designed with a view to carrying
out a series of studies on the regions of articulation of
anterior consonants in French: 12 electrodes were placed in
the retro-incisive region, from the neck of the central
incisors to the far limit of the first pre-molars, with the
remaining four electrodes placed on the lateral edges of
the palate.

In all three cases, the techniques used for placing
the electrodes were the same. The desired positions of the
electrodes were first marked with small circles on the
mould of the dental arch. When the plate is subsequently
placed on the model the positions can be marked on the
transparent plate. The electrodes were manufactured by
removing the protective enamel by flame from one end of
each of the 16 copper wires used (the diameter of the bare
wire is then increased until a copper ball of approximately 0,6 mm is obtained which is fixed in place, with
its linking wires by means of a special adhesive (methylic
butyl acetate). The wires are then gathered into two bun-
dles one each side of the dental arch, at the level of each
tuberosity and are placed under a thermo-shrinking sheath.
This sheath, itself held in place by the same adhesive,
takes the bundle of wires from the level of the neck of
the third molar up to the canines. When the plate is placed
in the subject's mouth, the sheaths leave the mouth from
the corners of the lips.

The present state of the palatographic plate. At this
stage of development (Fig. 2B), satisfactory solutions have
been found to most of the problems outlined above: both in

as far as respecting the palatal morphology is concerned and
for the thickness and stability of the plate. There are,
however, a number of possible difficulties during usage
caused by the copper balls or the wires breaking. Furthermore it proved impossible to assure perfectly hygienic conditions of use for such an apparatus. In order to increase
the strength of the plate and to protect the electrodes and
the wires we decided to make use of a second plate, also
made with the Biostar technique and stuck to the first using
ACRYSIVE (Fig. 2C.). It is possible to make use of the
stretching of the material which occurs when it is heated
but nonetheless the final thickness of the new plate was
close to 1 mm in several places. As the electrodes were
now sandwiched between two sheets of Imprelon the plastic
covering then was removed by means of a needlepoint. Once
the conductivity of each of the connecting wires had been
tested, the apparatus was ready for use.

   Possibilities of improvement. Without abandoning the
Biostar technique which has given entire satisfaction,
several possible improvements have been envisaged. It
should be possible in the very near future to return to a
plate of less thickness (0,5 mm) covered on the inner surface with a varnish or a resin protecting the wires and
the electrodes. Furthermore, the use of silver wires and
electrodes. should ensure a better conductivity of the
current. Our present researches, however, are aimed at
developing the use of electropalatography (for therapeutic
and pedagogical purposes). To do this it will be necessary
to reduce the cost of each plate. One solution would be to
construct a single "artificial palate" per subject and to
interchange the wires and electrodes from one plate to
another. Another possibility which we had already envisaged
in 1975 would be to use sheets of Imprelon with wires and
electrodes incorporated which could then simply be moulded
to the shape of each subject's palate.

The Linguo-palatal Contact Processing Unit

   The sine-wave generator. The electropalatographic
system we use was originally outlined by Kydd and Belt (1964)
and needs only a single source for the excitation signal.
This signal is an alternating current of 20 kH which is

passed through the subject's body by means of an electrode
which we place on his forehead by means of a suction contact as used for electrocardiography. The current is
supplied to the electrode by means of a sine-wave generator
which consists of an oscillator with a very stable frequency and an automatic gain-control amplifier. The output
current is limited to 100 microamps by means of a special
circuit. The output voltage of the generator varies with
an infinite resolution of 0 to 10 volts peak to peak.

The palatal electrode signal processing unit. One of
the numerous advantages of the KYDD and BELT system is to
allow the processing of signals from the palatal electrodes
(or palatal contacts) by means of a number of identical
relatively simple circuits. They consist of a voltage
amplifier of high input impedance (10 M ohm) followed by
a band-pass filter with a high Q factor adjusted exactly to
the frequency of oscillation of the generator. A threshold
detector, consisting of a hysteresis comparator produces a
pulse when the input signal is above a certain threshold
which is fixed at the same level for all the electrodes.
These pulses are then sorted by means of a temporal filter
and then, by way of opto-electric isolating circuits, fed
to a sampling and memorising system. The sampling frequency
is 100 Hz (thus giving a representation of linguo-palatal
contacts every 10 ms). The operator can store in the memory
the representation of the contacts at any moment he chooses.
Finally, various interfaces make it possible to send the
signals, in parallel, in three directions; (a) to a display
panel, (b) to a galvanometric recorded and (c) to a computer,
after multiplexing the various contacts.

The Operation of the Electropalatograph

The reliability of the detection of contacts. During
the first tests, which we began running, at the beginning of
our experiments on the tongue-electrode contacts, we noticed
that certain signals were obviously not caused by contact
between the tongue and the electrodes. In the case of some
subjects the operation of the system showed a great deal of
disturbance. To investigate this further we undertook a
series of measurements of the conductivity of the saliva of

various subjects. A few drops of saliva taken from ten
subjects were placed on two electrodes with a diameter of
1 mm and separated by 2,5 mm. The resistance between the
two electrodes was measured by an Impedance bridge (General
Radio Type) with an alternating excitation signal of 20 kH.
Our results brought to light considerable differences
between the conductivity of the saliva of various subjects.
A second experiment using the same material made it possible to measure the resistance between the emitting electrode
and the palatal electrode in actual contact with the tongue.
The results of these two measurements presented in the table
of Figure 3 show that in all but one case the total resistance of the circuit: emitting electrode - tongue - palatal
electrode is lower than the resistance between two adjacent
electrodes caused by the conductivity of the saliva. This
means that it is necessary to make a very precise adjustment of the signal level and for the amplitude to be
particularly stable. For this reason, we equipped the
generator with an automatic gain control which allows a
stability of 0,1% for the amplitude. The cut-off frequencies of the filters are adjusted exactly to the frequency
of the oscillator. In order to avoid loss of gain of the
filters caused by ageing of the components, we used a circuit known for the stability of his components. The threshold detector is a comparator to which we added a hysteresis
in order to prevent it from being set off erratically at
levels which are badly defined in relation to the threshold.
Finally, to prevent it being set off accidentally, which
despite all precautions is always possible, the comparator
is followed by a circuit which is a temporal filter, and
which eliminates any pulse which is below the period of the
oscillator, i.e. 25 micro secs.

Visualisation of the contacts. The visualisation of
the tongue-palate contacts is obtained by means of a panel
representing a photograph of the palate in the mouth at a
scale 4 x 1 (Fig. 4). In place of the electrodes, we fixed
light-emitting diodes. Such a panel, despite its spectacu-
lar nature, is in practice not very efficient. It is in fact
only used for pedagogical demonstrations where the subject
produces isolated articulations and makes use of the possibility of storing the signals in the memory. In this case,

electropalatography can be favorably compared to classic
indirect palatography. In order to achieve a long-term
memorisation of articulatory movements, we made use of a
video-recorder with a satisfactory pause. This method
was however lacking in precision since the pause on a video-
recorder is particularly difficult to position. This type
of recording was consequently rapidly abandoned. A more
efficient type of recording was made by the use of galvanometric recorders for the visualisation of the contacts
as a function of time. We consequently made use of two
Siemens L Oscillomink recorders with the same speed
(Fig. 5). This method is very efficient since it allows
for a high degree of precision but does not give a palatal
representation. We are, however, using this method for the
moment while waiting for the connection of the electropalatograph to our computer to be completed. The computer
we use is a S.E.M.S. T 1600. The information from the
contacts is sent via a 16 bit word after multiplexing.
After processing, the results can be visualised on a
TEKTRONIX 4012 screen and printed on a HOUSTON 8230 high-
speed line printer. The sampling frequency of the palatal
representation is fixed at 100 Hz, i.e., every 10 ms.

Intended Developments

     Since we consider that the full use of the electro-
palatograph implies that other measurements be made simultaneously, we have envisaged a number of developments of
the basic system. The first consists of the synchronic
recording of the palatal representation and the acoustic
spectrum, in order to establish correlations between articulatory realisations and the acoustic results. In order to
do this, we are at present connecting our computer to a
P.A.R. 4512 real-time analyser. This apparatus will make
it possible to obtain spectra of 128 resolution-points in
10 ms, timed by the sampling clock of the electropalatograph.
The second development will consist of the synchronisation
of X-ray films of the vocal tract at 100 frames per second
with the electropalatograph and the real-time analyser. We
will thus dispose of three simultaneous analyses. The
biggest obstacle at the moment is the distance separating
the hospital where our X-ray equipment is installed and our

computer. The solution we are examining at the moment would be to make use of three track instrumental recording with one track for the vocal signal, one for the synchronisation taken from the supply of the X-ray tube, and the third for the palatal contact information.

After a first phase of trial and error, understandable in such a complex field as the analysis of speech production, we managed to find a certain number of solutions to the problems we came across which will, we hope, make it possible to increase the number of applications of electropalatography. While a certain number of improvements are still necessary for the material to function satisfactorily, we feel that we have now reached a point where the decisive factor will be the method of interpretation of a vast amount of new data, and it is here that the phonetician-physiologist comes into his own.

REFERENCES

Fujii, I. (1970). Ann. Bull. Res. Inst. Log. Phon. U. Tokyo, 4:67-75.

Fukimura, O., Tatsumi, F., Kagaya, R. (1973). J. Phon., 1:47-54.

Hardcastle, W. J. (1972). Phonet., 25:197-215.

Hardcastle, W. J. and Roach, P. J. (1977). Phon. Lab. Univ. Reading, 1:27-44.

Kydd, W. L. and Belt, D. A. (1964). J. Speech Hear. Dis., 29:489-494.

Ladefoged, P. (1957). J. Speech Hear. Dis., 39:764-774.

Mollard, R. J. (1975). Thèse, Université d'Aix-Marseille II.

Palmer, J. M. (1973). Phonet., 28:76-85.

Rome, J. A. (1964). QPR, RLE, MIT, 94:190-191.

Scheu, R. (1968). L'inf. Dent., 48:3-7.

Shibata, S. A. (1968). Ann. Bull. Res. Inst. Log. Phon. U. Tokyo, 2:28-35.

Witting, C. (1953). Stud. Ling., 7:54-68.

ACKNOWLEDGMENTS: We express our gratitude to Mr. Tallet, Dr. R. J. Mollard and Mr. L. Seimandi--and to Mr. Daniel Hurst for this translation from the original text in French.

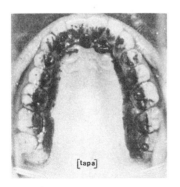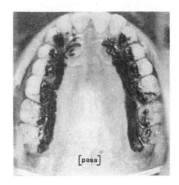

A. Direct palatography

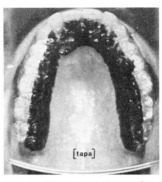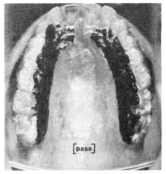

B. Indirect palatography (artificial palate made with a sheet
       of IMPRELON of 0,5 mm thickness).

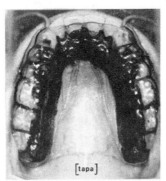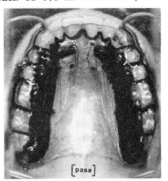

C. Electropalatographic plate (2 sheets of IMPRELON: 1 mm thickness).

Fig. 1: Effects of the thickness of the palatographic plate in
          phonetic realisations (/t/ and /s/ in French).

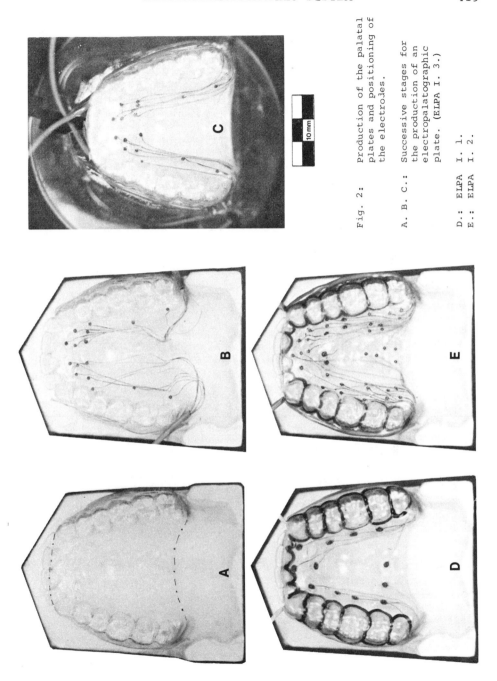

Fig. 2: Production of the palatal plates and positioning of the electrodes.

A. B. C.: Successive stages for the production of an electropalatographic plate. (ELPA I. 3.)

D.: ELPA I. 1.
E.: ELPA I. 2.

SUBJECTS	CONDUCTIVITY between two electrodes Ø 1mm separated by 2.54mm Kohm	RESISTANCE between frontal electrode and palatal contact Kohm
1	17	7
2	26	13
3	13	13
4	11	10
5	18	11
6	15	8
7	18	7
8	16	6
9	25	8
10	11	6

Fig. 3: Comparison of the conductivity of saliva and frontal-palatal resistance for different subjects.

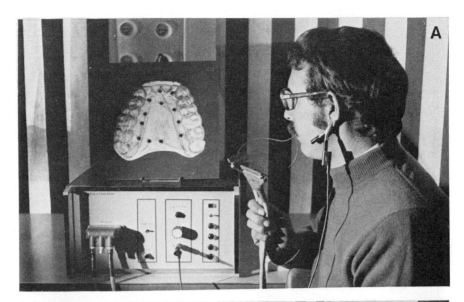

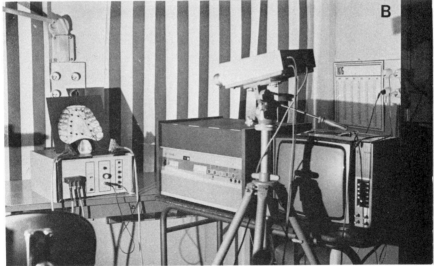

Fig. 4: Visualisation of the tongue-palate contacts by means of a panel (photography of the palate with light-emitting diodes):

A. Pedagogical direct demonstration.
B. Video-recording.

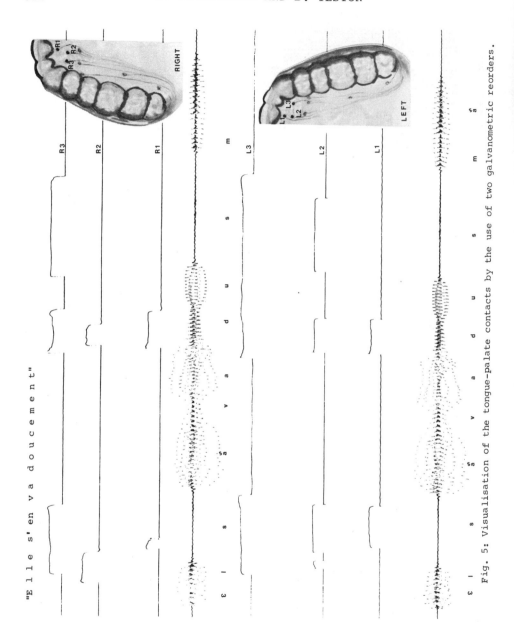

Fig. 5: Visualisation of the tongue-palate contacts by the use of two galvanometric reorders.

INADEQUACIES IN PHONETIC SPECIFICATIONS OF SOME LARYNGEAL FEATURES: EVIDENCE FROM HINDI

R. PRAKASH DIXIT
Louisiana State University

Some languages use voicing, others use aspiration, still others use voicing and aspiration together to distinguish their stop consonants. Hindi falls in the last group of languages. The intersecting categories of voicing and aspiration yield a four-way manner contrast in various stop consonants of Hindi, such as unvoiced unaspirated, unvoiced aspirated, voiced unaspirated, and voiced aspirated. Since both voicing and aspiration are considered to be laryngeal phenomena, they are phonetically specified in terms of laryngeal adjustment and action. However, phonetic specification of these features in terms of laryngeal adjustment and action has not always been adequate and satisfactory. A number of recent electromyographic (EMG), photoelectroglottographic (PEG) and fiber-optic investigations have produced a considerable body of data which can be utilized to reveal inadequacies in phonetic specification of these features. To that end, EMG and PEG evidence from Hindi is presented and discussed in this paper.

Figure 1 presents averaged EMG traces of the interarytenoid (IA) and the lateral cricoarytenoid (LCA) muscles for the experimental utterances /pipi/, /phiphi/, /bibi/, and /bhibhi/ which were produced in the frame sentence /didi - bolIye/. Over these traces are displayed averaged PEG traces for the same utterances. In Figure 2, averaged

EMG activity of the thyroarytenoid (TA) and the cricothyroid (CT) muscles for the utterances /apa/, /apha/,
/aba/, and /abha/ is shown. These utterances were produced
in the frame sentence /kya - hæ/. In these figures the
dotted lines represent the unvoiced unaspirated stop /p/,
the solid lines the unvoiced aspirated stop /ph/, the
broken lines the voiced unaspirated stop /b/ and the dashed-
dotted lines the voiced aspirated stop /bh/.

   Examination of Figures 1 and 2 reveals that all the
adductor muscles, the IA, LCA and TA, show marked suppression of EMG activity for the aspirated stops /ph/ and /bh/
as compared to that for the unaspirated stops /p/ and /b/.
Moreover, the adductor suppression for /ph/ is relatively
greater than for /bh/. On the other hand, the IA activity
is quite dissimilar from that of the LCA and TA muscles for
the two stops /p/ and /b/ in the unaspirated category of
stops. The IA suppression for /p/ is relatively greater
than for /b/, for which it is only minimal, while the
activity levels in the LCA and TA muscles for /p/ and /b/
are about the same. Further, the LCA and TA muscles show
only slight suppression of their activity for both /p/ and
/b/. However, the CT muscle shows an entirely different
pattern of EMG activity when compared to EMG patterns of
the IA, LCA and TA muscles. The levels of activity in the
CT muscle are consistently higher for the unvoiced stops
/p/ and /ph/ than for the voiced stops /b/ and /bh/. The
CT muscle appears to contribute to the maintenance of
voicing distinction in Hindi stops by facilitating elimina-
tion of gottal pulsing during closure periods of the unvoiced stops. No posterior cricoarytenoid (PCA) activity
could be recorded from the subject used for the present
study. However, the EMG activity of the PCA muscle seems
to be reflected in the PEG curves in Figure 1. These
curves show relative degrees of glottal opening during Hindi
stops /p/, /ph/, and /bh/. Hirose, Yoshioka and Niimi
(1977) have shown positive correlation between the degree
of glottal opening and the magnitude of PCA activation.
Hence, a reciprocal pattern of activity between the PCA
and the IA, LCA and TA muscles can be presumed during
Hindi stop consonant productions.

As a result of reciprocal activity of the abductor and adductor muscles of the larynx, the aspirated stops, both voiced and unvoiced, are produced with glottal opening in all phonetic environments (some of which are shown in Figure 1). The magnitude of glottal opening during the voiced aspirated stops is approximately half of that observed during the unvoiced aspirated stops. On the other hand, in the unaspirated category of stops, the voiced ones are produced with closed glottis, whereas their unvoiced counterparts are produced with either open glottis or closed glottis. That is, the unvoiced unaspirated stops are produced with open glottis in word-initial position before a vowel and with closed glottis in word-medial position between vowels. The extent of glottal opening during the unvoiced unaspirated stops is either as much as during voiced aspirated stops or smaller. The opening and closing gestures of the glottis are variously times for different stops, as shown in the PEG curves in Figure 1. Moreover, the voiceless stops exhibit relatively greater fold tension than their voiced cognates, as reflected in the activity levels of the CT muscle in Figure 2.

IMPLICATIONS FOR LARYNGEAL FEATURE THEORIES

These findings have serious implications for various feature systems which use binary features, such as (± voice), (± spread glottis), or scalar features like "glottal stricture," "voice onset time," etc., to differentiate voiced from unvoiced stops and aspirated from unaspirated stops. They not only point to the inadequacies in phonetic specification of some of the laryngeal features associated with stop consonant productions but also question the validity of some of those features. Chomsky and Halle (1968) have proposed four binary phonetic features: voicing, tenseness, glottal constriction, and heightened subglottal pressure. As defined by Chomsky and Halle, the tenseness involves greater articulatory effort which results from tension of the supraglottal musculature. This tension is supposed to eliminate vocal fold vibration by preventing the expansion of the supraglottal cavities during production of the stop consonants. The feature of voice

is defined as that state of the glottis during which the
glottis is neither constricted nor wide open. If the air flow
through the glottis is adequate, and if the vocal folds are
properly configured, voicing will occur. The feature of heightened subglottal pressure is related to the production of aspiration. According to Chomsky and Halle, "Heightened subglottal pressure is a necessary but not sufficient condition
for aspiration. Aspiration requires, in addition, that there
be no constriction at the glottis." On the other hand, the
feature of glottal constriction appears to be related to
those stops which differ from plosive stops in their air
stream mechanism.

Out of these four phonetic features only two, the voice
and glottal constriction, are laryngeal features. The tensity and heightened subglottal pressure are only indirectly
related to laryngeal function. It appears from the table
of phonetic features that only two features, the voice and
heightened subglottal pressure, are necessary to account
for the contrasts of voicing and aspiration in the stop consonants of Hindi. Tensity and glottal constriction are apparently redundant features. However, without the use of
the tensity feature with the feature of voice it was not
possible to reveal whether the voicing occurred or did not
occur during a certain stop consonant. Even when the state
of the glottis itself is favorable to voicing, whether voicing will occur during closure period of a stop depends on
the displacement of the supraglottal structures. Hence,
the specification (- tense) for the voiced stops and (+
tense) for the unvoiced stops is only to fit the fact that
voicing occurs during voiced stops and does not occur during unvoiced stops. The feature of glottal constriction,
which has minus values for all the stops of Hindi, appears
to have been used to show that they are produced with a different adjustment of the glottal aperture than are the implosives and the ejectives. The redundant use of the features of tensity and glottal constriction may be justified
on the above grounds. However, the specification (+ voice)
for both the voiced aspirated and voiced unaspirated stops
of Hindi is quite unjustifiable in the feature system proposed by Chomsky and Halle, since during voiced aspirates

the glottis is quite wide open whereas during voiced inaspirates the glottis is closed. Similarly, the specification (- voice) for the aspirated and unaspirated members of the unvoiced category of stops is also improper,
because the glottal opening during unvoiced aspirated
stops of Hindi is only slightly less than during breathing, while unvoiced unaspirated stops are produced with
either closed glottis or with glottal opening which is
never more than that observed during voiced aspirates.

The feature of heightened subglottal pressure related
to Hindi aspirated stops has found no support in the subglottal pressure data of Ohala and Ohala (1972), and Dixit
and Shipp (1975). Neither Ohala and Ohala nor Dixit and
Shipp found a necessary correlation between heightened subglottal pressure and Hindi aspirates. Thus, it is quite
obvious that Chomsky and Halle's use of the heightened subglottal pressure feature and some of the specifications of
the voice feature are contrafactual and inadequate.

Halle and Stevens' (1971) feature system is based on
"two independently controlled parameters: "the stiffness
of the vocal cords" and "the static glottal opening."
Various adjustments of these glottal parameters yield a set
of four laryngeal features: spread glottis, constricted
glottis, stiff vocal cords, and slack vocal cords (cf.
Table 1). The feature of spread glottis is defined as out-
ward displacement of the vocal cords from the position for
normal voicing, resulting from the adjustment of the arytenoid cartilages. The feature of constricted glottis is
described thusly: "Adduction of the arytenoid cartilages
relative to the position for normal voicing (accomplished,
perhaps, by fibers of the thyroarytenoid muscles, as well as
by the lateral cricoarytenoid muscles) can cause the vocal
cords to be pressed together and the glottis to narrow or to
close." On the other hand, stiffness and slackness of the
vocal cords are controlled "through adjustment of the
thyroarytenoid and cricothyroid muscles." These features
are used in terms of two binary oppositions each: (± spread
glottis), (± constricted glottis), (± stiff vocal cords),
and (± slack vocal cords). The combinations (+ spread,

+ constricted) and (+ stiff, + slack) are not permitted as
they are "logically and physiologically" impossible. It
appears from the description, given by Halle and Stevens,
of the laryngeal features of spread glottis and constricted
glottis in relation to the position for normal voicing that
during normal voicing or neutral position of the glottis
the arytenoid cartilages are partially apart. If this
assumption is true, then their neutral position of the
glottis runs counter to most of the experimental data that
have been reported in various recent EMG and PEG studies.
Most studies have shown that the arytenoid cartilages are
usually adducted during vowels and voiced stops which,
according to Halle and Stevens, are produced with neutral
position of the glottis. If the above assumption is incorrect, then Halle and Stevens' definition of the constricted
glottis is invalidated, because the already adducted arytenoids cannot be adducted any further. Hirose, Lisker and
Abramson (1972) have shown that the levels of activity in
the IA muscle, which is the adductor of the arytenoids, are
about the same for the plain voiced plosives and the voiced
implosives. It should be remembered that the implosives are
produced with the constricted glottis. Obviously, the IA
does not play any different role during implosives than it
plays during voiced plosives. (The above discussion may be
applicable to the neutral position of the glottis as described by Chomsky and Halle (1968) also.)

Similar objections, as were made against the Chomsky
and Halle specifications of the feature of voice, can be
made against Halle and Stevens' specifications of the feature of spread glottis for various stop consonants of Hindi.
The specifications (+ spread glottis) for both voiced aspirated and unvoiced aspirated and (- spread glottis) for
both voiced unaspirated and unvoiced unaspirated stops do
not seem adequate, because all these stops are produced with
different degrees of glottal stricture. Moreover, the unvoiced unaspirated stops, as indicated earlier, are produced with arytenoid abduction in word-initial position,
while in intervocalic position they are produced with adducted arytenoids. The use of the feature of constricted
glottis is quite similar in both Chomsky and Halle (1968)

and Halle and Stevens (1971) proposals. In terms of the
Halle and Stevens laryngeal feature system, the voiced and
unvoiced (both aspirated and unaspirated) stop consonants
of Hindi are specified as (– stiff vocal cords) and (+ stiff
vocal cords), respectively. These specifications find
strong support in the EMG data of the present study. The
data of this study have demonstrated that the CT muscle
shows high levels of activity during voiceless stops,
whereas during voiced stops the CT muscle activity is
relatively suppressed.

An alternative set of five laryngeal features:
glottalicness, voice onset, glottal stricture, pitch, and
cover feature, has been proposed by Ladefoged (1973). "All
these features are scales with, theoretically, an in-
finitely large number of phonetic values possible for each
of them." The first three features, which according to
Ladefoged, are "linguistic" features, have been used for
phonetic specification of different stop consonants in
various languages including Hindi. The feature of glottalicness has two values, the feature of voice onset has three
values, and the feature of glottal stricture has eight values.
Ladefoged has used the terms voiced plosives, voiceless
plosives, aspirated plosives, and murmured (breathy voiced)
plosives which correspond to the terms voiced unaspirated,
unvoiced unaspirated, unvoiced aspirated, and voiced aspirated, respectively. The 0 (zero) specification for the
feature of glottalicness indicates that this feature is redundant in relation to Hindi plosive stops. The values
shown for the features of voice onset and glottal stricture
are scalar values. With regard to Hindi stops, Ladefoged
assigns glottal stricture value 2 to the unvoiced unaspirated
stops and 3 to the voiced aspirated stops. In the light of
the present data, the above assignment of feature values is
contrafactual and inadequate, since in no case were the
Hindi unvoiced unaspirated stops produced with a larger
glottal opening than the voiced aspirated stops. It should
be recalled that the unvoiced unaspirated stops in intervocalic position were produced with a closed glottis and in
word-initial position with a certain degree of glottal opening which always was smaller than that found in the voiced

aspirated stops in any position. Furthermore, Ladefoged's
assignment of the same voice onset value for both the
unvoiced aspirated and the voiced aspirated stops is also
inappropriate. The dimension of voice onset cannot be
used in case of the voiced aspirated stops, as was rightly
acknowledged by Lisker and Abramson (1964), since such
stops in Hindi are produced with glottal pulsing throughout their total closure and aspiration duration. Ladefoged
has justified his use of the voice onset feature in case of
the voiced aspirated stops of Hindi by saying that the
voicing during articulatory closure of these stops is of
"the kind that would be expected from a small volume of air
flowing through the glottis while it is in the position for
a murmured sound and the articulatory closure is preventing
a high flow rate." These Hindi stops "are followed by comparatively long period of breathy voice after the release
of the closure and before the start of regular voicing in
the vowel." I do not deny that there may be differences in
voicing during the closure interval of a voiced unaspirated
stop and a voiced aspirated stop and that the voiced
aspirated stop is followed by a long period of breathy voice,
but this is beside the point. The point is that the voiced
aspirated stops of Hindi are produced with fold vibration
throughout their oral occlusion and aspiration period.
Hence, Ladefoged is unjustified in calling the voiced
aspirated stops of Hindi "delayed in voice onset."

REFERENCES

Chomsky, N. and Halle, M.   (1968).   New York, Harper and Row.
Dixit, R. P. and Shipp, T.   (1975).   Paper, Acoust. Soc. Am.
Halle, M. and Stevens, K. N.   (1971).   QPR, RLE, MIT,
      198-213.
Hirose, H., Lisker, L. and Abramson, A. S.   (1972).   SR
      31/32 Haskins Lab., 183-191.
Hirose, H., Yoshioka, H. and Niimi, S.   (1977).   Paper,
      An International Phonetic Science Congress, December
      17-19, Miami Beach, Florida.
Ladefoged, P.   (1973).   J. Phon., 1:73-83.
Lisker, L. and Abramson, A. S.   (1964).   Word, 20:384-422.
Ohala, M. and Ohala, J.   (1972).   Ann. Bul. (RILP), 6:39-46.

Table 1. Phonetic specification of Hindi stop consonants
in accordance with various feature systems.

	Unvoiced unaspirated	Unvoiced aspirated	Voiced unaspirated	Voiced aspirated
Chomsky and Halle (1968)				
Tense	+	+	−	−
Voice	−	−	+	+
Heightened P_S	−	+	−	+
Glottal constriction	−	−	−	−
Halle and Stevens (1971)				
Spread glottis	−	+	−	+
constricted glottis	−	−	−	−
Stiff vocal cords	+	+	−	−
Slack vocal cords	−	−	+	+
Ladefoged (1973)				
Glottalicness	0	0	0	0
Glottal stricture	2	1	5	3
Voice onset time	2	3	1	3

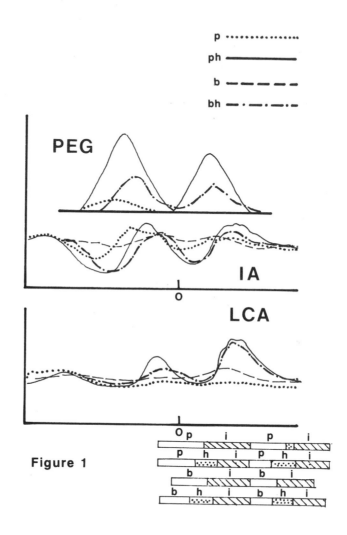

Figure 1

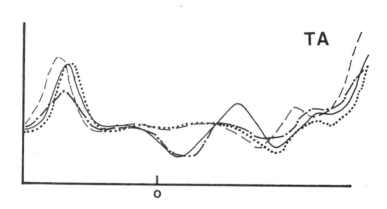

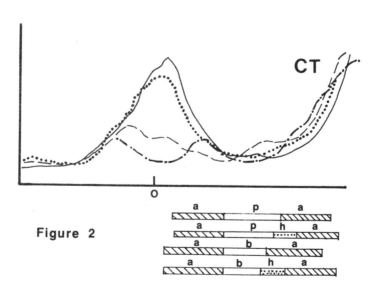

Figure 2

VOCALIC VARIABILITY IN PALATOGRAPHIC IMPRESSIONS

SOLOMON I. SARA
Georgetown University

This paper is in the nature of a report on data collected on palatographic impressions that were.done by
graduate and senior undergraduate students who participated
in a course in instrumental articulatory phonetics. The
data was collected over the last four years. All the students were native speakers of American English who were
linguistic majors. They were well acquainted with the phonetic details of articulation and have a good appreciation
of the difficulty of determining the differences among closely
related articulatory segments, e.g. /e, ɛ /. The vowel distinctions discussed in this report were clearly produced by
all the subjects and were so judged by all the participants
in the experiments without any noticeable pathological deviation from what is considered normal speech. Palatography is
one of the speech sciences. Since the days of its originator
Oakly Coles (Coles, 1872), it has been used sparingly despite
its ease and usefulness. Recently, however, various palatographic methods have been employed and there seems to be a
renewed interest in its potential as a contributor to our
knowledge of phonetics.

There are three palatographic methods in current use.
First, direct palatography is the method whereby the palate
is dusted with a removable powdery substance before the
utterance to be studied, then the palate is photographed
after the utterance. In this method the study of the palate
is based on the photographs of the palate (Keller, 1971).
Even though this method is more natural than the other methods,

it is quite cumbersome and needs at least two people for
good results, i.e., the subject and the experimenter.
Secondly, dynamic palatography which is a type of indirect
palatography whereby an artificial palate is fitted with
metal electrodes that can register tongue contact and/or
pressure during the articulation of sounds. ˙ The output from
this type of palate is fed into a computer terminal for
recording and analysis and can be connected to a CRT screen
for visual display and observation. This method of palatography gives the most accurate account of tongue-palate contacts. Thirdly, static palatography where an artificial
palate is inserted into the mouth for each utterance and removed for copying or study purposes. The data collected and
discussed in this paper were obtained with this last method
of palatography.

   A word on the procedures used here may be appropriate.
All the artificial palates used in these experiments were
made from pliable dental wax that was fitted by each student
over his or her palate. In order to make the palate fit
snugly and securely, its edges were extended over the upper
teeth. Such artificial palates insert and remove easily,
and when they are properly fitted, they can be left in the
mouth during speech and cause no great hindrance to speech.
The ease of manipulation was essential for the conduct of
these experiments. Once the subject was at ease with the
palate in place, and was able to speak properly, the experiment began. The actual procedure is very simple. The palate
is removed from the mouth and dusted with a powdery substance,
in this case with cornstarch; then the palate is inserted in
place, the lexical item is pronounced, the palate is removed
from the mouth. The palate may be photographed, the wipe-
offs traced on graph paper or simply studied as it is.

   The measurements in these experiments were done as
follows: Each subject traced his/her artificial palate onto
a stencil which was duplicated on graph paper. To trace the
tongue wipe-offs from the dusted palate onto the graph paper,
a clear plastic grid was made that corresponded to the
measurements on the graph paper that was used by the student.
This plastic grid was placed on the artificial palate that
was held level, and the wipe-offs from the palate were traced

on the corresponding duplicated palate traces on the graph
paper. Each utterance in these experiments was palatographed
and recorded at least three separate times and the measurements shown in Charts I-VI are the corresponding averages
from the multiple traces for each segment. Only three
measurements were taken for each segment as shown in Figure
1.

    Results: The data obtained from the experiments are
tabulated in Charts I-VI. There is no doubt that the results of the experiments are not uniform. The cause may be
partially due to the limitations of palatography itself.
Not all sounds are easily palatographed even if they are
palatal sounds. A good illustration of this would be the
back vowels. In addition, one is limited to a single tongue
gesture per utterance; and for best results for vowels one
is limited to either intoned vowels or to vowels in contexts
of labial and/or laryngeal consonants as seen from the
lexical list used in these experiments: peep /i/, /u/ hoop,
pip /ɩ/, /ɷ/ hoof, babe /e/, /o/ pope, pep /ɛ/, pop /a/.
Palatography is of limited use for the study of the back
vowels. In these experiments not all the subjects show
palatographic impressions for all the back vowels. Below
are the percentages of vowels missed by the subjects: /a/
8/18 i.e. 44%, /o/ 7/18 i.e., 39%, /ɷ/ 3/18 i.e. 17% and
/u/ 2/18 i.e. 11%. It seems, then, that palatography is not
a satisfying method for obtaining data from all subjects.
Some speakers may not be apt candidates for palatography.
Palatographic results are, however, much more promising when
applied to the front vowels.

    In order to characterize the different vowels, three
standard measurements were taken as shown in Figure 1. One
would expect comparable degrees of consistency for all the
measured vowels using any of these three measurements, but
such consistent results were not forthcoming. Chart III
(measurement c in Figure 1) shows that there is a tendency
for the high vowels to measure less distance to channel
narrowing than the more open vowels. There are, however,
seven exceptions to this tendency in the data. Chart II
(measurement b in Figure 1) shows that in moving from /i/ to
/a/ one expects a gradual retraction or lowering of the

tongue contact along the edges of the palate receding as
the vowel becomes more open. Chart II shows that this
measurement does not consistently reflect this feature in
moving from a high to a lower position. For example, only
15/18 i.e. 83% of the subjects show that /i/ is more forward than /e/. Two subjects show the reverse. Chart I
(measurement a in Figure 1) which measures the channel width,
more consistent results are obtained. With this measurement
16/18, i.e. 88.9% of the subjects have /i/ narrower than /e/
and 2/18, i.e. 11% have the same degree of narrowness for
both. There are no cases where /e/ is narrower than /i/.
The sameness of the degree of narrowness between these two
vowels can be attributed to their tenseness. From the results of these experiments the degree of narrowness has a
greater correlation with what is known about the positions
for the vowels and hence it is a more reliable measure of
their differences.

     Tense and Lax: Greater precision is needed when de-
limiting differences that distinguish between the tense and
lax vowels, e.g. /i,ɩ/, /e,ɛ/, /u,ɷ/. Tenseness and laxness
have been applied to these pairs of vowels, but the notions
themselves have escaped precise characterization. From the
data listed in Charts IV-VI, measurement "c" in Figure 1 is
summarized in Chart IV. These measurements do not give a
consistent reading for distinguishing tense·from lax. Even
though there is a tendency for the tense member to have a
shorter distance than the lax member, there are 14/50, i.e.
28% cases that show the reverse tendency. Chart V (measurement b Figure 1) gives slightly better readings in showing
that tenser members are farther front than the corresponding
lax members. There are, however, 11/51, i.e. 22% pairs that
give the reverse type of readings. The measurements that
give consistent readings for the relationships between these
pairs of vowels are shown in Chart V (measurement a Figure 1).
The degree of narrowing is consistently differentiated between the vowel pairs as the tenser member shows the narrower
channel and the laxer vowel the correspondingly wider channel.

     From the considerations of the above data, and the
variety of measurements taken, there is reason to maintain
that they are not of equal value. One can safely conclude

that the channel width, in all the cases studied above, gives the most consistent results in distinguishing the vowels. One is reminded here of Henry Sweet who exactly a century ago distinguished these vowels as narrow and broad, an insight that is born out by these measurements (Sweet, 1970).

REFERENCES

Butcher, A. and Weiker, E.   (1976).   J. Phon., 4:59-74.

Coles, O.   (1872).   Trans. Odont.Soc.Gr.Brit.,4:110-123.

Fujimura, D., Tatsumi, I. F. and Kagaya, R.   (1973). J.Phon., 1:47-54.

Keller, K.C.(1971).   Norman Oklahoma, SIL.

McGlone, R. E. and Proffit, W. D.   (1972).   Proceed. Inter. Cong. Phon. Sci., The Hague, Mouton, 375-379.

Sweet, Henry.   (1970, 1877).   College Park, Md., McGrath Pub. Co.

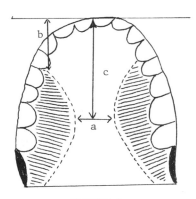

FIGURE 1

Chart I.   Channel width in millimeters. F=feminine
                                           M—masculine

Subjects	i	e	a	u	o
Fl	18	24	26	30	Ø
F2	15	27	45	33	35
F3	19	26	43	27	29
F4	19	19	Ø	Ø	Ø
F5	14	20	Ø	23	29
F6	25	27	32	27	27
F7	20	21	Ø	22	Ø
F8	10	18	34	17	24
F9	25	25	20	27	Ø
F10	21	28	28	29	28
F11	17	24	Ø	22	25
M1	12	17	Ø	23	Ø
M2	12	28	Ø	Ø	Ø
M3	12	19	29	24	29
M4	20	27	36	32	39
M5	20	25	34	36	32
M6	21	22	Ø	28	Ø
M7	26	30	Ø	33	38

Chart II.   Distance to front wipe off in millimeters.

Subjects	i	e	a	u	o
Fl	19	14	26	24	Ø
F2	22	26	51	48	54
F3	26	22	27	39	47
F4	35	38	Ø	Ø	Ø
F5	15	18	Ø	37	39
F6	18	25	37	32	32
F7	14	15	Ø	40	Ø
F8	12	15	53	24	48
F9	18	22	25	25	Ø
F10	20	26	46	39	41
F11	20	25	Ø	25	20
M1	21	21	Ø	23	Ø
M2	15	28	Ø	Ø	Ø
M3	10	16	38	30	46
M4	17	19	42	41	41
M5	10	19	27	31	27
M6	14	22	Ø	28	Ø
M7	27	19	Ø	36	35

Chart III. Distance to channel narrowing in millimeters.

Subjects	i	e	a	u	o
F1	31	27	39	37	∅
F2	30	31	51	50	52
F3	38	43	40	50	55
F4	45	50	∅	∅	∅
F5	31	39	∅	50	46
F6	30	35	45	37	40
F7	31	25	∅	63	∅
F8	24	25	55	38	53
F9	25	30	45	45	∅
F10	30	40	53	51	52
F11	30	30	∅	35	30
M1	27	34	∅	40	∅
M2	30	34	∅	∅	∅
M3	22	35	44	44	54
M4	46	45	57	55	55
M5	25	26	39	39	27
M6	32	37	∅	42	∅
M7	35	27	∅	45	55

Chart IV. Channel width in millimeters

Subjects	i	ɪ	e	ɛ	u	ɔ
F1	18	31	24	31	30	30
F2	15	33	27	29	33	32
F3	19	29	26	35	27	29
F4	19	26	19	25	∅	∅
F5	14	20	20	24	23	29
F6	25	27	27	30	27	27
F7	20	25	21	33	22	∅
F8	10	25	18	24	17	25
F9	25	28	25	28	27	33
F10	21	29	28	28	29	32
F11	17	28	24	30	22	26
M1	12	15	17	25	23	23
M2	12	28	29	32	∅	∅
M3	12	19	19	24	24	25
M4	20	31	27	36	32	33
M5	20	27	25	33	31	32
M6	21	28	22	29	28	∅
M7	26	34	30	38	33	40

Chart V.   Distance to front wipe off in millimeters

Subjects	i	ɫ	e	ɛ	u	ɷ
F1	19	25	14	23	24	21
F2	22	24	26	30	48	51
F3	26	23	22	12	39	46
F4	35	47	38	39	∅	∅
F5	15	15	18	18	37	39
F6	18	25	25	28	32	32
F7	14	19	15	25	40	46
F8	12	24	15	14	24	48
F9	18	28	22	28	25	23
F10	20	19	26	33	39	39
F11	20	13	25	20	25	20
M1	21	23	21	25	30	30
M2	15	28	18	20	∅	∅
M3	10	16	19	16	30	33
M4	17	19	19	31	41	38
M5	10	13	19	26	31	27
M6	14	21	22	23	27	∅
M7	27	32	19	39	36	36

Chart VI.   Distance to channel narrowing in millimeters

Subjects	i	ɫ	e	ɛ	u	ɷ
F1	31	33	27	32	37	30
F2	30	32	31	41	50	53
F3	38	41	43	36	50	55
F4	45	50	50	48	∅	52
F5	31	36	39	37	50	46
F6	30	34	35	41	37	40
F7	31	33	25	35	63	∅
F8	24	31	25	21	38	53
F9	25	30	30	33	45	38
F10	30	47	40	50	51	51
F11	30	30	23	30	35	35
M1	27	34	34	33	40	39
M2	30	24	34	37	∅	∅
M3	22	22	35	37	44	44
M4	47	46	45	43	55	57
M5	25	22	26	31	32	27
M6	32	35	37	37	42	∅
M7	35	40	27	42	45	40

A NEW PORTABLE TYPE UNIT FOR ELECTROPALATOGRAPHY

S. SHIBATA, A. INO, S. YAMASHITA, S. HIKI, S. KIRITANI
AND M. SAWASHIMA
National Center of Speech and Hearing Disorders,
Tohoku University and University of Tokyo

Electropalatography displaying the dynamic patterns of
tongue-palate contact during speech is a valuable method of
observing articulatory tongue gestures. In general, the
electropalatographic instrument consists of an artificial
palate with electrodes implanted and an electronic device
to detect and display tongue-palate contact patterns. On-
line use of a computer for this system has been used for
several years in the Research Institute of Logopedics and
Phoniatrics for basic research and in the National Center
of Speech and Hearing Disorders for speech training.
Recently, we have developed a portable type hardware electropalatographic unit for the wider application of this technique in both research and clinical fields.

INSTRUMENTS

Figure 1 shows a block diagram of the system using the
on-line computer at the Research Institute of Logopedics and
Phoniatrics. A similar system, with some modifications for
use in practical training, has been installed at the National
Center of Speech and Hearing Disorders. In these systems,
the square wave pulses are generated by the computer and fed
to a common electrode, which is attached to the ear lobe of
the subject. Each electrode on the artificial palate is
connected to one of the multiplexer input terminals. The
contact signal is fed into the computer via an analog to

digital converter. The contact patterns are stored in the
computer's memory, together with the sampled values of the
speech envelope.

Our new portable type hardware unit is shown in Figure
2. The unit is powered by a battery installed in it. The
size of the unit is 20 cm in width; 39 cm in depth; 16 cm in
height, and 5.2kg in weight. The upper front of the unit is
a display panel, which contains 62 light-emitting diodes.
The lower front part of the unit is a control panel with
push buttons. All functions of the unit are realized by
the digital hardware circuit.

The functions of the unit are explained in Figure 3.
In this unit, pulse signals are fed to 63 electrodes via a
distributor. The contact signal is picked up by a common
electrode which is placed on the back surface of the artificial palate so as to contact with the palatal mucosa. In
the normal mode, the contact patterns are displayed in real
time at a rate of 64 frames per second. At the same time,
patterns of 1 second each are recorded in a digital memory.
When the operation mode is switched to READ by a push button,
the stored patterns are read out and played back. The speed
of the play-back can be varied in 3 steps: real speed, slow
motion of 3 times and 10 times. A still display of a selected frame is possible via the STOP button. Frame by
frame inspection of the contact patterns are also possible
via the SINGLE STEP button. The contact signal can also be
recorded in a data recorded for later processing. The
possibility of using an ordinary audio cassette recorder is
also being explored. Contact signals played back in slow
motion can be fed to a small printer to obtain a hard copy
of the contact pattern.

A simplified technique for making the artificial palate
has also been developed as shown in Figure 4. Instead of
implanting each of the small electrodes on the plastic plate
by hand, the electrodes and lead-wires are printed on a thin
flexible film. This film is then pressed and attached to the
plastic palate. As is illustrated in the lower part of
Figure 4, the electrodes are printed on the oral side of the
film base and the lead wires are printed on the opposite side

which is attached to the plastic palate. The electrode and
corresponding leadwire are connected by use of a through-hole
metal coating method. The electrodes are located along an
equal-depth contour on the curved surface of the palate as
shown in the upper right portion of Figure 4. Of course,
there are individual differences in the shape and the size
of the palate. The shape and size of the palate also vary
according to the age of the subjects. In order to cover
these variations, several types of printed films are manufactured. By using our new technique, the problem of the
time consuming process of making artificial palates by hand
has been removed.

APPLICATION TO ARTICULATION TRAINING

Visual monitoring of tongue-palate contact patterns
gives the patient a powerful feed back route for detecting
and correcting his defective articulatory placements. In
the National Center of Speech and Hearing Disorders, this
method is being applied to articulation training for patients
with deaf or severe hearing impairment, cerebral palsy,
dysarthria, cleft palate and so-called functional articulation disorders. Although the training technique should be
varied according to conditions such as the age of the patient,
the type and extent of the disorders, and the underlying
pathology of individual cases, there are some common rules
in the use of this method.

The first step is a general orientation. The spatial
correspondence between various locations on the display and
those on the palate should be established. Second, the
kinesthetic sensation of the tongue gestures is trained by
placing the tongue in a position that gives certain configuration of the contact area, and also by moving the tongue
so that a certain dynamic change in the contact pattern is
achieved. In training articulatory placement, presentation
of an outline of the correct pattern (target pattern) superimposed on the display is of great help. Some examples are
shown in Figure 5. Systematic training programs using our
new electropalatographic system are now being developed.
(This system is manufactured by RION COMPANY, LTD. in Tokyo,
Japan.)

REFERENCES

Fujimura, O., Tatsumi, I. F. and Kagaya, R.   (1973).
     J. Phon., 1:47-54.
Sawashima, M.   (1976). Technocrat, 9:19-26.
Kiritani, S., Kakita, K. and Shibata, S.   (1977).   Univer-
     sity of Tokyo Press.

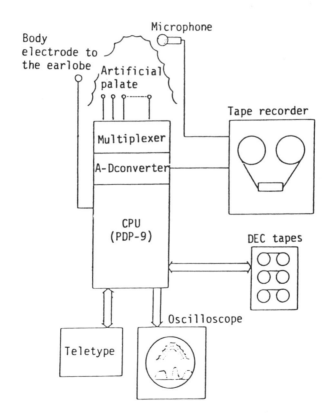

FIGURE 1

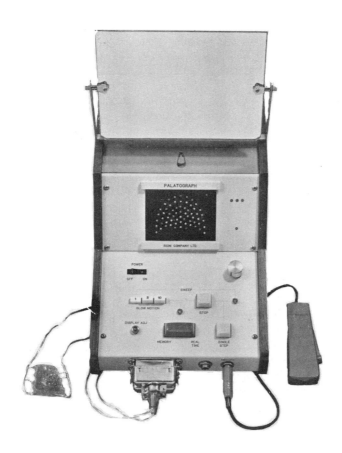

FIGURE 2

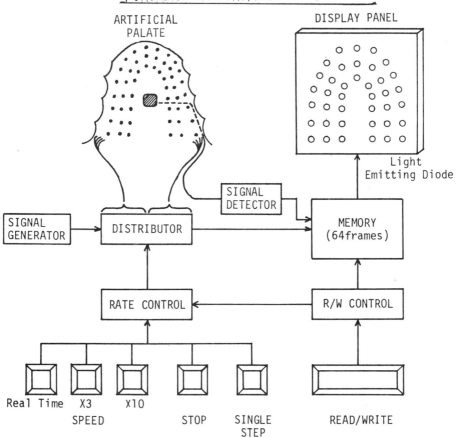

FIGURE 3

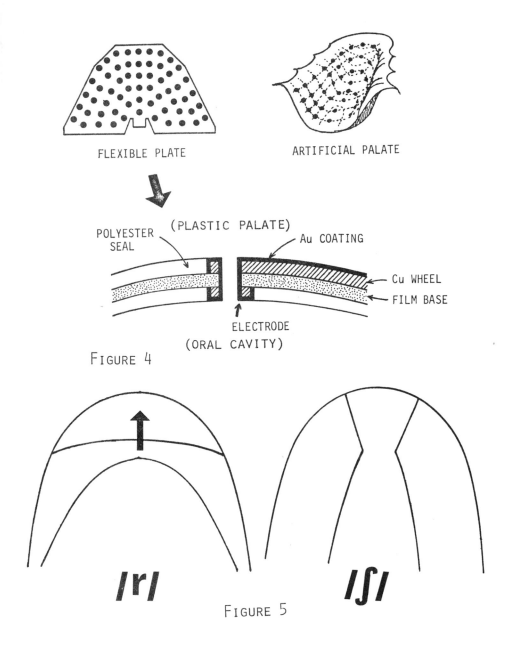

FLEXIBLE PLATE   ARTIFICIAL PALATE

(PLASTIC PALATE)

POLYESTER SEAL   Au COATING

Cu WHEEL

FILM BASE

ELECTRODE

(ORAL CAVITY)

FIGURE 4

/r/   /ʃ/

FIGURE 5

ASPIRATION IN SCOTTISH GAELIC STOP CONSONANTS

CYNTHIA R. SHUKEN
University of Edinburgh

The stop consonants of Scottish Gaelic provide a large amount of material of interest to the phonetician, particularly if the variety of extant dialects of the language is taken into consideration. This is especially true if one is interested in the investigation of the phenomenon (or, more accurately, the phenomena) known as aspiration. This term has been applied to a number of different types of phenomena in the description of Gaelic, some of which are voiced and some of which are voiceless. Those which precede consonants are referred to as preaspiration. Until now, Scottish Gaelic has always been described from the point of view of its phonological structure, usually with emphasis on its historical development and its relationship with other Celtic languages and, sometimes, its resemblance to Scandinavian languages. Through the phenomena widely known as preaspiration, it differs from other Celtic languages and resembles such Scandinavian languages as Icelandic and Faroese. The occurrence or non-occurrence of preaspiration, and the phonetic form which it takes when it occurs, also differentiates the dialects of Scottish Gaelic itself. There are only a few extant dialects where no form of preaspiration occurs at all, and these are dialects on the northern, eastern, and southern geographic periphery of the Gaelic-speaking area (referred to in the language as the Gàidhealtachd). There are two types of differences commonly mentioned by investigators describing Gaelic preaspiration. One is the phonological question of a biphonemic vs. a monophonemic interpretation—whether or not the preaspiration is part of the following consonant. It is

generally agreed by Celticists that it is only in the island
of Lewis, the northernmost island of the Outer Hebrides,
that preaspiration is actually part of the following stop
phoneme. In other dialect areas, the preaspiration element
is usually regarded as a separate phoneme; though recently,
the German phonetician Elmar Ternes, who studied the Gaelic
of Applecross on the west coast of Ross-shire on the main-
land of Scotland, reckons that some instances of preaspiration in Ross-shire must be interpreted as belonging to the
stop phoneme while others should not. This very brief
summary of the phonological complexity reflects great phonetic complexity.

The other breakdown of types of preaspiration has been
along phonetic lines. One phonetic realization is an ordinary palatal or velar fricative, and the other, which one
might wish to call true preaspiration, has been described as
being "h-like," as resembling post-aspiration, and is
generally transcribed with the letter h.

I have been looking at aspiration in only two dialects
of Gaelic, those of Lewis and Harris in the Outer Hebrides.
Although these places are actually part of the same island,
the dialects differ in many, many ways. Lewis has "h-like"
preaspiration which is always treated by analysts as part of
the following stop phoneme (though, to complicate matters,
one velar-fricative-plus-stop cluster does occur, and contrasts with a preaspirated velar stop). In Harris, pre-
aspiration-plus-stop sequences are generally considered to
be biphonemic; but the preaspiration is h-like before labial,
dental, and alveo-palatal stops, and is realized as a fricative before palatal and velar stops. I had two informants
from different parts of Harris and two from different parts
of Lewis. The data used consisted of lists of isolated words,
and a few short phrases. I felt that it was necessary to
analyze citation forms before looking at connected speech.

I used an electrokymograph and larynx microphone to look
at oral and nasal airflow and larynx vibration. These were
recorded on a four-track mingograph at 10 cm/sec. with time
recorded on the fourth track. The same lists were tape
recorded in the recording studio of the Linguistics Department of the University of Edinburgh, and a mingograph was

used to record a duplex oscillogram trace, along with intensity and an audio sound wave from these tape recordings.
This mingograph record was done at 20 cm/sec. in order to
obtain sufficient detail. Sound spectograms of some of the
items were made from the same tape recordings using a Kay
Sonagraph. Most of the spectrograms were done to 8000 Hz.
although some additional ones were made scale magnified to
4000 Hz. I wanted to compare the various sorts of information obtainable from different techniques in order to try
to build up as complete a picture of the sounds as I could.

Since in recent years discussions of aspiration have
centered around the measurement of voice onset time, or VOT,
this was the first parameter at which I looked. The majority
of my measurements were obtained for stops in the word-initial
position (and were mostly of post-aspiration rather than preaspiration, which I haven't finished measuring yet). Harris
and Lewis Gaelic both have only two series of stops in word-
initial position, series I usually being referred to as
unaspirated and series II as aspirated. Additional word-
initial series of voiced unaspirated and voiced aspirated
stops have been reported for other dialects, voiced aspirated
stops being voiced stops whose release is followed by a
period of breathy or whispery voiced phonation.

I shall try to summarize some of my findings. Briefly,
in word-initial position, series I stops showed low values
of voicing lag (with means ranging between 6.5 and 20 msecs.
for the four speakers), sometimes showed voicing beginning
simultaneously with the release of the stop, and a very few
cases of voicing lead. Series II stops on the whole showed
higher values of voicing lag than series I stops (with means
ranging from 51 to 75 msecs.), although there were some cases
of overlap between the ranges of the VOT values for the two
series, even within the speech of one speaker, as well as
within the corpus as a whole. In word-initial stop plus l,
n, or r clusters, VOT values for stops were consistent with
those obtained for word-initial stops followed by vowels.
Medially, where pre-aspiration rather than post-aspiration is
the significant factor, VOT values showed a more chaotic distribution. After other consonants, a variety of results were
obtained. Generally, very low VOT values were obtained for

all stops after voiceless fricatives. Laterals and the
various r-sounds become voiceless and fricative before
stops, as they do before a pause.

After nasal consonants, including word-initially after
enclitics with final nasals, a variety of things may happen.
In Lewis, the stop may disappear entirely; the nasal may
release into nasalized breathy or whispery voice; the nasal
may become partly or wholly voiceless and release into a
nasalized h or voiceless vowel or a fricative or even
occasionally into a short voiceless stop. In Harris, the
nasal can occasionally release into nasalized breathy voice,
as well as into a voiced or voiceless stop. Often, a voiced
nasal or a voiced stop following a voiced nasal, is followed
by voiceless aspiration or friction. The nasal can also become devoiced, and be followed by a voiceless fricative.
The choice of phonetic realization is at least partially
conditioned, but the degree of optionality has yet to be determined.

Figure 1 shows electrokymograms of the words cat
/kʰaht/ (a cat) and gob /kop/ (a beak) as said by one Harris
speaker. The top trace shows the nasal airflow; the second,
the oral airflow; the third, larynx vibration (this trace
lags 20 msecs. behind the top two); and the fourth, time,
with 20 msecs. between peaks of the waves. The top word
contains two series II consonants and the bottom contains
two series I consonants. You can see that there is no
difference in the amount of oral airflow of the post-
aspiration of the final consonants, where pre-aspiration
is the significant feature. But there is a significant
difference between the amount of airflow of the post-aspiration of the initial consonants and the pre-aspiration of the
final consonants. The post-aspiration of the /k/ in cat is
of long duration (about 70 msecs.), is voiceless, and is
produced with a large amount of airflow. A spectrogram of
that word shows high amplitude high frequency friction. The
postaspiration of the /k/ in gob, however, is short (15 msecs.)
and is characterized by a relatively small amount of airflow;
and friction which is fairly intense on a spectrogram up to a
frequency of around 2000 Hz. but which is very weak at higher
frequencies. It is also voiceless. The final /p/ in the same

word has no preaspiration. It may be voiced during the first
few milliseconds of its closure, although this does not show
up as clearly on the kymogram as it does in a spectrogram
because the voicing is of extremely low amplitude as well as
of extremely short duration. The preaspiration of the /t/
in cat is quite long and is primarily voiceless (although it
begins with a very brief voiced state), and fairly low amplitude friction occurs throughout the frequencies to 8000 Hz,
although it has concentrations at several frequencies.   It
shows a large amount of oral airflow.

    A very different sort of preaspiration is typical of
this Lewis subject, however (see Figure 2). The preaspiration in this speaker is typically voiced throughout most of
its duration, but this voicing shows a different shape of
larynx waveform from the voicing of the vowel which precedes
it. The presence of continuous voicing, however, does not
appear to affect the amount of oral airflow. It is possible
that this indicates either a very open glottis, or an increase in subglottal pressure, or both. This must remain
conjecture in the absence of direct information. The large
amount of airflow combined with periodic vibration of the
vocal cords implies a breathy or whispery-voiced phonation.
This accords not only with my own auditory impression, but
also with the impression which David Clement of the Gaelic
Linguistic Survey has of preaspiration in this dialect.
Breathy or whispery phonation occurs in this dialect after
voiced nasal consonants as well as before voiceless stops.
It also seems to occur non-contrastively at the end of vowels
before pause. Both the post-aspiration and the pre-aspiration
show fairly low intensity friction on a spectrogram, and
during the preaspiration the friction is limited to the lower
frequencies (below 2500 Hz.).

    Figures 3 and 4 show spectrograms of near-minimal
triplets focusing on word-final velar consonants or consonant-
clusters. The three words are bog /pok/ (soft), boc /pɔhk/
or /pɔxk/ (a roebuck), and bochd /pɒxk/ (poor). The velar
stop of the first word is never preaspirated in any dialect,
although it is always post-aspirated. That is, there is
always a period of audible friction following the release of
the stop. The stop often begins voiced. The third word

always contains a true velar fricative in every dialect.
It is the final element in the second word which varies from
dialect to dialect. In this Harris speaker, the fricative
before the velar stop is virtually identical in the second
and third words. If the stop in the second word was labial
or dental, the frictional phase would have been of considerably shorter duration than the one which occurs before
the velar stop. The second word said by the Lewis speaker
shows an extremely low amplitude, voiced period of preaspiration which contrasts markedly with the fricative of the third
word. The preaspiration is about 80 msecs. in duration, as
opposed to 150 msecs. for the fricative, and has energy only
at the frequencies of the first two formants of the preceding
vowel. A point of primarily phonological interest--Lewis
speakers seem to be the only ones who carry preaspiration
over into their English. This is often used as one of the
arguments in support of a monophonemic interpretation for
Lewis preaspiration.

In conclusion, the question still remains as to which
of these various phenomena one would wish to label as aspiration and which one would like to call something else. It is
certain that quite a number of different acoustic and physiological cues are often grouped together under the category of
aspiration in Scottish Gaelic. The examples I have shown here
are only a few of the more obvious ones. It is easy to see
that the difficulties with the phonological interpretation
lie at least partially in the complexity of the phonetic
material to be analyzed.

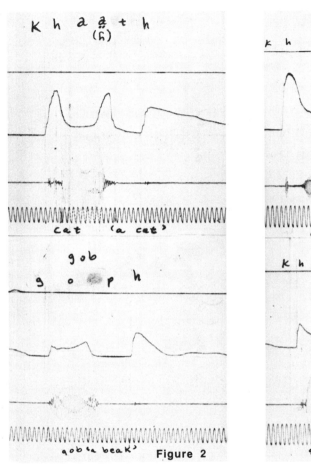

Figure 2

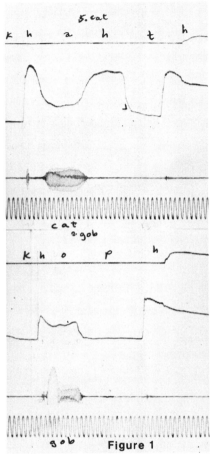

Figure 1

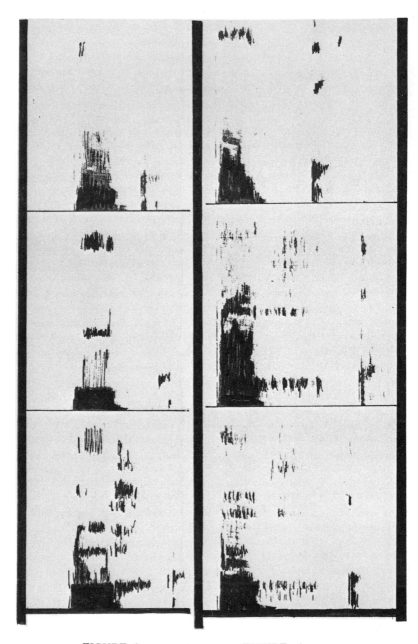

FIGURE 3   FIGURE 4

THE EFFECT ON FORMANT PATTERNS OF DIFFERENTIAL VOLUMETRIC CHANGE IN THE ORAL CAVITY

PETER S. VIG AND JAMES B. MCLAIN
University of North Carolina

The effect of changes in the volume or configuration of the oral cavity on speech quality and acoustics remains a focal point for the joint investigation of speech scientists and dentists. Applications to prosthodontics, orthodontics and most recently to orthognathic surgery have all stimulated the use of various research techniques to both subjectively and objectively look at changes in speech attributable to alterations in the oral morphology.

To date, no studies in the literature have investigated the changes in speech sounds as they relate to the volumetric displacement of the appliance with consideration given to the individual morphological characteristics of the adult subjects.

Several studies relate the thickness of an appliance or denture to measurable changes in speech (Petrovic, 1974; Martone, 1957; Hamlet, 1976; Allen, 1958; Agnello and Wictorin, 1972; Ylppo and Sovijarvi, 1962). Volumetric analyses of the appliances used to alter speech, however, are uncommon in the literature. Measurements of changes in speech due to the insertion of a dental appliance can be categorized as either changes in speech quality or as changes in the acoustical patterns of speech, which today can be measured using sound spectrography or computer analysis.

Speech Quality. Changes in speech quality can be ascertained by rating judgements and/or phonetic analyses (Amerman and Daniloff, 1971; Martone, 1957; Sim, 1966; Allen, 1958; Agnello, 1972; Garber and Speidel, 1977--in press). While these investigators indicate that adaptation occurs to varying degrees, the nature of such adaptations is not clear.

Acoustic Analysis of Speech. Most of the acoustical analyses of speech sounds have been generated since the 1950's which marks the development of the "Sonograph." Spectrographic recordings and analyses have been reported in the literature occasionally in conjunction with the alteration in size and/or shape of the oral cavity (Ylppo and Sovijarvi, 1962; Agnello and Wictorin, 1972; Petrovic, 1974; Hamlet et al., 1976). Ylppo and Sovijarvi studied selected consonant sounds using sound spectrography and palatography in edentulous patients with full and half dentures. Dimensional differences between the prosthesis and the edentulous arch in terms of arch length, arch width and arch height were also measured. Fourteen separate measurements were taken from the spectrographic recording and selected items of the data were analyzed as they pertained to the individual consonant sounds. Agnello and Wictorin, as previously described, studied the phonetic changes in edentulous patients following complete denture treatment. The spectrographic analysis of the four consonant sounds (/s/, /t/, /sh/, /th/) were compared to the judges' rankings of preferred speech. This comparison revealed that the spectrograms of preferred speech samples had discrete boundaries and segments (more precision in articulation) and also gave evidence of better coarticulation (whether or not the patient spoke with dentures). Non-preferred speech samples showed less definite formant patterns, less definite transitions from consonants to vowels, and more "noise-like" features. Petrovic utilized graphical representation of individual spectrographic wide band sections as provided by a CDC-3600 computer to analyze speech in full denture wearers. The coordinates of the graphical representation were: time (in intervals of 600

msec), frequency (0-7000 Hz), and l=log P (power spectral
density).   Petrovic concluded that unstable dentures produce speech distortions because of the use of articulatory
structures to improve retention; he also concluded that
after 15 minutes following insertion of a stable set of
dentures there was a change in the spectrographic pattern
of /a/.   Edentulous subjects produced no clear consonant
on the graphic representation.   This can be related to
Petrovic's statement that the articulation of consonant
sounds is affected by anterior tooth position, contour of
the anterior portion of the palate, vertical dimension of
occlusion, and appliance stability.

    Hamlet (1976) utilized subjects with natural dentitions
who were subsequently fitted with an experimental dental
appliance of 6 mm thickness in the anterior palate to study
changes in the first three formants of cardinal vowels.   The
appliance had the effect of lowering and retracting the
alveolar-palatal contour.   Subjects spoke a sentence for
recording before insertion of the appliance, immediately
after insertion, after one week of wearing the appliance
during waking hours, and five minutes after removal of the
appliance.   In addition to vowel formant frequencies; overall duration (speech rate), the fundamental frequency, and
the spectral characteristics of the fundamental were also
investigated.   Hamlet found that some formant changes present immediately after insertion were not compensated for
in a week of adaptation and that the vowels involved varied
with the subjects.   The duration was altered little except
in recordings made immediately after insertion.   The fundamental showed little change, while the spectral characteristics of the fundamental were altered with the appliance, but
differently for each subject.

METHODS

    Subjects.   The subjects were four adult males with
normal occlusions and without previous history of orthodontic or speech therapy and with normal hearing and a
natural dentition.

Appliances. Palatal acrylic appliances of four types
were constructed for each patient. Each appliance extended
to a line connecting the distal of the second molars and
covered the entire palate to the necks of the maxiliary
teeth. The appliances were retained in the mouth using
Adam's cribs on one first premolar and on both first molars.
The stability of the appliance was essential. Appliance #1
(THIN) was approximately 1.5 mm thick throughout. Appliance
#2 (THICK) was approximately 2 to 2.5 times the thickness of
the thin appliance (about 5 mm) and was uniform throughout.
Appliances #3 and #4 were composites of both appliances #1
and #2. Appliance #3 (THICK/THIN) was the thickness of
appliance #2 in the area from the lingual of the central
incisors to a line connecting the distal surfaces of the
canines and the thickness of appliance #1 from the distal
of the canines to the distal of the second molars. Appliance #4 (THIN/THICK) was the thickness of appliance #1 an-
teriorly and the thickness of appliance #2 posteriorly. The
transition between the thick and thin areas in both appliance
#3 and #4 was smooth with no steps or ledges. The volume of
each appliance was ascertained by observing its displacement of water in cubic centimeters.

Speech Samples. Tape recordings of the American
English vowels in the context of a word, in the context of
a sentence, and in isolation were made prior to the insertion of the appliance, immediately following insertion of
the appliance, after a 48 hour period of continuous wear,
and immediately following removal of the appliance. All
recordings were made on a Tandberg Model 3000 recorder in
an insulated sound studio. The carrier words used were:
HEED, HID, HAYED, HEAD, HAD, WHO'D, HOOD, HOED, HAWED, HOD,
HUD, and HERD. The carrier phrase for the twelve words was:
"Say the word _ _ _ _ again." Subjects were instructed to
maintain the same intonation and intensity throughout all
productions to the best of their ability. The appliance insertion sequence was randomized to control for errors resulting from a training effect.

Spectrograms. Wide band bar spectrograms were made for each production for the selected vowels in hod, heed, and who'd. Narrow band bar spectrograms were also made for reference purposes and to allow measurement of the Fundamental. All spectrograms were produced with the Voice Print Laboratories Model 700 Spectrograph calibrated to 1 mm per 50 Hz. This calibration provided a spectrum of 0 to 5000 Hz, which included the first three vowel formants.

Morphological Measurements. In order to relate the volume displacement of the four appliances to the individual oral cavity morphology of each subject the techniques described by Vig and Cohen (1973) relating Tongue Shadow Area (Ta) to Intermaxillary space Area Index (IMA) were used. This technique involves making standardized measurements from cephalometric films in which the dorsum of the tongue is visible. The measurements provide an index of oral cavity size by utilizing a two-dimensional representation (cephalometric x-ray) of the oral cavity. For the particulars of this measurement technique, as well as for the justifications for the associations made, the reader is referred to Vig and Cohen, 1974.

RESULTS

The gross data from the spectrograms was analyzed for all four subjects. While it is not possible to include all of the resulting figures here, a few should serve to illustrate the nature of the results. Figures 1-3 show the plotted F1, F2, and F3 formant frequencies for 3 vowels produced in a word. Similar plots were made for the other vowels in all modes. The figures are divided into sections representing the insertion, 48 hour adaptation, and removal of the four various appliances. The absence of certain data points, due to the non-visibility of certain formants or the distortion of the formant pattern, is represented by the omission of these data points from the figures. When a data point is missing for the insertion frequency (IN), a line is drawn from the 48 hour adaptation point (48 HRS) to the appliance removal point (OUT). This

convention is followed in a similar manner for other missing data points, with the exception that for a missing 48
HRS point an asterisk is used to distinguish the straight
line extending from IN to OUT from a line resulting from
three normal data points. Figures 4, 5, and 6 show the
mean formant frequencies in Hz for all 9 utterances for
each subject for F1, F2, and F3, respectively. In these
figures the data has been reduced for each subject over
each type of appliance mode. Figure 7 shows the relationship between Ta/IMA ratio and the mean values for F2 and F3
for each subject. Figure 8 shows the relationship between
IMA index rank by subject and mean F1 frequency rank by
subject. Figure 9 shows the relationship between the ranking of the variability in formant ranges of F1 + F2 + F3
and the IMA index rank by subject.

DISCUSSION

It is appreciated that such a small sample does not
permit broad generalizations. As all four subjects are
normal individuals in every respect and fall near the ideal
range in the spectrum of normal variation, dramatic differences were not anticipated between speakers' responses.
However, the results reveal a high degree of individual
variability in response, and also strong associations between morphology and function. Our findings indicate that
no correlation can be made between changes in palatal configuration or volume and the resultant change in formant
patterns between subjects if one does not control for the
morphologic variability of the subjects. When specific
consideration was given to the variations in individual
morphology certain correlations between formant frequency
behavior and oral morphology became evident.

We observed an inverse correlation between IMA index
rank and the ranking of the mean formant frequency of F1
(See Figure 9). This correlation gives support to the
theoretical consideration that F1 represents the oral cavity
portion of the vocal tract, i.e., as oral cavity size increased (increased IMA) the frequency which would emanate
from it would be decreased (mean F1 frequency). A definite

trend was also noted between the mean formant frequencies of
F2 and F3 and the ratio of Tongue Shadow Area over Intermaxillary Space Area Index. This also follows theoretical
considerations when one considers that as Ta/IMA increases
the effective "resonating chamber" size decreases and the
resultant frequency which is produced should increase.

Trends were also noted in the relationship between IMA
index rank and the maximum range of variability of Fl, F2,
and F3 (Figure 9), indicating that the larger IMA types show
greater ranges of variability of overall formant frequency
spread in all 13 different physiologic situations for both
the vowels ee and o. The reasons for the greater degree of
variability in the larger IMA types may be related to a
larger amount of variability in articulatory patterns in
these individuals allowed by a relatively large oral cavity.

SUMMARY

Four normal adult male speakers were fitted with four
separate palatal appliances of varying thicknesses and
known volumes. Cephalometric radiographs were made for
each subject and an Intermaxillary Space Area Index (IMA)
and Tongue Shadow Area (Ta) measurement were made for each
subject. The subjects wore the appliances for 48 hrs. each
and an interval of one week was used between appliances.
Recordings of the American English vowels were made and
spectrographic data was reduced to yield formant frequency
values. Data included control productions and three productions (in isolation, in a word, and in a carrier phrase)
of 3 of the 12 American English vowels. An inverse correlation between IMA index rank and the mean formant frequency
of Fl was observed, giving support to the theoretical concept that Fl represents the oral cavity portion of the vocal
tract. In addition, a direct correlation between mean
formant frequency of F2 and F3 and Ta/IMA ratio was observed. Trends were also noted in the relationship between
IMA index rank and the maximum range of variability of Fl,
F2, and F3.

REFERENCES

Agnello, J. G., and Wictorin, L. (1972). _J. Prosth. Dent._, 27:133-139.

Allen, L. R. (1958). _J. Prosth. Dent._, 8:753-763.

Amerman, J. D., and Daniloff, R. G. (1971). _ASHA Rep._, 13:559.

Hamlet, S. L., Geoffrey, V. C., and Bartlett, D. M. (1976). _J. Speech Hear. Res._, 19:639-650.

Martone, A. L. (1957). _Int. Dent. J._, 7:573.

Petrovic, A. (1974). _J. Oral Rehab._, 1:353-360.

Sim, J. M. (1966). Unpub. M. Sc. D. Thesis, U. of Washington, Seattle, 1966.

Vig, P. and Cohen, A. (1974). _Angle Orth._, 44:25-28.

Ylppo, A. and Sovijarvi, A. (1962). _Acta Odont. Scand._, 20:257-299.

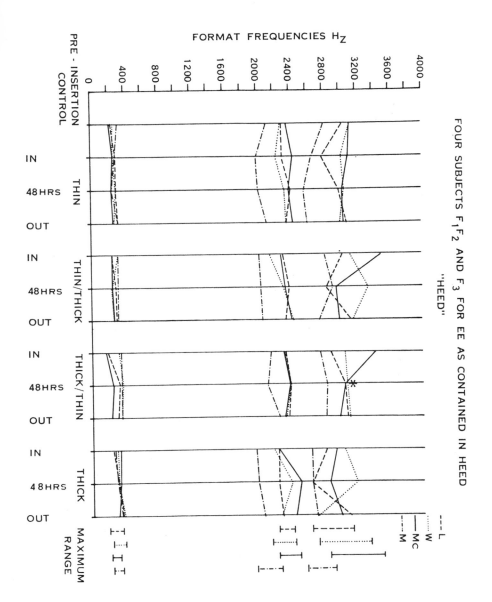

FIGURE 1

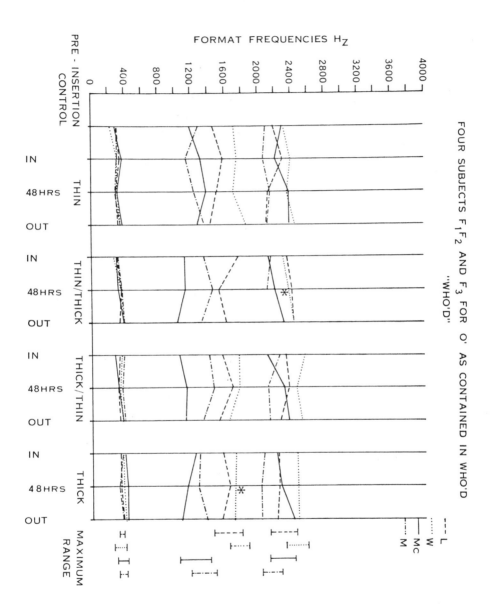

FIGURE 2

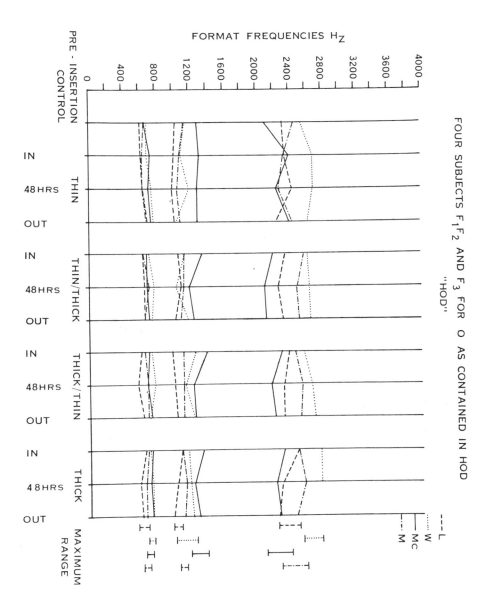

FIGURE 3

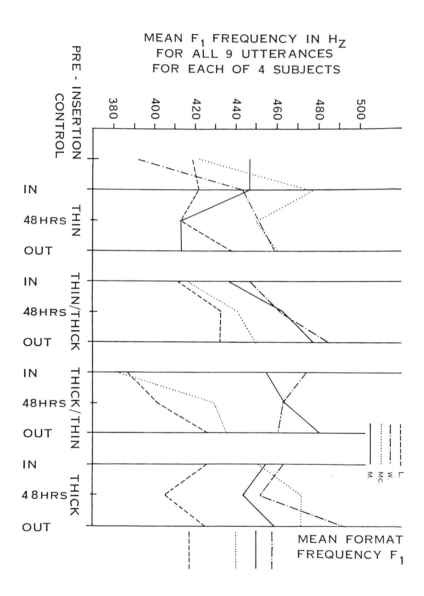

FIGURE 4

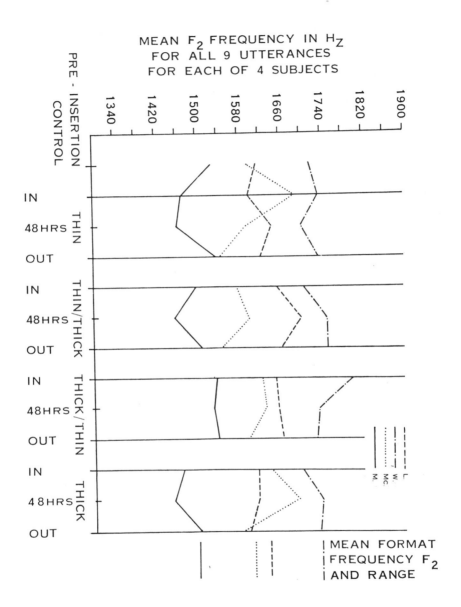

FIGURE 5

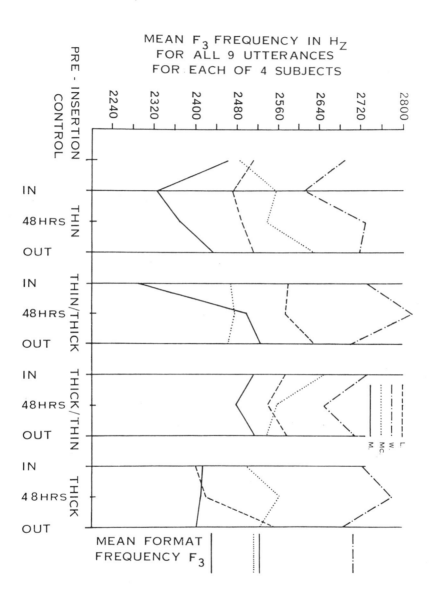

FIGURE 6

RELATION BETWEEN
(TONGUE AREA/INTERMAXILLARY SPACE INDEX)
AND THE MEAN FOR ALL VALUES OF F_2, F_3
IN ALL 9 UTTERANCES FOR ALL 13 MODES
(MEAN OF MEANS — SEE TABLE 3)

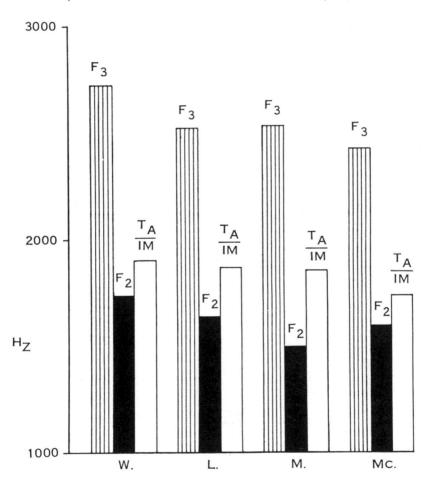

FIGURE 7

Figure 8. Mean value of F_1 ranked against IMA index. F_1 mean taken for all 13 modes, i.e., in all physiologic/morphologic situations for all sounds for entire experiment.

Subject	IMA Index Rank	F_1 Mean Rank	Reverse Rank F_1
L.	1	4	1
W.	4	1	4
Mc.	2	3	2
M.	3	2	3

IMA index, i.e., size of oral cavity is inversely related to F_1 mean. The bigger IMA--the lower is mean frequency of F_1.

Figure 9. Maximum ranges of $F_1 + F_2 + F_3$ for all 13 modes of (vis) "HEED" and "HOD"

Subject	HEED	Rank	HOD	Rank	Total	Rank	IMA Index Rank
L.	19.5	2	21.0	1	40.5	2	1
W.	12.5	4	14.5	3	27.0	4	4
Mc.	31.0	1	17.0	2	48.0	1	2
M.	19.0	3	11.0	4	30.0	3	3

1 Unit = 40 Hz.

CHARACTERISTICS OF ORAL AIR FLOW DURING PLOSIVE CONSONANT PRODUCTION BY HEARING-IMPAIRED SPEAKERS

ROBERT L. WHITEHEAD AND KENNETH O. JONES
National Technical Institute for the Deaf and
Brigham Young University

Information relative to the rate of air flow in consonant production in the hearing-impaired is limited. It appears that such information would be useful because of the reported mismanagement of the respiratory, laryngeal, and articulatory systems in the speech of the deaf. Such data would also aid in objectifying the description of the speech production process in the deaf and in the development of programs designed to modify speech patterns.

The purpose of the present study, therefore, was to investigate the peak rates of oral air flow in plosive consonant production as a function of the degree of hearing loss and speech impairment in hearing-impaired and normal-hearing populations.

PROCEDURES

Subjects for the study were divided into three groups. The first group included five normal hearing and speaking adult males. The second group included five adult males with intelligible speech, as measured by the NTID rating scales, and a mean pure tone hearing loss of 78.40 dB. The third group included five adult males with semi-intelligible speech, again as measured by the NTID rating scales, and a mean pure tone hearing loss of 96.20 dB. All of the deaf subjects had congenital hearing losses and were students at the National

Technical Institute for the Deaf (NTID). Although there were obvious differences in speech intelligibility, all subjects were able to correctly produce the test syllables. To insure correct production of the stimulus syllables, each utterance was monitored at the time data was collected. In addition, a phonetic transcription of each stimulus from the audio recording of each subject revealed correct production.

At NTID, the degree of speech intelligibility is judged by trained speech clinicians while the student reads the first paragraph of the Rainbow Passage. The judgment is made using a five point equal-appearing-interval scale. As noted, a rating of 5 or 4 indicates the listener was able to understand all or most of the message, while a rating of 3 indicates that approximately half of the message was understood. Ratings of 2 or 1 indicate the listener understood little or none of the content of the message. In the present study, the intelligible deaf subjects were all judged a five in speech intelligibility, while the semi-intelligible deaf were all judged a three.

The air flow data were obtained using a tightly fitting face mask and a pneumotach system (Hewlett-Packard). These signals were transduced by a differential pressure transducer (Statham, PM15E), amplified by a bridge amplifier (Honeywell Accudata 113) and recorded onto FM tape (Hewlett-Packard 3960) for playback ghrough a visicorder (Honeywell 1858). In addition, an audio signal was simultaneously recorded on a second channel of the FM tape recorder.

Air flow was measured during production of CV and VCV syllables consisting of the vowels /a/ and /i/ and the consonants /b/, /p/, /d/, and /t/. Each subject uttered each syllable three times in succession. The peak flow rate for each consonant was measured and an average determined for the syllable.

RESULTS

Table 1 presents the means and standard deviations of the peak flow rates for plosives in CV context for all three groups of subjects for the vowel /a/. In general, when

comparing the three groups of subjects, the air flow rates
for all consonants for the normal-hearing and intelligible
deaf groups were of similar magnitude. For the semi-
intelligible deaf group, however, the average peak flows
were greater for the voiced consonants and less for the voiceless when compared with the other subjects. As may also be
seen, for both the normal-hearing and intelligible deaf
groups, the peak flow rates for the voiceless consonants
were substantially higher than those for their voiced cognates. For the semi-intelligible deaf, however, there was
only a slight voiced/voiceless differentiation.

Table 2 presents the means and standard deviations of
the peak flow rates for plosives in CV context for all subjects for the vowel /i/. Again, as was demonstrated for the
vowel /a/, the obvious difference between groups is the
greater peak flow for the voiceless consonants when compared
with the voiced for the normal-hearing and intelligible deaf
groups. For the semi-intelligible deaf, however, there was
only a slight voiced/voiceless differentiation. In addition,
in almost all instances, for all three groups of subjects,
the peak flow rates for the plosives in the /i/ environment
were less than in the /a/ environment.

Table 3 presents the means and standard deviations of
the peak flow rates for the plosives in VCV context for all
three groups of subjects for the vowel /a/. As may be seen,
the results are very similar to those for the CV syllables.
In general, air flow rates were of similar magnitude in the
normal-hearing and intelligible deaf groups. In comparison,
higher flow rates were observed in the semi-intelligible
deaf group during voiced plosive production and, conversely,
lower flow rates were observed during voiceless plosive
production. Also, for the normal-hearing and intelligible
deaf groups, the flow rates for the voiceless consonants were
substantially higher than those for their voiced cognates.
For the semi-intelligible deaf, however, there was only a
slight voiced/voiceless differentiation.

Table 4 presents the means and standard deviations of
the peak flow rates for plosives in VCV context for all
subjects for the vowel /i/. Again, as was demonstrated for
the vowel /a/, the obvious difference between groups is the

greater peak flow for the voiceless plosive when compared
with the voiced for the normal-hearing and intelligible deaf
groups. For the semi-intelligible deaf, however, this voiced/
voiceless differentiation occurred to a slight degree only
for the lingual-alveolar plosives, while for the bilabials,
the flow rates for the voiced consonant exceeded those for
the voiceless. In addition, in almost all instances, for
all three groups of subjects, the peak flow rates for the
plosives in the /i/ environment were less than in the /a/
environment.

Table 5 presents the ratios of the mean peak air flow
rates for plosive cognate pairs in CV and VCV contexts for
the vowel /a/. For the normal-hearing and intelligible deaf
subjects, mean flow rates for voiced plosives were reduced
about 50% from the rate characteristic of its voiceless
counterpart. For the semi-intelligible deaf subjects, mean
flow rates were only slightly lower (71% to 96%) than for
the voiceless cognates.

Table 6 presents the ratios of the mean peak air flow
rates for plosive cognate pairs in CV and VCV contexts for
the vowel /i/. For the normal-hearing and intelligible deaf
subjects, mean flow rates for voiced plosives were reduced
from 40% to 62% of the rate characteristic of its voiceless
counterpart. For the semi-intelligible deaf, mean flow rates
were only slightly lower (82% to 95%) than for the voiceless
cognates. In one instance for the semi-intelligible deaf,
the mean flow rate for the voiced plosive was greater than
for the voiceless.

To test for significant differences in peak flow rates
for all combinations of plosives, an analysis of variance
procedure was employed for each of the three groups. The
resultant F ratio for the normal-hearing and intelligible
deaf groups were significant at the 0.01 level, while the F
ratio for the semi-intelligible deaf group was not significant
($p > 0.05$). Using the Duncan's New Multiple-Range procedure,
peak flow rates for voiceless plosives were found to be
significantly ($p < 0.01$) larger than those for their voiced
cognates for the normal-hearing and intelligible deaf subjects for both phonetic environments and for both vowels.
Among the semi-intelligible deaf speakers, no significant

(p > .05) difference between voiced and voiceless consonants were indicated. In addition, for each group of subjects, there were trends for greater peak flow rates for the plosives in the CV context when compared with the VCV context. These trends, however, were not significantly different (p > 0.05) for any of the three groups of subjects.

DISCUSSION

The results of the present study have revealed that normal-hearing speakers and intelligible speakers with severe hearing losses produced voiceless plosives with significantly greater oral air flow than voiced plosives. Semi-intelligible speakers with profound hearing losses, however, did not demonstrate a significant voiced/voiceless difference. Previous studies (Gilbert and Dixon, 1974; Hutchinson and Smith, 1974) of the rate of oral air flow during production of plosive consonants by hearing-impaired adults revealed a voice/voiceless difference similar to differences observed in the intelligible deaf subjects in the present study. It appears, therefore, that for hearing-impaired speakers, as the degree of hearing and speech impairment becomes more severe, the deviation from normal flow rates during production of plosive consonants becomes greater.

It has been suggested (Emanuel and Counihan, 1970) that air flow differences between voiced and voiceless production may be attributed to the flow resistence imposed by vocal fold action in voicing. For the semi-intelligible deaf subjects in the present study, it appears that even though each consonant was produced perceptually correct, there was an increased gottal resistance to flow for the voiceless consonants. There appears to be little data available relative to the laryngeal dynamics in voiced and voiceless consonant production in the speech of the deaf. It is possible that deaf speakers may be attempting voiceless plosive production with the vocal folds in an abnormal semi-adducted position, thereby adversely affecting flow rate. In this abnormal position, the vocal folds would not be set into vibration and thus the consonant production would be perceived as a voiceless phoneme.

Previous research conducted at NTID (Whitehead and Maki, 1977) has shown that semi-intelligible deaf speakers tend to initiate and produce speech at lung volumes substantially below those for normal-hearing speakers as well as with some dysynchronous respiratory movements. It is possible that air flow rates between voiced and voiceless plosives did not differ significantly among the semi-intelligible deaf speakers because they were attempting speech with a limited supply and faulty control of air and with poorly coordinated respiratory movements and laryngeal dynamics.

Although not significant, the present data on vowel and syllable effects on air flow rates of plosives for all three groups of subjects are similar to that reported for normal-hearing speakers by Emanuel and Counihan (1970). Thus, plosives in an /a/ vowel environment are produced with greater flow than plosives in an /i/ vowel environment. Also, plosives in CV context have greater flow than plosives in VCV context. The findings from the present study appear to imply that vowel and syllable effects on flow rates are a learned event as a function of the articulatory process and are not dependent on auditory cues.

In general, from the present study, it appears that deaf speakers with profound hearing losses and semi-intelligible speech demonstrate considerable problems in coordinating the respiratory, laryngeal, and articulatory system for speech. Much additional research in these areas is needed before an objective description of the speech patterns of the deaf may be made.

REFERENCES

Emanuel, F. W. and Counihan, D. T. (1970). Cleft Pal. J., 7:249-260.
Gilbert, H. R. and Dixon, H. P. (1974). Presented at Amer. Speech Hear. Assoc. Convention, Las Vegas, Nevada.
Hutchinson, J. M. and Smith, L. L. (1976). Aud. Hear. Ed., Dec/Jan, 16-25.
Whitehead, R. L. and Maki, J. (1977). Proc. Res. Conf. Speech Proc. Aids for Deaf, Gallaudet College, Washing- . ton, D. C.

TABLE 1
Ratio of Voiced to Voiceless Oral Air Flow Means

Syllables	Normal Hearing	Intelligible Deaf	Semi-Intelligible Deaf
ba/pa	0.46	0.44	0.96
da/ta	0.51	0.46	0.71
aba/apa	0.46	0.47	0.80
ada/ata	0.47	0.44	0.75

TABLE 2
Ratio of Voiced to Voiceless Oral Air Flow Means

Syllables	Normal Hearing	Intelligible Deaf	Semi-Intelligible Deaf
bi/pi	0.49	0.49	0.89
di/ti	0.62	0.50	0.95
ibi/ipi	0.56	0.50	1.02
idi/iti	0.58	0.40	0.82

TABLE 3

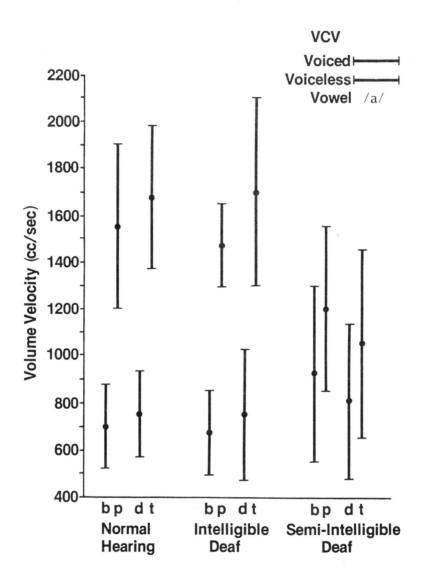

TABLE 4

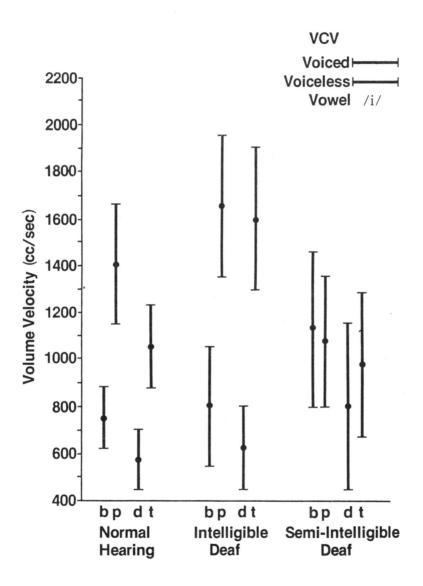

TABLE 5

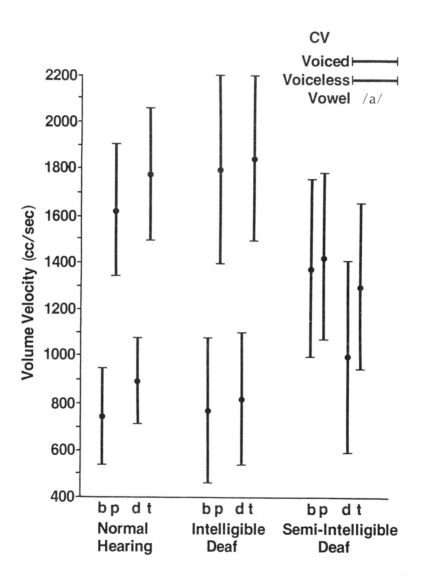

TABLE 6

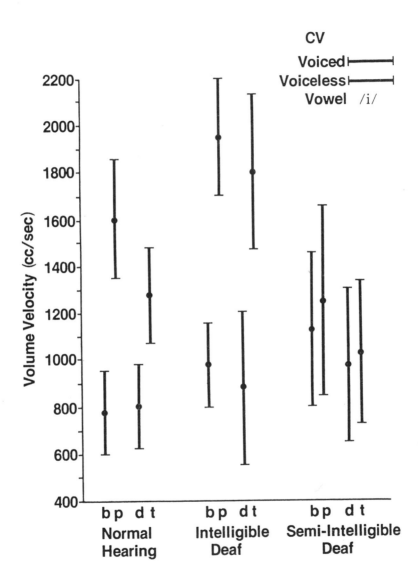

F. SPEECH PRODUCTION

THE PRODUCTION AND RECOGNITION OF SOUNDS IN ENGLISH WORDS SPOKEN BY YOUNG JAPANESE ADULTS

JOHN W. BLACK, YUKIO TAKEFUTA, AND ELIZABETH JANCOSEK
Ohio State University and Chiba University

Descriptions of Japanese phonology are plentiful and somewhat contradictory. Differing dialects of pronunciation along the archipelago confound the problem. School children memorize the specific combinations of phonemes or syllables of their language. These incorporate the following rules and when recited have the tonal properties of a jingle. The vowels are: /a, i, u, o, ɛ /. The approximate English equivalents of the consonants are: /k, s, ʃ, t, n, h, m, j, r(one-tap trill), w, b, g, d, p, z/. There are some irregularities: /s → ʃ / before /i/; /t → tʃ/ before /i/; /t → ts/ before /u/; /h → F/(bilabial) before /u/; /j/ precedes /a, u, o/ not/i,ɛ /; /w/ precedes only /a/; /n/ may stand alone, syllabic; /d → dʒ/ before /i/; /z → dʒ/ before /i/; /k, h, s, r, tʃ, m, n/ and a subsequent vowel may be linked by /j/. The effect is variously ascribed properties of a cluster and as affecting the subsequent vowel.

The linkage between the consonant and a vowel is so close that the more common terminology is to refer to the consonant as the prefix of the vowel. Thus, several of the English consonants are missing in Japanese. Kohmoto notes that of his list of "seven simple vowels" /i, e, æ, ə, a, u, o/ only /æ / and /ə/ are missing. The missing consonants are /l, f, v, θ, ʒ/. Kohmoto adds /tʃ, dʒ, ŋ/ calling them allophones of /t, z, g/, respectively. This system is referred to as the "50 sounds (syllables) of Japanese," although the number is figurative. The sounds fall into three classes, seion(pure),

dakuon or han-dakuon (less regular as vowel prefixes) and
yō on (clusters). A controversial topic in the sound system
of Japanese is the relation of the Japanese /r/ to English
/r, l/. No doubt the /r/ is present. Berendt and Takefuta
write of it as three sounds; a rounded initial sound
(alveolar flap), an unrounded consonant when spoken in an
English cluster (again, an alveolar flap) as pride, and
a vowel, almost /a/, as a final syllable. Kohmoto provides
a detailed parallel description of English and Japanese
sound systems. His description of /r/ agrees with that of
Berendt and Takefuta. He adds, quoting Jones that in Japanese
there is a kind of /l/, which is voiced alveolar lateral-flap
and a free variant of /r/. The Japanese /r/ carries over into
Japanese writing of English. Thirty 10-minute impromptu
themes describing the same picture, yielded these spellings
with only one example taken from the same student's paper:
recentry (multiple), frowers (multiple), dericious, especiary,
brossoms, Ann of Green Gabers, and chocorate. Conversely,
there was only one substitution of l for r; plinted. The r
was also intrusive (privarte). Other cues for possible
difficulties in English pronunciation included bairds (birds),
decites (decides), and chigarettes (cigarettes).

Speaking and understanding oral English are difficult for
Japanese adults, although study of English has been required
for more than a century. For the American listener Japanese
English has a foreign soundingness or accent. In a prior study
separate panels of American university students rated samples
of Japanese speech on foreign accent, articulation, rhythm and
melody. Judges used a 1-9 equal-appearing intervals scale with
1 representing high quality speech. The correlations between
foreign accent and articulation, rhythm, and melody were r, .79,
.89, and .93, respectively and with ratings of the latter three
variables pooled, .98. Japanese listeners have reason to be
phonemically sophisticated. All have learned to write their
language in two manners, in Kanji or characters and in Kana
or "phonetically." The present report is a summary and comparison of the errors of University students of Japan and the
United States in identifying the phonemes of English words
spoken by young Japanese adults. A misunderstood phoneme may
be attributed to either the speaker or listener; however, the
extent of the agreement among the errors of listeners tends

to imply where the fault lies. If many listeners agree that a particular error occurred one may infer that the sound was malproduced.

Twenty-four male students of Keio University who were beginning a six-week term of study at The Ohio State University spoke and recorded one list of Forms A and B of the Multiple-choice Intelligibility Test. Keio is a private university in Tokyo and is highly selective in its admission policy. Unlike some tests of intelligibility and speech discrimination, the Multiple-choice Test is not constructed to represent any set proportions among linguistic units. Rather, words read by 20 speakers were heard by 200 listeners who attempted to identify what they heard. The three errors that were most-frequently made were paired with the stimulus to form a closed response set of four possible responses. Twenty-four lists of 24 items were compiled. The lists were equal in the mean scores of the items and the standard deviations of these scores. This criterion ignored the phonemic content of the items or of a list of items. A few phonemes were not represented in Forms A and B, /j, ɔɪ, ð/. A typical list of stimulus words follows: swarm, canvas, quart, airport, bark, tassel, group, flicker, beef, legion, wonder, horn, threat, dear, garden, curtain, export, final, rage, city, all, knuckle, dress and screech. In the instance of the first word the possible errors were warm, form, storm.

In the United States the recordings were heard by 33 students at the end of an introductory course in phonetics. Each student worked independently, replaying his assigned recordings as often as desired. The students were restricted to the symbols used by Wise. Each list was transcribed by 3 students, making 72 transcribed lists. The present writers made a phonetic transcription of the words of the intelligibility tests in the manner of "platform pronunciation." This prescriptive "answer sheet" provided the criterion against which the transcriptions of the Japanese speakers were compared. Students at Chiba University provided another 72 transcriptions of the recorded material. The responses of Japanese and American listeners were summarized in two confusion matrices, one for consonants and one for vowels, in which only the phonemic "errors," that is, substitutions, omissions, and additions relative to the "correct" responses were tallied.

As a concession to practicality, a few phonemes were pooled, /w,ʌ/, /e,ei/, /o,ou/ and r-colored and non-r-colored vowels /ɚ,ə/ and /ɝ,ɜ/.The recordings were made in keeping with standard procedures for the intelligibility test. One series of three items might be "number one grew flicker beef." This was read as though it were a phrase of continuous prose, not with emphasis on each of the three test items.

      Two panels of American judges of 6 and 8 members heard the recordings and rated each sequence of items, such as "number two airport bark tassel," on foreign soundingness or foreign accent. The judges worked independently and used a 9-point scale with 1 representing little accent and 9 representing much. The ratings assigned to the 24 speakers were: Panel 1, range, 3.9-7.5, mean 6.1; Panel 2, range 3.7-8.0, mean 5.8. The reliabilities of the two panels were moderate, r = .78 and .72, respectively. Thus, in spite of the fact that the speech of the Japanese was intelligible it obviously seemed distant from expected English speech to American listeners. The transcribers were not professional linguists. Rather they were a sizeable group and varied, essentially 8 groups of three members. Tables 1 and 2 represent a pooling of their output. The writers of this report only checked that checked that the students were seriously completing their assignment. The transcribers were doubtless listening in terms of the features of their native language. In similar tasks even "experts" tend to show a bias toward their native language and the logic of their "expertise," for example anticipated distinctive features. This is a topic which Berendt and Takefuta emphasize: a listener hears a foreign language in the units of his native language.In working with stress and intonation Sledd and Lieberman, have independently found experts unreliable as criterion arbiters. Although an equal number of experts would have been preferable to the students, in either instance decisions would be based on the number of instances tallied, with rare events largely ignored.

RESULTS

   The confusion matrices for consonants and vowels are shown separately in Tables 1 and 2. The target sounds head the rows and the substitutions head the columns. Thus, the multiple

substitutions for /b/ were /p, d, v, f/. These data provided
comparisons between the two groups of listeners. For example,
continuing the reference to /b/, both groups of listeners
heard most frequently in error /v/ and /d/. They differed in
the instance of the third most frequent error response. An
incorrect response might be attributed to one or more causes:
(1) perhaps the target phoneme was badly produced, or (2)per-
haps the experience or the "set" of the listener represented
a compelling bias toward one phoneme, not another. In either
event, the phonemes occurred in meaningful, non-contextual
English words and were the same for two groups of listeners.
There was always some overlap between the most frequent errors of the two groups of listeners. As indicated in Table 3,
the same three consonants occurred most frequently among the
"errors" of the groups in response to seven consonants: /d,
t, g, k, t ʃ , ʃ , dʒ/. Two of the three most-frequent "errors"
were the same in response to 11 consonants:/b, p, n, l, r, h,
v, z, s, f, θ/. One of the three was duplicated in four instances: /m, ŋ , ʍ , ʒ /. A similar treatment of the multiple
"errors" in response to vowels did not show this much agreement between the Japanese and American listeners in any instance. The 2 groups of listeners made about the same total
number of consonantal errors,Japanese 663 and Americans 613.
The rank orders of the consonantal errors (Table 4)in the 2
sets of responses were similar (rho = .78). However the similarity of the 2 groups of listeners may be overstated. In
Table 1 of the response-cells with a minimun of 4 responses,
there is at least one cell per column with a 2:1 ratio between the errors of the 2 groups of equal numbers of listeners. This observation relates to substitutions in 17 of the
24 columns of the table. The notable exceptions to uniformity
are the responses to the sounds that do not occur in Japanese
/l, f, v, and θ/. Likewise among the vowels a 2:1 discrepancy
is evident in the error responses to all of the vowels and the
diphthong /ɑI/. Again the frequencies of the errors are readily linked with whether or not the sound exists in Japanese:
/I/ is replaced by /i/, /æ/ by /a/, /ʊ/ by /u/.

Masked errors made by American listeners suggest malprod-
uction on the part of the Japanese speakers. Hence, interest
focuses on the production of /r, l, p, t, d, s, b, v, f/.
If the errors made by Japanese listeners in excess of

those made by American listeners indicate special needs for auditory training, interest focuses on /p:k (read /p/ for /k/); r:w; l:w; s:0/. There are some voiced-voiceless interchanges, as /d,t/; some that attend similarity in sound as /m, n; s, θ); and some that go with linguistic changes, as the regressing of the bilabial fricative /F/ to /h/, illustrated in /Fari/ → /hari/ (needle).

Kohmoto lists common replacements of English consonants by Japanese speakers. These and the maximum substitutions shown in Table 1 follow:

Kohmoto	Present Maximum Substitutions
t → tʃ (read /t/ becomes /tʃ/)	t → d
d → dʒ	d → t
s → ʃ	s → 0
z → ʒ	z → s
ʃ → s	ʃ → dʒ
h → F	h → f
w → u	w → r
j → i	----

Most of the substitutions noted by Kohmoto are found in Table 1, but the best agreement between the two lists in the replacement for /h/.

DISCUSSION

Sapon and Carroll tested the aural perception of Japanese listeners. They used polysyllabic nonsense syllables spoken by Americans and appropriate for a multiple-choice response form. As in Tables 1 and 2 the investigators followed the error-matrix model of Miller and Nicely. Sapon and Carroll wrote "The delineation of patterns of confusion, or personal error has been attempted in recent studies by Miller and Nicely and Moser and Dreher and the present study would seem to confirm some of the findings presented by these investigators." The present writers agree with the results of Sapon and Carroll and the descriptions of Japanese pronuncations by Fujiware and Herhard we well as pre-World War II pronunciations. Errors are not random but tend to cluster. In Table 1, the stop consonants, stimuli and responses, are enumerated at the top, the nasal sounds, semivowels or glides and /r, l/ in the

central portion, and the fricative consonants at the bottom.
The table seems to suggest a rule and some exceptions. The
overriding rule is that confusions occur within these classes
rather than among them. The exception and extensions follow.
(1) /v/ is not in Japanese and is pronounced as a bilabial
voiced consonant, similar to /b/. (2) The regression of the
voiceless bilabial /F/ is incomplete and yields the voiceless
bilabial /p/ as well as the terminal point of its migration
/h/. As a related corollary of this, the voiceless, bilabial
/p/ may be misunderstood as a stop, voiceless, plosive /k/ or
as a voiceless, labio-dental, fricative /f/. (3) /m/ and /n/
are "interchangeable"; also /n/ and /ŋ/. (4) The affricative
sounds /tʃ/ and /dʒ/ are likely to be exchanged with each
other or with either of their component gestures.

The vowels of Table 2 are less systematically arranged
than the consonants. Americans made many more errors in
identifying vowels than the Japanese did, 625 vs. 376. Moreover, American students were not in agreement on what vowels
they believed they were hearing. They made responses in 112
of the available 225 error-response cells of Table 2 and 96
of these were multiple responses. As a generalization,
Japanese cannot produce in a manner recognizable to an American the vowels that are not approximate equivalents of ones
in the Japanese language, for example / æ I, ʌ /. The fact that
these sounds are identified more accurately by Japanese than
by Americans must give us pause.We have been asked recently,
"What's wrong with Japanese English?" The question was prefaced by the observation that British English, Hawaiian
English, Southern dialect, and General American are readily
accepted terms. Then, why not recognize respectfully
Japanese English? An implication of Table 2 is that one has
developed. Japanese listeners can identify Japanese English
vowels better than Americans can. Finally, a topic not to be
ignored in a comparison of Tables 1 and 2 is the differences
between vowels and consonants. One view is that the former
represent a continuum, a gradual gliding from one vowel to a
near neighbor in production. The same scheme would posit
that consonants are categorically one or another. The tables
are consistent with this view. The perceived consonant can
be named in accord with another person's identification of
it; the perceived vowel, less so.

There is a plethora of writing about the lack of success of the Japanese in teaching English despite that time, energy, and money that go into the effort. William Forbis quips, "English is damnably difficult for the Japanese. No one knows for sure whether it is difficult because it is taught badly, or whether it is taught badly so that it will be difficult." Here and elsewhere in Japan Today Forbis questions the willingness of the Japanese people to be "western." Nor is this surprising. Professor Lambert of McGill University emphasizes the role of anomia in learning a second language. This partial woeful trek from one culture to another as one "submits" to the second language may be unusually stressful in moving from the Kanji characters of the Japanese language to the Romanized alphabet of English. The phonologies of the two languages are dissimilar orally and aurally in a manner remindful of the differences in writing. The seriousness of misapprehensions of phonemes in communication can only be inferred from these results. Weaver notes as one of three levels of problems of communication, "How accurately can the symbols of communication be transmitted?" (The other two are the semantic problem and the effectiveness problem.) The data presented here support two conflicting conclusions. First, the words were intelligible. Second, the speech was unnatural for the listeners, a circumstance that might be noise in the Shannon-Weaver model and that might attenuate effectiveness.

Table 1. Confusion matrices of consonantal errors made by Japanese and American listeners. Number per group, 33; words per group, 1725. Entries in left side of cell are responses of Japanses listeners; in right side of cell, American listeners.

Response

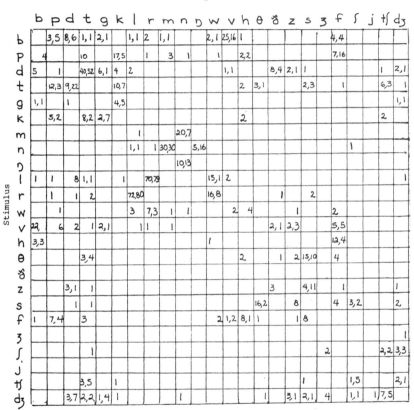

Stimulus	b	p	d	t	g	k	l	r	m	n	ŋ	w	v	h	θ	ð	z	s	ʒ	f	ʃ	j	tʃ	dʒ
b	3,5	8,6	1,1	2,1		1,1	2	1,1				2,1	25,16	1							4,4			
p	4		10	17,5			1	3	1			1	2,2								7,16			
d	5	1	40,52	6,1	4	2							1,1				8,4	2,1	1				1	2,1
t		12,3	9,22	10,7									2	3,1				2,3		1			6,3	1
g	1,1		1		4,5																			1,1
k	5,2			8,2	2,7								2								2			
m							1		20,7															
n							1,1		1	30,30	5,16							1						
ŋ											10,3													
l	1	1	8	1,1		1		70,79					15,1	2										1
r	1	1	2				72,80						16,8				1	2						
w		1					3	7,3	1	1			2	4			1	2						
v	22	6	2	1	2,1		1	1		1							2,1	2,3	5,5					
h	3,3												1						12,4					
θ			3,4											2			1	2	15,10	4				
ð																								
z		3,1	1														3	4,11	1					1
s			1	1											16,2			8	4	3,2				2
f	1	7,4	3												2	1,2	8,1	1	1	8				
ʒ																								1
ʃ			1																2			2,2	3,3	
j																								
tʃ			3,5	1														1	1,5				2,1	
dʒ			3,7	2,2	1,4	1				1						1	3,1	2,1	4		1,1	1	7,5	

Table 2. Confusion matrices of vowel errors made
by Japanese and American listeners. Number per group,
33; words per group, 1725. Entries in the left of each
cell are Japanese listeners; in right of each cell,
American listeners.

RESPONSE

STIMULUS	i	ɪ	e	ɛ	æ	a	aʊ	aɪ	ɔ	ɔɪ	ʊ	u	o	ʌ	ɜ	ɝ
ɿ		4,16	2,1	1,1	1						1	1	5			1
ɪ	10,57		2,2	9,9		3	1	3			1		3,1			1
e	2,2	2,4		13,15	1,13	7,6		3,12			1	2	2			1
ɛ	3,11	12,9	6,7		5,4	5,2	3,2	3,1	2		3	1,2	1,1	2		
æ		1	1,1	3,9		11,77	1,2	5,1	7		4	1,2	20,13	6		2,4
ə	1	2		3	1,4		1,2	2	3		1,1	13,19	3,4	8,2		2
aʊ						10,5			3	5		6,6	1			2
aɪ	3,4	3,5	6	2	1	3,6	1		1			1	1	1	1	4,1
ɔ								1			1	1,3	11,7	3		
ɔɪ																
ʊ		2,1			2,2	8,1						3,10	2,2	3		
u	5,1					3					5		4,3			
o		1		1,1	11,1				4,8	3,5	4	3,3		1,5	1,1	1,4
ʌ	1			1	12,11	26,28	2,2		16		10	1,10	4,3			2,6
ɜ	3,3	6		2	1	10,15	2		7			2	6,1	1,2		
ɝ			1		1,2	1	3,2		1		2	2	1	2,6	1	

Table 3. The three most frequent multiple errors made by each group of listeners arranged in the order of occurrence.

Stimulus	American Listeners 1	2	3	Japanese Listeners 1	2	3	Stimulus	American Listeners 1	2	3	Japanese Listeners 1	2	3
b	v	d	p	v	d	f	ɩ	I	e,ɛ,ʌ,ɝ		u	ɪ	e
p	f	k	b	k	t	f	I	ɩ	ɛ	aɪ	ɩ	ɛ	a,u
d	t	ð	g	t	ð	g	e	ɛ	æ	aɪ	ɛ	a	aɪ
t	d	k	p	p	k	d	ɛ	I	ɩ	e	I	e	æ,a
g	k	b	dʒ	k	b,d,dʒ		æ	a	ʌ	ɛ	ʌ	a	ɝ
k	g	t	p	t	p	g,h	a	o	ʊ	ʌ,æ	o	ɝ	ʌ
m	n	l	-	n	w	-	aʊ	o	a,ɔ		a	o	-
n	m	ŋ	l,r	m	ŋ	s	aɪ	a,e	I		ɝ	ɩ,I,a	
ŋ	n	-	-	n	-	-	ɔ	o	u	a,ʊ	o	ɝ	ʊ
l	r	d	m,t,k,dʒ	r	w	v	ɔɪ	-	-	-	-	-	-
r	l	w	tʃ	l	w	p,d	o	ɔ	ɔɪ,ʌ		a	ɔ	ɔɪ,u
w	f	r	v	r	l	f	ʊ	u	ʌ	æ	a	u	I,æ,o
v	b	p	f	b	f	g,ð,z	u	ʊ	o	ɩ,ɝ	i	o	a
h	f	b	-	f	b	w	ʌ	a	ɔ	æ	a	æ	o
θ	s	t	z	s	f	t	ɝ	a	ɔ	I	a	o	ɩ
ð	-	-	-	-	-	-	ɝ	o	ɛ,a,ʊ		a	o,ɔ	
z	s	d,t,f		s	ð,d								
s	z	θ,s		θ	f	s							
f	h,s	p		h,s	p	-							
ʒ	s	-	-	s	-	-							
ʃ	s	dʒ	tʃ	s	dʒ	tʃ							
j	-	-	-	-	-	-							
tʃ	t	dʒ	k,ʃ,s	tʃ	dʒ	k,ʃ,s							
dʒ	tʃ	ð,d		tʃ	ð,d								

Table 4. The rank order of consonantal error responses.

Responses	Japanese Listeners	American Listeners
b	6	5
p	12.5	15
d	14	6
t	3	3
g	17	13.5
k	8	13.5
m	4	4
n	7	9
ŋ	18	8
l	1	1
r	2	2
w	9.5	11.5
v	5	8
h	15.5	20.5
θ	9.5	20.5
ð	15.5	18.5
z	20.0	11.5
s	11	10
f	12.5	8
ʒ	22	18.5
ʃ	20	17
j	21	22
tʃ	16	17
dʒ	20	17

THE PRODUCTION OF LATERALS: SOME ACOUSTIC PROPERTIES
AND THEIR PHYSIOLOGICAL IMPLICATIONS

R. A. W. BLADON
University College of North Wales

The acoustic theory of the production of lateral sounds,
as it stands, follows the acoustic theory of vowels in tending
to seek, albeit rather cautiously and with some risk of over-
simplification, physiological correlates likely to be
affiliated with the various spectral properties (resonances
and antiresonances) which laterals exhibit. Fant's pioneer-
ing work Acoustic Theory of Speech Production (1960) on which
that theory is very largely based, was derived from data on
the two laterals in Russian, both postdental, one palatalized,
the other often called velarized but which in Fant's X-ray
tracings looks more pharyngealized. The objectives of my
work have been to extend this body of data to at least five
different lateral articulations, and to investigate the
implications of this fuller body of data (a) for the acoustic
theory of the transfer function of laterals and (b) for a
physiologically-based model of the lateral dimension of tongue
displacement.

The five lateral sounds under consideration are shown
in Figure 1, which summarizes some of their acoustic properties. All the laterals are voiced and non-fricative.
They are (left to right): /l̪/ a dental with some palatalization, as occurring in Irish, or French adjacent to close
front vowels; /l/ an alveolar tending to "clear," as observed
in RP English and German; /ɫ/ an alveolar with tongue-root

retraction or <u>pharyngealization</u>, as in American English and
Arabic; /ɭ/ a <u>retroflex</u>, tongue-tip making postalveolar
contact, as in Tamil and Swedish; /ʎ/ a <u>palatal</u>, tongue-tip
lowered, as in Castilian Spanish. For the present discussion,
frequency measurements have been averaged over each of three
vowel contexts of approximately /li, la, lu/ quality, and over
all male speakers. The data in Figure 1, derived from sweep-
frequency measurements, represent the central frequencies of
formants (filled data points) and of antiformants (unfilled
data points), and they match closely with similar data obtained by spectrographic measurements, which are not presented
here.

F2. The standard view that a palatalized /l̥/ derives
its F_2 from a half wavelength of the mid and back cavities
(behind the closure), and is thus comparable to /i/, is
apparently valid and extendable to the clear alveolar and the
palatal. As predicted, F_2 is highest when the cavity length
is smallest, namely for /ʎ/; and the dental's F_2 is higher
than the alveolar's, not because its total cavity length is
shorter (it is not), but because the dental we have recorded
is more palatalized. The mid-and-back cavity volume behind
/ɭ/ is considerably greater, and this might correlate with
the substantial drop in F_2. Dark /ɫ/ always has a very low
F_2, and this seems to be related to the uvular or pharyngeal
constriction which it shares with back vowels. So there are
no great surprises here.

F1. F_1 presents roughly a mirror-image to the F_2 frequency pattern, though with less variation (even allowing for
the perceptual distortion of the frequency scale in Hz). We
can confirm from all five laterals the general view that F_1
in laterals is uniformly low (Joos,1948;O'Connor <u>et al</u>.,1957;
Fant, 1960; Lehiste, 1964; Dalston, 1975). The traditional
affiliation of F_1 with the backmost cavity seems however to
have poor general applicability. X-ray tracings of laterals
of our kinds by Delattre (1965) and by ourselves show small
pharynx cavity volumes for /ɫ/, which does, as would be
expected traditionally, have a high F_1; and the largest
pharynx cavity volume occurs in the dental with its advanced
tongue body. However, a plot of approximate midsagittal
pharynx area against F_1 shows poor correlation over the five

laterals (r = -0.58). This is shown as the unconnected data points in Figure 2. As an alternative explanation, since the F_1 of laterals is relatively invariable, its source might appropriately be sought (as Fant has proposed) in the cross-sectional area of the lateral constriction. This kind of data is difficult to obtain. So we have recently been making estimates of that constriction area by aerodynamic methods, calculating it from measurements of intra-oral pressure and flow-rate. These give the results shown in Figure 2 as connected data points, suggesting an extremely strong correlation in all five laterals between increased lateral constriction area and increased F_1 (r = 0.99).

F4. F_4 is supposed, at least in some cases, to be a whole wavelength fundamental resonance of the whole cavity system behind the primary constriction. But that would predict a higher value for F_4 in the shorter cavity system, namely the alveolar one, which is not found. The role of the formant we have called F4 is apparently much more complex than has been described. First, consider the effect of anti-formants in these spectra. An antiformant in the range 2 to 3 kHz is invariably present in these laterals, often effectively cancelling the F3 in that frequency range. Thus F4 may be regarded as assuming some of the role of F3. In particular, F_4 in a lateral may be affected by the dimensions of the anterior mouth cavity: this would cause an upward shift in the dental's F_4, with its small front cavity, as observed. In any case F_4 may be associated in its own right with the frontmost cavity, as can be shown from independent evidence on lip-rounding in selected cardinal vowels--evidence which time does not allow us to present today. But there are then two reasons why F_4 in laterals, while perhaps tuned primarily by the back cavities, is seen to be appreciably shifted in response to front cavity modifications.

F3. F_3 will be considered in conjunction with the antiresonances or zeros. Existing acoustic theory in respect of lateral zeros must be treated with caution, because in spectrograms at least two and often three spectral minima below 5 kHz can be detected. Of these we will call Z2 an antiformant in the range 2 to 3 kHz which typically eliminates a formant 3. However, in the retroflex /ɭ/ and palatal /ʎ/

a strongish F3 is usually present, in the latter case along
with an F4 also. Why is F3 maintained in these laterals, but
rarely in the cases of the types surveyed by Fant? An explanation would seem to lie in the fact that the retroflex
and the palatal have a larger and better defined anterior
mouth cavity than do the other laterals.

Z2. If we turn to examine the detail of Z2, a variation
in frequency is visible which is only modest, but about which
we can be fairly confident, because measurement of a central
frequency of Z2 was strikingly easy from the sweep-frequency
data, which consistently showed a dramatic drop in amplitude
within a very narrow bandwidth (See Figure 3). However, it
is difficult to explain this Z_2 frequency as a function of
lateral constriction length, as is traditionally done. Fant
says (1960:164) that the antiresonance frequency is a quarter
wavelength of the shunting system, since that lateral cavity
can be approximated by a tube closed at its far (oral constriction) end. Our calculations of lateral cavity lengths
have been made from X-ray tracings of a wide variety of
laterals. As can be seen in Table 1, there is consistently
far greater variation in lateral cavity length (measured
from the point of maximum articulatory constriction to the
rear intersection of the tongue surface with the place of the
underside of the upper molars) than in the observed Z_2 frequency. Hence the correlation (r = 0.55) between measured
and calculated LCL is rather unimpressive.

Z1. A spectral minimum of a different nature occurs
between F_1 and F_2 at a centre frequency very close to 1000
Hz. Since this Z_1 frequency is so uniform across all laterals,
it has been suggested that Z1 may not be a vocal-tract filter
characteristic at all, but due to the voice source, specifically a subglottal shunt. Two serious objections to this theory
can be raised today: (1) other voiced sounds, such as nasals
(which commonly have a formant in the middle of the debated
range) and indeed vowels, would be expected to show the
supposed subglottal zero, but do not; and (2) our sweep-
frequency data consistently show the presence of Z1 in
laterals, even though for the experimental purposes these
are produced with a closed glottis. This seems to argue
strongly against the subglottal shunt theory. A physiological

explanation of Z1 remains elusive, but the sweep-frequency
data are revealing in another respect. For notice that the
spectral trough we have called Z1 is unlike Z2 in three ways.
Firstly, Z1 is of broad bandwidth; secondly, its amplitude
dips less far; and thirdly and most significantly, the Z1
amplitude is apparently a function of the distance F_2-F_1,
reducing as that distance increases. This does at least
explain why Z1 in conventional spectrograms is often difficult to detect when F_2-F_1 is small, as in /ɫ/ or /ʋ/.

In conclusion, in collating the results of a variety of
analysis techniques--aerodynamic, radiographic and acoustic--
we are attempting to provide some general phonetic evidence
towards physiologically-based speech production models, in
respect of the rather neglected dimension of lateral displacement of the tongue. At the same time, it has been shown that
the acoustic theory of the production of lateral consonants
requires some modification and extension, particularly in
respect of F_1, F_4 and the antiformants.

REFERENCES

Dalston, R. M. (1975). J. Acoust. Soc. Am., 57:462-469.
Delattre, P. (1965). London, Harrap.
Fant, G. (1960). The Hague, Mouton.
Joos, M. (1948). Baltimore, Waverly Press.
Lehiste, I. (1964). Bloomington, Indiana UP.
O'Connor, J. D., Gerstman, L. J., Liberman, A. M., Delattre,
    P. C. and Cooper F. S. (1957). Word, 13:256-267.

Table 1. Z_2 and lateral cavity length.

		Lateral cavity length (mm)		Z_2 (Hz)
		measured	calculated $LCL=\dfrac{c}{4.Z_2}$	
ḻ̩	dental with palatalization	55	34	2610
l	alveolar	52	33	2690
ɫ	alveolar with velarization	64	32	2740
ɭ	retroflex	9	20	4240
ʎ	palatal	30	32	2720

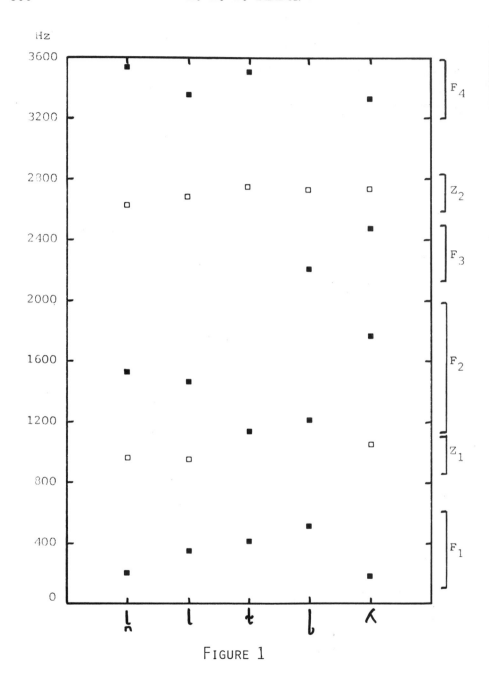

FIGURE 1

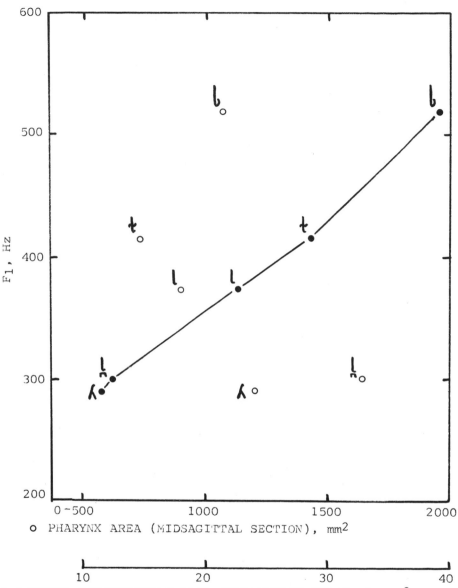

FIGURE 2

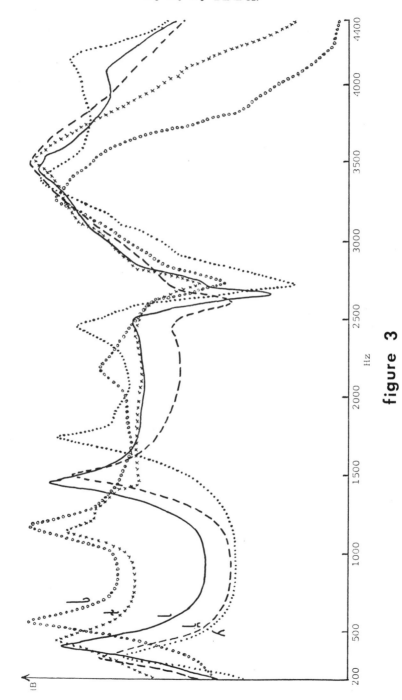

figure 3

AFRICAN CLICK SOUNDS, EARLY DESCRIPTIONS AND SYMBOLS

G. H. BRECKWOLDT
St. Louis University

In order to appreciate today's research on click sounds, it may be helpful to have some historical knowledge of the phenomenon as experienced and reported by early travellers, missionaries and scientists. For this reason a review of historical documents is given in the present paper. I previously conducted "A Critical Investigation of Click Symbolism" (from 1634 - 1970) and, in the form of a compendium (1972), presented it to the Seventh International Congress of Phonetic Sciences. I appealed to the Congress to recommend to the International Phonetic Association a revision of its existing click symbolism, which is incomplete and weak (Breckwoldt, 1972). I suggested a symbolism consisting of Latin capitals, each symbol being the first letter of the word giving the physiological definition of the specific sound. This symbolism proves compatible with the requirements listed in The Principles of the I.P.A., as printed on the inside of the booklet's cover (1970). To facilitate a classification of symbols we reprint my tabulation (1972); Figure 1.

None of the early Southern African travellers, who heard the click sound phenomenon in a native language, stayed unimpressed. Most of them gave a written description in words or symbolism of this to them most novel sound experience.

1634 The earliest notation appears to be Sir Thomas Herbert's (1634) obviously onomatopoeic "ist" which he suggests for any sound of a click nature.

<u>1662</u>   Johann Jacob Saar published an account of his travels,
in Nuremberg. Herein we find a passage in which the speech
sounds of the Hottentots are mentioned and in which the author
compares their clicks with clicks of turkeys (1662): "These
heathens are called Hottentots/.../ talk a disagreeable
language/as if they clucked/like Indian cocks (i.e., turkeys),
....When you come into the country they come running/ and
scream BROCQUA in their language: that is/ Bread...."

<u>1668</u>   is the year of publication of the first edition in
Amsterdam of Dr. O. Dapper's <u>Naukeurige Beschrijvinge</u>. Dapper
describes the speech of the Hottentots in more detail than
Saar. But the amazing thing is that Dapper also compares the
click-sounds with clucks made by turkeys; "they clap or clack
with the mouth in every other word, as if someone snapped his
thumb, so that their mouth almost works away like a rattle,
they hit and click with the tongue extremely loudly; thus it
seems that every word contains a different click. Some words
they can only utter with great difficulty, and it seems as if
they make the sounds from the back of the throat, like a
turkey cock, as do the people in Alpine Germany, who by
drinking snow-water are getting thyroid swellings at the neck.
For this reason our people have given them the name of Hottentot, because of this handicap and unheard-of stammering,
although this word is usually used in a nasty way of swearing
against someone who talks with a stutter or stammer. They now,
call themselves by the name of Hottentot, and sing and dance
in front of our people: HOTTENTOT brokwa, HOTTENTOT brokwa;
with which they want to say: "give the HOTTENTOT a morsel of
bread." Whether Dapper had read Saar's publication or not,
is unimportant; what is remarkable is that he tries to compare
the unusual speech sounds with some phenomenon or other with
which he is familiar. Thus his comparison with turkey clucks,
the snapping of a thumb or a voice or speech defect. It proves
that what is normal in one language may be a disorder in
another language and vice-versa.

<u>1685</u>   M. l'Abbé de Choisy's travels took place in 1685 and
1686. His book describing these was published in 1712; herein the following was written on the 8th of June, 1685: "The
people who live about forty miles around the Cape have been
named OUTENTOS by the Dutch, because in their language they
often use a word which sounds like that one."

<u>1686</u>   William ten Rhyne published at Schaffhausen his
<u>A Short Account of the Cape of Good Hope and of the Hottentots</u>
<u>Who Inhabit that Region</u> (1686):   "If one listens to them
(i.e., the Hottentots) talking, one supposes the age of
Pythagoras to have returned, in which birds were fabled to
have enjoyed mutual converse in speech.   In sober truth it
is noise, not speech, if one attends to the mode of expression of the Hottentots; for every single word is furnished
by a single click of the tongue against the echoing palate.
One would not be wrong in saying that this clicking of the
tongue against the palate is the main element in the sounds,
...."   Ten Rhyne gives short lists of words but, although he
mentions the clicks, he does not indicate them in any of the
words.   It is remarkable that also ten Rhyne is reminded of
birds, when he wants to describe the sound effect of click
noises (cf. Herodot, Plinius, etc. about this question).

<u>1691</u>   Nicolaus Witsen's diary contains Hottentot words.
Whenever Witsen thought he heard a click sound, he wrote a T,
a t', or a K' to mark it.   It is the merit of Witsen that he
was the first one who made a serious effort to symbolize the
different click sounds.

<u>1695</u>   J. G. Grevenbroek wrote (cf. I. Schapera: <u>The Early</u>
<u>Cape Hottentots</u>, 1933):   "I am of opinion that the
language of the natives has something in common with Hebrew,
for it seems to consist of guttutals, labials, dentals,
linguals and other sounds that fall with difficulty from the
lips and are hard for us to pronounce.   Grevenbroek compiled
a list of Hottentot words intended for travellers.   Among the
words, which he considers essential for communication, there
is a list of numerals.   These reveal that he used letters of
the Latin alphabet to represent click sounds.   Due to the lack
of linguistic knowledge or linguistic musicality Grevenbroek's
click transcription is inconsistent in a manner rather like
that of Witsen.

<u>1709</u>   Barthomäus Ziegenbalg, a Danish missionary, published
a book about his travels.   A letter herein, of the year 1709,
gives the missionary's following impression: "Their (i.e.,
the Hottentots') language is very uncouth and a sort of
Gibberish which no Body can learn.   They are otherwise of a

Temper good enough, and a suitable proportion of body; ..."
These superficial lines could have been written by almost
any tourist of any period.

1712   Johan Daniel Buttner (also spelt Büt(t)ner) left a
Manuscript, to be found in the Dessinnian Collection of the
South African Public Library of Cape Town. Figures 2 and 3
show photographs of Folio 67, recto and verso, of Buttner's
MS. as a typical example of this type of hand-written record
by a traveller of that period. The text preceding the symbol
description and word list says about the Hottentots: "They
have a curious language which is very difficult to learn and
cannot be learnt by any European. But European children born
here learn to speak it perfectly. I have tried hard to learn
it but have not managed to get the right teacher. In the
following I am going to give numerous words; but one has to
observe that one has to hit (or strike) with the tongue, because most of their words are hit with the tongue or uttered
from the throat. These are the symbols, which one must observe
in pronouncing: ∧ with this one the tongue has to hit hard
against the palate; ⌁ here one lets the tongue hit against
the palate and speaks the word half through the nose, half
through the mouth and O this one is spoken through the
nose. The promised word list follows (cf. Figures 2 and 3).
This list is interesting insofar as it shows Buttner's endeavor
to mark any type of click with a circumflex, viz. ∧ , nasal
and nasalized sounds with a circle, viz. O , and what to
him appeared to be an inbetween sound with an undulatory line,
viz. ⌁ . Buttner's effort to learn the Hottentot language
is laudable, but his approach to click sounds confuses rather
than clarifies. He is the first one to employ diacritical
marks to denote clicks.

1714   The Danish missionary Johann Georg Böving (or Bövingh)
published a 2nd edition of his travel book under the title of
Kurtze Nachrichten von den Hottentotten and discusses the
Hottentot language: "Those who do not speak the Hottentot
language think that it is queer and twisted, especially as the
speakers frequently smack their tongue and their speech frequently gets stuck either in their throat or larynx. As far
as I could grasp and observe there are many linguales and
gutterales in their language which cause the smacking. And

that the latter is a characteristic of their language is
obvious because smacks or clicks never occur when the Hottentot speaks Hollands." He continues saying that he is of the
opinion that it is not as impossible for a foreigner to learn
the Hottentot language as most people think. Thereafter he
remarks: "It is no true comparison to say that fast conversation of these heathens results in a gibber, comparable to the
noise made by turkeys, as some people have written (cf. Saar,
1662; cf. Dapper, 1668). It would be more befitting to compare their chatting to that of the Jews."

1719   Peter Kolb published his Reise an das Cabo du bonne
Esperance in Nuremberg. G. Hadley's translation of Kolb's
book was published in 1731 in London. The following quota-
tion therefrom shows Kolb's ideas about the Hottentot
language: "Some look upon it as the Disgrace of Speech; others
deny it the Name, as having Nothing of Sound or Articulation
that is peculiar to Man in it, but resembling, say they,
the Noise of irritated Turkey-cocks, the Chattering of Magpies
and the Hooting of Owls. And Dapper in particular says, 'tis
disagreeable to an European to hear it, much more to learn
it....But the unaccountable Motions and Postures of the Tongue
to which their own Language subjects them, renders them, for
the most Part, hardly intelligible when they come to speak
any other (language)." His collection of Hottentot words
proves that Kolb is the second person (cf. 1712: Buttner) to
use diacritical marks over Latin letters to symbolize click
sounds.

1726   In his travel account, dealing with the Cape of Good
Hope, François Valentyn proves to be another tourist who
complains that the language of the natives abounds in clucking
sounds, reminiscent of turkeys. He gives a list of words but
no click symbolism of any kind.

1790   There is a long interval between Valentyn and the next
traveller whose notes on clicks are worth studying. He is
le Vaillant, who refers to writers like Dapper, when he says:
"The Hottentot language has no resemblance, as several ancient
authors pretend, 'to the gabbling of turkeys when they fight,
to the cry of the magpie, or the screaming of an owl';....
It is equally false, that to hear Hottentots conversing
together, one would take them for a company of stammerers."

He describes three different clicks and gives each one a
symbol neither of the Latin alphabet nor of a diacritical
nature but of his own invention. Le Vaillant published a
word list of two printed pages. <u>Examples</u>: the elephant --
Λ -Goap; the rhinoceros -- V-Nabap and the giraffe -- Δ Na-ip.
From the latter it becomes obvious that he intended his click
symbols to fall into the three categories of <u>dental</u> (Λ),
<u>lateral</u> (V), and <u>alveolar</u> (Δ).

<u>1791</u>   Wolfang v. Kempelen published his famous book called
<u>The Mechanism of Human Speech, as well as the Description of</u>
<u>his Talking Machine</u> in Vienna. He makes the important state-
ment that for click formation it is essential that the
tongue "seals itself against the palate." But he mistakenly
considers clicks to be inspiratory. On the other hand this
idea is contradicted and rectified by his excellent example
of the opening of a tightly closed toothpick-box which illustrates the phenomenon of a rarefaction-release-noise, viz.
the click.

<u>1808</u>   Henry Lichtenstein published his book entitled
<u>Travels in Southern Africa in the Years 1803, 1804, 1805, and</u>
<u>1806</u> and in this devotes a section to the phenomenon of click
sounds. He says: "Nothing strikes so much as the croaking
in the throat, and clucking with the tongue" and believes
that the anatomy, i.e., the structure of the skull, the oral
cavity, etc., are responsible for the formation of the click
sounds. He does not give any proof or evidence of this, and
as we all know a European child growing up among Africans
learns the click-formation as perfectly as an African child.
In transcribing click sounds Lichtenstein distinguishes three
varieties like le Vaillant but does not take over the signs
invented by le Vaillant. He simply numbers them 1, 2, 3.
Where le Vaillant had done his best to describe as precisely
as possible each of the three clicks which he had recognized,
Lichtenstein unfortunately does not attempt to lay down a
definition.

<u>1824</u>   E. F. F. Chladni published his essay "About the Produc-
tion of Human Speech Sounds" (original title: "Über die
Hervorbringung der Menschlichen Sprachlaute") and shows the
most amazing insight into the physiology of click sound

production. He classifies clicks with the consonants and
discusses them separately from the expiratae. He states
that: "Clicks are consonants which are produced by a sudden
drawing back of the compressed lips, or of the tongue from
the palate, in a kind of suction (not through action of the
lungs, but through inner expansion of the mouth), in such a
way that when rarefaction of the inner air is suddenly dis-
continued, some outside air rapidly rushes into the air
cavity." As far as I have been able to ascertain, this is
the first instance in literature of a precise and concise
description of the characteristics of click sounds which,
according to Chladni are: (1) consonants, (2) independent
of the breath movement, (3) suction induced, (4) dependent
on rarefaction, and (5) the acoustic result of a sudden
rarefaction release.

<u>1914</u>   Ninety years later (1914:91), G. Panconcelli-Calzia
reminds his readers: "The opinion, still held today, that
clicks are inspiratorily formed, is faulty; one can breathe
calmly or deeply and at the same time uninterruptedly produce clicks." Panconcelli-Calzia is the first one, who in
the form of a kymograph tracing furnishes incontestable evidence of the fact that clicks are produced without any
dependence on the breath movement. He finds it necessary in
later publications (1919, 1924) to re-emphasize in word and
illustration that click formation is independent of breathing.

Between the days of Sir Thomas Herbert (1634), Chladni
(1824) and ours (1977) innumerable recorded, unrecorded,
published and unpublished researches into click sounds and
symbols have been undertaken. In "Sir George Grey's Library"
in Cape Town there lies a treasure of unpublished <u>ms</u>.waiting
to be studied. For the sake of keeping the size of the paper
within limits, and in order to dispense with the conventional
type summary, I am ending this with a synoptic presentation
(Breckwoldt, 1972) as shown in Figure 4.

REFERENCES

Bleek, W. H. I.   (1857).   Sir George Grey's Library, London
      and Leipzig.
Bleek, W. H. I.   (1862).   Cape Town, J.C. Juta.

Bövingh, Johann Georg. (1784). Hamburg, bei Caspar Johkel.
Breckwoldt, G. H. (1963). Unpublished Monograph, Johannesburg.
Breckwoldt, G. H. (1972). Proc. 7 Int. Cong. Phon. Sci.
Buttner, J. D. (1712). MS., Dess. Coll., So. Afr. Pub. Lib.,
    Cape Town, S.A.
Chladni, E. F. F. (1825). Annalen d. Phys., Jahrg., Stück 2,
    187-216.
Choisy, M. l'Abbé de. (1685). A. Trevoux, par la Compagnie,
    MDCCXII.
Dapper, O. (1676). Amsterdam Meures, 2nd edition.
Grevenbroek, J. G. (1695). From a Letter.
Grey, Sir George. So. Afr. Pub. Lib., Cape Town (cf. Bleek,
    1857).
Herbert, Sir Thomas. (1634). London, p. 16.
Jones, D. (1907). Le Maître Phon. (Nov.-Dec.).
Jones, D. (1921). l'Assoc. Phon. Inter. (cf. l'Ecriture).
Kolb, P. (1719). Nürnberg.
l'Ecriture. (1921). l'Assoc. Phon. Inter. (2nd edition).
Le Vaillant, M. (1790). Liège.
Lichtenstein, H. (1815). Vol. II translation by A. Plumptre.
    London.
Maitre Phonétique. (1969). London, Univ. College.
Panconcelli-Calzia, G. (1914). Berlin, H. Kornfeld.
Panconcelli-Calzia, G. (1919/20). Zeitschr. f. Eingeb.spr.
    Jahrgang X.
Panconcelli-Calzia, G. (1924). Berlin, Verlag von W. de
    Gruyter & Co.
Principles. (1949/70). I.P.A., London, Univ. College.
Saar, J. J. (1662). Nürnberg.
Schapera, I. (1933). Cape Town, van Riebeeck Society.
ten Rhyne, W. (1686). Schaffhausen.
Valentyn, F. (1726). Amsterdam, Dordrecht.
von Kempelen, W. (1791). Wien, J. V. Degan.
Wandres, C. (1918/19). Zeits. Kolo., IX:26-42.
Witsen, N. (1691). Diary of: Hottentottensprache.
Ziegenbalg, B. (1709). London.

n.b.: All translations of original texts into the English
    language were made by G. H. Breckwoldt.

man muss wohl observieren, als
man mit der Zunge schlagen
muss, denn ihre meisten wörter
werden fast allemahl mit der
Zunge geschlagen oder durch
die Kehle gesprochen. —
Dieses sind die Zeichen welche
man observiren muss in pronun,
,ciren —

Λ mit diesen muss man mit der
Zunge stark an den gaumen
schlagen. —

ɯ hier schlägt man mit der Zunge
gegen den gaumen, und spricht
das wort halb durch die nase,
und halb durch den mund. —

O dieses spricht man durch die
nase. —

Ich	Tiri
Du	Thaat
Er	Hackau
wir	Sikhim
ihr	Sikau
Sie	Hockoena —

Kom

FIGURE 2

kom hier	Ha alsee
Sehet oder Siehe	Moalsee
wo	Amma
hier	Heba
brood	Bree
hohlen	Heree
fleisch	Koo
wo gehet ihr hin	Amtsee
gehen	Kuhn
das auge	Mocqua
das bein	ouqua
der finger	oung
essen	oung
trinken	Kaa
schlaffen	Kooi
der vater	Soo, oder Nja.
die mütter	Sees
der bruder	Kang
die schwester	Kangkos
das kind	Koo
ein junge	Kaukoo
ein mägdelein	Trakoo

mein

FIGURE 3

1971	Proposed-phonetic-Symbols	B	ᵭ	D	A	A	P	R
	and their Definitions	Bilabial	Labio-Dental	Dental	Alveolar	Lateral Alveolar	(Pre) Palatal	Retroflex
	Historical Definitions	Labial	Denti-labial	Dental	Palatal	Lateral	Cerebral Guttural Cacuminal	Retroflex
	Orthography	⊙	⊙/	/	≠	//	!	///

figure 1

PUBLICATIONS & MANUSCRIPTS ON CLICKS

1971	Proposed-phonetic-Symbol.	B	ᵭ	D	A	A	P	R	
	and their Definitions	Bilabial	Labio-Dental	Dental	Alveolar	Lateral Alveolar	(Pre) Palatal	Retroflex	Symbols of undefined sounds
	Historical Definitions	Labial	Denti-labial	Dental	Palatal	Lateral	Cerebral Guttural Cacuminal	Retroflex	
	Orthography						!		

N.B.: In the following items from "Sir George Grey's Library" in Capetown are preceded by (G).

(G)	1638	Sir Th. Herbert				i s t				
	1662	J.J. Saar								
(G)	1664	G.F. Wrede								
	1668	O. Dapper								
	1686	W. ten Rhyne								
	1691	N. Witsen	inconsistent?			T, t', k'				
	1695	J.G. Grevenbroek	inconsistent?			Ch, Kh, Nh, nh				
	1714	J.G. Böving (Bövingh)								
(G)	1717	G.G. Leibnitz			t?		k?			
(G)	1719	P. Kolb		.	⌒	or	⌣			
(G)	1782	A. Sparman				t'				
	1790	F. le Vaillant			Λ	Δ	V			
(G)	1798	C.P. Thunberg			a		A	a'		
(G)	1801	J. Barrow						∪		
(G)	1905	van der Kemp								
	1808	H. Lichtenstein			t'¹	t'³	t'²			
	1824	E.F.F. Chladni								
(G)	1824	Kafir Books			c	(qc)	\	q		
(G)	1824	W.G. Burchell			'	"	'			
(G)	1829	J.L. Ebner								
(G)	1830	J.H. Schmelen			⌒					
	1838	Sir J. Alexander			.	.	.	'		
	1841	C.F. Wuras			··	.	.	.		

figure 4

(Continued on next page)

(Figure 4 continued from previous page)

		B	P̣	D	A	A	P	R	undefined
	1842	H.C. Knudsen			·		·	··		
	1846	H.C. Knudsen			·	?	·	·		
	1846	J. Ayliff			c		\	q		
(G)	1848	C.F. Wuras			·	?	ͻ	c		
	1850	Wuras (Appleyard)			f	\	ɥ	q		
	1850	J.W. Appleyard			c		\	q		
	1850	H.P.S. Schreuder			ϟ		ϟ	ϟ		
(G)	1853	R. Lepsius			c	ͻ	\	ɤ		
(G)	1854	R. Lepsius				ʾ		·		
	1855	R. Lepsius			(c)	(qc)	(x)	ʾ(q)		
(G)	1854	F.H. Vollmer			\	\	q	↙ʾ		
	1856	Rhenish Mission						↙		
	1857	J.G. Wallmann				ʾ		·		
	1857	H. Tindall			c	\	\	q		
(G)	1857	W.H.J. Bleek			c	ͻ	\	q		
(G)	1857	J.O. Rivers			ts	kt	kt	gkt		
(G)	1857	Motteno			1	4	2	3		
	1857 8	C.F. Wuras	∿	⌐	1 (Ł)	˥ (Γ)	⌐ (⌐)	⌐ (⌐)		
	1859	F.H. Vollmer						↙		
	1862	W.H.G. Bleek						·		
	1870	C. Callaway			c		\	q		
	1870	T. Hahn						·		
	1870	T. Hahn			Ⓓ ⅆ	Ⓖ ⅉ	ꙅ ⱬ	ⱳ ⱦ		
	1881	T. Hahn						·		
	1881	G. Bertin*	∥			ʾ		·		
	1888	I.P.A.: Table of phonetic symbols		·						
	1889	J.G. Kronlein						·		
	1891	H. Schinz						·		
	1894	G.H. Schils			δ	τ	æ	ʇ		
	1905	Ch. Sacleux	φ		δ	τ	\	ʇ		
	1905	W. Planert						·		
	1906	P. Passy			t\		c\	k\		
	1907	L. Schultze				·		·		
	1907	Anthropos-Script	d		ɪ	c	ɤ			
	1907	S. Passarge			1	2	4	3		
	1907	D. Jones	p\₂	·	t\₂		(t ̪)₂(c)	c\₂	x\₂	
	1909	C. Meinhof						·		

* Apart from the Labial Click and all original Lepsius symbols Bertin uses 3 self-invented clicks and undefined [s].

(Continued on next page)

(Figure 4 continued from previous page)

		B	P̪	D	A	A̠	P	R̪	undefined
1910	C. Meinhof	p̂		î	î	î	î		
1910	H. Vedder			/	/	// & ///	:		
1911	L.C. Lloyd			/	/	'/	:		
1913	W.L. Thompson						:		
1914	G. Panconcelli-Calzia	(p̂)		î	î	î	î		
1919	Sir H.H. Johnston			ʒ	ɔ	ʔ	ç		
1919-20	W. Bourquin ⎱	▭		⟁	⌐	▭	⌒		
	quoting: C.F. Wuras ⎰			⟋	⌐	⊔	∪		
1921	I.P.A.: "L'écriture phonétique internationale"			ʒ	ʖ	ʗ			ʖ
1923	C.M. Doke unvoiced ⎴			ʒʒh		ʖ ʖh	ʗ ʗh		
	voiced ⎬			ɤ		ɯ	ɘ		
	nasal ⎵			ŋ		ɴ	ʗ		
1924	C. Meinhof oral ⎴	p̂		î	î	ị̂	î		k̂ʼ
	nasal ⎵			n̂	n̂	n̂	n̂		
1925	C.M. Doke unvoiced ⎴			ʒ	↓	ʖ	ʗ	ψ	
	voiced ⎬			ɤ	↑	ɯ	ɘ	ʌ	
	nasal ⎵			ŋ	ʋ	ɴ	ʗ	ʈ	
1935	R. Stopa	∅	∅	⅃⅃	/	// & /ᵉ/	:	///	ǀ & //ǀ
1939	R. Stopa		⅃/	⅃⅃	/	// & //	:	///	
1938	D.M. Beach proposed spelling			/ (c)	/ (z)	// (x)	: (q)		
1938	P. Pienaar proposed orthography	°		/	/ˑ	//	:	///	
1958	G.H. Breckwoldt unvoiced ⎴	B	P̪	D	A	A̠	P	R̪	
.	voiced ⎬	B̬	P̬̪	D̬	A̬	A̬̠	P̬	R̬̪	
1971	nasal ⎵	B̃	P̪̃	D̃	Ã	Ã̠	P̃	R̪̃	

1971: proposed symbols and definitions		B Bilab.	P̪ Labio-dental	D Dental	A Alveol.	A̠ Later. alveol.	P (Pre) palatal	R̪ Retroflex	undefined
1921 "L'Écriture"	symb.			ʒ		ʖ	ʗ		ʖ
	Kafir			c		x	q		
1949/70 Principes	symb.			ʒ		ʖ		ʗ	ʖ velar (sic!)
	Zulu			c		x		q	
1969 "Maître"	symb.			ʒ		ʖ	ʗ		
	Zulu			c		x	q		

NASAL CONSONANT EPENTHESIS IN "SOUTHERN" FRENCH

E. DEAN DETRICH
Michigan State University

As in the United States, France also as a "Southern accent"; that is, a regional pronunciation characteristic of a particular geographical area. In this case the region is loosely termed the Midi. As in the Southern United States, we are dealing here with not one, but a whole series of regional accents which have certain traits in common. Southern States Americans have their drawl in common, and the Méridionaux, or people from the south of France share certain speech traits. Surely the most prominent phonetic trait of the accent du Midi (AM) which differentiates it from "Northern French," hereafter called "Standard French" (SF) (The Northerners won the wars) is the retention of the unstable vowel, schwa, in AM in phonetic environments where it is deleted in SF. Where in SF one might say "La petite Vivette elle-meme n'y entrait pas,"my informant,whose voice some of you may recognize says "La petite Vivette elle-même n'y entrait pas." In both AM and SF schwa is consistently deleted when contiguous to a pronounced vowel but in AM all interconsonantal schwas are retained while in SF they are deleted except in certain clearly defined phonetic environments. This retention of schwa interconsonantally in AM is often considered a blessing by students learning French as a second language.

In AM there is also a markedly different vocalic alternation in allophones of the mid-vowels. Most noticeable is the absence of the vowel /o/ in closed syllable. Hence SF "aube" /ob/, "rose" /roz/ and "chose"/ʃoz/ are pronounced /ɔb/, /rɔz/ and /ʃəz/ in AM.

The third principal phonetic difference between SF and
AM, and the subject of this paper, is the presence of nasal
consonant segments between nasal vowels and following consonants. This phenomenon does not obtain in SF, but is very
common in AM. In SF the following sentences would read:
"Notre pays, mon /m/ bon /m/ Monsieur, n'a pas toujours été
un endroit /n/ mort et sans refrains /ŋ/ comme il est
aujourd'hui. Auparavant, il s'y faisait un /n/ grand /n/
commerce de meunerie, et, dix lieues à la ronde /n/, les
gens /n/ des mas nous apportaient leur blé à moudre . . .
Tout autour du village les collines étaient convertes de
moulins à vent /ŋ/. De droite et de gauche, on ne voyait
que des ailes qui viraient au mistral par-dessus les pins /ŋ/
des ribambelles /m/ de petits ânes chargés de sacs, montant
/n/ et dévalant le long des chemins /ŋ/." In the speech of
my informant we hear a certain number of these epenthetic
nasal consonants, which shall henceforth be referred to as
EPN's.

In SF and in AM nasal vowels are followed by /n/ when
preceding a word beginning with a vowel and provided there is
a close syntactic link between the two words. This accounts
for the pronunciations:"on arrive"/ɔ̃na'riv/ and "en arrivant"
/ãnari'vã/. This exception aside, in SF nasal vowels and the
combination oral vowel,nasal consonant are mutually exclusive.
The masculine adjective "divin" /di'vɛ̃/ alternates with the
feminine form "divine" /di'vin/; "bon /bõ/ alternates with
"bonne" /bɔn/. When the nasal vowel is followed by a pronounced consonant there is a complete absence of nasal consonant pronunciation. This phenomenon is one of the traits
of SF pronunciation which is difficult for English speakers
who are learning French. The English speaker's tendency to
anticipate following consonants often leads him to insert a
nasal consonant between the nasal vowel and the following
consonant,accounting for the pronunciations "bonté"/bõn'te/
and "tõmber"/tom'be/. This same nasal consonant epenthesis
phenomenon obtains in AM(one more reason why English speakers
learning French find this dialect comforting),although not
necessarily in the same phonetic environments. The pronunciation of these ENC's sounds very novel both to native speakers
of SF and to those who have learned SF as a second language.
As we have seen in the case of the American "Southern drawl,"

we must not allow the novelty to obscure the facts. When a Yankee imitates a Southerner, his drawl is often excessive. Similarly when a speaker of SF imitates a speaker of AM, he generally inserts too many ENC's. Nasal consonant epenthesis in AM is frequent, but it is not pervasive. Close observation shows that these ENC's pose some thorny problems.

Though a brief recording of the speech of a student from Marseilles was analyzed in preparing this paper, the primary source of data was the recordings of the French actor, Fernandel, reading from Les lettres de mon moulin by Alphonse Daudet. Fernandel's perpetual role was that of the Méridional typique. Though he was an excellent comic actor, to a great extent his regional accent, the accent du Midi, was the raison d'être of his career. It was for this reason that he was chosen to read Daudet's letters concerning daily life in the Midi in the last century. Despite the abundance of ENG's in Fernandel's speech, there were problems in noting this occurrence. The presence or absence of these nasal consonants between a nasal vowel and a consonant was determined only by the ear of this author, and there were many judgement calls. Several factors made the discrimination of the ENC's difficult. First nasal vowels in AM have different qualities from those in SF. The /ɔ̃/ is more open, which tends to lead a person accustomed to hearing SF to perceive a consonant closing the syllable, hence a tendency to hear ENC's where there were none. In AM the nasal /ɛ̃/ has a higher pronunciation /ẽ/, which is occasionally diphthongized slightly to /ẽⁱ/. It is easy to perceive this nasal off-glide as a /ŋ/. What made the discrimination more difficult still was the fleeting nature of some of the occurrences of ENC's.

For these reasons the data classified in the following tables must be considered somewhat soft. When it is indicated that there was an 83% occurrence of a given ENC in a given environment, it must be born in mind that that figure reflects both the very prominent ENC's and the author's judgement of the very fleeting occurrences. Before considering the preconsontal ENC's let us discuss the data in Table 1. In AM when a nasal vowel is followed by a pause or by a word beginning with a vowel which is loosely bound syntactically to the preceding word (the terms "loosely bound" and "tightly bound" will be

explained shortly) there is an almost even distribution
between the absence of any nasal consonant and the presence
of /ŋ/. This consonant is often difficult to perceive, as it
is rarely released, and even when it is released, it is never
followed by the voyelle d'appui, schwa, as is almost always
the case after word final pronounced consonants in AM.
Occasionally when the /ŋ/ does not occur in this position,
there is a nasal off-glide in its place, as if the /ŋ/ was
attempted but not comsummated: "de loin en loin"
/də#lwẽⁱãlwẽⁱ/. This occurrence of /ŋ/ before pause and
before vowels is important to our consideration of the pre-
consonantal ENC's laid out in Table 2.

   Please read Table 2 in the following manner. In column A
there is a list of the consonants used in AM. They are listed
according to their frequency of occurrence following nasal
vowels, with /d/ having been found preceded by a nasal vowel
two hundred times while /n/ was found in that position only
seven times. In column B are found the different epenthetic
nasal consonants which occur before the corresponding consonants in column A. In columns C, D, E, F and G are the
various phonetic and syntactic environments in which the
presence or absence of the ENC's was noted. The symbols indicating phonetic and syntactic environments are to be interpreted as follows:

C. V́̃ __C ( )# means "between a stressed nasal vowel and a
   word final consonant": "chambre" /'ʃãmbrə/, "etendre"
   /e'tãndrə/, (V-vowel, C=consonant, ( )=optional,# = word
   boundary).
D. Ṽ __C means "between an unaccented nasal vowel and a
   consonant within a word": "bonté" /bɔ̃n'te/, "entendre"
   /ãn'tãndrə/.
E. Ṽ __#C means "between a word final unaccented nasal vowel
   and a following consonant." The presence of a single word
   boundary # is meant to indicate a close syntactic link
   between the two words. Such a close syntactic link occurs
   between two words generally when one modifies or comple-
   ments the meaning of another. Such is the case between ad-
   jectives and nouns,after determiners, after prepositions,
   between adverbs and a following modified word, in general
   within a groupe de sens or meaning group. Examples of E:
   "mon bon Monsieur" /mɔ̃m#bɔ̃m#m ə'sjø/, "un peu" / œ̃m#'pø/.

F. V̇ __#C means "between an accented word final nasal and
a following consonant." Here again we have a close syntactic link, but not as close as in E. Most instances
of the F environment occur between a noun and a following adjective, after a verb, and within a set expression,
(forme figée): "au fond de" (o#'fɔ̃n#də/, "pendant que"
/pãn'dãŋ#kə/.

G. Ṽ __##C means between a word final nasal vowel and a
consonant between words where there is a loose syntactic
link, generally between meaning groups. ". . .à tâtons
devant. . . /a#ta'tõ##dəvã/.

In each intersection of the matrix the number in parentheses indicates how many times the consonant in that row was
preceded by a nasal vowel in the phonetic or syntactic environment for that column. The percentage figure in each section
indicates in how many instances the concatenation of a nasal
vowel with a consonant resulted in an epenthetic nasal consonant.

An analysis of the data in Tables 1 and 2 leads to the
following conclusions. First, there are two nasal consonant
epenthesis rules in AM. The one, reflected in the data in
Table 1 and in column H of Table 2 inserts a velar(or perhaps
uvular) unreleased nasal consonant optionally after a nasal
vowel followed by a pause or followed by a loose syntactic
link (Ṽ__##). The second nasal consonant epenthesis rule inserts a nasal consonant between a nasal vowel and a following
consonant. The ENC copies the point of articulation from the
following consonant. This rule is highly constrained however,
both phonetically and syntactically. Phonetically it is constrained by features of the following consonant. Epenthesis
is more frequent before stop consonants (with the exception of
nasal consonants)than before continuants;among the stop consonants epenthesis is more frequent before voiceless consonants
than before voiced consonants;among the continuant consonants
there is insufficient data to say whether voicing is a variable;
there is no occurrence of ENC before the liquids; ENC's are
rare before nasal consonants, perhaps because of an abhorrence
of geminates. There is a slightly (perhaps insignificantly)
higher occurrence of ENC's after a stressed nasal vowel than
after an unstressed nasal vowel. Syntax also constrains the

second nasal consonant epenthesis rule. The occurrence of
ENC's within a word is much greater than between the words,
and between words the application of the rule is essentially
possible only if there is a close syntactic link. This positional hierarchy is represented left to right in columns
C, D, E, F and G of Table 2. The only real anomoly in this
scheme is the 25% occurrence of epenthesis in 1-G of Table 2,
where in five out of 25 potential cases of epenthesis there
were ENC's across a loose syntactic link. One possible explanation is that the instances of nasal vowel followed by
/d/ are far and away the most common in French, and since
epenthesis is frequent before /d/, perhaps the high frequency
combined with the abundance of instances of the environment
are causing nasal consonant epenthesis where we do not expect
it.

It was mentioned above that in SF nasal vowels alternate
morphologically with oral vowels followed by nasal consonants:
"bon/bonne" /bõ/-/bɔn/, "divin/divine" /di'vɛ̃/-/di'vin/. San-
ford Schane grasps this generality in his <u>French Phonology and
Morphology</u> (1968), a book which remains a standard reference
for those studying French phonology within the framework of
transformational linguistics. He describes SF as having an
underlying phonemic system using only oral vowels. Nasal
vowels are generated by a series of rules nasalizing oral
vowels in syllables closed by a nasal consonant, with subsequent vowel lowering and nasal consonant deletion rules. This
analysis allows us to capture the morphological pairs listed
above with abstract underlying representations as follows:
/bon/ /bon+ə/, /divin/ /divin+ə/. The same alternations
obtain in AM, and the same underlying representations could
function in both dialects. Moreover, AM buttresses the
analysis with its more frequent retention of the feminine
marker /ə/ in the pronunciation of these words. It would be
tempting to use AM to further buttress the hypothesis by maintaining that the ENC's are simply the underlying nasal segments which, rather than deleting after nasalization, assimi-
late by point of articulation to the following consonant.

Our analysis of the data concerning ENC's simply does not
point strongly in that direction. While not uncommon in AM,
ENC's are not pervasive in Fernandel's speech, and even when

he adopts a style with frequent ENC's, the environments in
which this epenthesis is obligatory are rare. Even in AM
there are more instances of nasal vowels not followed by
nasal consonants than there are nasal vowels followed by
nasal consonants, and when the consonants do occur, they
never agree in point of articulation with the underlying
nasal phonemens from which they should have sprung. However,
if these nasal consonants do not originate from underlying
nasal phonemes and are merely epenthetic consonants born of
the transition between two sounds, we have an interesting
linguistic predicament. This means that, if Schane's
description of French phonology (with which this author
agrees in part) is applied to AM, there must be underlying
nasal phonemes which nasalize preceding vowels, delete
entirely, and later in the string of phonological rules are
replaced by other nasal consonants.

This analysis is not quite so improbable or complex if we
understand that there are two quite different kinds of phonological rules which function in language. Bjarkman refers to
"a fundamental distinction between learned, abstract, and
obligatory phonological 'rules' and innate, phonetically motivated, and optional phonological 'processes' which together
comprise contradictory and competing types of phonological
operations." A similar distinction was drawn by this author
where he referred to "règles phonologiques apprises" and
"règles phonologiques acquises," that is, between "learned"
phonology and "acquired"phonology,in discussing the essential
difference between the rule of French phonology which deletes
word final schwas and the rule which deletes word final consonants. The latter rule is a highly marked and very idiosyncratic phenomenon. Some consonants never delete in phrase
final position; others delete word finally when followed by
another consonant, but not phrase finally; some delete
optionally in selected words and obligatorily in others.
This is actually a very complicated set of rules which is
learned by the speaker but which can potentially present
problems to the speaker throughout life. Consonant deletion
is a "règle apprise." Conversely schwa deletion is a "règle
acquise." This type of rule applies automatically and unconsciously; the speaker does not make a decision. Acquired
phonological rules often generate sounds that a speaker untrained in phonetics may deny having said or insist that he

does not hear. If you ask a French speaker to repeat precisely the sentence he has just said, he will very often
repeat in a more guarded style, changing it by deleting
fewer schwas, and yet be convinced that he has spoken exactly
the same utterance. Similarly in English students often do
not hear the /t/ in 'prince" but they do hear the /t/ in
"fisⱦ fight" precisely because the first /t/ is inserted and
the second /t/ is deleted by acquired phonological rules.

The "nasal vowel versus oral vowel + nasal consonant"
alternation in both SF and AM is generated by a learned rule,
but in AM there is the additional acquired rule inserting
epenthetic nasal consonants in specific environments. It
might well be a safe generalization to say that most of the
characteristics of "pronunciations" popularly called "accents"
are the result of acquired phonological rules, whether it
is the American "Southern drawl" or the accent du Midi.

REFERENCES

Bjarkman, P. C. (1977). (In press).
Daudet, A. (1869). Paris: Nelson.
Daudet, A. (Recording of Fernandel). Decca.
Detrich, E. D. (1975). Unpublished.
Schane, S. A. (1968). Cambridge, Mass.: MIT Press.

Table 1. Nasal vowels followed by vowels or pauses.

	no epenthesis	/ŋ/ or /n/
V__## $\frac{V}{\#}$	92	81

Table 2. Nasal vowels followed by consonants.

		Ṽ́_c(2)#	Ṽ_c	Ṽ_#c	Ṽ́_#c	Ṽ_##c	
1	d ⁿ	(42) 86%	(52) 83%	(23) 48%	(58) 47%	(25) 20%	4 ŋ
2	t ⁿ	(29) 90%	(86) 90%	(23) 65%	(7) 100%	(6) 0%	2 ŋ
3	s ⁿ	(18) 0%	(46) 15%	(33') 6%	(4) 0%	(17) 0%	5 ŋ
4	l		(4) 0%	(58) 0%	(11) 0%	(28) 0%	1 ŋ
5	p ᵐ	(1) 100%	(23) 87%	(47) 62%	(7) 100%	(6) 0%	2 ŋ
6	k ᵑ	(12) 83%	(15) 100%	(20) 85%	(14) 86%	(6) 0%	6 ŋ
7	b ᵐ	(18) 78%	(17) 87%	(18) 67%	(2) 100%		
8	f ᶬ		(20) 50%	(12) 42%	(2) 0%	(2) 0%	2 ŋ
9	ᵑ	(4) 0%	(18) 11%	(4) 25%	(1) 0%	(4) 0%	3 ŋ
10	m ᵐ		(1) 0%	(26) 23%		(4) 0%	1 ŋ
11	r ⁿ	(2) 0%	(10) 40%	(18) 0%	(3) 0%	(3) 0%	1 ŋ
12	v ᶬ		(3) 100%	(11) 9%	(2) 0%	(1)	
13	g ᵑ	(4) 100%	(4) 0%	(10) 80%			
14	ʃ ⁿ	(5) 0%	(10) 10%	(8) 13%			
15	z ⁿ	(1) 100%	(10) 10%	(1) 0%	(1) 0%		1 ŋ
16	n ⁿ		(1) 100%	(5) 20%	(1) 100%		1 ŋ

AN INSTRUMENTAL INVESTIGATION OF COARTICULATION
IN STOP CONSONANT SEQUENCES

W. J. HARDCASTLE AND P. J. ROACH
University of Reading

One of the important aims of research into coarticulatory processes in speech production is to establish the
various constraints on these processes, whether physiological, related to inherent characteristics of the speech
mechanism or linguistic, related to the phonological, syntactic and semantic rules of the language. By studying
details of coarticulatory effects in different phonetic and
grammatical environments, one can begin to shed more light
on these fundamental issues. A useful area of such study
is the coarticulation effects which take place during a
sequence of two stop consonants occurring for example in
environments such as -VCCV- and -VC#'CV- (where the symbol #
represents a word boundary and ' represents stress).
Phonetic observations reveal that in most of these cases,
the closure for the first stop is not released until the
closure for the second is formed (see Catford, 1977;
Ladefoged, 1975; Kozhevnikov and Chistovich, 1965). There
is thus a short period of overlapping or simultaneous closure
involving the articulatory organs participating in the production of the stops, the extent of such overlap depending
presumably on such factors as phonetic environment, placement
of stress and rate of utterance. The temporal relationships
between the stop closures (C1 and C2) are shown schematically in Figure 1 (using, as an example, the word "catkin").
It can be seen from the figure that closure for C2 does not

begin until closure for Cl is formed. This is an instance
of serial ordering and it is interesting to speculate on
how it is handled by the CNS. The aim of this experiment
is to provide some clues as to the nature of such control
by investigating the temporal relationships that obtain in
sequences of stop consonants in different phonetic and
grammatical environments.

METHOD

     Three male subjects were used: one subject (C) is a
speaker of Australian English and the other two, A and B,
are speakers of British English, the former's accent being
close to RP though with some northern characteristics and
the latter having a Midlands accent. The test material
consisted of single-word and two-word items containing all
possible combinations of two English voiceless stops, in
two different phonetic environments--after a front vowel (y̰)
and after a back vowel (v̰). The form of the test items used
can be seen in the left-hand column of Table 1. Lists containing the items in random order were presented to each
subject who read them through four times at normal conversational speed. Care was taken to ensure that the stress
was placed on the first syllable of each single word item
and on the first syllable of the second word in the two-word
items. Details of lingual closure were recorded by means of
an electropalatograph (see Hardcastle, 1972), hereafter
abbreviated as EPG; the device was connected to a computer
(see Roach and Hardcastle, 1976; Jones, 1977; Roach, 1977).
Labial movement was recorded by a cine-camera running at 100
f.p.s. and results from this were derived from frame-by-frame
analysis of the films. The experimental set-up is illustrated
schematically in Figure 2. Frame pulses from the camera are
fed into the computer which in turn determines the sampling
time in the EPG control. Information on tongue contacts with
the palate is processed by the computer, which provides a
print-out as shown. A frame counter is photographed with the
subject's lips and the frame number appears on each successive
palate diagram on the print-out. In this way it is possible
to synchronize the labial data in the film with palatal data
in the EPG print-out.

Diagrams such as that shown above for the sequence
/tk/ were made from the records obtained and the following
measurements were made: time from onset of closure for C1
on onset of closure for C2 ("C1-C2"); duration of the overlap in closure ("overlap"); and the sum of the closure
duration for C1 and the closure duration for C2 ("total
duration"). Preglottalization of the first stop, as
described by Roach (1973), was observed in many instances;
measurement of the duration and overlap of this laryngeal
closure was not made for this experiment, but it is our
intention to include these measurements in future research
of this type.

RESULTS

Subjects differed considerably in their production of
the test items. Figure 3 illustrates a typical EPG print-
out. In this diagram each successive frame represents an
interval of 10 msec. with Figure 3 showing a fairly typical
pattern for /tk/. In any case, one of the variations noted
related to alveolar closure. This "instability of alveolars"
(Gimson, 1960) has been frequently noted under conditions
of increased rate of utterance and is the subject of recent
research (e.g., Kohler, 1976 for German). However, complete
absence of a /t/ closure where one was expected was encountered
in only 6 out of a possible 96 cases.

Table 1 shows means for the two measurements C1-C2 and
overlap, for all repetitions of the test items by the three
subjects. In order to minimize the effects of any variations
in speech tempo which might influence the stop durations,
each value is expressed as a percentage of the total duration
of each stop pair. Because of the factorial design of the
experiment it was possible to carry out an analysis of
variance on each set of data (that is, data for /kt/, /tk/;
/kp/, /pk/; /tp/, /pt/). One of the clearest tendencies
seen in Table 1 and shown up in the analysis of variance
was for the C1-C2 values for /tk/ to be highly significantly
less than for /kt/ (at 0.1% level) for all subjects. The
analysis of variance showed in addition, however, a highly
significant three-way interaction effect involving /kt/,
/tk/ which is illustrated by Table 2.

The rather high value of Vt#kV can be attributed to the tendency for subjects B and C occasionally to release Cl before closure is formed for C2 thus producing a longer Cl-C2 value. Such significant differences in the Cl-C2 values were not found for the other stop combination pairs /kp/, /pk/; /tp/, /pt/. In the /kp/, /pk/ set, for example, there was considerable variation between subjects. This relationship is illustrated by the significant interaction for the Cl-C2 measure pooled across all environment as follows: (1) for /kp/, Sub. J = 30.3, Subj. B = 29.6 and Subj. C = 35.5; (2) for /pk/, Sub. A = 20.5, Subj. B = 39.5 and Subj. C = 41.4. Both subjects B and C show higher values for /pk/ than for /kp/ but for subject A the order is reversed.

The vowel environment appeared to have some slight effect on the Cl-C2 measure for stop combinations involving the bilabial. To illustrate this, Table 3 was compiled from means for V and V pooled across all subjects and both grammatical contexts for the stop combinations /kp/, /pk/; /tp/, /pt/.

This table shows that in the case where /t/ is the second stop in the sequence the front vowel environment causes a shorter Cl-C2 value. This can be explained by coarticulatory effects from the vowel on the alveolar stop, such coarticulation extending across an intervening bilabial closure. Similarly the back rounded vowel V seems to facilitate a faster labial gesture for the bilabial stop in /kp/, /tp/. The overlap measures revealed that in only 32 cases out of 272 was the first stop released before onset of the second closure. Subjects showed significantly different overlapping tendencies: the greatest overlap durations normally occurred with Subject A. Somewhat surprisingly perhaps, the grammatical environment (i.e., presence or absence of word boundary) did not appear to have a consistent significant effect on any measure.

CONCLUSIONS

One of the most interesting results of this experiment was the shorter Cl-C2 time for /tk/ compared with /kt/.

Kozhevnikov and Chistovich (1965) speculated that during stop sequences such as the above, motor commands to the appropriate muscles for both stops are issued simultaneously a low-level mechanism being responsible for the sequencing of closures. A suitable low-level mechanism may be, for example, a tactile feedback loop triggering the movement towards the second stop as soon as the appropriate sensory information is obtained from tongue-palate contact involved in the first stop. In the case of /tk/ the sensory information would be sent by mechano-receptors in the tongue as it makes contact along both sides of the palate and the alveolar ridge. From this position all that is necessary for a /k/ closure is a contraction of an intrinsic tongue muscle, the inferior longitudinalis, which has the effect of bunching up the middle posterior part of the tongue. Such a movement could take place relatively rapidly because the intrinsic muscles have fast contraction times and it is not necessary to move the whole body of the tongue appreciably. In the case of /kt/, however, the sensory feedback triggering takes place asthe back part of the tongue touches the velar region. The movement towards /t/ involves a shifting forwards and upwards of the body of the tongue using probably the genioglossus (an extrinsic muscle) and the superior longitudinalis. Because it involves repositioning the tongue body by the slower-contracting extrinsic muscles the movement towards the /t/ is relatively delayed. Such physiological constraints would not be present in other stop combinations as in these cases a separate articulatory organ, the lips, is involved, which can move independently of the tongue. One would expect, however, that the onset of alveolar closure would be faster than that of velar closure in /pt/, /pk/ because of the faster closing velocity of the tongue tip and blade (Kuehn and Moll, 1976). Such a tendency was observed. It is proposed to test this hypothesis by examining the coarticulatory effects discussed in this paper under conditions of altered tactile sensation.

REFERENCES

Catford, J. C. (1977). Edinburgh Univ. Press.
Gimson, A. C. (1960). M. Ph., 113.
Hardcastle, W. J. (1972). Phonet., 25:197-215.
Jones, W. R. (1977). Phonet. Lab., Reading Univ.
Kohler, K. (1976). Phonet., 33:1-30.
Kozhevnikov, V. A. and Chistovich, L. A. (1965). J.P.R.S., Washington.
Kuehn, D. P. and Moll, K. L. (1976). J. Phon., 4:303-320.
Ladefoged, P. (1975). New York, Harcourt Brace.
Roach, P. J. (1973). J. Inter. Phon. Assn., 3:10-21.
Roach, P. J. (1977). Phonet. Lab., Reading Univ.
Roach, P. J. and Hardcastle, W. J. (1976). Univ. Essex.

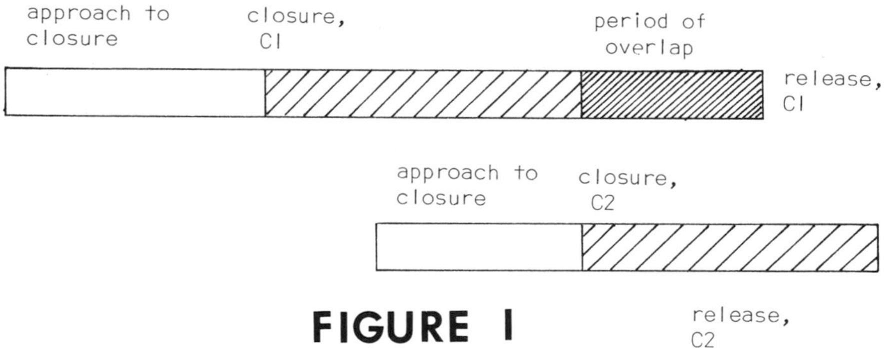

FIGURE I

Table 1.   Means for the measurements C1–C2 and overlap for
each subject, as percentages of total stop closure
duration.

Test Set	Item	Overlap (% Total Duration)			C1–C2 (% Total Duration)		
		Sub.A	Sub.B	Sub.C	Sub.A	Sub.B	Sub.C
I	VktV	23.3	10.9	25.6	27.0	33.2	36.5
	VktV	33.2	16.4	17.9	23.0	32.4	43.4
	Vk#tV	22.0	9.5	25.4	28.5	29.2	12.4
	Vk#tV	31.6	7.3	21.5	28.9	51.0	27.3
	Mean		20.3			31.1	
II	VtkV	34.4	6.2	5.0	6.7	29.3	10.0
	VtkV	27.6	2.7	21.2	17.7	38.4	17.7
	Vt#kV	28.4	8.2	10.2	13.3	29.0	30.5
	Vt#kV	29.7	8.5	30.5	10.0	0	1.9
	Mean		17.7			17.0	
III	VkpV	14.7	7.3	7.0	35.5	20.3	26.3
	VkpV	19.1	11.1	9.0	28.8	22.2	38.8
	Vk#pV	16.7	6.7	5.0	31.7	36.1	38.9
	Vk#pV	29.9	4.0	16.4	25.5	39.8	38.2
	Mean		12.2			31.8	
IV	VpkV	21.2	7.1	9.9	20.6	41.4	47.4
	VpkV	14.2	17.2	21.2	24.7	32.3	28.8
	Vp#kV	7.6	1.8	8.3	25.4	45.4	42.5
	Vp#kV	22.6	3.2	1.8	11.6	39.1	47.2
	Mean		11.3			33.8	
V	VtpV	28.7	6.3	20.6	21.0	39.9	20.6
	VtpV	34.2	16.7	7.6	18.3	20.7	39.4
	Vt#pV	32.3	12.3	19.2	16.8	27.8	19.0
	Vt#pV	30.1	10.3	6.9	23.3	30.5	30.0
	Mean		18.7			25.6	
VI	VptV	23.0	8.8	16.9	23.0	37.3	30.3
	VptV	26.1	22.4	27.6	21.7	27.6	23.1
	Vp#tV	16.4	19.5	20.6	20.8	26.4	31.1
	Vp#tV	28.8	14.9	20.9	17.8	26.7	29.0
	Mean		15.9			26.2	

Table 2. Three-way table of means, pooled for all subjects, showing effects on /kt/,/tk/ of different phonetic and grammatical environments.

	V=V̌	V=V̲
VktV	32.9	32.2
Vk#tV	35.7	23.3
VtkV	24.6	15.3
Vt#kV	3.9	24.3

Table 3.

	V̌	V̲		V̌	V̲
/kp/	32.3	31.4	/tp/	28.1	24.3
/pk/	30.6	37.1	/pt/	24.1	27.0

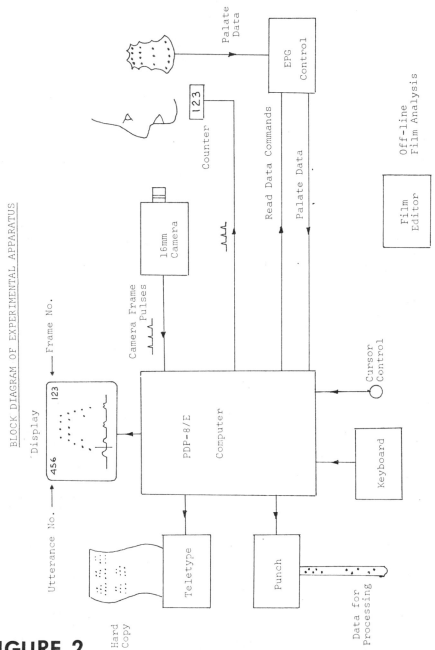

BLOCK DIAGRAM OF EXPERIMENTAL APPARATUS

FIGURE 2

Print-out of palatal data from [æ] to [ɪ] in "catkin" (Subj.C)

Alveolar closure

```
      342              343             ↓344             345             346
00......00       00......00       00......00      00....000      000...000
00....00         00....00         00....00        00....00       0000.000
0......0         0......0         00....00        00....00       00....00
........         ........0        0......0        0......00      00....00
........         ........         0......0        0......0       0.....00
........         ........         0......0        0......0       00...000
........         ........         00000000        00000000       00000000
......           ......           .00.0.          000000         000000
```

                                                 Velar closure   Alveolar release

```
      347             348             349           ↓350            ↓351
00000..000       00000.0000      00000.0000     0000000000      0000000000
0000.000         0000.000        0000.000       0000.000        0000.000
00....00         00....00        00....00       00....00        00...000
00....00         00....00        00....00       00....00        00....00
00....00         00....00        00....00       00....00        00....00
00...000         0000.000        00...000       00....00        00....000
00000000         00000000        00000000       00...000        00....00
.000000          000000          000000         000000          00...0
```

```
      352             353             354             355             356
0000000000       0000000000      0000000000     0000000000      0000000000
0000.000         0000.000        0000.000       0000.000        0000.000
000..000         000..000        000..000       000..000        000..000
00...000         000..000        000..000       00...000        00...000
000..000         000..000        000..000       00...000        00....00
0000..00         0000..00        00....00       00....00        .0....00
00.....0         0......0        0......0       0......0        ........0
0.....           0......          ......         ......          ......
```

Velar release

```
      357            ↓ 358            359             360             361
0000000000       00000.0000      00000.0000     00000.0000      000...000
0000.000         0000.000        0000.000       0000.000        0000.000
000..000         000..000        000..000       00...000        00....00
00...000         00..0000        00....00       00....00        00....00
00....00         00....00        00....00       0......00       0......0
......0          ......0         ......0        ......00        ........
........          ........        ........       ........        ........
......           ......          ......         ......          ......
```

```
      362             363             364             365             366
000....000       00.....000      00......00     00......00      00......00
0000.000         0000.000        0000.000       0000.000        0000.000
00....00         00....00        00....00       00....00        00....00
00....00         00....00        00....00       00....00        00....00
0......0         0......0        0......0       0......0        0......0
........          ........        ........       ........        ........
........          ........        ........       ........        ........
......           ......          ......         ......          ......
```

FIGURE 3

STANDARDISATION VS / DIVERSIFICATION DANS LA
PRONONCIATION DU FRANÇAIS CONTEMPORAIN

P. R. LÉON
University of Toronto

La phonologie classique a peu étudié les variantes du
système (phonématiques et surtout prosodiques) considérées
depuis Trubetzkoy, comme extra-phonologiques.

Cependant les variations ont été répertoriées par
catégories systémiques: variantes régionales (André Martinet,
1945; Fernand Carton, 1972; Denise François, 1970; Anne-Marie
Houdebine, 1974); variantes à l'intérieur d'un sociolecte
(Ruth Reichstein, 1960; Odette Mettas, 1971; Pierre Léon,
1973; André Martinet et Henriette Walter, 1975). Les
variantes stylistiques ont été étudiées principalement par
Ivan Fónagy (1976) et Pierre Léon (1971, 1976). Le fonctionnement de la variation a été observé en tant que causalité
interne (Martinet, 1955) ou externe, essentiellement d'ordre
expressif (Sommerfelt, 1930; Martinet, 1955; Fónagy, 1976;
Léon, 1974). Des études récentes ouvrent de nouvelles perspectives dans le domaine (Henriette Walter et al., 1977).
Aussi est-il devenu un lieu commun - voir les publications
françaises en linguistique appliquée des dernières années -
que de souligner la "diversité des français." Un numéro
spécial du Français dans le Monde (décembre, 1969) y a été
entièrement consacré.

Il faut bien admettre qu'on a surtout constaté jusqu'à
maintenant la diversité des français dans ses variations
dialectales. Il semble bien qu'on ait peu ou pas montré

les deux tendances en présence et leur fonctionnement:
(1) une <u>standardisation</u> de la prononciation par effacement
progressif des variantes régionales. (2) une <u>diversification</u>
résultant (a) du processus de standardisation plus ou moins
avancé selon les couches sociales; (b) d'une redistribution
des valeurs à l'intérieur de chaque couche sociale.

<u>La standardisation apparaît d'abord dans l'attitude des
sujets parlants.</u>

Elle s'effectue en direction d'un <u>modèle</u> (Léon, 1973) -
image générique et mythique à la fois - d'un français
idéalisé par les mass media. Représentation à travers hommes
politiques, artistes, etc. d'un "beau francais." Ce
français est défini comme "standard" ou "neutre" par la
plupart des sujets (étudiants et professeurs de 12 universités provinciales) dans une enquête en cours (Léon et Léon,
1977). Il ne s'agit plus désormais d'un modèle <u>parisien</u> dans
la conscience des sujets parlants. En effet, le français
teinté de parisianisme est rejeté hors du modèle idéal par la
majorité des sujets enquêtés; soit comme "snob," soit comme
"vulgaire" - (il s'agit alors du parisien "populaire,"
"faubourien," qualifié aussi parfois de "drôle"). Le français
régional est défini comme "standard" lorsqu'il se situe dans
"la bonne société" ou "la haute société" des <u>grandes villes</u>
de province, par les mêmes sujets. Ils décrivent la prononciation des campagnes environnantes comme "saine,"
"amusante," "provinciale," "campagnarde," "rurale," "drôle."

Le modèle défini par les provinciaux existe donc bien
hors de Paris. La standardisation implicitement reconnue
par l'attitude des interviewés oppose essentiellement les
catégories sociales suivantes: <u>citadins</u> ≠ <u>ruraux</u>; <u>favorisés</u>
≠ <u>défavorisés</u>. La même attitude semble se retrouver aussi
bien dans la France du midi que dans celle du mord. La
conséquence de la standardisation dans les grands centres
paraît amener la perte - totale? - due complexe de pro-
vincial. Subsiste toujours l'autre rapport dominant/dominé
qu'établit la double relation <u>ville</u> / <u>campagne</u> et <u>favorisé</u> /
<u>défavorisé</u> - rapport stigmatisé dans les termes dévalorisants
de "amusant," " drôle" ... On relève néanmoins des attitudes
revendicatrices prônant l'accent régional, voire le retour

au dialecte. Le phénomène n'existe-t-il pas beaucoup plus
chez les intellectuels que dans les autres couches des
populations régionales?

La standardisation apparaît ensuite dans le comportement
des sujets parlants.

On a effectué (Léon et Léon, 1976-1977) une série
d'interviews d'une trentaine d'heures dans 12 villes francaises réparties autour de l'hexagone. Enquêtes: chefs
syndicalistes. 34 échantillons ont été relevés au hasard
(de 30 sec. à 1 minute de parole) et écoutés par des universitaires français dans une dizaine d'universités (Paris et
province). Les réponses des auditeurs semblent (dépouillement en cours) confirmer une standardisation de la prononciation qui se manifeste par l'incapacité quasi-totale
à différencier des sujets issus de couches sociales
favorisées, citadines, jeunes et à un moindre degré
mobiles. Il semble que l'absence de mobilité puisse
être compensée par l'influence des mass media chez le
sujet réceptif et en contact permanent avec le monde ex-
térieur, comme c'est le cas dans le groupe étudié de mili-
tants syndicalistes. (C'est Anne-Marie Houdebine qui a
attiré notre attention sur le facteur mobilité géographique,
à la suite de son enquête sur le seuil du Poitou. Les catégories hommes / femmes n'ont pu être étudiées dans notre
enquête).

Le test d'audition de notre enquête met ainsi en lumière
deux nouvelles oppositions, à ajouter aux précédentes:
jeunes / vieux; mobiles / stables. On a donc maintenant
quatre couples de classes qu'il faudra étudier systématiquement: citadins / ruraux; favorisés / défavorisés; jeunes /
vieux; mobiles / stables. On peut dire à coup sûr que le
rural, défavorisé, âgé et sédentaire aura, par rapport au
français standard une prononciation marquée. A l'opposé,
le citadin, favorisé, jeune, mobile, a "toutes les chances"
d'avoir un accent standardisé.

Poids des facteurs sociaux en cause.

Les facteurs en cause peuvent se répartir inégalement.
On a ainsi l'exemple de deux chefs syndicalistes grenoblois

apparemment issus de milieux non <u>favorisés</u> mais pour qui deux
facteurs sans doute très importants ont joué (<u>jeunes</u>, <u>cita-
dins</u>). Ils ont donné une prononciation <u>non marquée</u> pour
tous les auditeurs. Un autre chef syndicaliste grenoblois
est âgé mais a toujours beaucoup voyagé et est issu d'un
milieu favorisé. Sa prononciation est perçue également
comme non marquée. A Strasbourg, on a un exemple d'un
accent très marqué chez un homme issu d'un milieu <u>défavorisé</u>,
<u>âgé</u>, alors qu'un <u>jeune</u>, du même milieu mais ayant voyagé et
étant devenu enseignant n'a aucune trace d'accent local. Il
est certain que les facteurs sociaux relevés ci-dessus n'ont
pas tous le même poids. Quel est ce poids? Seules des
enquêtes multiples et précises pourront le déterminer. Il
est différent dans la France du nord et dans celle du midi.
Le contexte <u>méridional</u> (facteur dialectal) semble plus important que celui de n'importe quelle autre région, en tant
que frein à la standardisation - toutes conditions égales par
ailleurs.

Relevé des variables linguistiques.

    L'enquête mentionnée ci-dessus a été menée selon une
procédure totalement différente de celles des enquêtes de type
Labovien. Ce sont les auditeurs qui ont jugé si le sujet
entendu appartenait à la catégorie non marquée (standard) ou
marquée (régionale). Les données sociologiques recueillies
sur les interviewers ont permis d'établir certaines corré-
lations. Les variables linguistiques en cause seront ex-
traites par la suite, par différentiation entre les groupes
identifiés. Certaines de ces variables (régionales) sont
déjà bien connues - (cf. pour le nord: F. Carton). Mais
il reste à établir pour chaque strate sociale leur importance
relative, autrement dit le degré d'accent, en fonction du
statut social. On se propose dans une enquête ulterienre
de déterminer, pour une même région, les différenciations
sociales indiquées par certains traits dialectaux. Lesquels? Dans quelles proportions? Plusieurs traits, tels
que le /r/ roulé, apical sont toujours indexés comme
"rural" et dévalorisant - de même une accentuation forte
et, à un moindre degré, la présence d'un double timbre
vocalique pour /i/, /y/, /u/, dans la France du nord.

L'exemple de l'accentuation.

Parmi les variables en cause, celle de l'accentuation a
paru l'une des plus importantes. Il nous a semblé intéressant d'examiner s'il pouvait y avoir une corrélation
entre la place et la nature de l'accent d'une part et,
d'autre part, le degré de standardisation de la prononciation dans le groupe observé. On aurait pu examiner le
problème en partant de quelques échantillons représentatifs
de sujets nettement marqués dans une catégorie ou une autre.
On a préféré, dans un premier temps, envisager le problème
en bloc en comparant la situation de l'accent dans ce groupe
avec celle décrite par Fónagy pour le français parisien
contemporain.

Pour l'exposé de la procédure de l'expérimentation, nous
renvoyons à notre article dans le volume sur l'accent.
(Fónagy et Léon, à paraître). Les résultats des tests
d'auditions des échantillons du corpus montrent que dans
52% des cas la place de l'accent n'est pas identifiable
pour 75% des auditeurs. Si l'on compare les résultats des
deux groupes, France du nord / France du midi, on s'aperçoit
que l'on obtient des différences non significatives. Pris
en bloc et comparés aux résultats de Fónagy, nos résultats
montrent que l'accentuation à la finale, considérée comme
une marque de provincialisme (Martinet, 1977) tend à dis-
paraître des français régionaux. Dans le type de discours
observé, l'évolution est même plus avancée qu'à Paris (75%
d'oxytonie dans la conversation, selon Fónagy). Il y a donc
là l'indice certain d'un processus de standardisation en
cours.

La différenciation entre l'accentuation du nord et
celle du midi semble s'opérer par une distribution différente
des paramètres accentuels. Le midi utilise moins la durée
et davantage l'intensité.

	Durée	Hauteur	Intensité
F N.	74%	63%	49%
F M.	70%	69%	53%

Pourcentage des marques acoustiques attestées dans les pro-
éminences accentuelles du corpus pour la France du Nord par
rapport à celle du midi.

Il nous faudra reprendre ces résultats en groupant les
locuteurs par catégories (+ ou - standardisé) pour tenter
de voir plus précisément le rôle de l'accentuation dans la
perception d'une déviation par rapport au français standardisé. Mais on peut cependant conclure des résultats
généraux exposés ci-dessus, que la perte de l'oxytonie des
français régionaux est un indice certain de leur évolution
vers la standardisation.

Diversification

Si les français régionaux se standardisent, les degrés
de standardisation introduisent une première diversification,
qui n'est en fait que le reliquat d'une situation antérieure.
Toutes choses égales par ailleurs, on peut dire que <u>le degré
d'accent dialectal est inversement proportionnel à l'importance du statut social</u>. La diversification s'opère donc à
ce stade par <u>les marqueurs dialectaux de classe</u>, déjà
mentionnés ci-dessus. Leur répartition pourrait se
schématiser ainsi:

Classe sociale	Type d'accent	Nombre de marques
favorisées	standard	non marqué
moyennes	régional	marqué à divers degrés
défavorisées	dialectal	très marqué

Mais de nouvelles variantes <u>sociolectales</u> apparaissent en
outre avec les <u>marqueurs "sociolectaux"</u> (marqueurs des
sociolectes) à l'intérieur de chaque classe sociale - ou
les débordant parfois. On peut classer dans cette catégorie:
les parlers identificateurs de <u>caste</u>: <u>prolétaire</u> / <u>bourgeois</u>;
<u>vulgaire</u> / <u>snob</u>, et <u>mâle</u> / <u>efféminé</u>. (On notera que ces trois
couples peuvent aussi bien ne former que deux paradigmes.
Plus exceptionnellement se combiner). Les parlers identificateurs <u>professionnels</u>: guide, sermonnaire, annonceur,
vendeur, publicitaire, etc.

Dans ce dernier sous-groupe, contrairement au précé-
dent les marqueurs peuvent être <u>permanents</u> ou <u>occasionnels</u>.
(L'entrée en fonctions, la "mise en scène", déclenche le
style verbal. Parfois, au contraire, tels chez certains
acteurs, le sujet ne cesse de jouer son "personnage").

Redistribution des variantes.

Plutôt que de voir dans les marqueurs sociolectaux de caste ou de profession de nouveaux traits phoniques, il est sans doute plus juste de considérer qu'il s'agit là d'une redistribution des variantes. Si l'on prend par exemple, le cas de l'accent dit tonique envisagé plus haut, on s'aperçoit que le déplacement de cet accent va constituer de nouveaux schèmes caractéristiques de certains types de discours (Léon, 1971; Fónagy, 1976, et à paraître; Lucci, à paraître).

Marqueurs sociolectaux et index sémiques potentiels.

Lorsqu'on essaie d'établir un classement des traits utilisés comme marqueurs sociolectaux, on s'aperçoit qu'un même trait peut se retrouver dans des catégories opposées. (Ces traits sont donc bien les signes d'un code, en nombre limité, mais susceptibles de produire un grand nombre de combinaisons). Ainsi le /ɑ/, postérieur, se retrouve à la fois dans le parler snob et rural. En réalité, ces traits représentent autant d'index sémiques qui ne s'actualisent qu'à l'intérieur d'un ensemble de traits convergents. On aura par exemple:

snob	/ɑ/	rural	/ɑ/
	/ɑ > õ/		/r/
	variations mélodiques et rythmiques importantes		renforcements articulatoires variations d'intensité accentuelle importantes

Nature des traits observés.

Ces traits sont-ils tous d'origine expressive? Tous motivés? On assiste souvent au passage d'une fonction émotive à une fonction identificatrice. C'est ainsi que l'accent banlieusard de plusieurs localités des environs de Paris semble bien né - en ce qui concerne la prosodie - d'un caractère enthousiaste, revendicateur, blagueur, volontiers ironisant. La courbe mélodique de l'ironie décrite par Fónagy (1971) ressemble étrangement à

l'intonation "faubourienne" et son rythme à une généralisation de l'accent d'insistance (Léon, 1974).

Dynamique de la variation.

    Le désir d'appartenir à un groupe socialement
prestigieux - politiquement, économiquement, artistique-
ment, etc. - semble le moteur essentiel de la variation.
On a tenté de le montrer dans le cas du prestige politique
attribué par les ruraux d'un village français à la classe
prolétaire parisienne (Léon, 1974). Cet exemple suffit à
prouver que le prestige ne va pas forcément en direction de
la classe la plus favorisée. D'autres axes seront, n'en
doutons pas, à découvrir.

    Quels sont les types de marqueurs qui sont les plus
susceptibles d'entraîner des changements phonétiques,
d'introduire des variations dans le système de la langue?
Est-il toujours sûr que le grand nombre de paires minimales
opposant /ã/ à /õ/ soit suffisant pour empêcher la confusion des deux nasales à Paris, comme le soutient Martinet
(1955)? La tendance actuelle dans certain parler "chic"
est à confondre les deux nasales au profit du seul /õ/.
"Les enfants sont en vacances" = /lezõfõsõtõvakõs/. Cette
tendance à l'arrondissement de /ã/ vers /õ/ est également
un phénomène d'hypercorrection courant dans les classes
sociales favorisées de régions où l'on rencontre habituelle-
ment /ɛ̃/ ou /æ̃/ là où le français standard possède /ã/.
Après le passage de /æ̃/ à /ɛ̃/, est-il impossible que le
système des nasales françaises se réduise aux deux seuls
phonèmes /ɛ̃/ et /õ/? La chose n'est théoriquement pas
invraisemblable quand on pense que le français canadien
neutralise, sans obstacle pour la communication, l'opposition /ɛ̃/ ∞ /ã/ dans des couples comme: vin ∞ vent (dans
plusieurs régions du Canada), alors que dans ces mêmes
regions l'opposition /ɛ̃/ ∞ /æ̃/ se maintient très bien. A
n'en pas douter, les facteurs sociaux pèsent d'un grand
poids sur l'évolution des variantes et la causalité externe
est ainsi assez puissante pour inverser parfois les forces
de la causalité systémique. Les résultats présentés au
cours de cet exposé ne sont que fragmentaires. On a surtout
emis des hypothèses et posé des problèmes qu'il faudra

vérifier à l'aide d'enquêtes complémentaires plus appro-
fondies et plus systématiques dans le contrôle des variables. Reste que l'hypothèse de deux forces vives:
standardisation et diversification semble devoir se confirmer et montrer que loin d'être opposées, ces forces sont
le plus souvent convergentes.

Une linguistique qui refuserait d'être discursive ne
mènerait qu'à l'abstraction et à l'irréalité. C'est un des
grands mérites de Martinet d'avoir su garder le fonc-
tionnalisme dans le réalisme. Et comme le rappelle fort
bien Anne-Marie Houdebine-(rapport d'Oviedo 1977 sur la
linguistique fonctionnelle et la sociolinguistique)- un des
grands principes de Saussure était aussi que la langue est
avant tout une réalité sociale.

BIBLIOGRAPHIE

Carton, F.   (1972).   Lille, Serv. reprod. theses.
Fónagy, I.   (1976).   Le Français Mod., 44:193-338.
Fónagy, I.   (à paraître).   Studia Phon.
François, D.   (1970).   Paris, SELAF.
Houdebine, A.-M.   (1974).   Annal. Sect. Ling., 37-58.
Léon, P. R.   (1971).   Paris, Didier.
Léon, P. R.   (1973).   Contrib. Canadiennes Ling. App., 55-79.
Léon, P. R.   (1974).   French Rev., 46:783-789.
Léon, P. R. et Léon, M.   (à paraître).   Studia Phon.
Lucci, V.   (à paraître).   Studia Phon.
Martinet, A.   (1945).   Paris, 2ème éd., 1971.
Martinet, A.   (1955).   Berne.
Martinet, A.   (1977).   Studia Phon., 13:79-88.
Martinet, A. et Walter, H.   (1973).   Paris, Expansion.
Mettas, O.   (1971).   Etud. Ling. Appl., 3:106-116.
Reichstein, R.   (1960).   Word, 16:55-99.
Sommerfelt, A.   (1930).   Norsk Tids. Sprog., 4:76-128.
Wagner, R.-L. et Quemada, B.   (1969).   Le Français dans le
     Monde, 69.
Walter, H.   (1976).   Paris, Expansion.

ON VOWEL-DIPHTHONG TRANSITIONS.

JOHN M. LIPSKI
Michigan State University

Phonologists have long been aware that there exist principled relations between single vowels and diphthongs, in addition to more sporadic and non-systematic patterns. Such relationships occur in bicausal fashion, with single vowels evolving to diphthongs, while diphthongs reduce to single vowels. To meet the ends of a phonological investigation of diphthongs, the Romance languages provide an extremely fertile territory for data collection, as the history of all the Romance group has exhibited a wide array of diphthongal formation and reduction. In this study, attention will be restricted to falling diphthongs, for several reasons. First, the evolution of diphthongs is often complicated by changes in accentual patterns, leading to a change in the value of syllabicity from one element of the diphthong to the other; such shifts turn rising diphthongs into falling diphthongs and vice versa. By restricting the domain of discussion to a single class of diphthongs, one may avoid the technical problems that arise when contemplating situations of shifting syllabicity. Moreover, an overview of diphthongal reduction, not only in the Romance group but in other languages as well, confirms the view that considered as an ensemble, falling diphthongs behave with greater consistency than rising diphthongs. One need only to peruse the studies of the formation of rising diphthongs in a variety of languages to become convinced that we are much further from a reasonable complete

theory of rising diphthongs, and therefore that it may be
premature to attempt to compress both classes of diphthongs
into a single theory. Moreover, the data also suggest that
two fundamentally different processes may be involved in
the formation and dissolution of the two classes of diphthongs, thus nudging our investigation toward the exclusive
study of falling diphthongs. Given the degree of consistency with which a model of the latter group may be formed,
it is at the moment unlikely that any immediately gains
would be realized from extending the model haphazardly to
the class of rising diphthongs.

     While there are no a priori restrictions on the phonetic
composition of falling diphthongs, the data available to us
militate in favor of considering only those diphthongs whose
non-syllabic element is /+high/, that is, a non-syllabic
version of one of the vowels /i/, /u/, /ɨ/, /y/, etc. Of
this group of vowels, only /i/ and /u/ have consistently
yielded semivocalic elements that stably coexist with a
syllabic element to form a diphthong; one may occasionally
find falling diphthongs whose non-syllabic mora is a /y/,
and rarely if ever do we encounter stable diphthongs ending
in a non-syllabic /ɨ/, although such combinations are often
heard as fleeting transitional sounds, which virtually defy
a detailed analysis.

     Before going on to propose a model for the phonology
of diphthongs, let us briefly consider a variety of cases
of the formation and reduction of falling diphthongs, largely
within the Romance group, to discover what kind of evidence
might be available to aid in the formation of a more general
model. Of the diphthongs ending in a /w/, only /aw/ sur-
vived the transition from Latin to Romance. In the over-
whelming majority of cases, reduction of /aw/ yielded an /o/
or perhaps a slightly lowered /ɔ/. In Portuguese, /aw/
became /ow/ retaining the final semivocalic element in
stressed position; later, in some words through a complex
process of morphological analogy, /ow/ became /oj/; thus
causam--coisa. In unstressed position, /aw/ simply reduced
to /o/.   Later cases of /aw/ in Romance, usually arising
from the vocalization of syllable-final velar l, also
yielded the same processes of reduction, giving /o/. In a

few dialects of Portuguese, /aw/ has reduced to /a/; this
apparently anaomalous development may be explained by the
excessive durational prominence of the first mora in the
dialects of these regions, a distribution clearly indicated
in experimental studies. This in fact indicates a further
point of indeterminacy in the study of (falling) diphthongs;
accurate results may be consistently obtained only when a
fairly equal distribution of acoustic energy and duration
exists between the syllabic and non-syllabic morae; when
one or the other enjoys excessive prominence, it tends to
swallow up the other element rather than participating in
a more equitable process of reduction.

The diphthongs /ow/ and /ɔw/, often indistinguishable
in speech, exhibit a tendency to reduce to /o/, to a higher
/o/ (in Galician) or to /u/ (for example, in French). One
most frequently finds this diphthong in Portuguese, where
reduction occurs in many areas, in Brazil, Portugal and
many insular dialects. The same reduction also occurs in
some dialects of Friulian. On the contrary, in modern
English, for example, /ow/ is rather stable, in fact
arising from an earlier simple vowel. The diphthong /uw/
is rarely observed in phonological opposition with /u/, at
least in Romance, although it is heard, as in English, as
a positional variant in various dialects. The only possible
reduction of this diphthong is to the expected /u/; any
other evolution would suggest the infoluence of non-phonetic
factors. Reversing the order of causality, we also find
spontaneous diphthongization of simple vowels, giving the
diphthongs mentioned above. For example, the diphthongization of /o/ to /aw/ (or its nasal counterpart) has been
observed in many dialects of Portuguese. It also occurred
in English, yielding the diphthong in words like house, etc.
English also provides ready examples of the diphthongization
of /o/ and /u/, as discussed earlier. Portuguese also
exhibits the same tendency, but here one must also contend
with the all-pervasive influence of the already-existent
diphthong /ow/, carrying over from Latin /aw/.

Turning now to diphthongs containing a front vowel plus
/w/ we consider the pair /ew/-/ɛw/, again often indistinguishable. In the absence of contravening factors, the general

tendency is the production of front rounded vowels. French
provides the most common examples of this route of evolution,
with /ew/ evolving to /ø/, /ɛw/ becoming / œ /, presumably
following a pattern in which the first stage was a diphthong
with a rounded first element. The same evolution has been
attested in various Surselvan and Italian dialects and in
the rapid speech of some dialects of Spanish and Catalan.
I have also observed this same reduction in Brazilian
Portuguese, and in at least one continental Portuguese
dialect restructuring along the lines of a front rounded
vowel may have occurred at an earlier period. In Leonese,
the intermediate stage /øw/ has been attested. In a few
Portuguese dialects, /ew/ has reduced to /e/, most likely
again due to the excessive durational prominence of the
first mora. It is also possible, however, that the /e/ is
the result of a process of delabialization of /ø/, particularly since these same dialects exhibit other instances
of unrounding. The same hypothesis may also be valid in
the case of the reduction of early Latin and Greek /ew/ to
/e/. The same reduction, in favor of front-rounded vowels,
is occasionally heard in some dialects of English, but the
relative scarcity of this diphthong makes accurate data
collection impossible. The diphthong /iw/ normally reduces
to /u/, a process to be observed in widely scattered dialects,
including Italian, Portuguese, old English, old Danish, and
even French. English words borrowed from French or German
forms containing /y/ normally substitute the pair /iw/-/ju/.
One may also observe the spontaneous formation of diphthongs
from front rounded vowels, although the complete delabialization of the first element is relatively rare, perhaps due to
considerations of relative markedness of the elements involved.
Faroese and Icelandic, for example, give evidence of turning
front rounded vowels into diphthongs, as do some dialects of
Chinese and Canadian French.

It is rather difficult to find usable data concerning
falling diphthongs ending in /w/ whose first element is
either a front rounded or back unrounded vowel. One may,
however, offer a few extrapolations based on the preceding
data, and such forms have frequently figured in posited
reconstructions of historical processes. One would, for
example, anticipate that /øw/ and / œw/ would reduce to

/ø/ or /y/, while /yw/ would reduce to /y/. I have observed, among some speakers of Rumanian, a tendency for
/əw/ to reduce to /o/, and for /ɨw/ to reduce to /ɨ/ or /ʉ/.
In addition, in some dialects of English, for example in
Canada, were the diphthong /aw/ has been centralized to /əw/,
it sometimes reduces to the centralized /ə/.

In general it appears that during reduction of a V̲w̲
type diphthong, the end result is a rounded vowel whose
frontness value approximately matches that of the first mora
of the diphthong and whose height value is at a point between the height values of the two moras of the diphthong.
Conversely, spontaneous evolution of a simple vowel to a
diphthong ending in /w/ follows the reverse process, implying
the bicausality alluded to earlier. The situation is strikingly similar for diphthongs ending in /j/. Turning first to
/aj/, one notices the general tendency to reduce to /æ/,
/ɛ/ or /e/, both in Romance and in other language groups.
Early Latin /aj/ reduced to /ɛ/ or /e/ in Romance. Later
stages of French developed the diphthongs /aj/ or /æj/,
which similarly reduced to vowels in the mid-front series.
The identical process occurred in Catalan, and may be
presently heard in the rapid speech of many dialects of
Latin American Spanish. In some peninsular dialects of
Portuguese, the diphthong /aj/, while not undergoing monophthongization, centralizes the first element /ə/.

The diphthongs /ɛj/ and /ej/ normally reduce to /e/ as
well, as would be expected. Similarly, /ij/, rarely found
in opposition to simple /i/, will reduce to the latter vowel.
Turning the tables, one notices a significant quantity of
spontaneous diphthongization which follows the reverse tendencies. In many dialects of Portuguese, for example, oral
and nasal /e/ have diphthongized to /aj/, a process also
typical of English. Spontaneous diphthongization of /e/ also
occurs in Portuguese and English, while the full range of
diphthongizations is found in English and many dialects of
Canadian French. Romance offers few usable examples of purely
phonetically-conditioned reduction of /ɔj/ and /oj/, or of
/uj/. In most instances, where such diphthongs have suffered
modification, the process of reduction has been contaminated
by a shift of stress to the second mora, thus creating a

rising diphthong or hiatus. In listening to the modern
spoken dialects, however, one may at times hear evidence of
a more balanced reduction of /oj/ or /uj/ in which phonetic
reduction has occurred before or instead of, a shift of
syllabicity. In Brazilian Portuguese, for example, /oj/
may reduce to a back or centralized /ɵ/ or /ɯ/. Similarly,
Spanish /uj/ may become /ɨ/ in rapid speech. In modern
Lithuanian, which has no back unrounded vowels, Russian /ɨ/
is borrowed as /uj/. Evidence from various dialects of
modern English also suggests that the reduction of /uj/ and
/oj/ will lead, ceteris paribus, to the formation of back
unrounded vowels. Regarding diphthongs ending in non-
syllabic /y/ or /ɨ/, few accurate data may be brought forward, but one would hazard the prediction that diphthongs
ending in /y/ would reduce to yield rounded vowels and
those terminating in /ɨ/ would produce unrounded vowels.
Significantly, in such languages as Canadian French and
Faroese where 'mixed' vowels have diphthongized, the same
process has occurred in the reverse direction, thus support-
ing our supposition.

We must now address the crucial question of the incorporation of such a model of diphthongal structure into modern
phonological theory. The issue involves more than the empty
question of formalization; indeed, since no single model of
phonology has so far proved adequate to account for all
available data on diphthongal evolution, one must consider
a few competing variants. Remaining within the framework
of generative phonology (if there is any such single theory
these days), one could attempt to rewrite the prose statement
as a single rule, a diachronic statement embodying the
structure of all possible falling diphthongs and simple
vowels. It is quite possible to write such a rule to describe
diphthong reduction, although the resultant configuration is
a notational nightmare. Proceeding in the reverse direction,
however, one encounters several problems, since current
generative phonological metatheory contains no formal
machinery for describing the potentially many-to-one relation between simple vowels and associated diphthongs. One
would either have to generate a complicated series of individual cases by a brute-force method, or possibly invoke
some considerations of relative markedness of certain combinations, perhaps in the form of irreversible implicational
statements.

In general, the theory of markedness has encountered
considerable difficulty in contemporary phonology, since
while most would agree on the intuitive notion of some segments being in a sense more 'marked' or less common than
others, formalization and incorporation of such notions into
a rigorous framework has so far proved an impossible task,
Chomsky and Halle notwithstanding. In the case of diphthongization, however, some interesting attempts have been offered.
Most significant is the well-known paper by Henning Andersen,
who considers each diphthong (in the most general sense) to
be the result of the change in the value of one particular
(necessarily binary) distinctive feature, regarded as the
primary diphthongization, while any other feature differences
between the two morae become secondary differences. Andersen
proposes that 'in a primary diphthongization, the opposite
values of the feature with respect to which a segment is
diphthongized are distributed over the duration of the segment
in the order unmarked-marked.' Andersen also claims that this
proposal accounts for the motivation between the structuration,
in individual child and adult grammars, of diphthongs and the
corresponding monophthongs. The proposal, intriguing as it is,
especially in view of the wide range of data which have been
considered, in addition to the obvious lack of common concen-
sus on what constitutes 'marked' segments. Andersen is unable
to offer an a priori method of determining which feature defines the primary diphthongization. His method in fact reduces
to an ex post facto determination based on already existing
diphthongs; it would appear from his examples that any feature
that can be specified as 'unmarked' in the first segment and
'marked' in the second will qualify. Thus, the diphthong
/iw/ is regarded as diphthongized with respect to the feature
(+grave), while the corresponding /ju/ is diphthongized with
respect to the feature of intensity. /uj/ is diphthongized
with respect to (flat), since (+flat) is the unmarked value
for (+grave) vowels. However, the same marking conventions
specify (-flat) as the unmarked value for /-grave/ vowels;
thus both morae of /uj/ should be 'unmarked' by these criteria. The same holds true for /iw/, if one chooses to
consider (flat) as the defining feature. Remaining within
the same system, it is difficult to see how an unmarked-
marked configuration could be arrived at for a diphthong
such as /øj/, unless one were to choose some very general

feature such as syllabicity, in which case /wi/ and /ji/, among others, would have to be considered marked-unmarked. The list could be continued indefinitely but the point is obvious; more than a posteriori considerations of markedness will have to be invoked to account for the interaction between single vowels and corresponding diphthongs. There is obviously a great deal of merit in incorporating some general considerations of naturalness in theories of diph-thongization, but they will have to go far beyond the rather limited boundaries of the presently available theories of markedness.

Returning to the initial question, the incorporation of the bicausal relations between simple vowels and diph-thongs into phonological theory, let us (perhaps only tem-porarily) abandon the battlefield of feature designations and markedness, and look more closely at the phonetic facts themselves. A diphthong ending in /w/ is a heterogeneous vocalic segment terminating with rounded lips; similarly a diphthong ending in /j/ terminates in an unrounded gesture. The simple vowels resulting from such diphthongs also end with the lips in identical configurations. Con-versely, diphthongs resulting from rounded vowels end in a rounded offglide, while those arising from unrounded vowels contain an unrounded semivocalic segment. The onset of a falling diphthong finds the tongue in a specified front-back position which is not significantly altered by the following glide, although due to the greater tongue movement involved, the glide /j/ may exert a slight assimilatory pressure. Thus the end product of diphthong reduction is a vowel whose frontness value is roughly that of the onset element. Finally, diphthongs involve a progressive change of aperture across the entire duration; the reduction of diphthongs yields a vowel of intermediate aperture, representing the movement of two poles toward the center, with both segments of the diphthong combining to characterize the final vowel. Thus, features of the onset, middle and offset of diphthongs appear in the reduced end product. Similarly, spontaneous diphthongization involves a constant change of aperture, centering about the point of the initial vowel. One need only view the spontaneous diphthongizations in Brazilian Portuguese, Canadian French or many dialects of English,

particularly in the American south, to observe the tremendous
potential for vocalic over-differentiation through diphthongization. The same bilareral causality has also been postulated
for many dialects of Chinese, and has been seen in certain
Scandanavian dialects. It suggests that in the overall
phonological structure of diphthongs and corresponding simple
vowels, certain features are more heavily weighted in terms
of the eventual outcome. There appears to be a hierarchy of
feature weightings which determine the eventual outcome of
monophthongization and also diphthongization. Ideally, it
should be possible to represent not only simple vowels but
also diphthongs as somehow more unified than they are depicted by present theories. If one remains only within the
class of diphthongs undergoing reduction, it might be possible to assign weight values to the various diphthongal
elements via a series of functions which would be considered
part of the phonological meta-theory. It is quite difficult,
however, to portray the opposition direction of causality,
which allows simple vowels to diphthongize. It is apparent
that there exist principled routes of evolution between
simple vowels and diphthongs, which suggests that each vowel,
at the phonological level, is not merely a simultaneous bundle of distinctive features, but a set of features divided
into sequential clumps, indicating the manner in which the
vowel may be phonetically realized; superficially, a simple
vowel would be a completely simultaneous realization of the
underlying phonological data, while a diphthong would be a
sequential realization. Clearly, the moment is not yet
mature for the proposing of another complete theory, since
we are already beset by a surfeit of theories based on
inadequate evidence, which nonetheless offer all-inclusive
claims. I would, however, like to modestly propose that
the phonological representation of all simple vowels be
amended to distribute the features as sequential arrays,
paralleling the phonetic structure of equivalent diphthongs.
Since, according to the data, several diphthongs may reduce
to the same vowel, it will be impossible to depict vowels at
the phonological level as fully specified diphthongs, nor
would it be wholly appropriate to do so. A more appropriate
representation would be to divide the phonological schmata
into two successive columns of features. The first column
would represent those features normally present in the

first mora of equivalent diphthongs namely values of frontness, while the second column would represent those specifications present in the off-glide of equivalent diphthongs,
or values of lip-rounding. The remaining principal feature,
tongue height, would be specified in both columns, or as
part of the entire segment. Since under normal patterns
of evolution diphthongs emerge with a <u>high</u> offglide, all
diphthongs, even those with (+high) first morae, involve
a progressive raising of the tongue across the expanse of
the diphthong. Diphthongs may thus be represented as the
same as simple vowels, except that each column would contain
a distinct value for tongue height. It has been suggested
that when a diphthong reduces to a simple vowel the tongue
height of the resulting vowel is approximately mid way between the two morae of the diphthong; therefore the two-
column phonological representation of simple vowels must
be supplemented by a universal meta-constraint which asserts
that in equivalent diphthongs the height values of the two
morae must be an equal quantity both above and below the
height value of the simple vowel. This could easily be done
employing numerical coefficients of vowel height; diphthongization could then be represented as merely a height-
varying function, with monophthongization being the opposite
process.

    The values of lip-rounding for the first element and of
frontness for the second would, under normal circumstances,
be specified by language-specific or universal redundancy
rules which dictate, for example, that front vowels are
unrounded and back vowels are rounded, as well as specifying
the most common glides /j/ and /w/. Only when redundancy
rules are violated would it be necessary to specify the values
directly in the representation of the diphthongs, but even in
such cases the added features would not appear in the representations for the equivalent simple vowel, since only the
frontness value of the first mora and the rounding value of
the second are directly tied to the phonological structure
of the equivalent vowel. At the phonological level, en,
vowel features would remain the same as in current descriptions, except for the two-column format. Diphthongization
would be regarded as a universal process which in effect
phonetically separates the two columns of underlying features
through a dynamic change in aperture, and perhaps through
other features as well.

REFERENCES

Andersen, H.   (1972).   Lang., 48:11-50.
Foley, J.   (1973).   Unpublished MS Thesis, Simon Fraser
     Univ.
Lipski, J.   (1963).   Vox Rom., 32:95-107.
Lipski, J.   (1974).   Rév. Roum. Ling., 19:415-435.
Lipski, J.   (1977).   Conf. Ling. Romance Lang., Cornell Univ.
Pulleyblank, E.   (1972).   Acta Ling. Hafn., 14:39-62.
Romeo, L.   (1968).   The Hague, Mouton.
Schurr, F.   (1936).   Roman. Forsch., 50:275-316.
Schurr, F.   (1956).   Rév. Ling. Rom., 20:107-144.

SPEECH ACROSS A LINGUISTIC BOUNDARY: CATEGORY
NAMING AND PHONETIC DESCRIPTION

LEIGH LISKER
Haskins Laboratories and University of Pennsylvania

By conviction, not apparently contradicted so far by
anecdotal evidence, almost any vocal tract, no matter what
the ethnic affiliation of its owner, is inherently able to
function "natively" in any language community, so long as
it, and the ear to which it is attached, are "normal" and
have been welcomed into that community at a "normal" age,
namely in infancy. Linguistic inabilities, including
phonetic, which are manifested in later life, are less
evenly distributed over individuals, but presumably are in
part culturally determined--some Americans, for example,
speak more acceptable (to the French) French than others,
but there is a recognized American-accented French. The
nature of these phonetic inabilities is not all that well
understood, for we are still not clear about what is perceptually based and what is a matter of more or less arbitrary category naming. Once acoustic signals are appre-
hended as speech, their attributes seem to be evaluated by
reference to a vocal tract that might have produced them,
and beyond that, they are labeled in terms of categories
given by the language in which that vocal tract is speaking,
which for the naive listener is the language in which he
is listening. Comparison of native and non-native labeling
of speech samples enables us to map categories of one language
on another, and also serves as some check on hypotheses
regarding the phonetic basis for category distinctions in
one or both of the languages being compared.

Let us consider the cross-language correspondences of
some stop consonant categories. English stops in initial
position have been characterized differentially in respect
to the phonetic features of voicing, aspiration and level of
articulatory force. The measure of voice onset timing (VOT)
has provided data to suggest that the /bdg/ and /ptk/ categories differ significantly, in the statistical sense, in
their VOT values. In addition, experiments in synthesis and
the systematic manipulation of normally produced speech
signals have yielded no strong evidence to discount the perceptual importance of this VOT dimension. Since the measure
relates to the features of both voicing and aspiration, this
leaves the force-of-articulation features out in the cold.
The relation between a postulated dimension of articulatory
force and other features recognized by the phonetician is a
somewhat obscure one, for it is not the case that force of
articulation is simply another phonetic dimension, like voice
or tongue height, for example. Rather it is a feature that
is brought into phonetic description in order to explain how
some of these other more readily observed and measured properties are generated, particularly where they occur as
properties of phonologically identical but phonetically
different events. Thus, the partially alternating properties
of aspiration and relatively longer closure duration of
English /ptk/ have been referred to a "fortis" level of
articulatory force, while the contrasting categories are
"lenis," a designation which is said to explain why initial
voiceless unaspirated and medial voiced stops are grouped
together in the /bdg/ set. In very much the same way, in
Korean, lenis articulation has been asserted (Kim, 1965) to
be the property underlying a phonological class that includes
voiceless stops with a moderate degree of aspiration (or
perhaps murmur, if we follow Ladefoged, 1971) as well as quite
ordinary voiced stops.

In some languages it seems that voiced and voiceless
stops are, ipso facto, lenis and fortis, respectively. However, there have been cited (Ladefoged, 1971; Catford, 1977)
languages in which the dimension of articulatory force is
said to operate quite independently of any voicing difference.
The argument for (or against) an independent fortis-lenis
dimension is complicated by the fact that some writers on the

subject have shown little tendency to restrict their choice
of physical indices of articulatory force to properties that
are clearly independent of voicing. Of course the terms
"fortis" and "lenis" have quite clearly a useful function, in
that, as qualifiers not well enough defined to be demon-
strably inapplicable to the stops of a specific language such
as English, they can serve (1) as category names acceptable
to those who are unconvinced that only a voicing contrast is
present, and (2) as the cover term for any observable features other than voicing that show significant differences
between distinct categories. Those already convinced take
a demonstration that any such difference exists as proof of
the fortis-lenis nature of the contrast. One investigator
who has written extensively on the subject has, after a long
hunt for indices that would yield the "right" answer,
finessed the question by supposing that the incontrovertible
evidence for a fortis-lenis difference is the fact that phonetically naive subjects regularly report /ptk/ to be harder
to produce than /bdg/, and that this difference rests on a
proprioceptive sensitivity to the greater intraoral air
pressures developed during /ptk/ (Malecot, 1971).

Despite all the doubt expressed about a dimension of
articulatory force as a phonological feature of specific
languages, it seems to me to be obviously true that a speaker,
say of English, is perfectly capable of regulating the
degree of force with which the lips come together during a
/p/ or /b/ (or /m/) occlusion, and the stops differing in
this feature can properly be said to differ in force of
articulation. Moreover, it does not appear unreasonable
to suppose that, despite intra- and inter-speaker variation
for a single language, there may be differences between
languages in the mean mechanical pressures exerted during
the production of such stop consonants. Thus, for example,
the initial voiceless stops of Dutch, which are unaspirated
in the standard dialect, appear to me to be produced with a
good deal of energy; in my judgment they can be plausibly
labeled (+fortis) as compared with the Dutch voiced stops,
or for that matter, as compared with the voiceless aspirates
of American English. The initial voiceless inspirates of
Korean, which Kim, 1965, asserts to be phonologically
(+tense)--the same thing as (+fortis)--also seem to me to be

produced with a good deal of energy, though perhaps less than
is involved in producing the phonetically comparable Dutch
stops.

The situation in English is more complex than I earlier
suggested. For one thing, the famous case of post-/s/ stops
is really not entirely clear--they are traditionally considered to be varieties of /ptk/: voiceless, unaspirated,
of uncertain degree of force, though perhaps fortis. If
they are fortis, then this attribute is not sufficient to
result in /ptk/-labelings by English-speaking listeners when
the /s/-noise is stripped away by tape-editing (Lotz et al.,
1960). If /ptk/ are distinctively (+fortis), and if the
post-/s/ stops are /ptk/, then removal of the /s/-noise should
yield /ptk/ rather than /bdg/. If it is argued that the
post-/s/ stops are neutral as to force of articulation, since
there is only a single set of stops--one for each place of
articulation--then we still have the problem of medial /ptk/
before unstressed vowel. These stops are also reported as
/bdg/ when editing puts their releases in initial position.
A survey of the phonetic literature on English indicates that
there is not complete agreement as to whether the /p/ of
rapid, for example, is fortis or lenis. If it is considered
to be fortis, while /b/ is lenis, this fortis quality does
not prevent listeners' identifying it as /b/ following removal of the pre-closure signal. A test in which listeners
were presented with the post-closure intervals from three
recorded tokens each of rapid and rabid yielded the result
that all stimuli were judged to begin with /b/. Moreover,
when listeners, on another occasion, were told how the
stimuli had been prepared, and were asked to guess the source
of each stimulus, those derived from rabid were correctly
identified 70% of the time, while those from rapid were
judged only 43% correct.

These results conform to the generally held belief that
English listeners accept initial stops as /ptk/ only if
voice onset lags release by some 35 msecs or more. There is
at present, I think, no commonly shared conviction as to what
listeners require in order to report a medial /ptk/.

If English post-/s/ stops and the post-release phases
of medial voiceless unaspieated stops are reported as /bdg/,

this does not necessarily invalidate the belief that the
English /ptk/-/bdg/ opposition is fortis-lenis in nature.
Thus, it might be supposed simply that medial /ptk/, although (+fortis) relative to medial /bdg/, are not sufficiently stronger than initial /bdg/ to be separated from the
latter when presented in a context allowing direct comparison with initial stops. On the other hand, it could also
be argued that once we have removed the pre-closure signal
of a word such as rapid we have deleted important cues to
the fortis nature of the stop, and that we cannot claim to
be presenting medial /p/ for identification in the kind of
test just referred to.

   If my impression that Dutch /ptk/ are produced with a
good deal of force has some basis in fact, and if at the
same time their VOT values are closer to those of English
(bdg/ than of /ptk/, it should be of some interest to see
how phonetically naive English-speaking listeners without
knowledge of Dutch will label the Dutch voiceless unaspirated
stops. The responses of eight such listeners are shown in
Fig. 1, and one possible interpretation of these data is that
Dutch /ptk/ are more fortis than is acceptable for initial
English /bdg/. Other interpretations are possible, to be
sure. First of all, it is impossible to make precise the
notion of "phonetically naive listener," or to defend the
assumption that a listener so described remained in that
blessed state throughout the duration of exposure to the test
stimuli. Secondly, it is possible that the identification
of Dutch /ptk/ with English /bdg/ depended crucially on the
fact that the competing stimuli were fully voiced stops.
In competition with both Dutch /bdg/ and voiceless aspirated
stops, Dutch /ptk/ might conceivably be identified with
English /bdg/. What is undeniable is that our listeners were
able to separate the two Dutch categories despite the fact
that both fall within the range of English /bdg/ in respect
to the timing of voice onset.

   The stop system of Korean allows us to determine the
labeling responses of naive English-speaking listeners to
voiceless unaspirated stops (called 'tense' by Kim, 1965)
when these are presented together with voiceless aspirates.
In addition, we can discover whether the so-called lenis

voiceless stops will be classed with English /bdg/ or /ptk/;
if the former, we may suppose it is on the basis of a shared
"lenisness," if the latter, it is because of the similarity
in VOT values. From the responses shown in Fig. 2, it
appears that Korean /p/ and /t/ are assigned largely to
English /pt/, despite the inclusion of voiceless aspirated
stops in the same test. Unlike the Dutch case, about 30%
of the responses were /bd/, a fact which we might attribute
either to the presence of the aspirates, or perhaps to a
possible difference in the force with which the Korean and
Dutch voiceless inaspirates are articulated. Korean /k/
is very differently labeled, although there is no reason
to think that it is less strongly articulated than /pt/.
If Korean /ptk/ are all articulated so as to produce strong
release bursts, then possibly the readiness to accept
Korean /k/ as English /g/ is explained by the fact that
English /g/, with its relatively long delay in voicing
onset, has a stronger burst than English /bd/.

The so-called middle category of Korean stops, the
"lenis" somewhat aspirated voiceless stops found in initial
position, are assigned entirely to English /ptk/. They are
either not lenis enough to satisfy the requirements for
English /bdg/· (although the "fortis" Korean /ptk/ did elicit
a significant number of /bd/ and especially /g/ responses),
or perhaps English /ptk/ are not especially fortis, at least
when there is some aspiration (even if it is "murmur").

To summarize: The labelings of English speakers asked
to assign English stop category names to Dutch and Korean
initial stops indicate that the voiceless unaspirated, and
possibly fortis, stops of the two latter languages are not
categorized on the basis of their VOT values, at least as
these are determined by acoustic measurement. If the features
determining their classification are not of laryngeal origin,
then we may suppose that other acoustic features, which might
be associated with a high level of articulatory force, are
responsible for the observed behavior. The evaluation of
Korean /p' t' k'/, on the other hand, suggests that a high level
of force is not a prerequisite for English /ptk/. Thus,
it appears that, assuming we accept the validity of asser-
tions regarding the fortis-lenis character of the foreign

stop categories dealt with, English initial /ptk/ may be
cued either by aspiration (i.e., a lag in voicing onset)
or by some other features, yet unspecified, produced by
fortis articulation, while English /bdg/ may require an
absence of both aspiration and the acoustic consequences
of fortis production. It is not entirely excluded that the
features which led our listeners to associate the Dutch and
Korean voiceless inaspirates with English /ptk/ are dependent
on the nature and timing of laryngeal adjustments during the
stop articulations.

REFERENCES AND ACKNOWLEDGMENT

Catford, J. C.   (1977). Edinburgh, University Press.
Kim, C. W. (1965). Word, 21:339-359.
Ladefoged, P. (1971). Chicago, Univ. Chicago Press.
Lotz, J., Abramson, A. S., Gerstman, L. J., Ingemann, F.,
     and Nemser, W. S. (1960). Lang. Speech, 3:71-77.
Malecot, A. (1970). J. Acoust. Soc. Am., 47:1588-1592.

This research was supported in part by the National Institute
of Neurological and Communicative Disorders and Stroke, Grant
NS-13870.

ENGLISH

	/ B	D	G	P	T	K /
/ B	99			1		
D		100				
G			100			
P	13			86	1	
T		9		2	89	
K /			3			96

DUTCH (row label, left side)

FIGURE 1

RESPONSES OF EIGHT ENGLISH-SPEAKING Ss TO TEN
TOKENS OF DUTCH /BA DA GA PA TA KA/; TWO
RESPONSES PER S PER TOKEN; Ss ASKED TO LABEL
WITH ENGLISH CATEGORY NAMES; PERCENTAGE RESPONSES.

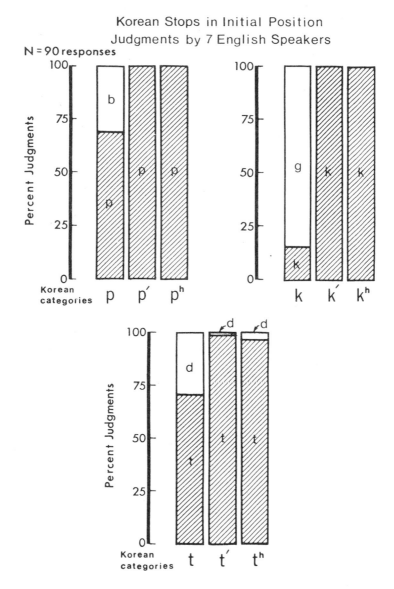

FIGURE 2.   Assignment by English-speaking listeners of Korean
             stop categories (three tokens of each) /ptk p't'k'
             p t k/ to the English categories /bdg ptk/.

COMPARATIVE ANALYSIS OF SYLLABLE AND ACCENT
BETWEEN ENGLISH AND JAPANESE

WILLIAM A. SAKOW
St. Margeret's College

One of my Japanese scholastic friends, a Professor of
English literature at a university in Japan, had a difficult
experience in England because he could not find a woman with
whom to discuss certain important subjects. Basically, his
knowledge of comparative phonetics and pronunciations between English and Japanese was not precise enough to use
effectively for his purposes. Surprisingly, his pronunciation of /smiθ/(Smith) created the problem. There appear to
be three key points upon which his difficulty was based;
they are discussed below.

The Fundamental Differences of Syllable Structures
Between English and Japanese. Most Japanese letters or words,
KANA, consist of V, or CV syllables and, hence, belong to an
open syllable class whereas a great number of English words
consist of CVC syllables and can be called "closed syllables,"
rather than open syllables. Therefore, according to Japanese
customs of pronunciation, /smiθ/→/sɯmiθɯ/ (/ɯ/ is an unvoiced Japanese spread /u/). Further, "devocalization of a
vowel" is quite common in Japanese, especially in the Tokyo
dialects, as two short, closed vowels /i,ɯ/, inserted
between voiceless consonants. From a syllabic point of view,
"Smith" must be pronounced with one syllable (with the stress
on /i/), like /smiθ/, while the Japanese are liable to
pronounce the word with three syllables, putting a pitch
accent on the first syllable, /sɯ/, like /sɯmiθɯ/. Thus,

my friend paid strict attention to the "th" /θ/ pronunciation, which was unfamiliar to him, but the "distance" may
seem peculiar to most Europeans but the Japanese single
letter (or word) has one-syllabled prominence, with the
small number of exceptions belonging to YOH-ON (/kja/).
Thus, to decide the number of syllables in a Japanese word
or sentence is easily accomplished simply by counting the
number of letters. For example, consider /nihon ŋo-no
onsetsɯ-wa, kantən desɯ/. This sentence consists of 16
letters and, hence, can be said to be constructed with 16
syllables, while /kjɯːkɯtsɯ/ ('narrow') is said to be a four-
syllabled word though five letters are included. This
relationship holds here because /kjɯ/ is a YOH-ON, and
estimated as one syllable even though it consists of two
letters. Among Japanese phoneticians, the word 'syllable'
is not popular but rather "HAKU" (a Japanese word) or "mors"
is used.

The Rhythm of a Word or Sentence Occurring from Different
Characters Between "Pitch Accent" and "Stress Accent." This
relationship is closely connected to syllable formation or
boundary, and even outstanding Japanese scholars of English
Language and literature have a tendency to use "pitch accent"
(high or low) carelessly. They do so even when they pronounce English words or sentences. These Japanese habits,
however, theoretically result from the "open-syllable"
structure. To apply 'stress accent' (strong or weak accent)
to Japanese sentences (i.e., succession of open-syllable
words) is almost impossible and the relationships between
closed syllable and pitch accent are the same.

Sentence Rhythm Between the Two Languages. Japanese
rhythm is syllable-timed and English, stress-timed. In a
syllable-timed rhythm, the periodic recurrence of movement is
supplied by the syllable-producing process, i.e., the chest-
pulses and, hence, the syllables recur at equal intervals
of time. The other type--stress-timed rhythm--the periodic
recurrence of movement is supplied by the stress-producing
process, i.e., the stress-pulses, and hence the stressed
syllables are isochronous. For example, read these two
sentences: "Rain, rain, go away." "Come again another day."
The first sentence contains five syllables and the second

contains seven syllables. Nevertheless, their spacing in
time is equal because there are four stressed syllables in
each of the sentences. Next, read these Japanese sentences:
"/āmejo, āmejo, hāɨete-kɯɨe/"; (11 syllables); "/mata kondo
kitto oidē-jo/"; (12 syllables). The first of the two sentences is "shorter" than the second, in accordance with the
number of syllables. The reasons why "Japanese is spoken
just like the peashooter, and English, like the Morse code"
seem to be understandable.

Comparative analysis of the sounds of English and
Japanese should lead us to a better understanding of both
languages. Moreover, it should provide us with the opportunity not only to revaluate our mother tongue, but also to
determine the nature of English sounds which are not intimate
to those of us who are Japanese. The syllable structures of
the Japanese Language are generally classified as Primary
syllables and Secondary syllables. Among many questions in
"Comparative Phonetics between English and Japanese," the
most important two appear to be (1) how should the Secondary
syllables of Japanese be treated, and (2) how should the
Sentence Rhythm of Japanese be explained? At present, very
little research has been carried out on these issues--i.e.:
their comparison with English Rhythm from the view of relationships between accents and parts of speech in Grammar.

In this regard, 'Japanese Syllable-formation' can be
specified as follows:
    A.   Primary Syllable or Mora.
        1. Vowel   (V)   /a/. /i/. /ɯ/...
        2. Consonant+Vowel   (CV)   /ka/. /sa/. /ta/...
        3. Glide+Vowel   (GV)   /ja/. /jɯ/. /jo/./wə/
        4. Consonant+Glide+Vowel (CGV) /kja/. /sja/

    B.   Secondary Syllable or Mora.
        5. Special Phoneme (Does not come at the beginning
            of the word).
            (a) HANERU-ON   (N)   /n/
                (Incomplete Nasal)   /anʃin/,piece of
                                          mind
            (b) TSUMARU-ON   (Q)
                (Chocking Sound)   /sekken/ (soap)

```
        (c) NOBASU-ON              (R)  /:/
            (Prolonging Sound)          /to:kjo:/ (Tokyo)
     6.  Diphthongs                (J)  /oi/
            JUH-BOIN                     /koi/ (carp)
     (Closing or falling diphthong = two syllables;
      Opening or rising diphthong = one syllable.)
```

To conclude. In English, scientific and theoretical
analysis of the relationships between rhythm and Grammar
have now reached a relatively high level. Content words are
generally pronounced with major stress and function words
with minor stress. However, in Japanese there are no differences of rule in accentuation between content and function
words.

ORIGINAL VOWELS IN AFRICAN LANGUAGES

ROMAN STOPA
Kraków, Poland

There is no doubt but that, out of the four fundamental characteristics of vowels (viz. colour, pitch, stress
and duration), colour constitutes linguistically the most important element. Colour, of course, relies on the various
shapes of the oral cavity which, in certain cases, is joined
by the nasal cavity or pharynx with the vibration of epiglot-
tis. Moreover, it can be stated a priori, that changing the
shape of the oral cavity (when considered from inside) relates to physiology; when it is considered outside it relates
to mimicry (mimicry by itself is one part of man's gesticula-
tory apparatus). Hence, it follows that the sources of the
movements which change the shape of the oral cavity are de-
posited in physiological symptoms of the psychic processes.
They are so strong that the human psyche, when dominated by
them, must be unloaded, must liberate the surplus of cumu-
lated energy in physiological expression of the speech organs
as well as in the respective gesticulation. It is in this
way we perceive the first 2 domains of the relative arrangement of the speech organs and those of the vowel colouring
in exclamations (or similar linguistic creations). Of course
the above mentioned unloadings -- or physiological and ges-
ticulatory liberation of surplus of energy and especially
emotional exclamations -- can play some overpowering if not
a decisive role in vowel colour. The third source of those
elements that determine the colour of the original vowels
in linguistic creations are spatial orientations. At this
juncture, let us consider the above mentioned domains of

human activity and see if the material offered by primitive
languages, and to a certain degree the material of developed
languages, justify such an interpretation of linguistic
phenomena.

In this paper the Bushman's emotional exclamations are
arranged according to two basic attitudes of the speaker:
(a) accepting the contents of the message (relative to a
given emotion) as a nice or agreeable one and (b) refusing
the contents (as unfavourable, hostile to the development of
organism) as something disagreeable, troublesome or painful.
Linguistically these attitudes are expressed in contradis-
tinction, in the opposition of the vowel belonging to the
front cluster /oca-uc/.[1]

In a short paper such as this one, only a few examples
of these relationships can be given. Thus, I will provide
only a brief discussion of the Bushman system for describing
pain and a few remarks about the use of clicks in the Bushman
language.

It is quite natural that, when experiencing pain, we
try to get away from its source. Therefore, as a physiological symptom having a vocal expression, a vowel of the back
cluster will appear, i.e.: /ocʌ-uc/, because flight
refers to some reflex "directed away." As examples: in
the language Nama, /hu:/ means "to flee or run away," note
the vowel of the back cluster. When mid-tone is used (not
the high tone of alarm), the long vowel points to "running
away." This is the result of mitigating the expression,
which in Nama is quite a common phenomenon; one that can be
observed in many other instances too.

In the Central Bushman (C₁) language, hie /oo/ means
"to die, death"; /o-ha/, /o-he/ means "dead." In the North

---

[1]Please note, for editorial convenience, the Zulu click
symbol "c" is substituted for the Bushman click symbol "/";
and the "q" for the "//" also.

Bushman (N$_2$) language, /o:ho/ means "alas" and /qnõ$^\prime$hõ"/
means "to cry." It is interesting to mention here that the
English word "boohoo," as well as the Polish verb "bu-czeć"
(to cry bitterly), are not far from the Bushman expression
of pain or cry, as they utilize the vowel /u/ of the back
cluster.

Let us return to Africa again. First, it would be
useful to look at the opposition of "joy" and "grief," in
general, in order to see if the Bushman vocabulary agrees
with the rules: the front cluster of primeval vowels are
for expressing "joy" and the back cluster are for expressing
"grief." When we look for signs of joyful experiences in
the movements of the whole body of primitive man, we find
them in kicking, jumping and dancing while painful feelings
appear as different behavior, i.e., falling down, bowing
with pain and writhing. Thus, in Southern or S$_1$ /≠ na:/ or
/≠ nai/ means "to kick or scrape with the feet," in the
S$_1$ /≠ naĩ:/ "to pour in" and in C$_2$ /≠ nai/ means "tsama
melon." The first word means also "to dance." Other expressions of joyful and sad experiences are found in the
S$_1$ /ckai/, /ckai/, i.e., "to light, to shine"; this is an
agreeable circumstance and produces a nice feeling in a
Bushman. On the other hand, in S$_1$ /cku/, /ckú/ -- "to bow
down (with pain), to be ill" -- is a sumptom of sorrow or,
even of great illness.

Standing upright and falling down constitutes another
example of the above cited supposition. Thus, we have the
S$_1$ /!khe:‹/, /!khai/ "to stand" and S$_1$ "/!khaü:/ "to lie
down or to fall down." Dancing, singing, clapping the hands,
a fire burning at the entrance of a hut are always circumstances of the same joyful situation and of the same agreeable experience. If we have, however, in S$_4$ /≠koa/ "to
dance" and S$_4$ /≠kaa/ "a pot," then the explanation is one
of cultural borrowing of pots, drums and of dances to the
sound of a drum (Bantu or Sudanic tribes).

When we look for opposed vocal symptoms of "joyful" and
"sad" feelings, we find them in the expressions for "singing"
and "howling" (complaining). The word for singing in S$_1$
is /!ku-tta/ but we see in the example that this kind of

singing has some special use: it sings that Krieboom
berries are upon the shoulders of the Blue Crane; they are
also on its neck which is called /!ku/, then /!kuttən/
or /!kutta/ depicts (in singing) the nice, agreeable
appearance of the Blue Crane. Of course, part of this
phrase, viz the plumage of the shoulders and neck, have
the respective means of the neck which, in turn, belongs
to the back parts of the body and is characterized by the
vowel of the back cluster /ocʌ-u/. The remaining words
with the meaning "to sing" show the vowel of the front cluster /ace-i/ except in the C_2 /qgwa/ which means "to sink, go
down, climb down" and probably points to "lighting a fire"
(C_2 /qgú + a/) as an agreeable circumstance of singing and
hence to the singing itself.

Now, let us look at the opposite words with the meaning "to howl." The cognate verbs are not only "to bark,"
but also "to blow, roll, burn, buzz, ease oneself" and the
nouns like "wind, whirlwind, buttocks." In S_1 /tʃu/,
/tʃũ/ denote "blowing" which word derives from S_1 /qgu:/
"to blow hard, roll." In N_2 /tʃũ/ means "to cry, howl";
it is connected with N_2 /qgu:/ "to bark," $N_{1\ 2}$ /dʒũ/ "to
blow" and N_2 /qgu/ "to wash." Even the leopard seems to be
named N_2 /qkum/ on account of its blowing or snorting when
it endeavours to frighten another animal. This feature -- of
of the attacking attitude of the leopard -- is similar to
wheezing which is expressed in C_2 by the word /qkuǐ/, and
to the panting of a thirsty dog that in S_2 is denoted by the
word /qkx'ui/, and even the word S_1 /qkhu:/ "to urinate."

After these rather general observations of the symptoms
of experiencing pain and joy, we have the fundamental
African material for words like the Polish /bole-ć/ and the
Latin /dole-o/. According to the rules for transforming
clicks into clicklike or expiratory consonants, the Bushman
source material will be found among the words with prepalatal
click /!/. As the labialization is not always respected in
Bushman (in Nama Hottentot, it has disappeared), the root-
words for /dole/ may be the same as for /bole-/ i.e., produced with the tip of the tongue raised to touch the palate
just behind the teeth of the upper jaw and corresponding
strictly to the position of the tongue producing the prepalatal click /!/. We have this relationship in Bushman:

(S₁) /!kõ:i/ "amiable, patient" and in the S₁, N₁, C₂
/!kaũ/ "to become bad, be in pain, be ill." Further examples showing the symptoms of a deep, acute pain are S₁
/!kũ:i/ "to burn, smart, pain, be warm, be burnt," S₁
/!kũ:i/ "to fall down," S₁ /!ku:/ "to fall down, dash
down, strike, hit on the ground," S₁ /!káu/, /!kã:u/ "to
call, bark, roar," S₁ /!kaũ/ "to become bad, be in pain,
be ill" and N₁ /!kau/, /!kauwa/ "to fall down, lie down."
Finally, the word /!nora/ "to roll" in Korana may point
to "rolling about" or "writhing the body" as a symptom of
great pain.

The following example will illustrate how some of these
words are used in actual situations. If in the course of
hunting, a Bushman is severely wounded, lies down and cannot
move or continue, his companions put him to a test. If he
is still alive they soon discover he is by pinching or
squeezing his limbs in order to evoke a cry of pain; in this
way, we can understand the connection between the Korana
words /kx'ui/ and /kx'úi/ "to hate, feel uneasy, vomit" --
and it is also a sign of being alive when someone is very
ill, i.e., /kx'úĩ/ "to recover" and /kx'uĩ/ "to live to be
alive." In C₂, as we have showed above, /qkx'wĩ/ denotes
the state of being alive; however, with the addition of the
lateral click, we now know that the "pinching test" proved
to be positive.

We have seen that, when considering the words for pain,
S₁ /!ku:i/ means "to burn, smart, pain," and S₁ /!ku:/,
/!ku'/ means an alarming pain (because its symptom is
bowing down). As to the relation between /o/ and /u/ in the
vowel back cluster, we have the opinion of that unfor-
getable informant of Hottentot, Samuel Blouw. He once indicated that, since /u-u/, is an exclamation of weeping and
of an acute pain, then /u/, being an extreme back position
of the tongue, is at the same time an expression of the
extreme pain. Thus pinching produces an exterior or a
tolerable pain, (therefore its vocal symptom is /kwi/);
hence a painful reflex /ku:/ or /ku:i/ is modified by
/wᴄu/, and thus the Bushman words such as /kwi/ "to speak,"
point to a milder kind of pain.

Many examples could be provided in order to complete
a reasonable description of the linguistic features of the
Bushman language. Such discussions, however, would require
a much more extensive forum than is this one. The above
should suffice to illustrate a few of the major relationships.

One additional comment -- concerning the use of the
click in Bushman -- would seem appropriate. Among the
clicks, the oldest are the labial "O," dental "/,"
lateral "//," and perhaps the alveolar "≠." I should like
to point out, however, that in the Northern Group: N_{1-3}
(which in some respects is even older than the Southern
Group: S_{1-6}), the labial click has disappeared or was
never ranked as a linguistic sign. This situation could
have resulted from an organic base established by the
Northern group -- a base which is characterized in the
anatomic build and psychic structure of the Northern Bushman
by a somewhat greater, stronger expressiveness that appears
in the predominance of back and energetic sounds, e.g.,
the retroflex click. This usage affords greater spontaneity
to the pronunciation of Northern Bushman -- in which case,
we receive an expression of a greater roughness or rudeness
of sounds in their speech.

In closing, it may be said that the following considerations emphasize the role of gesticulation, as well as that of
spatial orientation, in the determination of the root vowel.
Specifically, there are: (1) physiological symptoms, such
as those accompanying the feeling of fear or astonishment;
i.e., N_1 /kǒa/ /kau/, N_2 /kɔa:/ "to be afraid," N_1
/!goa-tʃi/ "fear," Nama /buru‹!guru/ "to thunder be
astonished"; (2) gestures which determine the root vowel,
i.e., S_1 /!kx'o/ or /!k'o/ "hole, a round opening," S_1
/ǂ/kx'ɔkən/ "to make fire by boring a hole in a piece of
dry wood," C_2 /xni C_1ni/, "long," and the Ewe /didi/, here
the vowel /i/ constitutes a part of the gesture of out-
stretched hands (the lips are stretched in the same direction
as are the hands) to denote length; (3) spatial orientation
was one of the original factors which determined the kind of
the root vowel.

VOWEL LENGTH IN MICMAC AND MALECITE

LASZLO SZABO
University of New Brunswick

Micmac and Malecite are two eastern Algonquian Indian
languages. I have investigated the question of vowel length
only in these two languages, not in the whole Algonquian
language family. However, since the question of vowel length
has not been clarified for the whole language family, the
results of this research might be interesting also for
Algonquianists working on languages other than Micmac or
Malecite. The reasons I compare these two languages are:
(1) they are very closely related to each other; (2) both
of them are spoken in New Brunswick, Canada, and so informants
are available.

When I speak about the length of vowels I do not mean
absolute duration. If we pronounce the English word garden
very slowly, then very quickly, we get two different absolute
durations for instance for the a in this word. I am speaking
about relative duration. In the Malecite word nit 'my friend,'
there is a long ī, in a other Malecite word: nit 'there,' the
i is short. The long /i/ and the short /i/ must be two phonemes
in Malecite. Moreover, a,o,e and i are mostly longer than ə
in Malecite; a,o,e and i can be short or long in this language,
but the ə is always short. This issue is what I am trying to
clarify: are the long ā,ō,ē and ī there in the same words in
Micmac and Malecite. Are the short a,o,e,i and ə there in the
same words in the two languages? At the same time I would
like to look also at the intensity of the vowel in question.
I have to do this because in some Algonquian languages the
vowel length means also intensity (stress), in other words,

in certain Algonquian languages long ā, long ō, etc., occur
in stressed syllables. In Micmac and Malecite long ā,ō,ē,ī
can be in stressed or unstressed syllables, and short
a,o,e,i,ə can be in stressed or unstressed syllables.

I collected a number of words in both languages, and
tried to compare them in the following way: (1) looking
for long ā,ō,ē,ī in stressed syllables, in words where the
length of these vowels is the same in the two languages,
(2) for ā,ō,ē,ī in unstressed syllables where it is the same
in the two languages, (3) for short vowels in stressed
syllables, (4) for short vowels in unstressed syllables, (5)
Finally, I will point out also differences in vowel length
between the two languages. In several cases, one of the two
languages has a long vowel, the other has a short vowel in
the same word.

One comment before examples are presented. The stress
is not phonemic in Micmac and Malecite. The length of the
vowels is phonemic. I have to involve the question of stress,
too, because of the belief of many Algonquianists that these
two things (length and stress) are automatically in the same
syllable. This is not the case in Micmac and Malecite.

Now, I would like to present words in Micmac and Malecite, following those five possibilities, mentioned above.
(My Micmac informant lives in Big Cove, my Malecite informant
lives in St. Mary's, N.B.)
1. (in stressed syllable)
   ā   Mc kāʿaʿoč 'crow   Mal kāhkakōhs 'crow'
              Mc kāʿan 'door'   Mal kākən 'door'
              Mc wāw 'egg'   Mal wāwən 'egg'
   ō   Mc w-tōsəl 'his daughter' Mal tōsəl 'his
                                                  daughter'
   ē   Mc ēpit 'woman'   Mal ēhpit 'woman'
   ī   Mc nik, kik, wik 'my your, his home'
         Mal nik, kik, wik 'my, your, his home'
                   Mc nītap 'my friend' Mal nītap 'my friend'
2. (in unstressed syllable)
   ā   Mc welākwel 'in the evening' Mal welākwīwik 'at night'
         Mc welimāt 'he smells good' Mal wəlimāhso 'he smells
                                                    good'

ō I could not find any words with unstressed ō which
   would be there in both languages.

ē   Mc wapēyek 'it is white' Mal wapēyo 'he is
                                                  white'

             Mc tekēk 'it is cold' Mal tkēyo 'it is cold'

ī   Mc n-pītən 'my hand'   Mal pīhtin 'hand'

             Mc təmikən 'ax'   Mal təmhīkən 'ax'

             Mc kīl 'you' Mal kīla 'you' (but: kīl
                                               'you')

3. (in stressed syllable)

   a   Mc ap 'again'   Mal apc 'again'

             Mc amu 'bee'   Mal amowes 'bee'

             Mc matnatəl 'he fights him' Mal matnal 'he
                                               fights him'

             Mc katew 'eel'   Mal kat 'eel'

             Mc awhti 'road'   Mal awht 'road'

             Mc apsatpat 'he has a small head' Mal apsatpe
                                               'small head'

             Mc (l)amihkwənhk 'inside of some sort of
                                               shelter'

             Mal lamikwam 'inside, in the house'

   o   Mc poktewick 'liquor' Mal poktēwick 'liquor'

             Mc mowin 'bear'   Mal mowin 'bear'

   e   Mc elminhto 'he is singing, going away'

             Mal elm- 'away,' elm-aphat 'he follows him'

             Mc mowen 'nobody'   Mal mawen 'nobody'

             Mc nekəmawhk 'they' Mal nekəmaw 'they'

   i   Mc wiyos 'meat'   Mal wiyōhs 'meat'

             Mc minišk 'berry'   Mal min 'berry'

             Mc pil awhti 'a different road' Mal pil-awht
                                               'a new road'

             Mc wikpi 'elm tree' Mal wikp 'black ash'

   ə   Mc təmhk 'first'   Mal təmhk 'first'

             Mc kəmotnes 'robber' Mal kəmotne 'he steals'
                                     kəmotnesk 'robber'

4. (in unstressed syllable)

   a   Mc sa'amaw 'chief' Mal sakəmak 'chiefs'
                                (but sākəm 'chief')

             Mc mecikatpat   Mal məciyatpe
               'he has a dirty head 'he has a dirty head'

   o   Mc amowiw 'a little bit' Mal amowi- 'a little'

   e   Mc kwospem 'lake'   Mal kwəspem 'lake'

i   Mc apikcīc 'mouse' Mal apikwsēhs 'rat'
           Mc apikcīlo 'skunk' Mal apikcīlo 'skunk'
           Mc welikiskək   Mal wəlikiskət
           'it is a nice day' 'it is a nice day'
ə   Mc əmhkəsənhk 'shoes' Mal maksən 'shoes'
           Mc wīsəs 'animal'   Mal wēyəhsis 'animal'
           Mc kəlaptan 'blacksmith' Mal kəlaptan
                                         'blacksmith'
           Mc səmākənis 'soldier' Mal səmaknəhs 'soldier'

5. (differences in vowel length)

a   Mc aᶜam 'snowshoe' Mal ākəm 'snowshoe'
           Mc peskonatek 'nine' Mal eskwənātək 'nine'
           Mc notepaᶜan 'my vehicle' Mal tapākən 'vehicle'
o   Mc kopit 'beaver'   Mal kwāpit 'beaver'
           Mc n-tol 'my boat' Mal tōl 'boat'
           Mc kesnokwat   Mal kesinōhkat
           'he is sick'   'he is sick'
e   Mc nekəm 'he, she' Mal nēkəm 'he, she'
           Mc mekweyek 'it is red' Mal mēhkwēyik 'it is
                                                  red'
i   Mc ēpicik 'women'   Mal ēhpīcik 'women'
           Mc mpison 'medicine' Mal pīson 'medicine'

(In all words presented in section 5, there is a short
vowel in Micmac, and there is a long vowel corresponding to
it in Malecite.)

   We do not have a complete comparative Micmac-Malecite
word list. But even this modest attempt at making a list can
tell us much about the vowel length in the two languages.
First, there are words with any of the four long and the five
short vowels in both languages. I could not find common words
with long unstressed o. But the stress is not phonemic in
these languages. It changes in the same sentence if the
informant repeats it again. I think we can neglect the stress
in the summary of this research, and concentrate now only on
the vowel length. This way we can say: there are common
words in the two languages with ā,ō,ē,ī, a,o,e,i,ə. Second,
in more than half of the words in our corpus, the long vowel
in one of the two languages corresponds to a long vowel in the
other language, and the same is true about the short vowels.
This means that the long a short vowels in Micmac and Malecite
cannot be the result of a recent change in the individual life

of Micmac or Malecite. This phenomenon must be very old, it
must be originated from the time when these two languages
lived together. (Of course, the other eastern Algonquian
languages, too, should be investigated to make a statement
about Proto-Eastern-Algonquian.) In a number of words,
vowels have become longer in the individual life of Malecite
(or shorter in Micmac).

Probably, there are long vowels and short vowels in many
other Algonquian languages. But a detailed research has never
been conducted into this question. At this moment it would
be hard to do such research for the whole language family
because reliable data about vowel length are not available
for many Algonquian languages. I think it would be worthwhile
to collect reliable new data about the vowel length in the
other Algonquian languages and try to clarify it in Proto-
Algonquian.